DICTIONARY
OF
BIOTECHNOLOGY

DICTIONARY
OF
BIOTECHNOLOGY

SECOND EDITION

James Coombs

stockton
press

Published in the United States and Canada by
STOCKTON PRESS, 1992
257 Park Avenue South,
New York, N.Y. 10010, USA

ISBN 1-56159-074-6

Second edition first published 1992 by
THE MACMILLAN PRESS LTD
London and Basingstoke

Associated companies in Auckland, Delhi, Dublin,
Gaborone, Hamburg, Harare, Hong Kong, Johannesburg,
Kuala Lumpur, Lagos, Manzini, Melbourne, Mexico City,
Nairobi, New York, Singapore, Tokyo.

A catalogue record for this book is available from The
British Library.

ISBN 0-333-57822-8

Printed in Great Britain.

A

A *See* adenine.

A Area in mathematical formulae, or descriptions. May be applied to parameters such as the area of fermenter surface, a heat transfer area in a heat exchanger, area across which diffusion occurs, area of a support medium in chromatography, area of a particle surface or internal pore surface, area of leaf surface in photosynthesis, etc.

A chromosome One of the chromosomes that make up the normal complement of the nucleus of a eukaryotic cell.

A line An inbred male sterile line used in the production of plant hybrids.

ABA *See* abscisic acid.

abattoir An animal slaughter house.

abaxial Descriptive of the surface of a leaf or other lateral organ which is furthest from the apex of the axis on which it is borne. Compare adaxial.

abomasum The fourth chamber of the ruminant stomach.

abortive transduction The transfer of bacterial genes into a new host by a viral vector that is not followed by integration of the new genetic material into the genome of the recipient cell. However, the transduced genes may persist for a time in the cell as a plasmid.

abrasion Pretreatment used in the malting of barley. The mild abrasion of the barley husk prior to treatment with gibberellic acid, by either steeping or spraying, that allows the acid to pass quickly to the aleurone layer, thus accelerating the malting process.

abscisic acid (ABA) A plant growth substance associated with leaf senescence, fruit drop, seed and bud dormancy, some aspects of apical dominance and inhibition of flowering in long-day plants under short-day conditions.

absolute filter A type of filter with pores of around 2 μm in diameter used to remove microbes from a stream of air.

absorbance A measure of the extent to which light is attenuated during passage through a coloured liquid or solid.

absorbent A substance used to absorb another.

absorptiometer A device used to measure the absorbance of a sample, usually a coloured liquid. It consists of a light source, a sample cell and a photomultiplier or other light-sensitive cell, coupled to a suitable meter or recorder. *See* spectrophotometer.

absorption coefficient See Lambert–Beer's law.

absorption spectrum The image recorded when electromagnetic radiation from a source emitting a continuous spectrum is passed through a substance. If the material is in the gaseous phase, bands will appear in the same position as the lines that appear in the characteristic emission spectrum of that substance. In solids or liquids, these bands are broadened and can be used to identify or quantify the material.

ABTS 2′-azino-bis-3-thylbenthiazoline-6-sulphonate; a chromogenic substrate used in immunological tests incorporating an enzyme-linked visualization system based on horseradish peroxidase (HRPO).

acceleration phase The phase of rapid growth of a microbial culture. The acceleration phase follows the lag phase and precedes the log phase, which begins when a constant maximum growth rate is reached.

acceptor site The active site of an enzyme or a site on an organism, tissue or cell recognized by a biological molecule and with which it reacts in a highly specific manner.

accessory cell A cell that presents antigen to a helper T lymphocyte cell, thus assisting in the induction of an immune response.

acellular An organism or tissue consisting of a mass of protoplasm that is not divided into cells. An example is the multinucleate hyphae of some fungi.

acentric Descriptive of a chromosome or chromosome fragment that does not possess a centromere.

Acer pseudoplatanus The sycamore tree; a source of both heterotrophic and autotrophic plant cell suspension cultures which have been widely used for research purposes.

acesulfame K A synthetic intense sweetener. It is about 150 times sweeter than sucrose.

acetaldehyde An intermediate in the formation of ethanol by glycolysis. It is formed by the decarboxylation of pyruvate in a reaction catalysed by pyruvate decarboxylase.

acetic acid An organic acid; the product of some types of fermentation. It is most familiar as the active principle of vinegar.

acetic acid bacteria Bacteria of the genus *Acetobacter* or *Acetomonas* that characteristically oxidize primary alcohols and aldehydes to the corresponding acids.

acetic anhydride An acid anhydride, the product of a dehydration reaction between two molecules of acetic acid.

Acetobacter A genus of the eubacteria. These bacteria are gram-negative rods with a highly aerobic metabolism and are used in the production of acetic acid (vinegar). They are also involved in beer contamination and wine spoilage.

acetoclastic bacteria Organisms that form methane exclusively from acetic acid in anaerobic digestion. They show very low growth rates, with doubling times of several days, and often represent the rate-limiting step in biogas production.

acetogenic bacteria Organisms that ferment longer chain fatty acids, notably propionic and butyric acids, to acetic acid. They are only able to grow in the absence of hydrogen.

acetone An important industrial solvent made by some bacteria, notably *Clostridium acetobutylicum*, as a result of fermentation.

acetone powder A protein preparation formed during the isolation of enzymes. The frozen material is homogenized in acetone at below $-30°C$, which prevents autolysis and/or inactivation of the enzymes by inhibitory substances.

acetone/butanol fermentation An industrial process, based on the fermentation of sugars (e.g., molasses), using *Clostridium acetobutylicum* to produce a mixture of acetone and butanol. This was the first fermentation to be carried out on a large scale using pure culture and aseptic methods. At one time, fermentation was the major source of these solvents. However, almost all plants were closed with the advent of the petrochemical industry. Interest in this process is now increasing as it may provide a means of producing co-solvents for addition to lead-free petroleum blends.

acetyl co-enzyme A (acetyl CoA) A complex of an acetyl unit with co-enzyme A produced during the oxidative decarboxylation of pyruvate and during oxidation of fatty acids. It functions as the link compound between glycolysis and the TCA cycle in respiration, is an intermediate of the glyoxylate shunt, and is involved in the synthesis of a wide variety of primary and secondary products including fatty acids, some amino acids and terpenoids.

acetyl-DL-amino acid The acetylated form of an amino acid produced by treating hydrolysed protein with acetic anhydride.

acetylcholine The acetyl ester of choline; a neurotransmitter in the peripheral nervous system of both vertebrates and invertebrates.

acetylene reduction test A sensitive technique used to measure the ability of an organism to fix nitrogen. It is based on the fact that the enzyme system responsible for the reduction of nitrogen gas (dinitrogen) is also capable of reducing acetylene to ethylene. Material under investigation is incubated in a closed flask in an atmosphere of acetylene. The gas phase is sampled periodically, and the constituent gases separated by gas chromatography.

acetylmuramic acid An amino sugar derived from D-glucosamine and lactic acid. It is a component of the mucopeptides found in bacterial cell walls.

acid hydrolysis A hydrolytic process in which a mineral or an organic acid is used as a catalyst. *See* hydrolysis.

acid medium A culture medium of between pH 1 and pH 5.

acid protease A protein-hydrolysing enzyme characterized by maximum activity and stability at pH 2.0–5.0. Acid proteases are low in basic amino acids and have a low isoelectric point. They are insensitive to sulphydral reagents, heavy metals and metal chelators, but are inactivated at pH values above 6.0. They are widely used in the food and beverage industries. Acid proteases of commercial importance are prepared from fungal sources and are of two types: pepsin-like and rennin-like enzymes. Pepsin-like proteases are generally prepared from *Aspergillus*, whereas rennin-like proteinases are produced from *Mucor*.

acid–base balance The ratio of acid to base in the blood. Blood usually contains bicar-

bonate and carbonic acid in the ratio of 20:1, which maintains the blood pH at 7.4. If this ratio changes owing to carbonic acid accumulation, the re-absorption of bicarbonate by the kidney is adjusted to compensate and maintain the correct ratio.

acidic Descriptive of pH lower than 7.0. *Compare* basic.

acidification A process in which the pH falls or acid is added to decrease the pH. In anaerobic digestion, problems may arise from acidification following shock-loading. Acid-producing bacteria are capable of faster rates of growth and metabolism than are methanogenic bacteria, which are also less tolerant of acid conditions. Hence, if the rate of acid production increases for any reason, the imbalance is enhanced as the acid producers grow faster and the acid-utilizing bacteria are inhibited. This can lead to the collapse of the biogas-producing system.

acidophilus milk A product obtained by the fermentation of milk with *Lactobacillus acidophilus*.

acidulant A type of food additive that imparts a sharp taste (e.g., citric acid, fumaric acid, malic acid).

acoelomate Any metazoan, such as the nematodes (threadworms), that lack a body cavity.

aconitase An enzyme of the TCA cycle that catalyses the conversion of citric acid to isocitric acid via aconitic acid.

aconitic acid An intermediate of the TCA cycle that usually only occurs as an enzyme-bound intermediate associated with aconitase. However, mutant strains of *Aspergillus* may produce large quantities of this compound.

aconitine A diterpenoid alkaloid formed by *Aconitum* and *Delphinium* that is highly toxic to man.

Aconta Algae that do not have a flagellate stage in their life cycle. This is characteristic of the red algae (Rhodophyta), which are an important source of many industrial polysaccharides including agar.

acoustic conditioning A method of aggregating particles in suspension by applying low-frequency (50–60 Hz) vibrations. Acoustic conditioning is used to improve the filterability of fermentation medium.

acquired immune deficiency syndrome (AIDS) A virus-mediated disease with a very high mortality rate. The name was first applied to a narrowly defined disease that was clinically recognizable by symptoms of Kaposi's sarcoma and *Pneumonocystis carnii* pneumonia. However, it is now known to include several other life-threatening opportunistic infections. AIDS is a group of disease processes secondary to a defect in cell-mediated immunity associated with a single, unique virus. The virus has variously been described as human T-cell lymphotrophic virus type III, lymphadenopathy associated virus, and AIDS retrovirus. However, it is now generally referred to as human immunodeficiency virus (HIV). The virus appears to be a retrovirus of the subfamily Lentivirinae which has previously been found in sheep, horses and goats. The spectrum of disease associated with AIDS virus is much greater than that defined originally and includes progressive encephalopathy (degeneration of the brain). On infection the virus infects a small number of mature T-helper lymphocytes as well as brain cells, where it is slowly replicated, in an integrated and an unintegrated form. Both types of cells form infectious virions. Treatment is difficult since the integrated virus becomes part of the genome of brain cells. The virus kills those T-helper cells in which it replicates, causing mild or profound immune deficiency according to the number of cells destroyed. The blood and plasma of an infected individual are highly infectious and the disease has been spread through blood transfusions and preparations of blood clotting factors as well as personal interaction. The virus shows antigenic drift, and antibodies when formed do not appear to affect the virus. Different isolates of the virus show a great variation in

the ENV gene, which codes for the envelope glycoprotein making it difficult to produce vaccines. *See* HIV.

acridine A mutagen that causes additions and deletions of base pairs, especially in plasmids and other extrachromosomal DNAs.

acridine orange Dimethylamino acridine hydrochloride; a dye used to stain nucleic acids. It fluoresces at 530 nm when intercalated into double-stranded DNA and at 640 nm when ionically bound to the phosphate backbone of single-stranded DNA or RNA.

acrocentric Descriptive of a chromosome in which the centromere is positioned towards one end.

acrylamide The monomer used in formation of polyacrylamide gels, which are employed in electrophoretic separation of proteins and nucleic acids.

ACTH *See* adrenocorticotrophic hormone.

actin A protein found in contractile systems, such as muscle and flagella.

actinomorphic Descriptive of flowers that are radially symmetrical.

actinomycetes A group of rod-shaped, filamentous, gram-positive eubacteria that lack cross walls and resemble miniature fungi (diameter less than 0.5 μm). This group include soil organisms that display oxidative metabolism (including *Streptomyces*, *Nocardia* and *Mycobacterium*), as well as parasitic or fermentative forms which include the genus *Actinomyces* proper. *Streptomyces* are used for the production of antibiotics and enzymes.

actinomycin D An antibiotic derived from *Streptomyces* that suppresses the synthesis of rRNA. *See* figure on page 5.

action potential A transitory reversal of the potential across the membrane of a nerve or muscle which changes from around −70 mV to +30 mV during the passage of an impulse along the cell.

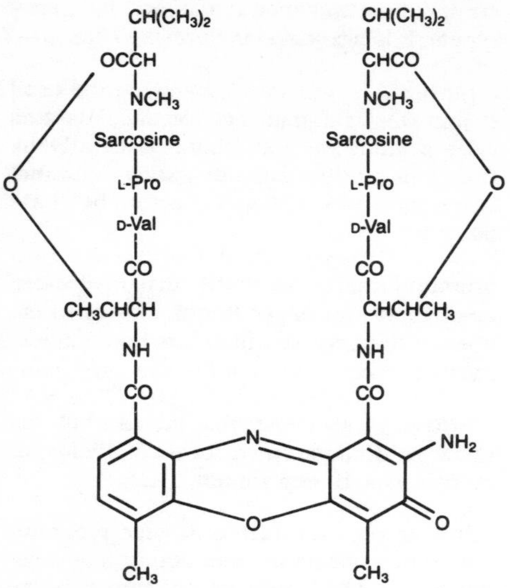
CH(CH3)2
OCCH
NCH3
Sarcosine
L-Pro
D-Val
CO
CH3CHCH
NH
CO
CH(CH3)2
CHCO
NCH3
Sarcosine
L-Pro
D-Val
CO
CHCHCH3
NH
CO
O
O
N
NH2
O
O
CH3
CH3

Actinomycin

action spectrum A plot of the intensity or magnitude of a biological reaction as a function of wavelength of electromagnetic radiation. Action spectra are usually plotted over the visible and/or ultraviolet regions. The magnitude of the response will, for a photomediated or light-dependent reaction, correspond to the absorption spectrum of the compound involved. Hence, the action spectrum can be used to infer a causal relationship between a given pigment or photoreceptor and a biological reaction.

activated carbon A finely divided form of carbon that has a high absorbency. Activated carbon is incorporated in percolating filters to enhance the removal of organic contaminants, and is used to remove colour from solutions or contaminants from gases.

activated sludge A mixture of aerobic organisms (biomass) produced in the activated sludge process of wastewater or sewage treatment.

activated sludge process A process used in sewage and wastewater treatment designed to increase the contact with a large concentration of actively growing microorganisms in the presence of sufficient dissolved oxygen so that growth of new biomass is balanced by the rate at which solids are washed from the system. The level of dissolved oxygen is maintained by agitation or air injection. The volumetric flow rate of waste sludge is kept constant and settled solids are recycled back to the early aeration stage in order to increase contact time and maintain a high level of biological activity.

activated support A matrix material that has been treated so that the surface contains a large number of chemically reactive groups.

activation energy The energy needed to form a transition state complex. This may be illustrated by considering the reaction

$$A + B = C + D$$

This reaction will only take place when molecules A and B form a transition complex AB, whose potential energy is greater than that of A + B. This transition complex can then decompose to yield the products C + D, whose potential energy is less than that of A + B since the reaction must be exogonic. The rate of reaction is proportional to the concentration of AB. The activation energy is the amount of energy required to bring all the molecules in 1 mole of A and B at a given temperature to the top of the energy barrier separating A and B from C and D. Enzymes increase the rate of reaction by lowering the activation energy.

activator A substance that is essential for a specific enzyme activity, but does not act as a substrate or contribute to the product. An activator may act through binding at a specific allosteric site on the enzyme.

active biomass The proportion of a cell culture that has microbiological activity.

active immunity Immunity that results from the production of antibodies within the body, rather than the introduction of antibodies by injection, for example. Active immunity gives a high resistance against subsequent infection and may be developed as a result of the disease itself or by immunization (using killed or attenuated vaccines or toxoids). The immunity takes several days to a couple of weeks to develop, lasts for a long time (possibly for life) and can easily be reactivated by a booster injection of the required antigen. Active immunization is used as a prophylactic.

active site The region of the enzyme with which the substrate binds during catalytic conversion to a product. The basic theory of enzyme activity assumes formation of an enzyme-substrate complex through binding at the active site. Electrostatic attraction, repulsion and other intermolecular physical forces contribute to a lowering of the activation energy, thus facilitating intermolecular conversions.

active transport A biological mechanism that results in the transport of molecules across a membrane against a concentration gradient. Active transport requires metabolic energy (usually ATP or an electrochemical gradient) and may be associated with a specific carrier protein or lipoprotein molecule.

acyclavir An antiviral agent (acycloguanosine) with a specific action against herpes virus. The phosphorylated derivative of acyclavir produced by a herpes virus-induced thymidine kinase inhibits herpes virus-induced DNA polymerase.

acylamino acid An amino acid to which an acyl group has been added.

Ada *See* zwitterionic buffer.

adaptation The fitting of an organism to its environment. It includes those processes whereby a microbial culture adapts to grow on a medium of a particular composition.

adaptive enzyme An enzyme that is formed in response to an outside stimulus during the process of adaptation. This term is now generally obsolete and has been replaced by inducible enzyme.

adaptive value A measure of the reproductive efficiency of an organism (or genotype)

compared with other organisms (or genotypes). It is also called selective value.

adaptor A synthetic oligonucleotide used to join DNA fragments to vectors. Adaptors have a blunt end that connects to a DNA fragment by ligation, and a sticky end that connects to a cleaved vector by base pairing.

adaxial Descriptive of the surface of a leaf or other lateral organ that is closest to the apex of the axis on which it is borne. *Compare* abaxial.

additive genes Genes that interact but that show no dominance, if they are alleles, or no epistasis, if they are not alleles.

additive recombination A gene recombination that occurs by insertion of a new sequence of DNA into an existing genome without any loss of DNA from the host genome.

additive variance Genetic variance due to additive genes.

add-on sequences Short, modifying DNA sequences that are added to the 5'-end of PCR oligonucleotides. For example, a restriction site is added to facilitate the insertion of the amplified PCR product into a cloning vector, or an RNA polymerase promoter is added to allow the sequence to be transcribed.

adenine A purine base that is a constituent of nucleic acids and co-enzymes, including NAD and FAD; a constituent of adenosine.

Adenine

adenosine A nucleoside comprising adenine linked to D-ribose through a β-glycoside bond. Phosphorylated forms of adenosine (AMP, ADP and ATP) are the major compounds involved in energy transfer in biological systems.

adenosine deaminase deficiency An often fatal genetic disease in which a mutant form of the gene for the enzyme adenosine deaminase is inherited. As a result the individual is unable to break down certain metabolites. These metabolites accumulate to levels at which they are toxic to lymphocyte cells, causing immune deficiency. Research has been carried out into the feasibility of correcting this condition by gene therapy, whereby retrovirus vectors containing cDNA for adenosine deaminase are transfected into a patient's bone marrow cells.

adenosine diphosphate (ADP) A nucleotide consisting of adenine, D-ribose and two phosphate groups. ADP is important in biological energy metabolism. *See* oxidative phosphorylation, phosphorylation, photophosphorylation.

adenosine monophosphate (AMP) A mononucleotide comprising adenine and D-ribose. Addition of one or two further phosphate groups leads to the formation of ADP or ATP, respectively. *See* cyclic adenosine monophosphate.

adenosine triphosphate (ATP) A nucleotide consisting of adenine, D-ribose and three phosphate groups. Two of the phosphates are linked by pyrophosphate bonds, hydrolysis of which results in a large change in free energy. ATP is important in biological energy metabolism, being produced by phosphorylation reactions in respiration and photosynthesis. Energy stored in ATP is used in synthesis of other molecules through linked reactions.

adenovirus A class of naked icosahedral viruses that contain double-stranded DNA associated with up to 12 different types of protein molecule. Adenoviruses cause acute respiratory diseases in man.

adenyl cyclase An enzyme that catalyses the formation of cyclic AMP from ATP.

adenylic acid A synonym for AMP. *See* adenosine monophosphate.

ADH Antidiuretic hormone. *See* vasopressin.

adipic acid A six-carbon dicarboxylic acid used in the production of nylon.

adipose tissue Fatty tissue consisting of aggregated cells containing large amounts of fats. In mammalian cells, the cell contents are often displaced by a single large fat droplet, particularly in subcutaneous cells, the mesentery and the mediastium. Adipose tissue provides an energy store, protection against damage of sensitive internal organs and thermal insulation.

adjuvant A substance that is not antigenic but, when mixed with an antigen, enhances antibody production. Adjuvants may be used therapeutically since they both help to

Adenosine nucleotides

produce antibody against small amounts of antigen and to prolong the period of antibody production. Adjuvants work by inducing an inflammatory response that leads to a local influx of antibody-forming cells.

ADP *See* adenosine diphosphate.

adrenal glands A pair of compound endocrine glands situated along the anterior or superior surface of each kidney in mammals. The adrenals are divided into two regions: an outer cortex, which has an embryonic origin as lateral mesoderm; an inner medulla, which develops from the neural crest. The cortex secretes several steroid hormones collectively known as corticosteroids. The medulla secretes the catecholamines adrenaline and noradrenaline.

adrenaline A catecholamine hormone, also known as epinephrine, secreted by the mammalian adrenal medulla. Its secretion is stimulated by the sympathetic nervous system under conditions of stress. Adrenalin stimulates blood flow to skeletal muscles and increases blood glucose levels.

HO — CH(OH)CH$_2$NHCH$_3$
HO —

Adrenaline

adrenergic Descriptive of a nerve fibre or nerve ending that releases adrenaline or noradrenaline as a neurotransmitter.

adrenocorticotrophic hormone (ACTH) A polypeptide hormone, comprising 39 amino acid residues, secreted in mammals by the par distalis of the pituitary gland. This hormone stimulates the production of corticosteroid hormones by the adrenal cortex and the production of melanin by pigment cells. Its secretion is regulated by a hypothalamic hormone known as corticotrophin-releasing factor and vasopressin, as well as by feedback mechanisms in which corticosteroids modulate the activity of the pituitary and hypothalamus.

adsorption (1) In physical chemistry, the adhesion of molecules to solids. This process forms the basis of adsorption chromatography, which is used to purify proteins and other macromolecules, as well as the basis of some methods of cell or enzyme immobilization. (2) In microbiology, the process whereby bacteriophage attach to specific receptors on the host cell prior to injection of their nucleic acid upon infection.

adsorption fermentation *See* extractive fermentation.

adventitious Descriptive of a structure that has arisen in an uncharacteristic position.

AE *See* amino ethyl group.

AEC *See* amino ethylcarbazole.

aeration (1) The introduction of air (or oxygen) into aerobic fermentation reactions. (2) The introduction of any gas, such as carbon dioxide, into a liquid.

aerator An apparatus used for aerating a liquid.

aerobe An organism that requires oxygen for respiration and hence growth.

aerobic bacteria *See* aerobe.

aerobic reactor A fermenter or bioreactor that is fitted with an aeration system for the culture of aerobic organisms.

aerobic respiration The overall process in which carbohydrates are completely oxidized to carbon dioxide and water using molecular oxygen. In the initial stage (glycolysis), which is common to both aerobic and anaerobic respiration, glucose phosphate is degraded to pyruvate. Pyruvate is then converted to acetyl-CoA, which enters the TCA cycle by combining with oxaloacetic acid to form citric acid. Citric acid is then metabolized to reform the acceptor molecule oxaloacetic acid in a cyclic process. This results in the release of two molecules of carbon dioxide and the passage of hydrogen atoms and their electron equivalents to an intermediate electron transport chain which ends with the formation of water from molecular oxygen. During passage through the series of redox couples which constitute the intermediate electron transport chain, energy is conserved in the form of ATP.

aerobic waste treatment A biological process in which aerobic microorganisms are grown on wastewater as a means of lowering the biochemical oxygen demand. Rapidly growing organisms use carbon compounds as a source of material for cell growth and metabolic energy, generating cell biomass and carbon dioxide. *See* activated sludge process, algal oxidation pond, deep shaft system, trickle filter.

aerogel A rigid, preformed matrix containing pores into which a solvent has been introduced. Because it is not a gel in the true sense the matrix will form aerogels in any solvent. Examples include porous glass beads and titanium spherules. Aerogels are used in chromatography for gel filtration or as carriers for ion-exchangers, or xerogel materials.

aerosol (1) A system consisting of fine droplets or colloidal particles dispersed in a gas. (2) A fine suspension of water droplets containing infectious organisms.

A-factor A factor produced by several *Streptomyces* species that is able to induce the production of streptomycin in certain A-factor-deficient mutant strains.

afferent Descriptive of a nerve or neurone that transmits information from peripheral receptors to the central nervous system. *Compare* efferent.

affinity A natural attraction towards any compound or object. The term is used in relation to the specific interaction that occurs between an enzyme and its substrate, or an antigen and an antibody, which can be exploited in techniques such as immunoassay, affinity labelling and affinity chromatography.

affinity chromatography A chromatographic technique that depends on the specific affinity of one molecule for another. For instance enzymes may be isolated by binding an analogue of their normal substrate to an inert matrix. If a solution of mixed proteins is passed through a column packed with such a matrix, the required enzyme will be retained or retarded because of its affinity for the bound substrate. The protein is then retrieved by eluting the column using a suitable solution with a pH or ionic concentration such that the binding affinity is reduced. The technique is also used to purify antibodies (especially monoclonal antibodies) by passing them through a column packed with a similar matrix to which a suitable antigen has been complexed.

affinity labelling A method of labelling nucleic acids for use as probes without employing radioactive materials. A group that does not impair the ability to hybridize with complementary sequences is coupled to the probe. Following hybridization the affinity-labelled duplex is reacted with a signal molecule which contains a binding site for the affinity label. Signal molecules include fluorescent antibodies, enzymes that produce colour changes and chemiluminescent catalysts. For instance, biotin can be chemically attached to the nucleotides of the probe DNA. Biotin is complexed by the protein avidin which may be labelled with a fluorescent marker. The sensitivity of the method can be increased by the addition of lengths of biotinylated nucleotides to the probes.

affinity partitioning The separation of a specific liquid from a mixture of liquids by introducing a ligand with an exclusive affinity for the desired liquid. The ligand and the liquid combine to form a new compound that is concentrated exclusively in a separate aqueous phase that is removed from the mixture. After removal, the new compound can be broken down and the desired liquid isolated.

affinity precipitation A system in which a precipitate is formed as a result of a reaction between two types of molecules through binding at a specific interaction site (e.g., enzyme and substrate, antibody and antigen).

affinity-isolated antibody A highly purified antibody prepared using an affinity column containing a matrix to which the antigen for the required product has been bound.

aflatoxins A group of highly toxic and often carcinogenic substances produced by the moulds *Aspergillus flavus* and *A. parasiticus* during their growth on foodstuffs or animal feeds. There is a potential hazard to health from consuming even very small amounts of these toxins (the LD_{50} may be less than 0.35 mg/kg body weight). The toxigenic *Aspergilli* species are widely distributed in nature and the likelihood of contamination is high, especially in grains and oilseed residues which are poorly dried or stored in damp conditions. The feeding of contaminated materials to cows can lead to contaminated milk. More than a dozen forms of aflatoxin have been identified. Chemically the aflatoxins are substituted coumarins, B1 being the most toxic and carcinogenic.

agammaglobulinaemia A condition in which individuals suffer from a congenital lack of gamma-globulin and form little or no antibodies. Such subjects are thus highly susceptible to repeated bacterial infections.

agamospermy Any type of apomixis other than vegetative propagation.

agar A complex polysaccharide produced by red algae, especially *Gelidium* and *Gracilaria* species. It contains the polysaccharides agarose and agaropectin. Agar is used in food manufacture and as a matrix for the culture of microorganisms. It is particularly suitable for the latter purpose since very few bacteria produce enzymes capable of liquefying the gel.

Agaricus bisporus The most widely consumed species of edible mushroom.

agaropectin A polymer similar to agarose, but containing D-glucuronic acid and small amounts of other sugars including sulphate esters.

agarose A polysaccharide gum obtained from seaweed composed of alternating (1,3)-linked D-galactose and (1,4)-linked 3,6-anhydro-D-galactose residues, as well as small amounts of D-xylose. Some of the D-galactose units are methylated at C-6. Agarose is used as a gel medium in chromatography or electrophoresis. It has a molecular fractionation range that extends into the region of viruses and microparticles.

agarose gel electrophoresis A separation technique using agarose gel as the stationary phase. Agarose gel electrophoresis is important in gene manipulation and sequencing, since it can separate DNA molecules on the basis of their molecular weights. The bands on the gel are detected using ethidium bromide so that levels as low as 0.5 mg DNA can be detected by examination in ultraviolet light.

agglutination The formation of clumps or flocs of microorganisms or cells, such as erythrocytes, due to the interaction of antigens on the cell surface with antibodies to form bridges linking the antigen determinants. Agglutination reactions are used in the identification of blood groups, bacteria, animal cell culture lines, etc.

agglutinin A substance (antibody) that causes agglutination.

agglutinogen An antigen present in a bacteria that causes production of an agglutinin when injected into an animal.

aggregation The clumping or flocculation of individual organisms or cells to form groups.

aging The biochemical and genetic changes that lead to the gradual senescence and death of a cell or organism.

agitation The mixing by shaking or other violent irregular action or motion.

agitator *See* impeller.

Agglutination

aglucone Non-sugar part of a glucoside.

aglycone A molecule containing a nucleophilic atom (usually oxygen present in an alcohol, phenol or organic acid) that replaces the hydroxyl group on the anomeric carbon atom (C-1 of aldoses or C-2 of ketoses) in the formation of glycosides. *S*-Glycosides and *N*-glycosides may also be formed.

agonist A competitive substance in any reaction.

agranulocyte A white blood cell that does not contain distinct cytoplasmic granules. Such cells include lymphocytes and monocytes.

agricultural alcohol Ethanol that has been produced by fermentation of a raw material derived from agriculture. The main sources of agricultural alcohol are sugar cane, maize, grapes, molasses, potatoes, spoilt fruit, wheat, cassava and rice.

agricultural wastes Products of agriculture which are not utilized by the established routes as food, animal feed, bedding, building materials, etc. These wastes can be divided into three groups: (1) woody or fibrous wastes such as straw, bagasse, wood wastes, etc.; (2) manures and other products of animal husbandry; (3) solid waste from food-processing operations.

agricultural wastes utilization A number of biological or fermentation processes are employed: the production of compost or silage; the production of methane by anaerobic digestion; the production of fuel alcohol (ethanol) and other solvents by yeast or bacterial fermentation; the production of glucose and fructose syrups using enzyme methods; the production of single cell protein, using fungi or bacteria, as an animal feed or human food. Most agricultural wastes contain high levels of cellulose, hemicellulose and lignin, which are not easily broken down. There are two approaches which can be used. The first is to treat the material with acid, solvents or other chemicals, or cellulolytic enzymes, following grinding or disruption by steam explosion. This will produce a sugar syrup which can then be fermented by conventional yeasts. The alternative is the development of specific strains of organisms which are able to grow on and/or ferment lignocellulose directly. Such direct conversion is best carried out using thermophilic organisms.

agriculture The cultivation of land to produce crops. In a broad sense, agriculture includes horticulture, forestry and the raising of farm animals.

Agrobacterium A genus of bacteria that includes *A. tumefaciens*, which is responsible for the production of crown gall tumours in gymnosperms and dicotyledonous plants. This disease is caused by a DNA plasmid (tumour-inducing or Ti plas-

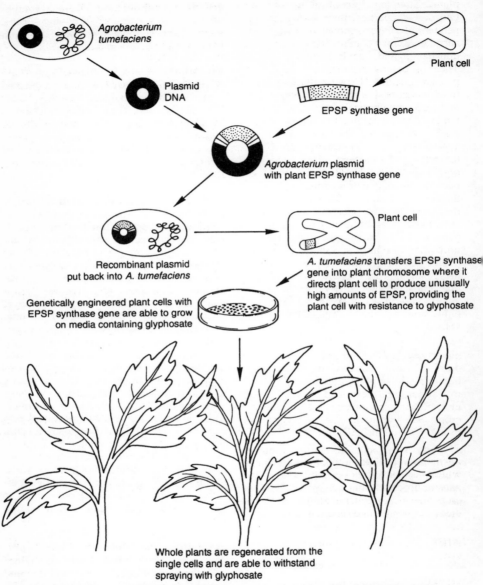

Agrobacterium tumefaciens

Plant cell

Plasmid DNA

EPSP synthase gene

Agrobacterium plasmid with plant EPSP synthase gene

Plant cell

Recombinant plasmid put back into *A. tumefaciens*

A. tumefaciens transfers EPSP synthase gene into plant chromosome where it directs plant cell to produce unusually high amounts of EPSP, providing the plant cell with resistance to glyphosate

Genetically engineered plant cells with EPSP synthase gene are able to grow on media containing glyphosate

Whole plants are regenerated from the single cells and are able to withstand spraying with glyphosate

Use of Agrobacterium in plant genetic manipulation (reproduced with permission from *A Revolution in Biotechnology*, ICSU Press).

mid). This is capable of independent replication within the cells of the plant host in the absence of the bacterium. The morphology of the tumours produced on infection varies depending on the bacterial strain and the plant species involved. The exact morphology depends on the extent to which the hormone system of the host plant is disrupted. Some tumours are undifferentiated, whereas others produce viable teratomatic plants. The plant cells of the tumour show two new properties: their growth is independent of phytohormones or plant growth substances; they contain one or more of the unusual guanido acids known as opines. The most common of these opines are octopine and nopaline. Crown gall tumours continue to synthesize opines in tissue culture, and plants regenerated from nopaline-containing tissue continue to synthesize nopaline. The ability of the tumours to synthesize opines is a property conferred on the cells by the bacteria which can use the opines as their sole nitrogen source. The bacteria do not penetrate into the plant cells that are converted to tumour cells, rather they penetrate the intercellular spaces and attach to the wall of healthy plant cells. The genetic information specifying bacterial utilization of opines and their synthesis by plants is borne on the Ti plasmids. Since these plasmids are capable of replicating in plant cells, they are widely regarded as suitable for use as a DNA vector in gene manipulation of plants. *See* plant cloning vehicle.

agrobiologicals Products based on or derived from various microorganisms, higher plants or algae that are used to control agricultural pests and diseases and to promote the nutrition and healthy growth of crops and livestock. *See* mycoherbicide, probiotic, viral insecticide.

agrochemicals Crop-protection chemicals, which may be synthetic, semi-synthetic or natural products, that are used to increase crop yields. Agrochemicals include pesticides, herbicides and fungicides.

AIDS *See* acquired immune deficiency syndrome.

air filter A device for cleaning air by removing fine particles. Air filters are used either to keep infective or contaminating particles out of a given area (e.g., a clean room) or a bioreactor, or to prevent the escape in a ventilation stream of pathogens or genetically manipulated organisms from a containment facility or fermenter.

air lift fermentation A process in which the cell suspension is kept mixed and aerated by introduction of air at the base of a central draught tube. This results in the vertical circulation of liquid. Large-scale air lift fermenters are used in the industrial production of single cell protein.

Air lift

air monitoring The measuring of the quality of an air stream. It is used to detect biological or non-biological materials, with the objective of preventing contamination and/or maintaining asepsis. Air may be monitored by collecting particles on ultrafilters and exposing these to nutrients so that trapped cells are recognized and counted on the basis of the colonies formed.

Ala An abbreviation for the amino acid alanine used in protein sequences and elsewhere.

alanine (Ala) One of the 20 common amino acids found in proteins.

Alanine $CH_3CH(NH_2)COOH$

alanine production Alanine is produced by direct fermentation, using a medium based on glucose or molasses, and bacteria such as *Corynebacterium, Brevibacterium, Arthrobacter, Microbacterium* or *Pseudomonas*. Alanine is also produced from aspartic acid using cultures of *Pseudomonas* or *Xanthomonas* with a high level of D-aspartic-β-decarboxylase activity.

albumen The water-soluble protein of egg

white. It comprises a number of conjugated proteins such as ovalbumin which contains a carbohydrate prosthetic group.

albumin One of a group of simple proteins soluble in water and coagulated by heat. Serum albumins occur in the blood.

Alcaligenes A genus of eubacteria. The bacteria are gram-negative rods, some of which are facultative anaerobes. These organisms may cause spoilage of milk, resulting in slimy milk or ropiness.

alcohol (1) The substance present in alcoholic beverages (i.e., ethyl alcohol or ethanol). (2) A class of chemical compounds having the general formula ROH, where R represents an alkyl group. The lowest molecular weight alcohol is methanol. Alcohols are widely used as industrial solvents and as precursors for the synthesis of various acids, esters, aldehydes and polymers including acetic acid, ethyl acetate, ethyl ether and polyethylene, respectively. Alcohols may also be used in internal combustion engines as fuels, octane enhancers or co-solvents in petroleum blends.

alcohol dehydrogenase An enzyme that catalyses the conversion of acetaldehyde to ethanol.

alcohol meter A device, based on a fuel cell, used for measuring the level of alcohol in a vapour. The peak current is proportional to the amount of ethanol in the vapour at the cathode.

alcohol production The production of alcohol by fermentation is mainly carried out using yeasts grown on sugar-containing substrates, which may be directly expressed juice or obtained by hydrolysis of starch. Such alcohol production can be divided into the production of alcoholic beverages for direct consumption (beers or wines), the production of alcoholic beverages for consumption following distillation to increase the alcohol content (spirits such as gin, whisky, vodka, brandy, etc.) or the production of alcohol for use as a chemical feedstock, fuel additive or fuel in its own right.

alcoholic fermentation An anaerobic metabolic process that occurs in certain yeasts, bacteria and fungi. Glucose is degraded to pyruvic acid by the glycolysis with subsequent production of carbon dioxide and ethanol (alcohol). This is the major route of production of potable, agricultural and fuel alcohols. Yeast-based alcoholic fermentations form the basis of large-scale fuel alcohol production (e.g., in Brazil over 11 billion litres are produced per year from sugar cane), as well as formation of beers, wines and spirits.

aldehyde One of a group of compounds of the general formula RCHO, where R is an alkyl group. Aldehydes yield alcohols when reduced and acids when oxidized.

aldo sugar *See* aldose.

aldolase An enzyme of glycolysis which catalyses the reversible conversion of fructose bisphosphate to one molecule of glyceraldehye phosphate and one molecule of dihydroxyacetone phosphate. It is an enzyme of glycolysis.

aldonic acid A compound produced from an aldose sugar oxidized at the C-1 position.

aldose A monosaccharide that contains an aldehyde group. *Compare* ketose.

aldosterone A hormone synthesized by the adrenal cortex of vertebrates that assists in the regulation of electrolyte balance.

alduronic acid A compound produced from an aldose sugar oxidized at the C-6 position.

ale A top-fermented beer; a beer produced using the yeast *Saccharomyces cerevisiae* which rises to the surface of the fermentation where it is recovered by skimming. Several types of ales are made which are distinguished on the basis of their colour and body. Pale ale has a low colour and a high level of hop bitterness. Mild ale (brown ale) is darker and sweeter. Stout is a very dark ale, full bodied, with a low level of hop bitterness.

algae Undifferentiated aquatic plants lacking true roots, stems or leaves that contain chlorophyll a and other characteristic pigments. The main groups are the eukaryotic Rhodophyta, Chromophyta, Chrysophyta, Phaeophyta, Euglenophyta and Chlorophyta. Some systems of classification include the prokarotes Cyanophyta under the general name of blue-green algae. However, other taxonomic systems place them as bacteria or cyanobacteria. Algae may cause serious problems owing to overgrowth in polluted water. A wide range of naturally occurring algae are used for the production of gums (e.g., agar, agarose, alginate and carrageenan). These gums are employed in microbial culture, food products, chromatography and electrophoresis. Algae may be cultured as a source of fish food, pigments, lipids and other chemicals (including hydrocarbons) or single cell protein. Some nitrogen-fixing blue-green algae are cultured as organic fertilizers, in the production of paddy rice for instance.

algal biomass Cultures of algae such as *Chlorella*, *Spirulina* and *Scenedesmus*, grown as a source of animal feed or food. *See* single cell protein (algal).

algal oxidation pond A large shallow confined stretch of water or a lagoon, which may cover several hectares, used for the treatment of wastewaters. Organic material and minerals are removed and converted into cell biomass by the combined action of bacteria and photosynthetic micro-algae. Oxygen produced in photosynthesis serves to keep the system aerobic, whereas carbon dioxide formed by bacterial respirations provides carbon for the algal growth. The system is restricted to areas of continued high sunshine and is suitable for areas of flat land close to the source of wastewaters.

algicide A substance used to kill algae or control algal blooms.

alginate An anionic polysaccharide; an acetylated polymer of mannuronic acid and guluronic acid. It is extracted on a commercial basis from brown seaweed. Microbial alginates are produced by a number of organisms including *Azotobacter vinelandii* and *Pseudomonas aeruginosa*. Alginates form viscous gels in the presence of calcium ions. Various grades of viscosity are available commercially. These differ in their ratios of guluronic acid to mannuronic acid. Alginates are used widely in food products, in textile printing and for the immobilization of microorganisms.

alginic acid *See* alginate.

alimentary canal The passage in animals, which extends from the mouth to the anus, through which foodstuffs pass to be broken down and absorbed into the body. The alimentary canal shows a great diversity of morphology and biochemical specialization to suit a wide variety of diets.

aliphatic Descriptive of organic molecules that occur as open chains, such as the paraffins or olefins.

aliquot A small sample of substance in solution of exact known volume.

alkaline Descriptive of a pH greater than 8.0.

alkaline hydrolysis A chemical hydrolysis carried out using an alkali such as sodium hydroxide.

alkaline media Culture media with a pH of between 8 and 10.

alkaline phosphatase An enzyme, commonly derived from *E. coli*, used in gene cloning experiments to remove terminal phosphate groups from restricted plasmids thus preventing recircularization. This enzyme is also used in enzyme-linked immunoassays with either chromogenic or fluorogenic substrates.

alkaline proteases Proteases that display optimum activity in the pH range 8–11. These include subtilisin Carlsberg, produced by *Bacillus licheniformis*, that is extensively used in biological washing powders.

alkaloid A nitrogen-containing compound. Alkaloids differ quite widely in structure and are classified on the basis of the type of heterocyclic group they contain: purine, pyrimidine, quinoline, isoquinoline, pyridine, reduced pyridine and indole. Alkaloids can act as analgesics (morphine), stimulants (caffeine, nicotine), muscle relaxants (strychnine), opiates (opium), vasoconstrictors (scopolamine), anaesthetics (cocaine), tranquillizers (reserpine) and psychedelic agents (psilocybin).

alkanes Saturated aliphatic hydrocarbons, components of oil. Normal (straight chain) n-alkanes containing more than 9 carbon atoms are readily metabolized by a variety of microorganisms through beta-oxidation to produce C_2 compounds. As the degree of branching increases their metabolism becomes more difficult and takes much longer. Their use as feedstock for the production of single cell protein (SCP) has been widely investigated and several large-scale plants for SCP production from alkanes have been built. Concern about possible toxic components and costs have led to closure of the largest plant.

alkenes Chemical compounds containing only carbon and hydrogen and having at least one unsaturated (double) >C=C< bond. This makes them chemically reactive. A common alkene used in commercial processes is ethene (ethylene, which is employed in the manufacture of polyethylene). Although in most instances polyethylene is produced from fossil fuel-based raw materials, a number of plants have been built that use fermentation ethanol as raw material.

alkyl group A univalent group or radical derived from an aliphatic hydrocarbon by removal of a hydrogen atom.

alkylation The replacement of a hydrogen atom in an organic compound by an alkyl group.

all or none Descriptive of a response that can be expressed in terms of either of two distinct states: no response or a maximal response, irrespective of the magnitude of the stimulus. A stimulus causing such a response usually produces no effect until a threshold value is reached.

allele One of two or more genes which occur at the same locus on homologous chromosomes and which become separated during meiosis and recombined following fusion of the gametes. When present in pairs, one (the dominant) may be expressed in preference to the other (the recessive). *See* heteroallele.

allelic exclusion The failure of one of the two allelic forms of a gene to be expressed in a diploid cell. This effect differs from normal genetic dominance, since the repressed allele may be expressed in other cells of the same organism.

allelochemical Non-nutritional chemicals produced by an organism that affect the growth, health, behaviour or population biology of other species. Characteristically, the response is one of attraction or stimulation at low concentrations, with the response becoming increasingly one of repellence or inhibition at higher concentrations. Many are based on monoterpenoids.

allelomorph The characteristic produced by an allele.

allelopathy An interaction between organisms in which the growth or reproduction of one is suppressed by chemicals released into the environment by the other.

allergen A substance that causes an allergic response.

allergy A hypersensitivity to food products, pollen, proteins, etc. that are normally harmless. The symptoms in response to an allergen are oedema and inflammation. Common allergies are hay fever, asthma and hives. Allergies may also develop following insect bite or sting, or inoculation. In all cases, the mechanism is similar. The individual is sensitized by exposure to an antigen and a period of time then elapses for antibody production to take place. Subsequently, when the individual is again exposed to a fairly large amount of the same antigen, the antibody–antigen reaction results in damage.

alloantigen An antigen found only in certain individuals within a species (e.g., antigens associated with different blood groups).

allograft A transplant of tissue between genetically different members of the same species.

allomone A chemical emitted by one species that modifies the behaviour of a different species, to the benefit of the emitting species. *See also* kairomone and pheromone.

allopatric Descriptive of populations or species that inhabit separate geographic regions. *Compare* sympatric.

allopolyploid Descriptive of an organism exhibiting polyploidy due to the addition of chromosome sets from two different species.

allosteric activator A compound that increases the activity of an enzyme by binding at an allosteric site. *See* allosteric inhibitor.

allosteric effector A compound that induces a conformational change in a protein, which changes its catalytic activity, by binding at a specific recognition site. The effector molecule may be a normal substrate for the reaction. If it can also function as a substrate, the position of the binding site that causes the conformation change differs from the position of the substrate binding site.

allosteric enzyme An enzyme that shows unusual kinetic properties in response to changes in substrate concentration and/or in response to the action of allosteric effectors that are not substrates. If the rate of reaction is plotted as a function of substrate concentration for such enzymes, the result will be a sigmoid curve rather than the usual right-angled hyperbola. Addition of the appropriate allosteric effector may cause a change in the kinetic profile to the usual hyperbolic form.

allosteric inhibitor A compound that reduces the activity of an enzyme by binding at an allosteric site. *See* allosteric activator.

allosteric protein A protein that undergoes a conformational change on binding of an allosteric effector.

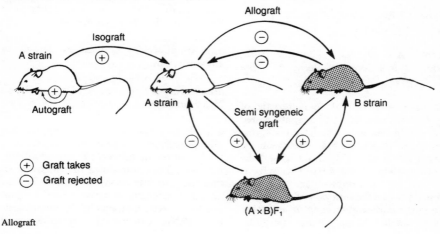

Allograft

allosteric transition A change in a protein from one conformation to another in response to an allosteric effector. If the protein is an enzyme, this transition is often associated with a change in catalytic activity. *See* allosteric enzyme.

allosterism The effect of binding of small molecules to an enzyme at a site or sites distinct from the active site. Binding results in changes in the catalytic properties of the active site.

allostery A property of many proteins, especially enzymes, that have at least two distinct binding sites. The occupation of one site by a molecule, which may or may not be a substrate for the enzyme, alters the specificity of binding at the other available site(s). Such changes, which may alter the affinity of the enzyme for substrate (K_m) or the maximum rate of reaction (V), depend on changes in the tertiary or quaternary structure of the protein. These changes may include the association of subunits. Allostery may also be associated with mechanisms which control the expression of genes. For instance, the regulatory protein that controls the activity of operon coding for inducible enzymes may be allosteric. Binding of the inducer molecule affects the protein's affinity for the operator sequence.

allotetraploid Descriptive of a tetraploid organism produced by alloploidy.

allotypes Different allelic forms of a particular immunoglobulin.

allozyme An alternative enzyme form encoded by a different allele at the same locus.

alpha-helix A structural characteristic of many proteins consisting of a right-handed helical configuration in which the backbone is derived from peptide bonds between the carboxyl group of one amino acid and the α-amino carbon of the next. The helix is stabilized by intramolecular hydrogen bonding between the nitrogen of one amino acid and the carbonyl oxygen of an amino acid four residues along, giving a periodic-

ity of 3.6 amino acids per turn of the helix. This formation contributes to the secondary and tertiary structure of the protein.

alpha-interferon *See* leucocyte interferon.

alternating double filter A wastewater treatment process that consists of two biological filters operating in series. Biomass accumulates in the first filter as it consumes most of the biochemical oxygen demand. The order of the filters is then reversed, before the first filter becomes plugged with biomass, which results in the rapid autolysis and consumption of the starved biomass.

alternation of generations A situation in which the life cycle of an organism contains two different types of organism that differ in ploidy, appearance and mode of reproduction. These differences, usually reflecting an alternation between sexual and asexual generations, are common in plants and parasitic animals. The sexual stage is termed the gametophyte generation and the asexual stage the sporophyte. In most plants, the alternation of generations is associated with alternations in diploid and haploid conditions and the intervention of meiosis and karyogamy. In some organisms the life cycle may consist of more than two generations which alternate regularly with one another.

alveolus A small sac such as occurs at the terminus of a bronchiole in the lungs or at the end of a duct in some glands.

am An abbreviation used to denote an amber mutant.

amastatin An immunomodulator produced by *Streptomyces*.

amber mutation A class of suppressible mutations that results in the creation of a UAG codon in mRNA. This codon normally signifies translation termination, so that polypeptide synthesis stops at the amber site. Such mutations can be suppressed in certain strains of *E. coli* possessing a tRNA with the AUC anticodon, and hence inserting an amino acid at the UAG site and permitting continued translation.

American Type Culture Collection (ATCC) An organization holding a large collection of microorganisms and cell lines, including type specimens.

Ames test A test for potential mutagens and frameshift carcinogens. Compounds are screened for their ability to revert a series of known frameshift mutants in the hisD gene of *Salmonella typhimurium*. The reverted cells can be recognized since they will grow into colonies, which can be counted, on a medium that lacks histidine.

amide An organic compound obtained by replacing a hydroxyl group by an amino group.

amido black A chemical stain used to determine the position of proteins, including products of antigen/antibody interaction, on gels following chromatography or electrophoresis.

amino acid analyser An automated analytical device designed to separate and quantify individual amino acids from a complex mixture which may have been obtained from a protein hydrolysate or a physiological fluid. In general, the analyser consists of an automatic loading device to which a large number of samples can be added, a separation stage (usually based on a chromatographic procedure) and a detection system (based on a colourimetric or fluorometric assay technique). Early systems relied on two columns of ion exchange resins which were sequentially eluted with buffers of varying pH with the liquid stream from the columns passing through a colourimeter after having reacted with ninhydrin. The results were obtained as a trace in which peaks of different height or area indicated the presence of the various amino acids. These could be quantified by using standards to calibrate the machine. More recent machines are fully automated single-column liquid chromatographs, using microprocessors for control and calibration as well as calculation of the results which may be printed directly.

amino acids Chemical compounds of the following general formula

where R is a hydrogen atom (glycine) or any of a number of different organic groups. These compounds are zwitterions (dipolar ions). Most amino acids found in biological systems are present in the L-optical configuration. Amino acids are the basic building blocks of proteins, as well as participating in central metabolism and contributing to the synthesis of a variety of secondary products and biologically active molecules including co-enzymes, hormones and neurotransmitters. Several hundred different amino acids are known, but only 20 are normally found in proteins. These may be classified on the basis of similarity in structure or route of biosynthesis as shown in the table. Other biologically important amino acids include ornithine and citrulline which are intermediates of the urea cycle, Y-aminobutyric acid which functions as a neurotransmitter, β-alanine which is a precursor of pantothenic acid, and D-glutamate which is found in bacterial cell walls. Protein amino acids:

1. Hydrophobic
   Alanine
   Valine
   Leucine
   Isoleucine
   Proline (or hydroxyproline)
   Phenylalanine
   Tryptophan
   Methionine

2. Polar
   Glycine
   Serine
   Threonine
   Cysteine
   Tyrosine
   Asparagine
   Glutamine

3. Acidic
   Aspartic

Glutamic

4. Basic
   Lysine
   Arginine
   Histidine

amino ethyl group [–NH(CH₂)₂NH₂] A reactive chemical group that may be bound to a support material such as agarose for use in affinity chromatography.

amino ethylcarbazole (AEC) A chromogenic substrate used in immunological tests incorporating an enzyme-linked visualization system based on horseradish peroxidase (HRPO).

amino purine A base analogue, which may be incorporated into the DNA of an organism in place of adenine, resulting in a mutation due to the incorrect base pairing in cell generations some time after the incorporation of the base analogue.

amino terminal The end of a protein or polypeptide bearing a free amino group. All polypeptides are synthesized beginning at this end and proceeding to the carboxy terminal. *Compare* carboxy terminal.

aminoacyl-tRNA A complex formed between a specific amino acid and a specific tRNA which facilitates the incorporation of amino acids into peptides in the correct sequence during protein synthesis by ribosomes. *See* aminoacyl-tRNA synthetase.

aminoacyl-tRNA ligase *See* aminoacyl-tRNA synthetase.

aminoacyl-tRNA synthetase (aminoacyl-tRNA ligase) An enzyme that catalyses the binding of an amino acid to a specific tRNA according to the following overall reaction:

amino acid + tRNA + ATP →
           aminoacyl-tRNA + AMP + PPi

This occurs in two stages: firstly

amino acid + ATP + enzyme →
           Enzyme.amino acid.AMP + PPi

followed by the transfer of the aminoacyl group to the 3'-terminal adenosine residue of the tRNA

enzyme.amino acid.cAMP + tRNA →
           aminoacyl-tRNA + enzyme + AMP

These synthetases may also catalyse the deacylation of aminoacyl-tRNA:

aminoacyl-tRNA → amino acid + tRNA
                         acid + tRNA

aminoglycoside antibiotic An antibiotic such as gentamicin, kanamycin, neomycin or streptomycin that binds to bacterial ribosomes preventing protein synthesis. Although aminoglycoside antibiotics are all effective bacteriocides, the toxicity of these antibiotics limits the extent of their clinical application.

6-aminopenicillanic acid A chemical compound produced by the action of a specific enzyme on penicillin.

amitosis A process in which a nucleus divides into two simply by constriction. Mitosis or meiosis are not involved and the daughter nuclei are not identical. Amitosis occurs in the embryonic membranes and cartilage of mammals, in the endosperm of flowering plants and in some protozoans.

ammonia (NH₃) A gas freely soluble in water that is readily absorbed by plants, usually as the ammonium ion. The major route of incorporation of nitrogen into all living organisms is by assimilation of ammonium ions either through the GS/GOGAT pathway or in the reaction catalysed by glutamate dehydrogenase. In both cases, the nitrogen forms an amino group in glutamic acid from where it is transferred to other compounds by transamination. A few types of bacteria and the cyanobacteria (nitrogen fixers) are capable of reducing atmospheric dinitrogen to ammonium. However, most bacteria and plants use nitrate, which they reduce to ammonia prior to assimilation into amino acids.

ammonium sulphate precipitation A technique, also known as salting out, used in the isolation and purification of proteins. The technique is based on the fact that the solubility of most proteins decreases at high electrolyte concentration, with the anion in the added salt being the more important. Multivalent ions are more effective than monovalent ions, hence the use of sulphate. The salt is added as solid, or as a concentrated solution, to a cell extract containing a mixture of proteins in solution, generally in the cold with control of pH close to neutrality. Different classes of proteins precipitate at various specific salt concentrations, enabling a preliminary fractionation, which can be followed by further purification using chromatographic methods. Tables are available that relate the amount of ammonium sulphate to be added to achieve a given percentage saturation as a function of the starting concentration.

amniocentesis A procedure for diagnosing genetic abnormalities in an embryo or foetus. A sample of amniotic fluid is withdrawn from the uterus of a pregnant female, the cells concentrated by centrifugation and examined for chromosomal and/or genetic abnormalities.

amniote A vertebrate (reptile, bird or mammal) characterized by having four extraembryonic membranes known as the yolk sac, amnion, allantois and chorion.

Amoeba A protozoa of the class Sarcodina characterized by an indefinite shape and the possession of pseudopodia which are used for movement and capture of food. Most species are aquatic. However, a number are endoparasites of vertebrates in which they can cause dysentery or fatal neurological disorders.

amoebocyte An amoeba-like phagocytic cell that occurs in the body fluids of coelomates.

amoeboid Descriptive of any single cell that has the appearance of an amoeba and moves, or engulfs particles, using pseudopodia.

AMP – *See* adenosine monophosphate

amperometric sensor *See* electrochemical sensor.

amphidiploid Descriptive of a tetraploid organism arising from a combination of different genomes: that is, by doubling of chromosomes of an interspecific hybrid.

amphimixis True sexual reproduction in which a zygote is formed through the fusion of two gametes.

amphipathic In chemistry used to describe compounds, such as fatty acids and phospholipids, that possess both a polar and a hydrophobic moiety. In aqueous solution, such molecules orientate with the polar groups at the surface of a sphere with the hydrophobic regions grouped together at the centre. The small drops of lipid so formed may be termed micelles.

ampholine A proprietary type of ampholyte specifically manufactured for use in electrofocusing.

ampholyte An amphoteric electrolyte.

amphoteric Descriptive of a chemical compound able to function either as an acid or as a base.

amphotericin B An antibiotic produced by *Streptomyces nodusus*.

ampicillin An antibiotic derivative of penicillin that inhibits cell wall synthesis in both gram-positive and gram-negative bacteria.

ampicillin resistance The ability to survive treatment with the antibiotic ampicillin, mediated by a β-lactamase which is secreted into the environment.

amplicon In molecular biology a vector used for cloning amplification.

amplification (1) To increase in size; used to describe processes in which an initial small reaction or signal is increased in size so that it can be observed, recorded or quantified. (2) In immunology, any of a large number of methods using radioactive, chromogenic, fluorescent or other markers that increase the ease of detection of the primary antigen/antibody reaction. (3) A treatment used to increase the ratio of plasmid DNA to that of bacterial DNA, for example, using chloramphenicol. (4) The replication of a gene library in bulk.

amplification plateau The linear or stationary phase of an amplification reaction (e.g., PCR) that occurs when the amplification fragment ceases to increase in size exponentially.

ampoule A glass tube, usually heat sealed, or closed with a rubber stopper, used to store biological materials.

amygdalin A glycoside capable of liberating hydrogen cyanide when acted upon by certain enzymes. Amygdalins occur in seeds such as almonds. They have the general structure mono- (or oligo-) saccharide–O–C(CN)ORR'.

amylase An enzyme that hydrolyses starch or glycogen. In general, amylases can be divided into two classes. (1) α-amylase, an enzyme that reduces the viscosity of a starch solution by attacking glucose–glucose bonds within the starch molecule at random to produce oligomers of variable size. It may be said that the starch is thinned. Such enzymes largely degrade amylose. However, the pure enzyme cannot attack the (1,6)-branch points of amylopectin. (2) β-amylase, an enzyme that catalyses the removal of two glucose units at a time from the terminal portion of amylose or the side chains of amylopectin. This enzyme does not attack the (1,6)-branch points of amylopectin and so the action of β-amylase results in the formation of so-called β-limit dextrins and a solution of maltose. A wide range of commercial amylases are produced from germinating barley, fungi such as *Rhizopus* species or *Aspergillus oryzae*, pancreatic extracts and bacteria such as *Bacillus licheniformis* or *B. subtillus*.

α-amylase An enzyme with endo-α-(1,4)-glucanase activity. Bacterial α-amylase is produced by submerged fermentation techniques using specially selected strains such as *Bacillus subtilis*. Fungal enzyme is produced by strains of *Aspergillus oryzae* or *A. niger*. This enzyme is used commercially in food preparations, thinning of starch slurries, production of glucose syrups and the initial treatment of starch for alcohol fermentations.

β-amylase An enzyme with exo-α-(1,4)-glucanase activity. β-amylase is prepared from germinating barley.

amylo process A process that was used to produce industrial alcohol (ethanol) from starch saccharified using strains of *Mucor* or *Rhizopus* following gelatinization and converting to alcohol by yeast fermentation. The process was operated in France in the early 20th century, and in a modified form using *Aspergillus niger* in the USA between 1930 and 1950.

amyloglucosidase An enzyme that catalyses the removal of one glucose molecule at a time from the terminal end of dextrins, breaking (1-4)-links. The enzyme does not attack (1-6)-links, so the end product is a mixture of mainly glucose plus some glucose oligomers. This enzyme is widely used in solution for the commercial hydrolysis of acid- or enzyme-thinned starch to produce glucose syrups.

amyloglucosidase production Amyloglucosidase is produced by submerged fermentation using strains of *Aspergillus niger*, or by solid substrate fermentations of *Mucor* or *Rhizopus*.

amylopectin A glucose polymer comprising up to 75 per cent of native starches, based on α-(1,4)-linked D-glucose molecules with numerous α-(1,6)-links which are introduced by the action of branching enzyme (Q enzyme). Molecules of amylopectin may have very high molecular weights of several million.

amylose A glucose polymer comprising up to 25 per cent of native starches, based on α-(1,4)-linked D-glucose molecules with chain lengths of 300–1000 units.

anabolic Descriptive of a biological reaction that results in net synthesis of more complex molecules.

anabolism The overall processes involved in biosynthesis, including the synthesis of proteins, nucleic acids, polysaccharides and other polymers from their monomeric precursors. The energy for these processes is derived from hydrolysis of ATP.

anaerobe An organism that can grow in the absence of oxygen.

anaerobic attached film expanded bed reactor An anaerobic digester in which the active biomass grows on the surface of solid particles that are kept in suspension by the upflow of the liquid being digested.

anaerobic bacteria *See* anaerobe.

anaerobic contact digester A continuous, completely mixed biological reactor in which the active biomass is recycled from the effluent after separation by centrifugation, decanting or sedimentation. *See* cell recycle.

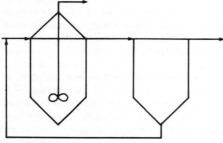

Anaerobic contact digester

anaerobic digester A fermenter or bioreactor designed to optimize the process of anaerobic digestion. The simplest types are: batch-fed, unstirred tanks, typified by the so-called Chinese digester; semi-plug flow reactors; and simple stirred tanks. In such reactors, the solids retention time and hydraulic retention time may be very similar. Such digesters are suited to wastes of a high solid content such as sewage sludge or animal manure. Wastes in which there is a high loading of soluble organic material (e.g., food-processing effluents) require more sophisticated reactor designs in which the objective is to maximize the solids retention time and minimize the hydraulic retention time. The term second generation digesters has been applied to such alternatives which include the anaerobic filters, sludge blankets, fluidized beds and two-stage reactors.

anaerobic digestion Strictly anaerobic bacterial fermentation in which complex organic biopolymers and other organic waste materials are broken down to produce a mixture of methane and carbon dioxide in approximately equal proportions (biogas). The process is used in the commercial treatment of sewage sludge, as well as in the disposal or treatment of farm wastes, industrial effluents or purpose-grown energy crops. Anaerobic digestion also results in the formation of gas mixtures of similar composition during biological decomposition of organic material in landfill waste disposal sites. The bioconversion of organic materials to methane is accomplished by a mixture of chemoheterotrophic, methanogenic and non-methanogenic bacteria. The actual mechanisms of gas production are complicated, and many details have still to be elucidated. However, taking a simple overview, the process may be described as follows. Complex organics are first hydrolysed to free sugars, alcohols, volatile fatty acids, hydrogen and carbon dioxide. This mixture is then oxidized to acetic acid, carbon dioxide and hydrogen which are converted to methane. The final gas composition by volume would, on a theoretical basis, be about 50 per cent carbon dioxide and 50 per cent methane. However, a greater proportion of carbon dioxide may stay in solution, giving a biogas that is enriched in methane up to 70 per cent with a calorific value of between 20 and 25 kJ per litre (500–700 Btu/ft^3). Volumes of gas produced and the time taken to evolve the gas (retention time) vary with the type of waste. In general, between 0.3 and 0.5 m^3 of gas might be expected from one kg of organic material (5–8 ft^3/lb).

A fundamental concern in process design is identification of the overall rate-limiting step which is related to the nature of the waste, the temperature and loading rate. Wastes high in insoluble material, such as paper, straw and other lignocellulosic materials, may require treatment for days (or even years as in landfill sites), whereas up to 95 per cent of the organic material (BOD) at loading rates of over 20 kg/day per cubic metre of reactor may be achieved with process effluents where the waste is in dilute solution. To achieve realistic rates of gas production in fabricated digesters, they must be heated. In general, an operating temperature of about 35°C is used (mesophilic). However, faster rates of gas production can be achieved at higher (thermophilic) temperatures – although this increases problems of temperature control, which is offset in some cases by the fact that the system is able to withstand overloading better and to recover faster from shock loading. In some industrial situations, waste process heat can be used for digester heating. If this is not available, part of the gas must be used for this purpose. In small systems where internal combustion engine generator sets are used to generate electricity, the engine coolant may be used to heat the digester. In anaerobic digestion, the reduction of sulphate to the highly toxic and corrosive gas hydrogen sulphide is energetically favoured over methane production. Hence wastes containing high concentrations of sulphur compounds pose particular problems in terms of gas clean-up or scrubbing prior to use. It is also necessary to scrub biogas to high methane content if it is to be used in pipe lines or compressed for use as a vehicle fuel.

anaerobic filter system A technology used in anaerobic digestion suited to liquid effluents with high levels of dissolved organic matter and relatively low levels of particulate solids. In an anaerobic filter, the biomass is retained by trapping or immobilizing on a fixed carrier which may be in the form of large plates, specially designed random plastic supports, or broken pieces of rock or similar material. The reactor may be run as a continuous process in either an upflow or a downflow mode. Retention of the cells on a support gives a high ratio of solids retention time to hydraulic retention time, permitting high rates of throughput.

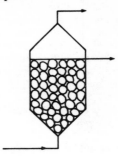

Anaerobic filter

anaerobic fixed film digester An alternative term for an anaerobic filter.

anaerobic reactor A fermenter or bioreactor which is run in the absence of air or oxygen.

anaerobic respiration A form of cellular respiration in which molecular oxygen is not involved; hence the substrate is not completely oxidized to carbon dioxide and water. Some authorities regard all fermentations carried out in the absence of oxygen as types of anaerobic respiration. However, it is preferable to regard anaerobic respiration as biological oxidations in which an inorganic compound other than oxygen is the ultimate electron acceptor. Such acceptors include nitrate, sulphate or carbonate. The ability to reduce nitrate to nitrite in the absence of oxygen is possessed by many bacteria and some fungi; the ability to reduce nitrite to nitrogen is restricted to a small number of bacteria known as denitrifiers. The end product of sulphate reduction is hydrogen sulphide, which may cause problems in anaerobic digestion systems. The decomposition of organic compounds with the production of methane and carbon dioxide is characteristic of the methane bacteria (e.g., *Methanobacterium* species) which can also reduce carbon dioxide to methane using hydrogen gas.

anagenesis The evolutionary change of a single lineage in the course of time. *See also* cladogenesis.

analgesic A drug that relieves pain.

analogue Data represented in a continuous form (e.g., by a needle on a dial). *Compare* digital.

analyser An instrument used to determine the nature and/or quantity of an element or compound. *See* amino acid analyser.

analyte The substance that is quantified or detected by an experimental procedure.

analytical balance A highly accurate device capable of weighing to fractions of a milligram.

anaphase The third stage of mitosis or of meiosis (I or II). During the anaphase, chromosomes migrate toward opposite poles of the cell.

anaphylaxis A shock reaction that may occur in a human or other mammal following re-exposure to an antigen. It is due to the inflammatory effect of histamine, bradykinin and serotonin released from mast cells in response to the antibodies formed.

anchorage-dependent cell A cell that will only grow and multiply if in contact with a suitable solid support. Many animal cell lines are anchorage-dependent. *See* microcarrier.

androdioecious Descriptive of plants that produce bisexual and male flowers on separate plants.

androgen A steroid hormone that contains 19 carbon atoms. Androgens are produced mainly by the testes, but also by the ovaries and adrenal cortex in mammals. They control the growth of male sexual organs, promote spermatogenesis and determine the development of male secondary sexual characteristics. The major natural androgens are dihydrotestosterone, testosterone and androsterone. Related synthetic compounds, known as anabolic steroids, are used for therapeutic purposes to increase body build and have been used to increase athletic ability.

androgenesis (1) The production of complete organisms (haploids) from anthers. (2) The manipulation of a male gamete in such a way that it undergoes embryogenesis.

andromonoecious Descriptive of higher plants having only male flowers.

androsterone An androgenic steroid excreted in urine. It is a metabolic product of androgens formed in the testes or adrenal cortex.

Androsterone

anemophily Wind pollination in plants.

aneuploidy A condition in which the chromosome number of a cell or organism is increased or decreased from the normal diploid number.

angiogenesis factor A protein that induces growth of blood tissues, important in wound healing (e.g., basic fibroblast growth factor, secreted by phagocytes).

Angiosperme A subdivision of the Spermatophyta that consists of the vascular plants that form seeds borne in an ovary. The angiosperms are divided into two subgroups: Dicotyledonae and Monocotyledonae.

angiotensin Either of two polypeptides (I or II) produced from a liver globulin. The polypeptides occur at elevated concentrations in people with high blood pressure. Angiotensin I is a decapeptide released under the influence of renin. Angiotensis I is enzymically converted to the octapeptide angiotensin II, which has a marked vasopressor action resulting in increased blood pressure.

angstrom (Å) A small unit of length equal to 0.1 nm.

anhydride A compound formed by abstraction of the elements of water.

animal cell culture The growing of specific cell types in an artificial medium. A suitable cell suspension may be obtained from cancerous or embryonic tissue. Nutritional requirements are complex; the cells must be supplied with a suitable mixture of amino acids, purines and pyrimidines (for the synthesis of proteins and nucleic acids), glucose (as a source of carbon and energy), vitamins and minerals as well as blood serum or serum proteins. Specific growth factors or hormones may also be needed. The cells must be maintained at a suitable pH (usually around 7.2), osmotic pressure and temperature (37°C). Low concentrations of antibiotics may be included to control bacterial contamination. Human cell line cultures are indispensable in the isolation and growth of certain viruses and in the production of antibodies and interferons, in cancer research and in antiviral chemotherapy. Recent techniques of cell culture have included the development of methods for culturing flat sheets of cells which can be used to treat severe burns.

animal cell line An animal cell culture produced as a clone (i.e., all the cells has the same genetic origin). A very wide range of cell types has been cultured, and the available cell lines run into thousands of different clones. The cells, which come from a human source or any other animal, may be cultures of primary tissue (kidney, muscle, skin, etc.), normal diploid cell strains (skin fibroblasts, foreskin cells, embryonic fibroblasts, etc.), transformed or cancer cell lines (melanoma, carcinoma, fibrosarcoma, etc.) or hybrid cell lines (hybridomas or interspecific hybrids, e.g., human × mouse).

animal feed A compounded product designed to provide animals in confined quarters or intensive growth conditions with all their nutritional requirements. Feeds may contain single cell proteins, added vitamins, amino acids, antibiotics

and growth stimulants (hormones) produced by fermentations.

animal pole The point on the surface of an animal ovum that is nearest to the nucleus.

animal tissue culture The culture of animal cells for the production of protein products or generation of replacement tissues, such as skin for use in treatment of burns.

anion A negatively charged ion which is attracted to the anode in electrophoresis.

anionic surfactant A type of soap or detergent with a negative charge. Anionic detergents include both alkyl and alkylaryl sulphonates and alcohol sulphates. Because of problems associated with biodegradation of those surfactants that contain aromatic rings or branched hydrocarbon chains, the base material used is often obtained by cracking long-chain naturally occurring paraffins which are reacted with sulphur trioxide. In general, the most effective detergent is obtained where the average number of carbon atoms is 18. Alcohol sulphates are formed by the reaction of long-chain fatty alcohols with sulphur trioxide.

anisogamy The fusion of dissimilar gametes.

anisotropic Descriptive of a structure having different dimensions along varying axes.

anisotropic membrane A membrane that has two different sides, for instance, a polymeric ultrafiltration membrane that has an open structure on one side and a microporous structure on the other.

anlage The group of cells from which a given part of the organism develops.

annealing The process, also called nucleic acid hybridization, by which two single-stranded polynucleotides form a double-stranded molecule, with hydrogen bonding between the complementary nucleotides of the two strands. Annealing can take place between complementary strands of DNA or

RNA to produce double-stranded DNA molecules, double-stranded RNA molecules, or RNA-DNA hybrid molecules. Lengths of DNA with sticky ends produced by the use of restriction endonucleases may be joined by a process of annealing followed by establishment of the necessary covalent links using DNA ligases.

Annelida A phylum of metamerically segmented worms including the Oligochaeta (earthworms) and Hirundinea (leaches). Leaches are used as a source of anticoagulants. Earthworms are cultured for a variety of purposes, including waste treatment, the production of compost and the production of animal feed protein. *See* vermiculture.

annual A plant that completes its life cycle in one year.

annulus A ring-shaped structure.

anoxic culture A culture of an organism that shows anaerobic respiration (i.e., one that uses inorganic material other than molecular oxygen as the terminal electron acceptor).

anoxic reactor A bioreactor in which an anoxic reaction is carried out, or an organism that shows anaerobic respiration is used.

ANS *See* autonomic nervous system.

antagonism The interaction of two biologically active substances performing in opposite ways in the same system, such that one partially or completely inhibits, or reverses, the effect of the other.

anterior Descriptive of the front part of an animal or the part of a lateral bud or flower in a plant that is furthest from the axis.

anther The portion of the microsporophyll that contains the pollen sacs in angiosperms (higher plants).

anther culture A technique by which haploid tissue cultures or plants are produced from anthers or pollen cells.

anthesis In higher plants, the production of a flower.

anthocyan A water-soluble plant pigment. Anthocyanins are flavonoids and comprise the anthocyanidin pigments and their glycosides, known as anthocyans.

anthrax A bacterial disease caused by *Bacillus anthracis*. The disease is usually limited to domestic animals, but man can be infected.

antibacterial agent A compound or organism that inhibits the growth of or kills bacteria.

antibiotic A natural substance of relatively low molecular weight, produced by a microorganism, which in dilute solutions inhibits growth or destroys other organisms. Toxicity is generally selective. Most natural antibiotics, whose structures vary widely, are derived from the Streptomycetes, an exception being penicillin. The major antibiotics include compounds which block bacterial cell wall synthesis (penicillins and vancomycin) and protein synthesis (neomycin, kanamycin, streptomycin and the tetracyclines). Substances of similar structure and mode of action may be synthesized chemically, or natural compounds may be modified to produce semi-synthetic antibiotics. Antibiotics are used in the control of disease in man and other animals, as well as in microbiology and gene manipulation for a variety of purposes. Antibiotics are added to culture media in order to control contamination by foreign bacteria or are used to exert a selection pressure that permits the clonal growth of bacteria containing antibiotic-resistance factors. Antibiotic-containing media are also used to select cells containing recombinant DNA where the antibiotic sensitivity of the vector is known, and in plasmid copy number expansion by suppression of cellular protein synthesis without effect on plasmid replication.

antibiotic modification The chemical conversion of a natural substance with antibiotic activity to a more stable derivative.

The product is described as a semisynthetic product.

antibiotic production Although six genera of fungi produce over 1000 distinct antibiotics, the main groups of antibiotics produced commercially on a large scale are the penicillins, cephalosporins, tetracyclines and erythromycins. These are produced from species of *Penicillium, Cephalosporium* and *Streptomyces.* Initially the products were obtained in fairly low yields from submerged batch fermentations of wild-type strains. However, considerable increases in yield have been obtained by development of improved media, adoption of continuous culture methods, and generation and isolation of mutant strains of the producing organisms. In order to overcome problems associated with the emergence of antibiotic resistance in many pathogens, methods of structural modification have been developed. *See* semisynthetic penicillins.

antibiotic resistance The property of a microorganism which enables it to grow in the presence of a specific antibiotic. Antibiotic resistance is usually associated with a particular mutation or genetic characteristic which may be carried on a plasmid or other vector and transferred from one strain to another. Resistance may be mediated through the action of various enzymes or changes in properties of cell membranes, or ribosomal structure.

antibiotic sensitivity A measure of the susceptibility of a given microorganism to inhibition by a particular antibiotic.

antibody A protein produced by blood plasma cells that bind specifically to a foreign substance. An antibody is synthesized in direct response to an antigen or to a hapten associated with a suitable carrier. The protein will react and combine with the antigen through interaction at two or more specific sites known as the combining sites of the antibody and the determinant site of the antigen. Antibodies are globulins, and are found in five major structural types: IgG; IgM; IgA; IgD; IgE. There are two different types of antibody.

(1) Humoral antibody is a free molecule that is released into the blood and other biological fluids and either combines directly with bacterial toxins or coats bacteria to enhance their destruction by phagocytosis.

(2) Cell-bound antibody is formed on the surface of sensitized lymphocytes and is responsible for the cell-mediated immune response. Most antibodies consist of two heavy and two light polypeptide chains linked by disulphide bonds.

antibody binding site The part of an antibody molecule that binds to an antigenic determinant.

anticoagulant A substance that prevents blood clotting.

anticodon A trinucleotide sequence (e.g., the recognition site on tRNA) that is complementary to a specific trinucleotide sequence codon (e.g., on mRNA) to which it complexes through base pairing.

antidiuretic   hormone   (ADH)   *See* vasopressin.

antifoam A compound added to fermentations in order to reduce the production of foams.

antigen A substance or entity, usually a protein, that induces the production of antibodies. The antigenicity of a compound depends on its structure and molecular weight.

antigenic determinant The structural portion of an antigen to which an antibody binds.

antigenic drift A gradual change in the type of antigens formed by an infective organism or virus. Succeeding generations or clones from various sources show variations in the genes coding for the antigen, as well as in the structure of the antigen formed (often a glycoprotein).

antigenic variation A change in the surface antigens of a microorganism that enables it to avoid being destroyed by the immunity of its host. *See* antigenic drift.

antigenicity The ability of a substance to be recognized and bound by a specific antibody.

anti-idiotype antibody An antibody that is induced by, and recognizes, the idiotype of another antibody.

anti-infective A protective agent which reduces the likelihood of disease developing following infection.

antilymphatic serum Blood serum containing antibodies produced by one species of animal against lymphocytes of another species.

antimetabolite A chemical compound that has a structure similar to a normal metabolic intermediate, but which cannot be metabolized, and so acts as a competitive inhibitor of a specific enzyme reaction.

antimicrobial agent A natural or artificial compound that prevents the growth of or kills microorganisms.

antimutagen A compound that protects against mutations or reverses the effects of mutagens.

antimycin A An antibiotic that blocks hydrogen transport between cytochrome b and cyctochrome c in the mitochondrial respiratory electron transport chain.

Antimycin A

antineoplastic agent A compound that prevents the growth of or kills cancer cells.

antioxidant A substance that inhibits or prevents oxidation.

antisense An inverted segment of a specific gene target in a constructed gene. A gene usually produces a message that can be interpreted by a cell (makes 'sense'). The inverted section cannot be interpreted and is therefore termed 'antisense'. The antisense gene interferes with the function of the targeted gene. Antisense technology is being investigated as a treatment for viral diseases, including cancer and AIDS. It is also applicable in agriculture, bioprocessing and other areas of therapeutics.

antiseptic A chemical compound that is used to destroy organisms that cause infection.

antiserum Whole serum (or the immunoglobulin fraction of blood) containing antibodies from an immunized animal or human. Antiserum containing high levels of antibodies to a specific antigen may be injected to give passive immunity against an infection.

antitermination factor (antiterminator) Specific protein that reacts with a termination signal (nucleotide sequence) to determine whether transcription stops at this site or whether it is read through, thus allowing expression of genes beyond the termination site.

antiterminator *See* antitermination factor.

antitoxin An antibody that reacts with a toxin and neutralizes it.

antitumour agent A compound that reduces the activity or growth of a tumour or cancer cell.

antiviral agent A compound that counteracts viral infections. Interferons are antiviral agents.

AP *See* alkaline phosphatase.

apical dominance The inhibition of the development of lateral buds by the growth of the apical meristem.

apical meristem A region of actively dividing cells that occurs at the tip of roots and shoots.

apocrine secretion The secretion of material by a cell as a result of the loss of part of the plasma membrane which then reforms.

apoenzyme The enzyme or protein part of an enzyme–cofactor complex that has lost the cofactor and is thus inactive.

apomixis In higher plants, the formation of a true seed without fusion of male and female gametes.

apparent viscosity The property or behaviour of a fluid expressed in terms of the ratio of shear stress to shear rate where this ratio is dependent on the rate of shear.

aquaculture The culture of aquatic organisms for use as models for research in physiology, neurology, medicine and ecology. The production of algal cultures or fish farming. Aquaculture is also known as mariculture when referring to saltwater organisms.

aquifer A stratum of water-filled rocks. It may underlie strata containing crude oil.

arachnoid mater The middle layer of the tissues that surrounds the brain and spinal cord in tetrapods.

arbovirus A class of enveloped viruses that cause diseases such as encephalitis and yellow fever.

archenteron The gut cavity which is formed by the infolding of the germ layer during gastrulation.

Arg An abbreviation for the amino acid arginine used in protein sequences and elsewhere.

arginine (Arg) One of the 20 common amino acids that occur in proteins. It is an intermediate of the ornithine/citrulline (urea) cycle.

Arginine $\quad \underset{H_2N}{\overset{HN}{\diagdown}} CNH(CH_2)_3CH(NH_2)COOH$

arginine production Arginine is produced using regulatory mutants of *Bacillus*, *Corynebacterium*, *Serratia* or *Brevibacterium*.

arid crops A crop plant that is adapted to conditions of low water availability. Such crops include the euphorbias, which have been suggested as a potential source of hydrocarbon fuels, and guayule, a plant that may be used for the production of rubber.

aril A fleshy outgrowth of the funicle found in some seeds. A number of compounds of economic importance, such as the spice mace from nutmeg and the very sweet protein thaumatin, occur in arils.

aromatic Descriptive of chemical compound with a cyclic arrangement of 6 carbon atoms as found in benzene.

arteriole A small artery.

artery A blood vessel that conveys blood from the heart. Arteries are characterized by a thick muscular wall.

artificial gene A double-stranded DNA molecule carrying a specific sequence that will code for a given amino acid sequence and that has been produced *in vitro*. It may be synthesized using an enzyme technique to form a strand of DNA on an mRNA template using reverse transcriptase and DNA polymerase to convert the single-stranded product (cDNA) to double-stranded DNA. Alternatively, an entirely artificial gene may be created, which will code for a novel amino acid sequence, by using a template formed from chemically synthesized oligonucleotides followed by enzymic polymerization.

artificial insemination The mechanical introduction of semen into the reproductive tract of a female. Using this technique a single male with desirable characteristics may be used to produce a large number of offspring.

artificial intelligence Descriptive of decision-making computer systems (e.g., expert systems, neural networks).

artificial selection The choosing of the parents for the following generation on the basis of one or more genetic traits. *Compare* natural selection.

ascites Hybridoma or myeloma cells, formed in experimental organisms, that contain high levels of proteins and specific antibodies.

ascitic tumour A tumour that grows in the fluid of the mammalian peritoneal cavity. Ascitic tumours can be engendered in experimental organisms as a source of monoclonal antibodies. *See* ascites.

Ascomycetes A group of fungi characterized by a sexual stage which results in formation of an ascus containing ascospores. The ascomycetes includes single-celled yeasts, as well as many soil organisms, plant pathogens and food-spoilage organisms responsible for powdery mildews and soft rots.

ascomycetous yeast A yeast that has a sexual stage resulting in the formation of ascospores.

ascorbic acid (vitamin C) A water-soluble compound structurally related to hexose. Plants and most animals are able to synthesize ascorbic acid. However, man, other primates and a few assorted species, such as the red-vented bubul and the Indian fruit bat, lack one of the enzymes involved (L-gulonolactone oxidase) and thus require ascorbic acid in their diets. A lack of this vitamin leads to scurvy in man. This is relieved by a diet rich in fruit (citrus fruit in particular) and vegetables. Although the precise metabolic role of vitamin C is not known, it appears to be associated with the synthesis of cartilage, bone and dentine. Claims have been made that a high intake of ascorbic acid can prevent or relieve infection by diseases, such as the common cold, however this has not generally been substantiated.

ascospore One of the haploid spores, formed by meiosis, in an ascus. Four or eight ascospores are found in each ascus.

ascus A sac-like spore-containing fruiting body produced by fungi which are members of the ascomycetes.

asepsis The absence of microorganisms that produce disease or contamination of other cultures, or processes characterized by the use of feedstocks and other materials that are free from such organisms. Asepsis may be achieved by sterilization of media and equipment. In fermentation, asepsis is achieved by using a sterile feed material and a closed bioreactor. Foreign organisms are prevented from entering the system by mechanical means. Total asepsis is hard to achieve on a large scale. Hence where there is a choice, short fermentation times should be used, with organisms that grow at high temperatures and extreme pH values, and on media that do not contain the nutrients required by many potential contaminating organisms.

aseptic techniques Methods applied when working with microorganisms in order to ensure the sterility of media, and to prevent the transmission of infection or contamination of cultures.

asexual reproduction A form of reproduction that does not involve the formation and fusion of gametes. Examples include vegetative propagation, budding and fission.

ash content The weight of material that remains after incineration of a sample of material at 450°C or 600°C.

Asn An abbreviation used to denote the amino acid asparagine in protein sequences and elsewhere.

Asp An abbreviation used to denote the amino acid aspartic acid in protein sequences and elsewhere.

asparaginase An enzyme that catalyses the conversion of asparagine to aspartic acid plus ammonia.

asparagine (Asn) One of the 20 common amino acids found in proteins.

Asparagine $H_2NCOCH_2CH(NH_2)COOH$

aspartame   L-α-aspartyl-L-phenylalanyl methyl ester; a colourless crystalline material that is 160 times sweeter than sucrose. This sweetener, which is used in carbonated beverages in particular, is derived from aspartate and phenylalanine, both of which are produced by a variety of biological routes using either enzymes or fermentations. *See* aspartic acid production, phenylalanine (Phe).

Aspartame

aspartate The salt of aspartic acid.

aspartic acid (Asp) One of the 20 common amino acids found in proteins. Aspartic acid is an intermediate of the ornithine/citrulline (urea) cycle.

Aspartic acid $HOOCCH_2CH(NH_2)COOH$

aspartic acid production L-Aspartic acid is produced from ammonium fumarate in a reaction catalysed by aspartase derived from bacteria such as *E. coli* and *Pseudomonas fluorescens*. *Alcaligenes* can produce aspartate from ammonium maleate.

aspergillosis Pulmonary infection caused by spores of the fungus *Aspergillus*. Also known as farmer's lung.

Aspergillus A genus of filamentous fungi. Various species are used for the production of enzymes: *A. alliaceus* (pectic enzyme); *A. awamori* or *A. oryzae* (amylase, protease); *A. phoenicis* (amyloglucosidase); *A. terricola* (protease); *A. niger* (amylase, amyloglucosidase, catalase, cellulase, lipase, pectic enzyme, protease, cellobiase, etc.). *A. niger* has also been used to produce single cell protein and citric acid. Infection of the lungs by *A. fumigatus* causes the disease aspergillosis. Other species, notably *A. flavus*, produce aflatoxins.

aspirin An analgesic and anti-inflammatory drug, the active ingredient of which is acetylsalicylic acid. It acts by inhibiting prostaglandin synthesis.

asporogenous yeast A yeast for which the life cycle is not known, or one that does not have a sexual stage.

assimilation The conversion of simple molecules into the complex constituents of the living body.

assortative mating Non-random selection of mates with respect to one or more traits. It is positive (negative) when individuals with the same form of a trait mate more (less) often than would be predicted by chance. *See* random mating.

asymmetric carbon A carbon atom to which four different atoms or groups of atoms are attached.

asymmetric PCR A PCR reaction in which two amplification primers are used to generate single-stranded DNA: an *excess primer* at a higher concentration; a *limiting primer* at a lower concentration. During an initial series of reaction cycles the two primers together produce double-stranded DNA. However, when the *limiting primer* is exhausted amplification continues for a further series of cycles during which single-stranded DNA is accumulated by primer extension of the remaining *excess primer*.

asymmetric primer ratio The ratio of excess primer to limiting primer used in an asymmetric PCR procedure.

ATCC *See* American Type Culture Collection.

ATEE *N*-Acetyl-L-tyrosine ethyl ester.

atom per cent excess The concentration of an isotope in a sample, expressed as the difference between the percentage of the atoms existing as the isotope in that sample and the percentage of the atoms existing as the isotope in the element found in its natural state.

atomic absorption spectroscopy A method used for the quantitative determination of metals. The sample is burnt in a flame through which ultra-violet light, generated from a lamp specific for the element under investigation, is passed. Attenuation of the beam is detected using a photomultiplier and converted into an electrical signal which is recorded on a chart or converted directly to concentration or amount using a microprocessor.

ATP *See* adenosine triphosphate

atrazine A triazine used as a herbicide that inhibits photosynthetic electron transport.

attached X chromosome A chromosome consisting of two homologous X chromosomes that are joined and that share a single centromere.

attenuated vaccine A vaccine produced using an attenuated strain of virus or bacterium.

attenuation (1) In physics, the loss of power that occurs when radiation is passed through matter. (2) In microbiology, the loss of virulence of a pathogenic organism that occurs when the culture is repeatedly subcultured under controlled conditions.

attenuator A sequence of bases that occurs in the leader sequence of some operons and controls transcription. Synthesis of RNA may be terminated at this site. The expression of the structural genes associated with the attenuator may be affected by the level of a specific metabolite.

Autoanalyzer Registered name applied to fully automated analytical systems marketed by Technicon. The Autoanalyzer is based on automatic sampling and continuous flow through a variable manifold (which can be adopted as required for colourimetric, enzymic or other reactions) to a detector (colorimeter, absorptiometer, fluorometer, etc.). The samples are kept separate by bubbles of gas.

autoclave An appliance, essentially a pressure cooker, used to obtain sterile media or to destroy microbially contam-

inated material such as used petri culture plates. The material is placed in a container which is sealed and heated, having been vented of air. Any living organism is killed by the superheated steam generated under pressure.

autograft A graft derived from the tissue of the recipient.

Autographa californica **nuclear polyhedrosis virus** Type species of the subgroup A of Baculovirus genus, nuclear polyhedrosis virus (NPV), originally isolated from the alfalfa looper. It is used as a cloning vector for expression of foreign DNA sequences inserted after the polyhedrin promoter.

auto-immune disease A disease in which auto-immunity is one of the contributory factors. Such diseases include Addison's disease and rheumatoid arthritis.

auto-immunity An abnormal condition in which individuals develop antibodies to constituents of their own cells or tissues.

autolysate A product of cell decomposition produced by autolysis.

autolysis The breakdown of animal or plant products as a result of the action of enzymes contained within the cells or tissue affected.

automated DNA synthesizer *See* oligonucleotide synthesizer, phosphoramidite method.

automated enzyme analysis A technique in which an instrument is used to carry out a number of assays based on an enzyme-dependent procedure. It is used to determine levels of substrates using specific enzymes or levels of enzymes using specific substrates. Analysers continuously record the reaction or record its extent after a fixed time. In the latter case, the maximum extent of the reaction should be set within the substrate/enzyme concentrations such that not more than 15 per cent of the substrate is used.

autonomic nervous system (ANS) The part of the nervous system in vertebrates that supplies cardiac and smooth muscle. It controls activities that under normal conditions are involuntary. Its activities are coordinated from higher centres located in the medulla oblongata and hypothalamus of the brain.

autonomously replicating sequence A DNA sequence contained in a vector that will, if present and inserted into a suitable host, induce the formation of copies of itself.

autopolyploid Descriptive of an organism in which the chromosome number of an otherwise normal organism has become multiplied.

autoradiography A technique in which an image of a radioactive specimen is obtained using a photographic or X-ray-sensitive emulsion. The emulsion is carried on a film or plate or, for microautoradiography, used to coat the sample directly. Ionizing radiation, emitted by radioactive compounds used as markers or labels, results in the production of image grains which are fixed using normal photographic developers. Whole or sectioned organisms, subcellular particles, nucleic acids, enzymes and low-molecular-weight metabolites may be subjected to autoradiography. In general, both macromolecules and other chemicals are separated by any of a number of electrophoretic or chromatographic techniques. The autoradiograph then reveals the position of the compound on the carrier matrix. In molecular biology, autoradiography is used to reveal the position of hybridized nucleic acids in blot tests.

autosome Any chromosome other than the sex chromosomes. These occur in homologous pairs in diploid cells.

autotroph An organism that utilizes carbon dioxide as its major source of carbon and obtains energy from the sun through photosynthesis (photoautotroph) or from organic or inorganic reduced chemicals (chemoautotroph).

auxin A plant growth substance. Auxins include both natural and synthetic substances. The natural auxins are indoleacetic acid (IAA) and indoleacetonitrile (IAN). Synthetic auxins, which are used for weed control or as herbicides, include naphthaleneacetic acid, indolebutyric acid and 2,4-dichlorophenoxyacetic acid. Natural auxins are formed in plant apices from where they diffuse through the tissue stimulating cell elongation in growth and tropic movements.

auxochrome The part of a chromophore that modifies its properties in relation to absorption of light. This includes groups such as amine, chloro, hydroxyl and methyl that either increase (hyperchromic) or decrease (hypochromic) the intensity of absorption or cause shifts to a longer (bathochromic) or shorter (hypsochromic) wavelength.

auxotroph A strain of organisms unable to synthesize a given organic molecule required for their own growth; growth occurs when the required compound is supplied in the food. *Compare* prototroph.

available electrons Those electrons present in any compound or element, which is used as a substrate, that are not involved in orbitals with oxygen and are thus available either for transfer of oxygen or synthetic reductive reactions. The number of available electrons per mole of substrate is equal to four times the total oxygen demand (TOD), since four electrons are required to reduce one molecule of oxygen.

avidin A glycoprotein component of raw egg white that can complex with biotin, producing a vitamin deficiency. It is used as a signal molecule in affinity labelling.

avidin–biotin reaction A binding reaction between the glycoprotein from egg white (avidin) and biotin (vitamin H) exploited in a number of assay methods (utilizing appropriate indicator molecules such as antibodies, enzymes, fluorescent dyes, electron-dense proteins, etc.) to localize specific macromolecular in cells, tissue sections and blots. For example, in ELISA techniques an enzyme conjugated to avidin can be used to bind to biotinylated antibody.

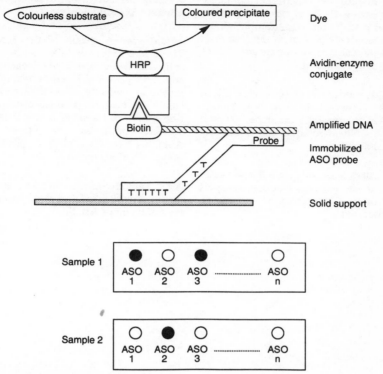

Use of avidin-biotin reaction in detection of amplified DNA

avidity The net combining power of an antibody molecule with its corresponding antigen.

axenic culture A microbial culture that contains only one species of organism.

axial mixing The disturbance of a liquid flowing through a vessel caused by parts of the liquid flowing at rates greater than, or less than, the average flow rate. Axial mixing is a common problem in bioreactors.

axial ratio (1) In crystallography, the ratio of the dimensions $a:b:c$ of a crystalline body, when b is one. (2) In colloids and macromolecules, the ratio of the length of the longest axis (L) to that of the shortest axis (D). This is determined by sedimentation or viscosity measurements. For a spherical particle $L/D = 1$, whereas for pro-

tein fibre such as myosin, L/D is around 100.

axon A long, unbranched projection arising from the cell body of a neurone.

azeotrope A liquid of fixed composition produced by condensation of the vapour obtained at constant boiling point (temperature) when a completely miscible liquid system is distilled. The composition and boiling point of the azeotrope varies with external pressure. For example, the ethanol: water mixture that is formed in a ratio of around 96:4 when bioethanol is distilled at standard atmospheric pressure.

azeotropic distillation The separation of an azeotropic mixture of two compounds in the liquid phase by the addition of another liquid. The additional liquid combines with the original liquids to form two new azeotropic mixtures with different compositions, allowing them to be separated by fractional distillation. For example, dehydrated ethanol (<99%) can be obtained from the ethanol–water azeotrope by addition of benzene or cyclohexane.

azeotropic mixture A mixture of liquids in which the composition of the liquid phase and the vapour phase are the same, so that it is not possible to separate the liquids by fractional distillation.

azide A salt of hydrazoic acid that acts as an inhibitor of the terminal electron transport chain, forming coordination complexes with cytochrome.

2′-azino-bis-3-thylbenthiazoline-6-sulphonate *See* ABTS.

Azotobacter A genus of the eubacteria. These free-living, rod-like, gram-negative soil bacteria are capable of nitrogen fixation and have been produced commercially as aids to composting or as 'biological fertilizer'. The bacteria produce a polysaccharide similar in chemical composition to the alginate produced by brown algae. Attempts have been made to produce this polysaccharide commercially.

AZT Azidothymadine; an analogue of thymadine that blocks DNA replication used in the treatment of AIDS.

B

B chromosomes Accessory chromosomes that are additional to the normal complement. They are found in many plant and animal species, including the important crop plants maize and rye.

B line A male fertile line used for maintaining male sterility in the production of hybrid seeds.

B lymphocyte A type of lymphocyte found in bone marrow in man. B lymphocytes are the precursors of antibody-producing plasma cells.

bacillus A rod-shaped bacterium of any genus.

Bacillus A genus of aerobic spore-forming, rod-shaped bacteria. *Bacillus* species are generally soil organisms and are chemo-organotrophic, being able to use a wide variety of organic compounds. Some species are pathogens. Most have simple nutrient requirements, requiring at most a few amino acids or B vitamins as growth factors. Three subgroups are classified on the basis of the spore form. In the first, the diameter of the spore is never greater than that of the cell. In the second, the spore is oval and thick-walled, and in the third group, the spore is spherical.

Bacillus licheniformus A species of bacterium that is used as a host organism for the industrial production of mammalian proteins by fermentation following introduction of a foreign gene using the technique of genetic engineering.

Bacillus popillae A bacterium that infects larvae of the Japanese beetle *Popilla japonica*. It has been used as a biopesticide to control the beetle.

Bacillus subtilis A bacterium widely used

in genetic engineering as a host for the replication of phages and plasmids.

Bacillus thuringiensis (Bt) One of a number of bacteria that are characterized by the formation of protein crystals in association with their resting spores. These crystals are highly toxic to the larvae of Lepidoptera (butterflies) and related forms. The crystals consist of a protein that is insoluble under acid conditions but dissolves when placed in alkaline conditions as occur in the larval gut. The dissolved protein attacks the gut cell wall, causing diffusion of the alkaline contents into the blood of the insect, resulting in paralysis of the insect. Any spores ingested at the same time may germinate, invade the tissue of the larva and cause death. Preparations of protein crystals and spores of a number of strains of *B. thuringiensis* are now produced as pest control agents, being effective against a range of caterpillars and mosquito larvae.

bacitracin A peptide with antibiotic properties formed by *Bacillus licheniformis*.

Bacitracin

back mixing The disturbance of a liquid flowing through a vessel caused by a proportion of that liquid flowing at a rate slower than the average flow rate. In bioreactors, back mixing reduces the throughput of the system.

back mutation A mutation that causes a

mutant gene to regain its wild-type function.

backcross A procedure in which progeny (F_1) are crossed with one of the parents. It is used as a test to determine whether an individual is homozygous or heterozygous for a particular gene. For homozygous parents described as AA (double dominant) and aa (double recessive) the ratio of Aa to AA to aa in the F_2 generation would be 2:1:1. The phenotypically identical AA and Aa may be distinguished by use of the backcross since the cross between the homozygous dominant F_1 and the homozygous recessive parent will produce offspring that are all Aa and show the dominant characteristic. In contrast, the cross between the heterozygous F_1 and the double recessive parent will produce offspring 50 per cent of which will show the recessive character.

backflushing A method for dislodging trapped particles on filters or membranes by reversing the usual direction of flow.

bacteria A division of the Protista consisting of single-celled prokaryotes. The bacteria and the cyanobacteria (blue-green algae) together form the Monera. The bacteria include the smallest organisms having a cellular structure; their average diameter is about 1 μm, but they range in length from 0.1 to 10 μm. Subgroups include the true bacteria (eubacteria), actinomycetes, chlamydobacteria, beggiatoa, myxobacteria, spirochaetes, mycoplasms and rickettsias. These organisms may be classified on the basis of their shape as a coccus, bacillus, spirillum or vibrio. The cells are generally enclosed within a rigid cell wall (which may be surrounded by a capsule or slime layer) and plasma membrane enclosing the cytoplasm which does not contain membrane-bound organelles as found in eukaryotic cells. The nuclear apparatus consists of a circular molecule of DNA, and ribosomes are present. Photosynthetic species do not have chloroplasts, the photosynthetic apparatus being associated with specific membranes or membrane-bound vesicles. Motile species possess one or several flagella. Most are saprophytes; some forms are pathogens of plants, humans, other animals and other microorganisms. Bacteria show a wide range of nutrient requirements and energy-related metabolism. Some require only minerals and a carbon source, such as glucose, others require complex media containing a wide variety of amino acids, vitamins and cofactors; some parasitic species will only grow on a medium of living animal tissue. Bacteria may be aerobic, anaerobic or facultative anaerobes. Bacteria are important in the breakdown of organic material in the soil, in nitrogen fixation and in rumen metabolism. Bacteria are used industrially in waste disposal processes, food processing, some fermentations, anaerobic digestion and production of antibiotics, as well as in providing a source of industrial enzymes and both bulk and fine chemicals.

bacterial chromosome A single DNA molecule up to 1 mm long, with a molecular weight of over 107 daltons, which may contain around 4000–5000 kilobases.

bacterial community A mixed culture of bacteria including populations of numerous different species.

bacterial population A group of bacteria belonging to the same species and exchanging genetic material among each other but having few contacts with other groups of the same species.

bactericidin An antibody that kills bacteria. *Compare* bacteriocide.

bacteriochlorophyll A type of chlorophyll that replaces chlorophyll a in the photosynthetic bacteria.

bacteriocide A toxic chemical that can destroy bacteria. Bacteriocides include the common disinfectants such as phenol, bleach (hypochlorite), as well as mercuric chloride and organic mercury compounds.

bacteriocin Any of the proteinaceous toxins liberated by many bacterial strains. These compounds are often named on the basis of the organisms which produce them:

for example, colicins are produced by E. coli and staphyloccins are produced by *Staphylococcus* species. Bacteriocins are active against closely related strains, while the producing cells remain immune. These proteins are encoded by plasmid genes rather than in the main bacterial genome.

bacteriolysis The destruction of bacteria by any means.

bacteriophage A subgroup of viruses that infect bacteria by insertion of their nucleic acid into the host. The smallest phage contain only 3 genes coded for on single-stranded RNA. Larger DNA-containing bacteriophage such as T4, which has *E. coli*

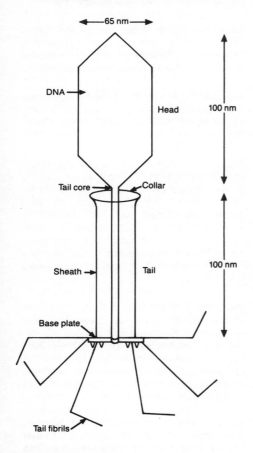

Structure of a bacteriophage

as a host, have a molecular weight of around 2.2×10^8 daltons and carry over 60 genes on a double-stranded DNA genome (which code for structural components of the phage) wound inside the head. Infection occurs after the phage becomes attached to the bacterial surface and the tail core is forced through the wall by contraction of the sheath. The nucleic acid is then injected into the bacterium through the hollow tail. Unlike viruses which infect eukaryotic cells, very few bacteriophage enter their hosts as whole particles. Infection may cause the host cell to switch metabolism entirely to formation of new bacteriophage, resulting in lysis of the host and release of new viral particles. Alternatively, the viral DNA may be inserted into the host chromosome and remain dormant, and be reproduced with the host chromosome as a prophage. *See* lysogen.

bacteriostat A chemical compound that inhibits the growth of bacteria without destroying them.

baculovirus A group of viruses that only infect arthropods. They are classified according to whether the virions become embedded (occluded) in inclusion bodies, and according to the shape and size of these bodies. The nuclear polyhedrosis viruses, characterized by polyhedral inclusion bodies, infect Lepidoptera, Diptera, Hymenoptera and Coleoptera. The granulosis viruses, which become occluded in capsule-shaped inclusion bodies, infect only Lepodoptera, whereas those that do not form inclusion bodies (non-occluded) infect a wide range of arthropods. The selectivity for their hosts, the ease of recognition and the fact that these viruses do not infect vertebrates make them of interest as potential biological pest control agents. They have also been widely investigated as expression vectors.

baculovirus expression vector A gene expression system based on the polyhedrin promoter from *Autographa californica* nuclear polyhedrosis virus.

bagasse The solid residues left after the juice has been squeezed from sugar cane. It

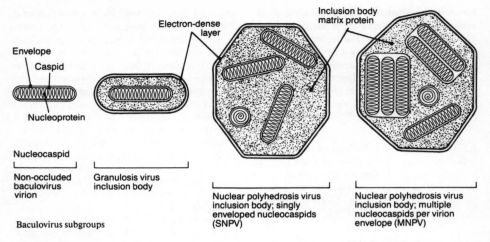

Envelope
Caspid
Nucleoprotein

Electron-dense
layer

Inclusion body
matrix protein

Nucleocaspid

Non-occluded
baculovirus
virion

Granulosis virus
inclusion body

Baculovirus subgroups

Nuclear polyhedrosis virus
inclusion body; singly
enveloped nucleocaspids
(SNPV)

Nuclear polyhedrosis virus
inclusion body; multiple
nucleocaspids per virion
envelope (MNPV)

is used as a fuel to supply energy for cane crushing and for the distillation of alcohol following the fermentation of cane juice or molasses.

bakers' yeast Strains of *Saccharomyces cerevisiae* propagated by pure culture methods using cane or beet molasses as substrate under highly aerobic conditions. The yeasts are harvested by centrifugation to produce a cream of about 20 per cent solids, which is pressed in a filter press or filtered in a rotary vacuum filter to produce compressed yeast. Alternatively, the yeast may be dried. In general, and in contrast to the yeasts used in brewing, distilling and wine making, these varieties of yeast are not proprietary.

bakery foods The main baked product that uses microorganisms in its production is bread. Most breads are made with wheat flour using bakers' yeast as a levening agent. The yeast gives off carbon dioxide produced during metabolism of sugars present in the dough, resulting in an aerated sponge-like structure which is fixed during the baking process. The yeast also contributes to flavour and the maturation of the dough, particularly through the formation of alcohol which influences the colloidal nature of the flour proteins.

balanced lethals A situation where several recessive lethal genes are carried at different loci, so that each homologous chromo-some carries at least one lethal gene. However, these genes are associated with inversions, so that no recombination occurs between the homologous chromosomes.

ball mill A rotating drum used to crush and grind materials through the action of a number of heavy balls that move freely within the drum.

banding A pattern of contrasting bands seen in chromosomes after staining or under phase contrast microscopy. Such bands are particularly visible in metaphase chromo-somes, where they may be enhanced by specific treatments with enzymes and/or heat combined with the use of basic dyes. Such chromosome banding techniques may be used to recognize specific chromosomes within a set.

Barr body A portion of heterochromatin identifiable by staining of the interphase nucleus of the homogametic sex (usually female) of some animals. The number of Barr bodies is one less than the number of X chromosomes, hence can be used to detect abnormalities characterized by deficient or multiple complements of sex chromo-somes. In humans, an apparent female having only one X chromosome will have no Barr body, whereas an abnormal female having three X chromosomes has two Barr bodies.

basal body A structure found at the base of a cilium or a eukaryotic flagellum associated with the assembly of microtubules in these organelles.

basal metabolic rate The rate of metabolism of an animal in its resting state. It is determined by measuring oxygen consumption.

base analogue A compound similar to or a derivative of a base found in nucleic acids. Analogues such as 5-bromouracil and 2-aminopurine are used as mutagens. These may be incorporated into DNA, in place of thymine and adenine, respectively, resulting in incorrect base pairings in cell generations some time later.

base calling The determination of a DNA or RNA base sequence.

base pairing The interaction, through hydrogen bonding, that occurs between opposite purine and pyrimidine bases in nucleic acids. Stable base pairs are formed between adenine and thymine (A + T) and between guanine and cytosine (G + C). The specificity of base pairing forms the basis of all interactions between nucleic acids and the transfer of information from one molecular species to another, as in the synthesis of RNA on a DNA template or the interaction between complementary nucleotide sequences of tRNA and mRNA in protein synthesis. It also forms the basis of recognition and control signals in protein synthesis.

base pairs Pairs of nucleotides linked through hydrogen bonding which occurs between complementary bases, A binding with T and G binding with C.

base ratio The ratio of the number of adenine and thymine bases (A + T) to the number of guanine and cytosine bases (G + C) found in double-stranded DNA. As a result of the specific base pairing, the amount of adenine is equal to the amount of thymine and the amount of guanine is equal to the amount of cytosine. For a given type of DNA or for the total DNA in a given species, the ratio (A + T) to (G + C) is constant, although it varies widely between species. For instance, in bacteria it ranges from over 2 to less than 0.4.

basement membrane A thin layer of mucopolysaccharides and fibrous material that acts as a barrier between epithelial cells and the underlying tissue.

base-specific ribonucleases An enzyme that cleaves a molecule of RNA at a specific base: for example, RNase T1 is specific for G residues, RNase U2 is A-specific, RNase PhyM cleaves at both A and U residues, RNase from *Bacillus cereus* cleaves at U and C residues. These ribonucleases are used in RNA sequence analysis.

basic Descriptive of pH greater than 7.0

basidiocarp The fruiting body of the higher basidiomycetes (e.g., mushrooms, toadstools and similar bodies).

basidiomycetes The most highly evolved group of fungi, characterized by the fact that spores are borne externally on a basidium within large fruiting bodies. This group includes the mushrooms, puff balls, bracket fungi, rusts, smuts, stinkhorns and other similar forms.

basidium A club-shaped structure formed from the terminal cell of a hypha which produces the haploid basidiospores in basidiomycetes. Pointed outgrowths, known as sterigmata, are produced on the basidium. There are generally four, but in some species only two form. The tip of each sterigma swells to produce the basidiospore. The young basidium has two nuclei which fuse, followed by meiosis to give four nuclei, one of which passes into each basidiospore.

basipetal A sequence of development in which the youngest parts are at the apex and the oldest at the base.

basket centrifuge A centrifuge containing a perforated basket lined with filter cloth, that retains solids whilst allowing the filtrate to pass through.

basophil A type of white blood cell that contains cytoplasmic granules that stain with basic dyes such as methylene blue. The cells contain histamine and the granules contain heparin. They comprise about 50 per cent of the white cells in human blood.

batch culture A discontinuous system used for culturing microorganisms, waste treatment or manufacturing products of value, characterized by a single loading or inoculation into fresh medium at the start of the process and a single harvesting stage at the end, usually when the substrate has been exhausted. Organisms grown in batch systems generally show the sigmoid growth curve, undergoing exponential growth for a few generations following an initial lag phase. Growth then ceases, and the cells may lyze, die or stop growing.

batch digester An anaerobic digester run as a batch culture.

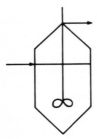

Batch digester

batch fermentation A fermentation system run as a batch culture.

batch process *See* batch culture.

batch recycle culture A discontinuous culture technique in which the cells are harvested at the end of the growth phase and reintroduced into fresh medium, which results in a new cycle of growth being initiated. This process is used in the manufacture of secondary products in order to increase the substrate use efficiency, since raw materials are not used to generate new cells for each cycle as in the case of a conventional batch process.

BDUR *See* bromodeoxyuridine.

bead mill A ball mill loaded with glass or ceramic beads used to rupture cells. Many bead mills are fitted with high-speed rotating discs to increase cell disruption, and with cooling jackets to limit temperature rises during the grinding process.

bead-bed reactor A reactor that consists of a glass column packed with glass beads providing a large surface area for cell growth. A growth medium is constantly pumped through the column and cells are harvested by trypsin treatment.

bed volume (V_t) The total volume occupied by the chromatographic packing material. In column chromatography, it can be determined by filling the tube to the original level of the bed with water and measuring the volume.

beer An alcoholic beverage produced by the yeast-based fermentation of malted grains with added hops. Ground malt is mixed with water to produce a mash, which is then heated to around 60°C, at which temperature the malt amylases liquefy the starch. This liquid is clarified and filtered to produce a sweet wort which is traditionally boiled in copper vessels with added hops. This sterilizes the solution and inactivates the enzymes, as well as flocculating numerous protein and phenolic impurities which are removed. During this process, the solution of sugars is concentrated to the required solids of around 12 per cent. An important reaction which occurs at the same time is the isomerization and hydrolysis of humulones, the bitter compounds from the hops. The cooled wort is then inoculated with yeast. There are two major types of beer, which are distinguished on the basis of the yeast used. The first are the lagers produced using a bottom yeast (*Saccharomyces uvarum*, which flocculates and settles as the fermentation proceeds). The ales produced using top yeasts (*S. ceriviseae* which rises to the surface during fermentation).

Beggiatoa Filamentous chemosynthetic sulphur bacteria.

belt press A mechanical device used to dewater sludge, pulp derived from the extraction of plant material, etc. The press consists of one or two endless belts which are rotated continuously under tension. The slurry is passed between the belts, or between the belt and a perforated drum, resulting in moisture being squeezed out leaving a semi-solid cake.

bench-scale Descriptive of a process, of possible industrial potential, in the early stage of development when it is still being investigated in the laboratory. The term may also be applied to small-scale experimental investigation or simulation of an industrial process. Such experiments may be performed in order to obtain data of use in the scaling up of the process through pilot plant work to an industrial plant.

Benedict's test A biochemical test for reducing sugars based on an alkaline copper sulphate solution and sodium citrate. Reducing sugars produce a coloured precipitate which varies from green through yellow to red with increasing amounts of sugar.

benzyl penicillin A semisynthetic penicillin.

6-benzyladenine *See* 6-benzylaminopurine.

6-benzylaminopurine A synthetic cytokinin, also known as 6-benzyladenine.

bequerel (Bq) A unit of radioactive decay equal to one disintegration per second.

berberine An isoquinoline alkaloid with antiseptic properties that is derived from plants including *Coptis japonica*, *Phellodendron amurense* and *Thalictrum rugosum*.

bestatin An immunomodulator produced by *Streptomyces olivoreticuli*.

beta-counter A device for quantifying the radioactive decay from a beta-emitting radioactive isotope. This can be either a

Geiger–Müller counter or a liquid scintillation counter.

beta-decay The disintegration of radioactive isotopes that results in emission of beta-particles. The beta-particles may be detected by use of a Geiger–Müller tube, by autoradiography or using a scintillation counter. This enables radioactive isotopes to be used as markers in studies of biological reactions since long-life radioisotopes are readily available for hydrogen (^{3}H), carbon (^{14}C), sulphur (^{35}S), phosphorus (^{32}P) and other elements of biological interest.

beta-interferon *See* fibroblastic interferon.

beta-lactamase *See* penicillinase.

beta-oxidation *See* fatty acid oxidation.

beta-pleated sheet An arrangement of protein molecules associated with secondary and tertiary structure, in which the polypeptide chains are linked by hydrogen bonds between amino and carbonyl groups.

BGG *See* bovine gamma globulin.

Bicine *See* zwitterionic buffer.

biennial A plant which has a life cycle that extends over two growing seasons (two years). In the first season, leaves are often in the form of a prostrate rosette and much of the assimilate is stored in an underground root which overwinters. In the second year, this stored material is used to produce an erect, flowering stem, which then produces seeds.

bilateral symmetry The property of an object in which only one plane, usually passing longitudinally along the mid line, divides it into two halves which are mirror images of one another.

bile A secretion of the vertebrate liver that contains cholesterol, bile pigments (biliverdin and bilirubin), bile salts (sodium salts of cholic acid combined with taurine or glycine) and lecithin. It is discharged into the small intestine through the bile duct.

binding site A specific arrangement of atoms or molecules that is recognized by, and forms the point of attachment for, an ion, compound, antibody, virus, cell or organism on another structure or organism.

binomial nomenclature A system for naming plants and animals devised by Linnaeus in the 18th century. Each species is given a generic name and a species name. The name of the discoverer is written in an abbreviated form after the species name. The exact procedure and rules for naming new organisms are laid down by International Codes of Nomenclature. These include the International Code of Nomenclature for Cultivated Plants, the International Code of Botanical Nomenclature and the International Code of Zoological Nomenclature. When a new organism is discovered it is named in Latin, a description is published in the same language and a holotype or type specimen is preserved. In general, the first or oldest name for a given organism takes precedence. Although a given animal or plant must have a name that is unique for the kingdom, in several instances the same name has been given to a plant and an animal. Other oddities occur where stages of the life cycle of a given organism have been placed in different genera or even phyla.

bioaffinity sensor A biosensor system that is based on molecular recognition, for instance an immobilized antibody that detects a specific antigen.

bioassay A procedure for determining the level or concentration of a substance by measuring its effect on a living system under controlled conditions. Compounds such as vitamins, hormones and plant growth substances, which occur in very low concentrations, are often determined using bioassays since such methods are several orders of magnitude more sensitive than conventional chemical analysis.

Bio-beads S A polystyrene support material used in gel filtration chromatography with lipophilic solvents. Produced as a copolymer of styrene and divinylbenzene, it can be used for fractionation of compounds with molecular weights of up to 1.4×10^6.

biocatalysis A catalytic process in which the catalyst consists of, or is derived from, living organisms. The term is applied in particular to processes in which the objective is the production of bulk chemicals or other products of commercial interest.

biocatalyst A catalyst that consists of, or is derived from, a living organism or tissue, or cell culture. Biocatalysts may be categorized as follows:
1. Cells
   (a) Growing. The use of growing cells in suspension as biocatalysts is generally termed fermentation. Such processes may be distinguished as batch, fed batch or continuous.
   (b) Non-growing. Non-growing systems include the use of suspensions, cells retained within a semipermeable membrane, or cells immobilized in or on a solid support. Such immobilized cells may be used in a fixed bed, expanded bed, fluidized bed or fully mixed system.
2. Enzymes
   (a) Soluble enzyme systems. Soluble enzymes of varying purity may be used in solution, generally in a batch system, and are lost at the end of the reaction.
   (b) Immobilized enzymes. Enzymes may be entrapped, adsorbed on to surfaces or cross-linked to support material and then used in fixed bed, expanded bed or fully mixed systems.

biochemical oxygen demand (BOD) The amount of oxygen, expressed in milligrams per litre of water, taken up, owing to the respiratory activity of microorganisms growing on organic compounds present in the sample when incubated at 20°C for a fixed period (often five days). It is a measure of the degree of organic pollution of water. *See also* chemical oxygen demand.

biochemistry The study of the chemical processes and compounds occurring in living organisms.

biochip A device which combines a small-scale biosensor with an integrated circuit.

biocide A chemical compound that kills most living organisms in an unspecific manner.

biocoenosis *See* nitrogen fixation.

bioconversion The transformation of matter, from one form to another, by living organisms or enzymes.

biodegradable Descriptive of substances that can be decomposed by the activity of microorganisms.

biodegradation A process in which material is broken down to its chemical constituents by the action of living organisms. The term is often restricted to the breakdown of wastes released into the environment. In general, biodegradation is regarded as a desirable process in contrast to biodeterioration.

biodeterioration Any undesirable change in the properties of non-living materials brought about by the biological activities of organisms resulting in the lessening of the intrinsic value of the materials to man. The change may be mechanical, physical, chemical or aesthetic and need not result in the chemical breakdown of the material. Almost any class of organisms may cause biodeterioration which includes the effects of microorganisms, insects, rodents, algae and birds. The processes of biodeterioration can be divided into three types. (1) Mechanical, which includes the gnawing and boring of non-nutritive materials such as insulation on cable, lead pipes, etc., by insects or rodents, or damage to buildings and other structures due to growth of plant roots. (2) Chemical, which includes both assimilatory and dissimilatory effects. The former are typified by the use of substrates in the material as a nutrient source and the latter are typified by situations in which the organism produces a metabolic product, such as an acid or toxin, which may corrode the material or render it unfit for use. (3) Fouling and soiling, such as the blocking of pipes, fouling of ships' bottoms, staining of surfaces, production of mycotoxin, etc.

biodiagnostic An analytical tool, often available in kit form, that depends on a specific biological response as the primary determinant. Biodiagnostics include enzyme, immunological and nucleic acid based test systems.

bioelectronics The investigation and application of processes that combine biosensors or other biological activities with electronic circuits.

bioengineering The science of manufacture and use of artificial replacements for various parts or organs of the body which no longer function normally because of damage due to disease or trauma.

biofilm A layer of microorganisms irreversibly adhered to the surface on which they are growing by secreted polysaccharides and glycoproteins.

biofilter An item of equipment used in the treatment of sewage and the purification of industrial wastewaters that uses active biomass growing on a solid support. Biofilters are circular or rectangular tanks made from concrete containing a graded biosupport medium, usually clinker, slag, stone or gravel, packed to a depth of 1.8 m. They include septic tanks, low-rate percolating filters, double filtration systems and high-rate filtration systems.

biofouling The blockage or coating of a system due to the growth of any organism.

biofuel A solid, liquid or gaseous fuel obtained from biological raw materials (biomass). The conversion process may be accomplished by thermo-chemical or biological means. The major biofuels produced biologically are biogas generated by anaerobic digestion (biomethanation) and fuel ethanol generated by a yeast-based fermentation of molasses, sugar cane juice or hydrolysed starch.

biofuel cell A device that uses biological reactions in association with the principles of a fuel cell. Biofuel cells may be classified as indirect or direct fuel cells. In an indirect cell, the electroactive species, such as hydrogen, is generated by anaerobic digestion or photolysis of water and subsequently oxidized at the anode of a conventional hydrogen/oxygen fuel cell. In a direct cell, a redox protein is used as an intermediate in the direct electron transfer from a substrate to an electrode. For instance, the complete oxidation of methanol, catalysed by methanol dehydrogenase and formate dehydrogenase, can be used to generate a current using a complex organic compound such as N, N, N', N'-tetramethyl-p-phenylaminediamine as a mediator. Such systems are still at the experimental stage, but have been demonstrated to give a steady current for over 24 hours. Biofuel cells could use the organic matter in food processing and other organic industrial waste streams as a substrate, thus combining water treatment with energy production.

biofungicide A preparation based on or derived from a living organism that is used to control diseases caused by fungi.

biogas A mixture of methane and carbon dioxide along with traces of other gases, such as hydrogen, nitrogen, hydrogen sulphide and water vapour, which is produced during anaerobic digestion or biomethanation.

biogas digester *See* anaerobic digester.

biogas plant An anaerobic digester together with ancillary equipment. These additional pieces of equipment include systems for storing and processing the influent (substrate), storing and/or treating the biogas produced, using the gas to produce heat or power, and storing and/or treating the effluent.

Bio-Gel P A cross-linked polyacrylamide support material used in gel filtration chromatography. The gel is prepared by copolymerization of acrylmide and N,N'-methylene-diacrylamide in aqueous solution. It is commercially available in ten porosities up to a molecular exclusion limit of 4×10^5 for globular proteins and 1.5×10^3 for linear polymers.

biogenesis The belief that living organisms can arise only from other living organisms and not from non-living material by spontaneous generation.

biohazard Any biological agent that represents a hazard to the environment. In particular spent broth, condensates or other wastes from systems in which pathogenic or genetically manipulated organisms have been grown. Inactivation by sterilization is required prior to disposal.

bioinsecticide An insecticide based on a microorganism, for instance *Bacillus thuringiensis* which is used to control mosquitoes and blackflies.

bioleaching The use of microorganisms in solution to recover metals from ores.

biological clock A hypothetical mechanism used to account for the occurrence of circadian and other biorhythms.

biological control Methods of controlling pests by interfering with their life cycle, attacking them with preparations of biological origin, or using their natural enemies to destroy them.

biological oxygen demand *See* biochemical oxygen demand.

biology The study of living things.

bioluminescence The production of light by living organisms by the enzymic oxidation of an ATP/luciferin complex in a reaction catalysed by luciferase. Bioluminescence occurs in many bacteria, algae, fungi, insects and many marine species, especially those found in deep water.

bioluminescence assay A method used to quantify the ATP content of biological samples. The method uses the luciferase/luciferin complex from the firefly. The assay is very sensitive and can be used for the detection and numeration of populations of bacteria and other microorganisms.

bioluminescence counter A sensitive device, based on a photomultiplier and associated electronic circuits, used to quantify the amount of light generated in a bioluminescence assay.

biomass (1) In microbiology, the cell mass produced during fermentation or the total weight of living matter in a population. (2) In renewable energy systems, the yield of organic matter that may be used as a source of energy and/or chemicals. Since this material is largely of plant origin, it is more correctly referred to as phytomass. However, the term biomass has a wider and general acceptance.

biomass concentration The weight of cells, expressed on a wet waste or dry weight basis, per unit volume of medium or fermenter volume.

biomass energy The use of biological materials, generally of plant origin, as a source of energy.

biomass fouling *See* fouling.

biomass hold-up The living microbial or cell culture mass present in a fermenter or bioreactor, or associated with support particles.

biomethanation The anaerobic fermentation of organic materials to produce biogas

(a mixture of methane and carbon dioxide). *See* anaerobic digestion.

biomethanation system A biogas plant or anaerobic digester integrated with an enterprise such as a farm, waste disposal, landfill site, sewage works or industrial factory.

biopesticide A pesticide in which the active ingredient is a virus, fungus or bacteria, or a natural product derived from a plant source.

biophotolysis The use of photosynthetic organisms to cleave water into hydrogen and oxygen.

biopolymer Any of the different types of large molecules formed by living organisms including nucleic acids, proteins, polysaccharides and lipids.

bioprobe A type of biosensor in which the catalyst is immobilized with the detection device. Examples include an enzyme electrode (where the catalyst is an enzyme) or a bioprobe electrode (where the catalyst consists of intact cells).

bioreactor A vessel used to carry out a biological reaction. The term may be applied to a reactor used for the culture of aerobic cells, or to columns or packed beds of im-

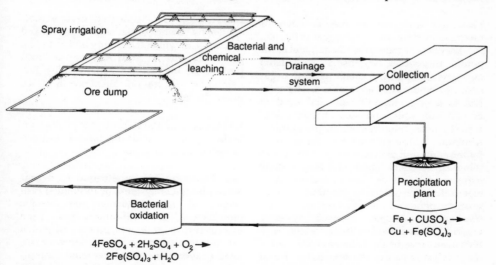

Bioleaching (reproduced with permission from *A Revolution in Biotechnology*, ICSU Press)

mobilized cells or enzymes. Bioreactors containing immobilized biocatalysts are used to carry out biological transformations such as hydrolytic reactions, isomerization, decolorization, etc. In some forms, the bioreactors may be used as biosensors. In such applications, a flowing stream of sample, buffer and reactants moves through the immobilized bed. Sensors are placed before and/or after the reactor and the difference determined.

bioremediation The use of microorganisms or plants to clean up environmental pollution. The term is often applied to the removal of oil, petrochemical residues or pesticides from soil or groundwater.

biorhythm A physiological or behavioural event displaying a periodic pattern of occurrence in a living organism or population. It is regulated by a hypothetical biological clock. The term includes circadian rhythms, menstrual cycles and annual rhythms of migration and hibernation.

bioscrubbing A process in which a packed bed of immobilized microorganisms or a growing culture is used to remove toxic materials or pollutants from a gas or liquid stream passed through the bed or culture.

biosensor A device that uses an agent of biological origin, or a biological principle, for detecting or measuring a chemical compound. In general, biosensors use isolated enzymes, immunosystems, tissues, organelles or whole cells as catalysts. The catalyst is usually immobilized and used in conjunction with a physico-chemical device. The latter monitors the chemical transformation of the substance under analysis by the immobilized catalyst, and translates it into an electrical signal. This may be done using a range of devices including redox electrodes, ion-selective electrodes, thermistors, photon counters, optical devices, mechanical systems, acoustic systems, calorimetric methods or fluorometers. Such biosensors may be described as bioprobes if the catalyst is part of the sensing device or bioreactors if the solution is monitored

before and after passing through the chamber containing the catalyst. Biosensors have advantages in terms of specificity, sensitivity, rapid response and the applicability to turbid or viscous samples. Use of biosensors enables repeated measurements with the same enzyme, cells, etc. This approach can be applied to the determination of a wide range of biological products and metabolic intermediates, including antibiotics, vitamins, amino acids and growth factors, as well as the determination of xenobiotics including biocides, detergents and synthetic organic compounds.

biosorption The removal of metal ions from solution by microorganisms.

biosphere The regions of the earth inhabited by living organisms.

biostat A continuous culture vessel in which the concentration of biomass is monitored and controlled at a constant level using a parameter other than turbidity, such as the level of a specific nutrient.

biosurfactant A compound produced by living organisms that increases the solubility of substances, such as oil, in water by reducing surface tension.

biosynthesis The synthesis of organic molecules by living organisms using linked reactions, in which the energy and reducing power are derived from ATP and reduced pyrimidine nucleotides generated by fermentation, respiration, chemosynthesis or photosynthesis.

biotargeted probe A probe based on antibodies or nucleic acids that binds to a specific cell macromolecule.

biotechnology The application of organisms, biological systems or biological processes to manufacturing and service industries. This definition has been extended to include any process in which organisms, tissues, cells, organelles or isolated enzymes are used to convert biological or other raw materials to products of greater value, as well as the design and use of reactors, fermenters, downstream processing, analytical and control equipment associated with biological manufacturing processes. Aspects of genetic engineering and bioengineering are also sometimes included in consideration of biotechnology, as are aspects of agriculture, horticulture and forestry where *in vitro* techniques of propagation or genetic manipulation are used. Biotechnologies can be divided into the traditional areas of fermentation for the production of potable beverages, foodstuffs, antibiotics and waste treatment, and the new biotechnologies, including the production and use of organisms which have been genetically manipulated for the large-scale production of single-cell protein, proteins, biologically active peptides, vaccines and other products of health care interest, as well as the use of hybridomas for the production of monoclonal antibodies for diagnostic and therapeutic use.

biotin A vitamin of the B complex that functions as a co-enzyme in some reactions associated with the fixation of carbon dioxide (e.g., fatty acid synthesis).

Biotin

The tight binding of biotin by avidin is used to amplify the detection of protein–protein or DNA–DNA interaction in biodiagnostics. *See* avidin–biotin reaction.

biotinylation The linking of biotin to macromolecules such as DNA or protein. For example, a DNA probe can be biotinylated by incorporating biotin derivatives of deoxyribonucleotides by nick translation. The hybridized product can then be detected by binding to an avidin enzyme complex. A substrate is provided for the enzyme (usually peroxidase or alkaline phosphatase) resulting in a coloured pro-

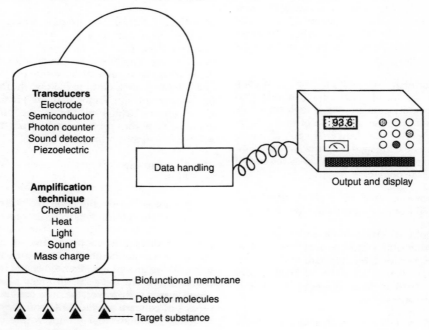

Biosensors – a unified concept

duct that indicates the position of the biotinylated probe.

biotype A group of organisms with the same genetic characteristics.

bisacrylamide The cross-linking agent employed in the formation of polyacrylamide gels used in electrophoresis.

bisexual A hermaphrodite.

Biuret test A biochemical test that produces a violet colour on addition of sodium hydroxide and a 1 per cent copper sulphate solution to a sample of protein. The reaction is the basis for a qualitative test for protein and when quantified provides a useful colourimetric method.

bivalent Two homologous chromosomes which become paired during meiosis.

black smoker A deep-sea hot vent. Bacteria have been found associated with such vents that can survive under pressure at temperatures of over 300°C.

blastocyst The embryonic stage of mammals that consists of about 64 cells (the outer trophoblast cells and the cells of the inner cell mass) and that implants itself into the uterine wall.

blastoderm A multinuclear embryonic stage that results from nuclear divisions, without division of the cytoplasm of the zygotic cell, and migration of nuclei to the periphery of the oocyte. A cellular blastoderm is established when cell membranes form around each of the nuclei at the periphery of the oocyte.

blastomere One of several small cells formed from a zygote following cleavage.

blastula A multicellular embryonic stage resulting from complete cleavage divisions that apportion the cytoplasm of the zygotic cell into that of a number of smaller cells. The blastular stage precedes gastrulation and organogenesis.

blinding The inactivation of a significant proportion of a filter's surface caused by particles slightly larger than the filter pore size becoming wedged in the pores.

blocking antibody An antibody that inhibits further antibody–antigen reactions.

blocking primer An annealed, non-extendable oligodeoxynucleotide that may arise during PCR.

blood The fluid which fills the vascular system. It consists of the liquid plasma containing both red corpuscles (erythrocytes) and white blood cells of several types, as well as platelets, proteins, salts, hormones and dissolved gases. It functions as a transport medium for respiratory gases, which may be transported in association with respiratory pigments, metabolites and excretory products. Components of the blood also contribute to the body's defence mechanism through production of antibodies and other activities of the white cells. Blood components are also involved in blood clotting following injury.

blood clotting See blood coagulation.

blood coagulation The process whereby blood is converted to a gel, or clot, following release from the circulation due to injury to the blood vessels. Coagulation is the result of the sequential activation of several soluble protein clotting factors (thrombin, thromboplastin, factor VIII, etc.) in the blood plasma which results in the production of a fibrous protein (fibrin) from the soluble precursor fibrinogen.

blood corpuscle See erythrocyte, white blood cell.

blood groups The classification of blood on the basis of the different antigens present on the surface of the erythrocytes. These antigens are distinguished by means of the specific serum antibodies that combine with them. Blood groups are inherited characteristics. There are over 20 different blood group systems. However, the most common groups of concern are the ABO and rhesus systems. There are four groups within the ABO system characterized by the presence of antigen A (group A), antigen B (group B), both antigens (group AB) or neither antigen (group O). The serum of group A contains antibody to group B, group B serum contains group A antibody, group AB contains no antibody and group O contains antibody to both antigens. If the wrong types of blood are mixed, the antigen–antibody reaction will lead to agglutination. Blood transfusions thus depend on the careful screening and matching of the blood used. Blood group antigens are also found in saliva, gastric juice and other similar body secretions.

blood plasma The clear, colourless fluid produced by centrifugation of uncoagulated vertebrate blood.

blood serum The clear, colourless fluid produced by centrifugation of coagulated vertebrate blood.

blood vascular system The continuous system of vessels and spaces through which blood is pumped around the body by the heart, or hearts, of an animal.

blood vessel A tubular structure that is part of the blood vascular system. Blood vessels include veins, arteries, venules, arterioles, capillaries and sinusoids.

blot transfer *See* northern blot, southern blot, western blot.

blue-green algae The Cyanophyta. *See* Cyanobacteria.

blunt end The end of a DNA molecule in which both strands terminate in the same position or base number. *Compare* sticky ends.

blunt end ligation In molecular biology, the joining of blunt-ended fragments of DNA using an enzyme such as T4 DNA ligase.

BOD *See* biochemical oxygen demand.

Bohr effect The effect of carbon dioxide on the capacity of the blood to carry oxygen.

Most respiratory pigments exhibit a negative Bohr effect since the volume of oxygen that the blood can hold is reduced when the pH is decreased as a result of dissolved carbon dioxide.

bombesin A protein produced by SCCL (small cell carcinoma of the lung) cells that acts as a growth factor for tumours.

bone The calcified connective tissue that forms the skeleton of higher vertebrates. The matrix of bone tissue contains about 35 per cent organic material (collagen fibres) and 70 per cent inorganic bone salts (mainly calcium phosphate known as hydroxyapatite). The bone minerals can be mobilized to provide the body with calcium or phosphate ions. This mobilization is controlled by calcitonin and parathyroid hormone.

botulism A serious, often fatal disease that results from ingestion of a toxin produced by the anaerobic spore-former Clostridium botulinum.

bovine gamma globulin (BGG) A type of serum protein, derived from cattle.

bovine papilloma virus A DNA virus causing warts on cattle. The virus is a potential vector for the transformation of mammalian cells. It replicates as a plasmid inside the host cell with a copy number of up to 200.

bovine serum albumin (BSA) A blood protein used as a standard in protein analyses.

bovine spongiform encephalopathy *See* BSE, spongiform encephalopathy.

Bowman–Birk inhibitors A group of protease inhibitors found in soya beans.

Bq *See* bequerel.

brandy An alcoholic beverage distilled from wine. Special types are recognized. Cognac, which comes from the Cognac region of France, is distilled in copper pots, in the presence of yeast shortly after fermentation has finished. The brandy is then stored for several years in oak barrels. Armagnac, which comes from another region of France, is obtained in a single distillation from wine that does not contain residual yeast.

Brevibacterium A fermentative bacterium used to produce amino acids.

brewers' yeast Strains of *Saccharomyces uvarum* or *S. cerevisiae* used in the production of beer.

brewing The art of producing beer. *See* ale, lager.

broad host range A plasmid or phage that is not specific to a single host species or strain and is able to replicate in a number of different hosts.

bromelain A glycoprotein with proteolytic activity obtained from pineapple stem.

bromodeoxyuridine (BDUR) A base analogue of thymidine.

bromophenol blue 3,3',5,5'-Tetrabromophenolsulphonephthalein; a dye used for visualization of proteins on gels following separation by electrophoresis.

5-bromouracil A base analogue used as a mutagen. This compound can be incorporated into DNA sequences in place of thymine and cause incorrect base pairing some time later.

broth A culture medium derived from a protein solution or hydrolysate; more generally, a suspension of cultured microorganisms.

broth conditioning A treatment applied in a fermentation process after harvesting in order to facilitate downstream processing. Processes such as pH modification, heat treatment or flocculation are applied to increase particle density and reduce viscosity and aggregation, leading to a reduction in fouling and facilitating the handling of solids.

brown algae The Phaeophyta; a commercial source of alginic acids.

brush border *See* microvillus.

BSA *See* bovine serum albumin.

BSE Bovine spongiform encephalopathy; one of a number of infectious diseases generally known as encephalopathies, which may be caused by an infective protein (prion). *See* spongiform encephalopathy.

Bt *See Bacillus thuringiensis.*

bubble column A type of fermenter or bioreactor used for the growth of plant cell cultures in liquid suspension. Air is bubbled into the bottom of a tall column, keeping the cells suspended in an expanded bed.

bubble point test A technique used to establish the integrity of filters, in which the gross flow of air through a prewetted membrane is detected. The sensitivity of the test decreases with increasing membrane area.

budding A mechanism of non-sexual reproduction found typically in yeasts, in which a small outgrowth develops into a new cell. This may remain attached to the parent cell or become detached.

buffer A chemical solution which is resistant to change in pH on the addition of acid or alkali. Buffer solutions commonly consist of a mixture of a weak acid and its conjugate base (e.g., acetic acid and sodium acetate) or a weak base and its conjugate acid (e.g., ammonium hydroxide and ammonium chloride). Traditionally, buffers based on inorganic salts (phosphate, carbonate) and organic acid salts (acetate, citrate, succinate, glycine, maleate, barbiturates, etc.) were used in biological experiments. In many cases these have been replaced by specific zwitterionic buffers. *In vivo* buffer systems are essential for maintaining the physiological pH of cytoplasm and extracellular fluids, with a phosphate buffer system being the main intracellular buffer, and a bicarbonate buffer the main extracellular one. Buffers are important in the isolation of subcellular particles, enzymes, proteins and nucleic acids from living material, as well as maintaining growth of cultured organisms, plant tissue cultures and animal cell lines. Buffers are also used in electrophoresis and some forms of chromatography.

bundle sheath A layer of cells which surrounds the vascular bundles of leaves. In C4 plants, the enzyme associated with the reductive assimilation of carbon dioxide through the photosynthetic carbon reduction cycle (rubisco) is restricted to the bundle sheath chloroplasts. In extreme C4 plants, such as sugar cane, maize and sorghum, these chloroplasts are larger than those of the mesophyll cells, and may have much reduced grana, or grana may be completely absent. In most leaves, the bundle sheath preferentially accumulates starch.

Bunsen coefficient (a) A unit defined as the volume of gas in millilitres, reduced to 0°C and 760 mm Hg pressure, dissolved in 1 millilitre of water.

buoyant density The equilibrium density at which a molecule comes to lie within a density gradient, formed from a solution of a material such as caesium chloride, when subjected to the force generated in an analytical centrifuge. The buoyant density of DNA increases with the content of cytosine plus guanine.

butanoic acid *See* butyric acid.

butanol An alcohol, produced in some bacterial fermentations, used as an industrial solvent.

buttermilk A fermented product obtained by culture of *Streptococcus lactis*, *S. cremoris* and/or *Leuconostoc cremoris* in pasteurized skimmed milk.

butyl alcohol *See* butanol.

butyric acid An organic acid produced in some bacterial fermentations.

C

C *See* cytosine.

C terminal The end of the chain of amino acids in a protein that contains a free carboxyl group (abbreviated to C).

C value A measure of the amount of DNA (expressed as picograms per cell) present in the haploid genome of an organism.

C$_2$ photosynthesis *See* photorespiration.

C$_3$ photosynthesis *See* C$_3$ plants.

C$_3$ plants The majority of oxygen-producing photoautotrophs. In C$_3$ plants, carbon dioxide assimilated during photosynthesis is fixed directly by the enzyme ribulose bisphosphate carboxylase and further metabolized through the photosynthetic carbon reduction cycle. The term C$_3$ arises from the fact that the first stable product of carbon metabolism recognized in radiolabelling experiments is the three-carbon compound 3-phosphoglyceric acid. Most aquatic plants, trees, shrubs and temperate herbaceous plants are C$_3$. Photosynthesis in C$_3$ plants is inhibited by oxygen. They are characterized by low levels of the enzyme phosphoenol pyruvate (PEP) carboxylase in green leaves. Also they display significant rates of photorespiration and have compensation points of around 40–100 ppm carbon dioxide. They show a discrimination against the heavy isotope of carbon (^{13}C) of around –30 per cent. Short-term photosynthetic yields are about 20–30 grams per square metre per day and annual productivities about 10–30 tonnes per hectare per year.

C$_4$ dicarboxylic acid cycle *See* C$_4$ plants.

C$_4$ photosynthesis *See* C$_4$ plants.

C$_4$ plants Higher plants in which the normal photosynthetic carbon reduction cycle is supplemented by another pathway of carbon assimilation. The term C$_4$ is derived from the fact that the first stable products obtained in the light – identified using ^{14}C labelling – are the four-carbon organic acid malic acid and the four-carbon amino acid aspartic acid. Most C$_4$ plants are tropical or subtropical grasses, although some temperate grasses and some dicotyledons with C$_4$ photosynthesis are known. C$_4$ plants may be recognized by a combination of morphological, anatomical, physiological and biochemical characteristics, which must all be present in a true C$_4$ plant. The photosynthetic tissue is arranged in two concentric layers around the vascular bundles. The enzymes associated with the photosynthetic carbon reduction cycle, in particular ribulose bisphosphate carboxylase/oxygenase (rubisco), are restricted to the inner bundle sheath layer. The outer, mesophyll layer contains high levels of phosphoenol pyruvate (PEP) carboxylase and chloroplast enzymes associated with the synthesis of PEP and the reduction or transamination of oxaloacetic acid to malate or aspartate, respectively. C$_4$ acids are translocated from the mesophyll layer to the bundle sheath layer. The fixed carbon is then released and re-fixed through the normal carbon reduction cycle in the bundle sheath. The three-carbon residue (pyruvate or alanine) is returned to the mesophyll layer and used to regenerate PEP. The entire C$_4$ cycle thus acts as a pump increasing the concentration of carbon dioxide in the vicinity of rubisco. In most C$_4$ plants, the chloroplasts are dimorphic, being larger in the bundle sheath, where they preferentially accumulate starch. In extreme C$_4$ plants, such as sugar cane, maize and sorghum, the bundle sheath chloroplasts have much reduced grana and abnormally low levels of photosystem II activity. As a result, the rate of oxygen production is reduced, lowering the oxygen/carbon dioxide ratio. Therefore C$_4$

plants are more resistant to inhibition by oxygen than C_3 plants. They display lower levels of photorespiration and may have carbon dioxide compensation points close to zero. They also display less discrimination against the heavy isotope of carbon (^{13}C) than either C_3 or CAM plants, giving values of around −15 per cent. C_4 plants are capable of the highest rates of photosynthesis, up to 80 grams per square metre per day, giving very high annual yields of up to 80 tonnes dry weight per hectare. C_4 plants may be classified according to fine details of their biochemistry which are correlated with anatomical differences. The first such distinction, as malate or aspartate formers, is based on the nature of the major C_4 acid produced. The second level of classification concerns the enzyme involved in decarboxylation of the C_4 acid in the bundle sheath. On this basis, NADP-malic enzyme, NAD-malic enzyme and PEP carboxykinase species may be recognized.

$^{13}C/^{12}C$ **ratio** The ratio between the heavy stable isotope of carbon and the normal isotope of carbon. This ratio can be used to determine whether a material is of biological origin or not, since living systems take up ^{12}C in preference to the heavy isotope. The ratio is also used as an indicator of the photosynthetic pathway by which carbon present in an organic compound has been fixed. The natural abundance of ^{13}C is around 1.1 per cent, and the differences in ratio found in plant tissue span only a small part of this value. In order to obtain an accurate result, the isotope composition is expressed in terms of deviations per mil (parts per thousand) from the ratio observed in a suitable standard. Plants discriminate against the heavy isotope, with C_4 plants discriminating less than CAM or C_3 plants. This technique can thus be used to distinguish the origin of food and fermentation products. For instance, natural honey (generally from insect-pollinated C_3 plants) can be distinguished from glucose syrup or high fructose syrup (generally made from maize – a C_4 plant).

C_p The heat capacity of a system.

cachetin *See* tumour necrosis factor.

caesium chloride A compound that forms high density solutions. It is used to facilitate the separation of nucleic acids by density gradient centrifugation.

calciferol *See* vitamin D.

calcitonin A polypeptide hormone that lowers plasma calcium levels and is an antagonist of parathyroid hormone. It is secreted by the cells of the thyroid or parathyroid glands of mammals, and by the ultimobranchial bodies of lower vertebrates.

calcofluor white A fluorescent stain used to study the regeneration of plant cell walls in protoplasts.

calibration The adjustment of an instrument, using authentic standards or known methods, to obtain an absolute result in subsequent determinations. Chromatographic, electrophoretic and centrifugal methods are calibrated using standards of known chemical composition, molecular weight or density.

CALLA *See* common acute lymphocytic leukaemia antigen.

calliclone A colony developed from a single plant cell that has been taken from a suspension culture and plated out.

callose A β-(1,3)-linked glucose polymer found in the sieve plate walls of sieve tubes. It is deposited in large amounts to seal off sieve plates during maturation, seasonal modification or response to wounding.

callus Actively growing undifferentiated (parenchymatous) tissue produced in higher plants in response to wounding and some infections. A callus may also be formed *in vitro* during artificial culture of plant tissue.

calmodulin A regulatory protein found in all eukaryotic cells that binds with absolute specificity to a number of enzyme groups involved in cyclic nucleotide transport, calcium ion transport, contractile processes, neurotransmission and some phosphatases. Such binding is directly dependent on the presence of calcium ions. This feature enables calmodulin to be used as an affinity product to or from which selective binding of elution of the above type of proteins may be effected with a high degree of specificity.

calorie A unit of energy equal to 4.1868 joules; equivalent to the amount of heat required to raise the temperature of one gram of water by one degree centigrade. The Calorie or kilocalorie, equal to 1000 calories, is often used to express the energy content of foods.

Calorie *See* kilocalorie.

calyx The sepals of a flower.

CAM photosynthesis *See* crassulacean acid metabolism plants.

CAM plants *See* crassulacean acid metabolism plants.

cAMP *See* cyclic adenosine monophosphate.

camptothecin An anticancer drug produced in the stem wood of the Chinese tree *Camptotheca acuminata*.

CaMV *See* cauliflower mosaic virus.

Canada balsam A gum dissolved in xylene that is widely used in the preparation of permanent mounts of tissue slices and other specimens for microscopic examination.

cancer Any of a wide range of malignant tumours that are capable of invasive growth and spread (metastase) through the body via the lymphatic system and/or the blood stream. Cancers may be divided into carcinomas, lymphomas, sarcomas, etc. on the basis of the type of tissue in which they arise.

CAP *See* catabolite gene activator protein.

capillary electrophoresis An electrophoretic separation technique that uses a capillary system as the stationary phase.

capped 5'-ends The 5'-ends of eukaryotic mRNAs that are modified after transcription to form ends with the general structure: 7-methyl-guanosine-(5')p-p-p-(5')2'-O-methylated nucleoside.

capping The process whereby terminal ends of nucleic acids are covalently bound to another type of molecule making them less chemically active or even inactive. *In vivo* capping of the 5'-end of mRNAs makes them less susceptible to attack by phosphatases and nucleases. Capping is also used to block the ends of partially formed intermediates during *in vivo* polynucleotide synthesis.

Caps *See* zwitterionic buffer.

capsid The external protein shell or coat of a virus particle.

capsomere An individual polypeptide that makes up the capsid of a virus.

capsule A coating, with limited solubility in water, that accumulates as loose, confluent layers outside the walls of many bacteria. The coatings are often polysaccharides and are generally known as gums or slimes. Carbohydrate capsules may be composed of dextrans, levans, alginic acid, xanthan gum, etc. Other bacteria form a cellulose capsule. However, some gram-positive bacteria produce polypeptide capsules which are composed only of glutamic acid, whereas others include amino sugars and uronic acid. Several of the gums are produced by controlled fermentation as industrial products for use as gelling agents or thickeners.

capture antibody An antibody that is immobilized on a solid matrix and that is able to bind selectively to a target antigen, thereby removing it from a sample.

carbaldehyde *See* formamide.

carbohydrate A compound consisting of carbon, hydrogen and oxygen with the general formula $C_x(H_2O)_y$. Carbohydrates are described as monosaccharides, disaccharides, oligosaccharides or polysaccharides depending on the degree of polymerization of the basic sugar units. They are the early products of photosynthesis and function as transport and storage materials in animals, plants and microorganisms. They are also components of food, animal feed and bacterial growth media, providing calories for growth and movement. Phosphorylated derivatives of monosaccharides are important intermediates in energy metabolism.

carbol fuscion An alcohol-soluble bacterial stain used in diagnosis. It is based on a mixture of basic fuchsin (*para*-rosaniline) and phenol.

carbon balance An analysis carried out on a fermentation or other bioreactor in which the distribution of carbon, supplied in the substrate, is determined in relation to the distribution into cell biomass, carbon dioxide and other metabolites on either a theoretical or an experimental basis as a means of investigating process efficiency.

carbon dioxide concentration The amount of carbon dioxide, expressed in terms of equivalent volume under standard conditions, moles or weight per unit volume of a gas or liquid phase.

carbon dioxide gas analyser An instrument used to measure the concentration of carbon dioxide. It may be used to monitor respiration, fermentation or photosynthesis. *See* IRGA.

carbon dioxide production rate The rate at which carbon dioxide is produced in the exhaust stream of a fermenter. It can be related to the rate of cell growth or fermentation.

carbon source The major substrate present in a culture medium which provides the bulk of the carbon structure of the growing culture of the organism. For photosynthetic and autotrophic organisms, the carbon source is generally carbon dioxide. For many heterotrophic organisms, the carbon source is usually glucose (derived from starch or cellulose) or sucrose.

carboxy terminal The end of any polypeptide or protein that bears a free carboxyl group. *Compare* amino terminal.

carboxydismutase *See* ribulose bisphosphate oxygenase/carboxylase.

carboxylase An enzyme that catalyses a reaction in which carbon dioxide is incorporated into another molecule. In plants, the major carboxylases are ribulose bisphosphate oxygenase/carboxylase (rubisco), which catalyses the primary assimilation of carbon dioxide in photosynthesis, and phosphoenol pyruvate carboxylase, which is active in the ancillary C_4 metabolism associated with C_4 photosynthesis and CAM plants.

carboxymethyl cellulose A cellulose derivative bearing substituted carboxymethyl groups which, depending on the molecular weight and the degree of substitution, may comprise a fully soluble polymer or an insoluble polymer or an insoluble weak ion exchanger used for separation of neutral and basic proteins.

carboxymethyl group ($-OCH_2COOH$) A weak acidic group that may be complexed with various polymers such as dextran, sepharose or cellulose to form a weak ion exchanger.

carcinembryonic antigen (CEA) An antigen that is released into the blood stream by cancer cells. CEA can be used as a prognostic indicator.

carcinogen An agent, which may be a chemical, ionizing radiation or a virus, that causes cancer. Most carcinogens are also mutagens.

carcinoma Any malignant tumour of epithelial origin.

cardenolide *See* cardiac glycoside.

cardiac glycoside A compound with important pharmacological effects on heart muscle. Cardiac glycosides are derived from plant tissue and contain a steroid aglycone which is either a C23 compound (cardenolide) or a C24 compound (bufa-dienolide). They arise by loss of carbon atoms from the side chain of sterol. The glycosidic part of these compounds is complex and contains unique sugars. The aglycones include digitoxigenin from foxglove and hellebrigenin from the rhizomes of the Christmas rose.

cardiac muscle The muscle of the vertebrate heart.

cariogenic Descriptive of a substance that causes tooth decay.

carnitine A compound associated with the transfer of fatty acids across the membrane of the mitochondria in fatty acid oxidation.

carotenes Structurally related plant pigments based on a tetraterpene structure, but lacking oxygen functions such as hydroxyl groups. The colour of these carotenoids is due to the presence of a long series of conjugated double bonds. Cyclization may occur at either or both ends as in β-carotene. The carrot is the classical source of 'carotene', which is a mixture of all the carotenes with β-carotene comprising more than 90 per cent of the total.

carotenoids Plant pigments based on a tetraterpene structure. A number of different carotenoids are associated with photosynthesis as accessory pigments or protective agents, preventing photo-oxidation of chlorophyll. The carotenoids may be divided into the carotenes (hydrocarbon tetraterpenes) and the xanthophylls (those containing oxygen functions, such as hydroxyl groups).

carpel The basic unit of the gynoecium of angiosperms, consisting of a single megasporophyll with its associated ovules.

carrageenan A gum that can be extracted from algae belonging to the Rhodophyceae. Carrageenans are mixtures of polysaccharides largely made up of D-galactose residues with (1,3)- and (1,4)-linkages. Many of the galactose residues are sulphated.

carrier (1) A matrix placed within a bioreactor or cell culture system to act as a support on which the active biomass or cells grow and become immobilized. Carriers are used as a means of retaining cell biomass within a fermenter or digester run in a continuous manner, or as a means of encouraging the growth and increasing the yield of animal cell lines that only grow when in contact with a suitable surface. Depending on the system, carriers range from large flat plastic plates, through specially designed plastic or ceramic rings, to pieces of broken rock, sand or specially selected spherules of microporous glass. (2) In genetics, individuals that carry a recessive gene for a hereditary disease but do not show symptoms of that disease. (3) In health care, individuals that carry the microorganisms responsible for a disease such as typhoid and do not show symptoms although they can pass the disease on to others.

cartilage Supportive tissue present in all vertebrates, consisting of a matrix deposited intercellularly with chrondroblasts. Several different types of cartilage occur: hyalin cartilage, consisting of chondroitin sulphate and collagen fibrils; fibrocartilage, composed mainly of collagen and elastic fibres.

cascade A continuous processing system consisting of a series of identical procedures in which the product of one stage is used as the feed for the next.

cascade fermentation A system in which the fermenting liquor is fed through a series of fermenters as the process proceeds. The process is also called an overflow continuous fermentation. In industrial-scale systems, up to ten fermenters are present in series. The cells are separated from the last fermenter by sedimentation or centrifugation. These cells, which are yeast in the case of alcohol production where the technique has been applied, are returned to the first fermenter, and any excess sold off as animal feed or disposed of. If insufficient yeast is recovered, further growth may be achieved by injection of air into the system or additional yeast is added from a starter culture tank. A number of patented modifications have been developed, which include methods of retaining or settling the yeast in intermediate tanks, in order to avoid physical removal and recycling of the cells. This overcomes having to acid-wash the yeast, which in conventional processes is usually performed to reduce the possibility of infection during recycling. With yeast, fermentation times of between 10 and 18 hours are achieved.

casein A phosphoprotein. Milk casein is mainly composed of three types of protein, one of which (x-casein) keeps the casein micelles present in milk in solution and protects them against flocculation by calcium ions.

catabolic Descriptive of an enzymic reaction that leads to the breakdown of a complex biological molecule into less complex components. Such reactions may either yield energy in the form of ATP or generate metabolic intermediates used in subsequent anabolic reactions.

catabolism The overall processes involved in the breakdown of complex organic compounds to provide energy in the form of ATP. Catabolism involves such processes as glycolysis, glycogenolysis, proteolysis and oxidation of fatty acids.

catabolite gene activator protein (CAP) A protein that combines at the promoter region of an operon in conjunction with cyclic AMP adjacent to the site of RNA polymerase binding. The interaction of CAP with the promoter facilitates the formation of the RNA polymerase–promoter complex, which exerts a positive regulatory control, enabling transcription to occur. Addition of glucose decreases the level of cyclic AMP and inactivates CAP, thus reducing the efficiency of transcription.

catabolite repression A control phenomenon in which glucose, or metabolites produced from glucose, inhibit pathways of enzyme synthesis. In microorganisms, catabolite repression enables preferential catabolism of glucose whenever it is available.

This is the result of the depressed activity of many bacterial operons (e.g., the lac operon of *E. coli*) in the presence of glucose. Active catabolism of glucose leads to a reduction in the intracellular concentration of cyclic AMP, thereby blocking an essential positive control signal for expression of glucose-sensitive operons.

catalase An enzyme that catalyses the decomposition of hydrogen peroxide to oxygen and water.

catalysis The promotion of a chemical reaction by addition of a substance or enzyme (catalyst) that partakes in, but is not permanently affected by, the reaction.

catalyst A substance that increases the rate of a chemical reaction, but remains unchanged at the end of the reaction. Enzymes are biological catalysts.

catechol 2-Hydroxyphenol; a chemical compound, the amine derivatives of which are important neurotransmitters. *See* adrenaline, noradrenaline.

catecholamine An amine derivative of catechol that acts as a hormone or neurotransmitter. The catacholamines include noradrenaline and adrenaline.

cathepsin A proteolytic enzyme located in lysosomes that causes autolysis following the death of a cell or tissue.

cation A positively charged ion which is attracted to the cathode in electrophoresis, or any positively charged ion, radical or molecule.

cation exchange capacity *See* exchange capacity.

cauliflower mosaic virus (CaMV) A plant virus, a member of the caulimoviruses which attacks Cruciferae and some Solanaceae. The genome of CaMV consists of a double-stranded circular DNA molecule of around 8000 base pairs. The circular molecule has several single-stranded dicontinuities or gaps which occur at specific locations in relation to the restriction sites, which have been mapped in detail from a number of isolates. The CaMV has been considered as a possible vector for transfer of foreign DNA into plant cells.

caulimovirus A group of plant viruses that contain double-stranded DNA. These viruses have a host range restricted to a few closely related plants. They are mainly transmitted by aphids. Infection leads to the formation of refractile round inclusions consisting of many viruses embedded in a protein matrix. The protein is virus-coded and can account for up to 5 per cent of the protein in infected cells. The best studied member of this group is the cauliflower mosaic virus (CaMV).

CD62 *See* PADGEM.

cDNA Complementary DNA; a single-stranded DNA that is formed from an mRNA template by the enzyme reverse transcriptase. Using radioactive nucleotides (generally ^{32}P), cDNAs can be obtained in a highly radioactive form and used as probes in hybridization assays to determine the number and location of genes in a chromosome, to construct physical maps of different genomes, to study the organization of eukaryote genes, and to locate coding sequences in a portion of DNA.

CDP *See* cytidine 5'-diphosphate.

CE cellulose *See* cellulose ion exchanger.

CEA *See* carcinembryonic antigen.

CELIA Competitive ELISA. *See* ELISA.

cell (1) A device for transforming chemical into electrical energy. (2) A small container with transparent, parallel sides used to hold a sample in spectrophotometry. (3) The basic structural and functional unit of all living organisms. All cells contain cytoplasm surrounded by a plasma membrane. Most bacterial and plant cells are enclosed in an outer rigid or semi-rigid cell wall. All cells arise from pre-existing cells by a process of division or fusion. The cells contain genetic material (DNA) which controls the inheritance of various characteristics as well as the machinery, in the form of ribosomes, required to translate this information into proteins. Two types of cell may be distinguished on the basis of the arrangement of the genetic material. Prokaryotes lack nuclei and have their genetic material lying free in the cell; in eukaryotes, the genetic material is separated from the cytoplasm and located in a nucleus. The cytoplasm contains the various enzymes necessary to catalyse all the anabolic and catabolic functions of the cell. In prokaryotes there is little separation of enzymes performing different functions, whereas in eukaryotes, enzymes or enzyme systems that catalyse conflicting reactions are enclosed within different membrane-bound organelles. These include those bounded by a double membrane (chloroplasts, mitochondria, plastids, the nucleus, etc.) and a large number of other organelles (lysosomes, peroxisomes, microbodies, spherosomes, Golgi bodies, etc.) bounded by a single membrane. In multicellular organisms the cells may be specialized for a particular function and grouped as tissues. Tissues with related functions are grouped to form organs.

cell affinity chromatography A method of obtaining defined, functionally homogeneous cell populations from mixed cultures using affinity chromatography. The affinity adsorbents are prepared by immobilizing proteins (antibodies, lectins, etc.) on to macrobeads. The sample is applied to a column packed with this material, impurities are washed out, and the cells selectively desorbed by washing in a buffer with excess competitive agent (e.g., free monosaccharides for elution from immobilized lectins).

cell body The central part of a neurone which contains the nucleus.

cell breakage Any mechanical procedure used to break cells in order to liberate their contents. Techniques used involve pressure or mechanical shock, sonication, shaking, blending, ball milling or hammer milling, etc.

cell counter An automated device designed to enumerate the number of cells in a sample. The simpler type of cell counters consists of a mechanism to draw a known volume of a suitably diluted cell culture through a detection device. The detector comprises a plate with a small hole in it across which an electric potential is maintained. As any cell or particle passes through the hole a pulse is generated, which is an amplified and logged using an electronic counter. More sophisticated cell counters include flow cytometers.

cell counting A method used to enumerate the number of cells in a culture sample. This is done manually or using an automated cell counter. The manual methods are either direct or indirect. A direct count is obtained by making a suitable dilution and counting the cells under a microscope, using a haemocytometer, in order to get a statistical representation. Indirect methods involve diluting the cells and plating out on nutrient agar plates, and subsequently counting the number of colonies that have grown on the plate. Usually one discrete colony will grow from each viable cell in the original culture.

cell culture *See* tissue culture.

cell cycle The growth cycle of an individual cell. Starting from a cell that has just undergone mitosis, and thus has only one chromatid and half the normal DNA content, the first phase is termed G1. This is followed by the S phase in which each chromatid is duplicated and the G2 phase in which duplication is complete but mitosis has not been initiated again. Mitosis then occurs in the M phase.

cell disruption A procedure used to liberate the content of cells. These may be mechanical and result in cell breakage or depend on cell lysis induced by addition of solvent which affects the cell membrane, antibiotics or antimetabolites which disrupt or disorganize cell wall growth.

cell division A process by which a cell divides into two daughter cells. *See* amitosis, meiosis, mitosis.

cell fusion A technique whereby cells or protoplasts are induced to fuse, often in pairs, in such a way that a new single cell is formed. Initially this will contain chromosomes from both of the precursor cells. If the cells are genetically compatible, the nuclei may also fuse and a viable hybrid cell result. In some cases, one or more chromosomes are expelled to form mini-nuclei, leaving a nucleus capable of division. It is possible to induce the development of such a product of cell fusion to produce a viable multicellular organism. Cell fusion occurs naturally in sexual reproduction where two gametes fuse to form a zygote.

cell immobilization *See* immobilization.

cell mediated immunity (CMI) Immunological reactions initiated by T lymphocytes and mediated by effector T lymphocytes and macrophages.

cell membrane The outer layer or boundary of the cytoplasm of a living cell, composed of protein and lipids. Several different models have been proposed for the structure of cell membranes. These include suggestions that the proteins are embedded in a bimolecular lipid layer formed by orientation of the lipid molecules owing to the different hydrophobic or hydrophilic properties of the fatty acid portion or the polar ends which may contain galactose, glucose or acetylgalactosamine or other similar groups.

cell recycle A process used in fermentation and anaerobic digestion in which the cells are removed from the product or effluent stream and recycled into the reactor, which is run in a continuous, cascade or batch mode. The technique is of value when the cells are being used to produce a secondary product or treat effluents where: (1) cell growth is not required; (2) the growth of cells causes diversion of substrate into unwanted biomass; (3) the rate of cell production or growth, or cell concentration is a rate-limiting step.

cell sorter A mechanical device designed to separate mixtures of cells. *See* flow cytometry.

cell wall A rigid or semi-rigid outer covering surrounding the protoplasts of plant cells and most prokaryotes. In plants, the wall consists of several layers; a primary wall composed of cellulose microfibrils running through a matrix of hemicelluloses and pectic substances surrounded by a secondary wall composed of cellulose which is generally lignified to a varying extent. Cell walls of the fungi may contain varying amounts of chitin. The cell walls of prokaryotes are strengthened by mucopeptides and may be surrounded by a mucilagenous capsule.

cell-free translation The translation of mRNA in a cell extract solution (commonly derived from rabbit reticulocytes or wheat germ) that contains added tRNAs, amino acids, creatine phosphate and creatine phosphatase.

cellobiase An enzyme that hydrolyses cellobiose to glucose. It is produced from cultures of *Aspergillus niger*.

cellobiose A disaccharide, consisting of two β-(1,4)-linked molecules of glucose, obtained by hydrolysis of cellulose.

cello-oligosaccharide A short chain of β-(1,4)-linked glucose units produced during enzymic hydrolysis of cellulose.

cellulase A complex enzyme system that hydrolyses cellulose to sugars of lower molecular weight, including cellobiose and glucose. Early work on cellulase suggested that a two-step process was involved. This concept was based on the fact that some organisms can hydrolyse native cellulose, whereas others can only degrade soluble derivatives. This suggests that a component (C1) initiates hydrolysis by a preliminary activation or disaggregation of cellulose chains, and a second component (Cx) was responsible for depolymerization to soluble oligosaccharides. It is now known that C1 is a β-(1,4)-glucan cellobiohydrolase, and thus acts on the chains formed by Cx action; it is an exoenzyme. The cellulase system also contains an endoenzyme known as

β-(1,4)-glucan glucanohydrolase and a β-glucosidase. The endoglucanase acts on the interior of the polymer to generate new reducing ends. The second enzyme acts on the non-reducing ends to release cellobiose. The β-glucosidase hydrolyses cellobiose, and to a lesser extent, other cello-oligosaccharides.

cellulolytic activity The ability of an enzyme to degrade cellulose. The methods are used to assay the activities of complete cellulase systems and of the individual components as follows. Complete cellulase: release of reducing sugars from cotton; loss of weight of avicel; decrease in turbidity of solutions of filter paper; release of dye from dyed cellulose; clarification of cellulose-agar or decrease in tensile strength of fibres of solka-floc. Endoglucanase: release of reducing sugars from carboxymethyl cellulose; decrease in viscosity of solutions of hydroxyethyl cellulose; clarification of agar. Exocellobiohydrolase: production of reducing sugar from amorphous cellulose; production of cellobiose from oligosaccharides; release of *p*-nitrophenol from *p*-nitrophenyl-β-D-cellobioside. Exoglucohydrolase: release of reducing sugar from amorphous cellulose; production of glucose from cellobiose; release of *p*-nitrophenol from *p*-nitrophenyl-β-D-glucoside.

Cellulomonas A rod-shaped, gram-positive, thermophillic, aerobic bacterium that is capable of decomposing cellulose. It has been investigated as an organism for the production of single-cell protein from cellulosic wastes.

cellulose A high-molecular-weight polysaccharide comprising long unbranched chains of (1,4)-linked β-D-glucose residues. Cellulose is found in cell walls of higher plants and some fungi as microfibrils, in which the cellulose chains form crystalline micelles separated by regions of randomized amorphous cellulose. It is probably the most abundant carbohydrate, being freely available as a lignocellulose complex in wood, forest and agricultural wastes, and in waste paper. Development of an effective, economic process for separation of cellulose from such materials and hydrolysis to glucose in order to provide low-cost fermentation substrate, is a major challenge to biotechnologists. *See* cellulase.

cellulose hydrolysis *See* enzymatic hydrolysis.

cellulose ion exchanger A substituted cellulose derivative that is used in bead form as a weak ion exchanger. The most frequently used products are DEAE-cellulose (diethylaminoethyl) and CM-cellulose (carboxymethyl), which are weak base (anion) and weak acid (cation) exchangers, respectively. These are prepared from cellulose by substitution of some primary and secondary hydroxyl groups of the anhydroglucose units with diethylaminoethyl or carboxymethyl groups, respectively, joined through ether linkages. These exchangers have an open structure, readily penetrated by large molecules, and a large surface area giving them a high capacity for absorption of protein. The binding is usually freely reversible. DEAE-cellulose is used for chromatography of acidic and slightly basic proteins at pH values above their isoelectric point. The most useful range is pH 6–8. CM-cellulose is used for separation of neutral and basic proteins, which bind at around pH 4.5. Desorption of proteins from the ion exchangers is accomplished by changing the pH or increasing the ionic strength of the eluant. The most weakly held proteins are displaced at low salt concentrations and the more tightly bound at higher concentrations. Similar products such as PAB-cellulose (*p*-aminobenzoyl) or ECTEOLA-cellulose (substituted mixed amines), may be used for the chromatography of nucleic acids.

cellulosic Descriptive of a substance that is formed of or relates to cellulose.

centiMorgan (cM) Unit of distance in a genetic linkage map as measured by recombination frequency. One cM corresponds to a meiotic recombination frequency of 1 per cent.

central dogma A set of rules that describe the ways generally used in information transfer in cellular processes.

$$DNA \xrightarrow{\text{transcription}} RNA \xrightarrow{\text{translation}} protein$$

The central dogma assumes that information can be transferred from DNA to RNA, and from RNA to protein, but cannot be passed on from protein. However, unusual processes have been observed in certain viruses which employ other ways of storing, transferring and expressing information. The extent of the possibilities is as follows:

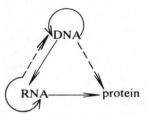

central nervous system (CNS) The part of the nervous system responsible for the integration of nervous activity in vertebrates. It consists of the brain, spinal cord and peripheral nerves.

centric fission The formation of two chromosomes by the splitting of one chromosome at (or near) the centromere.

centric fusion The fusion of two acrocentric or telocentric chromosomes into one metacentric chromosome.

centrifugal contactor A device for separating liquids. The centrifuge bowl consists of concentric channels with spirally wound baffles that facilitate the concentration of the heavier liquid towards the periphery of the bowl and the lighter liquid towards the axis.

centrifugal evaporator A centrifugal device used to increase the concentration of products in a solution, which is fed into one side of a rotating disc or cone whilst heat is applied on the other. The vapour is removed by condensation.

centrifugal force *See* relative centrifugal force.

centrifuge A mechanical device, usually driven by an electric motor, that enables a rotor to be driven at high speed resulting in the production of high gravitational forces. Centrifuges are analytical or preparative and vary from simple low-speed bench systems to high-speed refrigerated ultracentrifuges. The samples are placed in discrete tubes within the rotor or contained within a rotating cylindrical shell or series of concentric plates. *See* density gradient centrifugation, ultracentrifuge, zonal centrifuge.

centriole An organelle located close to the nucleus in the cells of most animals and the lower plants. Centrioles are not found in prokaryotes or vascular plants. During nuclear division the centrioles migrate to opposite poles of the newly formed spindle so that one passes to each daughter cell.

centromere The point of attachment for chromosome movement during cell division. The centromere becomes attached at the equator to a spindle fibre that is responsible for the directional chromosome movement. Centromeres are composed of heterochromatin.

centromeric DNA Short, highly repetitious sequences of DNA associated with centromeres.

cephalosporin An antibiotic structurally similar to penicillin because of the presence of a β-lactam ring.

CH$_3$COCH$_2$ ... NHCO(CH$_2$)$_3$ CHNH$_2$COOH

Cephalosporin

cerebroside A phospholipid associated with the myelin sheath of nerves.

chain termination method A method of DNA sequencing also known as dideoxy sequencing.

Chakrabarty patent The first patent for a recombinant organism. This patent was allowed by the United States Supreme Court in 1980. US patent 4259444 is for '*a bacterium from the genus* Pseudomonas *containing therein at least two stable energy-generating plasmids, each of said plasmids providing a separate hydrocarbon degradative pathway*'.

challenge The administration of an antigen to establish the state of an acquired immunity.

character A trait or form that is recognizable in the phenotype; the expression of a dominant allele.

charon vector A vector constructed from a lambda phage. Most charon vectors are replacement vectors.

chart recorder An instrument that converts a variable electrical signal into a trace on paper, thus providing a visual representation of the signal.

chasogamy A characteristic of higher plants in which the flowers open after pollination and fertilization.

cheese A hard or soft product formed from milk coagulated as a result of microbial action. The basic processes consist of: (1) setting milk by the addition of starter cultures and coagulant to prewarmed milk; (2) cutting the coagulum; (3) cooking the cut coagulum; (4) removing whey from the curd; (5) allowing the curd particles to knit; (6) slating; (7) pressing; (8) ripening or curing the cheese. Starter cultures for hard (cheddar) cheese are usually *Streptococcus lactis* or *S. cremoris*, whereas soft (cream) cheese may use *Lactobacillus bulgaricus* or *S. thermophilus*. Many cheeses are ripened by the growth of mould, which may penetrate the whole cheese (blue cheese) or may appear only on the surface (Camembert). Fungi used in such processes include *Penicillium roquefortii* and *P. camembertii*.

chelate A chemical structure in which a central polyvalent metal ion is combined with a ring of organic compounds or radicals.

chelating agent An organic compound that is capable of complexing with a metallic ion to form a chelate.

chelation The formation of a chelate.

chemical clarification The removal of suspended particulate material from a solution or solvent. This may be aided by the addition of inorganic or organic compounds ranging from simple salts, through polyelectrolytes based on polyacrylamide, to quaternary ammonium compounds or even natural products such as blood. The objective is to make fine particles join together to form flocs which will float to the surface or precipitates which will sink. If the particulate matter is of biological origin it will often be charged. Addition of charged ions or polymers of these types leads to clumping of the material due to mutual attraction of opposite charges on the particulate material and the additive. Inorganic treatments include addition of alumina, calcium phosphate or lime which may be followed by injection of carbon dioxide or sulphur dioxide which results in the formation of precipitates of carbonates or sulphates, respectively, that trap the particles. Such processes may be termed carbonatation (addition of lime and carbon dioxide), phosphatation (addition of phosphoric acid) or sulphatation (addition of sulphur dioxide).

chemical fusogen A chemical, such as polyethylene glycol (PEG), that is used to facilitate the fusion of two cells or protoplasts, for example, in the formation of hybridoma.

chemical oxygen demand (COD) A measure of the amount of oxygen, expressed in milligrams per litre, required to oxidize organic matter (in a sample of polluted water, for example) using a chemical method. The chemical oxygen demand includes the biochemical oxygen demand and is usually of a greater magnitude.

chemical potential The change in free energy due to a change in the molar concentration of a solute, when the temperature and pressure of the system, and the concentration of all other constituents remain constant.

$$\mu_i = (\delta F/\delta n_i)_{T,P,n_j}$$

where F is Gibbs' free energy, n is the number of molecules, n_i refers to the particular solute and n_j collectively to all other constituents. The letters outside the bracket denote variables held at constant value.

chemiluminescence The emission of light as the result of a chemical reaction. It occurs because of the interaction of components added to liquid scintillation cocktails, giving spurious results. This may be associated with peroxidation and can be overcome by leaving the samples in the dark for about 24 hours prior to counting.

chemiluminescent labelling A technique used to label DNA probes. Two different probes are constructed that are complementary to adjacent segments of a gene. Each probe carries part of a chemiluminescent system. When brought together the two probes hybridize in the same region and emit light which can be detected using a photomultiplier.

chemiosmotic theory A biochemical mechanism suggested as the route of phosphorylation (formation of ATP) linked to electron transport in either respiration or photosynthesis. According to this hypothesis hydrogen ions are pumped across the inner mitochondrial membrane, or across the chloroplast thylakoid membrane, as a result of the passage of electrons through the electron transport chain. This requires that the proteins and other intermediates of the electron transport chain are arranged so that hydrogen ions are only taken up on one side of the membrane and discharged on the other side. The electrochemical gradient so formed (the proton motive force) is the driving force for phosphorylation. The proton motive force is composed of two elements: (1) a pH difference or gradient across the membrane of about 1.5 pH units; (2) an electrical potential difference of about 0.15 V. The formation of ATP, which requires the removal of the elements of water between the two reactants, is catalysed by an ATPase built into the membrane. The ATPase is a complex molecule consisting of a stalk and a head piece, which contains the ATPase activity. When ADP and ortho-phosphate bind to the ATPase the H^+ and OH^-, removed in the formation of ATP, are pulled in opposite directions under the influence of the electrochemical gradient and react with the opposite ion species to form two molecules of water. This move-ment is favoured by the stalk of the ATPase which passes through the membrane pro-viding a channel for passage of the OH^- ions. *See* electron transport chain.

chemisorption Adsorption involving chemical bonding between a substance and the surface to which it is adsorbed.

chemoautotroph An organism that obtains energy for growth by oxidation of various reduced compounds of sulphur, hydrogen, ammonia or nitrite.

chemolithotroph An organism that obtains energy by oxidizing inorganic compounds such as nitrite, hydrogen or iron (Fe^{2+}).

chemometrics The application of maths, statistics and computing to the analysis of chemical data.

chemostat A fermentation vessel or bio-reactor in which steady-state growth is maintained by providing the cells with a constant input of nutrients. The rate of growth can be regulated by the level of a specific nutrient and the dilution rate (rate of removal of organisms from the vessel) matched to the cell growth rate.

chemotaxis Migration of cells in response to a chemical stimulus, i.e. movement towards or away from high concentrations of certain chemicals.

chemotherapeutic agent A chemical agent for treating disease; a curative drug.

chiasma The point of close association be-tween chromosomes of a homologous pair at the diakinesis stage of meiosis. Chias-

mata result from the crossing-over of DNA at an earlier stage of the meiotic cycle.

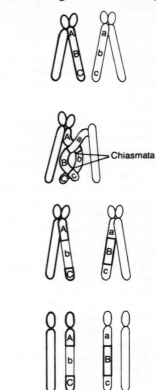

Crossing-over between the chromotids of homologous chromosomes

chill haze A precipitation of proteins, often together with polysaccharides, tannins and various other compounds, that occurs dur-ing the cold storage of beer. Chill haze can be treated by the application of proteases.

chillproofing The treatment of beer in cold storage with proteases, such as bromelain, to break down and solubilize the proteins that cause chill haze.

chimaera *See* chimera.

chimera (1) A segment of tissue which has a genetic make-up that is different from that of the surrounding cells of the same organ-ism. (2) An animal or plant whose tissues are of two different genotypes. This may be achieved by grafting, by mixing cells of very early embryos or as a result of hybridization through normal crossing methods.

chimeric antibody An antibody that contains proteins from different species (e.g., murine/human monoclonal antibodies).

chimeric gene An artificial gene produced by combining DNA sequences from several different sources. For instance, the sequence for a small peptide can be spliced with the sequence coding for an inducible enzyme. If the chimeric gene is then inserted into a suitable host, amplified and expressed, the resulting hybrid protein can then be hydrolysed to produce the required peptide product.

chi-square test A statistical test used to determine the probability that a given set of experimental values will be equalled or exceeded by chance alone.

Chlamydia trachomatis A human pathogen that causes infertility and blindness. Research is being carried out into the production of genetically engineered vaccines to protect against this disease.

Chlamydomonas reinhardtii A motile unicellular algae widely used in genetic and cell biology studies.

chloramphenicol An inhibitor of protein synthesis that acts by binding on to the 5OS subunits of bacterial and chloroplast ribosomes, preventing peptide bond formation. It is used to optimize replication of plasmids in cells of *E. coli*.

$$O_2N - \bigⵛ\!\!\!\bigcirc\!\!\!\bigⵛ - CHCHNHCOCHCl_2$$

with OH above the first CH and CH_2OH below.

Chloramphenicol

chloramphenicol resistance Ability to survive treatment with chloramphenicol. It is mediated through acetylation of the antibiotic, leading to inactivation.

chloretone (trichlorobutanol) A chemical that is used at 0.05 per cent in weakly acidic solutions to prevent microbial infections of packed chromatography columns and gel suspensions.

chlorhydrin A chemical compound that is an intermediate in the production of alkene oxides from alkenes.

chlorine A gaseous element that is reactive, corrosive and poisonous.

chlorophyll A green pigment composed of a tetrapyrrole (porphyrin) ring containing magnesium complexed with a molecule of the long-chain alcohol phytol. Chlorophylls are the primary photosynthetic pigments found in all autotrophic organisms. Several distinct structural forms occur: chlorophyll a (found in all oxygen-producing photoautotrophs); chlorophyll b (found in higher plants and green algae); chlorophylls c and d (found in various algal groups); bacteriochlorophyll (found in the green and purple bacteria). Various forms of chlorophyll a and b may be distinguished by their absorption spectra. These differ *in vivo* from those of isolated chlorophylls in solution in organic solvents. Differences are the result of the association of chlorophyll molecules, or chlorophyll dimers, with specific proteins and include the so-called reaction centre complexes P700 and P680, which form the energy traps of photosystem I and photosystem II, respectively.

Chlorophyta The green algae, including such genera as *Chlorella*, which are widely used in studying photosynthesis and the control of the cell cycle in plants. *Chlorella* and other green algae may be cultivated as a source of single cell protein, plant pigments such as carotenoids, fine chemicals and vitamins. Green algae are also used in waste treatment processes associated with algal oxidation ponds.

chloroplast A plastid bound by a double membrane that is associated with photosynthesis in plants. In higher plants, the chloroplasts are green (owing to chlorophyll), 3–10 μm in diameter and shaped like a biconvex lens. The outer envelope encloses a complex lamellar structure embedded in an amorphous protein stroma. The internal volume can thus be divided into three distinct regions with different functions: (1) the stroma containing soluble enzymes associated with the dark reactions of carbon assimilation and further metabolism; (2) the membrane system, made up of thylakoids, bearing the photosynthetic pigments, the intermediates of the electron transport chain and many of the components associated with the production of oxygen, the formation of ATP and the reduction of NADP – collectively known as the light reactions; (3) the lumen of the thylakoids, an aqueous region containing proteins, magnesium ions and other charged inorganic molecules that result in the formation of a potential gradient across the thylakoid membrane. Movement of ions across the membrane produces changes in potential and changes in pH and magnesium concentration which control the activities of some of the enzymes associated with the dark reactions of carbon assimilation. Chloroplasts also contain DNA and ribosomes that code for and synthesize some of the chloroplast proteins; others are encoded by nuclear genes and formed by cytoplasmic ribosomes. In C_4 plants, the activities of photosynthesis are divided between the chloroplasts of the mesophyll cells and the bundle sheath. Such chloroplasts differ in structure and/or function. Chloroplasts store starch (in C_4 plants, this property is largely associated with the bundle sheath chloroplasts) and lipids. The chloroplasts of algae vary in terms of pigmentation (used in primary classification), lamellar structure, storage products and the presence of pyrenoids.

chloroplast aminoacyl-tRNA synthetase Any of a number of aminoacyl-tRNA synthetases which have been isolated from chloroplasts. These enzymes are specific for the chloroplast tRNAs.

chloroplast DNA *See* chloroplast genome.

chloroplast genes Genetic information carried on the DNA contained within the chloroplast. Since the chloroplasts are cytoplasmic and during fertilization cytoplasm comes only from the ovum, characteristics coded for in the chloroplasts do not show Mendelian inheritance; characteristics are only passed on through the female line. Considerable information is now accumulating concerning the chloroplast genome. For instance, the gene for the large subunit of rubisco is located in an 11.5-kilobase *Bam* HI fragment consisting of 1687 nucleotides with 178 nucleotides in an untranslated 5'-leader sequence. Such material has been cloned into *E. coli*, and the products of the genes from a number of different plants including spinach, maize and *Chlorella* have been investigated. These studies may lead to means of increasing photosynthetic productivity by modification of the properties of the catalytic binding site with a reduction in the magnitude of photorespiration. The genes coding for membrane proteins have also been investigated in some detail. The proteins that have so far been shown to be coded for by chromosome genes include chlorophyll a protein 2, chlorophyll a protein 3, cytochrome b559, cytochrome f and several proteins of the coupling factor complex. Such studies may increase productivity by modification of the regulatory aspects of light harvesting and electron transport.

chloroplast genome The genetic information of the chloroplast, which occurs as multiple copies of a circular double-stranded DNA molecule. This DNA codes for rRNA, tRNA and a number of proteins, including the large subunit of rubisco and some membrane proteins (e.g., photosystem I chlorophyll protein). The mechanism of replication of chloroplast DNA is semi-conservative and involves rolling circle intermediates.

chloroplast mRNA A messenger RNA which is only translated on 70S ribosomes.

chloroplast proteins The soluble stroma proteins and the insoluble lamellar proteins. These are encoded by nuclear genes and chloroplast genes. The enzyme rubisco is the best studied of the stroma proteins. It consists of large subunits encoded by chloroplast genes and small subunits encoded by nuclear DNA. The membrane proteins have been studied using mutants that lack certain components, and over 50 separated of which 30 are implicated in the photosynthetic function of the membrane. Of these, 9 or 10 are coded for by nuclear DNA (these include chlorophyll a/b protein 2, plastocyanin, ferredoxin, ferredoxin-NADP reductase and several subunits of coupling factor) and 7 are known to be coded for by chloroplast genes. *See* chloroplast genes.

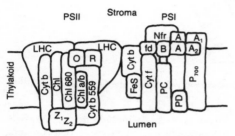

Possible arrangement of thylakoid proteins in PSI and PSII

chloroplast ribosome A 70S ribosome found in eukaryotic chloroplasts. Protein synthesis on 70S ribosomes is inhibited by chloramphenical, but not by cycloheximide; the reverse is true for 80S cytoplasmic ribosomes. Chloroplast ribosomes dissociate into 50S and 30S subunits. Chain initiation on 70S ribosomes requires *N*-formylmethionine rather than methionine. About 50 proteins are associated with the 70S ribosome, some of which are synthesized by the cytoplasmic system.

chloroplast rRNA The rRNA that consists of various forms of 23S, 16S, 5S and 4.5S with a G + C content of 55.8 per cent.

chloroplast tRNA A tRNA found in the chloroplast. These tRNAs differ in structure from the cytoplasmic tRNA and are coded for by the chloroplast DNA. The structure of these molecules is closer to that of prokaryote tRNA than eukaryote cytoplasmic tRNA. The chloroplast tRNAs are not aminoacylated by cytoplasmic aminoacyl-tRNA synthetases.

chlorosis The yellowing of plant leaves resulting from a loss of chlorophyll. This may be due to nutrient deficiency, the effects of pests and disease or of chemicals (e.g., herbicides, fungicides or pesticides), a response to pollutants, or lack or excess of light.

chlortetracycline An antibiotic produced by *Streptomyces aureofaciens.*

cholesterol An animal sterol that occurs as a component of plasma membranes. Excess cholesterol in the blood has been implicated as a contributory factor in cardiovascular disease.

choline A basic compound found as a constituent of phospholipids such as lecithin and the neurotransmitter acetylcholine.

Choline $(CH_3)_3 + NCH_2CH_2OH$

cholinergic Descriptive of a nerve fibre that releases acetylcholine as a neurotransmitter.

chondroitin A mucopolysaccharide comprising repeating units of D-glucuronic acid and *N*-acetyl-D-galactosamine. Chondroitin sulphates are important components of cartilage and bone.

chondroitin sulphate *See* chondroitin.

Chordata A major phyllum of animals that includes all those organisms possessing a notochord and a dorsal nerve cord. Vertebrates are members of the Chordata.

chorionic villus biopsy A method of obtaining cells and DNA from a developing foetus during the early stages of pregnancy (between seven and ten weeks). A catheter tube or forceps are used to remove a few of the villi that project from the surface of the chorion, a membrane of embryonic origin that surrounds the foetus. This method allows much earlier prenatal diagnosis of genetic disease than amniocentesis. *See* figure on page 70.

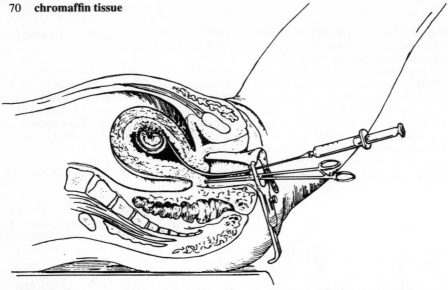

Chorionic villus biopsy by suction through a catheter tube. (Reproduced with permission from *A Revolution in Biotechnology*, ICSU Press)

chromaffin tissue The tissue of the adrenal glands that secretes catecholamines.

chromatid A longitudinal half chromosome that results from duplication during interphase. Mitotic chromatids are identical, but meiotic chromatids may differ as a result of cross-over. Chromatids of the same chromosome become separated during anaphase of mitosis (non-sexual division) and during anaphase II of meiosis (sexual division).

chromatin Structural material of which chromosomes are made. It consists of DNA and proteins.

chromatofocusing A technique used for the purification of macromolecules. It combines chromatographic and electrophoretic principles.

chromatographic detector An instrument used to monitor and quantify the products eluted from a chromatography column. The techniques used may be based on the physical, chemical or biological properties of the molecules and may involve prior conversion by chemical or enzymic means to produce a coloured or fluorescent complex.

Physical methods include the use of spectrophotometric devices, colorimeters, spectrophotofluorimeters, refractometers, polarimeters, etc. Biological molecules may be monitored using enzyme-linked reactions specific for the required class of compound. Such detectors often include a flow cell so that the fluid passes continuously from the column through the detector. Several types of detector have been developed specifically for use with gas/liquid chromatographs. These include flame ionization and electron capture devices or, where information is required on the exact structure of the compounds, a mass spectrometer. Many are linked to microprocessors for control of the chromatographic analysis, as well as direct computation of results.

chromatography A technique used to separate or analyse mixtures of liquids, gases, compounds in solution or particles. Different types of chromatography are defined in terms of: the principles of separation (absorption, ion exchange, permeation, affinity); the support material (silica, cellulose, starch, acrylamide or agarose gel, cellulose paper, cellulose acetate, etc.); the physical form of the matrix used (paper, thin layer, column). Sophisticated automated chromatographic techniques include gas/liquid chromatography (GLC) and high performance (formerly high pressure) liquid chromatography (HPLC). The basic principles of all forms of chromatography are similar. The system consists of three components: the sample; a solid matrix (stationary phase); a fluid (mobile phase). The mixture is placed at the top of the column or at the edge of a gel slab, sheet of paper or thin layer support. The mobile phase is then passed through the stationary phase. The various components in the sample are carried through the stationary matrix at different rates by the mobile phase, resulting in separation. Using column chromatography, the components are removed completely (eluted) and the mobile phase is then passed through a suitable detector where a response, proportional to the concentration of the various materials is used to establish the position and the quantity of the material. Using paper or thin layer chromatography, the chromatograms are run with a suitable solvent and for such a time that the compounds of interest are spread across the sheet but not eluted. The resolution of a mixture may be increased by running such chromatograms twice at right-angles to each other in different solvents. This is known as two-dimensional (2D) chromatography. Once the matrix is dried, the compounds are visualized and identified on the basis of their reaction with various chemical sprays, which may be combined with the use of ultraviolet light or fluorescence. Where radioactive tracers have been used, the compounds may be located using autoradiography. An indication of the nature of such samples may be obtained by comparing their behaviour with standards (pure, authentic samples). The position of a given compound on a chromatograph may be defined in terms of its R_F. This is a measure of the ratio of the distance travelled by the compound to the distance moved by the solvent front. In column systems, the compounds may be characterized in terms of the ratio of the volume of liquid used to elute the sample to the volume of liquid used to elute the complete mixture. Alternatively, where the mobile phase consists of a solvent

in which a gradual change in molar concentration or pH (a gradient) has been used, the compounds may be characterized on the basis of the concentration or pH at which they are eluted. Although chromatography separates components of a mixture and can indicate their chemical nature by comparison with standards, the only way to prove conclusively the identity of the separated compounds is to subject them to further chemical and physical analysis.

chromatography column A tubular container used to hold and support the solid stationary phase in chromatographic separations. The columns are made of glass, plastic or metal, and vary in size and length according to the technique used. Very long, narrow columns are used for gas chromatography; liquid chromatography columns usually have a length/diameter ratio of between 10:1 and 100:1. Large-scale gel filtration or ion exchange columns may be wider than they are long in order to reduce pressure drop and compression effects on the packing.

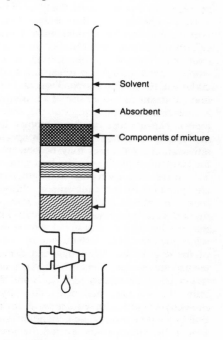

Column chromatography

chromatophore A cell or organelle that accumulates coloured pigments. Chromatophores include the chromoplasts found in plants and the melanophores of animals. The term is also used to describe the membrane vesicles associated with photosynthesis in prokaryotes.

chromedia The solid or stationary phase used in chromatography.

chromogenic substrate A substrate that is converted into a coloured product by an enzyme, used in techniques such as ELISA and immunoblotting.

chromomere A small granule formed from tightly coiled euchromatin, that stains deeply during prophase of mitosis and meiosis. When chromosomes pair during zygotene of meiosis, the chromomeres of homologous chromosomes become aligned.

chromosome The DNA-bearing structure that carries the inheritable characteristics of an organism. In eukaryotes, the genetic material is contained within a membrane-bounded nucleus during interphase. During cell division this material becomes contracted to form the chromosomes which, when stained with basic dyes, are visible under the light microscope. Typically they may be arranged in the form of a cross with a central non-staining region (the centromere). The number of chromosomes in a nucleus is constant for any given species, although chromosomes may be present in the haploid, diploid or polyploid number. They differ from each other in length, shape and position of the centromere, although pairs of homologous chromosomes in diploid cells are visually identical. They may be distinguished as sex chromosomes, which are associated with the determination of the sex of the individual, and the rest termed autosomes. The chromosomes consist of DNA associated with RNA and proteins known as histones. The DNA molecules bear linear sequences of nucleotide bases which carry the genetic information in hereditary units termed the genes. The DNA is organized into small particles

known as nucleosomes which aggregate to form chromatin. During cell division each chromosome differentiates into two visually identical strands – the chromatids. The mechanism of division of the chromosomes ensures that genetic material is not lost during division. The chromosome of prokaryotes is not contained within a membrane and does not show secondary structure, nor is it associated with protein; instead the genetic material generally consists of a circular molecule of DNA. In some viruses, the chromosome consists of a linear or circular portion of RNA.

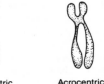

Metacentric   Acrocentric   Telocentric

Chromosomes

chromosome complement The group of chromosomes in a normal gametic or zygotic nucleus. It consists of one (monoploid nucleus) two (diploid nucleus) or more (polyploid nucleus) chromosome sets. *Compare* karyotype.

chromosome map A graphic representation of the relative positions of genes on chromosomes, plasmids or viral genomes. Such maps indicate the physical structure based on microscopic examination (cytological map), the position of genes in terms of linkage units (linkage map) or the nucleotide sequences. *See* mapping.

chromosome mutation A change in the structure or number of the chromosomes; also called an aberration or abnormality.

chromosome polymorphism The presence in a population of more than one gene sequence for a given chromosome.

chromosome set The normal gametic complement of chromosomes for a diploid individual.

chromosome walking An analytical technique used in the mapping of genes depending on the sequential isolation of overlapping molecular clones so as to span large chromosome intervals. Cloned fragments of gene are radiolabelled and used as a probe in hybridization experiments *in situ* with cytological preparations of polytene chromosomes. A random set of cloned DNA is localized in this way, and one is chosen that is close to the region of interest. The genomic library is then screened with this chosen clone as a probe to identify other clones with which it overlaps. This overlapping can be to the right or to the left. Repetition of this procedure, accompanied by the use of hybridization *in situ* to check the extent and direction of progress, allows the investigator to 'walk along the chromosome' in the region of interest.

chrysolaminarin A storage polysaccharide found in the yellow-brown algae (Chrysophyceae) consisting of β-(1,3)-glucans. This material is similar in structure to laminarin found in the brown algae and callose formed by higher plants.

chymosin The major milk-clotting enzyme in rennin. It is approved for use when manufactured using recombinant DNA technology based on *E. coli* K-12 carrying the bovine prochymosin gene. Chymosin is used as a substitute for rennin in the dairy products industry.

chymotrypsin An exopeptidase secreted by the vertebrate pancreas in the form of an inactive precursor, chymotrypsinogen, which is activated by trypsin.

cibacron blue 3G-A A dye used in dye–ligand chromatography for protein purification. It is also known as reactive blue 2 and procion blue H-B.

CIF *See* computer integrated fermentation.

cilium A hair-like organelle that protrudes from the surface of ciliated cells. Cilia form an organ of locomotion, or where they line a body cavity, a means of inducing flow of liquid. Cilia are structurally identical to the eukaryotic flagellum, but shorter (5–10 μm).

circadian rhythm A change seen in any biological or metabolic function that shows periodic peaks and troughs of activity based on or approximating to a 24-hour cycle. Such activity may be synchronized to the natural light/dark changes of night and day.

circular restriction map A pictorial representation of the position of the sites recognized by various specific restriction enzymes on circular genomes from bacteriophage, viruses, chloroplasts, mitochondria, bacteria or cyanobacteria.

***cis* configuration** (1) In chemistry, one of the configurations seen in compounds that exhibit *cis–trans* isomerization. (2) In genetics, the location of two alleles on the same chromosome, as defined by the *cis–trans* test.

cisterna A flattened sac-like vesicle such as found in mitochondria, the endoplasmic reticulum and the Golgi apparatus.

***cis–trans* test** A test used to define the unit of genetic function that determines whether independent mutations of the same phenotype occur within a single gene or in several genes involved in the same function. When two mutations occur in the same chromosome they are termed *cis*, whereas when they occur in different chromosomes of the same homologous pair they are *trans*. If each mutation occurs in a different gene, the resultant phenotype will be normal in both the *cis* and *trans* diploids. If both mutations occur on the same chromosome, only the *cis* diploid is normal. Since this test has been used to define the unit of genetic function, a structural gene sequence has been termed a cistron.

cistron A length of DNA that codes for mRNA associated with the expression of a specific polypeptide. The term excludes DNA which codes for rRNA or tRNA, or regions of the genome having a regulatory function. The cistron may also be regarded as a nucleotide sequence in DNA specifying a single genetic function as defined by the complementation test, a nucleotide sequence coding for a single polypeptide or a gene.

citric acid A white crystalline organic compound soluble in water. It occurs in citrus fruit and is an intermediate of the TCA cycle. Citric acid is produced commercially by fermentation using fungi such as *Aspergillus niger* grown in aerated submerged culture. Mutant strains are used or metabolic inhibitors are added to block the TCA cycle. Citric acid can also be produced by yeasts such as *Candida lipolytica* grown on long-chain n-alkanes.

citric acid cycle *See* tricarboxylic acid cycle.

cladistics In taxonomy, the study of evolutionary groupings.

cladogenesis The splitting of an evolutionary lineage into two or more distinct lineages which may be new species.

clarification The removal of suspended particulate material from a solution. Clarification may be a necessary part of either pre- or post-fermentation processing of feed solutions or product streams: for example, where byproducts of food processing, such as molasses are used as feed. Juice obtained from sugar beet by diffusion, or expressed from sugar cane, as well as starch hydrolysate obtained from a wide variety of crops such as maize, wheat, potato or cassava may also need clarification. Removal of particulate material may be necessary to reduce the solids load passing through the system, in order to reduce fouling of heat exchangers in particular, to increase the purity of the final product, to remove potential inhibitory materials or to recover a desired product. Techniques used include filtration, settling, decantation, centrifugation, chemical clarification, electrolytic techniques and precipitation.

clarifier (1) A settling tank used in continuous processes. (2) A liquid–solid centrifuge.

class A group consisting of closely related orders, or a single order. The sub-phylum Vertebrata (vertebrates), for instance, includes the classes Amphibia (amphibians), Aves (birds), Mammalia (mammals) and Reptilia (reptiles).

classification The placing of individuals into a category or group based on their characteristics. Early classification systems were based on phenotypic appearance. Increased knowledge of the cytogenetics and biochemistry of organisms may require revision of earlier classifications if the system is to reflect evolutionary relationships (phylogenetic classification) or genetic relationships. Natural classification of biological organisms is based on the concept of the species which are grouped into genera, then families, orders, classes and phyla. At each stage of the hierarchy the number of similarities between members of the group becomes less.

clavulanic acid An antibiotic produced by *Streptomyces* that inhibits the β-lactamases produced by penicillin-resistant bacteria.

clean room A room in which contamination is reduced to a specific maximum level in order to facilitate the manufacture of sterile and high purity products, to protect personnel, equipment and products from microbial contamination and to prevent escape of hazardous particles into the environment.

cleanliness class A standard of cleanliness into which clean rooms are classified based on the number of particles per unit area present. Classes are identified by a specific maximum permissible particle concentration per cubic foot at a reference particle size of <0.5 μm. Classes range from 1 to 100,000 particles per cubic foot. In the pharmaceutical industry, class 100 (i.e., 100 particles per cubic foot), as specified by US Federal Standard 209D, is the highest cleanliness requirement. This corresponds to Class E in the UK, Class 4000 in France and Class 3 in Germany.

cleared lysate A centrifuged cell extract that has had cell debris, subcellular particles and most of the chromosomal DNA removed.

clearing A process used in the preparation of fixed samples for inspection using light microscopy. This is carried out using clove oil or xylene, following dehydration through a series of water/ethanol mixtures of increasing alcohol content.

cleavage The mitotic division of a zygote that follows fertilization and produces a ball of smaller cells known as blastomeres. At this stage there is no net growth of the developing embryo.

cleisogamy A condition found in higher plants in which the flower fails to open.

climacteric A period of high metabolic activity in plants associated with the production of ethylene and the hydrolysis of stored carbohydrates. It occurs during the ripening of fruit. Chemical control of the climacteric can be used as a means of commercial storage of fruit. Such control includes keeping the unripe fruit in an atmosphere high in carbon dioxide or ethylene, or low in oxygen. Alternatively, the fruit may be coated with a thin layer of a suitable lipid or sucrose ester which achieves the same effect by limiting the escape of carbon dioxide from the inner regions of the fruit, which in turn depresses the enhanced respiration associated with the climacteric.

cline A gradient in the frequencies of genotypes or phenotypes along a stretch of territory.

clonal propagation The cloning of plants from a single plant cell or protoplast.

clone A group of organisms that are genetically the same since they have been produced by an asexual process or sexually by inbreeding of pure lines. In prokaryotes or eukaryotic cell culture, the term is used to describe a population of cells descended from a single parent. In molecular biology, the term is applied to multiple copies of identical DNA sequences that are produced

when they are inserted into cloning vehicles (plasmids and other vectors) and replicated using gene manipulation.

cloning The production of a number of genetically identical individuals. In genetic engineering, a process for the efficient replication of a great number of identical DNA molecules. This can be achieved by inserting the required material into a phage or plasmid vector which is then used to infect a suitable host, within which the genetic material is replicated to form a large number of copies.

cloning vehicle *See* vector.

closed mating system A breeding programme in which no outside individuals are allowed to introduce gametes into the population. Hence progeny are produced by known parental combinations.

Clostridium A genus of obligate anaerobic, spore-forming bacteria. *Clostridium* species include the pathogens responsible for tetanus (*C. tetani*) and botulism (*C. botulinum*). *C. welchii* (*C. perfringens*) and *C. histolyticum* may cause serious disease through wound infection. *C. botulinum* does not grow in the human body, but is able to cause serious disease when the toxin produced during growth on foodstuffs is ingested. A number of other species are of industrial or commercial importance. These break down cellulose in anaerobic digestion or are used as a source of cellulase, acetic acid or ethanol (*C. thermophyllum, C. thermoaceticum*), the production of enzymes (*C. felsineum*) or the production of organic solvents such as acetone and butanol (*C. acetobutylicum, C. butyricum*). A number of species are capable of nitrogen fixation (*C. pasteurianun, C. acetobutylicum, C. butyricum, C. welchii*). Many species of *Clostridium* are highly specific in terms of the organic substrates which they can use. They may be grouped on this basis according to whether they use sugar and/or starch, cellulose but no other carbohydrate, amino acids, uric acid and other purines, and mixtures of acetic acid and ethanol.

clotting factors A group of 12 or more proteins that are inactive in normal blood plasma but become activated when blood is removed from the circulation, as in injury. Clotting factors also include the various non-protein components of blood clots (calcium ions, platelets and phosphoglycerides).

CLSM Confocal laser scanning microscope; a laser scanning microscopy system that focuses on a single plane of light through a biological substance, allowing high-resolution, three-dimensional images to be built up.

cM *See* centiMorgan.

CM *See* Carboxymethyl group.

CMC 1-Cyclohexyl-3-(3-morpholinoethyl) carbodiimide methano-*p*-toluene sulphonate.

CMI *See* cell mediated immunity.

CMP *See* cytidine 5′-monophosphate.

CMV *See* cytomegalovirus.

C/N ratio The ratio of carbon to nitrogen in a feedstock, substrate or culture medium. Various systems require a C/N ratio which falls within certain specific limits in order to optimize the process and ensure its reliability.

CNS *See* central nervous system.

coacervation The separation of lyophilic colloids into two immiscible phases of different concentrations.

coadaptation The harmonious interaction of genes; the selection process by which harmoniously interacting genes become established in a population.

coagulant An agent that causes coagulation.

coagulation The changing from a fluid to a solid mass. In biological systems, coagulation is often the result of denaturing proteins in solution.

coagulum A curd or clot formed as a result of coagulation. The term is used in the manufacture of cheese to refer to the initial product of milk solidification brought about by microbial or enzyme action.

cobalamine The biologically active form of vitamin B_{12} which is required as a coenzyme for the synthesis of methionine and nucleotides, as well as in fatty acid oxidation.

coccus Descriptive of any spherical bacteria.

cocktail In liquid scintillation counting, the mixture of solvent, solutes and scintillators to which the sample is added for assay.

COD *See* chemical oxygen demand.

code A set of rules for transferring information from one alphabet or language to another.

codeine An analgesic derived from the plant *Papaver somniferum*.

coding strand That strand of double-stranded DNA from which the information for making a protein molecule is derived.

codominant Descriptive of alleles whose gene products are both manifest phenotypically.

codon A group of three nucleotides that codes for an amino acid. *See* genetic code, transcription, translation.

coefficient of selection The intensity of selection, as measured by the proportional reduction in the gametic contribution of one genotype compared with another.

coenocytic Descriptive of fungal hyphae that do not have cross walls, so that many nuclei are distributed throughout a continuous tract of cytoplasm.

co-enzyme An organic molecule associated with a protein that takes part in the catalytic reaction, but is only loosely associated with the enzyme in solution. Co-enzymes may be regarded as dissociable prosthetic groups. Their protein partners are termed apoenzymes. Neither the apoenzyme nor the co-enzyme is, in itself, a complete catalyst. In the course of the catalysed reaction, the co-enzyme may be changed chemically in the same way as a substrate and dissociate from the apoenzyme. However, all co-enzymes can be regenerated in associated reactions and can complex again with the apoenzyme. Some co-enzymes function with many different apoenzymes, and hence play an important role in coupling different biochemical reactions. Co-enzymes of importance in central metabolism include the pyrimidine nucleotides (NAD and DADP), co-enzyme A, flavin adenine dinucleotide (FAD) and pyridoxal phosphate.

co-enzyme A (CoA) A co-enzyme consisting of pantothenic acid linked to a mononucleotide based on adenine. It is an intermediate involved in the transfer of acetyl groups (with which it combines to form acetyl-CoA) and other fatty acyl groups which are bound to a thiol group on the molecule. CoA plays an important role in fatty acid synthesis and oxidation, as well as in the first step of the TCA cycle:

acetyl-CoA + oxaloacetic acid → citric acid

co-enzyme Q A substituted benzoquinone (ubiquinone) that plays a role in the respiratory electron transport chain, where it receives hydrogen or electrons from a flavoprotein and is reduced to a quinol, which then reduces the next member of the chain (a cytochrome).

Ubiquinones (coenzyme Q)

cofactor A non-protein compound that is essential for catalytic activity. An enzyme–cofactor complex is termed a holoenzyme.

The protein on its own is termed an apoenzyme. Cofactors may be organic compounds (co-enzymes) or metals ions such as magnesium, manganese, calcium, zinc, potassium, etc. Cofactors tightly associated with the protein in the holoenzyme are generally termed prosthetic groups.

cofactor recycling The regeneration of cofactors such as NADP, FAC and ATP during a commercial catalytic process utilizing enzymes or electrochemical oxidation–reduction.

cohesive termini (cohesive ends) DNA molecules with single-stranded ends that show complementarity, making it possible, for example, to join end to end with introduced fragments.

coimmobilized enzymes Complementary enzymes that are immobilized together to enhance the efficiency of a catalytic reaction. For example, the enzyme glucose oxidase is inactivated by the hydrogen peroxide it produces. However by coimmobilizing glucose oxidase with catalase (an enzyme which breaks down hydrogen peroxide) this inactivation can be prevented.

Col E1 A plasmid that encodes for colicin, a protein (bacteriocin) which kills *E. coli*. By necessity this plasmid also carries a gene that confers on host cells immunity to colicin. E1.RSF 2124 is a derivative of Col E1 which carries a transposon specifying ampicillin resistance.

col factor *See* colicin.

col plasmid A plasmid that carries genes for colicins.

colchicine An alkaloid obtained from the roots of the autumn crocus (*Colchicum autumnale*) that interferes with the formation of microtubules and thus inhibits the formation of the spindle during nuclear division. As a result, cells of dividing tissue treated with colchicine will show polyploidy, or at least a doubling of chromosome number. Colchicine is used to produce artificial polyploids as part of a breeding programme. A specific use is in the production of a fully homozygous diploid line in plant breeding by treating haploid tissue generated from anther cultures.

Colchicine

cold room A controlled temperature facility usually maintained at around 4°C, used for the preparation of enzymes and other temperature-sensitive compounds.

cold sterilization The use of ionizing radiation for sterilization.

coleoptile A protective sheath associated with the plumule of embryonic grasses.

colicin Proteins with antibiotic properties produced by enteric bacteria such as *Eschericha* or *Salmonella* which are bacteriocidal for closely related bacteria. They are encoded by plasmid colicin factors (col factors). *See* bacteriocin.

coliform bacteria A group of rod-shaped gram-negative eubacteria. They are divided into several genera on the basis of their metabolic characteristics. The coliform bacteria may be aerobic or obtain their energy by fermentation to produce organic acids (e.g., *Escherichia*) or organic acids and butylene glycol (e.g., *Klebsiella*). Other coliforms are characterized by their inability to use lactose (e.g., *Salmonella*, *Shigella* and *Proteus*) and their ability to produce gas when fermenting sugars (e.g., *Salmonella* and *Proteus*). Studies on *E. coli*, and to a lesser extent *Klebsiella*, have provided much of the information available on the molecular biology and gene manipulation of prokaryotes, as well as many other aspects of microbial metabolism. The genera *Salmonella* and *Shigella* include most of

the agents of intestinal disease in man (bacillary dysentery, typhoid and paratyphoid, as well as 'food poisoning'). *E. coli* is an inhabitant of the human gut and is generally harmless. However, some strains can cause serious infections. Monitoring of coliforms is used as a means of determining water quality and faecal contamination.

colinearity The linear correspondence between the order of amino acids in a polypeptide chain and the corresponding nucleotide sequence in the DNA molecule.

collagen The main structural protein in the white fibres of connective tissue. It is composed of units made up of three polypeptide chains (tropocollagen). Collagen is characterized by a high hydroxyproline content.

collandria evaporator A natural circulation evaporator that consists of short, vertical bundles of tubes set between two fixed sheets, bolted to the tube flanges. Steam flows outside the tubes in a steam chest and the product is heated and flows upwards by natural circulation, through the tubes and back down a large central pipe as it cools.

colloid A stable suspension of very small particles dispersed in a liquid medium.

colloid mill A mill used to grind a substance into particles of a size such that they will form colloids when suspended in a liquid.

colon The large intestine.

colony A group of cells produced from a single individual when microorganisms are cultivated on solid media such as an agar plate.

colony hybridization *See* Grunstein–Hogness method.

colony lift A procedure for transferring colonies from an agar plate to a filter for subsequent screening. A sterile filter paper is pressed against the surface of an agar plate bearing microbial colonies; some cells become attached to the paper and can be used to inoculate a second agar plate. The position of colonies which develop on this second plate will be the same as those in the original culture dish. If the nutrient or antibiotic content of the second dish differs from that of the first, colonies can be selected that are enzyme-deficient or resistant (or sensitive) to a particular antibiotic.

column reactor A bioreactor or fermenter where the height is several times the diameter. Typically a column packed with a fixed bed is used for immobilized cells or enzymes. *See* air lift fermentation, deep shaft system, tower fermenter.

commensalism An association between two organisms in which either or both of them appear to derive some benefit, and neither suffers any harm. The relationship is a casual one in which there is no metabolic interdependence. *Compare* parasite, symbiosis.

common acute lymphocytic leukaemia antigen (CALLA) A surface glycoprotein that is expressed in 80 per cent of non-T cell leukaemias.

common variable immunodeficiency (CVI) A group of disorders characterized predominantly by antibody deficiency and by various defects in cell-mediated immunity.

compensation point A set of conditions that result in a balance between the rates of photosynthesis and respiration, such that there is no net gas exchange. Two types of compensation point exist. The light compensation point is that light intensity at which the uptake of carbon dioxide (or evolution of oxygen) in photosynthesis is identical to the rate of respiratory carbon dioxide production (oxygen consumption). The carbon dioxide compensation point is the concentration of carbon dioxide reached when an illuminated plant is placed in a closed atmosphere, reflecting the balance between carbon assimilation by photosynthesis and carbon dioxide evolution mainly due to photorespiration. Most C_3 plants have carbon dioxide compensation points of about 50–100 ppm of carbon dioxide,

whereas the value for C_4 plants is normally about 5 ppm and extreme C_4 plants may have carbon dioxide compensation points of zero. These low compensation points are the result of the ability of the C_4 species to refix photorespiratory carbon dioxide, produced in the bundle sheath cells, using phosphoenol pyruvate carboxylase, during its passage through the mesophyll cells. This ability is reflected in much higher rates of photosynthesis being achieved by C_4 plants.

competent In embryology, descriptive of a cell that retains the ability to differentiate into any other type of cell if subjected to the right stimulus.

competition In biology, used in respect of competition between organisms for the same resources (such as nutrients, water, light, etc.) when these are in short supply.

competitive EIA A type of enzyme immunoassay in which an antigen in a test sample competes with an enzyme-labelled antigen for the limited binding sites of an antibody immobilized on a solid matrix, or the sample antigen competes with an immobilized antigen for limited binding sites on a free enzyme-labelled antibody.

competitive ELISA *See* ELISA.

competitive inhibitor A substance which inhibits an enzyme reaction by complexing with the enzyme at the same binding site as the substrate.

complement A group of blood proteins that combine with antibodies to cause lysis of bacterial and other cells. It consists of nine different components (known as C1 to C9) some with enzyme activity. The activation of the C1 molecule leads to the subsequent sequential activation of the other components.

complement fixation The ability of an antigen–antibody complex to bind the components of complement.

complement fixation test A test used in the diagnosis of syphilis and some viral infections that enables antibodies to be detected in the presence of known antigens and vice versa.

complementary bases Pairs of bases (purines and pyrimidines) that associate through hydrogen bonding in double-stranded nucleic acid. The following base pairs are complementary: guanine and cytosine; adenine and thymine, adenine and uracil.

complementary DNA *See* cDNA.

complementary sequences Two sequences of nucleotides that are capable of base pairing throughout their length.

complementary strands Two single strands of DNA in which the nucleotide sequence is such that they will bind as a result of base pairing throughout their full length.

complementation The situation in which a normal wild-type phenotype is formed when two homologous chromosomes, known to bear a mutant gene, are brought together in a diploid cell.

complementation test A genetic test to ascertain whether two gene mutations occur in the same functional gene and to establish the limits of the functional gene; also called the *cis–trans* test.

completely mixed bioreactor A stirred tank fermenter or a continuous single-stage, once through microbial process that does not involve recycle of the cell biomass. The contents of the bioreactor are mixed by intermittent or continuous stirring of the liquid. This is achieved by mechanical means (using an impeller) or by recycling liquid or passing a gas through it.

complexity The number of units in a non-repeating sequence of nucleotide pairs in a prokaryotic genome or a haploid complement of chromosomes.

composting A process used to hasten the aerobic decomposition of organic wastes (horticultural, agricultural or municipal)

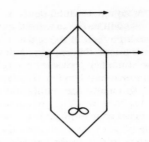

Completely mixed continuous digester

resulting in the production of a humus rich soil. The decay process is the result of the combined action of invertebrates, including insects and worms, as well as bacteria and fungi. Industrial composting technologies include various techniques for aerating the compost, as well as the addition of cultures of bacteria (including nitrogen fixers), cellulolytic or lignolytic fungi, or earthworms in order to increase the rate of decomposition.

compound A substance composed of one type of molecule only.

computer integrated fermentation (CIF) A real-time process data management system that integrates itself and computer assisted software tools into the overall fermentation process. CIF can control several fermenters simultaneously, allowing data exchange between different processes.

concanavilin A A lectin, isolated from the legume *Canavalia ensiformis*, that binds specifically to the glucose and mannose residues on the surface of transformed cells, producing agglutination.

concatemer A DNA structure made up of linearly repeated unit length DNA molecules.

concatemeric Descriptive of DNA molecules or sequences (not necessarily identical) covalently linked in series.

concentration The amount of a particular compound in a defined volume.

concentration gradient A solution in which the ratio of solvent to solute changes from one region to another in a defined manner. A continuous concentration gradient is formed by mixing a concentrated solution with a less concentrated solution, or pure solvent, in a continuous manner. A stepwise gradient is produced by layering a series of gradually less concentrated solutions one above the other in a suitable container, often a centrifuge tube.

conditional lethal mutation A mutation that kills the affected organism under one set of environmental conditions (restrictive condition) but is not lethal under another set of conditions (permissive condition).

conductimetric sensor A sensor that measures changes in conductivity in the proximity of a membrane-linked enzyme, caused by the presence of a substrate; the conductivity changes being proportional to substrate concentration.

cone A light-sensitive cell present in the retina.

confocal laser scanning microscope *See* CLSM.

congenic strains Inbred strains of an organism that differ in only a short segment of the genome.

congenital Descriptive of a disorder (genetic or otherwise) present at the time of birth.

conglutination The aggregation by conglutinin of bacteria or red blood cells that have been sensitized with antibody and sublytic amounts of complement.

conglutinin A serum protein derived from ruminants that binds to immune complexes in the presence of calcium ions, enhancing the process of phagocytosis.

conidium The haploid vegetative spore of an ascomycete fungus such as *Neurospora*. When conidia of one mating type come in contact with the protoperithecia of the opposite mating type, cell fusion followed by nuclear fusion occurs to produce diploid

cells that develop into asci as meiosis takes place.

conjugated protein A protein that contains or is linked to other non-protein moieties: for example, metalloproteins (contain metals), lipoproteins (contain lipids) and nucleoproteins (contain nucleic acids).

conjugation (1) The fusion of gametes or any union of two individuals that results in the exchange of genetic material. (2) In microbiology, the process by which DNA is transferred from bacteria of one mating type to bacteria of another during cell to cell contact.

connective tissue A matrix of cellular and fibrous tissue, found in vertebrates, in which more highly organized structures are embedded.

consanguinity The sharing of at least one recent common ancestor.

consensus sequence An average sequence derived from a number of related sequences, each nucleotide of which is the most frequent at that position in the set under consideration. For example, the promoter region of eukaryote structural genes and the recognition site for RNA polymerase.

consistency A general term for the property of a material to resist flow, defined as the ratio of shear stress to shear rate.

consortium A group of interdependent (micro)-organisms, collectively able to grow on certain substrates but unable to do so individually.

constitutive enzyme An enzyme that is synthesized under all conditions of growth, and does not require a specific substrate to induce its synthesis. *Compare* inducible enzyme.

constitutive equation An equation relating stress, strain, time and sometimes other variables such as temperature.

contact angle The angle between the interface of a solid and a fluid. This angle is used to determine interfacial tension and can also be used to assess the surface properties of various cells.

contact inhibition The cessation of cell division in, and immobilization of, a culture once it has formed a continuous monolayer over the surface on which it is growing.

contact insecticide A substance that kills an insect by penetrating the body surface and that does not need to be ingested.

contact reactor A continuous stirred tank reactor (CSTR) in which the active biomass is removed from the effluent by settling, filtration or centrifugation and recycled back into the main tank.

containment A policy of preventing the distribution of an organism or compound outside a given boundary. Containment is essential in respect of pathogens, radioactive materials, toxins, metabolic inhibitors, drugs, carcinogens, mutagens, some products of gene manipulation, oncogenic and pathogen viruses, and similar potentially dangerous materials. In many cases, legislation exists that restricts the movement of materials and type of facilities or conditions under which such compounds can be used.

containment facility A building, room or cabinet designed to prevent the escape of a dangerous material. The extent of precautions, limits to access and structural design vary according to the type of material and the potential danger if the material was released.

contaminate The addition of impurities or foreign organisms to a pure substance, cell or microbial culture.

contamination The introduction of an impurity or foreign organism into a sample or culture. The contaminant may be a chemical substance or a living organism or virus. Chemical contamination can cause problems where the chemical is an inhibitor of metabolism or cell growth, or in bioassays or enzyme assays where it interferes with or produces spurious results. Contamination of food products by organisms can cause disease. Contamination of experimental cultures or fermentation reactions by foreign organisms can produce spurious results, give poor yields or products contaminated with harmful byproducts. Contamination with radioactive materials can cause radiation hazards or invalidate experimental results.

continuous cell recycle reactor A fermentation system in which cells are continually removed from the effluent and returned directly to the fermentation vessel. The fermenter may be a simple continuous stirred tank fermenter. The cells are often separated by centrifugation. Cell recycle maintains a high cell concentration and hence a high volumetric productivity, and enables high concentration feeds to be used. A low rate of cell growth may be necessary to maintain a viable culture. The disadvantage of higher capital costs is counterbalanced by improved productivity and reduced equipment size. Several alternatives to the centrifuge for cell harvesting have been investigated. These include simple settling systems where the cells are thermally shocked to halt gas production temporarily and allowed to settle from the fermenter overflow. Alternatively, naturally flocculating organisms may be used. A related technique uses a simple partial recycle fermenter in which the overflow is taken from a vertical pipe rising through the fermenter base and jacketed by a baffled sleeve which tends to reduce the agitation of that region, so allowing the cells to separate partially from the media rising to the overflow nozzle.

continuous culture A technique that is used to maintain a culture of bacteria or cells in a condition of stable multiplication and growth. This is usually achieved by supplying a fermenter or bioreactor with a continuous supply of nutrient solution at the same rate as cells are washed out of the reactor by spent medium. *See* chemostat.

continuous fermentation A fermentation process in which the cells are kept in a state of exponential growth, or in which stationary cells continually produce a secondary product. In general, a suitable medium will be fed into the fermenter at the same rate as the effluent is removed so that conditions remain constant. If the objective is the production of cell biomass, the dilution rate will be adjusted to match the doubling rate of the cells. If the objective is to produce a secondary product, the cells will be retained in the fermenter by some device and the feed rate adjusted to the rate at which the substrate is being further metabolized to form the required end product.

continuous process A processing method in which reactants are added and products removed at equal rates, and thus the operating conditions of the process are constant.

continuous stirred tank reactor (CSTR) In fermentation, a reactor consisting of a vertical, baffled cylinder containing a rotating shaft with flat-blade impellers. The impellers create agitation and facilitate the mixing of reactants and aeration. Air is introduced through an open pipe or ring sparger at the base of the cylinder. The term is also applied to other stirred tank reactors, including anaerobic digestion.

continuous variation A phenotypic characteristic that shows variation, but which cannot be classified into two (or several) clearly distinct classes. The variation between one individual and the next may be slight, whereas if the extremes are taken a large difference can be seen. Continuous variation usually reflects the interaction of numerous genes associated with the particular trait.

continuous-flow reactor A reaction vessel in which there is continuous supply of reactants, continuous removal of products and mixing or recycling of unreacted materials.

contractile vacuole An organelle associated with osmoregulation. It is characteristic of the freshwater protozoans.

controlling element A transposable element found in eukaryotes, detectable through the abnormal activity of the standard genes that it affects.

conversion The process by which one allele of a gene participating in a cross is lost and is replaced by the other allele during recombination. Conversion results from the formation of heteroduplex DNA during recombination and the subsequent repair of non-complementary bases in the heteroduplex DNA.

conversion efficiency *See* per cent yield.

cooling coil A tubular heat exchanger in which the surface area is increased by winding a long thin tube, often made of copper, stainless steel, etc., in a circular manner. This may be inserted into or used to jacket a fermenter or bioreactor. Cooled water is passed through the coil as a means of removing metabolic heat and maintaining constant reactor temperature.

cooling tower A mechanical device used to lower the temperature of cooling water, or as a means of cooling hot process water from evaporators, vacuum pans, steam turbines, etc., so that the water may be recycled and re-used or discharged to the environment at an acceptable temperature. As water falls through the tower, which is arranged so that maximum surface area is provided, heat exchange occurs between the water and the atmosphere.

cooling water Water used as a medium for the removal of process or metabolic heat. The water is cycled between a heat exchanger associated with the reactor and a cooling tower or refrigeration plant. The maximum temperature of the available cooling water is of importance in sizing of the cooling surfaces required to maintain the temperature of any particular process, and the operating costs for cooling systems depend on the temperature of the water. Cooling water temperatures depend on the origin of the water, the climatic conditions and the type of cooling system used (cooling tower or refrigeration).

Coomasie brilliant blue A stain used to reveal the position of proteins on gels, following separation by electrophoresis or chromatography.

copy number The characteristic number of plasmids that develop in a single bacterial host cell after the introduction of a specific vector.

cordial A beverage produced from distilled spirit and aromatic flavourings containing not less than 2.5 per cent sugar by weight and a fairly low alcohol content.

coriolin Any of a number of antineoplastic antibiotics produced by the fungus Coriolus consors.

corn steep liquor A liquor generated in the early stages of wet milling of corn (maize). The grain is submerged in water where the microbial and enzyme reaction contributes to the swelling and softening of the grain, allowing subsequent separation of the starch, oil and protein. Soluble components are leached out of the grain to form the corn steep liquor which may be concentrated and used as a component of fermentation media or as an animal feed.

corn syrup See glucose syrups, high fructose syrup.

corolla The petals of a flower.

coronary vessels In vertebrates, the paired blood vessels that supply the heart muscle.

corpus luteum A structure formed within the graafian follicles of the mammalian ovary following ovulation. It has a temporary endocrine function, secreting progesterone, a hormone that prepares the uterus for implantation. If fertilization does not occur the corpus luteum disintegrates.

correlation The degree of relationship between two attributes or measurements made on the same group of objects or organisms.

correlation analysis A statistical procedure used to determine the degree of correlation between two sets of values or measurements.

correlation coefficient A measure of the degree of correlation having the value of +1 for perfect positive correlation, the value of −1 for perfect negative correlation and the value of 0 for complete lack of correlation.

cortex An outer zone of tissue in any organ, usually visually distinct from the inner medulla.

corticosteroid A steroid containing 21 carbon atoms with a double bond at C4 and a ketonic group at C3 and C20, synthesized in the mammalian adrenal cortex. A number of corticosteroids show hormonal activity related to homeostasis and survival under stress.

corticosterone A glucocorticoid hormone found in small mammals. It is the main glucocorticoid in rodents.

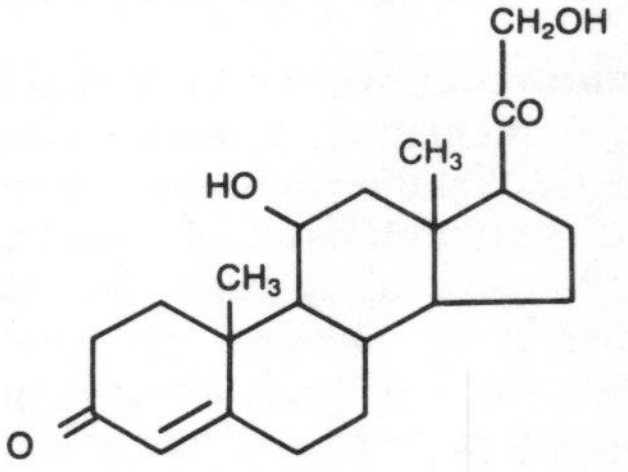

Corticosterone

corticotrophin A synonym for adrenocorticotrophic hormone (ACTH); a straight-chain polypeptide hormone secreted by the mammalian pituitary gland during periods of stress. Its main effects are on the stimulation of the synthesis and release of corticosteroid hormones.

cortisol The main glucocorticoid hormone produced by the adrenal cortex of many mammals including man.

cortisone A glucocorticoid used to treat rheumatoid arthritis.

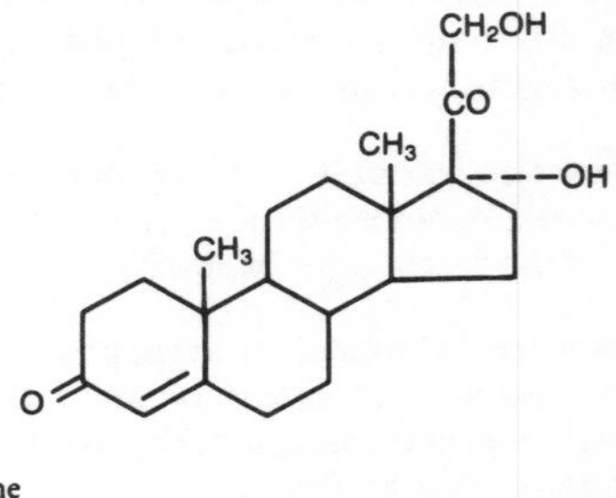

Cortisone

Corynebacterium glutamicum A fermentative bacteria used to produce amino acids.

cosmid A synthetic self-replicating particle constructed from a plasmid that contains a fragment of lambda-DNA coding for the sequence of the cos site (recognition site) for the lambda-packaging system.

Cot curve A plot of percentage reassociation of denatured DNA as a function of Cot units.

Cot unit The product of the concentration of the nucleic acid and time of reaction. It may be expressed in terms of moles of nucleotides times seconds per litre. It is used in the measurement of reassociation of heat-denatured DNA. The rate at which denatured DNA reassociates is dependent on the genome size, the variety of differing base sequences and the extent of repeated sequences in the molecules under investigation. Only complementary single strands will pair hence various types of DNA may be characterized in this way. The percentage of DNA renatured at any given Cot value may be determined either by chromatographic separation of the double-stranded DNA, or by measurement of the change in absorption of ultraviolet light by the solution. Upon renaturing, the hyperchromicity decreases in proportion to the amount of double-stranded DNA formed. The rate of annealing of any given sequence depends on its complexity or the frequency of its occurrence in any strand. Short, simple or highly repeated sequences will renature quickly, whereas unique sequences will renature slowly, or not at all. Hence, a Cot curve of eukaryotic DNA will often show four distinct regions which relate to palindromic sequences, highly repetitious DNA, moderately repetitious DNA and unique sequence DNA.

cotyledon The embryonic leaf or leaves of angiosperms or gymnosperms. The number of cotyledons is used as a method of classification of vascular plants. The angiosperms are divided into two groups known as dicotyledons (two seed leaves) or monocotyledons (one seed leaf). Gymnosperms have a variable number of cotyledons (up to 12).

Coulter counter An automatic cell counter that measures the changes in resistance that occur when cells (e.g., bacteria or blood cells) suspended in a saline solution are drawn through a glass orifice. The size of the change in resistance, which occurs every time a cell passes through the orifice, is proportional to the volume of the cell. Therefore, the Coulter counter is able to determine the proportions of different size fractions in a given sample as well as the total volume of cells.

counter ions Buffering cations.

counterstaining A technique in which a specimen that has already been stained to show one type of component is stained with a second stain which highlights the background of another type of cell constituent. For instance, a cell may be stained to show the nucleus and then counterstained to colour the cytoplasm.

coupled reaction The linking of an exogonic reaction and an endogonic reaction in such a way that there is only a small net change in free energy, resulting in an overall reversible reaction. In living organisms, anabolic reactions are coupled with catabolic reactions resulting in the build up of complex molecules, but with an overall loss of energy as metabolic heat.

coupling efficiency A measure of the activity of immobilized cells or enzymes divided by the activity of an equivalent quantity of free cells or enzymes.

coupling factor A complex, membrane-bound, multi-subunit structure with ATPase activity, associated with phosphorylation in both respiration and photosynthesis. Coupling factor is found on the membranes of mitochondria and chloroplasts.

covalently closed circular DNA Circular double-stranded DNA, without any discontinuities or nicks, which occurs as a super-coiled molecule. *See* super-coiled DNA.

cpDNA Chloroplast DNA.

Crabtree effect A form of substrate inhibition seen in yeasts such as *Saccharomyces cerevisiae* in which media with a glucose content of over 5 per cent totally inhibit the formation of respiratory enzymes, even in the presence of air.

crassulacean acid metabolism (CAM) plants Higher plants in which the photosynthetic carbon reduction cycle is supplemented by a second carbon assimilation pathway based on an initial fixation of carbon dioxide by the enzyme phosphoenol pyruvate carboxylase. Many CAM plants live in arid environments, and CAM metabolism may be associated with a need to conserve water. In the classic CAM plant, the stomata are only open in the dark (at night) when carbon dioxide is incorporated into malate. In the light (day time), the stomata close and malate is decarboxylated releasing carbon dioxide internally. This carbon dioxide is then refixed through the normal photosynthetic carbon reduction pathway.

Creutzfeldt–Jakob disease *See* spongiform encephalopathy.

crista A projection of the internal membrane of a mitochondrion.

critical micelle concentration The lowest surfactant concentration at which the formation of micelles occurs.

cro protein A protein formed in bacterial cells infected with bacteriophage. The cro protein blocks synthesis of a repressor molecule which prevents the lytic cycle of replication occurring.

cross The combining of gametes from two individuals or the result of such a procedure.

crosscurrent flow A pattern of flow that occurs in a continuous process where the main reactant stream is crossed by a series of secondary streams flowing into it at right angles. The concentration of product in each successive product stream diminishes as the mass of reactant in the main stream gradually decreases.

cross-fertilization A process in which zygotes are produced by gametes from different individuals.

crossflow filtration A filtration process in which the fluid travels parallel to the membrane surface reducing the possibility of blinding or precipitation on the membrane surface.

cross-hybridization Hybridization of a probe to imperfectly matching (less than 100 per cent complementary) molecules.

cross-linker Equipment that uses ultraviolet light to facilitate the transfer of DNA and RNA fragments from electrophoresis gels to nitrocellulose or nylon membranes.

cross-linking Formation of covalent bonds by bases in two complementary and opposite DNA strands by mitotic poisons such as the antibiotic mitomycin C.

cross-over The exchange of chromatid segments between a homologous pair during meiosis. This results in an exchange of DNA that produces genetic recombination through the breakdown of established linkage groups. The phenomenon is closely correlated with chiasmata frequency although the locality of the primary DNA cross may not be the same as that of the visible chiasma. The probability of a cross-over occurring in any region of a chromosome is primarily a function of the distance between the two loci, although other factors such as centromere proximity, distance to another cross-over, and chromosome structural abnormalities can decrease cross-over frequency.

cross-over units The distance in terms of probability of cross-over occurring between two linked loci on a chromosome.

cross-over value A number that indicates the degree of crossing-over between genes at two loci, and hence the degree of linkage between them. It is expressed in terms of the percentage of recombinants in the total number of offspring from a given cross. Cross-over values are used in the production of linkage maps which show the relative position of the genes on a chromosome. If two genes are far apart, the probability of cross-over is much higher than that for two genes situated at adjacent loci.

cross-protection The infection of an organism by one type of virus that prevents infection by another similar virus.

cross-reaction The reaction of a substance other than a target antigen with an antibody during an immunoassay, causing inaccuracies in experimental results.

crossing-over *See* cross-over.

crown gall A symptom of infection or description of the disease caused by *Agrobacterium tumefaciens* found in dicotyledonous plants. It is of particular interest in genetic manipulation since it is associated with a specific plasmid (the Ti plasmid) which may be used as a vector for introduction of new genes into plant cells.

crude extract A preparation made from biological material in which the cells have been disrupted and the cellular debris removed by centrifugation or precipitation, but little (if any) further attempt has been made to purify the sample.

cryobiology The study of the effects of low temperature on living organisms and their preservation.

cryogen A freezing mixture.

cryogenics The study of the behaviour of materials at low temperature or the application of low-temperature techniques.

cryopreservation A technique used to store living organisms at low temperatures (e.g., using liquid nitrogen). In particular, bacterial, fungi and yeasts may be stored in this way in culture collections.

cryoprotectants Protective agents (e.g., dimethyl sulphoxide, glycerol, sucrose) that are added to cell suspensions before cryopreservation. They protect the cells from the stresses of freezing and thawing.

cryptic plasmid A plasmid to which phenotypic traits have not yet been ascribed.

crystal violet A stain used to identify bacteria.

CSTR *See* continuous stirred tank reactor. *See also* bioreactor, fermenter, stirred tank fermenter.

CTP *See* cytidine 5′-triphosphate.

cultivar (1) In horticulture, a particular strain or selected clone of a given species. (2) In general taxonomy, a grouping below the subspecies level.

culture A collection of microbial cells. If all the cells are identical, the culture is said to be pure; pure culture is synonymous with clone. If the culture contains different microbes, it is said to be mixed.

culture collection A collection of authentic pure cultures of microorganisms and cultured cell lines.

culture optimization An iterative procedure whereby the composition of nutrient media and growth conditions are changed a little at a time in order to identify those conditions under which maximum growth rate occurs.

curdlan An uncharged microbial polysaccharide of glucose found in *Alicaligenes faecalis* and various *Agrobacterium* species. It forms a non-reversible gel on heating. It has uses in the food industry and enzyme immobilization and acts as an antitumour agent.

curds The solid coagulated product derived from milk when treated with rennet, used as a culture medium for *Lactobacillus* and other organisms.

curie A unit of radiation defined as the quantity of radon in radioactive equilibrium with 1 g of radium, equal to 3.7×10^{10} disintegrations per second. In biological work, the microcurie is often used, although the official SI unit is now the becquerel.

curing agent A chemical catalyst added to the components of a polymer to effect polymerization.

custom synthesis A service provided by a chemical manufacturer who produces small amounts of specialist materials designed to the needs of the client. Two areas of custom synthesis commonly contracted are the production of radiolabelled molecules for tracer work and the production of specific oligonucleotide sequences.

cut A break through both strands of DNA, as distinct from a nick which is a break in a single strand.

cuticle An outer layer of fatty materials secreted by the epidermis of plants. The cuticle protects against water loss.

cutin A complex mixture of fatty acids that makes up the cuticle of higher plants.

cuvette A glass or similar vessel used to hold samples in spectrophotometric analysis.

CVI *See* common variable immunodeficiency.

Cyanocobalamin (vitamin B$_{12}$)

Cyanobacteria Photosynthetic, oxygen-producing prokaryotes, previously known as the blue-green algae.

cyanocobalamin (vitamin B$_{12}$) A highly complex organic compound comprising a tetrapyrrole to which cobalt is chelated, with cyanide and a nucleotide coordinated to the cobalt. Vitamin B$_{12}$ can be absorbed from the intestine only in the presence of intrinsic factor, which is secreted by the gastric mucosa. The active form of the vitamin is cobalamin.

cyanogen bromide A reagent that breaks down proteins into peptides by cleavage of specific methionine residues. It can also be used to cross-link proteins to matrix materials to form affinity matrices.

cyanophyte *See* cyanobacteria.

cyclic adenosine monophosphate (cyclic AMP, cAMP) A form of the mononucleotide AMP that serves as a metabolic regulator in animals and bacteria and possibly plants (in phytochrome-related reactions). Cyclic AMP mediates the action of hormones such as prostaglandins, catecholamines and many pituitary hormones, which act by stimulating the formation of cyclic AMP from ATP.

cyclic AMP *See* cyclic adenosine monophosphate.

cyclodextrin (CD) Any of a number of oligosaccharides based on glucopyrinose units that are linked to form a ring structure. The three natural CDs, α, β and γ, contain 6, 7 and 8 units, respectively. The molecule consists of an apolar, electron-rich, hydrophobic interior with exterior sites available for hydrophilic interactions at the entrances to the internal cavity. Substitution at the 2, 3 and 6 hydroxyl groups markedly increase their aqueous solubility enabling CDs to be used as carriers for molecules that are entrapped in the centre cavity. Applications include drug delivery and diagnostics.

cycloheximide (actidione) An antibiotic that inhibits DNA and protein synthesis on

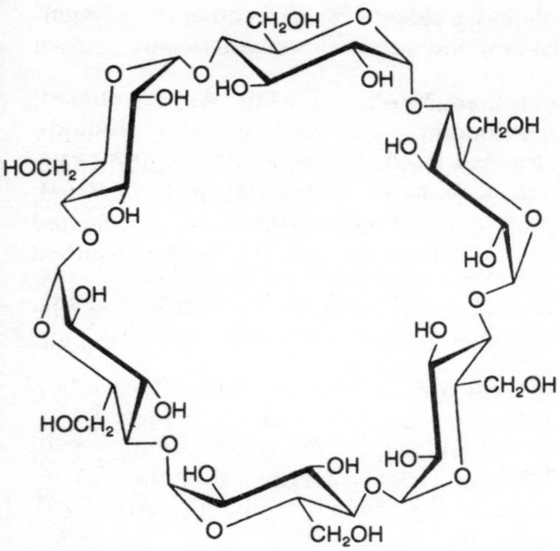

α-cyclodextrin

eukaryote cytoplasmic ribosomes, but has little effect on bacterial or chloroplast protein synthesis. This property enables it to be used in tests to determine if yeast cultures (used in the production of beer, for example) are contaminated with bacteria and some wild yeasts which are less sensitive than the cultured species of *Saccharomyces* (and *S. uvarum*, in particular). It may also be used in experimental studies concerning the function of chloroplastic ribosomes in combination with the use of chloramphenicol.

cyclosporin A drug used in organ transplant surgery that suppresses the immune response system.

Cys An abbreviation for the amino acid cysteine used in protein sequences and elsewhere.

cysteine (cys) A sulphur-containing amino acid. One of the 20 common amino acids found in protein.

Cysteine contributes to the secondary and tertiary structure of proteins since disulphide bridges may be formed between two cysteine molecules in the same or adjacent polypeptide chains.

Cysteine   HSCH₂CH(NH₂)COOH

cystic fibrosis The most common genetic disease of Caucasians, inherited as an autosomal recessive gene situated on the long arm of chromosome 7. This disease leads to increase mucous viscosity and impaired ciliary action in the lungs, as well as pancreatic abnormalities; these in turn frequently lead to dietary problems and pneumonia.

cystine A chemical compound that consists of two cysteine molecules joined by a disulphide bond.

cytidine A nucleoside consisting of cytosine linked to D-ribose through a β-glycosidic bond.

cytidine 5′-diphosphate (CDP) A nucleoside diphosphate based on cytosine.

cytidine 5′-monophosphate (CMP) A nucleotide based on cytosine.

cytidine 5′-triphosphate (CTP) A nucleoside triphosphate based on cytosine formed in a specific reaction catalysed by CTP synthetase for which UTP is the substrate:

$$UTP + ammonia + ATP \rightarrow CTP + ADP + Pi$$

CTP is one of the bases found in nucleic acids.

cytocentrifuge A centrifuge used to remove cellular components from body fluids.

cytochrome A conjugated protein associated with electron transport and redox couples in plants, animals and bacteria. Cytochromes contain haem as the prosthetic group. The terminal electron transport chain of oxidative respiration contains at least five different cytochromes, and three distinct forms are found in the intermediate electron transport chain between photosystem I and photosystem II in photosynthesis.

cytochrome oxidase A copper-containing complex associated with cytochromes a_1 and a_2 in the terminal electron transport chain of oxidative respiration. This complex reduces molecular oxygen. It is inhibited by carbon monoxide, cyanide and hydrogen.

cytochrome P$_{450}$ An intermediate in electron transport chains, found in microsomes for example. It is associated with desaturation of fatty acids and hydroxylation of steroids. ATP is not produced during electron transfer through these electron transport chains.

cytogenetics A branch of biology that links chromosome form and function. It may be used as a means for the diagnosis of inherited disease.

cytokine A polypeptide secreted by cells that affect the functions of other cells. Cytokines play an important role in the interactions between cells in the immune system. *See* interleukin, lymphokine, monokine.

cytokinesis The division of cytoplasm that follows nuclear division. In plants, it begins with the formation of the phragmoplast in early telophase and results in cell plate formation.

cytokinin A naturally occurring plant growth substance: a kinin.

cytology The study of the microscopic structure of cells.

cytolysis Lysis or destruction of cells. Certain T lymphocytes sensitized to specific antigens are capable of destroying target cells bearing these antigens; a group of lymphocytes called NK cells can destroy target cells without specific sensitization.

cytomegalovirus (CMV) An enveloped icosahedral virus that contains double-stranded DNA. It is related to herpes virus and may cause congenital deformities if present during pregnancy.

cytoplasm A term used to include all the living parts of a cell, bounded by the plasma membrane, but excluding the nucleus.

cytoplasmic inheritance Inheritance other than that associated with the nuclear DNA in eukaryotes, or the main chromosomal DNA of prokaryotes. In eukaryotes, cytoplasmic inheritance is mainly associated with the transmission of mitochondria and/or chloroplasts from one maternal generation to the next. In prokaryotes, it is generally due to the transmission of plasmids from one generation to the next.

cytosine (C) A pyrimidine base, derivatives of which are constituents of nucleic acids and nucleotides.

Cytosine

cytosol The part of the cytoplasm that does not contain any membrane or particulate structures.

cytotoxic drug Any drug that kills cells. The term is sometimes used specifically to refer to compounds that kill cancer cells.

D

2,4-D *See* 2,4-dichlorophenoxyacetic acid.

D loop A structure formed at the start of DNA replication in which a short length is displaced from its complementary strand by a length of newly formed DNA.

DAB *See* diaminobenzidine.

DAF *See* decay accelerating factor.

DAGT Direct antiglobulin test.

dalton The unit of atomic mass; equal to 1.660×10^{-27} kilogram or one-twelfth of the mass of a single neutral atom of carbon 12 (the most common isotope of carbon).

Dane particle A particle which can be isolated from the blood of people infected by hepatitis B. A Dane particle has a diameter of 42 nm, representing a virion. It consists of an envelope and a 27 nm nucleocapsid containing a molecule of DNA of about 3.2 kilobases which encodes for both the surface antigen (HBsAG) and the core antigen (HBcAG). *See* hepatitis B.

dark field microscopy A microscopic technique in which a sample is illuminated by an oblique beam of light concentrated by a condenser. Light only enters the field of view after it has been scattered or reflected by the sample and thus creates bright images on a dark background.

dark reaction The carbon assimilation through the photosynthetic carbon reduction cycle (PCR) and associated pathways, including the C_4 cycle and C_2 photorespiratory cycle. The dark reactions are catalysed by soluble enzymes found in the stroma of the chloroplasts, and use ATP and NADH generated in the light reactions of photosynthesis as a source of energy and reducing power.

dark repair The repair of DNA that occurs in the absence of visible light. The process consists of the removal of thymidine dimers, which are the result of exposure of DNA to radiation, and their replacement by normal sequences of bases. The dark repair reactions are catalysed by a specific DNA polymerase.

Darwinian fitness The relative fitness of one genotype compared with another, determined by its relative contribution to the following generations.

data logger A device that accepts an electrical signal, which may be analogue or digital, and converts this to a numerical output.

dating technique A method that examines the biological, chemical or physical characteristics of matter in order to determine its geological age. With biological material, the technique of carbon dating is often used. In this technique the residual level of radioactivity due to the presence of ^{14}C is measured. It is used to determine the origin of food products and of wines and spirits. Such products should be derived from fermentation or extracted from natural products. However, often a synthetic substitute can be obtained, at a much lower cost, from the products of the petrochemical industry. The radioactive carbon content of the synthetic material will be zero, because decay will have occurred for millions of years. In contrast, newly assimilated carbon fixed through photosynthesis will have a significant content of radioactive carbon. The standard for present-day material is 19 dpm per gram of carbon for material originating from C_3 plants and about 25 dpm for material originating from C_4 plants; the difference reflects the fact that C_4 plants discriminate less against the heavier isotopes of carbon. Carbon fixed prior to the advent of the atom bomb (older trees and beverages such as old port wine) will have a lower count of 12–15 dpm per gram carbon.

daughter In microbiology or molecular biology, one of the products arising from division of a cell or replication of a molecule of DNA. In such processes, two individuals or molecules will be produced which are genetically identical to the parent cell or molecule.

day-neutral plant A plant in which the tendency to flower, or not, is not influenced by the length of day (or more strictly the length of time the plant remains in a condition of total darkness). *See* long-day plant, phytochrome, short-day plant.

DE *See* dextrose equivalent.

DEAE-cellulose *See* diethyl amino-ethyl group.

dealkylation The removal of an alkyl group from a complex molecule.

deaminase An enzyme that catalyses the removal of an amino (–NH$_2$) group from a chemical compound (usually an amino acid or amine).

deamination An enzyme-catalysed process in which an amino (–NH$_2$) group is removed from an amino acid or other amine.

death phase The phase in a microbial culture during which the number of viable cells decreases. It follows the stationary phase. *Also see* deceleration phase, stationary phase.

debranching enzyme An enzyme that hydrolyses the (1,6)-links found in amylopectin and similar polysaccharides.

decant The separation of a solid from a liquid by pouring off the liquid from a settled solid; the process of pouring a fluid from one container to another.

decarboxylase An enzyme that catalyses the removal of a carboxyl group from a compound (often an organic acid).

decay accelerating factor (DAF) A membrane glycoprotein of erythrocytes, leukocytes and platelets that accelerates the breakdown of complement enzymes. DAF inhibits the amplification of the complement cascade on host cell surfaces, thus protecting them from autolysis. *See* complement.

deceleration phase The phase in a microbial culture (preceding the stationary phase) during which the rate of growth diminishes owing to substrate depletion and the accumulation of toxic or inhibiting byproducts. *Also see* death phase, stationary phase.

deciduous Descriptive of plants which shed their leaves each year.

decontamination The removal of a hazardous material such as a radioactive isotope or a pathogenic organism enabling an area to be entered, or the object re-used, without having to resort to protective clothing or precautions.

deep jet fermenter A fermentation system in which the contents are mixed and aerated by injection of a high-pressure air stream into the top of the reactor. This type of system is suitable for the production of cell biomass (single cell protein) or for fermentations that become highly viscous, since they do not employ stirrers, baffle plates or draught tubes. Such systems are

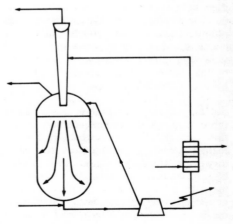

Deep jet aeration

also easier to keep aseptic, since they do not require the formation of an aseptic seal around a rotating shaft as in the case of a stirred tank system. The term may also be applied to a system in which the jet consists of part of the liquid being recycled and is reinjected at high pressure to cause agitation. Such a system is used with anaerobic organisms or in true fermentations.

deep shaft system A type of aerobic wastewater treatment that uses a deep tank usually sunk into the ground. The construction of such tanks may be based on a well-drilling procedure. The well is fitted with a lining and an inner cylinder to form a small downcomer and a bigger riser compartment. The advantage of such systems lies in the increased oxygen transfer rates which are achieved because of the greater solubility of oxygen under the high hydrostatic pressure generated by the tall water column.

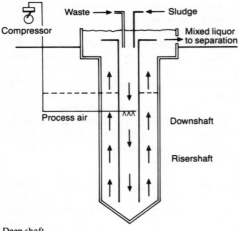

Deep shaft

deficiency In genetics, a chromosome aberration that arises from the loss of a gene or series of genes by deletion.

deficiency disease A disease resulting from a diet which lacks an essential nutrient, such as a vitamin, essential amino acid or trace element.

defined medium A culture medium of known composition containing specific

concentrations of pure chemicals. Also known as a synthetic medium.

degenerate codons Nucleotide triplets which although containing variations in the third letter will code for the same amino acid as others with the same initial letters. *See* wobble hypothesis.

degeneration An effect whereby the productivity of a microbial strain used in a commercial process diminishes after repeated transfer from one culture media to another. It is often caused by genetic mutation.

dehydration The drying or removal of water. It is used as a means of preserving biological material or preparing specimens for examination under a microscope. Dehydration, using careful freeze-drying techniques, is used to preserve bacteria, yeasts and fungi in culture collections.

dehydrogenase An enzyme that catalyses oxidation–reduction reactions by transferring hydrogen from one compound to another; a type of oxidoreductase.

deionization The removal of ions from a solution. This is usually achieved using an ion exchange resin, or a mixture of such resins.

deionized water A pure water of low conductivity from which cations and anions have been removed using ion exchange resins. If very pure deionized water is required it is usual to distil the water prior to treatment with resin.

del factor The fractional reduction of a viable organism count resulting from the application of a certain temperature over a certain period of time during a sterilization procedure.

$$\text{del factor} = N_0/N_t$$

where N_0 is the number of organisms present prior to sterilization and N_t the number at the end of the procedure.

deletion A chromosome aberration in which a section is lost during nuclear division. In some cases, deletions can be recognized at prophase in meiosis since a loop is formed to allow normal pairing on each side of the deleted region.

demeclocycline An antibiotic produced by *Streptomyces aureofaciens.*

denaturant gradient gel electrophoresis (DGGE) A separation technique based on the melting properties of DNA molecules, that is sensitive to single base differences between nucleotide sequences. When a DNA melting curve is produced, discrete portions (melting domains) are observed. The temperature or equivalent denaturant concentration at which each occurs depends on the precise sequence of the molecule. DGGE involves the electrophoresis of fragments though a gel impregnated with a concentration gradient of DNA denaturant. When a fragment reaches the denaturant concentration equivalent to the temperature at which its lowest domain melts, it begins to branch and its passage through the gel is retarded. By selecting an appropriate concentration gradient, fragments with differing nucleotide sequences can be separated.

denaturation A change in conformation and a loss of secondary and tertiary structure resulting from the loss of non-covalent bonding that occurs when proteins and nucleic acids are exposed to extreme temperature or pH, non-physiological concentrations of salt, detergents, organic solvents or other chemical agents. It can lead to unfolding of the polypeptide chain in proteins and dissociation of the helical structure in nucleic acids. The changes may be associated with changes in solubility, physical properties and biological activity. Changes may be reversible.

denatured DNA DNA that has been converted from double-stranded to a single-stranded form by breaking the hydrogen bonds joining the two complementary strands. *Compare* native DNA.

denatured protein A protein that has lost its natural configuration by exposure to a destabilizing agent such as heat.

dendrite A short process that arises from the cell body of a neurone and makes synaptic contacts with other neurones; the input region for excitation from one neuron to the next during the transfer of a nerve impulse.

denitrification The reduction of nitrates to nitrites, nitrous oxide or nitrogen catalysed by facultative aerobic soil bacteria under anaerobic conditions.

densitometer A device used to scan chromatographic plates or electrophoretic gels to evaluate the amount of various compounds present on the plate or gels. The essential parts consist of a light source, a sample holder and a detector (photomultiplier). The sample is passed continually through the light (visible or ultraviolet) beam and the changes in density, reflected light or fluorescence (depending on the mode of operation) are recorded on a chart or using a data logger. The samples being scanned are often stained using a suitable dye prior to analysis.

density gradient A carefully contrived solution or mixture of solutions of suitable salts, sugars or polymers treated in such a way that the concentration, and hence the density of the solution, varies either in a continuous or a discontinuous manner. Density gradients are used to enhance the separation of components of different density using centrifugation. *See* density gradient centrifugation.

density gradient centrifugation A process in which components of a mixture are separated by centrifugation through or in a density gradient. The gradient may be discontinuous or continuous. Sucrose is often used in the formation of discontinuous gradients; solutions of differing concentration are layered one above the other in a suitable tube. The sample is then placed on top, and the tube spun in a centrifuge. The heavier material travels through a greater number of the layers. Hence, the various fractions come to rest at the different interfaces. Continuous gradients, which may be based on caesium chloride, are often run to equilibrium such that a given molecule takes up a position where its density matches that of the gradient. Density gradient centrifugation is used in molecular biology for purification of molecular species and/or determination of molecular weight. *See* buoyant density, svedberg unit.

deoxynucleotide triphosphates *See* ATP, CTP, GTP, TTP.

deoxyribonuclease *See* DNase.

deoxyribonucleic acid *See* DNA.

deoxyribonucleotide A nucleotide in which the sugar component is deoxyribose. Deoxyribotides are formed from the corresponding D-ribose containing diphosphate and formation is catalysed by a multi-enzyme complex with thioredoxin as a cofactor.

deoxyribose A deoxysugar derived from the pentose ribose by removal of an atom of oxygen from the C-2 position. Deoxyribose is an important intermediate in DNA.

deoxysugar A sugar in which an atom of oxygen has been removed from one of the hydroxyl groups.

depolarization A reduction in the potential difference across a membrane.

depollution A process that results in the removal of a polluting substance. The term is often used in a collective manner to include all aspects of aerobic and anaerobic biological waste treatment processes.

derepression The expression (activation) of a repressed gene.

dermatophyte A fungus that causes skin disease.

dermis The inner living layer of vertebrate skin.

desalting A procedure in which salts are removed from a mixed solution of high-molecular-weight biological molecules. This is achieved by gel filtration, dialysis or

ultrafiltration. Similar techniques are used for removing other small molecules from solutions of proteins or nucleic acids (e.g., removal of phenol in extracts of nucleic acids or excess stain in fluorescent labelling of antibodies).

desiccant A chemical compound, such as calcium chloride, sodium hydroxide, concentrated sulphuric acid, silica gel, alumina gel or molecular sieves, used to remove water from a sample or to keep the air in a container dry. Many of the complex reagents and chemical compounds used in biochemistry are subject to decomposition by hydrolysis. Hence, they are stored in the presence of a desiccant in order to reduce such loss to a minimum.

detention time The length of time a liquid or solid component of the mixed liquor in a fermentation process remains in the fermenter or bioreactor. *See* mean detention time.

determined Descriptive of a cell that has reached a stage of development where its structural and metabolic fate is irreversibly established.

detritus Fragments of decomposing organic matter or any debris in general.

deuteromycetes The Fungi Imperfecti; a subdivision of the fungi that arbitrarily contains all organisms for which a true sexual stage is lacking, or has not been recognized. They are difficult to classify and lack any common phylogenetic relationship.

deutoplasm The yolk or other nutritive substance within an ovum.

dextran An uncharged polysaccharide formed by bacteria (e.g., *Acetobacter* species and *Leuconostoc mesenteroides*, and yeasts). It consists of branched chains of D-glucose residues. It is characterized by its viscous, near-Newtonian behaviour, and its ability to complex divalent ions. Dextran is used in the production of media for gel filtration chromatography (Sephadex), plasma volume expanders, ion exchangers and flow improvers. It also causes fouling problems and distorts crystal shape, producing long needles, in sugar processing. Dextran is produced commercially by growing *Leuconostoc mesenteroides* on sucrose-based media.

dextran beads Proprietary products made from cross-linked dextrans that are used as media for gel filtration chromatography, as support media for the culture of anchorage-dependent cells, for the immobilization of affinity groups, production of ion exchangers or immobilization of enzymes.

dextranase An enzyme that catalyses the hydrolysis of dextran to glucose.

dextrin A short-chain polysaccharide formed during the breakdown of starch.

dextrorotatory Descriptive of an optically active substance that rotates light to the right.

dextrose A trivial name for glucose.

dextrose equivalent (DE) An expression of the extent of hydrolysis of a polysaccharide (usually starch) to glucose. It is measured by determining the reducing sugar content of a syrup and comparing this with an authentic sample of pure glucose and expressed as a percentage. A completely hydrolysed sample of starch would thus have a DE of 100.

DGGE *See* denaturant gradient gel electrophoresis.

diabetes mellitus A disorder of glucose metabolism caused by a lack of the hormone insulin normally produced by the pancreas.

diafiltration The continuous recycling of a solution through a membrane filter with the constant addition of fresh solvent, in order gradually to remove membrane-permeating particles.

diagnosis The process of determining by examination the nature and circumstances of a diseased condition; the conclusions reached from such an examination; more generally any scientific procedure that allows a precise result or classification to be reached.

diagnostic Descriptive of a diagnosis; a symptom or characteristic having value in diagnosis. In health care and experimental biology, the term is used to describe a test or procedure that may be either qualitative or quantitative and is designed to reveal the presence or amount of specific substances (such as metabolites, enzymes or antibiotics), thus indicating a disease or pathological condition.

diagnostic enzyme An enzyme used as a specific diagnostic agent in order to obtain a qualitative or quantitative indication of the presence of a given compound which serves as the enzyme substrate.

diagnostic kit A package that contains all the required reagents, in suitable form, to carry out one or more specific assays which may be based on immune, chemical or enzyme-catalysed reactions. To be accepted for use in health care, such procedures and reagents require validation and acceptance by health authorities.

diagnostic procedure The overall series of reactions that is carried out in order to complete a diagnosis.

diagnostic reagent A chemical, buffer, enzyme, antibody preparation, etc. that is used for the purpose of diagnosis or as a component of a diagnostic kit.

diagnostics The science of diagnosis.

diakinesis A stage in the prophase of the first division of meiosis in which the centromeres move further apart and the double chromosomes take on the appearance of rings. The chromosomes continue to contract and the nucleolus begins to disappear.

dialysable Descriptive of a low-molecular-weight solute that can be removed from a solution through a semipermeable membrane during dialysis or ultrafiltration. The exact molecular weight at which a solute may be removed by dialysis depends on both the shape of the molecule and the type of membrane used.

dialysis The separation of substances of different molecular weight by diffusion through a selectively permeable membrane. A technique used to remove low-molecular-weight compounds such as salts from solutions of high-molecular-weight compounds such as proteins. The mixed solution is placed in a sealed semipermeable membrane which is immersed in water or a suitable buffer. Low-molecular-weight compounds diffuse through the membrane whereas the high-molecular-weight materials are retained.

dialysis fermentation A technique in which the cells are retained within a fermenter using a membrane at some point. The substrate and/or the product can diffuse through the membrane, thus maintaining a high biomass concentration in the reactor. Such systems may be used in series with separate stages of an overall conversion processes occurring each side of the membrane. Dialysis fermentation may be carried out as a batch technique using a simple dialysis flask fermenter. This process is readily adapted to continuous culture. In a simple continuous dialysis system, a culture of actively fermenting cells is maintained in a confined zone of the fermenter. Substrate enters the fermentation zone by diffusing through a dialysis membrane from the medium zone. Fermentation then takes place and the product diffuses back through the membrane into the medium zone, where it is recovered in an overflow. Cells cannot escape the fermentation zone, so that extremely high cell densities can be achieved. For this system, the fermentation rate is limited by the rate at which substrate can diffuse across the membrane surface. Although this rate is slow, it can be increased by applying a pressure differential across the membrane.

diaminobenzidine (DAB) A chromogenic substrate for horseradish peroxidase.

diastase A popular name for crude enzyme preparations with amylase activity.

diastole The phase of the heart cycle when all parts are relaxed.

diatomaceous earth Deposits of the skeletons of prehistoric diatoms that are mined and processed for use as adsorbents.

2,4-dichlorophenoxyacetic acid (2,4-D) A synthetic plant growth regulator with auxin-like activity used as a herbicide.

Dicotyledonae The larger subgroup of angiosperms. The group includes hardwood trees, shrubs, agricultural crops and many herbs of commercial importance as sources of fine chemicals.

dictyosome A membrane structure found in eukaryotic cells that together with associated vesicles make up the Golgi apparatus.

dideoxy sequencing A technique used for determining the nucleotide sequence of nucleic acid. After isolation in a single-stranded form, it is hybridized with DNA. This is then incubated with mixtures of deoxynucleotides and 2′,3′-dideoxynucleotides in the presence of the enzyme DNA polymerase. The procedure capitalizes on two properties of DNA polymerase: (1) its ability to synthesize a complementary copy of a single-stranded DNA template; (2) its ability to use 2′,3′-dideoxynucleoside triphosphates as substrate. Once the analogue is incorporated, the 3′-end lacks a hydroxyl group and is no longer a substrate for chain elongation. Hence the growing DNA chain is terminated. In practice, the Klenow fragment of the DNA polymerase I, which lacks the 5′-3′-exonuclease activity of the intact enzyme, is used. DNA synthesis is carried out in the presence of the four deoxynucleoside triphosphates, one or more of which is labelled with ^{32}P, in four reaction mixtures each of which contains one of the dideoxy compounds. In each final reaction mixture, on completion, there is a series of fragments of new DNA, each having a common 5′-end but varying in length to a base-specific 3′-end. These can be resolved by electrophoresis, visualized by autoradiography and the sequence read.

dielectrophoresis *See* electrofusion.

diethyl aminoethyl (DEAE) group $[OC_2H_4N(C_2H_5)_2]$ An ion exchange group incorporated into polymeric carriers, such as dextran or cellulose, in the formation of weak ion exchangers of importance in the separation and purification of proteins and other compounds of biological origin.

differentiation The general process by which unspecialized cells become specialized to carry out a particular function in the tissues or organs of multicellular organisms.

diffuser A device, such as a perforated plate, inserted in a fermenter and through which air is introduced. The purpose of the diffuser is to give a widespread output of small bubbles in order to favour the rapid and effective dissolution of oxygen in the medium.

diffusion The process whereby two miscible fluids or solutions will disperse and mix when arranged with a common area of contact. Diffusion is due to a random movement imposed on the molecules by intermolecular collision. Molecular diffusion is important in many biological and bioengineering transfer processes. Mass transfer by diffusion in the steady-state is defined by Fick's law which states that the mass rate of transfer per unit area is proportional to the gradient of concentration:

$$Q = -D(dC/dx)$$

where Q = the quantity flowing in a specified time across unit area, D = a diffusion coefficient and dC/dx = the concentration gradient in the direction of flow. It is a steady-state equation which holds when the quantity to be transferred is large in comparison with the rate of transfer, and hence the conditions at any point in the system do not change significantly with time. More complex treatment is required when the concentrations vary significantly with time:

$$dC/dt = -D(d^2C/dx^2)$$

The general principle stated in Fick's law is equally applicable to mass, heat and momentum. The form of D can be derived for each process:

Transfer	Physical operation	Diffusion coefficient
Momentum	Viscous flow	$\mu = \rho[bc]\lambda$
Heat	Thermal conduction	$k = \rho[bc]\lambda C_v$
Mass	diffusion of mass	$D = [bc]\$k$

where ρ = density, $\sqrt{c^2}$ is root mean square velocity, λ = mean free path, C_v = specific heat at constant volume, μ = viscosity and k = thermal diffusivity.

diffusional limitation The phenomenon by which the rate of diffusion of substrate into and products out of an enzyme, cell, tissue or aggregate of immobilized cells becomes limiting. Increased size of biological particles, microbial flocs, immobilized organisms or enzymes, etc. leads to diffusional limitations on substrate ingress and/or product egress, which in turn leads to reduced overall specific rates of reaction.

digester *See* anaerobic digester.

digestion (1) The breakdown of complex foodstuffs by mechanical and chemical means into simpler molecules that can be absorbed into the body. (2) The breakdown of samples of material for experimental or analytical purposes *in vitro*. For example, samples of proteins or carbohydrates may be digested with either enzymes or dilute acids prior to analysis of the constituent amino acids or sugars.

digital Data represented as discontinuous numerical units. *Compare* analogue.

digital DNA sequence scanner A computerized system for determining DNA sequences; autoradiographic films are scanned and the visual information is then digitized allowing the image to be manipulated on a VDU.

digoxin A heart stimulant derived from the foxglove *Digitalis lantata*.

dihybrid An organism that is heterozygous for two pairs of alleles at independently assorted loci (e.g., AaBb). A parental combination that results in a 9:3:3:1 ratio of progeny.

dihybrid cross A cross between individuals that have different alleles at two gene loci.

dihydroxyphenylalanine (L-DOPA) An amino acid that is a precursor of the catecholamines: dopamine, adrenaline and noradrenaline. It is administered in the treatment of Parkinson's disease in order to raise the levels of brain dopamine which are deficient.

dikaryon A heterokaryon with two nuclei per cell.

dikaryosis Cells containing two nuclei that differ in size, appearance or genetic make-up.

dilution cloning The isolation of clones by repeatedly plating out increasingly dilute cell suspensions until colonies derived from a single cell are achieved.

dilution rate In continuous fermentation, a measure of the rate at which the existing medium is replaced with fresh medium. The dilution rate is the reciprocal of the hydraulic detention time.

dimension A physical property of an object or substance of which the fundamentals are mass (M), length (L), temperature (θ) and time (T). These may be used to define other dimensions which are important in the engineering description of processes.

dimensionless groups Any of a number of specific combinations of physical properties expressed in terms of ratios such that the dimensions cancel producing a group that is wholly numeric. Such quantities are ratios of equivalent properties of a system and are important in certain aspects of chemical engineering. The value of dimensionless groups lies in the fact that they are not confined to the characteristics of a specific system. For example, the behaviour of a fluid in one size of pipe can be determined in another more convenient size with another liquid provided that the dimensionless group (in this case the Reynolds number) is the same for both.

Quantity	Definition	Dimensions
Velocity	Distance moved in unit time	LT^{-1}
Acceleration	Change of velocity with time	LT^{-2}
Force	Product of mass and acceleraton	MLT^{-2}
Density	Mass per unit volume	ML^{-3}
Momentum	Product of mass and velocity	MLT^{-1}
Energy	Product of force and distance	$ML^{2}T^{-2}$
Pressure	Force per unit area	$ML^{-1}T^{-2}$
Viscosity	Pressure per unit velocity gradient	$ML^{-1}t^{-1}$
Kimematric viscosity	Quotient of viscocity and density	$L^{2}T^{-1}$
Heat	—	$ML^{2}T^{-2}$
Specific heat	—	$L^{2}T^{-2}\theta^{-1}$

dimethylsulphoxide (DMSO) A compound that partially denatures the DNA double helix. It is used in tissue culture to induce the expression of certain genes.

dimorphic Descriptive of species that exist in two distinct forms. These distinct forms may represent different stages of the life cycle of two different sexes. The term may also be applied to parts of the body or subcellular organelles where two structures of similar function differ in appearance (e.g., dimorphic chloroplasts as found in some C_4 plants).

dioctyl plithalate (DOP) A substance used to test the integrity of filters (e.g., fermenter inlet and exhaust filters).

dioecious Descriptive of plants in which the male and female flowers are produced on separate individuals.

diosgenin A substance used in the synthesis of antifertility steroids. Diosgenin is derived from the yam *Dioscorea deltoidea*.

diphtheria A serious disease caused by *Corynebacterium diphtheriae*. It is cured by treatment with an antitoxin derived from the blood of animals injected with a purified toxoid. Recovery from the disease is followed by lasting immunity.

diphtheria toxin The toxin produced by *Corynebacterium diphtheriae*. It is a single polypeptide of molecular weight 62,000 which contains two disulphide bridges associated with a loop of 14 amino acids involved in the toxicity and immunogenic specificity of the molecule.

diplanetism Possessing two types of zoospores, hence two swarming stages in the life cycle. Diplanetism is characteristic of some Phycomycetes.

diplobiont An organism that has both haploid and diploid somatic stages in the life cycle.

diploblastic Descriptive of animals of which the body wall is composed of only two cell layers.

diploid Description of a nucleus, cell or organism that contains $2n$ chromosomes (i.e. twice the haploid number) which pair normally. All chromosomes except the sex chromosomes occur in homologous pairs which are structurally and genetically similar in respect to the number and position of gene loci. Most animals are diploid, as are the sporophyte generations of plants which show alternation of generations.

diplont An organism that has a diploid somatic state.

diplotene A stage in the prophase of the first division of meiosis in which the two chromatids of each chromosome become visible. The paired chromosomes begin to separate from one another, although points of attachment (chiasmata) are visible.

dipole A pair of equal and opposite electrical charges or magnetic poles present on the same molecule or object.

disaccharide A carbohydrate that consists of two monosaccharides joined by a glycosidic link (e.g., sucrose, cellobiose, maltose, lactose).

disc centrifuge A centrifuge that consists of a bowl containing a stack of perforated, truncated cones used primarily for clarification and breaking-up of emulsions.

disease A condition in which the normal functioning of an organism is disturbed by some agent. The cause may be infection with another organism (pathogen), a genetic disorder or the effect of a chemical compound.

disease resistance The ability to prevent infection by disease-causing agents. In animals, disease resistance is largely associated with the immune system and activities of the white blood cells and lymphocytes.

disjunction The separation of pairs of homologous chromosomes and their movement to opposite poles during anaphase I of meiosis.

dispase A commercial enzyme preparation that breaks down connective tissue.

dissolved carbon dioxide The amount of carbon dioxide, expressed in terms of equivalent volume under standard conditions, moles or weight, in true solution in unit volume of culture medium or other liquid.

dissolved oxygen electrode A sensor used to measure oxygen in solution. It consists of a cathode covered by a selectively permeable membrane.

distal Descriptive of the part of a limb or other organ that is furthest from the point of attachment.

distillation A process used in the purification of volatile compounds. Heat is applied to a mixture and the vapour condensed in a distillation column. However, the separation of two liquids by simple vaporization and condensation is not effective, except in the case of liquids with widely differing boiling points. Better separation is achieved by a series of simple distillations, but this is not practicable. The same result may be obtained using a fractionating column through which the vapour is passed and contacted with part of the condensate flowing back down the column. Greater separation is obtained if most of the vapour condensed at the top of the column is returned as a reflux.

distilled spirits Ethanol obtained by distillation of a beer or wine.

distillers' grains A dried material, often used as animal feed, obtained from the solids fraction following distillation of alcohol from grain-based fermentations. Distillers' grains are rich in protein, vitamins, minerals, organic acids, fats and fibres. The solids are obtained by centrifugation or by filtration and pressing, followed by drying in a horizontal rotary drier to about 10 per cent moisture. Dried products are called distillers' light or dark grains, depending on whether the syrup produced from the liquid portion of the spent grains has been added back.

distillers' solubles A solid, or high solids liquid, produced by concentrating the spent liquor obtained during recovery of distillers' grains. The solubles may be added back to the solids to produce 'dark grains'.

distribution coefficient (k_{av}) In gel filtration chromatography, the fraction of the total gel volume that is available to the solute.

$$k_{av} = (V_e - V_0)/(V_t - V_0)$$

where V_e = the elution volume, V_0 = the void volume and V_t = the bed volume. There is a linear relationship between k_{av} and log molecular weight of many substances, including globular proteins. Gel filtration can be used in a column calibrated with standard proteins to determine the approximate molecular weight of an unknown protein sample.

disulphide bond A chemical bond, formed in protein, between the sulphur atoms of two molecules of cysteine. Such bonds are important in determining the tertiary structure of proteins and the shape of catalytic sites. In enzyme isolation, sulphydral reagents may be added to protect such bonds and prevent loss of enzyme activity.

dithiothreitol *threo*-2,3-Dihydroxy-1,4-dithiolbutane; a sulphydryl compound used to protect sulphydryl groups in proteins during the isolation and assay of enzymes.

diuresis Excessive discharge of urine.

diuretic A substance that increases the volume of urine produced.

diurnal rhythm A change in biological activity that occurs with a periodicity of about 24 hours, showing a change in behaviour between day and night.

divalent Descriptive of an ion having a valency of two. Divalent ions are extremely important cofactors in many enzyme reactions especially those associated with oxidation–reduction reactions.

diverticulum A blind-ending tube branching off from a canal or cavity.

division (1) The separation of genetic material to form daughter nuclei, as in meiosis and mitosis. (2) A unit used in the classification of plants consisting of a number of classes; it corresponds to a phylum in animals.

DMSO *See* dimethylsulphoxide.

DNA Deoxyribonucleic acid; a complex biological polymer that carries and transmits the genetic information in most organisms – an exception being the RNA viruses. The basic structure of the DNA molecule is formed from nucleotides based on purines (adenine and guanine) and pyrimidines (cytosine and thymine). Adjacent nucleotides are linked by phosphodiester bonds between the phosphate of one and the 3'-carbon of the next to form two helical single strands. DNA occurs in both a double-stranded and a single-stranded form. Of these the double-stranded form is important as it carries the genetic information in most organisms. The basic structure of double-stranded DNA is a double helix in which two single strands of DNA are arranged in an antiparallel direction such that the 3'-end of one strand is paired with the 5'-end of the complementary strand. The two strands are joined by hydrogen bonding between complementary bases arranged perpendicularly to the long axis of the helix. Adenine only pairs with thymine, and guanine only pairs with cytosine. Each turn of the helix comprises 10 base pairs which are at a distance of 0.34 nm. The length of a full turn is thus 34 nm. Interaction also occurs between the bases in a vertical direction where the parallel position of the apolar heterocyclic structures within a polar environment leads to stacking of the bases, giving additional strength to the structure. *See also* base pairing, DNA replication. (*See* following two figures.)

DNA filter assay An analytical procedure used to recognize recombinant DNA in cloned cells. The transformed cells only represent a small percentage of the total population of cells present in a culture. The culture is diluted and plated on petri dishes at such a concentration that individual colonies form from each cell. A replicate of the pattern of cells on the plate is taken using a cellulose nitrate filter. The cells are lysed, and the filter heated to bind the DNA on to the filter in a denatured form in a position equivalent to that of the cell colonies on the petri dish. The filter is then treated with the probe which combines by DNA hybridization only at positions of transformed DNA. These are then located using autoradiography or fluorescent antibodies, as appropriate. *See* affinity labelling, southern blot.

DNA

DNA gyrase An enzyme involved in the replication of DNA. It relaxes the tension of supercoiled twists by breaking a phosphodiester bond in one of the parental strands ahead of the replication fork, creating a swivel in the opposite strand about which the molecule rotates. Once the tension has been removed, gyrase then catalyses the reformation of the phosphodiester bond.

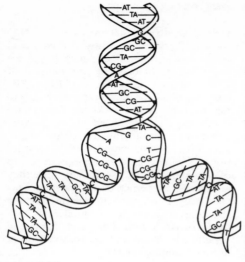

DNA double helix.

DNA ligase An enzyme that catalyses the synthesis of DNA and can seal single-stranded nicks between adjacent nucleotides in a double-stranded DNA chain. *In vitro* the enzyme joins covalently the annealed cohesive ends produced using certain restriction enzymes. It also catalyses the formation of phosphodiester bonds between blunt-ended fragments of DNA. The enzyme is widely used in gene manipulation.

DNA modification Alteration of DNA by the addition of various side groups (often methyl groups) brought about by specific enzymes.

DNA phage A phage in which the genetic information is carried as DNA.

DNA polymerase An enzyme that synthesizes a new DNA strand if provided with a growing point in the form of a pre-existing primer which is base-paired with the template and bears a free 3'-OH group. Different enzyme types occur that are associated with either DNA synthesis or DNA repair.

DNA polymerase I A DNA polymerase isolated from *E. coli* which is used in gene manipulation and genetic engineering. It is used to convert single-stranded tails to double-stranded form (i.e., converting the sticky ends of restriction fragments to blunt ends). It is also used to convert single-stranded cDNA to duplex cDNA. The polymerase I molecule is susceptible to protease action which splits into two specific fragments. The larger (Klenow) fragment has polymerase activity and 3'-5'-exonuclease activity, but lacks 5'-3'-exonuclease activity, and is sometimes employed as an exonuclease. The polymerase is also used in nick translation to prepare radioactive hybridization probes.

DNA polymerase III An enzyme identified in *E. coli* that functions at the replication fork by extending synthesis on both the leading and lagging strands. On the lagging strands, it utilizes a primer synthesized by an RNA polymerase.

DNA probe A short length of DNA of known sequence or origin that is labelled in such a way that it can be subsequently recognized. The label may be an isotopic marker, such as radioactive phosphate, or a chemical compound that can act as a binding site for an affinity label. The probe is used in DNA filter assay.

DNA repair An enzyme mediated process catalysed by ligases and polymerases that reduces the damage caused to genetic material by radiation and other mutagenic agents.

DNA replication The formation of new DNA molecules, the information passed on with great accuracy to the daughter molecules. During this process, each strand of the double helix serves as a template for the synthesis of a complementary strand, thus producing two molecules identical to the parent strand. Three separate replication methods are known. In prokaryotes, replication is carried out by the rolling circle method or theta-replication, both methods being suited to replication of circular DNA molecules. In eukaryotes, the replication of linear molecules is initiated at specific points by the formation of replication bubbles. There may be several hundred such initiation points per molecule. Once a bubble forms, it grows in size as replication proceeds in both directions. As replication continues, adjacent bubbles fuse to form larger bubbles and Y-shaped intermediates (replication forks). Replication then proceeds by a semi-conservative mechanism (i.e. each daughter contains one new and one old strand). As the two complementary strands of DNA are antiparallel, the movement of the replication fork coincides with the 3′ to 5′ direction in one template strand and to the 5′ to 3′ direction in the other. However, all enzymes catalysing the DNA synthesis are specific for the direction of template and can only copy from the 3′-end to the 5′-end. The explanation as to how DNA growth can occur in opposite directions at the same time was suggested by Okazaki, who postulated that many small DNA fragments are formed (synthesized in the correct direction) and then joined together to form longer chains corresponding to parts of the template. These short fragments of around 100 to 2000 residues are now known as Okazaki fragments. Following binding of the fragments to the template in the correct position, a maturation process occurs in which the Okazaki fragments are joined together. At the same time, a continual unwinding of the parent DNA takes place at the replication fork. This is catalysed by unwinding protein.

DNA sequencing The determination of the order in which the bases are arranged within a length of DNA. A number of different techniques are used. These include either enzymic digestion with restriction endonucleases or chemical hydrolysis. *See* dideoxy sequencing, Maxam–Gilbert chemical sequencing.

DNA synthesizer *See* oligonucleotide synthesizer.

DNA unwinding enzyme An ATP-dependent enzyme involved in the early stages of DNA replication. It unwinds the parental strand to create the two template strands.

DNA-dependent RNA polymerase *See* RNA polymerase.

DNA-PRINS *See* PRINS.

DNase An enzyme that breaks down DNA. Most DNases require a divalent cation as cofactor (e.g., Ca^{2+}, Mg^{2+}, etc.), hence activity can be blocked by the addition of EDTA during isolation of DNA. The enzymes break the phosphodiester bonds in the sugar–phosphate backbone. Both endonucleases and exonucleases are known. These show specificities for either single-stranded or double-stranded DNA. Restriction endonucleases are an important group of enzymes with DNase activity since they are specific for certain base sequences. This specificity is of value in determining the structure of genes and in preparing fragments of DNA with sticky ends for use in gene manipulation and the construction of artificial cloning vectors.

DNase-free reagent *See* nuclease-free reagent.

domain A portion of a protein that has a discrete structure or a function that is independent of the rest of the protein.

dominant Descriptive of one of a pair of alleles that is expressed in the phenotype irrespective of the nature of the other (recessive) allele.

donor An organism from which organs, tissues or other cells are transferred to another individual.

DOP *See* dioctyl plithalate.

DOPA *See* dihydroxyphenylalanine.

dopamine A neurotransmitter, low levels of which are associated with Parkinson's disease. Overproduction of dopamine is associated with psychological disorders such as schizophrenia.

dopastin A hypotensive produced by *Pseudomonas*.

dormancy A state of low metabolic activity found in the resting and overwintering stages of the life cycles of many organisms; an adaptation to adverse conditions.

dorsal The upper surface of an organism; the surface of a chordate that is nearest the notochord.

dot-blot A semi-quantitative procedure for simultaneously detecting a specific base sequence in a large number of DNA and RNA samples. The samples are dotted on to a nitrocellulose filter by adsorption and incubated with a radiolabelled probe specific to the desired base sequence. The filter is then washed and dried and the desired sequence detected by autoradiography.

double digestion The use of two different restriction endonucleases in conjunction to cleave a DNA molecule.

double fertilization The simultaneous process of zygote formation and endosperm initiation found in angiosperms. It arises from the fertilization of both the egg cell and a polar nucleus by generative nuclei from the pollen tube.

double helix Description of the structure of DNA. *See* DNA.

double recessive An individual that is homozygous for a recessive characteristic which is therefore expressed phenotypically.

doubling time The time taken for the number of cells, or the weight of active biomass, in a cell culture to double. *See* generation time.

Down's syndrome A condition, characterized by physiological, behavioural and mental defects, due to the presence of an extra copy of the genetic material contained in chromosome 21.

downstream processing In fermentation processes, any technique used in the recovery of the end product. Such techniques include precipitation, chromatography, electrophoresis, centrifugation, distillation, concentration and drying.

DPN Diphosphopyridine nucleotide; the now obsolete name for NAD.

drift *See* random genetic drift.

drilling mud A mixture of water, fine clay particles and polymers pumped into an oil well during drilling. The mud acts as a carrier to bring pieces of rock to the surface, as well as lubricating and cooling the drilling bit. Polymers, such as xanthan gum, are of value since the viscosity drops in the region of the bit, because of the effect of shear forces. The polymer then re-gels to carry the heavy debris to the surface.

driselase An enzyme mixture consisting of cellulase and fungal pectinase that is used to break down plant cell walls.

drop counter A mechanical device used in conjunction with a fraction collector in order to determine and control the size of each sample taken. The effluent stream from a chromatography column, for example, falls in drops through a light beam. Each drop induces an electrical pulse which is counted. The collector is set to move on to the next tube once a predetermined number of drops have been counted.

Drosophila The fruit flies. They are used in genetic research.

Drug A chemical substance administered to a living organism with the intention of preventing or curing disease or otherwise enhancing the physical or mental well-being of humans or other animals; a habit-forming substance or narcotic.

Drug resistance The ability of a microorganism to grow in the presence of a drug, usually an antibiotic. It is used as a selective marker in order to verify bacterial transformation, as well as for monitoring insertion of a specific DNA fragment into a vector. *See* antibiotic resistance.

drug resistance gene A gene that codes for an enzyme which enables the host cell to resist the effects of a drug. In general, the enzyme hydrolyses the drug or modifies its structure in some way. Drug resistance genes include the genes conferring antibiotic resistance which are carried on plasmids.

drum drier A device used to remove water from solids. Drum driers generally consist of a rotating cylinder that is heated directly or indirectly. It may be batch fed or continuous. In a continuous system, the inside may be fitted with a series of baffles which gradually move the contents from the input to the output end as the cylinder rotates.

drum filter A device used for dewatering solids. Drum filters usually consist of a rotating, perforated metal drum. This is treated with a filter aid or covered with filter paper or a similar porous membrane. A vacuum is applied to the inner volume of the filter which is rotated in a bath of liquid or placed in a liquid stream. The liquid is sucked into the central cavity and the solids retained on the outer surface, from which they are continuously removed on to a conveyor or into a hopper by means of a scraper.

dry cell weight The weight of cells contained in an aliquot obtained after drying to constant weight in an oven at 105°C. Dry weights are often expressed in terms of grams of material per litre or cubic metre of fermenter volume.

dsRNA A form of RNA found mainly in RNA-containing virus or virus-like agents, and particularly in plant virus types (other than CaMV). Usually plants do not contain substantial amounts (by molecular weight) of RNA. In many crop-infecting viruses, RNA is the infecting agent. Deletion can be used as a method of establishing virus-free planting stock or identification of diseased material.

ductless gland *See* endocrine gland.

Dunaliella bardawil A unicellular algae that produces large amounts of glycerol (up to 85 per cent dry weight) when grown in highly saline solutions.

duplex An autopolyploid in which the dominant allele at a given locus is present twice.

duplex DNA A synonym for double-stranded DNA.

duplication (1) The formation of new chromatids during interphase following mitosis. (2) A chromosome mutation in which a segment of a chromosome is doubled during nuclear division. The duplicated region may become attached to another chromosome.

dye exclusion test A method of determining the proportion of viable cells in a suspension using a stain, such as trypan blue, that only stains non-viable cells. A drop of stain is added to a drop of the cell suspension on a slide and left for a few minutes. The excess stain is then rinsed away and the slide examined under a microscope.

dynamic video imaging A technique in which an ultrasensitive CCD (charged couple device) camera is scanned across a microscopic field of view twenty five times per second, enabling cytological activity to be monitored.

dynamic viscosity A measure of the ability of a material or solution to resist deformation or its resistance to flow defined as the ratio of shear stress to shear rate in steady flow.

dynein A protein with ATPase activity found in microtubules and flagella.

dynorphin One of a number of enkephalins; a peptide with opiate activity of sequence Tyr–Gly–Gly–Phe–Leu–Arg–Arg–Ile–Arg–Pro–Lys–Leu–Lys–Trp–Asp–Asn–Gln.

dynorphin B An enkephalin with the amino acid sequence Tyr–Gly–Gly–Phe–Leu–Arg–Arg–Gln–Phe–Lys–Val–Val–Thr. *See* dynorphin.

E

E. coli *See Escherichia coli.*

Eadie plot A method of treating data from investigations of enzyme kinetics in order to obtain straight line plots from which the various kinetic constants can be calculated. In such plots, the value obtained by dividing the substrate concentration ([S]) by the observed velocity (v) at that substrate concentration is plotted as a function of substrate concentration. This gives a slope with a value equal to the reciprocal of the maximum velocity and an intercept on the x-axis equal to the negative of the K_m.

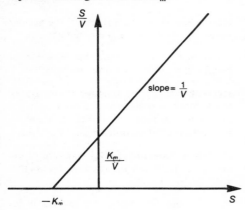

Eadie plot

EC *See* enzyme classification.

ecdysis The periodic shedding of the rigid exoskeleton. The process, which occurs in arthropods, permits further growth.

ecdysone A steroid hormone produced in arthropods that controls ecdysis.

ECG *See* electrocardiogram.

Eco RI A restriction enzyme derived from *E.coli* that has a recognition site of G'AATTC. It is widely used in gene ma-

nipulation since the cloning vector pBR322 has only one cleavage site recognized by this enzyme.

ecology The study of living organisms in relation to the environment.

ecosystem A unit that consists of all the living organisms in a community together with the environment, particularly its chemical and physical features, in which the animals and plants are living. It is the fundamental unit for ecological studies. The organisms are grouped as primary producers, herbivores, carnivores and decomposers existing at different trophic levels. The characteristics of the abiotic component of the ecosystem determines the type of organisms found in a given area.

ecotype A subspecies that has become specially adapted to certain environmental conditions (i.e., a specific ecosystem).

ectoblast The prospective ectoderm, before separation of the germ layers.

ectoderm The outer germ layer formed in metazoan embryos. It develops into the epidermal tissue and nervous system.

ectoplasm A thin outer layer of cytoplasm that can be distinguished in many animal cells and amaeboid cells, in particular.

ectotrophic mycorrhiza A basidiomycete fungus that grows in association with a host plant. The fungal hyphae penetrate between the cells of the cortex to form a mesh work termed the Hartig net. The association causes suppression of root hair development at the root tips and can cause other morphological changes in the roots. The fungus assists in the mobilization of phosphate and other ions from the soil to the host plant which supplies carbohydrate and other nutrients necessary for the growth of the fungus. Such mycorrhizal association may be essential for the plant to thrive, especially on poor soil.

edaphic factor A physical, chemical or biological characteristic of soil that affects plant growth.

Edman chemistry A sequence of chemical reactions generally used as the basis for spinning cup, solid phase, gas phase and myco-sequencing of proteins. Each complete cycle of reactions results in the removal of one amino acid from the N-terminal end of a peptide and the generation of a new peptide that is one amino acid shorter. The overall reaction consists of two steps. In the first coupling reaction, phenylisothiocyanate is coupled under basic conditions to the amino end of the peptide to form a phenylthiocarbamyl peptide. In the second cleavage reaction, treatment with strong anhydrous acid removes the derivatized amino acid as its anilinothiazoline. The latter is usually then converted into the more stable phenylthiohydantoin (Pth) amino acid derivative for subsequent analysis.

EDTA *See* ethylenediamine tetraacetic acid, disodium salt.

EEC *See* enteropathogenic *E. coli.*

EEG *See* electroencephalogram.

effective population size The number of reproducing individuals in a population.

effective yield The volume of cells produced in continuous-culture from a specific quantity of substrate.

effector A cell or organ that performs an action in response to a stimulus from the nervous system.

effector molecule A substance that binds to a regulatory molecule to create a complex capable of activating or inactivating a gene.

efferent A nerve or neurone that transmits information from the central nervous system to the peripheral effectors.

effluent A mixed liquor flowing out of a reactor. The term may be used more specifically to refer to a liquid, with or without suspended particles, or a solid discharge from a reactor or process plant that does not represent the required product and is thus regarded as a waste and will require further treatment or will cause pollution problems.

egosterol A precursor of vitamin D found in plants. Animals may convert it to vitamin D when exposed to ultraviolet radiation.

EIA *See* enzyme immunoassay.

elaioplast A plastid that stores fats or oils.

ELAM-1 Endothelial leukocyte adhesion molecule-1; a glycoprotein involved in cell to cell binding. It is induced by bacterial endotoxins or inflammatory cytokines such as TNF.

elastin The structural protein of the yellow fibres of connective tissue in metazoans.

elastomer A polymer that has elastic properties. It may be natural or synthetic.

electroblotting The transfer of separated DNA, RNA or protein molecules from a gel matrix to a nitrocellulose filter or sheet by the process of electrophoresis.

electrocardiogram (ECG) A record of the changes in electrical potential associated with cardiac activity.

electrochemical sensor An analytical device based on either a potentiometric or an amperometric electrode. In a potentiometric electrode, the response (in millivolts) is a logarithmic function of the concentration. This forms the basis of ion-selective electrodes. In an amperometric sensor, the response (in microamps) is a linear function of the concentration. The current measured arises from the diffusion of the species being measured towards the electrode as a result of it being consumed at the electrode surface. The oxygen electrode works on this principle.

electrodialysis A technique used for the deionization of solutions. The sample is placed in a compartment limited by ion-specific semipermeable membranes, across which a potential is applied. Charged ions move to the relevant electrode, whereas larger molecules or uncharged compounds are retained within the chamber. Electrodialysis is used on a large scale for desalination of sea water. It is also used for deionization of whey permeates, cell hydrolysates, etc.

electroencephalogram (EEG) A record of the changes in electrical potential that occur in the brain of vertebrates, mainly as a result of activity in the cerebral cortex.

electroendosmosis The flow of buffering cations (counterions) in solution towards the cathode during electrophoresis to counteract the movement of charged groups present in the supporting media (e.g., sulphate groups in agarose).

electrofusion A technique used to induce fusion in some animal cells and protoplasts. The cells are aligned by exposure to a low-level non-uniform electric field. This process, termed dielectrophoresis, generates dipoles within the cells. The attractive forces between the dipoles lead to the orientation of the cells. The cells are then subjected to a microsecond high-voltage discharge. This results in microscopic holes in the cell membranes where the cells touch. The holes expand and allow the contents of the cells to mix and some of the cells to fuse together.

electrolysis The decomposition of a compound by an electrical current or the destruction of tumours, hair roots, etc. in a similar manner.

electrolyte (1) A conducting medium in which the flow of electrons is accompanied by the flow of matter. (2) a substance which when dissolved in water dissociates into ions forming a conductor of electricity.

electromorphs Allozymes that can be distinguished by electrophoresis.

electron microscope An instrument used to obtain pictures of magnified objects. Since the wavelength of the electrons used as a radiation source is much shorter than that of light, the electron microscope has a much higher degree of resolution than the light microscope. The system must be operated under high vacuum to minimize electron scatter through collision with air molecules. The image is visualized by the interaction of the beam with a fluorescent screen or a photographic film to produce an electromicrograph. The type of sample used differs with the type of electron microscope. In the transmission microscope, the electron beam is passed though the specimen which will have been prepared in the form of an ultrathin section in the case of larger organisms. Such sections are fixed with glutaraldehyde, dehydrated and stained with electron-dense materials such as uranyl acetate, osmium tetroxide, lead citrate, etc. Small particles such as viruses, cell fragments and nucleic acids may be mounted whole on a grid and shadowed with metal (e.g., platinum or gold) or negatively stained with other electron-dense material. Samples used in scanning microscopes may be larger. The preparation may be dehydrated or the sample may be coated with electron-dense material.

electron transport chain A series of protein and enzymes capable of accepting electrons or hydrogen atoms and transferring them through a series of oxidation–reduction reactions. Electron transport chains occur both in aerobic respiration and in photosynthesis. The chains are associated with the inner membrane systems of the eukaryotic mitochondria or prokaryotic cell membranes and chloroplasts. In mitochondria, the electron is taken from a reduced carbon compound which is an intermediate of the TCA cycle and oxygen is the final electron acceptor. The components of the chain include dehydrogenases with associated flavanoid prosthetic groups, quinones and cytochromes. In chloroplasts, the major electron chain links photosystem I and photosystem II. Intermediates of the chain again include quinones, cyctochromes and other proteins with metal prosthetic groups. Much of the energy associated with the passage of the electrons through the chain is conserved in the form of ATP by oxidative phosphorylation or photophosphorylation. *See* photosynthesis, terminal electron transport chain.

electrophoresis A technique for separating molecules based on their differential mobility in an electric field.

electrophoretic analysis Separation of macromolecules by electrophoresis on the basis of their charge/mass ratio and molecular conformation. The technique may be used to characterize complex mixtures or determine molecular weight of macromolecules under specific conditions. Double-stranded DNA has a uniform charge/mass ratio hence migration in an electrical field is proportional to length of a fragment. Single-stranded DNA and RNA require denaturation to destroy regions of self-hybridization. Proteins require denaturation with sodium dodecyl sulphate and mercaptoethanol to give a uniform structure and charge for accurate molecular weight determinations.

electrophoretogram A pictorial representation of a column or plate following separation and visualization of a complex mixture using electrophoresis. The position of the compounds is usually revealed by staining with a dye and the result photographed. This is because the gels or colours that develop may not be very stable or easy to keep for a long time.

element A substance comprising one type of atom only.

ELISA *See* enzyme-linked immunosorbent assay.

elongation The formation of a peptide chain during which a ribosome moves along a molecule of mRNA from the 5'-end to the 3'-end. A specific aminoacyl tRNA binds to each codon, as it comes into contact with the ribosome, in a position that places the amino acid it carries at the functional centre where the peptide bond is formed.

elongation viscosity A measure of the ratio of the rate of extension as a function of the tensile strength of a fluid.

eluant A solution used for the elution of compounds from a solid matrix.

elution The removal of a compound from a solid matrix using a suitable solvent. In liquid chromatography, the term is applied to the process by which various compounds are removed in sequence from the solid phase by passing a liquid through the material packed in a column.

elution profile A diagrammatic representation of the amounts of material eluted from a liquid chromatography column, and the sequence and position in which they occur. For a given column the position, defined by the elution volume, will be indicative of the identity of the compound. The elution profile is obtained by passing the eluant through a flow cell attached to a suitable chromatographic detector. Samples may also be taken from a series of aliquots using a fraction collector, and the nature and amount of a compound or enzyme in each tube assayed. For instance, the elution stream from an ion exchange column can be passed through a continuous flow cell in a colorimeter monitoring at 280 nm. This will give an elution profile for the various protein fractions. The tubes on the fraction collector corresponding to high protein content may be assayed for the presence of a specific enzyme and the total activity calculated. An aliquot of the same sample may also be assayed for protein content using the Lowry assay. The total and specific activity of the protein recovered can then be calculated.

elution volume (V_e) In chromatography, a measure of the volume of liquid required to remove a given component of a mixture from the column.

EMA *See* enzyme membrane immunoassay.

emasculate (1) In general, the removal of the male reproductive organs. (2) In plants, the removal of the pollen sacks or complete male flowers to facilitate artificial pollination in order to achieve specific crosses or hybrids.

Embden–Meyerhof–Parnus pathway *See* glycolysis.

embedding A stage in the preparation of biological samples for microscopic examination. After dehydration the sample is immersed in a suitable wax, resin or polymer, which impregnates the material, and is then allowed to set. The embedding agent supports the sample during sectioning. For light microscopy the support material may then be removed (e.g., by dissolving wax in xylene) and the sample stained. For electron microscopy, the sample is stained with electron-dense material prior to embedding.

embryo The structure that develops in animals and some plants (bryophytes, pteridophytes and angiosperms) from a zygote through repeated division of cells which differentiate into tissues and organs. In animals, the embryo may be protected during development within an egg. In plants, the embryo is protected by the seed or fruit.

embryo culture The aseptic culture of a zygote embryo excised from the seed or ovule of a plant.

embryo sac A structure produced from the megaspore mother cell in angiosperm ovules. The embryo sac contains one or more polar nuclei, one of which may be fertilized by a pollen tube nucleus to form the endosperm.

embryo transfer A technique by which embryos are collected from a donor female and transferred to a recipient female which serves as a surrogate mother for the remainder of pregnancy. Such techniques have been applied to nearly every species of domestic animal, to many species of wild life and exotic animals, as well as to humans and other primates. The techniques are now sophisticated and include non-surgical procedures for obtaining the embryo at an early stage of development, cryopreservation and micromanipulation of the developing embryo. Gene manipulation techniques may be used to introduce new genetic material into the zygote at a very early stage. A donor is selected and, if necessary, treated with hormones to produce superovulation. The donor is inseminated naturally or artificially, and the embryos collected. They may then be sexed, split or manipulated prior to being inserted into the host which must be in oestrus. The technique has been applied to increase the number of rare animals, since the embryo need not develop in the same strain or even species. It is also used for genetic improvement, production of twins in cattle, disease control, and import and export (where embryos can be shipped in a frozen state, or using a small mammal as a carrier). Embryo transfer is employed to overcome some types of infertility or to salvage the genetics of terminally ill animals.

embryogenesis (1) The formation of an embryo from a zygote. (2) In plant tissue cultures, the induction of a cell suspension to form embryos.

embryology The study of the formation and development of embryos.

embryonal stem (ES) cell A cell obtained from an embryo during the early stages of development which can be grown in culture.

EMIT *See* enzyme mediated immuno test.

emulsifier A compound that assists in the formation and stabilization of an emulsion.

emulsion Any colloidal suspension of one liquid in another liquid. In photography, the term is used to refer to the light-sensitive layer on a photographic film, paper or plate, consisting of one or more silver halides in gelatin.

enamel The outer layer of tooth; composed largely of calcium phosphate in the form of apatite.

enantiomers Two molecules of the same elemental composition and basic structure which differ in configuration about an asymmetric carbon atom, one configuration being the mirror image of the other. One enantiomer will rotate a beam of polarized light to the left (laevorotatory or *l*-form) and the other rotates the light to the right (dextrorotatory or *d*-form).

encapsulation The surrounding of one compound or substance with a thin coat of another. The term microencapsulation is used where the final product is a very fine powder. Microencapsulation is used as a means of preservation.

end plate The area of membrane of a muscle cell below the nerve ending at a neuromuscular junction.

end plate potential A potential formed in the muscle cell membrane at the neuromuscular junction following release of the neurotransmitter from the nerve ending.

end-product inhibition A type of allosteric regulation in which the activity of an enzyme is decreased by the product of the reaction. *Compare* feedback inhibition.

endergonic Descriptive of a chemical reaction in which heat is absorbed.

end-filling The blunting of the sticky end of a DNA fragment by the addition of a complementary polynucleotide strand.

end-labelled nucleic acid Nucleic acid containing a radioactive (^{32}P) label at one end. It is prepared by removing the 5′-phosphate using bacterial alkaline phosphatase and incubating with (α-^{32}P)ATP and T4 polynucleotide kinase, or at the 3′-end by addition of a (α-^{32}P)3′-deoxyadenosine (cordycepin) 5′-triphosphate using terminal deoxyribonucleotide transferase.

endocrine gland An organ or group of cells that produces a hormone and secretes it directly into the blood or circulatory fluid. The glands are found in all vertebrates and some invertebrates. Vertebrate endocrine glands include the pituitary, pineal, thyroid, parathyroid, cells of the pancreas and alimentary tract, gonads and adrenal bodies, as well as the placenta in mammals. Endocrine glands that are derived from embryonic mesoderm secrete steroid hormones,

whereas those derived from endoderm or exoderm secrete modified amino acids, peptides or proteins.

endocrine system All the glands in an animal that produce, or are capable of producing, hormones.

endocrinology The study of the endocrine system and the role and action of hormones.

endocytosis The engulfing of material by a cell by extensions of the plasma membrane or ectoplasm to form a vesicle or vacuole. The engulfed material may then be digested following fusion with lysosomes containing the required enzymes.

endoderm The inner cell layer of metazoan embryos. It forms part of the alimentary canal and lines the respiratory tract.

endodermis A layer of cells that surrounds the vascular bundles of plants. It is distinguished by the formation of a casparian strip in each cell.

endogamy The formation of a zygote from gametes produced by closely related parents. *Compare* exogamy.

endoglucanase An enzyme that cleaves a polysaccharide such as cellulose at a point within the macromolecular substrate, rather than at the end. *Compare* exogluco-hydrolase.

endogonic reaction A chemical reaction that requires an external source of energy for it to occur. The energy is needed in order to join atoms to form molecules. *Compare* exergonic reaction.

endomembrane system A system of cytoplasmic membranes found in eukaryotic cells. It participates in the synthesis, transport and storage of chemical compounds within the cell and facilitates export from cells. It includes the plasma membrane and tonoplast of vacuoles.

endomitosis A process in which the chromosome number doubles but nuclear division does not take place, resulting in a polyploid.

endonuclease An enzyme which cleaves nucleic acids by hydrolysis of internal phosphodiester bonds in an unspecified manner. *See* restriction endonuclease.

endoparasite An organism living parasitically in another.

endopeptidase *See* proteinase.

endoplasm The inner cytoplasm of a cell that contains the bulk of the organelles. It may be enclosed by ectoplasm.

endoplasmic reticulum A system of membranes found in most eukaryote cells that is continuous with the outer membrane of the nucleus. It is termed rough endoplasmic reticulum when ribosomes are present and smooth endoplasmic reticulum when ribosomes are absent.

endorphin A protein produced mainly in the pituitary gland that prevents pain, invoking a feeling of euphoria. It acts on the same sites in the brain as morphine. It is sometimes known as 'endogenous morphine'.

endosome An intracellular vesicle formed during endocytosis.

endosperm A nutritive tissue found in seeds of some angiosperms. In many seeds it is absorbed during embryo development, whereas in others it expands to form the storage tissue of the ripe seed. It represents part of the gametophyte tissue since it develops from the embryo sac as a result of double fertilization. Commercial oils derived from many important agricultural crops are obtained from endospermic seeds.

endospermic Descriptive of seeds with a well developed endosperm.

endospore A highly resistant resting structure formed within the vegetative cell of eubacteria of the genera *Bacillus* and *Clostridium*.

endosporic Descriptive of a situation in which spores are produced within a sporangium.

endothelial leukocyte adhesion molecule-1 *See* ELAM-1.

endothelium A single layer of cells that lines the internal cavities of vertebrate blood and lymph vessels. It is derived from embryonic mesoderm.

endothermic reaction A chemical change in which heat is absorbed; a reaction with a positive enthalpy change.

endotoxin A toxic compound that is formed within the cells of bacteria such as *Salmonella*, *Vibrio cholerae* and *Shigella*, all of which cause dysentery. If isolated and injected under the skin of animals these toxins produce an inflammatory response.

endotrophic mycorrhiza Fungus that forms an association with both woody and herbaceous plants, penetrating the cortex of the roots both inter- and intracellularly. The fungi assist in the uptake of mineral nutrients (phosphate in particular), whereas the plant host supplies the fungi with sugars and other nutrients for growth.

end-specific probe A probe derived by the amplification of one end of a DNA sequence using inverse PCR.

energy balance An analysis carried out on a process or reaction system, in which all inputs and outputs of energy are determined experimentally or by calculation. Such balances may be used to determine the overall efficiency of the system or to identify areas for process improvement.

energy crop Selected plant species grown and harvested specifically as biomass to be used as a source of energy and converted into a fuel or bulk chemical. The major energy crops include fast-growing or coppiced trees (willows, poplars and eucalyptus species), sugar crops (sugar cane and sugar beet), starch crops (maize or cassava), inulin crops (chicory or Jerusalem artichoke), aquatic plants including algae and water weeds (water hyacinth and emergent species such as rushes and reeds).

enhanced oil recovery *See* tertiary (oil) production.

enhancement A situation in which the biological response of a system to two stimuli applied at the same time is greater than the sum of the individual effects. The term is applied specifically to photosynthesis where the illumination of oxygen-producing photoautotrophs using a mixture of red and blue light produces oxygen at a faster rate than with either on its own.

enhancer A promoter element that increases the efficiency with which a nearby gene is transcribed into mRNA.

enhancing antibodies Blocking antibodies that bind to tumours preventing their destruction by cytotoxic T lymphocytes.

enolase An enzyme that catalyses the interconversion of phosphoenol pyruvate and 2-phosphoglyceric acid. This reaction is one of the intermediate steps in glycolysis.

enrichment culture A method used to isolate a specific type of microorganism from a mixed culture or inoculum taken from the wild. The composition of the medium, aeration or lack of oxygen, pH, temperature, illumination, nutritional cofactors, etc. are adjusted to favour the faster growth of the required organism and discourage the growth of unwanted species.

ensile The preservation of green animal fodder by fermentation in a pit or enclosed heap.

enteric fever Typhoid.

enterokinase An enzyme with peptidase activity, secreted by vertebrate intestinal glands, that converts trypsinogen to the active form trypsin.

enteropathogenic Descriptive of an organism that has the potential to cause intestinal or diarrhoeal disease.

enteropathogenic E. coli (EEC) Strains of *E. coli* that cause diarrhoea. They may be divided into two groups: toxigenic EECs produce toxins that cause dehydration and shock; invasive EECs penetrate the epithelial cells of the intestine and produce stools containing blood and mucus.

enterotoxaemia A severe systemic poisoning associated with bacterial toxins in the intestinal tract.

enterotoxin A protein with a molecular weight of 28,000–34,000 produced by Staphylococci that act on the viscera causing cramps, nausea, diarrhoea and vomiting. The usual cause of infection with such bacteria is food poisoning associated with milk products and meats.

enthalpy A thermodynamic expression for heat content defined by the equation:

$$H = U + pV$$

Where H = enthalpy, U = internal energy, p = external pressure and V is volume. In biological systems, the pressure, temperature and volume usually remain constant, hence the change in enthalpy δH is equal to the change in internal energy δU. During a reaction, heat may be given out (negative δH) or taken from the surroundings to the reactants (positive δH). These are termed exothermic and endothermic reactions, respectively.

entomology The study of insects.

entomophily Pollination in higher plants in which insects act as vectors.

entrained bed reactor A bioreactor or fermentation system in which the active biomass is supported by a fine particulate carrier that is kept in suspension in a recirculating liquid flow at high velocity.

entrapped cells A system in which cells are trapped in a solid matrix. This is one method of immobilizing cells for use in a bioreactor or biosensor. The cells may be trapped in a biological polymer (e.g., calcium alginate) or a chemical polymer (e.g., polyurethane foam). The trapped cells will often retain their viability if provided with the correct nutrients for growth. Such cells may grow through the matrix forming small colonies, or cells may leak out into the medium. These effects can be prevented by nutrient limitation. Preparations in which whole cells are trapped in a matrix, retaining some enzymic activity, but which are not capable of continued growth if given the right nutrients are referred to as trapped enzymes.

entrapped enzymes *See* entrapped cells.

entropy A thermodynamic property of systems that defines the degree of randomness of the constituents. The greater the order, the lower the entropy. The second law of thermodynamics states that the entropy of the universe as a whole is increasing. The change in entropy of a system is defined by

$$\delta S = \delta q/T$$

where δq = heat absorbed by the system and T = temperature at which the heat is absorbed. At first sight, biological systems might appear to be in conflict with the concept since the entropy of a living system decreases during growth. However, this can only occur because of the input of energy through linked reactions, which are ultimately driven by light energy derived from the sun, whose entropy is increasing as required by the second law.

environment The sum of the biological, chemical and physical properties of the surroundings in which a particular organism lives.

Enzacryl gel A cross-linked polyacryloyl-morpholine support material that forms gels in both water and organic solvents and can be used in a wide range of gel filtration applications. It is prepared by copolymerization of acryloylmorpholine and *N,N*-methylene diacryl amide in aqueous solution. It can be used to separate materials with molecular weights of up to 10^5 in water and lower-molecular-weight compounds in

solvents such as chloroform and tetrahydrofuran.

enzymatic hydrolysis A hydrolytic process in which the catalytic agent is an enzyme. *See* hydrolysis.

enzyme A protein that is capable of catalysing a reaction in which various substrate(s) are converted to product(s) through the formation of an intermediate enzyme–substrate complex. As with other catalysts, enzymes are responsible for accelerating the rate of a chemical reaction. However, they are not capable of altering the equilibrium of the reaction or the direction in which it proceeds on the basis of the thermodynamics of the overall actions catalysed. In general, enzymes will catalyse only one type of reaction (*see* enzyme classification, enzyme reaction mechanism) and will operate on only one type of substrate. This specificity depends on the structure of the peptide chain and, in particular, on the arrangement of amino acids and other constituents, such as metal ions or prosthetic groups, at the active site. It may be possible for an enzyme to catalyse a reaction in a direction that is not favoured by the free energy change by: (1) linking the reaction with a second exogonic reaction in such a way that there is an overall increase in free energy; (2) altering the equilibrium by rapid removal of one of the products, again through linking to either a second enzyme reaction or an active transport mechanism.

enzyme activation A mechanism in which the activity of an enzyme is increased by a direct effect on the enzyme, rather than being due to new protein synthesis. It may be brought about through the binding of an activator molecule at an allosteric site on the enzyme resulting in a change in the enzyme configuration, which leads to a change in the shape of the active site. Alternatively, the enzyme may be activated through a chemical modification, which may in itself be catalysed by an enzyme. For instance, a wide range of enzymes are activated by a mechanism involving ATP-dependent phosphorylation. A number of plant enzymes, in particular, are activated by light, through a mechanism that involves reduction of a sulphur or similar group by reduced pyridine nucleotide or ferredoxin. Other types of activation mechanisms include ATPase-dependent changes in levels of divalent cations (Mg^{2+}, Ca^{2+} or changes in intracellular pH or redox potential.

enzyme activity An expression of the ability of a given enzyme preparation to catalyse a specific reaction. It may be defined in terms of the number of moles of substrate converted, or the number of moles of product produced, in unit time per unit weight of protein (e.g., micromoles per milligram protein per minute).

enzyme amplification A technique used to visualize or quantify an immunoreaction in an assay procedure in which the enzyme label in the immunoassay is used to provide the trigger substance for a second system that can produce a large amount of a coloured product

enzyme analysis A technique in which a specific reaction catalysed by an enzyme is used to determine either the amount of enzyme or substrate present in a sample that may be highly complex. The advantage of the method relies on the high specificity of the enzyme, hence accuracy is dependent on enzyme purity and on the lack of inhibitors and interfering compounds. The design of such techniques is based on the assumption that the reaction shows Michaelis–Menten type kinetics. (i.e., at high substrate levels, rates of reactions are proportional to enzyme concentration, whereas at high enzyme and low substrate levels they are proportional to substrate concentration). The rate of reaction is usually measured over the initial period and extrapolated to zero time. This is because observed activity can change owing to substrate being consumed or because end products may inhibit the reaction.

enzyme assay (1) A method for determining the activity of an enzyme sample. (2) An assay used to determine the amount of a specific substance in a sample, where the means of detection is dependent on an enzyme-catalysed reaction. *See* enzyme analysis.

enzyme classification A system of rules by which enzymes are classified on the basis of the substrate they react with and the type of reaction catalysed. Many enzyme, especially the more common ones, are known by short trivial names and usually end in the suffix -ase. However, this can lead to confusion, and hence the use of a specific name according to the rules of the international enzyme classification system is preferable. This system provides both a systematic name and a four-part number code. The first number of the code places the enzyme into one of six groups, indicating the type of reaction involved. The next two numbers indicate the groups involved in the reaction and the fourth number provides the absolute identification of the enzyme. The main groups are as follows (further details can be found by reference to each class elsewhere in the dictionary):

1. oxidoreductases
2. transferases
3. hydrolases
4. lyases
5. isomerases
6. ligases

enzyme commission nomenclature The terminology generally agreed for use in relation to enzymes. The Commission on Enzymes of the International Union of Biochemistry has recommended various conventions for use in enzyme kinetics. The symbols v, V, K_m, K_s and K_i are used for observed velocity, maximum reaction velocity (with enzyme saturated with substrate), Michaelis constant, substrate constant and inhibitor constant, respectively. The term Michaelis constant and the symbol K_m are used to denote the substrate concentration at which the velocity is equal to one-half the maximum velocity, whereas the terms 'substrate constant' and 'inhibitor constant' denote the equilibrium (dissociation) constants of the reactions:

$$E + S = ES$$

and

$$E + I = EI$$

Velocity constants are written as k, whereas the system of numbering rate constants for systems involving consecutive steps is that forward reactions are numbered in order with a positive suffix (i.e., k_{+1}, k_{+2}, etc.) and back reactions are numbered k_{-1}, k_{-2}, etc.

enzyme equilibrium An expression which describes the state of an enzyme-catalysed reaction in terms of the rates of forward and back reactions. A reversible reaction is in equilibrium when the rates of the forward reaction and the reverse reaction are the same so that there is no net change in concentration of the reactants. All equilibria involving combination of enzymes with substrates or inhibitors are expressed in terms of dissociation constants rather than association constants; other equilibrium constants are written as association constants. For the following reaction:

$$A + B = AB$$

the equilibrium constant is given by:

$$K = [AB]/[A][B]$$

enzyme extraction The removal of enzymes from contaminating materials in order to increase their specific activity. Techniques fall into two groups: those used to separate enzymes from solid substrate culture; those used to release enzymes from the interior of microbial cells. Where enzymes produced in solid fermentation are of the extracellular type, they may be removed by countercurrent washing. If enzymes are intercellular, the cells must be broken using chemical or biochemical methods such as autolysis, treatment with solvents, detergents, etc. Alternatively, physical methods are used such as homogenization or ball milling for dried sources. The result is a dilute enzyme solution that requires concentration and separation.

enzyme fermentations A process in which a microorganism is grown as a source of an industrial enzyme on a large scale. Industrial enzymes are produced by either solid substrate cultivations using fungal sources or conventional batch submerged culture techniques for bacterial sources. *See* solid substrate fermentation, submerged culture.

enzyme hydrolysis *See* enzymatic hydrolysis.

enzyme immobilization The conversion of a soluble enzyme to a bound or insoluble form. The technique has two advantages: expensive enzymes can be recovered and used again; the enzyme can be used in a variety of configurations of bioreactors that permit continuous operation. These include packed bed continuous-fed columns and expanded bed systems. A wide range of techniques is used for enzyme immobilization. These techniques are similar in many ways to those used to produce preparations of immobilized cells and include adsorption, entrapment, cross-linked systems and encapsulation or membrane enclosure. Immobilized enzymes are mainly used in the production of high fructose syrups (also known as HFCS or isoglucose). Other commercial uses include production of semi-synthetic penicillins, the hydrolysis of starch using amyloglucosidase, and the resolution of DL-mixtures of amino acids.

enzyme immunoassay (EIA) A type of immunoassay in which an enzyme reaction is used as a label. The enzyme chosen is one that can catalyse the conversion of an otherwise undetectable compound into one that can easily be detected using visual, spectrophotometric or other similar means. EIA is usually used to describe assays in which the antigen is labelled. Enzymes used include horseradish peroxidase (HRPO), alkaline phosphatase (AP) or β-galactosidase. Typically, using a microtitre plate system, highly purified antigen is fixed to the walls of the measuring well to form a solid phase. A serum sample suspected of containing antibodies specific to this antigen is dispensed into the well. On incubation, these antibodies bind specifically to the solid phase. Labelled antibodies to serum (e.g., human IgG) are incubated with the antigen–antibody complex. An enzyme substrate is then added and the presence of specific anti-bodies is indicated by a colour reaction or fluorescence which is measured using a microplate reader.

enzyme induction The synthesis of an enzyme in response to an inducing agent which stimulates expression of the genes encoding the protein with a specific enzyme function.

enzyme inhibition A mechanism whereby an enzyme is inactivated by chemical agents. Enzymes are inhibited by binding of chemicals at either the active site or at con-trol (allosteric) sites. Irreversible inhibition is caused by substances reacting with groups usually associated with the active site (e.g., through covalent bonding) so as to modify or destroy the structure perma-nently. Reversible inhibition may be termed competitive, non-competitive or uncom-petitive. These effects are distinguished by the changes in kinetic behaviour that are evoked when the levels of substrate and/or inhibitor are changed. Competitive inhibi-tion occurs when the inhibitor binds at or near the active site. In general, the effect can be reversed by increasing the ratio of sub-strate to inhibitor. Non-competitive inhibi-tion occurs when the inhibitor binds to some other part of the enzyme. This binding may occur at an allosteric site, in which case it results in a change in the shape of the enzyme which alters the binding character-istics of the active site. Non-competitive inhibition is not altered by changing the level of substrate. Feedback inhibition often works through an allosteric mechanism. In the case of uncompetitive inhibition, the inhibitor reacts with forms of the enzyme that do not themselves combine with the substrate. These cannot then be converted back into the form that is able to react with the substrate. Uncompetitive inhibition is rare in reactions involving single substrates, but is common in multi-substrate reactions.

enzyme kinetics The study of the rates of enzyme-controlled reactions. At low sub-strate concentrations the rate of reaction is proportional to the substrate concentration (first order), but at high substrate concen-

Outline of a non-competitive ELISA antigen test

The sample containing antigens is added to the antibodies bound to the solid phase matrix

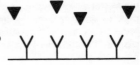

Binding occurs; unbound material is washed away

A second, enzyme labelled, antibody is added, and binds to the antigen from the sample

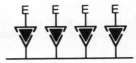

Addition of substrate produces a colour reaction

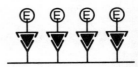

The amount of colour is related to the concentration of antigen in the sample

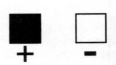

tration the reaction becomes saturated, reaches a maximum rate and is independent of substrate concentration (zero order). For an ideal enzyme reaction which involves a single substrate and a single product, the system is described as follows:

$$E + S \underset{k_{-1}}{\overset{k_{+1}}{\rightleftharpoons}} ES \xrightarrow{k_{+2}} P + E$$

For which $v = V[S]/(K_m + [S])$

where $K_m = (k_{-1} + k_{+2})/k_{+1}$

When the velocity of an enzyme reaction is determined and plotted as a function of sub-strate concentration, the result is a right-angled hyperbola. The shape of this makes it difficult to determine the value of V and

K_m. A number of different types of kinetic analyses have been devised in order to overcome this problem (*see* Eadie plot, Hoftstee plot, Lineweaver–Burk plot). Enzymes subject to allosteric inhibition or activation display kinetics that deviate from the classic Michaelis form. These may be described in terms of the Hill plot where

$$V = \frac{VS^n}{K_m + S^n}$$

enzyme membrane immunoassay (EMA) A homogeneous assay in which the enzyme label is entrapped by liposomes.

enzyme mediated immuno test (EMIT) A type of homogeneous immunoassay in which the enzymic activity of a conjugate is altered after binding.

enzyme production The processes whereby industrial enzymes are manufactured. Some enzymes are formed at all times (constitutive enzymes), whereas others are only formed when needed (inducible enzymes). Few enzymes are produced by wild-type organisms in the quantities required for a viable commercial operation. Enzymes may be produced by extraction of very small amounts from very large quantities of cells or tissues, making them suitable for medical, diagnostic, analytical or research purposes. However, methods are available to overcome the control mechanisms that exert an inhibiting effect on the production of large amounts of enzymes by microorganisms. These techniques are divided into two categories: (1) manipulation of the genetics (use of mutagens and selection, or more recently gene manipulation) in order to alter the regulation mechanisms or produce more copies of the gene responsible; (2) manipulation of the environment (addition of inducers, or removal or avoidance of end product repressors). This can be done using a mixed culture, the second organism removing the end product which represses the first.

enzyme reaction mechanism The basic principles involved in the physical and chemical reactions associated with an enzyme-catalysed reaction. An enzyme functions by lowering the activation energy of a reaction. This is brought about by formation of a complex between the substrate and the enzyme. Most enzymes function according to the induced fit principle whereby binding of the substrate to the enzyme causes a change in shape, resulting in the alignment of catalytic groups. The electrostatic and hydrophobic interactions assist in the alignment and subsequent reaction.

enzyme recovery The methods used in the recovery of industrial enzymes. In enzyme production by fermentation, the output of product is often low. It is necessary therefore to concentrate and partially purify the product. The overall process consists of enzyme extraction, followed by concentration and drying. Techniques used in concentration include ultrafiltration, precipitation, adsorption techniques using ion exchangers, affinity columns, etc. or the use of gel filtration. Commercial enzyme preparations are available in solid or liquid form. Solid preparations are obtained by spray drying or freeze drying, or granulation in the presence of maltodextrin as a carrier. Liquid preparations may be stabilized by addition of divalent cations, buffers, glycerol, substrates or inhibitors. A few commercial enzymes are supplied in an immobilized form.

enzyme regulation Enzymes may be regulated at two levels: (1) at the level of gene expression and protein synthesis through induction and repression; (2) at the enzyme level through enzyme inhibition or activation as a result of the binding of effector molecules at allosteric sites on the enzyme.

enzyme repression A mechanism that prevents the synthesis of an enzyme by the formation of repressors that bind to DNA preventing transcription.

enzyme separation Techniques used for the separation and purification of enzymes. These include solids separation, membrane separation, precipitation, absorption chromatography and gel filtration.

enzyme unit The amount which will catalyse the transformation formation of one micromole of substrate in a given time (e.g., one minute) under defined conditions of temperature, pH and substrate concentration.

enzyme-linked immunosorbent assay (ELISA) A sensitive analytical technique in which an enzyme is complexed to an antigen or antibody. A substrate is then added which generates a colour proportional to the amount of binding. This method can be adapted to a solid phase. An antigen is added to an antibody-coated tube. The antigen is added and forms the required complex. The enzyme-labelled antibody is then added, and this also forms a complex with the antigen. Excess antibody is removed by washing and the necessary substrates added to generate the colour.

enzymic hydrolysis *See* enzymatic hydrolysis.

eosinophil A white blood corpuscle that contains large granules which stain with acid dyes such as eosin. They comprise about 2–3 per cent of the white cells in human blood. The number of cells may increase in response to parasitic infection, allergy or skin disease.

EPDM Ethylene-propylene-diene-caoutchouc; a material used for the manufacture of gaskets in sterile centrifuge systems.

ephemeral Descriptive of a plant which completes its life cycle from germination to seed production and regermination several times in a year.

epicotyl The short axis of the plumule of a germinating seed.

epidemiology The branch of medicine dealing with the distribution of diseases.

epidermis The outermost layer of cells of an animal or plant.

epididymis A convoluted tubule in which vertebrate spermatozoa mature and are stored.

epigeal A condition in plants where the cotyledons are raised above the ground during seed germination.

epigenetic The absence of factors in the genotype that exerts an effect upon the phenotype.

epimers Two monosaccharides that differ only in their configuration about one carbon atom.

epinephrine *See* adrenaline.

epiphyte A plant that grows attached to the surface of another plant, but is not parasitic upon it.

episome A genetic element found in bacterial cells that is able to replicate either autonomously or when integrated into the chromosome: equivalent to a plasmid.

epistasis Interaction between two nonallelic genes so that one of them (epistatic gene) interferes with, or even inhibits, the phenotypic expression of the other (hypostatic gene).

epithelium A continuous layer of cells that covers internal or external surfaces of organs in vertebrates. It is derived from embryonic ectoderm and endoderm.

epitope The part of a non-immunoglobulin antigen to which the variable region of an antibody binds.

EPO *See* erythropoietin.

EPSP synthase *See* glyphosate tolerance.

equatorial plate The plane of the equator of the spindle produced during metaphase in mitosis and meiosis. In mitosis the centromeres of the chromosomes lie on the equatorial plate, whereas in meiosis the centromeres of the homologous pairs of chromosomes are attached to the spindle on opposite sides of the equatorial plate and equidistant from it.

erepsin A mixture of proteases secreted by mammalian intestinal glands.

ergosterol A plant sterol which functions as a precursor for vitamin D in animals. The conversion in some animals is dependent on ultraviolet light.

erythroblast A nucleated bone marrow cell that gives rise to erythrocytes.

erythrocyte A red blood cell. In mammals, unlike other vertebrates, the cells are anucleate. The cells contain a solution of haemoglobin, the respiratory pigment responsible for oxygen transport.

erythromycin An antibiotic produced by *Streptomyces erythraeus*. Erythromycin is used as an alternative to penicillin in the treatment of Staphylococcal and Streptococcal infections.

erythropoietin (EPO) A hormone that stimulates the production of erythrocytes.

ES cell *See* embryonal stem cell.

Escherichia coli A motile, rod-shaped, gram-negative bacterium, a member of the Enterobacteriacae that inhabits the colon of man. Some strains can cause infections of the urinary tract, food poisoning, etc. *E. coli* is widely used in research on molecular biology, gene manipulation and microbial biochemistry and physiology.

essential amino acid An amino acid that is not synthesized by higher vertebrates and must therefore be obtained direct from the diet. Essential amino acids for man are isoleucine, leucine, lysine, methionine, phenylalanine, threonine, tryptophan, and valine.

essential element The major constituents of living organisms include: carbon, hydrogen, oxygen, nitrogen, phosphorus, sulphur, potassium, magnesium, calcium and iron.

essential fatty acids Unsaturated fatty acids required for the growth of mammals. They are constituents of phospholipids and glycerides in cell membranes. Linoleic acts as a precursor for synthesis of both linolenic and arachadonic acids.

essential oil An oil obtained from plants, possessing the smell, flavour and other properties of the plant, and vaporizing completely when heated. Essential oils are used in making perfumes and flavours.

esterastin An immunomodulator produced by *Streptomyces lavendulae*.

ethanolic fermentation *See* alcoholic fermentation.

ethidium bromide A stain used to visualize DNA fragments on electrophoresis gels. It fluoresces in a hydrophobic environment on exposure to radiation in the 250–310 nm range.

ethyl ethane sulphonate An alkylating agent that acts as a mutagen, giving high yields of mutants at high survival rates. The mutagenic reactions are stopped by addition of sodium thiosulphate or by dilution during plating.

ethyl methyl sulphonate *See* ethyl ethane sulphonate.

ethylene (C_2H_4) An unsaturated hydrocarbon gas that acts as a plant growth substance. It is associated with the ripening of fruit and the climacteric (rise in respiratory activity), plays a role in the breaking of seed dormancy and can inhibit growth of some plant organs.

ethylenediamine tetraacetic acid, disodium salt (EDTA) A chelating agent that binds divalent cations such as Mg^{2+}, Ca^{2+} Mn^{2+} and Fe^{2+}.

etiolation Characteristic pattern of growth found when higher plants, or their seeds, are grown in continual darkness. In particular, etiolated plants show a lack of chloroplast development, do not possess chlorophyll, have elongated internodes and reduced lignification. Exposure to light reverses these effects and leads to rapid synthesis of chlorophyll leaves, development of chloroplasts, leaf expansion and retardation of internode growth. The light response may be mediated through phytochrome.

etioplast A plastid found in the leaves of etiolated plants. The etioplast will, if exposed to light, develop to form a chloroplast. It is characterized by the presence of a prolamellar body which consists of a pseudocrystalline array of membranes.

eubacteria Bacteria characterized by the possession of a rigid cell wall and, in the motile forms, flagella.

euchromatic Descriptive of chromosome regions or whole chromosomes that have normal staining properties and that undergo the normal cycle of chromosome coiling.

euchromatin The bulk of the chromosomal material in the nuclei of plant and animal cells. It is distinguished from heterochromatin by its staining properties and genetic character.

eugenics The concept of improving the human race by genetic selection.

eukaryotes Higher organisms in which the genetic material is enclosed by a membrane forming a distinct nucleus. Nuclear DNA is associated with proteins and is present in definite structures (chromosomes) which are visible during cell division. The cell mass contains other organelles such as mitochondria and chloroplast (sites of respiratory and photosynthetic metabolism). All eukaryotes require oxygen for growth. During cell division meiosis permits the transmission of genetic material to daughter cells.

Eumycophta The fungi, comprising four groups: Deuteromycetes, Phycomycetes, Ascomycetes and Basidiomycetes.

euploidy A condition in which the chromosome number of a cell or organisms is an exact multiple of the haploid number so that all chromosomes are present in equal numbers and there are no unpaired ones.

euryhaline Descriptive of organisms that can tolerate a wide range of salinity.

eutrophic Descriptive of a body of fresh water that contains a high level of inorganic nutrients and has a high rate of primary productivity.

eutrophication The process by which the concentration of inorganic nutrients in a body of water increases. It may be associated with pollution by run-off from agricultural land where excess fertilizer or animals' wastes have been applied.

evaporation The removal of a liquid by conversion to the vapour. In the processing of biological material, evaporation is generally used as a means of removing water from solids or non-volatile organic products. The energy that is required for evaporation can be a significant part of total manufacturing costs.

evaporative cooling A decrease in temperature of a body or volume of liquid that results from the use of heat from within the body or solution to supply the required latent heat of evaporation to permit evaporation of vapour from the surface.

evaporator An apparatus designed as a means of removing liquid; in biological systems the liquid is usually water. The evaporation of water is often carried out under less than atmospheric pressure since this results in a lowering of the boiling temperature. For economy, multiple effect evaporators are used. In such systems, several evaporators are connected in series in such a way that steam from the boiling solution in the first effect serves as a source of heat for the second effect. The second effect is operated at a lower pressure than the first and thus boils at a lower temperature. Steam and condensate from the second effect may then go on to a third effect and so on through the multiple effect system. Usually three or four effects are used, although in some processes, six or seven effects are found.

evergreen Descriptive of plants that produce or shed leaves throughout the year in such a way that the branches are never bare.

evolution The development of complex organisms from simpler ancestral types. It is caused by gradual changes in a population, resulting from inherited variations in individuals in successive generations.

exchange capacity A measure of the number of ions that can be exchanged with a standard weight of an ion exchanger (e.g., equivalents per gram of dry resin).

excretion The elimination from the body of waste metabolites including carbon dioxide, water and nitrogenous compounds (e.g., urea, uric acid, allantoin, etc.).

exergonic reaction A chemical reaction in which there is a net release of energy. *Compare* endogonic reaction.

exocellobiohydrolase An enzyme that cleaves cellobiose units from the end of polysaccharide molecules such as cellulose.

exocrine gland A ducted gland found in vertebrates. These glands are classified as complex or simple depending on the type of duct.

exoenzyme An enzyme localized on the outer side of the cell membrane. In bacteria, for instance, exoenzymes may be released from the outer medium or lie in the space between the cell wall and the cell membrane.

exogamy The production of a zygote through fusion of gametes from parents that are not closely related. *Compare* endogamy.

exoglucohydrolase An enzyme that cleaves glucose units from the ends of polysaccharide molecules such as cellulose. *Compare* endoglucanase.

exon The part of the DNA of a gene that encodes the information for the actual amino acid sequence of the protein. In many eukaryotic genes, the coding sequences consist of a series of exons alternating with intron sequences. Following transcription, the introns are excised, and the exon sequences are spliced together to form the mRNA used in protein synthesis.

exonuclease An enzyme that cleaves nucleic acids at one of the ends. *Compare* endonuclease.

exonuclease III An exonuclease that is specific in removing nucleotides from the 3'-ends of duplex DNA.

exonuclease lambda An exonuclease from the lambda phage that is used in molecular biology to remove nucleotides from the 5'-ends of duplex DNA, usually to create an improved substrate for terminal transferase.

exoparasite An organism living parasitically on the outer surface of another. *Compare* endoparasite.

exopolysaccharide An extracellular gum produced by microorganisms. Exopolysaccharides include alginate, dextran, polytran, xanthan gum and many others. They have a variety of different physical properties and a wide range of industrial uses.

exoskeleton A skeleton, such as the cuticle of the arthropods, that lies outside the body tissues.

exothermic reaction A chemical change in which heat is given off; a reaction with a negative enthalpy change. *Compare* endothermic reaction.

exotoxin A toxic compound that is secreted by a bacterium. In human disease, exotoxins are produced in tetanus, diphtheria and botulism.

expert systems A computer program used to solve problems in a manner similar to that used by a human experienced in a specific subject. They are applied to problem solving in areas where expertise is of heuristic nature rather than numerical, where many decisions must be taken and algorithms cannot be defined or are too complex for an appropriate timescale, to enable real-time application or implementation. *See also* inference engine, knowledge base, knowledge management.

explant A tissue sample used to initiate a tissue culture.

exponential growth A type of growth in which increase in population is proportional to the number of individuals present.

exponential phase of growth That stage of microbial growth when all foodstuffs and other requirements are present in excess, and the rate of growth is limited only by intrinsic properties of the organism. As each cell divides into two at regular intervals, the population numbers repeatedly double in an 'exponential' fashion.

expression (of genes) The actual synthesis of specific proteins on the basis of inherited (or acquired) genetic information. In molecular biology, a recombinant gene inserted using a vector is said to be expressed if the synthesis of the protein it codes for can be demonstrated. *See* protein synthesis.

expression vector A vector carrying an inserted gene that is expressed in the host organism.

extracellular Descriptive of a structure or substance present outside the cell. *Compare* intracellular.

extrachromosomal genetic element *See* plasmid.

extractive fermentation A fermentation system in which the product is continuously removed by extraction with a solvent that is insoluble in water, not harmful to the organism, simple to recover (e.g., by distillation) and in which the fermentation product is considerably more soluble than it is in water. The fermenter may be fed nutrient continuously or intermittently. One advantage of this type of reactor is that products may be removed before they reach concentrations that limit the rate of fermentation by feedback inhibition. The disadvantage is that few, if any, solvents with the required properties have been identified.

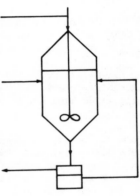

Extractive
fermentation

F

F_1 Designation of the first filial generation produced in a breeding programme through crossing of the parental generation P_1.

F_2 Designation of the second filial generation obtained in a breeding programme through crossing of the F_1 generation.

F factor A plasmid or episome found in some bacteria that enables them to undergo conjugation. *See* fertility factor.

F plasmid A conjugative plasmid that determines mating type (F+ or F−) in enterobacteria and mediate transfer of chromosomal genes between these bacteria.

Fab fragment Fragment antigen binding; part of an immunoglobulin molecule containing the antigen-binding site and produced by treatment with the enzyme papain. It is composed of one light chain and part of one heavy chain joined by a disulphide bond. *See also* antibody.

facilitated diffusion A biological process in which the rate of uptake of a material across a membrane is increased by a carrier protein in the membrane. Facilitated diffusion cannot increase intracellular concentrations of a substance above those occurring in the external medium, but rapid removal of the material being taken up results in a positive diffusion gradient into the cell. *Compare* active transport.

facilitated membrane transport The active conveyance of a substance across a membrane by a carrier molecule.

FACS *See* fluorescence-activated cell sorter.

factor VIII A protein associated with blood clotting in humans. A deficiency results in the most common hereditary bleeding disorder, haemophilia A, that occurs in over 90 per cent of cases. Factor VIII has been manufactured using recombinant DNA techniques, replacing natural product isolated from blood, following incidence of transmission of HIV.

factor IX A protein associated with blood clotting in humans. A deficiency results in the less common hereditary bleeding disorder, haemophilia B, that occurs in less than 10 per cent of cases.

facultative anaerobe An organism, generally a bacterium or fungus, that can adapt its metabolism to survive and grow either in the presence or in the absence of oxygen.

FAD Flavin adenine dinucleotide; a riboflavin derivative that functions as a prosthetic group in flavoproteins participating in oxidation–reduction reactions.

Flavin adenine dinucleotide

false recombinant An experimental artefact that occurs in recombination studies based on PCR. The occurrence is due to the failure of some target DNA sequences to be amplified.

family A group of closely related or similar genera. Families are named after the type genus that is characteristic of the whole family. Families are divided into subfamilies and grouped into orders.

farmer's lung *See* aspergillosis.

fat A general name for triglycerides that occur in animal storage (adipose) tissue and some plants.

fate map A map of an embryo, identifying the cells whose progeny will give rise to specific adult tissues and organs.

fatty acid A long-chain (hydrocarbon) carboxylic acid. Fatty acids are components of many lipids including glycerides. Long-chain fatty acids are insoluble in water. However, their sodium and potassium salts are soluble as soaps. The most common naturally occurring fatty acids are monocarboxylic acids which have an even number of carbon atoms (16 or 18) and which may be saturated or unsaturated (possess *cis* double bond(s) between the carbon atoms). In polyunsaturated acids (i.e., those with more than one double bond) the double bonds are arranged in a methylene-interrupted system ($-CH=CH-CH_2-CH=CH-$). Fatty acids may be described using a numbering system in which a number before the colon indicates the number of carbon atoms in the fatty acid, whereas that after the colon is the number of double bonds present. In the case of unsaturated fatty acids, this is followed by a number in parentheses that indicates the position of the double bonds. Each number is the lower numbered carbon atom of the two connected by the double bond; c or t indicates that this double bond has a *cis* or *trans* configuration, respectively. The common fatty acids are listed below using this nomenclature:

Common name	Structure
Lauric	12:0
Myristic	14:0
Palmitic	16:0
Stearic	18:0
Oleic	18:1(9c)
Linoleic	18:2(9c,12c)
α-Linolenic	18:3(9c,12c,15c)

Palmitic and stearic acids are the most abundant fatty acids in animal fatty tissue. Oleic acid is the most widely distributed of the unsaturated fats, whereas linolenic is an important constituent of the chloroplast membrane lipids. Over 200 minor fatty acids have been isolated from various biological sources. These are either similar to those listed above with varying chain length or may be unusual, containing non-conjugated double bonds in an unusual position, conjugated double bond systems, allenic double bonds, triple bonds, oxygen functions (hydroxy, keto, epoxy groups) or branched chains.

fatty acid oxidation Part of the process of catabolism of stored food reserves in animals and fatty seeds. Since these reserves generally comprise triglycerides, the first step is hydrolytic cleavage of the three ester bonds to yield glycerol and fatty acids. Glycerol is then phosphorylated, oxidized to dihydroxyacetone phosphate and passed into the glycolysis pathway. The long-chain fatty acids are broken down two carbons at a time in the process of beta-oxidation and glyoxysomes. This process generates ATP since it produces reduced substrates (e.g., NADPH), which are re-oxidized via the terminal electron transport chain with the generation of ATP, and acetyl-CoA, which can be metabolized through the TCA cycle. The fatty acid is first converted to its co-enzyme A derivative in a reaction that requires energy in the form of 2 molecules of ATP. This acetyl-CoA derivative is then oxidized to an unsaturated form, with the reduction of an FAD-containing flavo protein. The flavo protein can be re-oxidized via the terminal electron transport chain providing more ATP. The double bond of the fatty acid derivative is hydrated, and oxidized in a reaction linked to NADP reduction. The final step involves the addition of a second co-enzyme A molecule to produce one molecule of acetyl-CoA and one fatty acid-CoA which is two carbons shorter than the initial substrate. The cycle can then be repeated until the fatty acid has been completely converted to acetyl CoA. The gross yield from one molecule of palmitic acid is 131 ATP molecules, but the net value is 129 since

2 molecules of ATP are used in the activation of palmitic acid. This shows the value of fats as an energy reserve in biological systems.

fatty acid synthesis Long-chain fatty acids synthesis is divided into three distinct phases: (1) acetyl-CoA is carboxylated to yield malonyl-CoA; (2) the two-carbon units derived from decarboxylation of malonyl-CoA are condensed to form a fatty acid of intermediate chain length, eventually palmitic acid (C_{16}) (this is a multi-step process catalysed by a multi-enzyme complex termed fatty acid synthase); (3) the wide range of longer-chain, saturated and unsaturated, fatty acids is derived from palmitic acid by the concerted action of fatty acid elongation and desaturation systems.

FBS *See* foetal bovine serum.

FCS Foetal calf serum. *See* foetal bovine serum.

FDA *See* fluorescein diacetate.

fed batch system An anaerobic digester or fermenter operated in a batch mode to which substrate, in either solid or concentrated liquid form, is added several times during the run.

feedback inhibition A control mechanism in which the activity of an enzyme associated with an early stage of a multi-step pathway is inhibited by a metabolite produced by a reaction further along the sequence. The mechanism of control may be due to binding of the product at an allosteric site on the enzyme.

feedback repression A mechanism whereby the biosynthesis of an enzyme is inhibited when an end product of its pathway accumulates or is added to a culture medium.

feeder layer method The cultivation of single protoplasts in which protoplasts of one type or origin are grown on sheets of filter paper laid out over feeder-plant cells that provide growth factors facilitating cell wall synthesis.

feedstock The raw material or substrate used as a source of carbon in a bioreactor.

Fehling's reaction A chemical test for reducing sugars and aldehydes. Fehling's solution consists of Fehling's I, an aqueous solution of cupric sulphate, and Fehling's II, potassium sodium tartrate and sodium hydroxide. Equal volumes of I and II are added to the sample solution which is then boiled. Reduction of the cupric salt produces a brick red precipitate of cuprous oxide. In the absence of a reducing compound the solution remains blue.

fermentation (1) In metabolism, the degradation of organic substances by organisms or cells to proved chemical energy as ATP in reactions that do not require molecular oxygen. In anaerobic cells, it is the only energy-producing process. (2) Descriptive of processes in which cells or other microorganisms are cultured in a container (bioreactor or fermenter) in liquid or solid medium for experimental or commercial processes. The term was originally applied only to anaerobic cultures, but now is often used to describe all cultures of microorganisms or cells in fabricated vessels.

fermented dairy products A wide range of processed foods prepared by growing microorganisms on whole or separated and/or reconstituted milk. Products include acidophilus milk, butter milk, cream cheese, yoghurt, etc.

fermenter A vessel or bioreactor designed for fermentation. The most common configuration is the completely stirred tank reactor (CSTR). Fermenters can vary in size from less than a litre for bench-scale or experimental systems to thousands of litres for commercial systems; the only similarity is that they are closed tanks. Materials used for their construction include wood, copper, concrete, plastics, aluminium, mild steel and stainless steel. A liner of wax or resin is often used to protect against corrosion if the basic construction is of cheaper material. The shape of tanks varies considerably from domed, square, rectangular, horizontal cylindrical, vertical cylindrical to conical, many designs having been developed for specific types of fermentation or techniques. A standard general-purpose fermenter consists of a cylindrical glass (laboratory scale) or metal (pilot and commercial scale) cylinder with a height/diameter ratio of 2:1 and either a cone-shaped or sloping bottom to facilitate emptying. The fermenter also has a number of ports for addition of nutrient, removal of products and insertion of measuring and control probes. Larger systems have inbuilt (steam) systems for cleaning and sterilization. The tank may be fitted with openings for venting or collection of gases. Where necessary, agitation and aeration facilities are provided. The most common means of agitation is of a combination of baffle plates fixed inside the fermenter tank and an intermeshing motor-driven rotor, but alternative methods may be necessary when the viscosity of the culture is high. These are based on the recirculation of the liquid or gas stream, or injection of air at high pressure. Air (or oxygen) injection is used with all aerobic organisms. In general, this is sparged into the base of the fermenter. The metabolic processes associated with the growth of organisms generate heat, and heat may also be transmitted through the stirring device. In many cases, it may be necessary to control the temperature of the fermenter by cooling. This is usually done using an outer jacket or internal cooling coil through which cold water is passed. In some systems, the fluid is circulated through an external heat exchanger and returned to the vessel. Systems in which mesophilic or thermophilic organisms are used may require heating rather than cooling, again using jackets, coils or external heat exchangers. Large fermenters rather than being housed are set out in the open, and in some climates, this will necessitate external insulation. In large systems, access is aided by the provision of catwalks.

fermenter agitation A method of mixing or stirring the contents of a fermenter in

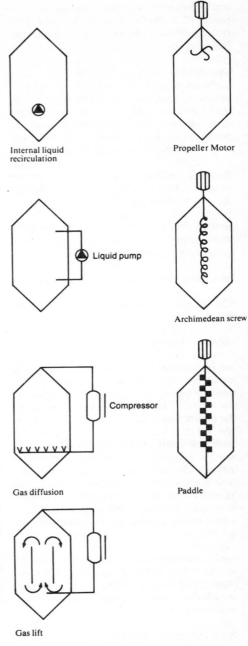

Internal liquid recirculation

Propeller Motor

Liquid pump

Archimedean screw

Compressor

Gas diffusion

Paddle

Gas lift

Fermenter agitation

order to prevent settling of the organism or product, to facilitate rapid gas exchange (oxygen uptake in particular), and to establish uniform temperature and nutrient distribution. The most common means of agitation are the use of an impeller rotating at high speed. The fermenter may also be equipped with internal baffles to increase the degree of agitation of the broth by the creation of turbulence. Other methods of mixing include the injection, or recycling, of gas streams or liquid streams.

fermenter control Advanced fermentation processes may be equipped with a wide variety of automatic control and/or monitoring facilities using microprocessors. These include: (1) control of temperature, pressure and pH by closed loop feedback; (2) control of foaming by on/off addition of an antifoam; (3) automatic sequencing to ensure correct adherence to protocols for sterilization, cleaning and filling, as well as harvest operations; (4) control of dissolved oxygen concentration; (5) automatic feeding of nutrients in response to dissolved oxygen concentration or biomass level, or to feed nutrients automatically according to a preset schedule; (6) control of the respiratory quotient in order to optimize cell mass production.

fermenter cooling On a commercial scale, the most common methods of removing heat generated during fermentation are the use of cooling towers or refrigeration to provide cold water which is passed through a jacket or internal coil associated with the fermenter. In hot climates, where natural water supplies are at a temperature similar to or above that of the optimum for cell growth, cooling can be a major problem. A cooling tower is not very effective in summer, when cooling requirements are greatest, because humidity is often quite high. The alternative – refrigeration – is relatively expensive. A large internal cooling coil wastes a great deal of fermenter volume and decreases oxygen transfer rate and mixing quality, particularly for viscous broths. A jacket is limited in area to the dimensions of the fermenter. Hence recirculation through external heat exchangers may be used.

fermentograph An automated device used to measure the production of carbon dioxide in order to assess the activity of bakers' yeast in a sample of dough.

ferredoxin An iron–sulphur protein. Ferredoxins have a very noted negative redox potential and are constituents of electron transport chains. A ferredoxin is associated with the reduced side of photosystem I in photosynthesis, donating electrons to NADP in a reaction mediated by ferredoxin-NADP oxidoreductase.

Proposed model for the active centre of ferredoxins

fertility factor An episome capable of transferring a copy of itself from its host bacterial cell (an F^+ cell) to a bacterial cell not harbouring an F factor (an F^- cell) during conjugation. The F factor may become integrated with the chromosome of the F^+ cell. When this happens the F factor causes transfer of part (or rarely all) of the chromosome to the F^- strain. Strains with an integrated F factor are termed Hfr.

fertilization The fusion of the nuclear material and cytoplasm of two haploid gametes to form a single cell, the diploid zygote. Fertilization usually provides the stimulus for cell division and differentiation to form an embryo.

fetal *See* foetal.

fetus *See* foetus.

feulgen stain A dye employed in histology to stain chromosomes which can then be observed using light microscopy. The stain reacts with DNA.

FIA *See* fluoroimmunoassay.

fibrin An insoluble fibrous protein that forms the matrix of blood clots. It is produced by the action of the enzyme thrombin on the plasma protein fibrinogen. This results in the release of two small polypeptides leaving the fibrin monomer, which then polymerizes.

fibrinogen A plasma protein that acts as a precursor of fibrin. It is a soluble dimeric protein consisting of three pairs of polypeptide chains. Fibrinogen is converted into fibrin by the action of the enzyme thrombin.

fibrinolysis The dissolution of blood clots brought about by the enzyme plasmin.

fibroblast A cell type present in vertebrate connective tissue that secretes a collagen precursor (tropocollagen) and mucopolysaccharides which constitute the connective tissue ground substance. Tropocollagen is polymerized into collagen fibres in an extracellular process. Fibroblasts which are flat, elongated or triangular in shape can readily be grown by tissue culture.

fibroblastic interferon An antiviral protein, also known as beta-interferon, produced by fibroblasts in mammalian connective tissue. It is isolated from foetal tissue or from the prepuces of circumcised infants. Fibroblastic interferon can also be prepared from cells maintained in culture, where the cells form monolayers on suitable supports such as microbeads which give a high surface area thus increasing yields.

fibronectin A connective glycoprotein secreted by a variety of cells. It forms a fibrillar matrix that helps to link cells to other extra cellular proteins (e.g., collagen). Transformed cells and tumours do not have fibronectin bound to their surfaces and therefore have certain abnormal properties. Transformed cells can, to a certain extent, be normalized by the addition of fibronectin. Therefore it is sometimes referred to as large external transformation-sensitive protein (LETS).

ficoll A synthetic polymer made by copolymerization of sucrose and epichlorhydrin that is widely used as a density gradient centrifugation medium. It is also used as an immunologically inert carrier for low-molecular-weight haptens in immunological studies.

field inversion gel electrophoresis (FIGE) *See* pulsed field gel electrophoresis.

FIGE Field inversion gel electrophoresis.

filial generation The progeny obtained in cross breeding. *See* F_1 and F_2.

filter aid Materials such as diatomaceous earth or Kieselguhr added to a fluid to increase the rate at which it may be clarified by filtration.

filter press A filtration device in which the filtration rate is increased by the application of above atmospheric pressure at the filter surface.

filtration A process used to separate particles of various sizes, or solids from liquids, in which the mixture is passed through a perforated plate or membrane. A wide range of filter plates and membrane designs has been developed for sterilization or in order to separate biological products from fermentation media. These are classified in terms of both flow pattern and pore size. *See* crossflow filtration, microfiltration, ultrafiltration.

fimbriae A small proteinaceous outgrowth from the cell wall occurring in some yeasts.

fingerprinting *See* fingerprinting technique, genetic fingerprinting.

fingerprinting technique A method used to determine the structure of proteins or nucleic acids in which partial hydrolysis is followed by production of a two-dimensional map using gel electrophoresis and/or chromatography. Fingerprinting techniques are also used to compare the structure or sequences of molecules from different sources or to identify a molecule or genome by comparison with a known standard.

fission. A process of asexual reproduction found in single-cell organisms in which nuclear division is followed by the formation of a cross wall, or by constriction of the original cell wall to form two or more daughters of equal size and similar genetic make-up.

FITC *See* fluorescein isothiocyanate.

fitness The ability of an organism to survive selection pressures in a given environment, dependent on its genetic make-up.

fixation A preservation procedure used in the preparation of specimens for microscopic examination. Ethanol and acetic acid are often used for preparation of samples for light microscopy, whereas glutaraldehyde, which crosslinks proteins, is used for electron microscopy. Lipids and membranes may be fixed using osmium tetroxide.

fixed bed reactor A bioreactor in which the active biomass or enzymes are immobilized on a fixed carrier stream. The reactor may be run as a filter system, a packed column or a plug flow system.

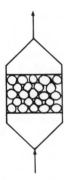

Fixed bed
reactor

fixed film A layer of active biomass immobilized, or growing, on the surface of a fixed carrier.

flagellin A protein constituent of the wall of prokaryotic flagella.

flagellum A long hair-like organelle that projects from cells and is generally used in locomotion. In prokaryotes, flagella are hollow structures with walls formed from helical rows of spherical protein (flagellin)

subunits. Eukaryotic flagella may be used for either locomotion in motile reproductive stages or circulating internal fluids in some multicellular organisms, and are larger than those found in prokaryotes and have a structure similar to that of cilia. Nine outer pairs of microtubules (distinguished as A and B) are continuous with the A and B microtubules of the basal body. Two central microtubules end in the transition zone between the flagellum and basal body.

flanking regions *See* inverse PCR.

flash-ferm process A modification of the vacu-ferm process of ethanol production in which fermentation is carried out in an atmospheric pressure fermenter so that the yeast's oxygen maintenance requirement can be cheaply met with sparged air. Carbon dioxide produced in the fermentation process can be directly vented from the fermenter and thus need not be compressed with the vapour product as in the vacu-ferm. To remove ethanol, beer is rapidly cycled through a small auxiliary flash vessel where it boils. Ethanol is recovered as the flash vessel over-head vapour product and ethanol-depleted beer is returned to the fermenter for further fermentation. The problem of contamination is greatly reduced as only the small flash vessel is under vacuum. Energy requirements for this process are also slightly lower than for vacu-ferm systems.

flavanone *See* flavone.

flavin A derivative of riboflavin that functions as the prosthetic group in flavoproteins.

flavin adenine dinucleotide *See* FAD.

flavin mononucleotide *See* FMN.

flavone A flavonoid that activates transcription of *Rhizobium* nodulation genes.

flavonoid Compounds based on two benzene rings joined by a three-carbon chain. Flavonoid glycosides are important plant pigments and include the anthocyanins, benzalcoumarans, chalcones, flavones and flavonols, as well as the colourless leucoanthocyanidins and isoflavones.

flavoprotein A protein conjugated with a flavin prosthetic group that functions as a dehydrogenase in the respiratory electron transport chain.

floating gas holder *See* gas holder.

floc A loose association of suspended solids composed of particles ranging in size up to a few millimetres. The term may be applied to bacterial cultures in which the cells tend to aggregate in this way.

flocculating agent A compound, such as a long-chain polyelectrolyte, that encourages the formation of flocs.

flocculating yeasts A yeast that has a natural tendency to form flocs when grown in suspension culture. Such yeasts are of value in continuous fermentation systems since the cells may be removed from the effluent stream and recycled using simple sedimentation rather than more expensive centrifugation.

flocculation The physicochemical process by which suspended solids assemble into a floc.

florigin A hypothetical plant growth substance supposedly associated with the onset or regulation of flowering.

flotation A technique used for the separation of solids from water in which a stream of air or other gas is blown through the liquid, as a result of which small bubbles become attached to the solids which thus float to the surface where they may be removed by skimming.

flow (1) To move along in stream or to circulate. (2) In fluid mechanics, a deformation of which at least part is non-recoverable.

flow cell A device used with analytical equipment that enables continuous readings to be taken or a liquid stream to be monitored continuously. For instance, a fluorometer, spectophotometer, scintillation counter, colorimeter, pH meter or similar instrument may be fitted with a small glass cell with an inlet and outlet fixed in such a way that the sample passes continuously through it.

flow cytometry An automated technique used to separate and analyse individual classes of cells, microorganisms or organelles from mixed populations. The process is carried out using a fully automated instrument, the activities of which can be divided into two parts: recognition and separation. Cells are injected into a flow stream that fragments into droplets. These are carried past an excitation source (usually a laser beam) where measurements are made rates of between 10^5 and 10^6 per second. Multiple parameters can be measured for each cell by using stains or fluorescent compounds. Emitted and scattered light emanating from the cell–laser interaction are used to characterize the cells. The intensity of scatter at different angles yields information about cell size, shape, density, viability and surface morphology. This information is fed into a computer, and cells with the desired characteristics can be physically sorted out by charging and electrostatic deflection of the liquid droplets in which they are carried. In most applications, fluorochromes, often carried on monoclonal antibodies, are used to label specific classes of cells at different cell components. A wide range of parameters can be measured using this technique, including DNA content, karyotyping and detection of cell surface markers. In particular, this technique has been used to measure populations of T and B lymphocytes. The method has applications in cancer research and clinical onclogy, as well as screening for chromosome abnormalities such as aneuploidy.

flow meter A device used to determine the volume of liquid or gas passing through a system.

flow sorter A device for sorting cell types. *See* flow cytometry.

flower The reproductive body of an angiosperm formed from modified sporophylls which form the perianth, androecium and gynoecium borne on a receptacle.

fluid A substance that is capable of flow. This term includes gases, liquids and suspensions of solid particles. Gases are compressible fluids, whereas liquids in general are not compressible. By definition, fluids are not self-supporting and hence must be contained in vessels and transported through pipes.

fluid mixing The interchange of molecules between regions of different concentration in a fluid or fluids. Mixing may be due to diffusion or turbulent flow. Diffusion is independent of any laminar flow where molecules move from faster to slower moving layers. In turbulent flow, there is a forces multidirectional transfer which proceeds at a much greater rate. Such turbulence may be introduced by the use of impellers or other mixing devices. In many processes, the presence of laminar regions in a mixed system is the major limit to mass transfer.

fluid transport In biochemical processes, fluids may be transported under gravity, but more often under pressure created by pumps. Behaviour of fluids during transport depends on both the physical characteristics of the fluid and the pressure applied. The absolute boundary of the fluid is considered to adhere to its containing pipe; hence there is no flow in the extreme boundary film. Adjacent layers flow with increasing velocity at a rate depending on the applied pressure, the viscous forces operating in the fluid and the distance of the layer under consideration form the boundary. This is termed laminar flow and is maintained up to a certain mean velocity above which the flow becomes turbulent, except in the region of the boundary where it remains laminar. The thickness of this boundary layer depends on the degree of turbulence in the main flow.

fluidized bed A bed of small particles freely suspended in an upflow of a fluid (in biological systems usually water or a water/ air mixture). At the point of fluid minimization the fluid dropped across the bed equals the total weight of particles in the bed, corrected for their buoyancy in the liquid. Increase in liquid flow results in the expansion of the bed until at high velocity the particles may become entrained and lost from the reactor.

fluidized bed reactor A fermenter, anaerobic digester or bioreactor in which the active material is associated with a bed of a particulate nature kept in suspension by the upward flow of the fluid phase.

Fluidized bed reactor

fluorescein diacetate (FDA) A stain that is deacetylated following absorption by living cells and becomes fluorescent, thus allowing viable cells to be identified when examined under ultraviolet light.

fluorescein isothiocyanate (FITC) A type of fluorophore.

fluorescence A physical process in which light is emitted from certain chemical compounds following absorption of radiation. A given compound will absorb radiation of wavelengths corresponding to its absorption spectrum, and the light emitted will be at a lower-energy, longer wavelength.

fluorescence photometry A system for *in vitro* quantification of low-level intracellular ions.

fluorescence-activated cell sorter (FACS) An instrument used to separate cells that fluoresce from those that do not, as they pass through a narrow orifice. Cells may be bound to a specific fluorescein-conjugated antibody to facilitate their separation.

fluorescence-activated flow sorting A technique in flow cytometry in which the cells are recognized by their fluorescent characterisitics. The cells may be made to fluoresce using antibodies (often monoclonal) to antigens on specific cell types. The antibodies are linked with a fluorochrome.

fluorescent antibody A monoclonal or polyclonal antibody that is labelled with a fluorochrome.

fluoroacetic acid A derivative of acetic acid in which one of the hydrogens on the methyl group is replaced by an atom of fluorine.

fluoroacetyl-CoA A metabolic intermediate formed between co-enzyme A and fluoroacetate, catalysed by the acetyltransferase that usually results in the formation of acetyl-CoA. Fluoroacetyl-CoA reacts with oxaloacetic acid, in the reaction catalysed by citrate synthetase to form fluorocitrate, a potent inhibitor of the TCA cycle.

fluorochrome A chemical compound that will absorb light and re-emit it as fluorescence.

fluorogenic Producing a fluorescent signal.

fluorogenic EIA An enzyme-based immunoassay in which the signal is generated through conversion of a non-fluorescing substrate to a fluorescing one. The use of a fluorogenic substrate (e.g., 4-MUP, 4-MUG) together with alkaline phosphatase (AP) or β-galactosidase gives a very sensitive assay.

fluoroimmunoassay (FIA) An immunoassay in which a fluorophore is used as a label.

fluorometer An instrument designed to measure fluorescence. Typically a fluorometer consists of a light source, a sample holder and a photomultiplier arranged with the source at right angles to the detector. A dif-

fraction grating is inserted between the sample and the source, and between the sample and the detector. These are adjusted so that the excitation beam can be distinguished from the fluorescence emission. The instrument is used in scanning mode to determine excitation or emission spectra for identification, or at fixed wavelengths to quantify the amount of a known substance.

fluorophore A fluorescent reagent.

fluoruracil An analogue of uracil that blocks the synthesis of RNA.

Fluorouracil

FMN Flavin mononucleotide (oxidized form); a derivative of riboflavin that functions as a prosthetic group in flavoproteins and acts as an acceptor in oxidation–reduction reactions. $FMNH_2$ is the reduced form. *See* flavonoid.

foam A two-phase (gas/liquid or gas/solid) or three-phase (gas/liquid/solid) system formed by the aggregation of minute bubbles. For stability, a liquid foam agent requires the presence of a surface-active agent that lowers the free surface energy of the solution relative to the pure liquid. Hence, the addition of surfactants can assist in the production of a foam. Low concentrations of proteins may have a stabilizing effect on such foams. Many microorganisms in culture produce compounds with surfactant properties, which coupled with proteins, polysaccharides and lipids may result in serious problems associated with foam production in both stirred and aerated systems. Control of such foam production is important in fermentations. Foams are of advantage in the immobilization of cells or enzymes since they may be formed with a high ratio of entrapped biocatalyst to support material or provide a large ratio of surface area per volume.

foetal Associated with or derived from a foetus, (e.g., foetal tissue).

foetal bovine serum (FBS) A growth media supplement used for *in vitro* cultivation of hybridoma and related mammalian cells.

foetal calf serum (FCS) *See* foetal bovine serum.

foetus The embryo of a mammal at a stage where all the features of the adult form are recognizable.

foldback DNA A single strand of DNA that contains an inverted repeat sequence of bases so that it is able to fold back and hybridize with itself. Such self-hybridization occurs very rapidly when DNA that contains long palindromic sequences is placed in conditions that favour renaturation.

folic acid Pteroylglutamic acid; a complex molecule formed from glutamate and *p*-aminobenzoic acid linked to a substituted pterin. It is a vitamin of the B group. Folic acid deficiency leads to megablastic anaemia in mammals. It is a precursor of tetrahydrofolic acid, a co-enzyme that mediates in the transfer of C_1 groups in methylation and similar reactions, and is involved in the synthesis of purines and pyrimidines (precursors of nucleic acids).

follicle A small cavity or gland, such as the hair follicles found in mammalian skin.

follicle-stimulating hormone A glycoprotein hormone secreted by the pituitary gland under regulation of the hypothalamus. In female mammals, it stimulates the growth of young graafian follicles in the ovary, whereas in males it stimulates the production of sperm in the seminiferous tubules.

food chain The process by which energy is transferred from plants through a series of organisms within a given ecosystem. Each stage of the chain is known as a trophic level. The first level is represented by plants which trap solar energy through photosyn-

thesis. The second level is represented by herbivores which are consumed by carnivores.

food poisoning An acute illness caused by consumption of contaminated food, usually presenting gastrointestinal symptoms. Poisoning is due to toxins produced in the food prior to consumption and produced during growth of the causative organisms in the gut.

foot and mouth disease A highly contagious disease that afflicts about 30 species of cloven-hoofed animals worldwide. The disease, which is a particular threat to cattle, sheep and swine, is often controlled by eradication of infected animals.

foot and mouth vaccine A vaccine against foot and mouth disease prepared by inactivation of virus previously grown in baby hamster kidney cells. The multiplicity of virus forms and subtypes requires the use of polyvalent vaccines, or vaccine appropriate to a given region or outbreak. Problems associated with the current vaccines include lack of stability, the need to store under refrigeration and the possibility that the use of live vaccines can lead to outbreaks of the disease. Hence there is interest in using molecular biology techniques to produce more stable, safer vaccines. Treatment of the virus with trypsin results in the cleavage of the protein known as VP1 and a significant decrease in infectivity. Large doses of VP1 may give swine some protection against infection, since this protein induces low immunogenic activity. The coding sequence for this protein has been isolated and cloned into a plasmid in *E. coli*, and the amino acid sequence established.

foot and mouth virus A member of the *aphthovirus* genus of the family piconaviridae. Foot and mouth virus contains a single strand of RNA with a molecular weight of 2.6×10^6 surrounded by a capsid constructed of 60 copies of four polypeptides known as VP^1, VP^2, VP^3 and VP^4. The virus occurs as seven different types and over 60 subtypes.

footprinting A method used to detect regions of a DNA sample that are conjugated with a specific protein. Two DNA samples, one with and one without protein, are fragmented by an endonuclease and are then run on parallel electrophoresis gels. Because the conjugated regions of DNA are resistant to the action of the endonuclease, they will not be fragmented. Therefore, bands associated with fragments containing those regions will not be formed in the DNA sample with added protein.

foreign DNA DNA that is not found in the normal chromosome complement of the organism concerned. It may be introduced into a vector by complexing with native DNA using techniques of gene manipulation, and hence into the new host. Foreign DNA may also be introduced into host cells following virus infection.

formaldehyde (HCHO) A gas that is an effective bacteriocide against non-spore-forming organisms. It is generally available as a 40 per cent solution in water (formalin) and used at a dilution of 0.1–0.5% formalin in water.

formalin *See* formaldehyde.

formamide CH_3NO; also known as methanamide or carbaldehyde. Formamide is used as a solvent for animal glues and water-sol gums. It is also used as a solvent to facilitate the melting of double-stranded DNA or RNA. It is extensively used in molecular hybridization.

formate A salt of formic acid.

formic acid (HCOOH) The simplest carboxylic acid.

formulation A mixture made up to a prescribed recipe. Often used in relation to a prophylactic.

forphenicine An immunomodulator produced by *Streptomyces fulvoviridis*.

forward mutation A mutation from the wild type to the mutant condition. *Compare* back mutation.

fouling The deposition of material in the wrong place at the wrong time. In bioreactors and cooling systems in particular, the fouling of heat exchanger surfaces by growing biomass, protein, polysaccharide or other similar materials with insulating properties is of particular concern. Similar fouling may also occur during downstream processes such as concentration, drying and distillation.

founder effect Genetic drift due to the founding of a population by a small number of individuals.

Fourier transform infrared spectroscopy *See* infrared immunoassay.

fraction I protein *See* ribulose bis-phosphate oxygenase/carboxylase.

fraction collector A device that collects sequential samples. The term is often applied to an instrument in which a series of test tubes is located in sequence to collect the effluent from a chromatography column. The size of each fraction collected before the cell moves on is based on automatic measurement of time, volume of liquid or the number of drops which pass in front of a photodetector.

fragment antigen binding *See* Fab fragment.

fragmentation sequencing A DNA sequencing technique in which target DNA is fragmented into short oligonucleotides that are then hybridized to form thousands of immobilized oligonucleotide probes. The frequency of fragments hybridized to each probe can then be measured and the information processed by a computer to deduce the original sequence.

frameshift A shift in the reading frame used to translate the base sequence of mRNA. It is caused by the addition or deletion of one or more bases, resulting in an alternative peptide being formed. The amino acid sequence of this peptide may be nonsensical.

frameshift mutation A mutation caused by either the insertion or deletion of a number of nucleotide pairs in DNA. The effect is to change the reading frame of codons in an mRNA molecule during protein synthesis, causing an abnormal amino acid sequence to be synthesized from the site of the mutation onward.

free energy A thermodynamic function representing the energy evolved or absorbed during a reversible reaction. It is defined as:

$$G = H - TS$$

where H = enthalpy, T = temperature and S = entropy. For chemical processes, the main concern is with the change in free energy (δG) which for biological reactions can be expressed as:

$$\delta G = \delta U - T\delta S$$

where U = change in internal energy. If δG for a reaction is negative, the reaction proceeds to equilibrium (where $\delta G = 0$) naturally. The value of δG is a function of such conditions as temperature, concentration and pressure.

freeze etching A process used in electron microscopy in which the extent of detail in a freeze-fractured specimen is increased by allowing some of the ice to sublime prior to production of a shadowed replica.

freeze fracturing A method used in the preparation of specimens for examination under the electron microscope. The frozen specimen is fractured under vacuum, revealing the plane of membranes and organelles which may then be shadowed by metal deposition demonstrating the surface structure. The resultant image is close to that of the material in the natural state because neither fixatives nor dehydration are involved.

freeze preservation A technique used for the long-term preservation of microbial cultures in culture collections. The cells are frozen slowly at around one degree per minute to −20°C and then rapidly to the storage temperature; glycerol may be added

as protective agent. The frozen culture is then stored at liquid nitrogen temperatures.

frequency-dependent selection Natural selection whose effects depend on the frequency of the genotypes or the phenotypes.

Freund's adjuvant A mixture of waxes, mineral oil and inactivated turbecle bacilli used as an adjuvant, in the form of an emulsion, with an aqueous antigen. When the mixture is injected subcutaneously, it forms a granulomatous lesion containing a high local concentration of lymphocytes, histiocytes and epitheloid cells which increase the local production of the required antibody.

Friend cell An erythroid cell line derived from leukaemic mouse cells induced by injection of a specific virus. Treatment with dimethylsulphoxide may induce the formation of haemoglobin in these cell lines.

Frings acetator A device for commercial production of vinegar using submerged culture techniques. Frings acetator is a tank fermenter fitted with a cooling coil and automated controls. Air is supplied in a controlled manner through a Frings aerator.

Frings aerator A device designed to control precisely the aeration rate needed in the continuous production of vinegar using submerged culture techniques. It consists of a hollow body turbine surrounded by a stator. The body has 6 openings for the escape of air that open against the direction of rotation. Liquid is forced through these openings and brought into contact with the air that is passed into the hollow body. The air/liquid emulsion is thrown out radially to give a uniform distribution throughout the fermenter and to achieve the uniform distribution of air needed to ensure continued survival of the *Acetobacter*.

Frings alkograph An automated instrument used to measure the percentage ethanol for control of vinegar fermentations.

frozen embryo transfer A technique of embryo transfer in which the embryos are stored or transported in a frozen state.

fructofuranosidase A synonym for the enzyme commonly known as invertase. It hydrolyses sucrose to glucose and fructose.

fructose A ketohexose sugar that usually exists in the L-pyranose form. However, in combination with other sugars (as in sucrose), fructose is more common in the D-furanose form. The production of fructose from hydrolysed corn starch as high fructose corn syrup (HFCS) is the largest industrial use of immobilized enzymes. Such syrups have generally replaced the use of sucrose in carbonated beverages in the USA and elsewhere. In solution fructose exists as an equilibrium mixture as follows:

fructose-1,6-bisphosphate A phosphorylated derivative of fructose that plays an important role in central metabolism, being the starting point for glycolysis and an intermediate in carbon assimilation, starch synthesis and sucrose formation.

fruit The ripe ovary of a flower together with any accessory parts that may develop with it. Fruit formation follows fertilization of the ovules and proceeds as the seeds develop and ripen.

frustule The silica shell of a diatom. Fossil remains of diatoms are used, in the form of diatomaceous earth, as a filter aid.

fucoxanthin A brown xanthophyll pigment present in brown seaweeds in particular.

fumaric acid A chemical compound that occurs naturally in most cells. It is an intermediate in the TCA cycle.

fumigation A disinfection technique in which a toxic gas is released into a closed environment. Fumigants such as methyl bromide are used to treat imported grains and fruit. A clean room may be fumigated by boiling formalin, to release formaldehyde, using about 12 millilitres per cubic metre of room volume.

fungi A group of non-photosynthetic eukaryotic, thallophytic organisms. Traditionally they have been classified as non-green plants. However more recent classification schemes place them in a separate kingdom that is separated as follows: Ascomycota, Basidiomycota, Fungi Imperfecti, Zygomycota, Omycota, Chytridomycota. The last three divisions correspond to the class of fungi previously known as the Phycomycetes. In previous classifications, where the groups were regarded as classes, the same prefixes were used but ending in -mycetes (e.g., Ascomycetes). The fungi (which include the single cell types generally termed yeasts) are used in the production of a wide range of materials of commercial importance. These include antibiotics, cellulase, amylases, proteases, single-cell protein, solvents, organic acids, etc. Fungi are also important as mycorrhiza in symbiotic relationships with higher plants and in the breakdown of organic material in composting and sewage dispersal. Some fungi are human or animal pathogens. Problems of commercial importance are largely related to the activities of fungi as agents of plant disease (mildews, rusts and smuts), food spoilage (aflatoxin) and contamination, and their widespread ability to attack structural materials (wet or dry rots).

Fungi Inperfecti The Deuteromycetes; a division of the fungi in which a sexual reproductive stage does not exist or has never been observed. The exact taxonomic relationship of these fungi is uncertain. The Fungi Imperfecti may represent unidentified stages of fungi known in other forms or degenerate forms where the capacity for sexual reproduction has been lost.

fungicide A chemical or biological agent that kills fungi.

furanose A monosaccharide that has a five-membered ring structure consisting of four carbon and one oxygen atoms.

fusaric acid A hypotensive produced by *Fusarium*.

Fusarium Graminaria A fungus, the cells of which grow as filamentous aggregates. It is used for producing single-cell protein.

fusel oil A mixture of higher alcohols formed during yeast-based fermentations to produce ethanol. The higher alcohols are synthesized by transamination of amino acids present in the wort to the corresponding aldehydes followed by their reduction to the alcohols.

fusiform Spindle-shaped, rounded and tapering from the middle towards the end.

fusion The combination of two distinct cells or macromolecules into a single integrated unit.

fusion protein A protein encoded by two fused genes. It is often deliberately engineered to facilitate genetic studies or manipulations.

fuzzy control Process control using fuzzy set theory (also called fuzzy logic). In fuzzy set theory, standard logical values false (0) and true (1) are replaced by continuously graded values between 0 and 1. This allows linguistic qualifiers (e.g., high, low, good enough, very high, large, etc.) to be represented in computer systems (particularly artificial intelligence, including expert systems).

G

G *See* guanine.

G phase A phase of the cell cycle. In G_1, following mitosis, only one chromatid is present, hence the cells have only half the normal amount of DNA. In G_2, duplication is complete but mitosis has not yet occurred.

GA_3 *See* gibberellic acid.

GABA *See* gamma aminobutyric acid.

GAG Glycosaminoglycan.

gal (galactose) operon A transcriptional unit containing genes for the three enzymes that convert galactose into glucose-1-phosphate and uridine di-phosphate glucose. It is regulated in a manner similar but not identical to the lac operon.

galactan A polysaccharide based on galactose (e.g., agar, carrageenan).

galactose An aldohexose sugar that is a constituent of the disaccharide lactose found in milk, as well as occurring in glycolipids, glycoproteins and plant cell wall components. D-galactose is an epimer of D-glucose.

D-galactose

galactosidase An enzyme that converts lactose (milk sugar) to glucose and galactose, and also uses other galactose-containing compounds as substrates. The enzyme exists in several forms that are highly specific for the galactose residue, but much less specific for the aglycone. The enzyme also acts as a transferase in the formation of oligosaccharides. Some strains of *E. coli* produce large amounts of this enzyme. Commercial preparations are generally obtained from lactose-fermenting yeasts such as *Saccharomyces fragilis*, or fungi such as *Aspergillus niger*, grown on a lactose medium or on whey.

galactosyl diglycerides Plant lipids that occur in the chloroplasts. Both mono- and di-galactosyl diglycerides are found. They are almost exclusively esterified with the di- and tri-unsaturated fatty acids, linoleic and α-linolenic acids, with the latter generally predominant. The galactosidic linkage with glycerol is β, whereas that between the two galactose residues is α.

gametangium A structure found in plants that produces and houses the gametes (e.g., an antheridium, archegonium or oogonium).

gamete A specific haploid cell produced during sexual reproduction that fuses with another gamete to produce a zygote from which the next generation develops. In general, such fusion occurs between male gametes (spermatozoa) and female gametes (ova). The female gametes are often sessile, whereas male gametes are generally motile.

gametogenesis The formation of gametes.

gametophore A structure specialized to bear either antheridia or archegonia.

gametophyte The life form that bears the sex organs in those plants that exhibit alternation of generations. The gametophyte generation, which alternates with a sporophyte generation, is the dominant form in more primitive plants such as the bryophytes, but it becomes reduced in size and longevity in more advanced vascular plants, the sporophyte becoming dominant. In pteridophytes, it is reduced to a small prothallus, whereas in angiosperms, the gametophyte is represented by the pollen grain and embryo sac.

gamma aminobutyric acid (GABA) An amino acid that acts as an inhibitor of neurotransmission. It is found in nervous tissue and in the brain in particular.

gamma counter A device used to measure the amount of gamma-rays emitted by a sample. The device generally consists of a well formed from a suitable transparent plastic impregnated with a scintillator. The sample, contained in a vial, is placed in the well. *See* scintillation counter.

gamma globulin A type of serum protein that is distinguished on the basis of its electrophoretic mobility and that includes both serum immunoglobulins and other proteins without antibody activity.

gamma-interferon *See* immune interferon.

gamma-ray Electromagnetic radiation with wavelength of less than 0.1 μm that is emitted from some radioactive substances. *Compare* X-ray.

ganglion Nervous tissue containing many synapses and cell bodies encapsulated in connective tissue. Ganglia are found close to areas of high sensory input or motor output. In vertebrates, they are found in the autonomic nervous system, the spinal region and the corpus striatum. In invertebrates, they form the central nervous system in association with connective nerve fibres. The most anterior (cerebral) ganglia are associated with sense organs and may be the most dominant centre of the nervous system, equivalent to the vertebrate brain.

ganglioside A type of glycolipid found in nerve-cell membranes, composed of a fatty acid-substituted sphingosine molecule linked to an oligosaccharide that contains D-glucose, D-galactose, *N*-acetylgalactosamine and/or *N*-acetylneuraminic acid.

gas absorption coefficient *See* Bunsen coefficient.

gas chromatograph An instrument for carrying out gas chromatography. Modern designs are very sophisticated microprocessor-controlled systems. Basically, a gas chromatograph comprises a column (around 1 metre long for conventional systems, but over 100 metres long for capillary systems) contained in a temperature-controlled, programmable oven and fitted with an injection port for introduction of the sample. Inert carrier gas from a cylinder is passed through a flow regulator and the injection port where it picks up the sample and carries it through the column, in which separation takes place, to the detector. The column packings and detectors used vary depending on the nature of the material being analysed. A common detector used with biological materials is the flame ionization detector in which a hydrogen/nitrogen mixture is used as the carrier and is burnt in the detector at a jet above which a collector electrode is placed. Addition of organic compounds to the flame results in the production of ions which are collected at the electrode and amplified. The signal is then displayed on a paper recorder, cathode ray tube or passed to an electronic integrator/calculator. The results appear as a series of peaks. The amount of a given substance is determined by peak height or area. The nature of the compound can be deduced by comparison of the retention volumes of unknowns with authentic standards. However, unknown compounds can only be conclusively identified by further analysis, often using a combined gas chromatography/mass spectrometry system.

gas chromatography A very sensitive analytical technique used in the analysis of complex mixtures of volatile substances. The chromatographic process depends on the relative speeds at which the various components pass through a long, narrow tube packed with inert material, which is coated with a non-volatile liquid. This rate in turn depends on the partition coefficients of the various components. Low-molecular-weight compounds and gases may also be separated on columns packed with porous materials. By heating the column in an oven in a programmed way, compounds of varying volatility are vaporized in sequence. The process is also known as gas/liquid chromatography (GLC).

gas holder A device for the storage of (bio) gas. This may be an expanding flexible bag, a membrane over an otherwise open digester or a floating gas holder. A floating gas holder is a cylinder closed at its upper end and sealed at the lower end by a liquid, generally water, contained in a tank. The gas is stored at low pressure within the cylinder, above the water level, with the cylinder rising and falling to accommodate the varying gas volume.

gas lift A mixing and aeration device used in fermentation consisting of a vertical draft tube immersed in a liquid from the lower end of which compressed gas is expelled.

gas oil The oil that remains after petrol and paraffin have been distilled from crude petroleum. It has been used as a substrate for the production of single-cell protein by yeasts such as *Candida (Endomycopsis) lipolytica*.

gas/liquid chromatography *See* gas chromatography.

gasohol A mixture of petrol (gasoline) and alcohol (ethanol) used to power motor vehicles.

gas-phase sequentor A device used for determining the amino acid sequence of proteins in which gas-phase reagents are used at critical points of the Edman degradation. The sample is treated with gas-phase base and acid for the coupling and cleavage attachment of the sample to a carrier which may be dried on to a thin disc of glass filter paper coated with polythene.

gastric glands Cells found in the stomach mucosa that secrete gastric juice.

gastric juice A solution of hydrochloric acid, proteolytic enzymes and mucus secreted by gastric glands.

gastrin A polypeptide hormone, secreted by the mucosa of the stomach, that stimulates the production of hydrochloric acid.

gastrula A stage in the development of animal embryos that follows the blastula.

gastrulation The conversion of a blastula to a gastrula in embryo development with the differentiation of germ cell layers and the formation of the archenteron which opens to the exterior through the blastopore.

GC *See* gas chromatograph.

GC (G + C) content A measure of the amount of the bases G + C expressed as a percentage of the total. The higher the GC content, the higher the buoyant density.

GDP *See* guanosine 5′-diphosphate.

Geiger–Müller tube (counter) A device for measuring the activity of a radioactive source or sample. Radiation passes into a partially evacuated tube, filled with an ionizable gas and a quencher, containing an electrode at a high potential with respect to the case of the tube, which is earthed. The radiation results in ionization of the gas and a discharge. The rate of discharge is proportional to the number of disintegrations per minute of the sample, and hence the amount of radioactivity can be determined from the observed counts per minute multiplied by various correction factors for self-absorption, counter geometry, etc. The device is less sensitive and more difficult to calibrate than a scintillation counter, which has largely replaced the Geiger counter for routine experimental work using beta-emitters. However, such systems are still used in radiation monitors and other safety applications.

gel A physical mixture of solid and liquid consisting of an inert polymer matrix saturated with a liquid component.

gel chromatography *See* gel filtration.

gel electrophoresis An analytical or separation technique in which charged compounds are separated under the influence of an electrical field (electrophoresis) with a gel being used as the support matrix. Precast gels of starch, agar, agarose or polyacrylamide are used in slab form or in a narrow column. Separation depends on the mass/charge ratio of the compounds and their interaction with the porous structure of the gel.

gel filtration A form of chromatography used for separation of molecules on the basis of molecular weight. The sample is passed through a column packed with small porous hydrophobic beads. Large molecules pass straight through the column, but smaller molecules enter the pores and are retarded to a degree that relates to the properties of the gel and the molecule in question. Fractionation occurs because different volumes of the stationary phase are available to different solutes. In practice, other forces of attraction may retard many types of molecules. The technique is used for desalting proteins (ammonium sulphate precipitates) and the separation and purification of peptides, proteins, polysaccharides and nucleic acids. Commercial support materials include (trade or registered names in brackets): cross-linked polyacrylamide (Bio-Gel P); cross-linked dextran (Sephadex); polystyrene gel (Bio-Beads S, Styragel); cross-linked polyacrylolyl morpholine (Enzacryl).

gel resin An ion exchange resin with a low affinity for macromolecules owing to its lack of definite pore structure, but with a high capacity for small ions. Gel resins are used in water softening and purification procedures.

gelatin A substance obtained by boiling the bones, skins, ligaments, etc. of animals in water. Similar substances may also be obtained from plant residues. The material forms the basis of the manufacture of gels and glues, and is used as a solid support for culture of some microorganisms.

gellan A polysaccharide formed from glucose, rhamnose and glucuronic acid residues with between 3 and 4 per cent *O*-acetyl groups. It is produced by an aerobic strain of *Pseudomonas elodea*.

geminiviruses A group of single-stranded DNA plant viruses.

gemma A small unicellular or multicellular propagation unit formed by plants.

gemmule A small protected cell mass formed internally by some sponges that can survive unfavourable conditions in a state of dormancy.

gene A unit of hereditary material that forms a discrete part of the chromosome of most organisms encoding information in the form of a DNA sequence. The concept of the gene and its accurate definition have changed as more information concerning the genetic code and the way it functions has become available. In the earliest sense, the gene was regarded as the smallest particle of inheritance that was passed on from generation to generation in an unchanged manner. The concept of particulate inheritance assumed that characters mixed in a genetic cross can be resegregated and are not lost in an inseparable blend. This concept formed the basis of Mendel's laws of inheritance which were based on observations of alternative forms of the same gene (alleles). Genes located on separate chromosomes show independent assortment. However, genes present on the same chromosome do not segregate as readily and show linkage. Such linked genes can be separated by crossing-over, with the probability of crossing-over decreasing as the loci of the genes become closer. This effect can be used to produce linkage maps that place the genes in a linear array along the chromosomes. Such observations led to the concept of the gene as the shortest length of chromosome separable from adjacent segments by recombination, or the shortest length of chromosome that could undergo mutation. However, these definitions no longer hold true since the shortest length of chromosome that can be mutated is in fact a single base pair (much less than a gene). In turn, this led to the one gene–one protein hypothesis that was later modified to the concept of one gene–one polypeptide. This polypeptide may be produced through transcription and translation of the information contained in the chromosomal DNA associated with a specific gene. However, even this concept is not satisfactory, although correct for 'structural genes'. In addition, many other types of gene are now known that code only for the synthesis of nucleic acids (such as tRNA or rRNA) or have a role in the regulation of other genes. Many gene sequences, in eukaryotes in particular, are interrupted by lengths of DNA (introns) that are not used in the coding of amino acid sequences of proteins. The gene as a hereditable unit may now be defined in terms of a base sequence in DNA, whereas the gene as a unit of function is best defined by the *cis–trans* test.

gene amplification (1) An increase in the number of copies of a specific gene carried in a given cell. (2) A temporary large increase in numbers of a gene during a single period of development.

gene bank A collection of cell cultures, seeds, frozen sperm or ova, etc. kept as a means of holding representative genomes of any type of organism.

gene cloning The technique whereby multiple copies of a plasmid or other cloning vehicle are produced by inserting the plasmid into a suitable host capable of producing multiple copies and growing in a bulk culture. The bacterium *E. coli* is often used as the host organism for this purpose. The term gene cloning is sometimes used instead of genetic engineering or gene manipulation.

gene dosage The number of copies of a specific gene present in the genome of a eukaryote cell or organism. In diploid cells, the usual number of nuclear structural gene copies is two. However, much higher numbers of non-structural genes or structural genes carried in the plastids and mitochondria may be found.

gene engineering *See* gene manipulation.

gene expression The synthesis of a normal, complete functional polypeptide or protein from an appropriate gene. Formation depends on accurate transcription and translation as well as, in many cases, post-translational processing and compartmen

talization of the nascent polypeptide. A failure of any one of these processes to be performed correctly can result in a gene not being expressed.

gene flow The introduction of new genes to a population from an outside source by interbreeding, thus increasing the degree of genetic variability.

gene frequency The frequency with which a given allele occurs within a specific population.

gene isolation The removal of the genetic information, in the form of a DNA sequence, from a selected organism in order to study its structure or insert it into a vector during gene manipulation. It is often difficult, or impossible, to isolate eukaryotic DNA. An indirect method is to start with mRNA; the required messenger is often abundant in cells that specialize in the synthesis of a particular protein. For instance, insulin mRNA is found in the β-cells of the islets of Langerhans in the pancreas. This messenger does not contain the introns of the corresponding gene that have been excised. The RNA can be translated using reverse transcriptase to produce a complementary DNA strand, which can then be used as a template to produce a double-stranded DNA, using DNA polymerase. The resultant DNA will correspond to the original DNA sequence of the required gene, without the introns. It is necessary to ensure that the copy DNA contains all the regulatory signals for its translation and transcription. This can be achieved by inserting it into a suitable plasmid.

gene library A random collection of cloned fragments in a number of vectors of the same origin that ideally includes all the genetic information of that species; sometimes called a shot-gun collection.

gene machine An idiomatic description of an automated oligonucleotide synthesizer.

gene manipulation The formation of new combinations of hereditable material by the insertion of nucleic acid molecules pro duced outside the cell into any virus, bacterial plasmid or other vector system so as to allow their incorporation into a host organism in which they do not naturally occur, but in which they are capable of continued propagation. In most countries, there is a precise legal definition of gene manipulation as a result of legislation to control it. The process is also referred to as genetic manipulation, genetic engineering or recombinant DNA technology, but is also termed molecular cloning or gene cloning since a line of genetically identical organisms can be propagated and grown in bulk.

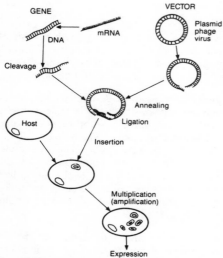

GENE

VECTOR

Plasmid phage virus

DNA

mRNA

Cleavage

Annealing

Host

Ligation

Insertion

Multiplication (amplification)

Expression

Gene manipulation: insertion of a new gene into a host organism using a suitable vector and the technique of recombinant DNA

gene manipulation techniques The transfer of DNA coding for a specific gene from one species (or synthesis of a completely artificial gene in the laboratory) and its insertion into another organism. It is important that the new DNA is integrated with the host DNA so that it is replicated and passed on when the cell divides. If this does not happen, the new information will gradually be diluted out.

In order to be replicated, DNA molecules must contain an 'origin of replication' (replicon). In bacteria and viruses, there is usually only one replicon per genome. Fragments of DNA are not replicons, hence will be diluted out of a cell. Even if a DNA molecule contains a replicon, it may not function in a host cell. The DNA for the required gene is combined with a replicon to produce a vector or cloning vehicle. The best vectors are small plasmids, bacteriophages or viruses. Since these particles are replicons in their own right, their maintenance does not necessarily require integration into the host genome and their DNA can be isolated readily in an intact form. The techniques for inserting the foreign DNA into a vector are conceptually simple. The required length of DNA is selected and purified. For eukaryotes this may involve the production of cDNA from a mRNA using reverse transcriptase. The plasmid to be used as a vector is selected and purified. The DNA and plasmid are treated with restriction endonucleases in order to produce complementary sequences at the cut ends (sticky ends). The DNA fragments are then joined to create artificial recombinants *in vitro* using enzyme techniques. The most common joining technique uses *E. coli* DNA ligase which seals single-stranded nicks between adjacent nucleotides. This enzyme is employed since when the termini created by restriction endonuclease associate, the joint has nicks a few bases apart in opposite strands. The DNA ligase repairs these nicks to form an intact duplex. An alternative method uses the T4 DNA ligase, which is capable of joining blunt-ended DNA molecules. This method is generally used in combination with linker molecules. A third method of joining DNA molecules makes use of the annealing of complementary homopolymer sequences. This method involves the addition of oligo-(dA) sequences to the 3′-ends of one population of DNA molecules and oligo-(dT) blocks to the 3′-ends of another population. The two types of molecule can then be annealed to form mixed dimeric circles. The terminal homopolymeric extensions can be synthesized using a terminal deoxynucleotidyl transferase from calf-thymus. DNA with exposed 3′-hydroxyl groups may be formed by pretreatment with phage lambda exonuclease or a restriction enzyme such as Pst I.

The plasmid with the new DNA, which must contain some type of genetic marker (usually resistance to a specific antibiotic which the chosen host cell does not possess), is then used to infect (transform) a host such as a mutant *E. coli* which lacks restriction enzymes that might attack the plasmid used in infection. The infectivity is increased if the *E. coli* is treated with calcium chloride. Less than 1 per cent of the *E. coli* may be transformed, producing further copies of the plasmid. These cells may be recognized since they will grow to form colonies on an agar plate treated with the antibiotic for which they have resistance, whereas the wild-type (untransformed) cells will not grow. The selected cells from the antibiotic-treated plate may then be grown in bulk liquid culture if so required. Similar techniques are used to introduce new genes into eukaryotes. The techniques of splicing the new genetic material into a vector will be the same. However, the choice of vector, the means of obtaining the required DNA and the means of introducing the vector into the new host may vary. *See* plasmid, vector.

gene pool The total available genes within an interbreeding population at any given time.

gene sequencing A technique used to determine the sequence of bases in the length of DNA coding for a particular polypeptide. *See* DNA sequencing.

gene synthesis The production of base sequences in lengths of DNA which can subsequently be expressed as peptides, after insertion into a suitable host.

gene therapy A technique adopted to overcome genetically linked disorders or disease. Where such disorders are known to be associated with a simple incorrect base sequence in a gene, or the failure to produce a certain polypeptide, it may be possible to use gene manipulation techniques to correct this defect. This can be done by micromanipulation of ova or of embryos at an early stage of development.

genecology The study of the genetics of plant and animal populations in relation to their ecology.

generation time The average time between one cell division and the next in a prokaryotic cell or the time between the prophase of one cell division and that of the next in a population of eukaryotic cells. Generation times vary from about 20 minutes for rapidly growing bacterial cultures to over two days for some plant tissue cultures. This may be expressed mathematically as follows for the exponential phase of growth:

$$\mu = v \times \ln 2$$

$$t_d = g$$

where μ = specific rate of growth, v = rate of cell division, t_d = doubling time of biomass and g = doubling time of cell number (generation time). *See also* doubling time.

generative nucleus A nucleus that gives rise by mitosis to the two male gametic nuclei found in the developing pollen tube of angiosperms, one of which fuses with the egg cell to form the zygote. The other combines with the two polar nuclei of the embryo sac to form a triploid nucleus that may divide many times to form the endosperm (storage tissue) of endospermous seeds (e.g. maize).

genetic code The code, based on the arrangement of nucleotides in nucleic acids, that stores the information for all genetically determined characteristics of living organisms. The information is passed from one generation to the next by producing exact replicas of the code. The code is expressed through the synthesis of specific proteins, the amino acid sequence of which reflects the coded information. The code is based on groups of three bases (codons) which correspond to specific amino acids as follows:

genetic deficiency The result of a chromosomal aberration in which a piece of a chromosome is lost. Deletions are often lethal in homozygous conditions. The genetic loss associated with such deficiencies can be

1st base	2nd base				3rd base
	U	C	A	G	
	phe	ser	tyr	cys	U
U	phe	ser	tyr	cys	C
	leu	ser	STOP	STOP	A
	leu	ser	STOP	trp	G
	leu	pro	his	arg	U
	leu	pro	his	arg	C
C	leu	pro	gln	arg	A
	leu	pro	gln	arg	G
	ile	thr	asn	ser	U
	ile	thr	asn	ser	C
A	ile	thr	lys	arg	A
	met	thr	lys	arg	G
	val	ala	asp	gly	U
	val	ala	asp	gly	C
G	val	ala	glu	gly	A
	val	ala	glu	gly	G

determined using the complementation test. In humans, a heterozygous deficiency in the short arm of chromosome 5 is associated with microencephaly, severe growth abnormalities and mental retardation. Deletion of part of chromosome 22 is associated with chronic myeloid leukemia. Heterozygous deficiencies in human chromosomes 4, 13 and 18 are associated with severe physical and mental handicaps. Such deficiencies may be recognized cytologically by the appearance in heterozygous individuals of a characteristic buckling when the two homologous chromosomes pair at meiosis.

genetic disease A disease associated with the presence of certain alleles or abnormalities in an individual's genotype. *See* adenosine deaminase deficiency, Down's syndrome.

genetic drift The chance variation in genetic make-up of populations which is not imposed by pressures of natural selection.

genetic   engineering   *See*   gene manipulation.

genetic fingerprint The characteristic pattern of bands on a map created by the elec-

trophoretic separation of a DNA sample derived from the tissue (usually blood), of a given individual, which has been treated using endonucleases. *See* fingerprinting technique, genetic fingerprinting.

genetic fingerprinting The production of genetic fingerprints to provide forensic evidence or to establish the paternity of children. Because a child inherits 50 per cent of its genes from its biological father and 50 per cent from its mother, half the bands on its genetic fingerprint will match with those of each parent. Thus the fingerprint can be used to identify a child's true father in contested palimony and immigration cases. Similarly a sample of blood or semen found at the scene of a crime can be matched to a genetic fingerprint produced from the blood sample of a suspect. Screening of large numbers of suspects in this way has led to the conviction of several murderers. The legal legitimacy of the technique is based on the fact that the chances of two people coincidentally sharing the same genetic fingerprint is more than 40 million to one.

genetic   manipulation   *See*   gene manipulation.

genetic map A diagram indicating the position or the distribution of genes on a genome or chromosome. For small viruses, it is possible to determine the number of genes present and compare the genetic map with the physical structure and coding potential. In larger genomes, not all the genes may have been detected, and there may be gaps in the genetic map. The map of the genome of SV40, DNA codes for five proteins: VP1, VP2, VP3, t antigen and T antigen. Some of these proteins contain identical amino acid sequences and are coded for by the same stretch of DNA. The mRNAs specifying the five proteins account for almost the entire length of the genome. In contrast, in maps of eukaryotic chromosomes, there are large regions of DNA that do not code for amino acids, as well as many repeated regions.

genetic marker A gene conferring a specific characteristic, such as resistance to an antibiotic, which can be recognized and used to select cells. For example, if the gene conferring resistance to the antibiotic tetracycline is inserted into a new host bacterium using a suitable plasmid vector and the complete culture is plated out on agar medium containing this antibiotic, only the cells with the marker gene will survive. Hence colonies of these cells can be recognized and isolated. These cells will also contain other characteristics that were contained in sequences linked to the marker gene in the vector.

genetic modification A process that results in a change in the genetic make-up of a population. Methods of inducing genetic modification include: conjugation (mediated by wild-type plasmids) in prokaryotes; *in vivo* rearrangements of transposable elements; *in vitro* gene recombination techniques; protoplast fusion; the use of mutagens; hybridization by normal breeding techniques. In prokaryotes, the use of mutagens is still the most widely practised technique for the production of improved commercial strains. In eukaryotes, the most usual technique is still conventional breeding and hybridization.

genetic recombination The exchange of genes between two chromosomes. This occurs naturally in the process of crossing-over. *In vitro* genetic recombination requires the extraction of DNA, or the production of copy DNA from a suitable mRNA, from one source and the insertion into another. *See* gene manipulation.

genetic variance The fraction of the phenotypic variance that is due to differences in the genetic constitution of individuals in a population.

genetically engineered interferon An anti-viral peptide produced by bacteria or yeasts to which the gene needed for the peptide's production has been introduced by gene manipulation. Although it has proved difficult to isolate the mRNA coding for the various interferons – leucocyte (IFN-α), fibroblast (IFN-β) and immune (IFN-gamma) – the gene sequences for these

compounds are now known. The IFN-β mRNA contains 836 nucleotides, including 72 and 203 nucleotides, respectively, in the 5'- and 3'-untranslated regions, 63 nucleotides coding for a peptide that is responsible for protein secretion and 498 nucleotides coding for the sequence of 166 amino acids. The IFN-α mRNA contains 865 nucleotides, of which 242 are located in the 3'-untranslated region; again the main sequence is 498 nucleotides. The polypeptide product of these genes is a glycopeptide with a molecular weight of 20,000. Such genes have been cloned in *E. coli*, animal cells and yeasts. Introduction of these genes into yeast gives higher yields, since the mechanism of glycosylation in yeasts is similar to that in animal cells.

genetics The study of the nature and transfer of hereditable information that controls the development of living organisms and the distribution of this information during reproduction and growth. *See* Mendelian inheritance.

genitalia The external reproductive organs of animals.

genome A single haploid set of chromosomes of any organism.

genotype The genetic characteristics or description of an organism that are defined by the base sequence in the genome or the chromosome complement.

gentamicin C An aminoglycoside antibiotic produced by *Micromonospora purpurea*

genus A unit of classification. A genus includes those closely related species that have an obvious series of characteristics in common. In the binomial system of nomenclature of living organisms, the first name given is that of the genus, followed by the species name.

geophyte A plant that produces over-wintering perennating organs, such as corms, bulbs and rhizomes.

geotropism A tropic movement observed in plants. It is the manifestation of the response to gravity.

germ A idiom for microorganisms, generally indicating bacteria and viruses, often those associated with human disease.

germ cell An animal cell set aside early in embryogenesis that may multiply by mitosis to produce the germinal epithelium; a gamete.

germ layer One of the main layers of cells found in the early stages of development of animal embryos. In gastrula of triploblastic organisms, the three layers known as the ectoderm, mesoderm and endoderm can be distinguished. In contrast, diploblastic organisms display only an ectoderm and an endoderm layer.

germ plasm Hypothetical material thought to be transmitted in an unchanged form from generation to generation through the gametes. The term is now obsolete. It is loosely correlated with the theory of genes.

germinal epithelium A cell layer found in ovaries and testes that gives rise to the reproductive cells.

germination The onset of growth in a seed or spore. It often follows a period of dormancy.

gestation period The time from conception (fertilization) to birth (parturition) occurring in viviparous animals.

Gibberella fujikuori The fungus from which gibberellic acid is commonly derived.

gibberellic acid (GA$_3$) A plant growth substance based on a diterpenoid structure. It is one of the gibberellins most often used in agriculture, horticulture and experimental work.

gibberellins A class of plant growth substances first isolated from the fungus *Gibberella fujikuroi* growing on rice. The first isolates were GA$_1$, GA$_2$ and GA$_3$. However, more than 30 gibberellins have now been identified which differ according to the substituted groups on a diterpenoid skeleton. Spraying the aerial part of higher plants with gibberellin often results in internode elongation. Gibberellins can make genetically dwarf varieties grow to a normal height and stimulate flowering in some long-day plants, as well as stimulating fruit and leaf growth. The synthesis of α-amylase in germinating barley (malt) is stimulated by gibberellins, which can also cause dormancy to break in some seeds and plant tubers.

Gilson respirometer *See* manometry.

gin A flavoured grain spirit. The flavour is produced by adding juniper berries, coriander seeds, cardamom or angelica to the still. Gin is also produced by adding such flavours to previously distilled spirit.

gland A structure that secretes specific chemical substances. In animals, glands are usually multicellular. Their products include hormones and gastric juices (endocrine glands), sebaceous fluids, sweat, etc. (exocrine glands). In plants, the glands may be single-celled and external (e.g., stinging cells), external and multicellular (e.g., nectaries, hydathodes) or internal and multicellular (e.g., latex, resin tubes, etc.). Plants may also contain single cells that accumulate tannins, gums, etc.

GLC *See* gas chromatography.

glia Accessory cells in nervous tissue that do not have a nervous function, but are derived from embryonic neural tissue. They provide both mechanical and metabolic support to nerve cells and may have a function in the regeneration of damaged neurones.

Gln Abbreviation used in peptide and protein sequences, and in general, to denote the amino acid glutamine.

globulins A group of proteins that are soluble in salt solution, but insoluble in water.

They include the serum- or gamma-globulins and are common in seeds as storage proteins, such as arachin from ground nuts.

glomerulus A structure comprising many capillaries encapsulated by the expanded end of a uriniferous tubule in the vertebrate kidney. Glomeruli remove salts and water from the blood stream.

GLP *See* good laboratory practice.

Glu Abbreviation used in peptide and protein sequences, and in general, to denote glutamic acid.

glucagon A polypeptide hormone synthesized and secreted by the α-cells of the islets of Langerhans of the mammalian pancreas. It consists of a straight chain containing 29 amino acids. Glucagon produces high blood glucose levels by stimulating glycogenesis, gluconeogenesis from protein, lipolysis and ketogenesis. The hormone also stimulates insulin secretion by the β-cells of the pancreas.

glucan A polysaccharide based on D-glucose units, including cellulose, amylopectin and dextran.

glucocorticoid One of several corticosteroid hormones. They promote the deposition of glycogen in the liver, the formation of glucose from protein and the mobilization of fat reserves, and inhibit carbohydrate utilization by tissues. These steroids, which possess a ketonic or hydroxyl group at positions C-3 and C-20, include cortisol, corticosterone and cortisone, as well as synthetic analogues that are used for therapeutic purposes.

gluconeogenesis The formation of glucose from non-carbohydrate metabolic intermediates through reversal of glycolysis.

gluconic acid An organic acid. In a phosphorylated form it is an early intermediate of the pentose phosphate pathway. Gluconic acid is produced by the incomplete oxidation of glucose in fermentations using *Pseudomonas florescens*, acetic acid bacteria or fungi. It is used in food products, pharmaceuticals and other industrial products.

glucosamine An amino sugar that occurs in the D-form in heparin, hyaluronic acid and other structural polysaccharides.

glucose An aldohexose, trivially known as dextrose. This reducing sugar is the most common monosaccharide, occurring in nature in the D-form in either the α- or β-configuration. It is a component of a wide range of storage and structural polysaccharides, including cellulose, starch, dextran, glycogen and sucrose. Glucose is a major energy source in both aerobic and anaerobic respiration. It may be metabolized via glycolysis and the TCA cycle to carbon dioxide and water, or fermented to a wide variety of organic compounds including ethanol, acetic acid, organic acids and amino acids. Glucose is prepared commercially by hydrolysis of starch using either dilute acid or a mixture of amylase and amyloglucosidase. Such techniques are employed to produce a variety of glucose syrups or solid glucose. Solid glucose may contain water of crystallization, in which case it is referred to as the monohydrate. Pure anhydrous glucose is only used in medical applications. Glucose is used as the major raw material (source of carbon) in many industrial fermentations.

D-glucose

glucose equivalent *See* dextrose equivalent.

glucose isomerase Commercial preparation of bacterial enzymes used in the industrial production of isoglucose or high fructose corn syrup (HFCS) from starch hydrolysates. These enzymes are developed from the discovery that some bacterial enzymes can bring about isomerization of a free aldo-pentose (a five-carbon sugar) to the ketoform. The first such enzyme isolated (xylose isomerase) required arsenate as a cofactor and could not be used commercially. Subsequently enzymes were discovered in *Streptomyces phaechromogenes, S. albus, S. rubiginosus, Bacillus coagulans* and other organisms that required cobalt as a cofactor. Patents have been taken out on similar enzymes from the following genera: *Arthrobacter, Aerobacter, Actinoplanes, Nocardia, Micromonospora, Microbispora* and *Microcellobospora*. Early processes (1972) used heat-fixed cells, mixed with filter aid, or the DEAE-cellulose absorbed isolated enzyme of *S. rubiginosus*. This was the first large-scale use of immobilized cells or enzymes. Such enzyme preparations had fairly low activities and half-lives of about 200 hours. Subsequently the enzyme has been immobilized on a variety of supports, including alumina and titania, with activities increased over 200 times and half-life extended to over 1200 hours. Immobilization with cobalt on the carrier has eliminated the need for use of soluble cobalt and the purification problems associated with its use.

glucose isomerization Both glucose and fructose have the same empirical formula, but differ in the arrangement of the individual atoms in the molecule. In alkaline solution, glucose undergoes a Lobry de Bruyn–Aldeberda van Ekenstein transformation, forming an equilibrium mixture with fructose. The conversion of glucose to fructose occurs in all living organisms but involves the phosphorylated intermediates. The conversion of the free form of glucose to fructose may also be catalysed by enzymes isolated from bacteria. The use of this enzyme in isomerization of glucose derived from starch-based glucose syrups to an equilibrium mixture of glucose and fructose is now a major industry. *See* glucose isomerase, high fructose syrup.

glucose oxidase An enzyme that converts glucose to gluconic acid and hydrogen peroxide in the presence of oxygen. It is highly specific for β-D-glucose. The enzyme is a glycoprotein, with about 10 per cent carbohydrate and containing two mol-

ecules of FAD per protein molecule. Glucose oxidase is commercially prepared from *Aspergillus niger* or *Penicillium amagasakiense* in submerged culture. Glucose oxidase is used to remove glucose or oxygen from a solution. In food processing, it is employed to remove residual glucose in order to reduce non-enzymic browning. In beverages, it is used to remove residual oxygen from products such as fruit juice, mayonnaise and packaged dehydrated foods. It is also used in an enzyme assay for glucose.

glucose-6-phosphate dehydrogenase (EC 1.1.1.4) A soluble enzyme that catalyses the first step in the pentose phosphate pathway of carbohydrate metabolism. It converts D-glucose-6-phosphate to 6-phosphogluconate.

glucose syrups A mixture of glucose and higher saccharides produced by acid or enzyme hydrolysis of starch. The starting material is often corn starch. However, starches from potato, wheat and cassava are also used. The syrups are classified according to their dextrose equivalent (DE). The DE is a measure of the extent of hydrolysis of the starch. Acid hydrolysis produces a random mixture of oligosaccharides of varying chain length and may be used to produce syrup of 43 DE. Enzymes (amylase and amyloglucosidase) are preferred as a means for the production of syrups of higher DE, since acid produces both colour and reversion products. The basic composition of various commercial syrups can be resolved using liquid chromatography and shown to comprise glucose, maltose, maltotriose, maltotetrose and maltopentose. Lower DE syrups contain higher oligosaccharides and dextrins. The normal commercial preparations are 43, 63 (produced by blending), 90 and 95 DE. Speciality syrups, such as a high maltose or a high fructose syrup, may be produced using other enzymes.

glucosinolate Any of a number of related plant growth-regulating compounds found in plants, including rapeseed, which have deleterious affects on animals. Glucosinolates consist of a β-thioglucose group, a sulphinated oxim and an organic side chain. Over 100 glucosinolates have been described in which the side chain consists of alkyl, aryl or indolyl groups. The alkyl types can also contain extra sulphur atoms producing sulfinyl, sulfonyl or thioglucosinolates. The presence of glucosinolates limits use of rapeseed in animal feeds because of the effect on the thyroid gland (goitrogenic effect). Other effects are on adrenal gland, kidney or liver, and in poultry, taint and decoloration of eggs. The thyroid enlarging effect is due to vinylthiooxazolidon which is a breakdown product of the hydroxybutenyl glucosinolate progoitrin, the major component in rapeseed. Plant breeding endeavours to produce rapeseed with low glucosinolate content.

glutamate dehydrogenase (EC 1.4.1.3) An enzyme that catalyses the conversion of L-glutamic acid to α-ketoglutaric (oxoglutaric) acid and ammonia coupled with the reduction of NAD(P). It is found in the mitochondria of most cells, and is involved in the deamination and transamination of amino acids.

glutamate synthase An enzyme that catalyses the formation of two molecules of glutamic acid from one molecule of glutamine and one molecule of α-ketoglutarate (2-oxyglutarate). It is of importance in the assimilation of ammonia and in nitrogen metabolism associated with the C_2 of photorespiration. The enzyme is also known as glutamate oxyglutarate amino transferase (GOGAT).

glutamic acid (Glu) One of the 20 common amino acids occurring in proteins. Glutamic acid and the amine derivative (glutamine) are involved in the primary assimilation of nitrogen (as ammonia) in many microorganisms and plants, as well as in transamination and deamination.

Glutamic acid $HOOCCH_2CH_2CH(NH_2)COOH$

glutamic acid production Glutamic acid is produced by fermentation of carbohydrate using a number of different bacteria, which although put in separate genera are similar. The main organism used is *Corynebacterium glutamicum* (*Micrococcus glutamicus*). The bacteria require biotin and lack the enzyme α-ketoglutarate dehydrogenase. With biotin supplied, the cells produce lactate; at suboptimal levels, over 50 per cent of the carbon supplied may be converted directly to glutamate, with little production of any other byproduct.

glutamine (Gln) One of the 20 common amino acids occurring in proteins. It is of importance in the assimilation of nitrogen as ammonia in microorganisms and higher plants, as well as in the metabolism of nitrogen associated with the C_2 pathway of photorespiration.

Glutamine $H_2NCOCH_2CH_2CH(NH_2)COOH$

glutamine synthetase (GS) An enzyme that catalyses the formation of glutamine from glutamic acid and ammonia using energy from ATP. This is the primary reaction involved in the assimilation of nitrogen by many microorganisms and by higher plants.

glutathione A tripeptide (Glu–Cys–Gly) that acts as a hydrogen acceptor in a number of reactions including the formation of disulphide bridges.

glutelins Proteins that are soluble in dilute acids and bases, and insoluble in neutral solvents. They include plant storage proteins in cereals (e.g., glutenin from wheat).

gluten A reserve protein found in seeds, such as wheat. It consists of a mixture of glutelin and gliadin.

glutenin A seed reserve protein, a component of gluten. In ungerminated wheat, the enzyme β-amylase is attached by disulphide linkage to glutenin. The enzyme is activated following its release from the glutenin, with the formation of active –SH groups.

Gly An abbreviation used to denote the amino acid glycine in protein sequences and elsewhere.

glycan A synonym for polysaccharides.

glycerides Fats and oils formed as mono-, di- or tri-esters of glycerol with fatty acids.

glycerol A trihydric sugar alcohol; an important component of many lipids.

glycine (Gly) The simplest of the 20 common amino acids occurring normally in proteins. It is important in the synthesis of purines, porphyrins and creatine, as well as in nitrogen metabolism associated with the C_2 pathway of photorespiration.

glycocalyx A collective term for polysaccharides that occur outside the cell walls of bacteria.

glycogen A storage polysaccharide consisting of branched chains of D-glucose. In vertebrates, it is found mainly in the liver and in muscle. It is readily degraded to glucose by amylases or phosphorylases.

glycogen phosphorylase An enzyme that catalyses the conversion of glycogen to glucose-1-phosphate.

glycogenolysis The breakdown of glycogen to glucose-1-phosphate. It occurs mainly in the liver and in muscles, and is activated by hormones such as adrenaline and glucagon.

glycolic acid A two-carbon carboxylic acid produced in a phosphorylated form in the oxygenase reaction catalysed by rubisco. It can be a major product in algae carrying out photosynthesis under conditions of low carbon dioxide and/or high oxygen.

glycolipid A lipid that contains one or more carbohydrate moities. These lipids include the cerebrosides and gangliosides in animals, and the galactosyl diglycerides and sulpholipids in plants. The lipid portion is usually glycerol phosphate, glycerol or sphingosine, and the carbohydrate is D-galactose, inositol or D-glucose.

glycolysis The metabolism of glucose to lactic or pyruvic acid with the production of ATP. Under anaerobic conditions lactic acid accumulates, whereas in aerobic conditions the sequence from glucose to pyruvate forms the first part of the respiratory process. The overall process involves the sequential interaction of 10 or 11 cytoplasmic enzymes with the net production of two molecules of ATP per molecule of glucose degraded. In animals, glucose is normally derived from glycogen. In plants, glucose is generally derived from starch, but translocated as sucrose. Other hexose molecules may enter the glycolysis chain if converted to any of the early phosphorylated hexose sugar intermediates (glucose-6-phosphate, fructose-6-phosphate or fructose-1,6-bisphosphate). Fructose-1,6-bisphosphate is split into an equilibrium mixture of glyceraldehyde-3-phosphate and dihydroxyacetone phosphate, which is oxidized to diphosphoglyceric acid, with the uptake of inorganic phosphate and the reduction of NAD. The diphosphoglycerate is then converted to 3-phosphoglycerate (with ATP being formed in a substrate-level phosphorylation reaction at the same time) and thence through phosphoenol pyruvate to pyruvate. ATP is also formed during this last interconversion. Under anaerobic conditions, pyruvate is reduced to lactate or through acetaldehyde to ethanol. Some bacteria convert pyruvate to diacetyl or 2,3-butanediol via acetolactic acid and acetoin. In aerobic respiration, the pyruvate is converted to acetyl-CoA which enters the TCA cycle.

glycopeptide A compound formed from a peptide covalently linked to a carbohydrate.

glycoprotein Compounds in which carbohydrate side chains are covalently linked to a protein. Common side chains include D-galactose, D-mannose and N-acetyl-D-glucosamine. Cell surface glycoproteins play a role in cell recognition. Other biologically important glycoproteins include enzymes, hormones and antigens.

glycosaminoglycan (GAG) See mucopolysaccharides.

glycoside A derivative of pyranose sugars in which the hydroxyl group on the aldehyde carbon is substituted with another group, such as a methyl group or phenolic compounds. Many plant secondary products occur in the form of glycosides.

glycosidic linkage The basic type of bond that links the monosaccharide units of disaccharides and polysaccharides. It is produced by elimination of the elements of water:

$$R'-OH + R''-OH \rightarrow R'-O-R'' + HOH$$

glycosyl transferase *See* glycosylation.

glycosylation The addition of an oligosaccharide group to a protein. It takes place within the lumen of the endoplasmic reticulum and is mediated by membrane-bound glycosyl transferase.

glyoxal (HOCCHO) A reagent used in molecular biology to denature RNA and DNA. It reacts specifically with guanosine residues preventing base pairing, eliminating secondary structure of the nucleic acid.

glyoxylate A two-carbon aldehydic acid of importance in the glyoxylate cycle and in photorespiration (C_2 pathway).

glyoxylate cycle A modified form of the TCA cycle found in microorganisms, algae and plants under circumstances where fats are being rapidly metabolized (e.g., in fat-storing seeds during germination). The fatty acids are broken down to acetyl-CoA, pass through the glyoxylate cycle, and thence to glucose via a reversal of glycolysis. The key enzymes of the glyoxylate cycle are isocitratase and malate synthetase. Isocitratase catalyses the reversible aldol fission of isocitrate to succinate and glyoxylate, whereas malate synthetase catalyses the condensation of acetyl-CoA with glyoxylate to form malate. The action of these two enzymes enables acetyl-CoA to enter the TCA cycle avoiding oxidation. The succinate so formed is converted to oxaloacetic acid, via fumarate and malate, and thence through phosphoenol pyruvate and pyruvate to reverse glycolysis.

glyoxylate shunt *See* glyoxylate cycle.

glyoxysome A microbody that contains enzymes associated with the glyoxylate cycle. These bodies contain both isocitratase and malate synthetase, as well as enzymes associated with related reactions including citrate synthetase, aconitase, malate dehydrogenase, glycollate oxidase and catalase.

glyphosate *N*-(Phosphonomethyl)glycine. A broad spectrum, post-emergence, translocated herbicide.

glyphosate tolerance A resistance to the herbicidal agent glyphosate that inhibits the enzyme EPSP synthase. This resistance can be engineered in plants by infecting them with *Agrobacterium* cells containing recombinant Ti plasmids carrying the EPSP synthase gene.

GMP Good manufacturing practice.

GMP *See* guanosine 5'-monophosphate.

GMP-140 *See* PADGEM.

goblet cell A cell type present in epithelial tissue that synthesizes and secretes mucus glycoproteins.

GOGAT *See* glutamate synthase.

goitre Enlargement on the thyroid gland.

goitrogenic Descriptive of a substance causing goitre.

Golgi apparatus A cytoplasmic organelle found in most eukaryotic cells, consisting of a stack (dictyosome) of flattened membranes (cisternae) together with vesicles that bud off laterally from one end of the stack. In many secretory cells, the Golgi body ramifies throughout the cytoplasm, whereas in others it consists of many discrete dictyosomes. The Golgi apparatus is involved in the concentration and transport of materials that collect in the cisternae and are transported through or from the cell in the vesicles. In plant cells, the Golgi bodies are involved in cell wall formation and contribute to cell plate formation. The proteins, slimes, gums and waxes secreted from many cells are released from Golgi vesicles.

Golgi body *See* Golgi apparatus.

gonad An animal organ in which spermatozoa or ova are formed (e.g., testis or ovary).

gonadotrophin Mammalian hormone that stimulates the gonads and regulates reproductive activity. There are three gonadotrophins secreted by the pituitary gland. These include the glycoproteins luteinizing hormone and follicle-stimulating hormone, and the protein prolactin. Secretion is regulated by separate hypothalamic mechanisms. Chorionic gonadotrophin, a glycoprotein, is secreted by the chorionic villi of the placenta in mammals and functions in the early maintenance of the corpus luteum.

good laboratory practice (GLP) An integrated approach to experimental work which through regular calibration of equipment, adoption of standard methods and recording of all results, combined with regular internal checks and review systems ensures the accuracy and repeatability of results. Required in the development and commercial production of pharmaceutical and other products of biotechnology.

graafian follicle The structure within the mammalian ovary in which the oocyte develops. A graafian follicle matures periodically, under the control of pituitary gonadotrophins, releases the ovum and then forms the corpus luteum. Graafian follicles act as endocrine glands producing oestrogens.

gradient The change in a variable quantity with distance or time. Gradients of pH, concentration or density are used in centrifugation, chromatographic separation systems, electrophoretic analysis and other laboratory procedures.

gradient centrifugation *See* density gradient centrifugation.

gradient former A mechanical device used to generate solutions of varying pH, density, viscosity or concentration used in separation and analytical techniques. A typical device consists of two chambers linked at the bottom. A concentrated solution in one is progressively diluted with solvent either by gravity flow or use of a peristaltic pump. Simple gradient formers are generally used to make linear gradients. The formation of more complex gradients requires a programmable device. *See* gradient programmer.

gradient programmer An electronic device used to produce density gradients or elution gradients. The machine consists of two or more channels, generally peristaltic pumps, dispensing the required liquids of differing pH, concentration or composition, at controlled rate. Gradients of any shape can be constructed.

graft (1) The transplanting of a part of one plant or animal on to the body of another. (2) The material so transplanted.

graft hybrid A plant chimera produced by grafting in which a mingling of the tissues of the stock and the scion occurs.

graft rejection The process whereby a host rejects tissues or cells derived from another organism. The mechanism of rejection is usually due to the production of specific antibodies against the new tissue which contains antigenic sites.

grain neutral spirit A pure ethanol/water mixture distilled from a yeast-based fermentation of grain used in the production of potable spirits such as gin and vodka. The starting material is usually maize or wheat.

grain spirit *See* grain neutral spirits.

gram stain A differential staining procedure of great value in the identification of eubacteria. A heat-fixed smear of bacteria is stained with a solution of crystal violet followed by a dilute iodine solution and then cleared in ethanol or acetone. Gram-negative bacteria are completely decolorized by the solvent; gram-positive bacteria retain the stain. The procedure may be used in conjunction with a counterstain such as saffranin, which stains the negative cells, enabling them to be distinguished on microscopic examination. Gram-positive organisms are penicillin-sensitive.

gramicidins Structurally related antibiotics consisting of basic cyclic polypeptides, produced by *Bacillus brevis*. These antibiotics are uncouplers of oxidative phosphorylation in intact cells and cell-free preparations. They also act as cationic detergents and lead to the disorganization of protoplast membranes, permitting leakage of their contents.

L-Val —— L-Orn —— L-Leu- —— D-Phe —— L-Pro
|
L-Pro —— L-Phe —— L-Leu —— D-Orn —— L-Val

Gramicidins

gram-negative bacteria *See* gram stain.

gram-positive bacteria *See* gram stain.

grana A region of stacked appressed membranes (thylakoids) that occurs in the chloroplasts of some green algae and most higher plants.

granulocyte A white blood cell characterized by distinct cytoplasmic granules which are visible under a light microscope and may be stained with acid or basic dyes. All granulocytes are polymorphs. They include basophils, eosinophils and neutrophils.

grapes The berries of the vine *Vitis* species used in the production of wine and brandy. Most wine is produced from *V. vinifera* or *V. rotundifolia*.

GRAS An abbreviation for 'generally regarded as safe', a designation given to some food materials, drugs, etc. in the USA in particular. GRAS status may be given to compounds that are closely related to compounds already being used for a similar purpose, or compounds that have a long history of widespread safe use although they have not been subjected to detailed testing.

green algae *See* Chlorophyta.

greening The process of chlorophyll synthesis and development of the photosynthetic apparatus that occurs when leaf tissue previously kept in the dark is exposed to light. *See* etioplast.

grey matter The part of the central nervous system of vertebrates that contains the cell bodies, dendrites and axon terminals of neurones. It lacks myelinated fibres.

GRF *See* growth hormone releasing factor.

griseofulvin An antifungal antibiotic used to treat fungal skin diseases, derived from *Penicillium patulum*.

ground meristem The part of the apical meristem in higher plants that gives rise to ground tissues.

ground tissue Regions of the plant stem and roots formed of parenchyma, sclerenchyma or chlorenchyma that comprise the cortex, medullary rays and pith of stems and roots.

growth An increase in dry weight or bulk of an organism associated with development. In most organisms, it involves cell division, expansion, differentiation and morphogenesis.

growth curve A pictorial or graphical representation of the increase in weight, size, cell number or similar characteristic of an organism or cell culture with time. In most cells or organisms, growth follows a sigmoid curve showing a lag phase followed by periods of exponential growth, senescence and eventual death.

growth factor An element or compound that is essential for the healthy nutrition and growth of an organism or cell culture. Growth factors include vitamins, minerals, essential amino acids, etc.

growth hormone A protein hormone, secreted by the pars distalis of the mammalian pituitary gland. It stimulates growth

growth hormone releasing factor (GRF) A compound that is involved in control of the release of human growth hormone from the pituitary gland.

growth kinetics Mathematical descriptions of the change in cell or product related parameters associated with the growth of microorganisms in fermentation or other culture systems. Such descriptions may be applied to continuous or batch cultures. For batch cultures the increase in cell number with time during the exponential phase of growth may be described as follows:

$$N_t = N_0 \times 2^n$$

$$n = (\log N_t - \log N_0)/\log 2$$

$$v = n/t = 1/g$$
$$= (\log N_t - \log N_0)/(\log 2(t_t - t_0))$$

where N_t = number of cells at time t_t, N_0 = number of cells at time t_0, n = number of cell divisions, v = rate of cell division, g = generation time and t = time.

Growth may also be expressed in terms of the specific growth rate related to various other culture parameters as follows:

$$\mu = \mu_{max}[S/(K_s + S)]$$

$$\mu = \mu_{max}[1 - e^{-S/K_s}]$$

$$\mu = \mu_{max}[S^n/(K_s + S^n)]$$

$$\mu = \mu_{max}[S/(K_s \times X + S]$$

where μ = specific rate of growth, μ_{max} = maximum specific rate of growth, S = substrate concentration, K_s = saturation constant (substrate concentration when μ = 0.5 μ_{max}) and X = biomass concentration.

Where fermentation is carried out using a media containing insoluble substrates growth kinetics may be expressed in terms of cell biomass corrected for insoluble material:

$$\bar{X} = [S_{ed} - (S_{ed}/DW)_0 \times DW]/(S_{ed}/DW)_1$$
$$- (S_{ed}/DW)_0$$

where $\bar{X}$ = average concentration of biomass, S_{ed} = residual sediment, DW = total dry mass of media, 0 = before inoculation, 1 = during course of process.

Growth kinetics may be expressed in similar terms for continuous fermentation or other continuous cell culture processes as follows:

$$dX/dt = \mu X - DX = X(\mu - D)$$

$$D = f/V_0$$

where μ = specific growth rate, D = dilution rate, f = feed rate of medium = discharge rate of culture broth, V_0 = working volume.

Under steady-state conditions in a chemostat, μ is equivalent to D and $dX/dt = 0$.

If $\mu > D$, the cell concentration increases, whereas if $\mu < D$, cell concentration decreases until washout occurs.

For single-stage, continuous fermentation with constant recycling of biomass and feeding of medium under sterile conditions ($X_0 = 0$) then:

$$\mu = D[1 + \alpha(1 - X_2/X_1)]$$

$$D = f_{fr}/V_0$$

$$\alpha = (f - f_{fr})/f_{fr}$$

where μ = specific growth rate of total biomass, α = ratio of recycling, f_{fr} = feed rate of fresh medium, f = flow rate of medium leaving the fermenter, X_1 = concentration of cells in outflow and X_2 = concentration of cells in the recycle stream.

For single-stage, continuous fermentation with constant recycling of biomass then:

$$X = [Y_{X/S}(S_0 - S)]/[1 + \alpha(1 - X_2/X_1)]$$

where X = concentration of biomass during steady-state conditions, $y_{X/S}$ = yield coefficient with respect to substrate, S_0 = concentration of substrate in inflowing medium and S = concentration of substrate at outlet. *See also* growth rate, Monod kinetics.

growth rate A measure of the rate of growth of an organism or culture. Most microorganisms grown in liquid culture show periods of exponential growth which may be extended for long periods in continuous culture. For such fermentations the increase in cell mass can be expressed in terms of the specific growth rate constant (μ):

$$dP/dt = \mu \times P$$

or

$$dP/P = dt \times \mu$$

where P is the cell mass and t is the time.

On integration $\ln(P_t/P_o) = \mu \times t$; for $t = 1$ hour, $\mu = \ln(P_t/P_o)$ or $2.31 \times \log (P_t/P_o)$. This is the specific growth rate for exponential growth, and for continuous fermentations its value is identical to the dilution rate. The relationship between generation time and μ is:

$$\text{generation time (h)} = (2.303 \times \log 2)/\mu$$

Hence, for a generation time of one hour, the specific growth rate constant is 0.693.

growth retardant A natural or synthetic chemical substance that inhibits plant growth.

growth substance A chemical compound that affects plant growth and development at low concentrations. Growth substances include abscisic acid, auxins, kinins and gibberellins, as well as a wide range of uncharacterized compounds.

Grunstein–Hogness method A multi-step method for the identification of clonal colonies in a microbial culture. The Grunstein–Hogness method is based on the binding of a radiolabelled DNA probe to a specific sequence of nucleotides.

GS/GOGAT pathway The major route of ammonium assimilation in bacteria and plants catalysed by the two enzymes glutamine synthetase (GS) and glutamate synthase (GOGAT). The first reaction leads to the formation of glutamine from ammonia and glutamic acid. The second reaction involves the transamination of the amino

group from glutamine to a molecule of α-ketoglutarate, resulting in the formation of two molecules of glutamic acid – one of which is a net product, whereas the other can be recycled as substrate for assimilation of further ammonia.

GTP *See* guanosine 5'-triphosphate.

guanine (G) A purine base that is a constituent of nucleic acids and nucleotides.

Guanine

guanosine A nucleoside comprising guanine linked with D-ribose through a β-glycosidic bond.

guanosine 5'-diphosphate (GDP) A nucleoside diphosphate based on guanine.

guanosine 5'-monophosphate (GMP) A nucleotide based on guanine.

guanosine 5'-triphosphate (GTP) A nucleoside triphosphate based on guanine; one of the bases found in nucleic acids.

guard cell One of the pair of epidermal cells that surround the stoma in higher plants. The cell walls are differentially thickened. Hence, changes in turgor, resulting from movement of potassium in and out of the cell vacuoles, cause the stoma to open and close.

gum A chemical substance that swells in water to form a sticky gel or mucilage.

gut Synonym for the digestive tract.

guttation The exudation of water from plant tissues. The process is often associated with a specific body, the hydathode.

Gymnospermae A division of the vascular plants characterized by the fact that they bear naked seeds on a sporophyll or frond. They contain three subgroups, the most common of which are the conifers and the cycads. Conifers are an important source of timber and paper pulp; whereas cycads are an important source of starch.

gynandromorph An individual exhibiting both male and female sexual differentiation.

gynoecium The female reproductive organs of flowers.

gyrase An enzyme that causes negative supercoiling of *E. coli* DNA during replication. *See* DNA gyrase.

H

H chain *See* heavy chain.

habituated culture A plant tissue culture that has evolved the irreversible ability to synthesize auxin and can thus proliferate without the need for exogenous supplies in the culture medium.

haem An iron-containing porphyrin that serves as a prosthetic group in proteins such as haemoglobin, myoglobin and cytochromes. The four pyrrole nitrogen atoms of protoporphyrin IX are chelated to divalent iron.

haemagglutinin *See* agglutinin.

haematology The study of blood and blood-related disorders.

haemerythrin An iron–protein complex found in the blood corpuscles of some invertebrates. It functions as a respiratory pigment.

haemin The oxidized form of haem in which the iron is in the trivalent form.

haemocoel Part of the vascular system in molluscs and arthropods.

haemocyanin A copper–protein complex that occurs in solution in the blood of some molluscs, arachnids and crustaceans. It functions as a respiratory pigment.

haemocytometer A microscope slide with a small depression, forming a chamber of known volume, marked with a grid. It is designed for statistical counting of cells in suspension.

haemoglobin A respiratory pigment found in the erythrocytes of vertebrates. It also occurs in some invertebrates and in the root nodules of leguminous plants. Haemoglo-

bin consists of two pairs of associated polypeptide chains, each of which contains a haem group. The amino acid sequences of the polypeptide chains vary, resulting in many different types of haemoglobin. All human haemoglobin contains 2 α-chains, whereas the other pair varies. Most adult haemoglobin also contains 2 β-chains (haemoglobin A). About 2 per cent of the population differ in the form of the ancillary polypeptide chains, which are known as δ-chains (haemoglobin A2). Foetal blood contains haemoglobin F, with gammachains. The iron atom in haem is in the ferrous state (Fe^{2+}) and binds oxygen without a valency change to produce oxyhaemoglobin. This is bright red, but becomes blue as oxygen is lost. Treatment of haemoglobin with oxidizing agents oxidizes the iron to the ferric form (Fe^{3+}), forming methaemoglobin which cannot bind oxygen. Carbon dioxide is bound to haemoglobin through interaction with the polypeptide chains.

haemolysin An antibody that can activate complement to cause lysis of erythrocytes.

haemolysis The rupture of the plasma membrane of red blood cells with the release of haemoglobin.

haemophilia A hereditary disease in which there is a failure in the ability of the blood to clot normally, resulting in a condition in which any injury causes profuse bleeding. The most common form (haemophilia A) is due to a defect in clotting factor VIII. Since the gene for this protein is on the X chromosome, it is more common in males who inherit it from their carrier mothers. Genes for factor VIII have been cloned.

haemopoiesis The differentiation of bone marrow and lymph cells into erythrocytes and white blood cells. Erythrocytes and polymorphs are formed in the bone marrow. Lymphocytes and monocytes are formed in lymphoid tissue.

hairpin loop A region of double helix formed by base-pairing within a single strand of DNA or RNA which has folded back on itself.

halide A salt derived from a halogen.

halogen Any of the electronegative elements fluorine, chlorine, iodine, bromine or astatine. Halogens form salts (halides) with metals.

halogenation The introduction of a halogen atom into a molecule. Iodination, using radioactive iodine, is frequently employed as a means of labelling protein.

halophyte A plant that can withstand conditions of high salinity. Halophytes typically inhabit salt marshes. Many have a succulent appearance and have some xeromorphic characteristics. Acquisition of halophytic characteristics would be of value if they were introduced into crop plants, without deleterious effects, since it would permit the use of saline or brackish water for irrigation.

hamanatto A fermented product of soybeans produced using *Aspergillus oryzae*.

hammer mill A mechanical device used to shred or disrupt solid materials, for example, in the crushing of sugar cane or the grinding of grains for conversion to glucose syrups. The mill consists of a number of fixed or flailing blunt blades that rotate at high speed about a central axis within a cylinder. Material is passed in at one end of the cylinder and emerges from the other in a macerated state.

hanging drop culture The culture of cells in a drop of solution hanging from the lower surface of a slide for the purpose of microscopic examination of the growth process.

haplobiont An organism that has only one somatic state, haploid or diploid.

haploid (monoploid) Descriptive of a nucleus, cell or organism that possesses a single set of unpaired chromosomes, the haploid number (n). A haploid cell cannot undergo meiosis. Gametes are haploid. In plants that show alternation of generations, the spores and gametophyte generation are haploid, as are the spores of many fungi and algae.

haplont An organism that exists in the haploid state.

hapten A low-molecular-weight compound that reacts specifically with an antibody, but does not stimulate antibody production unless complexed with a carrier protein.

hapteron A plant structure that acts as a holdfast; the basal region of algae in particular which is modified to serve as a means of anchoring the plant to a suitable surface, thus preventing dispersal through water due to currents and waves.

haptonasty The rapid response to touch shown by some plants, such as the insectivorous (fly traps) and sensitive plants (*Mimosa pudica*).

haptotropism A plant growth response to touch in which cells in contact with a solid object grow shorter than those not subjected to the touch stimulus. This results in the part of the plant, a tendril or stem for example, coiling around the object thereby providing support.

Hardy–Weinberg equation *See* Hardy–Weinberg law.

Hardy–Weinberg law The law states that the frequency of alternative alleles of the same gene in a population are constant from one generation to the next so long as: (1) the population is large; (2) crosses occur at random; (3) there is no selection pressure favouring a specific form; (4) there is no mutation; (5) there is no migration of part of the population. In a population at equilibrium, the genotype frequencies for a single gene with two alleles (A and a) are p and *q* respectively, in diploid individuals (AA, Aa or aa). The frequency of homozygous AA is p^2, the frequency of homozygous aa is q^2 and the frequency of heterozygous Aa is $2pq$. Hence $p^2 + 2pq + q^2 = 100$ per cent. This is known as the Hardy–Weinberg equation.

Hartig net A meshwork of fungal hyphae formed between the cortical cells in the roots of those plants that form an association with ectotrophic mycorrhizae.

harvest index The ratio between the amount of useful (harvested) biomass and the total standing crop. In traditional long-stem grains such as wheat, only 40 per cent of the total biomass was grain. Modern short-stemmed varieties may have a harvest index of over 0.5, giving a marked increase in economic yield, although total biomass (standing crop) remains the same or actually decreases.

HAT medium A selective tissue culture medium, containing hypoxanthine, aminopterin and thymidine, in which only certain types of cells are able to survive.

haustorium An outgrowth produced by parasitic plants that penetrates the host tissue and acts as a means of absorbing nutrients. Haustoria are found in parasitic fungi and form from the roots of parasitic angiosperms, such as dodder.

haversian canals Channels found in compact bone that permit the passage of blood vessels and nerves.

HBSS Hanks balanced salt solution.

HDP *See* helix-destabilizing protein.

heat exchanger A mechanical device used to bring two fluids of differing temperature into close contact (without mixing) so that heat may be efficiently transferred from the fluid at the higher temperature to that at the lower temperature. A wide variety of designs is used, the principal objective being to provide a large surface area for heat exchange. The main types are plate exchangers and tubular exchangers. In the former, the two fluids pass either side of a flat metal plate; in the latter, fluid passes through spiral pipes or a series of parallel tubes immersed in a tank containing the second fluid. In both cases, the construction of the heat exchangers may be such that they form an integral part of another process. For instance, in a jacketed fermenter, the fermenter wall is the heat exchange surface, or in a fermenter with an internal coil, the vessel forms the container for the second fluid. (*See* figure on page 163.)

heat of fermentation The heat that is produced as a result of the metabolic activity of organisms growing in a fermenter. In an anaerobic fermentation, between 5 and 10 per cent of the total heat value of the substrate may be released as heat, whereas for an aerobic system, depending on the substrate, over 50 per cent of the energy content may be released as heat.

heat of vaporization The amount of heat needed to change a liquid into a gas. It is equal to the difference in enthalpies of the liquid and vapour state:

$$\Delta H = H_{vapour} - H_{liquid}$$

ΔH is always positive for an evaporation and negative for a condensation.

heat removal *See* heat transfer.

heat transfer The movement of heat from one body or region to another. Heat transfer occurs by conduction, radiation or convection. In most biological chemical engineering processes, heat transfer is achieved using heat exchangers which are important in the cooling of bioreactors used in aerobic fermentation and the heating of anaerobic digesters or other reactions carried out at mesophilic or thermophilic temperatures. In heat exchangers, in general terms, the rate of heat transfer is proportional to the surface area and the temperature gradient between the fluids as well as the conductivity of the materials concerned.

heat-shock gene Any gene that can be turned on or off (i.e., expressed or

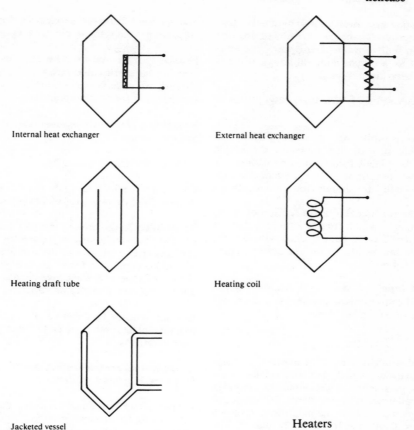

Internal heat exchanger

External heat exchanger

Heating draft tube

Heating coil

Jacketed vessel

Heaters

repressed) by short exposure to a higher (or lower) temperature than that at which the organism usually grows. The term is also applied more specifically to a set of genes found in *Drosophila* that are affected by exposure to a heat shock of about 37°C.

heavy chain (H chain) Longer of the two types of polypeptide chain present in all immunoglobulin molecules. The heavy chains are linked, usually covalently, with two light chains to form the basic immunoglobulin molecule.

heavy hydrogen Deuterium or tritium.

heavy isotope Any isotope that has a higher atomic weight than the usual (i.e. most abundant) natural isotope. The term is usually applied to stable isotopes.

heavy metal Any of a number of elements that are in general toxic to biological systems. These include lead, mercury, cadmium, etc.

heavy water Water in which the hydrogen has, to a large extent, been replaced by deuterium or tritium.

HeLa cells A human tissue cell line, derived from a carcinoma, widely used in cell biology since the cells are easily grown in culture. May be found as contaminants in, or totally supersede, other supposedly pure lines of mammalian cells.

helicase An enzyme preparation derived from snails used to break down the walls of yeast cells.

Heliothis zea nuclear polyhedrosis virus A subgroup A baculovirus isolated from the cotton bollworm *H. zea*. It has been marketed as a biopesticide, although use has now been discontinued.

helix A spiral of regular repeating turns or units.

helix-destabilizing protein (HDP) A specific protein that binds to the single strands of DNA formed at a replication fork during transcription. HDP prevents the separated daughter strands from re-annealing.

helper (inducer) T cells A class of white blood cells which are a functionally distinct group of T cells that associate with B cells, increasing their tendency and ability to produce antibody.

hematopoietic stem cell An undifferentiated self-renewing cell that is a precursor for a variety of cell types.

heme *See* haem.

hemicellulose Any of a number of polysaccharides, which include xylans, mannans, galactans and glucomannans, found in the cell walls of higher plants. The degree of polymerization of hemicellulose is much lower than that found in cellulose. The chains may be branched, but do not form crystalline regions.

hemizygous Descriptive of a region of a chromosome that is not paired in the diploid state, such as the unpaired region of the X chromosome. In haploid cells, all chromosomes are hemizygous.

HEPA filter *See* high efficiency particulate air filter.

heparin A sulphated mucopolysaccharide composed of D-glucosamine and D-glucuronic acid. It acts as an anticoagulant by neutralizing the action of thrombin and prevents the activation of prothrombin to thrombin.

heparinase An enzyme that breaks down the anticlotting agent heparin. It is used to reverse the effects of heparin if, for example, a patient starts to bleed excessively.

hepatic portal system The vein in vertebrates that carries blood from the intestine to the liver. It serves as a transport system for absorbed foods other than fats.

hepatitis B A virus that causes serious liver disease in man.

Hepes *See* zwitterionic buffer.

herbicide A chemical or biological agent designed to kill unwanted plants (weeds).

heritability In the broad sense, the fraction of the total phenotypic variance that remains after exclusion of the variance due to environmental effects. In the narrow sense, the ratio of the additive genetic variance to the total phenotypic variance.

hermaphrodite Descriptive of a plant or animal that has both male and female reproductive organs.

Hermissenda crassicornis A species of sea slug used in genetic studies.

herpes virus Icosahedral viruses that are responsible for diseases such as herpes and chicken pox. They include the cytomegalovirus which may cause congenital handicaps in the foetus of infected mothers.

heteroallele An allele that differs from other alleles of the same gene by nucleotide differences at different sites within the gene. This contrasts with 'true' alleles, of which only four are possible at each site within the gene (AT, TA, GC and CG).

heterochromatin A specific fraction of the chromosomal material that is out-of-phase in being highly contracted when the bulk of the chromosomes, the euchromatin, is extended and uncoiled during cell division. It contains few, if any, coding sequences.

heterocyst A modified cell type found in some filamentous cyanophytes that develops thick walls and becomes the site of dinitrogen fixation. The heterocysts are deficient in photosystem II activity, and thus do not form oxygen. Because of this, problems of protecting the oxygen-sensitive nitrogenase from inhibition are avoided.

heteroduplex A DNA double helix in which the complementary strands differ slightly in sequence so that there is some mismatching. Heteroduplex molecules occur naturally during genetic recombination between homologous chromosomes.

heteroecious Descriptive of fungi such as

the rust *Puccinia graminis* that require two hosts in order to complete their life cycles.

heterofermentation The fermentation of glucose (or another sugar) by a lactic-acid-forming microorganism, producing carbon dioxide and ethanol (or other products), in addition to lactic acid. *Compare* homofermentation.

heterogametic sex The male or female type of a species that contains both an X and a Y chromosome, or in some species only one

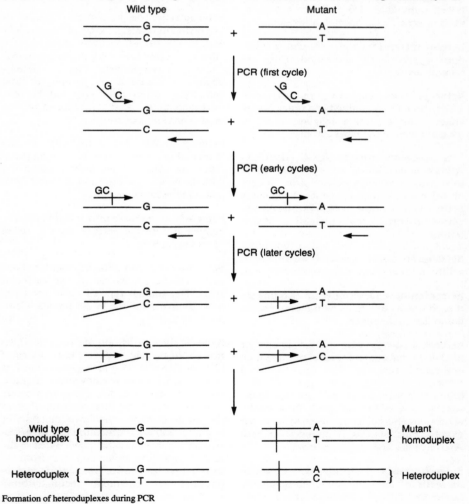

Formation of heteroduplexes during PCR

sex chromosome (XO). In humans, this is the male (XY); in other animals, the female may be heterogametic. The gametes produced by the heterogametic sex will contain either an X or a Y chromosome in the ratio of 1:1, or in the case of XO organisms, 50 per cent of the gametes will contain X and 50 per cent will possess no sex chromosome. The chromosome complement of the gamete from the heterogametic sex thus determines the sex of the zygote and hence the offspring. *Compare* homogametic sex.

heterogamic Descriptive of matings between individuals from different populations or species. *Compare* homogamic.

heterogeneous Descriptive of varied structure or chemical composition. *Compare* homogeneous.

heterogeneous assay An immunoassay in which the antigen–antibody complex is separated from the other reagents prior to measurement of the label activity.

heterogeneous nuclear RNA (HnRNA) A-high-molecular-weight type of RNA formed as the primary transcription product of eukaryotic structural genes. It contains both exon and intron sequences, and is converted to mRNA by elimination of the introns.

heterograft A graft derived from a donor of a different species from that of the recipient.

heteroimmune Descriptive of two phages if each is sensitive to its own repressor, but not to that of the other.

heterokaryon A cell, fungal hypha or mycelium that contains nuclei of more than one genetic make-up. The usual form is a dikaryon with two nuclei per cell each derived from a separate mating strain. In the sexual phase of the life cycle, these nuclei act as gametic nuclei and fuse to form the zygote. This process is common in both Ascomycetes and Basidiomycetes.

heterokaryosis A phenomenon in which the cells of an organism contain several nuclei that differ in genetic make-up. Het-erokaryosis results from the fusion of the cytoplasm of two gametes without nuclear fusion. It occurs in some fungi and may be a prerequisite for sexual reproduction.

heterokont Descriptive of a motile spore or cell in which the flagella are of unequal length.

heteromorphic Descriptive of organisms in which the same species exists in several distinct forms, for example, the gametophyte and sporophyte found in those species that show alternation of generations.

heterophylly The production of leaves of two different forms. In some plants, the juvenile leaves differ from those of the adult; in others, variable forms are produced in response to environmental factors. Heterophylly is common in xerophytes and halophytes, where the leaves may become thick and fleshy or much reduced in size under conditions of stress.

heteropyknosis An irregularity in the degree of condensation or in staining properties in some chromosomes compared with the bulk of the chromosomes and chromatin in the same nucleus.

heterosis An increase in size and vigour, as compared with the parents, seen in many hybrid organisms.

heterospory A condition in vascular plants in which the spores are of two different sizes. The smaller type of spore produces male prothalli and the larger female. *Compare* homospory.

heterostyly A condition of plants in which flowers of the same species have styles of different lengths. This arrangement ensures cross-pollination by insect vectors. In primroses, for instance, the pin-eyed flowers have long styles and short anthers, whereas the thrum-eyed flowers have short styles and long anthers. Pollination can be effective only between anthers and styles of the same length. The pollen and style from the same form of flower may also contain physical or chemical incompatibility mechanisms.

heterothallic yeasts Yeasts with complex sexual compatibility systems in which specific mating types are required. At least four mechanisms occur. The simplest is a biallelic, bipolar system with two mating types termed a and α. In more complex systems, a sex determinant occurs at one locus, but there are three or more alleles, resulting in a number of mating types (e.g., A1, A2, A3, etc.). A third mechanism is found in those yeasts that form ascospores. In basidiomycetous yeasts, three compatibility systems are known; some species resemble that described above. Other systems are tetrapolar and involve two unlinked loci and two allelic pairs. Hence a fertile mating would require A1, A2, B1, B2.

heterothallism A condition in which cross-fertilization between gametes from different mating types is essential irrespective of whether each thallus produces gametes of both sexes. The thalli are self-sterile.

heterotroph An organism that obtains its nourishment from preformed organic matter. *See* heterotrophic.

heterotrophic Descriptive of organisms that require preformed organic substances as a source of energy and/or building blocks for growth. Most heterotrophs (bacteria, fungi and animals) are chemotrophic (i.e., they derive energy from the organic material). A few heterotrophs, including the purple non-sulphur bacteria, use carbon compounds for growth, but obtain the energy from light.

heterozygote A cell or organism having two different alleles at a given locus on homologous chromosomes.

heterozygous Descriptive of a nucleus, cell or organism that contains two different alleles for any one gene. If a gene exists in two allelic forms A and a, the heterozygous form is Aa. A cross between two such heterozygous organisms will, in theory, give F_1 progeny which have the following genetic make-up: Aa 50 per cent, AA 25 per cent and aa 25 per cent. This will be expressed in the phenotype as dominant to recessive in the ratio of 3:1. To observe these ratios, it is essential that the number of offspring under consideration is sufficiently large to be statistically significant.

heuristic Descriptive of decisions based on trial and error or experience.

hexose A monosaccharide that contains six carbon atoms.

hexose monophosphate pathway *See* pentose phosphate pathway.

HFCS High fructose corn syrup. *See* high fructose syrup.

Hfr cell *See* fertility factor.

hGH Human growth hormone. *See* growth hormone.

HGPRT *See* hypoxanthine-guanine phosphoribosyl transferase.

high added value Descriptive of any process in which the economic value of a product is many times the cost of the raw materials required for its production.

high efficiency particulate air (HEPA) filter A type of high specification air filter.

high fructose syrup A syrup composed of the hexose sugars glucose and fructose in roughly equal amounts. High fructose syrups are produced from starch using enzymes. It is mainly produced in the USA, where 6 million tonnes are produced from corn starch. This product is commonly referred to as HFCS (high fructose corn syrup). In Europe, the product is often termed isoglucose, and may be derived from other starches. The standard syrup produced by enzyme processes alone has a composition of around 42 per cent fructose, 51 per cent glucose, 5 per cent maltose and 2 per cent higher oligomers. It is sold as a clear, colourless liquid of around 70 per cent solids. The fructose content is limited by the composition of the starting glucose syrup, which reflects the combination of acid and/or enzymes used in its preparation, and the equilibrium mixture reached in the isomerase-catalysed reaction. The demand by the food industry for products with a higher fructose content (55 per cent, 70 per cent or even 90 per cent) has led to the development of combined techniques using enzyme isomerization followed by separation on ion-exchange columns, with the glucose and/or oligomer streams being returned for further treatment.

high fructose syrup production High fructose syrups are produced by the action of glucose isomerase on a syrup containing a high content of glucose, derived by hydrolysis of starch. Corn starch produced by wet milling is the usual starting material. Starch slurry (about 33 per cent solids) is liquefied using bacterial amylase and saccharified using amyloglucosidase to produce a syrup which must be over 94 DE. This syrup is decolorized and deionized with carbon and/or resins, and concentrated to 45 per cent solids. The concentrated syrup is then passed through a column containing either immobilized cells of an organism with a high glucose isomerase content or the semi-purified enzyme immobilized on a carrier. Since the activity of the enzyme decreases with time, it is usual to have several columns working in parallel.

high mobility group protein A low-molecular-weight non-histone protein that binds strongly to DNA. High mobility group proteins are associated with the organization of chromosome structure.

high performance crystal spectroscopy (HPCS) A near infrared analytical technique using crystal optics to change the refractive index of light as it passes through crystal wedges rather than the traditional moving mirrors. HPCS is therefore less sensitive to vibration, temperature or humidity changes than conventional systems. *See* spectroscopy.

high performance liquid chromatography (HPLC) An analytical system in which liquid chromatography is scaled down and automated in such a way that rapid, reproducible analyses of complex mixtures can be carried out. Packings differ from those used in standard liquid chromatography in that the particle size of the beads of the matrix is very small. This enables small columns with a high number of theoretical plates to be used. The small size results in rapid analyses, whereas the high number of theoretical plates provides greater resolution. The column has an injection port through which very small (microlitre) samples are introduced on to the column. The column is eluted with a mobile phase pumped through the column in a highly controlled manner. Gradients of pH or eluent composition may be generated by the equipment to improve separation. The column effluent is passed through a suitable detector such as a fluorometer or a differential refractometer. The signal from the detection system may be processed directly by a microprocessor to give a readout of the amount of compound present. As with other chromatographic systems, the HPLC has to be calibrated with authentic samples and does not provide a means of absolute identification of the chemical identity of the components of the mixture. If larger scale columns are used, the techniques may be adapted to preparative methods. The term high pressure liquid chromatograph (now obsolete) was used in the early stages of development of the technique since the quality of the columns was such that high pressures were needed to force the liquid through.

high performance ultrafiltration (HPUF) A type of high performance liquid chromatography that uses a gel filtration column.

high pressure liquid chromatography *See* high performance liquid chromatography.

high rate biological filter An advanced technique for the aerobic treatment of waste water and sewage. In such filters, the traditional gravel is replaced with specially designed plastic media, often in the form of rings. This has three advantages: (1) flow rates can be higher since there is more room for the active biomass; (2) construction can be based on lighter (hence cheaper) materials since the same weight of inert solid carrier does not have to be supported; (3) the filters do not clog so easily, as these systems have a much greater void volume.

high rate digester An advanced anaerobic digester designed to have a high ratio of solids' (biomass) detention time to hydraulic detention time. Such digesters show high volumetric productivities and can accommodate high hydraulic throughput. High rate digesters include contact digesters, anaerobic filters and sludge blanket systems.

Hill plot A procedure for fitting the Michaelis–Menten plot to a sigmoid curve. This is used as a method for treating the results obtained from kinetic experiments where the enzymes show deviations from Michaelis–Menten kinetics (i.e., they have allosteric properties). A straight-line plot is obtained by plotting $\log V/(V - v)$ as a function of $\log S$, where V = maximum velocity, v = observed velocity and S = substrate concentration. The slope (n) indicates the number of interacting sites on the enzyme or enzyme complex.

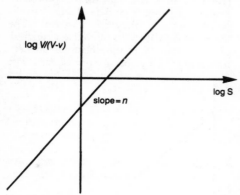

Hill plot

Hill reaction A light-induced electron flow associated with evolution of oxygen observed in chloroplasts incubated *in vitro* with either artificial or natural electron acceptors. The Hill reaction can be demonstrated using ferricyanide, dichlorphenolindophenol or NADP.

hindbrain The posterior part of the neural tube of embryonic vertebrates associated with auditory sensation. The hindbrain develops into the medulla oblongata of the brain stem, as well as forming the cerebellum.

His Abbreviation used to denote the amino acid histidine in protein sequences, etc.

histamine An amine derived from the amino acid histidine by decarboxylation. It is released from tissue following injury, causing inflammation (dilation of blood vessels), contraction of smooth muscle and stimulation of gastric secretion.

histidine (His) One of the 20 common amino acids occurring in proteins. It is a precursor of histamine.

$$\text{CH}_2\text{CH(NH}_2)\text{COOH}$$

Histidine

histidine production Histidine may be produced by fermentation of phosphoribosyl pyrophosphate to histidinol, by a histidine auxotrophic mutant, followed by conversion to L-histidine. Direct production using mutants of *Corynebacterium glutamicum* is also possible.

histiocyte A phagocytic cell found in connective tissue characterized by granular cytoplasm that stains with neutral red. Histiocytes are irregular in shape, contain vacuoles and are capable of amoeboid movement. They are active in inflammatory conditions and accumulate near sites of tissue haemorrhage.

histochemistry The study of the chemistry of living cells using such techniques as microscopy, staining and chemical analysis.

histocompatibility A sufficient similarity between tissue types such that a graft of tissue from one individual is accepted by another.

histocompatibility antigen An antigen that initiates the immune response leading to rejection of a graft by the host. Such antigens are genetically determined glycoproteins which occur in cell membranes of lymphocytes and macrophages in particular. In humans, the antigens that cause the strongest immunological response are the HLA system.

histocompatibility molecules Cell membrane glycoproteins that mediate cellular interactions of the immune system. There are two types of histocompatibility molecules: Class I, found on virtually all nucleated cells and in high concentrations on lymphocytes; Class II, found on accessory cells and B lymphocytes.

histogen The regions in a plant in which tissue is undergoing differentiation.

histogen theory The concept that the apical meristem of plants consists of three distinct parts (histogens) which give rise to specific tissue layers. The outer dermatogen forms the epidermis, the middle periblem forms the cortex, and the inner plerome gives rise to the internal tissues.

histogenesis The process by which undifferentiated cells develop into specialized cells of a tissue.

histogram A plot of frequency distribution in which equal intervals or arbitrary values are marked on the horizontal axis and the frequency corresponding to each selection is indicated by the height of a rectangle having the interval as its base.

histology The study of the structure of tissues using stained sections, light microscopy and electron microscopy.

histone A protein associated with nucleic acids in the chromatin of eukaryotic cells. Histones are characterized by high levels of the basic amino acids arginine and lysine. There are five major groups of histones: H1, with a very high lysine content and a molecular weight of around 21,500; H2A, lysine-rich with a molecular weight of about 14,000; H2B, lysine-rich with a molecular weight of about 14,000; H3, arginine-rich with a molecular weight of about 15,000; H4, arginine-rich with a molecular weight of about 11,000. Histones H2A, H2B, H3 and H4 form the cores of the nucleosomes found in chromatin, whereas H1 links the neighbouring nucleosomes.

histone modification An alteration in the structure of histones brought about by phosphorylation, methylation or acetylation of some amino acid side chains.

HIV Human immunodeficiency virus; causative agent of AIDS. This name was adopted in 1986 to prevent confusion arising from the use of alternatives HTLV-III or LAV (lymphadenopathy associated virus).

HLA system Human leucocyte antigen; a complex group of antigens that define human tissue histocompatibility in the same way that the ABO blood typing antigens define blood transfusion compatibility.

HMG protein *See* high mobility group protein.

HnRNA *See* heterogeneous nuclear RNA.

Hofstee plot A technique used to generate a straight-line plot from data obtained in experiments on enzyme kinetics. The observed velocity (v) is plotted as a function of v/S, where S is the substrate concentration at which velocity v is observed. The

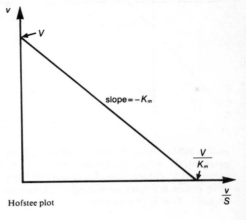

Hofstee plot

slope of the line is equal to $-K_m$ (the negative of the Michaelis constant). The intercept on the y-axis is equal to the maximum velocity (V).

Hogness box Analogous to the Pribnow box. *See* TATA box.

Holliday model A proposed mechanism for recombination in eukaryotes. It suggests that exchange of single strands of DNA occurs between homologous chromatids during crossing-over. Cutting of the single-strand bridges yields recombined sections of DNA.

hollow fibre reactor A fermentation system in which the cells are separated from the medium using semipermeable membranes arranged in the form of hollow fibres. This provides an extremely large surface area so that rapid substrate diffusion and high fermentation rates are possible. The hollow fibre reactor is arranged like a shell in a tube heat exchanger; a bundle of 1000 of the fibre tubes can be packed into a single 1-cm diameter shell. The shell side is then inoculated with growing cells. Medium is fed into the fibre tubes at one end of the reactor, and the substrate (e.g., glucose) diffuses out and is fermented. The product (e.g., ethanol) diffuses back into the tubes and is carried out at the far end of the reactor. The hollow fibre reactor can achieve cell densities approaching the maximum cell packing density and corresponding high volumetric productivities. However, hollow fibre reactors are costly and membrane plugging may be a problem.

holoenzyme A complete enzyme complex consisting of the protein structure (apoenzyme) and any non-protein cofactor.

holophytic Descriptive of organisms that form complex organic substances from simple inorganic precursors by photosynthesis.

holotype An organism used as the type specimen, or example, in the description and naming of a new species or variety.

holozoic Descriptive of organisms that feed on solid organic matter or other organisms.

homeogenetic induction The induction of differentiation in an undifferentiated cell by an adjacent differentiated cell.

homeostasis The maintenance of constant physical and chemical conditions within the body of a living organism.

homeotic mutation A mutation that causes one body structure to be replaced by a different one during development.

homofermentation The fermentation of glucose or another sugar by a microorganism, producing only lactic acid. *Compare* heterofermentation.

homogametic sex An organism that contains two X chromosomes in its somatic cells. Hence it produces gametes of one type only (X). *Compare* heterogametic sex.

homogamic Descriptive of matings between individuals from the same population or species. *Compare* heterogamic.

homogeneous Descriptive of similar or uniform composition or structure throughout.

homogeneous assay An immunoassay in which it is not necessary to separate the antigen–antibody complex from other reagents prior to measurement of the label activity. *Compare* heterogeneous assay.

homogenizer A machine used to homogenize, mix, emulsify and disperse plant and animal tissues.

homograft A graft tissue or organ derived from the same species as the recipient. *Compare* heterograft.

homoiothermic Descriptive of warm-blooded animals (i.e., birds and mammals). They are able to maintain a constant body temperature. *Compare* poikilothermic.

homologous chromosomes Two chromosomes that become paired during the prophase of meiosis.

homologous recombination The integration of a nucleoside sequence at a specific location on a chromosome.

homopolymer tailing A technique whereby lengths of oligonucleotides comprising only one nucleotide (A or T) are joined on to the ends of DNA molecules. If oligo-(dA) sequences are added to the 3'-ends of one population of DNA molecules and oligo-(dT) blocks are added to the 3'-ends of another, the two types of molecules can anneal to form mixed dimeric circles. The reaction is catalysed by a terminal deoxynucleotidyl transferase.

homospory Descriptive of vascular plants in which spores are all one size, producing hermaphrodite prothalli. *Compare* heterospory.

homothallic yeasts Yeasts that are capable of self-fertilization since a single spore or cell can carry out a complete life cycle. Homothallic yeasts are found in both the ascomycetes and basidiomycetes. *Compare* heterothallic yeasts.

homothallism Descriptive of a thallus that is self-fertile. *Compare* heterothallism.

homozygous Descriptive of a diploid nucleus, cell or organism that contains two identical alleles for any gene. The alleles may be either dominant or both recessive. A cross between two individuals homozygous for the same trait will breed true, forming a pure line. *Compare* heterozygous.

hops The female flowers of the vine *Humulus lupulus* which are used in the production of the bitter flavour of beers. The essential oil from hops, which gives them their aromatic properties, contains a mixture of hydrocarbons, mainly terpenes, and comprises about 1 per cent of the total dry weight. The bitter components are resins, which account for about 15 per cent of the dry weight. The bitter compounds are mainly humulones, cohumulones and adhumulones.

hormone (1) A chemical substance secreted by an endocrine gland. (2) A plant growth substance.

horseradish peroxidase (HPO, HRPO) An enzyme used as a label in immunoassays.

host An organism that supports the growth of another organism which may be parasitic.

host restriction The degradation by restriction enzymes of foreign DNA introduced into a bacterial cell.

hot polymerase A thermostable DNA polymerase derived from *Thermus thermophilus* that has optimum activity at 75°C.

hot spot A region of a DNA molecule that is much more susceptible to mutation than other regions of similar size.

HPCS *See* high performance crystal spectroscopy.

HPLC *See* high performance liquid chromatography.

HPO *See* horseradish peroxidase.

HPUF *See* high performance ultrafiltration.

HPV *See* human papillomavirus.

HRPO *See* horseradish peroxidase.

5HT 5-Hydroxytryptamine. *See* serotonin.

HTLV *See* human T cell lymphotrophic virus.

Hughes press A device in which frozen cells are forced through an orifice under high pressure in order to disrupt them prior to downstream processing.

human cell line A culture of cells derived from human tissue. *See* animal cell culture.

human growth hormone (hGH) A hormone that is used to treat dwarfism. The hormone also has anti-wasting properties and is being investigated as a treatment for muscle injuries and conditions caused by AIDS and cancers. *See also* growth hormone.

human immunodeficiency virus *See* HIV.

human macrophage chemoattractant protein-1 (MCP-1) *See* MCAF.

human macrophage/monocyte chemotactic and activating factor *See* MCAF.

human papillomavirus (HPV) A pathogen associated with a range of urethrogenital diseases and cancers. *Also see* papillomavirus.

human T cell lymphotrophic virus (HTLV) Any of several viruses, members of the Oncornavirinae, that cause leukemia in humans (e.g., HTLV-I, HTLV-II, HTLV-III). Some authorities have suggested that AIDS is caused by HTLV-III (*see* HIV).

humectant A substance that absorbs water (e.g., glucose syrup). Humectants are added to various products (e.g., baked foodstuffs, glues) to help maintain moisture content.

humic acid A high-molecular-weight organic acid produced by decomposition of plant material. Humic acid occurs in peats and soils and can cause the discoloration of water and the fouling of adsorbents.

humulone Any of a number of acidic terpenes known as alpha acid resins obtained from hops that confer the bitter taste on beer.

humus A colloidal material formed in the soil by decomposition of organic matter.

hyaluronic acid A mucopolysaccharide comprising repeating units of N-acetyl-D-glucosamine and D-glucuronic acid. It occurs in extracellular spaces of connective tissues associated with joints. It has lubricating properties.

hybrid An organism produced by the crossing of individuals or species that are genetically different. Hybrids between species may be sterile since the unlike chromosomes are not capable of pairing during meiosis. F_1 hybrids, of plants in particular,

are produced to take advantage of higher yields associated with hybrid vigour.

hybrid inviability Reduction of somatic vigour or survival rate in hybrid organisms.

hybrid protein A polypeptide formed by the expression of a hybrid gene.

hybrid sterility Reduction or suppression of the reproductive capacity in hybrid organisms.

hybrid vigour *See* heterosis.

hybrid-arrested translation A method that enables a cloned DNA to be correlated with the protein which it encodes. It is based on the fact that mRNA will not direct the synthesis of protein in a cell-free translation system when hybridized with its DNA complement. Hence, the proteins synthesized by a cell-free system, including a particular hybridized mRNA, can be compared with those of a system in which no hybridization with DNA has occurred. The difference indicates the nature of the protein encoded by the mRNA in question.

hybridization (1) A process in which a strand of nucleic acid joins with a complementary strand through base pairing. The technique is used to locate or identify nucleotide sequences and to establish the effective transfer of nucleic material to a new host. (2) The mating or crossing of two animals, plants or fungi of dissimilar genetic origin or make-up to produce hybrids.

hybridization oven An oven used to provide a constant temperature for DNA, RNA or protein hybridization. A typical oven has a temperature range of 30–70°C and contains 6–12 glass tubes that are constantly rotated to maintain the homogeneity of the hybridization suspension.

hybridoma A hybrid cell, or chimera, produced by the fusion of a myeloma (antibody-producing tumour) cell and a plasma cell. A hybridoma clone produces the one specific antibody of the parent plasma cell (monoclonal antibody).

hybrid-released translation A method that enables a cloned DNA to be correlated with the protein for which it encodes. Cloned DNA is bound to a cellulose nitrate filter and hybridized with an unfractionated preparation of mRNA. The filter is washed and the hybridized messenger eluted by heating in a buffer with formamide. The recovered mRNA is then translated in a cell-free system, and the radiolabelled polypeptide products analysed by gel electrophoresis.

hydathode A secretory organ found on leaf margins, for example, through which guttation occurs.

hydraulic detention time *See* mean detention time.

hydrazine A reagent used in amino acid analysis. When heated with proteins or peptides under anhydrous conditions, it converts all amino acids except the carboxyl terminal residues to hydrazides. The terminal amino acid can thus be recognized, and the nature and relative amounts determined using an amino acid analyser.

hydrocarbon A chemical compound that contains only carbon and hydrogen.

hydrocortisone A synonym for cortisol.

hydrogen bond An electrostatic attraction between an electronegative atom within a given molecule and a hydrogen atom attached to another electronegative atom.

hydrogen ion Ionized hydrogen of the form H^+.

hydrogen ion concentration The number of grams of hydrogen ions in a litre of solution; a measure of the acidity or alkalinity. *See* pH.

hydrogen peroxide (H_2O_2) A chemical compound that very readily loses some of its oxygen, and is thus a good oxidizing agent.

hydrogen production *See* photobiological hydrogen production.

hydrogen sulphide A colourless, flammable, cumulatively poisonous gas. The gas, at very low concentrations, smells of rotten eggs. It is produced by a mixed population of anaerobic microorganisms present in anaerobic digesters where the feedstock has a significant content of sulphur in any form. In particular, hydrogen sulphide is produced in digestion of farm manure and industrial effluents from fermentation plant where molasses clarified with sulphuric acid is used. The gas rapidly corrodes copper and can cause damage to both internal combustion engines and boilers if not removed by gas scrubbing.

hydrogenase An enzyme complex that catalyses the formation of molecular hydrogen. Enzymes that *in vivo* act as nitrogenases may also show hydrogenase activity.

hydrogenation (1) The combining or treating with hydrogen. (2) In chemistry, the catalytic saturation of double bonds in unsaturated molecules.

hydrogenotrophic Descriptive of anaerobic bacteria that are able to use hydrogen gas to reduce carbon dioxide to methane in the production of biogas.

hydrolase An enzyme that catalyses a reaction involving the addition or removal of a molecule of water. Hydrolases are one of the main groups (EC 3) used in enzyme classification:

3.1 act on ester bonds
3.2 act on glycosyl compounds
3.3 act on ether bonds
3.4 act on peptide bonds
3.5 act on C–N bonds
3.6 act on acid anhydride bonds
3.7 act on C–C bonds
3.8 act on halide bonds

hydrolysate A solution derived by the chemical or enzymic hydrolysis of a polymer, cell extract or culture. An autolysate is a specific example of a cell hydrolysate. Hydrolysates are used in analysing the chemical composition of macromolecules and polymers or as a source of nutrients. For example, yeast hydrolysates are used as a source of vitamins and amino acids.

hydrolysis The catalytic breakdown of macromolecules or polymers into constituent building blocks with incorporation of the elements of water. The hydrolysis of proteins yields amino acids, that of carbohydrates monosaccharides and/or disaccharides, that of nucleic acids nucleotides, and that of fats glycerol and fatty acids.

hydrophilic Descriptive of having an affinity for water. *Compare* hydrophobic.

hydrophobic Descriptive of having a lack of affinity for water. *Compare* hydrophilic.

hydrophobic interactions Attraction that occurs between non-polar molecules in aqueous solution.

hydrophyte A plant that grows in a watery habitat.

hydroponics A technique used for the growth of plants in a shallow layer of liquid culture medium that contains the necessary inorganic nutrients. The technique is used in the large-scale production of tomatoes and other horticultural crops.

hydrotropism The growth response to water shown by plant roots in particular.

3'-hydroxyl terminal The end of a single strand of nucleic acid or a single-stranded oligonucleotide that has a free 3'-hydroxyl group. *In vitro* such ends may be capped with other groups in order to render them less open to attack by phosphatases or nucleases.

5'-hydroxyl terminal *See* 3'-hydroxyl terminal.

hydroxylapatite A form of calcium phosphate gel that is used for chromatography. One use is in the purification of plasmid DNA, which binds to the gel so that contaminating RNA and protein can be washed through. The plasmid DNA is then selectively eluted from the column.

hydroxytetracycline An antibiotic produced by *Streptomyces rimosus*.

5-hydroxytryptamine *See* serotonin.

hymenium The cell layer that contains the asci or basidia in fruiting bodies of fungi.

hyoscyamine An anticholinergen derived from the plant *Hyoscyamus niger*.

hyperchromic effect An increase in absorbance of ultraviolet light at 260 nm associated with the denaturation or hydrolysis of double-stranded DNA to single-stranded DNA and/or free nucleotides. It is caused by the suppression of the free rotation of the bases in a polynucleotide structure. *Compare* hypochromic effect.

hyperchromicity *See* hyperchromic effect.

hyperplasia An increase in the number of cells in a tissue due to increased cell division. This occurs in normal growth, as well as in response to wounding or tumour growth.

hyperpolarization An increase in the membrane potential.

hypertonic Descriptive of a solution that has a higher osmotic pressure than another to which it is compared. *Compare* hypotonic.

hypertrophy An increase in the size of a tissue or organ due to an increase in size of the individual cells.

hypervariable region Part of the variable region of light chains and heavy chains of immunoglobulins which is more variable than other parts in terms of amino acid substitution, deletions and insertions.

hypha A tubular filament that forms the vegetative stage of most fungi and many algae.

hypochlorite A salt of hypochlorous acid. A mixture of such salts – household bleach – is used as a general antibacterial agent for cleaning and sterilizing surfaces.

hypochlorous acid (HClO) An acid, solutions of which have a strong bleaching action.

hypochromic effect A decrease in absorbance of ultraviolet light at 260 nm associated with the joining of free nucleotides into single-strand nucleic acid or the formation of double-stranded DNA. *Compare* hyperchromic effect.

hypochromicity *See* hypochromic effect.

hypocotyl The part of the shoot axis of a higher plant that lies below the cotyledons.

hypodermis (1) A layer of cells that lies below the epidermis proper in stems or leaves of certain plants. (2) The layer of loose connective tissue that lies just below the dermis in mammals.

hypogeal Descriptive of plants that develop below the surface of the ground.

hypogyny Descriptive of plants with a superior gynoecium.

hyponasty A growth response of plants that results in an upward curvature due to the more rapid growth of cells on the lower side.

hypostatic Descriptive of a gene whose effect is suppressed by the effect of another nonallelic gene.

hypotensive An agent that reduces hypertension (blood pressure).

hypothalamus Part of the brain that contains regions controlling many functions such as sleep, feeding and various behaviour patterns. It is the head of the autonomic nervous system with separate centres for both the sympathetic and the parasympathetic regulation.

hypotonic Descriptive of a solution that has a lower osmotic pressure than one to which it is being compared. *Compare* hypertonic.

hypoxanthine-guanine phosphoribosyl transferase (HGPRT) An enzyme that catalyses the transfer of the phosphoribosyl moiety to hypoxanthine and guanine, two of the constituents of nucleic acids.

I

IAA *See* indoleacetic acid.

IAGT *See* indirect antiglobulin test.

IAN *See* indoleacetonitrile

ICMA *See* immunochemiluminometric assay.

ICSH Interstitial cell-stimulating hormone. *See* luteinizing hormone.

ideoblast A cell that differs from the surrounding cells within a composite tissue.

ideogram A diagram or photograph of the complete chromosome complement of a cell. It is characteristic of an organism in terms of chromosome number and chromosome appearance.

ideotype A hypothetical organism that contains all the ideal characteristics for which one might breed.

idiophase The phase of a culture during which secondary metabolites (i.e., metabolites that have no obvious role in central metabolism) are produced.

idiotroph A microorganism that has a mutation in its biosynthetic pathways associated with the production of secondary product(s). For instance, in the production of antibiotics, such mutants are not capable of making one part of the antibiotic. Hence for antibiotic production to take place the medium must be supplemented with the missing moiety. When the mutant is fed analogues of the missing part, new antibiotics are produced.

idiotype The region associated with the antigen binding site that characterizes a specific antibody.

IDP *See* inosine 5'-diphosphate.

IELIA *See* inhibition enzyme-linked immunoassay.

Ig *See* immunoglobulin.

Ile Abbreviation used to denote the amino acid isoleucine in amino acid sequences and elsewhere.

IMAC *See* immobilized metal-affinity chromatography.

imago The adult, sexually mature form of an insect arising during development from the imagal cells and imagal discs of the larva.

imbibition The adsorption of water by colloids, gels and similar substances. It is a physical process rather than a metabolic one. Imbibition is common in plants, and in seeds in particular. As water is imbibed the substance of the cotyledons or endosperm swells causing a high imbibition pressure. This leads to rupture of the seed coat and release of the developing root and/or plumule. Increases in the fresh weight of expanding cells in the meristematic region of developing plants are also partly due to imbibition and partly due to osmosis.

immobilization A physical or chemical process used to fix enzymes, bacteria, cultures of plant or animal cells, or organelles derived from these sources, on to a solid support or trap them in a solid matrix. Such systems are then employed as biocatalysts in continuous flow systems (e.g., packed column reactors or expanded bed systems). Various methods of immobilization exist. (1) Enclosure in semipermeable membranes. This is a gentle method, but there is no stabilization of the cells or enzymes. Also there is the possibility of the membranes becoming fouled. (2) Entrapment in polymeric material. A wide range of materials have been used, including cellulose acetate, acrylamide, alginate, carrageenan and collagen. Each material has its own advantages relating to cost of materials and gentleness of the reaction procedure, and disadvantages relating to the effects of heat, solvents and chemical intermediates on the cells or enzymes, as well as the instability of the gel when treated with chelating agents. (3) Adsorption into charged supports. This is quite easily done, and there is some stabilization of enzyme activity. However, the linkage is not permanent and can result in some leakage of the cells or enzyme. (4) Absorption into porous supports. This is a gentle technique and is quite easily performed, but again there are problems with loss of catalysts from the system. (5) Covalent attachment to activated support material. This can give good results, although there may be some enzyme inactivation as a result of the bonding procedure. (6) Cross linkage of protein or cells with or without the use of support material. Again some inactivation may occur.

immobilized cells *See* enzyme immobilization.

immobilized enzymes *See* enzyme immobilization.

immobilized metal-affinity chromatography (IMAC) A protein purification technique in which metal ions immobilized on a support matrix bind with electron donor groups on the surface of protein molecules. Following this adsorption process the protein can be eluted by, for example, changing the pH or adding chelating agents.

immortalization The overriding of senescence mechanisms by a malignant cell allowing it to be subcultured indefinitely.

immune Protected from a disease.

immune interferon (INF-gamma) A type of interferon produced by human T lymphocytes when stimulated by viral infection or in *in vitro* experimental systems by a variety of inducers including protein A (enterotoxin) from *Staphylococcus*. INF-gamma is manufactured from lymphoblastoid cells isolated from new-born hamsters or from human blood lymphocytes.

immune modulator A compound that interferes with the production of an antibody in response to an antigen. Immune modulators are used to reduce the possibility of a host rejecting a heterograft.

immune precipitate A precipitate formed as a result of the interaction of an antibody and an antigen.

immune response The events that occur in humans and other vertebrate animals when the body is invaded by foreign protein. It is characterized by the production of antibodies and may be stimulated by an infectious organism or parasite (bacteria, yeast, fungi, protozoa, etc.), transplanted material, vaccine, sperm or even the host's own tissue.

immune suppression The impairment of the immune response.

immunity The ability to resist infection or reject foreign tissue (protein) conferred by the formation of specific antibodies in animals. Active immunity is due to development of an immune response following stimulation of the immune system by an antigen. It may develop after exposure to infection or be induced by vaccination. Immunity is characterized by the production of humoral antibody or lymphocytes containing cell-bound antibodies.

immunization A technique used to induce immune resistance to a specific disease in humans and other mammals by purposeful exposure to an antigen in order to raise antibodies to that antigen. It is achieved by injection of a mixture of antibodies to the disease (passive immunity) or by vaccination which stimulates the immune system to produce specific antibodies. Vaccination confers longer-lasting active immunity, whereas passive immunity confers only temporary protection since the externally derived antibody is be metabolized by the recipient.

immuno label A compound used to facilitate measurements based on immunoassays. These include radioisotopes (e.g., carbon, cobalt, iodine, phosphorus, tritium), fluorescent molecules, phosphorescent molecules, luminescent molecules, infrared absorbers and enzymes linked to chromogenic or other chemical markers.

immunoadsorbent An affinity matrix consisting of an antibody preparation linked to an insoluble support.

immunoaffinity Similarity in the immune properties of two or more substances; the mechanism of attraction between an antibody and an antigen.

immunoassay An assay method that uses antibodies (monoclonal or polyclonal) to detect and quantify proteins, bacteria and other biological molecules. *See* enzyme immunoassay, enzyme-linked immunosorbent assay, immunodiagnostic, radioimmunoassay.

immunoblotting A technique in which antibodies linked to marker enzymes are used to detect specific proteins blotted on to a nitrocellulose sheet, usually following electrophoretic separation. Also known as western blot.

immunochemiluminometric assay (ICMA) An immunoassay visualized using a chemiluminescent substrate.

immunochromatography A type of immunoassay in which the analyte and analyte–enzyme conjugate are mixed together and then applied to chromatography paper on which antibody has been immobilized.

immunocytochemical method A method that uses a signal compound linked to a specific antibody to locate a single protein in a cell. The cells are reacted with the labelled antibody and then examined under the microscope (after development of the colour), examined for fluorescence or subjected to autoradiography, as appropriate to the labelling technique used.

immunodiagnostic An analytical test based on the highly specific interaction between an antibody and an antigen. The interaction is linked to a method of quantifying the result. Most immunodiagnostics are based on radioimmunoassays. Other methods include immunodiffusion, immunoelectrophoresis and affinity labelling, etc.

immunodiffusion A technique used to investigate immunological reactions in which an antibody and an antigen diffuse toward each other across an agar gel. Compatibility is indicated by the precipitation of antibody–antigen complexes.

immunoelectrophoresis An analytical technique used for the identification of antigens separated from a mixture of proteins (e.g., blood serum) by electrophoresis. A specific antibody or antiserum is diffused into the support medium (e.g., cellulose acetate paper or agarose gels) and forms a visible precipitate when it meets the antigen. A number of different techniques are used which produce a different type of image (e.g., zone, rocket, fused line, fused rocket, crossed immunoelectrophoresis, etc.).

immunofluorescence An analytical technique in which a fluorescent dye is complexed with a specific antibody to the protein of interest. The antibody complexes with the protein, and the complex formed is recognized using a light microscope or devices such as automated cell sorters where the fluorescence is recorded by a photomultiplier. The technique is used to locate a given protein or enzyme in a tissue section, to identify membrane-bound proteins, or to identify or enumerate the number of a specific type of cells in a mixed population. In combination with computer-based counters or image analysers, very detailed information can be obtained owing to the specificity of the label and the sensitivity of detection devices.

immunogen A substance that stimulates the immune response.

immunogenetics The study of genetic

aspects of the type and formation of immunoglobulins (antibodies).

immunogenicity The ability of a substance to induce antibodies that bind to it.

immunoglobulin A protein of the globulin-type (usually gamma-globulin) that possesses antibody activity. Immunoglobulins are divided into five classes on the basis of the heterogenicity of the types of antibodies contained: IgG (with four subgroups); IgA (with two subgroups); IgM (with two subgroups); IgD; IgE. IgG and IgM fix complement, but only IgG crosses the placenta and binds to macrophages. The major components of blood serum antibodies are IgG (molecular weight 150,000) and IgM (molecular weight 900,000).

immunogold labelling A technique that uses an antibody–colloidal gold complex in order to label tissues. The gold can then be detected by electromicroscopy.

immunological tolerance A tolerance towards a particular antigen in an individual human or mammal. It results from a failure of the immune response. The tolerance may be due to genetic factors, exposure to antigens during foetal life, exposure to ingested antigens or an overall failure of the immune response as in certain diseases such as AIDS.

immunology The study of the nature and behaviour of the immune response and immune system in humans and other animals.

immunomodifier A chemical or biological agent that alters the immune response, for instance, by stimulating the formation of antibody-producing cells or by altering the cell properties by binding to outer cell membranes.

immunomodulator A compound that influences immune responses.

immunoradiometric assay (IRMA) *See* radioimmunoassay.

immunotoxin An artificial product obtained by fusing an antibody with a toxin of plant or bacterial origin. Such compounds are used to deliver potential pharmacological agents to specific areas and to tumour cells in particular.

immunoturbidimetry A technique that uses an assay in which insoluble antibody–antigen complexes are formed, enabling the analyte to be quantitatively measured by turbidimetric methods.

IMP *See* inosine 5′-monophosphate.

impeller A multibladed device, rotated at high speed, in a fermenter in order to assist the rate of oxygen transfer and to keep the cells in suspension.

implantation The process whereby the fertilized ovum of mammals becomes implanted in the endometrium of the uterus at the start of pregnancy.

imprinting A learning process found in animals, and birds in particular, that results in a specific response to a certain object. Often the response, which occurs at an early age, results in the object being followed. In nature this response is induced by the parent. However, under artificial conditions an animal can learn to follow other animals or objects.

impulse A signal that is propagated through the nervous system along the axons of neurones. It is the result of changes in the cell membrane properties which cause a potential gradient across the membrane. The characteristic changes in potential associated with an impulse (action potential) can be recorded using microelectrodes. The threshold stimulus required to produce an impulse is induced by a local depolarization, resulting in an end-plate potential, excitatory postsynaptic potential or receptor potential, according to the site where it occurs. Once initiated the change is propagated along the membrane, first as an inward movement of sodium ions, which reverses the potential from -70 mV to $+30$ mV, then as an outward movement of potassium ions, which restores the resting potential. Following the passage of an impulse, the membrane cannot be excited again until it recovers to the resting state. All the impulses are the same size, hence information is dependent on the frequency and total number of impulses invoked by a specific stimulus.

in situ In its original place (*Latin*).

in situ **hybridization** An analytical technique in which a radiolabelled DNA or RNA probe is hybridized with fixed cellular material. Cells are squashed on a microscope slide and the chromatin denatured so that it becomes single stranded. The probe is then applied, and it hybridizes with complementary sequences. An autoradiograph of the preparation reveals the location of the DNA sequences involved in the hybridization on specific chromosomes.

in utero Descriptive of a foetus that is still being carried in the womb.

in vitro Descriptive of an event or enzyme reaction under experimental investigation occurring outside a living organism. Parts of an organism or microorganism are used together with artificial substrates and/or conditions.

in vitro **packaging** The packaging of a recombinant DNA molecule within an infective bacteriophage to increase the efficiency of its transfection into the bacterial host cells in which it is to be cloned.

in vivo Descriptive of an event or enzyme reaction under experimental investigation occurring in the normal way (i.e., within a living organism).

inbreeding The mating of closely related individuals. Inbreeding results in a progressive decrease in the degree of heterozygosity of the population which is reflected by a decrease in the variation found in the phenotypes of a given population. Inbreeding may also result in the expression of harmful recessive characteristics. Many organisms have evolved patterns of social behaviour, mechanical features or biochemical reactions that prevent or dis-

courage inbreeding. In contrast, many of the crop plants and animals selected by man are tailored to fit by deliberate inbreeding with selection for preferred characteristics and rejection of organisms showing unacceptable traits from the breeding stock.

inbreeding coefficient The probability that the two genes (alleles) at the locus are identical by descent.

inbreeding depression A loss of vigour associated with self-crosses or crosses between closely related individuals.

incipient species Populations that are too distinct to be considered as subspecies of the same species but not sufficiently differentiated to be regarded as different species; also called semispecies.

inclusion body A structure, consisting of many virus particles embedded in a protein matrix, formed in plant cells infected by caulimoviruses.

incompatibility The result of a mechanical, genetic or physiological interaction between two organisms of opposite sexes that prevents or results in a failure of fertilization. In plants, incompatibility mechanisms exist to prevent self-pollination in flowers or individual plants that bear both male and female flowers. In this case the mechanism is genetic and caused by interaction of the pollen grain and stigma which may prevent or slow growth of the pollen tube. In fungi, a genetically based mechanism results in heterothallism. The physiological interaction between the tissues of two organisms that results in the failure or rejection of a graft or blood transfusion may also be termed an incompatibility mechanism.

incomplete dominance A characteristic of two allelic genes which interact in such a way that the phenotype of a heterozygous individual differs from the phenotype expressed by either of the homozygous alternatives.

incubation The maintenance of a bacterial,

tissue or cell culture at constant temperature, favourable for cell growth, under controlled conditions.

incubator A controlled-environment system (e.g., a cabinet or room) used for the maintenance of bacterial and other cell or tissue cultures. In addition to temperature control, the incubator may be equipped with facilities for controlling the gas composition and humidity of the atmosphere (under aerobic, microaerobic or anaerobic conditions). The term is also applied to a similar controlled-environment device used to hatch eggs or to maintain premature babies.

independent assortment The segregation of two or more pairs of alleles that lie on different chromosomes. Independent assortment does not occur if the alleles are linked on the same chromosome, although some assortment may take place as a result of crossing-over.

indican An anionic microbial polysaccharide produced by *Beijerinckia indicus* ATCC 19361. It is composed of glucose, mannose, rhamnose, uronic acid and acetyl groups. It has high viscosity, forms gels on heating, is soluble in methanol, and suspends and stabilizes emulsions. It is used as a gellant for water, methanol, methanol/ethanol mixtures and ethylene glycol.

indicator species A plant or animal whose presence, or absence, suggests that certain environmental conditions prevail.

indigenous Descriptive of an organism that is native to a particular habitat.

indirect antiglobulin test (IAGT) A technique used to measure the ratio of immunoglobulin G antibodies to red blood cells in a serum sample. The sample is incubated with red blood cells, which are then washed and incubated with a known quantity of IgG antibodies. The relative degree of agglutination that occurs is related to the concentration of antibodies present in the serum sample.

indoleacetic acid (IAA) A plant growth substance or growth hormone; the most common of the naturally occurring auxins. Auxins are synthesized mainly in the meristem tissues of shoots and root apices, developing leaves, flowers and fruits. They are then translocated to their site of action. Lateral movement occurs in response to stimuli such as light and gravity, resulting in changes in growth rate causing negative or positive phototropism or geotropism. The vertical movement in the root or shoot is polarized (i.e., movement is more rapid in one direction than the other). In shoot tissue, auxins move basipetally (from apex to base), whereas in roots the movement near the apex is basipetal but over the rest of the root length it is acropetal (base to apex). These movements result in differential concentration gradients, with various tissues responding differently. The concentrations of IAA that cause maximum stimulation of growth are about 5×10^{-10} M for roots and about 10^{-6} M for shoots. The main target cells of the auxin are those in the process of differentiation close to the meristems where IAA stimulates the synthesis of all types of RNA and protein.

indoleacetonitrile (IAN) A natural plant growth substance that displays auxin-like activity.

inducer A natural compound, or synthetic analogue, that binds to and inactivates the repressor in an operon. This results in the operator becoming unblocked and the promoter site becoming accessible to RNA polymerase. The enzyme can then attach to the promoter site and transcribe the whole length of the operon producing a polycistronic mRNA which contains the messages for all the proteins encoded in the structural genes of the operon.

inducible enzyme An enzyme that is formed in the presence of, or in response to, an inducing agent. The inducer may be the substrate for the enzyme induced. The mechanism of induction depends on the effect of the inducer on transcription and translation rather than on the enzyme itself.

induction (1) An increase in the rate of synthesis of an inducible enzyme in response to a small molecule, the inducer. (2) The experimental elicitation of phage development from a prophage by a lysogen.

inert Non-reactive.

inert support A non-reactive matrix. Inert supports are used: (1) for the immobilization of chemicals in solid support synthesis or sequencing; (2) for affinity groups in affinity chromatography; (3) for immobilized cells or enzymes; (4) for the growth of anchorage-dependent cells; (5) as a packing material for biological filters and anaerobic filters. Inert supports vary in size from microscopic beads to large sheets several metres square, depending on their use. Materials used in their manufacture include carbohydrates, plastics, silica, glass and titania.

INF-α *See* leucocyte interferon.

INF-β *See* fibroblastic interferon.

INF-γ *See* immune interferon.

infection The process by which a host organism becomes invaded by a pathogenic virus, bacterium or other microorganism or disease agent.

inference engine In expert systems, the inference engine interprets the represented knowledge and infers new knowledge.

inferior Descriptive of a flower in which the gynoecium lies below the other floral parts.

inflammation A response of an animal to injury. It results in a dilation of the blood capillaries, a decrease in blood flow and an accumulation of leucocytes at the site of damage.

inflorescence A structure in higher plants consisting of a group of flowers borne on the same stem.

influent The liquid feedstock loaded into a bioreactor or fermenter.

infrared immunoassay (IRIA) An immunoassay in which a transition metal carbonyl metallic label is detected by Fourier transform infrared spectroscopy.

infrared (IR) light Descriptive of electromagnetic radiation contiguous with the visible region, but of longer wavelength than red light.

infrared spectrometer An instrument used in analytical chemistry. It consists of a radiation source, a sample holder, a diffraction device and a detector. The sample, in a solvent or as a solid in a pellet of potassium bromide, is scanned and the absorbance recorded as a function of wavelength. The resulting spectrum provides information on the interatomic bonds, which have characteristic frequencies that fall within the infrared range. For instance, carbonyl resonance occurs in the region of 1700 cm and hydroxyl resonance occurs in the region of 3300 cm.

infundibulum The neural stalk of the pituitary gland.

infuse (1) To introduce one substance into another. (2) To make an extract of the soluble parts of a material such as plant leaves.

infusion (1) A liquid extract obtained from a substance by soaking or steeping it in water. (2) The introduction of saline or another solution into a vein, artery or tissue. (3) The solution used as in (2).

infusorian (1) A microscopic aquatic protozoan possessing cilia. (2) Any of the microorganisms that develop in an infusion of decaying organic matter.

ingest To take food, or other foreign material, into the body.

inheritable Capable of being passed on from one generation to the next. It is a characteristic of the genotype rather than the phenotype.

inherited characteristic A condition or trait which is passed on from one generation to the next. Inherited characteristics must be encoded within the DNA sequences of the chromosomes or genomes of the parents.

inhibition (1) The blocking of an enzymic, physiological or metabolic process by an inhibitor. In general, inhibition is due to the binding of a chemical to a specific site on a specific enzyme. Such inhibition may be competitive with the substrate (binding at the active site on the enzyme) or may be non-competitive (binding at an allosteric). Other mechanisms of inhibition involve local changes in pH or chelation of essential metals or co-factors. (2) In the nervous system, the prevention or reduction of the activity of an effector by the action of either presynaptic or postsynaptic impulses. *See* inhibitory postsynaptic potential.

inhibition enzyme-linked immunoassay (IELIA) An assay in which the activity of an enzyme is suppressed by the addition of an antibody.

inhibitor A substance that retards or prevents a chemical or physiological reaction or response.

inhibitory postsynaptic potential A local hyperpolarization of the postsynaptic membrane caused by a neurotransmitter released from the presynaptic membrane of an inhibitory synapse.

initial cell A meristematic cell that undergoes mitotic division to produce two cells. One of these cells becomes differentiated, the other undergoes further division in the meristem.

initiation In molecular biology, the first step in translation. It is generally controlled by an initiation codon.

initiation codon A specific sequence of bases (AUG or GUG) to which a molecule of tRNA carrying a methionine residue binds in the first step of protein synthesis.

initiation complex A combination of mRNA, a ribosome that binds to the specific initiation site of the mRNA and an initiator tRNA which interacts with an initiation codon. Some proteins (initiation factors) also contribute information to the initiation complex and are then rapidly released.

initiation factor *See* initiation complex.

initiator tRNA A specific form of RNA which carries a free or formylated methionine residue and interacts with the initiation codon to start the synthesis of a protein molecule. The methionine, which is required for such initiation, is removed from most proteins before or shortly after synthesis is terminated.

inoculation (1) The introduction of a small number of individual microorganisms into a culture medium with the expectation of a larger number ultimately developing by growth and reproduction. (2) The injection of a vaccine to stimulate the production of antibodies against a disease.

inoculum A starter culture of an organism, or a mixture of organisms, added to a medium to initiate the production of a larger number.

inosine 5'-diphosphate (IDP) A nucleoside diphosphate based on inosine.

inosine 5'-monophosphate (IMP) A nucleotide based on inosine, the first compound with a purine ring structure formed during biosynthesis and a precursor of the bases adenine and guanine which are formed at the ribotide level. IMP is produced using the nucleoside phosphohydrolase which splits the link between the three-carbon of the ribose moiety and the phosphate link. The staring material is isolated from biomass of *Candida utilis*. IMP is used as a flavour enhancer in meats, soups and processed foods. It has a synergistic effect with glutamate, yeast extracts and hydrolysed vegetable proteins.

inosine 5'-triphosphate (ITP) A nucleoside triphosphate based on inosine.

5'-inosinic acid   *See*   inosine 5'-monophosphate.

inositol A polyol formed from glucose-6-phosphate in plants. The stereoisomer *myo*-inositol is important as a constituent of the phosphoglyceride phosphatidylinositol which occurs in membranes.

insecticide A chemical or biological agent manufactured and formulated with the purpose of killing insect pests.

insects The largest class of Arthropoda, characterized by the possession of six legs and two pairs of wings (which may become vestigial). They are important as pests of crop plants (aphids, beetles, Lepidoptera larvae) and as parasites that may transmit disease (fleas, mosquitoes, tsetse flies). Insects have been widely used in genetic research (Drosophila). They are also of economic importance in biological control (ladybirds, various wasps), production of food (honey) and as pollination vectors for many commercial crops (fruit in particular).

insert A length of DNA that is linked into another length of DNA or a cloning vehicle using gene manipulation techniques.

insertion element A DNA sequence that is inserted into the genome more or less randomly and that moves from chromosome to chromosome within the same cell or organism, at a frequency much greater than that of true mutations. Such sequences are referred to as jumping genes or transposons. These sequences carry active promoters or terminators of mRNA synthesis. They also provide the location of site-specific episome integration.

insertion sequence selection A method by which cells containing a foreign gene, which has been inserted by gene manipulation, can be distinguished and selected from the general cell population. Where antibiotic resistance markers are not available, this is done using genetic selection if the insertion sequence includes a gene coding for an enzyme of a biosynthetic pathway. The vector is used to infect mutant cells, which are not capable of growth or producing a recognizable metabolite (such as a pigment). The added gene comple-ments the auxotrophic mutation and only the transformed cells grow or produce the specified metabolite. These cells can thus be isolated and grown in bulk. Immunochemical methods are also used to detect a clone capable of synthesizing a foreign protein. A replicate plate is produced and the cells are lysed, releasing the antigen from positive colonies. A sheet of polyvinyl that carries the antibody is then placed in contact with the surface of the plate. The location of the antigen–antibody complex, and hence the position of the transformed colonies on the original plate, can then be detected by reacting the plate with radioiodine-labelled IgG followed by autoradiography. The cells can also be identified by transferring a replica of the culture plate on to a cellulose nitrate filter. The cells are removed by treatment with alkali and proteinase leaving denatured DNA attached to the filter. This DNA is fixed by baking at 80°C and hybridized with radioactive RNA probes, the positions of which are detected by autoradiography.

insertional vector A cloning vehicle in which a foreign DNA is inserted without loss of any of the original DNA sequence.

instar The interval in the life cycle of an arthropod between any two moults.

insulin A protein hormone secreted by the β-cells of the islets of Langerhans in the pancreas of mammals. Secretion is stimulated in response to hyperglycemia (high levels of glucose in the blood). The hormone stimulates catabolism of glucose and blocks glycogenolysis. Insulin, which has a molecular weight of 5800, was the first protein to be fully sequenced. It consists of two polypeptide – A (21 amino acid residues) and B (30 amino acid residues) – which are linked by disulphide bridges between cystine residues. It is produced from a single precursor polypeptide known as proinsulin which is cleaved in the pancreas. An inability to form insulin results in the disease diabetes mellitus. This disease may be treated by injection of insulin in conjunction with careful attention to diet in order to control blood sugar levels. Problems of immune response can arise since insulins of animal origin differ slightly in their amino acid sequences compared with human insulin. Hence the production of human insulin, or the conversion of other forms of insulin to the human form using gene manipulation, molecular biology and enzymology, is of particular significance.

integration (1) The insertion of a plasmid or viral DNA into the chromosomal DNA of a host following infection. (2) The modulation of a nervous signal such that the output from an effector is appropriate to, rather than proportional to, the size of the input signal from a receptor.

integument A protective covering in a plant or animal. In plants, the integument(s) form an envelope around the ovule. Most angiosperms have two integuments, whereas only one is found in gymnosperms. A small pore, the micropyle, occurs at the head of the integuments which after fertilization becomes the testa. In animals, the term may be applied to a variety of coverings, such as scales, skin or cuticle.

intercalation The insertion of planar molecules between adjacent base pairs of DNA or RNA, inhibiting replication and transcription.

intercellular Descriptive of a substance or fluid that occurs or lies between the cells of a tissue. *Compare* intracellular.

intercistronic region An untranslated sequence of bases found in a polycistronic mRNA which separates the sequences coding for each particular protein. These untranslated sequences may have a control function.

interesterification A reaction catalysed by sodium metal or sodium alkoxide that results in the random migration of the fatty-acyl residues among the acyl-glycerol molecules.

interference A measure of the degree to which one cross-over by a chromatid affects the probability of a second cross-over by

that same chromatid occurring. Positive (negative) interference indicates that a cross-over decreases (increases) the probability of a second cross-over.

interferon A protein with anti-viral activity formed by animal cells in response to infection by viruses. Interferons are classified on the basis of their origin: leucocyte interferon (alpha-interferon or IFN-α); fibroblastic interferon (beta-interferon or IFN-β); immune interferon (gamma-interferon or IFN-γ). Each class is subdivided into a number of different, distinct types which differ in their amino acid sequence, although these sequences are highly conserved with over 70 per cent of the amino acid positions being identical. The protein chains are about 165 residues long. The structure of the interferons was unknown until recombinant DNA techniques were used to clone the animal genes responsible for their formation in bacteria. mRNA from interferon-producing human leucocytes was isolated and reverse transcriptase used to produce the relevant cDNA which was cloned in pBR322. The sequence was determined using hybridization methods. Interferons are synthesized as a more rapid response to viral infection than the formation of serum antibodies and are associated with the body's protective mechanism against and recovery from viral infection. Hence interferons have attracted interest as potential therapeutic agents against viral diseases and some forms of cancer. Considerable research and commercial effort have been applied to the production of interferons, although the exact potential for therapeutic use has yet to be established. *See* fibroblastic interferon, genetically engineered interferon, immune interferon, leucocyte interferon.

intergenic region Aa part of a DNA sequence that does not code for amino acids. In prokaryotes, such regions may contain the replicon.

intergenic suppressor A mutation that suppresses the phenotype of another mutation in a gene other than that in which the suppressor mutation resides.

interkinesis The period between two mitotic divisions or the period between the first and second divisions of meiosis.

interleukin A protein synthesized and secreted by activated macrophages that stimulates both immune and inflammatory responses. Over-production of interleukins can contribute to autoimmune diseases such as rheumatoid arthritis and multiple sclerosis.

intermediate filaments Immunologically distinguishable structural components of cells which, being specifically expressed in malignant cells, can be used for tumour characterization using labelled (fluorescent or enzyme) monoclonal antibodies.

intermolecular hydrogen bonding Hydrogen bonds formed between separate molecules. *Compare* intramolecular hydrogen bonding.

internal energy (U) The difference between the heat absorbed from the surroundings (q) and the work done by the system on its surroundings (w):

$$U = q - w$$

The internal energy represents the sum of the bond energies in the molecules plus energy associated with such factors as vibration and rotation. The absolute value of U is difficult to obtain; changes in U (δU) can be measured.

internal environment The fluids associated with a body that lie outside the actual cells. The composition is kept constant by homeostasis, thus ensuring that the cells are supplied with nutrients and oxygen and maintained under stable conditions.

internal rate of return In accounting, the discount rate that equates the present value to the expected net cash flows or receipts to the initial cash outlay.

internal volume (V) In gel filtration chromatography, the internal volume of solvent within the gel.

interneurone A nerve cell that lies between the afferent and efferent neurones of a reflex arc. In vertebrates, interneurones are confined to the central nervous system.

internode A part of an organism or structure that lies between two joints. In plants, the internode is the part of the stem that lies between two nodes. In many plants, the apical meristems contain many nodes which are regions of cells division and leaf attachment. Growth of the stem occurs through division of meristematic cells in the node region followed by expansion of the cells in the internodes. In animals, the term internode refers to the myelinated region of the axon of a neurone that lies between two nodes of Ranvier.

interphase The part of the cell growth cycle when the cell nucleus is not undergoing division either by meiosis or mitosis. The chromosomes are duplicated during interphase.

intersex An abnormal organism that does not have the complete sexual characteristics associated with either a male or a female of that species. An intersexual individual may be intermediate between male and female in characteristics or may be a true hermaphrodite. Intersexuals arise either from abnormalities of the hormone system or in the number or structure of the sex genes.

interstitial cell stimulating hormone *See* luteinizing hormone.

intervening sequence A portion of a gene in eukaryotic DNA, separating two portions of nucleotide sequence, that is transcribed but does not appear in the final mRNA transcript; a synonym for intron.

intracellular Descriptive of an event, substance or organelle that occurs within a cell. *Compare* intercellular.

intragenic suppressor A mutation that suppresses the phenotype of another mutation in the same gene as that in which the suppressor mutation resides.

intramolecular hydrogen bonding Hydrogen bonds formed between atoms within the same molecule. *Compare* intermolecular hydrogen bonding.

intraspecific selection In breeding, a form of competition that occurs between members of the same species. It results in the selection and survival of some varieties with a specific characteristic and the elimination of others.

introgressive hybridization In plant breeding, the cross between two different species. This produces fertile offspring that may back-cross with the parents leading to the movement of genes from one species to the other. The result is a range of phenotypes, some with the characteristics of the parents and some with intermediate characteristics.

intron A region of DNA of several hundred base pairs in the eukaryote gene that is not expressed in the protein molecule or in mature RNA. It is also referred to as silent DNA. Introns divide the DNA of a single eukaryote gene into a number of non-contiguous stretches. Introns are also found to a lesser extent in some prokaryotic genomes and may be associated with a regulatory function. The initial heterogeneous nuclear RNA (HnRNA) produced by transcription of the nuclear DNA contains sequences complementary to introns and sequences complementary to the conserved coding sequences or exons which carry the actual information for translation in protein synthesis. The mRNA molecules are formed from the HnRNA by the removal of the sections corresponding to the introns by specific enzymes in the nucleus. The residual exons are then spliced by ligases to produce the intact mRNA carrying the sequence for the particular protein or peptide coded for by the gene.

intussusception A process by which the plant cell wall increases in area as a result of the addition of new material (cellulose fibres) between those already present.

inulin A polysaccharide formed of fructose units added to a molecule of sucrose. It has a mixture of chain lengths with up to about 30 units. Inulin is a storage compound found in Compositae such as Jerusalem artichoke, chicory and dahlias. That isolated from artichokes has been used for production of commercial ethanol and suggested as raw material for production of acetone–butanol mixtures for use as cosolvent in lead-free petrol using *Clostridium acetobutylicum*.

invagination (1) In embryology, a double-layered pocket formed by the in-folding of one layer of cells within another. (2) The inward movement of a portion of the wall of a blastula in the formation of the gastrula. (3) Any area in which a tissue folds within another.

inverse PCR A technique for the amplification of an unknown DNA sequence that flanks a core region of known sequence. First the DNA sequence containing the core sequence is digested by restriction enzymes to a size appropriate for amplification and then it is circularized using a DNA ligase. The PCR primers homologous to either end of the core region are orientated such that the polymerization reaction proceeds across the unknown flanking sequence.

inversion An abnormality in chromosome structure that results from a portion of the chromosome becoming detached, rotating through 180° and then becoming attached again.

inversion polymorphism The presence of two or more chromosome sequences, differing by inversions, in the homologous chromosomes of a population.

invert sugar A mixture of glucose and fructose provided by the action of dilute acid or enzymes on sucrose. Invert sugars are used as the substrate for some fermentations, as well as in the food and beverage industries. The first application of an immobilized enzyme was the use of invertase bound to a charcoal support to produce invert syrup in the 1940s.

invertase An enzyme, also known as

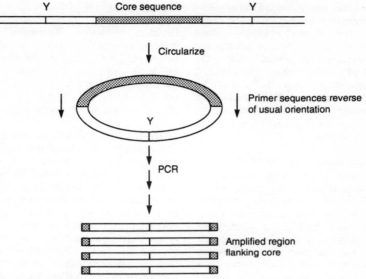

Amplification of flanking regions by inverse PCR

sucrase and fructofuranosidase, that catalyses the hydrolysis of the terminal non-reducing fructose residue from fructose polymers or sucrose. The hydrolysis of a sucrose is also catalysed by enzymes with α-D-glucosidase activity. Commercial preparations are obtained from the yeasts *Saccharomyces cerevisiae* or *S. carlsbergensis* often as a byproduct of brewing. Invertase is used in the production of invert syrups and in the confectionery industry.

inverted repeat sequence A sequence of bases in a molecule of nucleic acid that is identical to another sequence in the same molecule, but in which the order of bases is reversed. If one is read from the 5′-end and the other from the 3′-end, the order of bases will be the same.

iodination The replacement of a hydrogen atom by an atom of iodine. The process, using radioactive iodine, is often employed as a means of labelling proteins, especially for use in radioimmunoassays.

iodine value A measure of the amount of unsaturated fatty acid present in a fat, oil, resin or other natural product. It is the weight of iodine absorbed by 100 grams of

the substance under consideration.

ion An electrically charged atom, radical or molecule formed by the loss or gain of one or more electrons.

ion exchange The competitive substitution of ions at a common phase and certain types of solids. The solids may be of natural occurrence (e.g., clay particles or aluminosilicates, known as zeolites) or artificial ion exchangers based on polymers such as cross-linked polystrene resins or biological molecules such as dextran, cellulose or agarose reacted with suitable reagents to introduce anionic or cationic groups.

ion exchange chromatography A laboratory or full-scale industrial process in which the ion exchangers are used to fractionate mixtures of charged molecules which may be inorganic, low-molecular-weight organic compounds or macromolecules. Macromolecules are usually separated using ion exchange celluloses or similar materials, whereas more stable compounds such as sugars or amino acids are separated using ion exchange resins. The exchanger is usually packed into a long column, the dimension varying from a few centimetres to several metres depending on the application. The sample is loaded on to the resin, uncharged and unbound material is then washed off, and the bound compounds are eluted in sequence by adjusting the ionic strength or pH of the eluent. Alternatively, ion exchangers can be used in a batch mode. The sample is mixed with the resin. The required material is then recovered by washing the resin with a solution of suitable pH and ionic strength.

ion exchange resin A material that consists of a cross-linked polymeric structure to which ionized or ionizable groups are attached. The most common are the polystyrene resins and the methacrylic resins which are very stable. The polystyrene resins are formed by copolymerizing styrene and divinylbenzene, with ionic groups being attached to confer the required property. The second type of matrix is formed by copolymerizing methacrylic acid and divinylbenzene. The properties of the resins vary with the nature of the ionizable groups, the extent of cross-linkage and particle size. The ion exchange groups are based on sulphonic acid, carboxyl, phosphate or quaternary nitrogen groups. These resins are used for deionizing water and other solutions, and for chromatography of organic molecules. For separation of proteins and compounds that are easily hydrolysable, cellulose ion exchangers are preferred.

ion exchanger *See* cellulose ion exchangers, ion exchange resin.

ion exchanger conditioning A process used to clean an ion exchange resin and convert it to the required form. Depending on the application, the resin may be converted to the free base (or free acid) or converted to the metal salt (sodium, potassium, calcium, etc.). Usually solutions of sodium hydroxide or hydrochloric acid, followed by washing with water, are used to prepare the free base. If a particular form is required, a solution of a suitable salt is then passed through the resin column.

ion fluorescent probe A probe that can detect and quantify intracellular ions (e.g.,

Ca^{2+}, Na^+, Mg^{2+}, K^+, Cl^-).

ionizing radiation Radiation, such as X-rays, gamma-rays, neutrons, alpha-particles, etc., that damages the structure of DNA. This property is exploited to induce deliberate mutations.

IR Abbreviation for infrared (light).

IRGA Infrared gas analyser, which consists of three parts: the infrared (IR) source, a gas sample cell and the detector. The presence of carbon dioxide or other IR absorbing gases in the cell will decrease the intensity of radiation reaching the detector, resulting in a decrease in the output signal proportional to the gas concentration. Two types of IRGA are produced. In a dispersive system the source radiation is passed through a monochronometer and a selected narrow band of radiation is passed through the cell. Hence, the sample may be scanned over a range of wavelengths and gases other than carbon dioxide measured. A nondispersive instrument uses broad-band radiation as emitted by the source. The IR source is typically an electrically heated coil of nichrome alloy. Many instruments are dual beam, passing equal amounts of radiation through two parallel cells, the analysis cell and a reference cell.

IRIA *See* infrared immunoassay.

IRIS system An anaerobic digestion process similar to the anaerobic contact system in which biomass separation and cell recycle occur within the same tank. The term is derived from the name of the developers – the Institut de Recherches de l'Industrie.

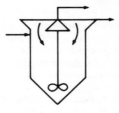

IRIS
digester

IRMA *See* immunoradiometric assay.

irradiation (1) A ray or beam of ionizing or electromagnetic radiation. (2) The exposure of material to radiation (light, ultraviolet, infrared, gamma-rays, X-rays, beta-particles or alpha-particles.

islets of Langerhans Endocrine cells found in small groups throughout the pancreatic tissue of vertebrates. There are three types of cells: α-cells which produce glucagon; β-cells which produce insulin; D-cells which produce gastrin.

ISO International Standards Organization.

isoamylase An enzyme (amylopectin 6-glucananhydrolase, EC 3.2.1.68) that cleaves α-(1,6)-linkages when present in branch points of oligosaccharides and polysaccharides. Isoamylase requires a minimum of 3 glycose units on the side chain. Isoamylase occurs in yeasts and bacteria, and is produced commercially from cultures of *Cytophaga* or *Pseudomonas*.

isoantigen An antigen that stimulates the production of antibodies in a genetically distinct, different member of the same species.

isoelectric focusing An analytical or separation procedure similar to gel electrophoresis. It is used to separate proteins and other charged molecules on the basis of their isoelectric point. A series of ampholytes is used to establish a pH gradient within a support gel. The charged molecules migrate through the gel until they reach an equilibrium point at which they carry no net charge and thus are not affected by the electric field across the gel.

isoelectric point The pH at which the various groups on a large molecule are ionized in such a way that the molecule carries no net charge and will therefore not migrate in an electric field. *See* isoelectric focusing.

isoenzymes Various forms of an enzyme that catalyse the same reaction but differ slightly in amino acid composition or structure such that they may be separated from one another by electrophoresis or chroma-tography and may be distinguished by variations in their amino acid sequence and the DNA in which they are encoded. In some instances, apparent isoenzymes may be artefacts of separation techniques due to the partial denaturation of part of the protein or to formation of complexes with charged molecules such as phenols during isolation. Any variation in the charge/mass ratio that results from such causes will generate spurious isoenzymes where electrophoretic techniques are used.

isogamy In sexual reproduction, the fusion of gametes that are very similar in appearance.

isoglucose *See* high fructose syrup.

isograft A graft that is derived from a donor which is genetically identical or very similar to the recipient.

isokont Descriptive of a flagellated spore or cell in which the flagella are of identical length.

isolate (1) The act of purifying a compound from a mixture or a pure line or strain from a mixed culture. (2) The substance isolated.

isolation mechanism In sexual reproduction, a method of preventing interbreeding between populations so that each population develops independently into a separate species.

isoleucine (Ile) One of the 20 common amino acids found in proteins. It is an essential amino acid for humans.

Isoleucine $\quad \underset{CH_3}{\overset{CH_3CH_2}{>}} CHCH(NH_2)COOH$

isomer A chemical compound having an identical composition to other compound(s), but with the atoms arranged differently.

isomerase A enzyme that catalyses intramolecular rearrangements. Isomerase are one of the main groups (EC 5) used in enzyme classification:

5.1 racemases and epimerases
5.2 *cis–trans* isomerases
5.3 intramolecular oxidoreductases
5.4 intramolecular transferases
5.5 intramolecular lyases
5.99 other isomerases

isomerization The changing of one isomeric form to another.

isomorph An organism that is very similar in appearance to another, genetically unrelated, organism.

isomorphism Descriptive of an organism or species in which both sexes or all generations in the life cycle are morphologically similar. The term is applied to plants in particular.

isoniazid Isonicotinic acid hydrazide; an inhibitor of transamination and specifically the conversion of glycine to serine in plants. It is therefore an effective inhibitor of the photorespiratory (C2) pathway.

isonicotinic acid hydrazide *See* isoniazid.

isopropanol An alcohol used as an industrial solvent produced in certain types of fermentation.

isopropyl alcohol *See* isopropanol.

isopycnic gradient separation A technique in which macromolecules are separated by centrifuging through a gradient of increasing density. The macromolecules move until they reach the region where their density is equal to that of the gradient.

isoschizomers Pairs of restriction endonucleases, obtained from different sources, that cut DNA at the same recognition site, although not necessarily at the same point in the recognition sequence.

isotachophoresis A specialized form of electrophoresis in which the separation is based on differences in electrophoretic mobility.

isotonic Descriptive of a solution of a substance in water that has the same osmotic pressure as another solution, which need not be of similar chemical composition. For instance, a glucose solution or culture medium is designed to be isotonic with a cell suspension or culture in order to prevent osmotic damage.

isotope Various forms of the same element having the same number of protons, but differing in the number of neutrons and hence in mass. Two types of isotopes exist: stable and unstable (radioactive). Isotopes are valuable in analytical and diagnostic work. Radioactive isotopes are detected and quantified on the basis of the ionizing radiation emitted (alpha-particles, gamma-rays and beta-particles). The most useful radioactive isotopes are the low-energy beta-emitters with a reasonable half-life. These include tritium ^{3}H, ^{14}C, ^{32}P and ^{35}S. The radioactive isotopes of nitrogen and oxygen are either not available or of such short half-life that they can only be used under special circumstances. Stable, or heavy, isotopes are detected using mass spectrometry. Heavy isotopes used in biology include deuterium ^{2}H, ^{15}N and ^{18}O. *See* radioactive tracer.

itaconic acid An organic acid, produced by fermentation using certain strains of *Aspergillus niger* that are overproducers. Itaconic acid improves the properties of fibres, paints, surface coatings and carpet backings, and is used in the manufacture of adhesives.

ITP *See* inosine 5′-triphosphate.

J

jejunum The region of the mammalian small intestine that lies between the ileum and the duodenum.

Jerusalem artichoke A plant (*Helianthus tuberosus*) related to the sunflower capable of producing high levels of carbohydrate, in the form of the fructose polymer inulin, in its underground tubers. It has been widely investigated as a potential raw material for the production of fuel alcohol (ethanol), acetone–butanol for use as a cosolvent or oxygenate in petroleum mixes, or as a source of fructose syrups.

jet loop fermenter A fermentation system in which agitation and gas absorption are achieved by recirculation of the broth with re-injection into the main fermenter vessel under pressure.

joule (J) A unit of energy equal to 0.28846 calories. *See* calorie, SI units.

juglone A naphthoquinone derived from walnuts.

jumping gene *See* transposon.

juvenile hormone One of several terpenoids which inhibits metamorphosis and promotes the growth of larval structures in insects. The hormones are secreted by the corpora allata.

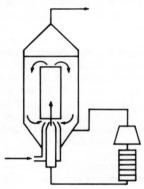

Jet loop fermenter

Juvenile hormone III

K

k_L Mass transfer coefficient for oxygen movement from the gas to the liquid phase in fermentation. Usually used in a combined form as $k_L a$.

K_m Michaelis constant or Monod coefficient. *See* enzyme kinetics.

$k_L a$ *See* volumetric oxygen transfer coefficient.

kairomone A chemical emitted by one species of animal which modifies the behaviour of a different species of animal to the benefit of the receptor species.

kanamycin An inhibitor of protein synthesis. It acts by binding on to 70S ribosomes causing the mRNA to be misread. It is mainly used with gram-negative organisms.

kanamycin resistance The ability to survive treatment with kanamycin mediated by an enzyme that modifies the antibiotic and prevents its interaction with ribosomes.

karykinesis The division of a cell nucleus in which the genetic complement of the daughter cells is identical to that of the parent cell. *See* mitosis.

karyogamy In sexual reproduction, the fusion of the nuclear material of the gametes or especially in some fungi the fusion of the nuclei of a heterokaryotic cell.

karyotype Descriptive of the chromosome complement of a cell or organism. Since each organism has a distinctive karyotype in terms of chromosome number and chromosome appearance, it represents a characteristic that can be used in the identification of a species or the parents of a hybrid, as well as in the recognition of a polyploid.

karyotyping The identification and classification of organisms, cells or tissues on the basis of their chromosome content.

Kautsky effect In photosynthesis, the transient pattern of fluorescence that occurs on illumination of a leaf previously kept in the dark.

Kb An abbreviation for kilobase.

kefir A fermented milk product produced in the USSR using a mixture of symbiotic yeasts, lactobacilli, leuconostocs and lactic streptococci.

kelp A number of different genera of large brown seaweeds, some of which are used as a source of alginic acid. Kelp has also been suggested as a source of biomass for use in anaerobic digesters for the production of biogas. Studies have been carried out in which high concentrations of kelp were grown on floating islands.

keratin A structural protein with a high sulphur content that is found in hair, feathers, horn, nails, etc., as well as in the outer layer of the epidermis of vertebrates.

keratinization The accumulation of keratin by a cell.

kestose A non-reducing trisaccharide formed by the condensation of sucrose and fructose with (2,6)- and (2,1)-linkages. The related trisaccharide iso-kestose is similar, with (2,1):(2,1)-linkages.

keto acid An acid containing a ketone group. In biological systems, organic acids with such a group in the α position are important precursors in amino acid production (e.g., α-ketoglutaric acid).

keto group A group of the form $>C=O$ in organic chemical compounds.

keto sugar *See* ketose.

ketogenesis The formation of ketone bodies from acetyl-CoA produced in fatty acid oxidation.

α-ketoglutaric acid A dicarboxylic acid, an intermediate of the TCA cycle and a precursor of the amino acid glutamic acid.

ketohexose A six-carbon ketose.

ketone A compound in the class of chemicals having the general formula RCOR'.

ketone bodies Compounds such as acetoacetate, hydroxybutyrate and acetone formed in the liver during fatty acid oxidation by condensation of acetyl-CoA. Ketone bodies normally pass into the blood and are transported to peripheral tissue where they are metabolized.

ketose A monosaccharide that contains a ketone group or its equivalent.

ketosis An abnormality metabolism which results in over-production of ketone bodies. This may be associated with diabetes or prolonged starvation. The condition leads to acidosis and coma.

kettle boil The heating of wort to inactivate enzymes, precipitate impurities and concentrate the sugar solution prior to inoculation with yeast.

keV An abbreviation of kiloelectron volt.

kidney Organ, usually paired, that performs the functions of excretion and osmoregulation in vertebrates. The individual units of the kidneys (nephrons) consist of a narrow uriniferous tubule terminating at the Bowman's capsule which encloses a knot of capillaries, the glomerulus. The capsule plus the glomerulus forms the corpuscle (malpighian body). The uriniferous tubules drain to paired ureters which open into the bladder or cloaca. The mammalian kidney is divided into an outer cortex in which the corpuscles are concentrated and an inner medulla which contains the collecting ducts. Water, salts, sugars, nitrogenous wastes and other low-molecular-weight compounds are filtered into the Bowman's capsule. Much of the water, together with mineral salts and glucose, is re-absorbed and the remaining water and nitrogenous compounds excreted as urine.

kieselguhr A type of diatomaceous earth that is used as a filter aid.

kilo (k) A prefix indicating that a number is multiplied to the power of 10^3.

kilobase (kb) A sequence of 1000 bases or base pairs in DNA, other nucleic acids or oligonucleotides. The term is used to define the size of the genome of a specific organism or of various fractions of nucleic acids following extraction or cleavage using restriction enzymes.

kilocalorie (Cal) A unit of energy; 1000 calories. It may be referred to as the large calorie or Calorie, as used in food and nutrition.

kiloelectron volt (keV) A unit of energy of 1000 electron volts. The energy of electron sources such as in X-ray machines or electron microscopes is usually expressed in terms of kiloelectron volts.

kilogram (kg) A unit of weight; 1000 grams.

kinase An enzyme that catalyses the phosphorylation of an organic compound; an enzyme which converts a zymogen to the active enzyme form.

kinetic viscosity A description of the flow behaviour of a fluid expressed in terms of the ratio of the dynamic viscosity to the density of the material measured at the same temperature.

kinetics The study of the rate of chemical reactions. *See* enzyme kinetics.

kinetin A synthetic plant growth substance; one of the family of kinins. It delays leaf senescence in some species.

kinetosome The basal body of structures such as cilia.

kinin (1) In animals, any of a number of polypeptides (e.g., bradykinin) that occur in blood and cause contraction of smooth muscle and dilation of blood vessels. (2) A type of plant growth substance derived from purines that stimulates plant cell division, working synergistically with auxin. The balance between kinin and auxin also affects morphogenesis and cell expansion. Natural kinins (e.g., zeatin) are known as cytokinins or phytokinins. Synthetic analogues include kinetin (6-furfurylaminopurine) and benzyladenine (6-benzylaminopurine).

kit A package containing all the specialized reagents, enzymes, buffers, cloning vectors, linkers, primers, etc. Required to carry out a particular diagnostic procedure or technique in molecular biology. In general, the kit provides the right proportions of the various components, packaged in a manner to make the best and most cost-effective use of expensive or difficult-to-obtain components. Some components may be pre-weighed, partially pre-fabricated or attached to solid supports in order to overcome the need to engage in time-consuming preparative steps.

Kjeldahl method An analytic technique used to determine the amount of nitrogen in a sample. It is often used for the determination of total protein in a sample on the basis of the nitrogen content. The sample is digested with concentrated sulphuric acid in the presence of potassium sulphate, copper sulphate and sodium selenate under reflux for about eight hours. The sample is then transferred quantitatively to a distillation apparatus the neck of which is immersed in a solution of boric acid. Sodium hydroxide is added to the digestion products and steam passed through the mixture so that ammonia distils over into the boric acid solution. The absorbed ammonia is then determined by titration with standard hydrochloric acid (1 ml of 0.01 M HCl corresponds to 0.14 mg of nitrogen). This method measures *total* nitrogen. Most proteins have a nitrogen content of about 16 per cent, thus to convert the nitrogen value into a weight of protein it is multiplied by 6.25.

Klebsiella pneumoniae A gram-negative bacteria that is capable of fixing atmospheric nitrogen. *K. pneumoniae* is widely used as a model system for studies on the molecular biology and genetics of nitrogen fixation (nif) genes.

Klenow fragment *See* DNA polymerase I.

Klinefelter's syndrome A group of symptoms found in humans due to the presence of one extra X chromosome in the male karyotype (XXY).

Kluyveromyces A genus of yeast used in the production of biomass (single-cell protein).

knowledge base In expert systems, the representation of knowledge by rules, objects, frames and procedures.

knowledge management In expert systems, a module used to implement and handle the knowledge in the knowledge base.

Koji A fungal protease derived from *Aspergillus oryzae* grown on rice as a solid substrate fermentation.

kojic acid 5-Hydroxy-2-hydroxymethyl-gamma-pyrone; a product of glucose metabolism generated by some moulds and bacteria, including *Aspergillus* and *Acetobacter*.

koumiss A fermented milk product produced in the USSR. It is similar to kefir, except that it is produced from mares' milk.

Kranz-syndrome The group of anatomical, morphological and biochemical characteristics that distinguish plants with the C_4 pathway of photosynthesis from those with the C_3 pathway. These characteristics include the presence of a chloroplast-bearing bundle sheath surrounded by a radially arranged mesophyll layer.

Krebs cycle *See* tricarboxylic acid cycle.

Kuru *See* spongiform encephalopathy.

L

L chain *See* light chain.

L form A form of bacteria in which the ability to form the cell wall has been lost. L forms can divide and give rise to L-form colonies on suitable media.

label An element, isotope or chemical compound that is attached to a biological molecule, organelle, subcellular fragment or cell in order to follow the latter's metabolism or fate. In general, labels fall into three classes: (1) isotopic labels, which may be radioactive or heavy isotopes; (2) immune labels, which may be antibodies or antigens; (3) coloured or fluorescent dyes. *See* affinity labelling, fluorochrome, radioactive labelling.

laboratory scale Descriptive of the process carried out using only small amounts (i.e., milligrams or grams) of reagents in order to validate the nature of the products and the characteristics of the reaction.

lac (lactose) operon A transcriptional unit that codes for the three enzymes required for the metabolism of lactose by *E. coli*. In addition to the three structural genes coding for the enzymes β-galactosidase, galactoside permease and galactose acetylase, the lac operon contains a promoter site, an operator site, a site for interaction with a catabolic activator protein (CAP) and a gene coding for the synthesis of the repressor protein. These genes occur in a control region consisting of 122 nucleotides that enables the structural genes to be switched on, or induced, by a change in metabolite availability (i.e., substitution of lactose for glucose in the growth medium).

β-lactam A four-element ring that occurs in the base structure of some antibiotics notably penicillins and cephalosporins.

lactam group *See* cephalosporin, penicillin.

β-lactamase *See* penicillinase.

lactase *See* galactosidase.

lactation The production of milk by the mammary glands. This is promoted by hormones produced by various glands including the pituitary, thyroid and adrenal glands, as well as by the placenta and ovaries. Secretion is stimulated by prolactin (produced by the pituitary) and adrenal corticosteroids, whereas milk ejection requires the action of oxytocin and vasopressin.

lactic acid A three-carbon organic acid produced during some fermentations and during the breakdown of glucose under anaerobic conditions.

lactic acid bacteria A trivial name applied to a diverse group of bacteria, which are characterized by the production of lactic acid during fermentation of carbohydrate. Genera include genera *Lactobacillus* and *Streptococcus*. These bacteria are of particular importance in food fermentation including dairy products (cheese, buttermilk, yoghurt and sour cream), pickles, fermented sausage and sour dough bread. Lactic acid is the main product produced by homofermentative species, whereas a mixture of lactic acid, ethanol, acetic acid, glycerol and carbon dioxide is produced by heterofermentative species.

lactic heterofermentation A type of fermentation occurring in some microorganisms, the end products being lactic acid, ethanol and carbon dioxide. The metabolic pathway may be referred to as the phosphoketolase pathway. Initially carbon dioxide is produced during conversion of glucose-6-phosphate to xylulose-5-phosphate. Xylulose-5-phosphate then is cleaved to glyceraldehyde-3-phosphate, which is converted to lactate and acetyl-phosphate. Finally ethanol is formed via acetaldehyde.

lactic homofermentation A type of fermentation that produces lactic acid as the end product through metabolism of glucose via glycolysis with the reduction of pyruvate to lactate.   ,

lactifers Cells or vessels containing latex, found in vascular plants.

Lactobacillus A genus of rod-shaped, gram-positive bacteria characterized by the production of lactic acid as an end product of metabolism, through a heterofermentative route or a homofermentative route. Members of this genus are widely used in the production of fermented milk products including cheese and acidophilous milk. These bacteria are also involved in beer and wine spoilage.

Lactobacillus plantarum A species of bacterium that is used for vitamin assays and the fermentation of pickles and sauerkraut. It is also used in the starter cultures for various dairy products and in the production of silage.

lactogenic hormone *See* prolactin.

lactoglobulin A crystalline protein obtained from milk.

lactosamine A disaccharide that occurs in many of the carbohydrate groups attached to the surface of proteins.

lactose 4-*O*-β-D-Galactopyranosyl-D-glucopyranose; a disaccharide comprising galactose and glucose. Lactose occurs in milk.

laevorotatory Descriptive of a chemical compound with optical activity. In solution, it bends polarized light to the left. *Compare* dextrorotatory.

lag phase The initial part of the characteristic growth curve found in most living systems. In microbial cultures, inoculation of a new medium may not result in immediate growth. Cell numbers remain stationary or increase only slowly while the cells become acclimatized to the new conditions of growth. The lag phase may be avoided if an active culture, in the exponential phase of growth, is introduced at a fairly high concentration into fresh medium of a similar composition to that used previously.

lager A beer produced using a bottom yeast (*Saccharomyces uvarum*). This yeast tends to flocculate and settle as the fermentation proceeds.

lagging strand In replication of DNA, the strand of the duplex that reads from the 5'-end to the 3'-end and thus cannot be copied directly.

LAM-1 Leukocyte adhesion molecule-1; a glycoprotein that occurs on neutrophils and leukocytes. LAM-1 is involved in cell-to-cell binding.

lambda phage Bacteriophage lambda; a genetically complex, but extensively studied virus of *E. coli* and other enterobacteria, that has been developed as a cloning vehicle. The DNA of this phage is a linear duplex molecule of 49,000 pairs. At each end are short, single-stranded 5'-projections of 12 nucleotides, that are complementary in sequence and by which the DNA adopts a circular structure when it is injected into its host cell. Functionally related genes are grouped together. These include a central portion that is not essential for phage growth and that can be deleted and replaced without impairing the infectious growth cycle. In the lytic cycle, transcription occurs in three stages: (1) gene transcription establishes the lytic cycle; (2) gene products replicate and recombine the DNA; (3) gene products package the DNA into mature phage particles. Derivatives of the wild-type DNA have been produced that have a single target site for construction of insertional vectors, or two sites for production of replacement vectors. Hence the usual enzyme techniques of DNA cutting and rejoining can be used to insert sequences coding for other genes. The infectivity of such recombinant DNA can be increased by packaging it back into a phage particle.

Lambert–Beer's law An expression for the measurement of optical density or extinction coefficients:

$$\log(I_0/I) = E = \varepsilon c d$$

where E = extinction, ε = molar extinction coefficient, c = concentration of substance, d = length of light path, I_0 = intensity of the incident beam and I = intensity of transmitted beam

lamella A thin, plate-like structure. In plants, lamellae are the layers of closely appressed membranes that occur in the chloroplasts. They are associated with the light-dependent bio-physical and photochemical reactions. In higher plants, the lamellae generally appear in section to be stacked as grana, linked by intergranal membranes, whereas in the bundle sheath of extreme C_4 plants and in most algae, such stacking is not seen. It now seems that the complex internal system of lamellae is derived from the folds and connections of a continuous sheet of membrane that divides the volume within the chloroplast envelope into two compartments, each forming a separate continuum. One compartment is the stroma proper; the other represents the intracisternal volume enclosed within the membrane. If this hypothesis is accepted, the term lamella loses much of its original meaning.

lamina The flattened photosynthetic blade of a leaf, or similar flattened terminal portion of the thallus of lower plants.

laminar flow A description of the flow behaviour of a fluid through a pipe in which the molecules move parallel with the pipe surface. It is also known as streamline flow. In the laminar layers, transfer of momentum, heat or mass can only occur by diffusion.

laminaribiose A disaccharide of glucose linked through 3-O-β-links, produced during the hydrolysis of storage polysaccharides from the brown algae.

laminarin A polysaccharide formed from linear chains of β-(1,3)-linked glucose units. It is a major storage compound in brown algae.

lampbrush chromosome A form of chromosome that occurs in the oocytes of many vertebrates. These chromosomes are larger and less condensed than the normal ones. They bear a large number of paired loops arising from the chromomere which gives them the characteristic appearance from which the name is derived.

landfill gas A mixture of methane (50–65 per cent) and carbon dioxide (30–40 per cent) together with traces of nitrogen, hydrogen and a wide range of volatile organic compounds generated by anaerobic bacteria present in landfill waste disposal sites. This gas can cause problems because of its smell, as well as being a possible hazard since it is flammable if diluted with air to 5–15 per cent methane content. Control measures may be needed to prevent gas migration through land drains, cracks, etc. In some cases, the gas is extracted and cleaned to provide fuel gas, which is of similar quality to natural gas. Gas production from large sites is measured in terms of thousands of cubic metres per day.

landfill site An area of land where domestic solid refuse and similar waste is discharged and buried.

large external transformation-sensitive protein (LETS) *See* fibronectin.

large scale Descriptive of a process carried out using the amounts of material (i.e., kilograms or tonnes) that are similar to those required for commercial production of the product.

laser scanning A technique in which the image is built up by scanning a laser across a microscopic object. *See also* CLSM.

latent period The time that elapses between the reception of a stimulus and the onset of a response.

latent virus A virus that remains within the host without producing any obvious effects. Activity may be induced, resulting in multiplication and the production of disease symptoms, long after the initial infection.

latex A liquid found in certain plants that contains a variety of secondary products, often including terpenes, terpenoids and alkaloids. High-molecular-weight products found in latex include rubber. Other polyisoprenes include gutta and chicle (the original chewing gum base). Latex accumulates in specific cells or vessels known as lactifers.

latex agglutination A serological test in which the antigen or antibody is adsorbed on to polystyrene latex particles. When incubated with the other reactant (antibody or antigen, respectively) a positive reaction is indicated by aggregation of the latex particles that can be detected visually.

latex cells *See* lactifers.

lauric acid Dodecanoic acid; a long-chain fatty acid widely distributed in animal and vegetable fats and oils.

LD$_{50}$ A measure of toxicity of a chemical substance or of the susceptibility of organisms to radiation or viral infection. It is the dose of a specific chemical, level of radiation or titre of virus that is lethal to 50 per cent of the treated population.

L-DOPA *See* dihydroxyphenylalanine.

leachate An aqueous solution containing organic or inorganic material. It results from the percolation of water through various types of solid. For example, rain water running through a landfill waste disposal site will become contaminated with water-soluble organic materials present in the original waste, as well as low-molecular-weight compounds formed by the action of anaerobic organisms. In the same way, water percolating through deposits of mineral ore that contain sulphur bacteria has significant concentrations of metal salts in solution. *See* microbial leaching.

leader peptide A short peptide synthesized *in vitro* by translation of the leader sequence of some bacterial mRNAs. These peptides are not formed *in vivo*.

leader sequence A length of mRNA, extending from the 5'-end to the beginning of the coding region of the first structural gene, that is not translated during protein synthesis. It may contain ribosomal binding sites or an attenuator.

leading strand In replication of DNA, the strand read from the 3'-end to the 5'-end, which can be replicated directly.

leaf A lateral appendage of the stem of plants. It functions in photosynthesis and transpiration. Leaves produce lateral buds in their axis. Types of true leaves include cotyledons, scale leaves, bracts and some floral parts (petals, sepals). In some plants (xerophytes), the leaves may be much reduced in size, with the leaf functions being taken over by other organs such as cladodes or phyllodes.

leavening agent A compound or system used in baked food products to produce carbon dioxide. Production of such gas causes the mix or dough to rise. Chemical leavening is carried out using baking powder (a mixture of sodium bicarbonate and acid salts). An alternative is to use a fermenting yeast culture. Baked goods prepared using fermenting yeast have a better flavour because of the reaction of fermentation products with other ingredients. However, the leavening power of yeasts is low in dough systems of high osmotic pressure. Hence, breads, rolls and buns are usually leavened with yeasts, whereas cakes and biscuits are leavened using chemical agents.

LECAMs Leukocyte endothelial cell:cell adhesion molecules; glycoproteins that occur on the surface of platelets or endothelial cells in response to inflammatory or thrombogenic agents and promote cell-to-cell adhesion. *See* ELAM-1, LAM-1, PADGEM.

LEC-CAMs *See* LECAMs.

lecithin Diacyl glyceryl phosphorylcholine or phosphatidylcholine; a type of phospholipid.

lectins Proteins isolated from plant tissue that are capable of binding to the antigenic glycoproteins on the surface of cells, causing the cells to agglutinate. Lectins can agglutinate red blood cells, in certain cases, with a high degree of specificity such that they may be used in typing of human blood. Lectins may also preferentially agglutinate certain malignant cells. Lectins may be formed as antibodies by the plants to counteract soil bacteria or to protect against fungal attack. High concentrations of lectins are found especially in the seeds of some legumes, being localized in the cytoplasm of the cotyledons and embryonic cells. Varying levels are found in root, shoots and leaves. The lectin of soya bean has been studied in detail and the oligosaccharide moiety shown to include mannose and D-*N*-acetylglucosamine. Not all lectins are glycoproteins, for example, concanavalin A is a pure protein. They are also called phytoagglutinins.

leghaemoglobin A component of the nodules in nitrogen-fixing plants. It occurs in the bacteroid membrane, although it is synthesized on the plant genome. It is a haemoglobin-like molecule with a high affinity for oxygen and functions to protect the nitrogenase inside the bacteroid from detrimental effects of oxygen while providing adequate oxygen in the bacteroid membrane to allow respiration to proceed to generate the ATP required for nitrogen fixation.

legume (1) The trivial name for a member of the plant family Leguminosae. Members of this family are of interest since they are capable of entering a symbiotic relationship with nitrogen-fixing bacteria. (2) The fruit formed from a monocarpellary ovary in the plant family Leguminosae.

legumin A storage protein (along with vici-

lin) found in seeds of legumes. The protein has twelve components, each with an average molecular weight of 33,000. It contains more acidic and basic residues than vicilin, and three times as many tryptophan residues.

Leishman's stain A stain used in haematology. It stains some blood cells red-pink.

lenticel A region of loosely packed cells which occurs in the outer layer of the covering of the roots and stems (periderm) of woody plants. The cells function as a means of gaseous exchange.

Lepidoptera Moths and butterflies; an order of insects, characterized by a covering of bright scales over the wings and bodies. They are of particular importance since the larvae (caterpillars) feed on plant leaves and stems, and are thus serious plant pests. Caterpillars are unusual in that their intestinal pH is alkaline, hence the toxic spore protein formed by the bacteria *Bacillus thuringiensis* may be used as a selective pest control agent.

leptotene A stage in the prophase of the first division of meiosis.

lethal dose *See* LD$_{50}$.

lethal gene An allele introduced by gene or chromosomal mutation that produces such a degree of change in an essential protein that it can no longer fulfil its proper function. If dominant, it leads to the early death of the developing embryo in all carriers. Death only occurs, however, when present in the homozygous form if it is recessive.

lethal mutation *See* lethal gene.

LETS Large external transformation-sensitive protein. *See* fibronectin.

Leu An abbreviation used to denote the amino acid leucine in protein sequences and elsewhere.

leucine (Leu) One of the twenty common

amino acids found in proteins and an essential amino acid for man.

Leucine $(CH_3)_2CHCH_2CH(NH_2)COOH$

leucocyte A white blood cell. A number of different types of non-pigmented, nucleate, amoeboid cells occur in the blood of animals. They are generally divided into two groups: polymorphs (basophils, neutrophils and eosinophils) characterized by a granular cytoplasm; lymphocytes and monocytes. In vertebrates, leucocytes protect the body against infection.

leucocyte adhesion molecule-1 *See* LAM-1.

leucocyte endothelial cell:cell adhesion molecules *See* LECAMs.

leucocyte interferon (α-interferon, INF-α) An antiviral protein isolated from blood. Normal leucocytes cannot be cultivated, hence mass production is hampered unless gene manipulation techniques, transformed cells or hybridomas are used.

Leuconostoc A genus of microaerophilic, spore-forming, gram-positive cocci that produce lactic acid. *Leuconostoc* species also produce large amounts of an extracellular polysaccharide (dextran) and are used in the commercial production of dextran, as well as in the production of a number of fermented dairy products.

leucoplast An unpigmented plastid.

leucosin A storage polysaccharide [β-(1,3)-glucan] found in the Bacillariophyceae (diatoms). Leucosin is structurally related to laminarin and chrysolaminarin.

leukaemia A malignant disease, characterized by the abnormal proliferation of leucocytes. Some forms of leukaemia may be associated with a viral infection.

leukotriene A compound derived from arachidonic acid by the action of lipooxygenases that are produced by mast cells and neutrophils. Leukotrienes have various functions: some cause the constriction of smooth muscle, others increase vascular permeability and cause aggregation and degranulation of neutrophils.

levan A polysaccharide formed from chains of β-(2,6)-linked fructosefuranose units branched through β-(1,2)-links.

Lewis x A tetrasaccharide that occurs on cell surface glycoproteins and cell surface glycolipid carbohydrates. It is the ligand for LECAMs.

LFG *See* landfill gas.

LH *See* luteinizing hormone.

LHCP gene The gene that encodes the light-harvesting chlorophyll a/b binding protein.

library *See* gene library.

lichens Thallophytic plants formed through the symbiotic association of a fungus (mycobiont), which is either a basidiomycete or an ascomycete, and an alga (phycobiont). The morphology of the plant body is quite distinct from that of either of the constituents.

life cycle The sum of the various stages through which an organism passes from conception to death; the description of the various stages through which an organism passes from the fertilized egg cell of one generation to the same stage in the next generation. In the simplest life cycles, the offspring is formed by simple asexual binary division. The most complex life cycles, as found in some parasitic organisms, may involve the development of a number of distinct morphological and reproductive stages. In those organisms that have sexual reproduction, an alternation of generations may be recognized, with both a haploid and a diploid genetic state; either may be dominant. *See* diplobiont, diplont, haplobiont, haplont.

ligament The fibrous tissue connecting bones in movable joints of vertebrates. The ligaments are made up of bundles of nonextensible collagen fibres and lie inside or outside the capsule that encloses the joint.

ligand A neutral molecule or charged ion that complexes with a metal ion to form a complex ion.

ligase An enzyme that catalyses the condensation of two molecules coupled to the breakdown of a pyridine triphosphate (ATP, GTP, UTP, etc.). Ligases are one of the main groups (EC6) used in enzyme classification;

6.1 forming C–O bonds
6.2 forming C–S bonds
6.3 forming C–N bonds
6.4 forming C–C bonds

They are also known as synthetases. *See* DNA ligase.

ligate (1) To bind. (2) In affinity chromatography, a specific biological entity that is bound to an immobilized ligand.

light The visible region of the electromagnetic spectrum, of wavelength 400–770 nm.

light chain (L chain) Shorter of the two types of polypeptide chain (approximate relative molecular mass = 22,000) present in all immunoglobulin molecules. The light chains are linked, usually covalently, with two heavy chains to form the basic immunoglobulin molecule.

light reactions *See* photosynthesis.

lignans A group of naturally occurring phenylpropanoid dimers. The C_6–C_3 units are joined by carbon–carbon bonds between the middle carbons of their side chains.

lignification The replacement of much of the water in the matrix of higher plant cell walls at the end of the cell growth period by lignin.

lignin A complex, highly ramified three-dimensional polymer of phenylpropane (C_6–C_3) residues. In higher plants, lignin is a major constituent of the cell walls of the

supporting tissues. The structural variations of the individual phenylpropane residues found in lignin are few, but the variations in the manner in which they are linked are numerous. The order of linkage is random and involves no template, hence the structure of each molecule may be unique and cannot be defined. However, it is possible to deduce a hypothetical partial structure based on the nature of the different types of building units, which on mild oxidation can release vanillin, *p*-hydroxybenzaldehyde and syringaldehyde. Gymnosperm lignin yields mostly vanillin and dicotyledonous lignin yields mostly vanillin and syringaldehyde, whereas monocotyledonous lignin yields all three aldehydes. The lignin molecules are probably linked covalently to polysaccharides of the cell wall matrix. The separation of lignin from other constituents (cellulose and hemicellulose) is a major problem that prevents the easy use of the very large amounts of agricultural and forestry wastes, which are generally available at low cost, as substrates for microbial growth.

lignocellulose The complex mixture of lignin, cellulose and hemicellulose that occurs in wood and woody parts of herbs and trees. Most intractable wastes are lignocellulose.

lignocellulose processing A technique, or combination of techniques, used to upgrade the value of lignocellulose by breaking it down to simpler molecules of value. Biological processing involves either direct methods (composting and anaerobic digestion) or more complex processes to generate sugar or alcohol streams. The latter can be divided into three stages: (1) pretreatment by a physical process (steam explosion, milling, grinding, radiation treatment) that reduces the particle size; (2) acid, alkali or organic solvent treatments that separate the fractions to produce lignin, cellulose and sugars or degradation products from the hemicellulose; (3) hydrolysis of the cellulose using cellulase from fungi such as *Trichoderma*. Alternative approaches rely on thermophilic organisms to ferment the cellulose or hemicellulose directly.

lignocellulose waste Forestry and agricultural waste with a high lignocellulose content. These wastes represent a major source of raw material that could be exploited by application of biological techniques to produce food, animal feed, chemicals or liquid and gaseous fuels.

limiting factor An environmental factor or nutritional imbalance that restricts the growth of an organism, culture or population. Although in general limiting factors may be regarded as deficiencies, in some cases growth may be limited if the level of a given component exceeds the limits of tolerance for the organism.

limiting primer *See* asymmetric PCR.

limnology The study of fresh water ecosystems, including biological, physical and chemical aspects.

Lineweaver–Burk plot A mathematical analysis used to treat data obtained from simple enzyme reactions. It enables straight line graphs to be obtained from experimental data derived by measuring rate of reaction as a function of substrate concentration. This is achieved by taking a reciprocal version of the Michaelis–Menten equation:

$$\frac{1}{v} = \frac{K_{\mathrm{m}} + S}{VS}$$

where v = observed velocity, S = substrate concentration, V = maximum velocity and K_{m} = Michaelis constant. For a plot of $1/v$ against $1/S$, the intercept on the y-axis is equal to $1/V$ and the slope of the line is equal to K_{m}/V. Results obtained from allosteric enzymes do not give straight lines.

linkage The occurrence of two or more genes on the same chromosome. Such linked genes do not show independent assortment, although linkage can be broken by crossing-over during meiosis. This leads to recombination (i.e., the formation of new linkage groups in the gametes and hence a new genotype in the progeny).

linkage analysis The determination of the

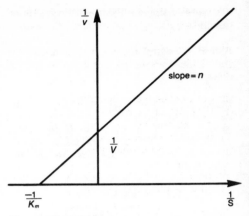

Lineweaver-Burk plot

frequency of crossing-over or recombination of DNA sequences. It is used as a means of establishing the position of a gene, or sequence, in a chromosome or length of DNA. *See* linkage map.

linkage disequilibrium Non-random association of alleles at different loci in a population.

linkage group A set of gene loci that can be placed in a linear order, representing the different degrees of linkage between the loci. The term is applied to all the genes on the same chromosome, hence the number of linkage groups is equal to the haploid number of chromosomes.

linkage map A map constructed from genetic data, derived from crossing-over experiments. It identifies the relative position of loci on a chromosome.

linked enzyme assay A diagnostic procedure in which two or more enzymes are used to catalyse a series of reactions enabling identification and/or quantification of a specific substrate (or levels of a specific enzyme) and the visualization of the result. A common technique is to link one enzyme assay with a second enzyme reaction which results in either the oxidation or reduction of NAD or NADP. The rate of oxidation or reduction of the co-enzyme is then followed by measuring the change in absorbance at 320 nm.

linked genes Genes that are carried on the same chromosome in a nucleus, cell or organism.

linker A chemical compound that is covalently bound to a length of probe DNA to enable subsequent reaction with a signal compound; a chemical compound used to join the first protected nucleotide in solid support synthesis of nucleotides to the support matrix. *See* affinity labelling, oligonucleotide synthesizer.

linoleic acid A long-chain fatty acid containing 18 carbon atoms and two double bonds. It is common in plant lipids

linolenic acid A long-chain unsaturated fatty acid containing 18 carbons and three double bonds. It is a major component of chloroplast lipids.

lipase An enzyme that catalyses the hydrolysis of fats to glycerol and fatty acids. It is more correctly described as a non-specific acyl hydrolase that catalyses the hydrolysis of ester bonds in monoglycerides, glycerophospholipids, diglycerides and monogalactosyl diglyceride. Commercial enzymes are produced from *Candida cylindracea*.

lipid bilayer *See* cell membrane.

lipid micelle A structure formed through the aggregation of lipids in aqueous solution resulting from the orientation of the hydrophobic fatty acid chains at the centre of a sphere with the polar groups directed outwards.

lipid monolayers A thin film of lipids, one molecule thick, which forms on aqueous surfaces, resulting from the orientation of the lipid with the polar groups in the liquid and the fatty acid chains above the surface.

lipids One of the four major classes of compounds found in living organisms. Unlike the others (carbohydrates, proteins and nucleic acids), lipids are difficult to define in a specific way, other than by the fact that they tend to be soluble in organic solvents and insoluble in water. They include fats, waxes, phospholipids, glycolipids, steroids, terpenes and a number of different types of pigments. The major group contains those lipids whose structure is characterized by the presence of fatty acid moieties (acyl lipids). These may be divided into neutral lipids (glycerides and waxes) and polar compounds (phospholipids and glycolipids). Of the acyl lipids, glycerides accumulate as food reserves and are of commercial importance as 'fats and oils'. Phospholipids and glycolipids are structural components of membranes.

lipogenesis The synthesis of fatty acids or lipids.

lipoic acid 6,9-Dithiooctanoic acid; a fatty acid with an eight-carbon chain with a disulphide bridge. It acts as a cofactor in enzyme reactions associated with the oxidative decarboxylation of pyruvate and α-ketoglutarate.

lipolysis The hydrolysis of lipids, and the breakdown of triglycerides in particular, to produce fatty acids which are used in oxidative catabolism. In vertebrates, hormones such as adrenaline and ACTH increase the rate of lipolysis of triglycerides in adipose tissue.

lipophilic *See* hydrophobic.

lipophobic *See* hydrophilic.

lipopolysaccharide A complex substance comprising a polysaccharide based on glucose, galactose, *N*-acetylglucosamine and other sugars linked to lipids. Lipopolysaccharides form, together with lipoproteins, the main constituents of the cell walls of gram-negative bacteria. Lipopolysaccharides are responsible for the antigenic specificity of bacteria.

lipoprotein A protein that is conjugated with a polar lipid.

liposomes An artificial phospholipid vesicle. Macromolecules such as nucleic acids and drugs can be enclosed by liposomes.

lipotrophin (LPH) A product of the mammalian pituitary gland that contains peptides (α- and β-LPH) structurally related to the melanocyte-stimulating hormone. They stimulate lipolysis.

liquefaction A series of biological and/or physico-chemical processes that results in the conversion of insoluble solid organic material into liquid or soluble form. Examples of liquefaction using biocatalysts include the hydrolysis of cellulose or starch to form glucose solutions.

liqueur An alcoholic beverage produced from aromatic extracts of fruit or other plant material to which sugar is added.

liquid chromatography A separation technique in which a mixture of compounds in solution is passed through a column packed with a solid matrix. The sample is loaded on to the column, and various components are eluted sequentially in the effluent from the column. Such systems may be used with packing materials for gel filtration, affinity chromatography, absorption chromatography, etc. Fully automated systems are available as high performance liquid chromatographs.

liquid manure Animal waste from intensive animal husbandry units where no bedding material is used. It is usually collected as a slurry.

liquid nitrogen Nitrogen that has been liquefied using cryogenic techniques. It is used as a refrigerant to keep lyophilized stock cultures frozen at $-130°C$ or as a coolant for instruments such as electron microscopes.

liquid scintillation counter *See* scintillation counter.

liquid-phase protein sequencing *See* spinning cup sequenter.

lithotroph *See* autotroph.

litre (l) A unit of volume equal to 0.26418

gallons (imperial, 0.0353 cubic feet or 1.0567 quarts). It is the volume of one kilogram of water at standard temperature and pressure.

liver An organ found in vertebrates that serves as the site of intermediary metabolism. It receives products of digestion absorbed from the gut via the hepatic portal vein. The liver stores carbohydrates as glycogen and also stores fats. Storage compounds are broken down and metabolized to provide energy. Other functions include the deamination of amino acids with the formation of nitrogenous excretory products, the breakdown of red blood cells, detoxification of poisonous substances and the production of bile, which is stored in the gallbladder. The liver is the site of synthesis of fibrinogen and prothrombin.

load cell An instrument for measuring the weight of a large vessel such as a fermenter. The cell consists of a solid or tubular metal cylinder with gauges on its surface that measure changes in electrical resistance proportional to the compressive strains exerted by a given load.

loading The introduction of a feedstock into a reactor or a sample for analysis into an analytical instrument, or on to a gel or similar support material in a chromatographic or electrophoretic technique.

locus The region of a chromosome that is associated with the expression of a particular gene. The alleles of any one gene occupy the same loci on homologous chromosomes.

log phase growth *See* exponential phase of growth.

long terminal repeats (LTR) Identical sequences, hundreds of base pairs long, that are found at either end of DNA molecules, especially the genomic DNA of retroviruses.

long-day plant A plant that apparently flowers in response to an extended period of light. The critical factor is in fact the period of uninterrupted darkness to which the plant is subject; a single flash of white or red light during a prolonged period of dark will stimulate flowering in long-day plants. This effect can be reversed using a flash of far red light, indicating that a phytochrome response is involved.

loop fermenter A bioreactor in which the culture medium is continuously recycled through two chambers, or through a side arm attached to a single vessel, as an aid to mixing and mass transfer.

low-pressure liquid chromatography An automated system for carrying out liquid chromatography.

Lowry method The most widely used chemical method of protein analysis. A sample containing up to 500 μg of protein is dissolved in a solution of sodium carbonate, copper sulphate, sodium hydroxide and sodium potassium tartrate, followed by addition of the phenol reagent. The dark blue colour produced, by interaction of the reagents with tyrosine in the protein, is compared colorimetrically with the colour generated using standards, usually bovine serum albumin (BSA).

LPH *See* lipotrophin.

LTR *See* long terminal repeats.

luciferin   4,5-Dihydro-2-(6-hydroxy-2-benzothiazolyl)-4-thiazolecarboxylic acid; a substrate for the light-emitting reaction responsible for the luminescent properties of many organisms. Luciferin forms a complex (luciferyl adenylate) with ATP which is then bound by the enzyme luciferase. During oxidation the activated luciferin emits light. The overall reaction is used to detect living organisms or to quantify very low levels of bacterial contamination, for instance, through the detection of the light emitted using a photomultiplier system.

lumen (1) The central cavity of a duct or tube. (2) The inner space of a plant cell.

luminescence Light emission by a chemical reaction occurring at ambient temperature.

lung A vertebrate organ with a moist invaginated epithelial surface across which respiratory gas exchange takes place.

luteinizing hormone (LH) A glycoprotein secreted by the pars distalis of the pituitary, secretion being controlled by the hypothalamus. In females, the hormone promotes the maturation of the graafian follicles with the production of oestrogens and is essential for ovulation and the formation of the corpora lutea. In males, it stimulates androgen production by the interstitial cells of the testes.

lyase An enzyme that catalyses the addition of groups to double bonds or the formation of double bonds. Lyases are one of the main groups (EC 4) used in enzyme classification:

> 4.1 C–C lyases
> 4.2 C–O lyases
> 4.3 C–N lyases
> 4.4 C–S lyases
> 4.5 C–halide lyases
> 4.99 other lyases

Lyme disease A vector-borne disease transmitted by ticks. Lyme disease develops in three stages: a rash accompanied by non-specific flu symptoms; cardiac and neurological disorders; arthritic symptoms that are often permanently debilitating. The disease is treatable with antibiotics in the early stages.

lymph The colourless fluid found in the vessels of the lymphatic system. It is derived from the interstitial fluid and contains both salts and lymphocytes, but has a lower protein content than blood plasma.

lymph node A structure comprising lymphoid tissue that lies in the course of the main lymphatic vessels and acts as filters for the removal of foreign bodies such as bacteria, thus preventing them from entering the blood stream. Lymphocytes are formed in the cortex of the lymph nodes.

lymphatic system A closed system of vessels through which the lymph is transported from the interstitial fluid to the blood stream. The flow of lymph in mammals is maintained by muscular activity.

lymphocyte A white cell arising from tissue of the lymphoid system. There are two types of lymphocytes: B cells and T cells. These cells are capable of being stimulated by an antigen to produce a specific antibody to that antigen and to proliferate to produce a population of such antibody-producing cells.

lymphocyte activation factor *See* lymphokine.

lymphocytic leukemia A form of blood cancer in which a clone of white blood cells continuously increases in number.

lymphoid tissue Tissue found in vertebrates that is responsible for the production of lymphocytes. Lymphoid tissue may be organized in the form of organs such as the lymph nodes, the thymus, spleen or tonsils, or may occur as aggregations of cells in the respiratory and gastrointestinal tract.

lymphokine Any of a number of soluble physiologically active factors produced by T lymphocytes in response to specific antigens. Important in cell mediated immunity, lymphokines include interferon, macrophage arming factor, lymphocyte inhibition factor, macrophage inhibition factor, chemotactic factor and various cytotoxic factors.

lymphoma A malignant growth that arises in the lymph nodes.

lyophilization Freeze drying. It is used as a method of end product recovery and as a means of preserving cultures of various microorganisms. The bacteria, yeast or spores are frozen and the water is removed by sublimation under vacuum.

lyophilized culture A preparation of microorganisms produced by freeze drying. The desiccated cultures are sealed under vacuum in glass ampoules and stored at

about 4°C. The tube may subsequently be opened and the organisms recultured.

Lys An abbreviation used to denote the amino acid lysine in protein sequences and elsewhere.

lysine (Lys) One of the twenty common amino acids found in protein and an essential amino acid for man.

Lysine $H_2N(CH_2)_4CH(NH_2)COOH$

lysine production Lysine is produced by fermentation, generally using molasses as substrate. Some methods use a double fermentation in which diaminopimelate is produced by a strain of *E. coli* and is then decarboxylated by *Aerobacter aerogenes*. Direct production of lysine is possible using *Corynebacterium glutamicum* or *Brevibacterium flavum*.

lysis The destruction of a cell by rupture of its outer membrane or envelope.

lysogen A strain of bacteria carrying a prophage.

lysogenic bacteria *See* lysogen.

lysogenic pathway The sequence of development of a phage that results in the production of a lysogen. In this form of development, almost all of the genes carried by the phage are repressed. This requires the insertion of the phage genome into the host genome, as well as activation of repressor synthesis. The repressor represses the synthesis of the products of other genes and regulates its own synthesis, with the concentration of repressor controlling the rate of synthesis of its own mRNA. *Compare* lytic pathway.

lysogeny A relationship between a bacteriophage and a host bacterium in which infection does not initiate the synthesis of more phage material. Instead the phage becomes attached to a specific site on the chromosome of the bacterium, thus forming a lysogen, and is reproduced together with the chromosome being transmitted at each cell division to the daughter cells. In this prophage stage, the virus genome is repressed and the phage DNA becomes indistinguishable in behaviour from a specific region of the bacterial chromosome. Spontaneous vegetative development of the phage leading to cell lysis may occur in a small proportion of lysogenic cells, releasing a number of phage particles, or this transformation can be induced by mutagens or ultraviolet radiation. Lysogenization may cause a hereditary modification of a particular bacterial property such as the ability to produce diphtheria toxins in *Corynebacterium diphtheriae*.

lysosome An organelle found in eukaryotic cells that contains hydrolytic enzymes including lipases, proteases, phosphatases and nucleases. In animals, the function of lysosomes is to digest organic matter brought into the cell by endocytosis and degenerating intracellular components. The products of digestion are released into the cytoplasm and re-used. Many of the hydrolases characteristic of animal lysosomes

have also been found in the vacuoles of cells from a variety of members of the plant kingdom. Hence, the plant cell vacuole may be considered to function as a lysosome. Lysosomes may be derived from vesicles of the Golgi apparatus.

lysozyme An enzyme that catalyses the hydrolysis of a β-(1,4)-glycosidic bond between the N-acetylmuramic acid and N-acetylglucosamine residues of the mucopeptide found in the cell walls of many bacteria. This action weakens the covalent structure of the wall and reduces its resistance to osmotic swelling, as a result of which the cells burst.

lytic cycle A sequence of events that occurs when a susceptible bacterium is infected by a virulent phage. Following infection of the host by the viral chromosome, a series of enzymes are formed which, in conjunction with the pre-existing metabolic machinery of the infected cell, catalyse the formation of more phage nucleic acids and protein. In the late stage of the infection, the structural

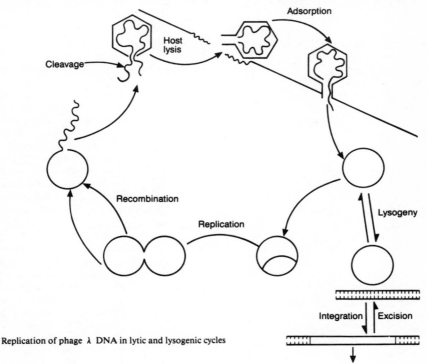

Replication of phage λ DNA in lytic and lysogenic cycles

subunits are assembled within the infected cell to form new virions. At the end of this latent or vegetative phase of development, the host cell is lysed (i.e., bursts) to release the phage, which may then infect other cells and repeat the cycle. Why the lytic pathway is followed in some infected cells and the lysogenic pathway in others is not known, although the mechanism of control is known. *See* lytic cycle control.

lytic cycle control A mechanism whereby the pathway of transcription of phage DNA is controlled in such a way that either the lytic pathway or the lysogenic pathway is followed. If a protein (cI repressor) is formed the lysogeny results, if cro protein is formed progeny are formed.

lytic pathway The sequence of reactions involved in the expression of the phage genes that results in the completion of a lytic cycle. The genes of the phage are regulated to permit controlled DNA replication, recombination, and synthesis and assembly of the progeny phage. In the prophage stage, all the genes required for progeny production are repressed by a repressor protein which acts by binding to operator genes. In the absence of repressor, transcription is initiated at two promoter sites, one of which produces the N protein which prevents termination by interacting with the RNA transcriptase. This allows synthesis of mRNA required for the production of structural proteins, assembly of the virus and lysis of the host cell. *Compare* lysogenic pathway.

M

M phase The part of the cell cycle during which mitosis occurs.

Mab *See* monoclonal antibody.

macerozyme A pectinase-rich enzyme preparation derived from *Rhizopus* species that is used to break down plant cell walls, particularly in the preparation of protoplasts.

macrobead A large particle used as the stationary phase in affinity columns where large molecules or whole cells are being separated.

macrolide A high-molecular-weight molecule that is not a polymer of smaller subunits of similar chemical form. For example, the term is applied to the antibiotic erythromycin, which is the most widely used of the macrolide group of antibiotics, characterized by a large lactone ring linked with novel amino sugars. Erythromycin inhibits protein synthesis and is active against gram-positive organisms.

macromolecule A high-molecular-weight polymer. Proteins, carbohydrates and nucleic acids are all macromolecules.

macronutrient *See* major element.

macrophage A motile white cell type found in vertebrate tissue, including connective tissue, the spleen, lymph nodes, liver, adrenal glands and pituitary, as well as in the endothelial lining of blood vessels and the sinusoids of bone marrow, and in the monocytes. They display phagocytic activity and process antigens for presentation to lymphocytes, which then prepare antigen-specific antibodies.

macrophage chemoattractant protein-1 (MCP-1) *See* MCAF.

macrophage chemotactic and activating factor *See* MCAF.

magnetic enzyme immunoassay (MEIA) An immunoassay in which a magnetic solid support is used to enable the reactants to be removed for quantitative measurement using a magnetic field rather than by centrifugation.

magnetic immunoassay An analytical technique in which an antibody is immobilized on a magnetic microcarrier. This is added to a sample, allowed to react with an antigen and recovered by applying a magnetic force to the bottom of the tube containing the sample, rather than using centrifugation.

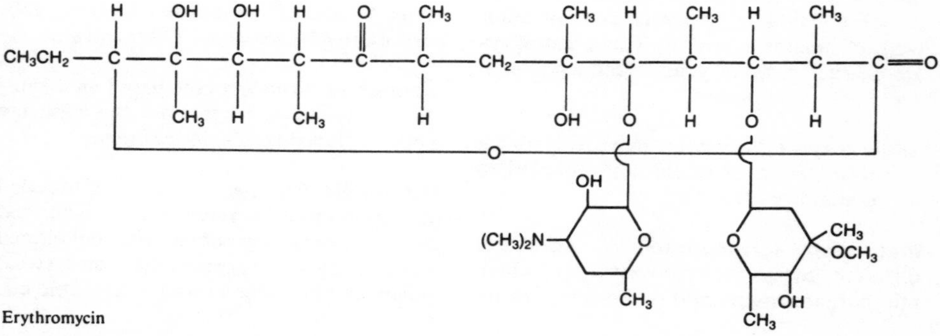

Erythromycin

211

magnetic microcarrier A type of microbead that has magnetic properties and can be used in magnetic immunoassay.

maintenance energy Energy required by an organism or a cell culture in order to survive in a viable condition, but without further increase in size or cell number. This may be expressed in terms of the weight of substrate, or energy in joules, required per dry weight of cells or body mass. The value for a given organism is independent of growth rate.

major element An element that is essential for life and is required for the formation of the major structural parts of living organisms. Major elements include carbon, nitrogen, oxygen, hydrogen, sulphur, phosphorus, calcium and, in some instances, silicon (e.g., in the frustule of diatoms).

malate A salt of malic acid.

malate dehydrogenase An enzyme that catalyses the reversible reduction of oxaloacetic acid to malic acid in a reaction linked to the oxidation–reduction of NAD(P).

malic acid A four-carbon dicarboxylic acid that is an intermediate of the TCA cycle.

malic acid fermentation A metabolic process that results in the degradation of malic acid to ethanol. There are two possible pathways based on malic enzyme or malate dehydrogenase. In the former, malic acid is decarboxylated to pyruvic acid, and then to acetaldehyde and ethanol. In the latter, the malic acid is oxidized to oxaloacetic acid, decarboxylated to pyruvate and metabolized to ethanol as above. These pathways are characteristic of yeasts such as *Schizosaccharomyces pombe*.

malic enzyme An enzyme that catalyses the decarboxylation of malic acid coupled to the reduction of NAD(P).

malo–lactic fermentation A number of different metabolic pathways by which microorganisms convert malic acid directly to lactic acid plus carbon dioxide. It is of importance in the production of wine, where it is catalysed by lactic acid bacteria.

malpighian body A part of the nephron found in vertebrate kidneys comprising a Bowman's capsule and a glomerulus.

malpighian layer A layer of cells found in the epidermis of vertebrates that often contains granules of the pigment melanin, which is responsible for skin colour. The malpighian layer may be divided into a lower region, adjacent to the basement membrane, in which the cells are in a state of active mitosis and an upper layer of cells containing keratin.

malt A mixture of starch hydrolysis products produced from germinating barley. Barley (*Hordeum distichum* or *H. hexastichum*) is sprouted under controlled conditions and then dried in a kiln.

maltose 4-*O*-α-D-Glucopyranosyl-D-glucopyranose; a disaccharide comprising two molecules of glucose produced by the action of β-amylase on starch. Maltose occurs in high concentrations in germinating seeds. The sugar is of importance as a constituent of malt produced from germinating barley.

Maltose

Mamestra brassicae **nuclear polyhedrosis virus** A baculovirus isolated from the cabbage moth *M. brassicae*. *See* mamestrin.

mamestrin A biopesticide based on the nuclear polyhedrosis virus of the cabbage moth produced by Calliope, France.

Mammalia The mammals; warm-blooded (homoiothermic) vertebrates, characterized by the possession of a well-developed brain. They also possess hair and sweat glands in their skin, as well as a double circulation maintained by a four-chamber heart. With the exception of the primitive Monotremata, they are viviparous. The young are fed by milk secreted from the mammary glands.

mammalian cell cloning The gene manipulation of mammalian cells. One vector that has been widely investigated is the papovavirus SV40. This is suitable since it consists of a single small, covalently closed circular DNA molecule, the entire nucleotide sequence of which has been determined. The genomic regions responsible for the viral functions have been established, and information is available on the replication and expression of the viral genome. The virus can replicate either vegetatively (in the cytoplasm of the host) or as an integral part of the cellular chromosome. Improved SV40 vectors, which retain the regions implicated in initiation, termination, splicing and polyadenylation, have been constructed.

mammary gland The milk-producing gland characteristic of female mammals.

mannan A major constituent of the hemicellulose of soft (coniferous) woods. Hydrolysis yields mannose, glucose and galactose in the ratio of 3:1:1. It consists of a main chain composed of mannopyranose and glycopyranose residues in the ratio 3:1 linked together by β-(1,4)-glycosidic links. Single galactopyranose residues form β-(1,6)-links to some of the mannose residues of the main chain.

mannitol A sugar alcohol derived from mannose or fructose. It occurs as a storage compound in brown algae and lichens.

mannose An aldohexose sugar, an epimer of glucose, occurring frequently in polysaccharides.

mannuronic acid A uronic acid structurally related to the hexose mannose. It is a constituent of alginate and other plant gums, as well as occurring in plant cell wall matrix polysaccharides.

manometry A technique used to measure gas exchange in small pieces of tissue or cell suspensions. The sample is enclosed in a gas-tight vessel, kept at constant temperature, and gas evolution or consumption is determined by measuring the change in volume at constant pressure or the change in pressure at constant volume. Alkaline solutions or pyrogallol may be added to a central well in order to absorb carbon dioxide or oxygen as appropriate. Standard devices include the Warburg manometer and the Gilson respirometer.

map In genetics, a pictorial representation of the location of genes, location of restriction sites or physical appearance of genomes or chromosomes, a record of the sequence of bases in a gene or genome. *See* linkage map, physical map, restriction map.

map units In linkage maps, a 1 per cent recombination frequency is defined as 1 map unit, or one centimorgan.

mapping A process used in the production of a map. These processes may include breeding experiments to produce linkage maps, the use of endonucleases to produce restriction maps, DNA sequencing or observations on dividing cells made under the light microscope.

marker (1) In genetics, an allele, the inheritance of which can be followed during a genetic cross to provide a reference point to enable the mapping position of other genes to be determined. (2) In analysis, a molecule of known size or identity run on electrophoretic gels or chromatographic media in order to provide an indication of the position of equivalent compounds. (3) In immunology, a specific antigenic conjugant used to identify a particular class of lymphocytes. (4) In cytology, a characteristic of a cell or cell line that enables separate identities to be determined in mixed cell cultures or tissues. This includes specific staining properties or nuclear characteristics.

mash A mixture of water, malt and other ingredients produced in an early stage of brewing.

mass balance An analysis carried out on any process in which the weight of inputs are correlated with the weight of products on either a theoretical or an experimental basis.

mass flow A postulated mechanism to account for the movement of materials through the phloem of higher plants. The driving force is a difference in hydrostatic pressure resulting from the osmotic effects of variations in the solute concentration at the source (the loading ends of the sieve tubes) and the sink (storage tissue).

mass selection Artificial selection practised by choosing individuals with maximum (minimum) expression of a given trait as parents of the following generation. This is repeated several times.

mass spectrometer An instrument used to determine the structure and identity of complex organic molecules. A mass spectrometer is used to determine the isotopic ratio in a given compound or to monitor the amount of a heavy isotope in an isotopically labelled sample. The sample is bombarded with a stream of high-energy electrons, which leads to its fragmentation in a characteristic way for a given compound. The fragments, which are of varying weight and charge, are then passed through a magnetic field where they are separated on the basis of their mass/charge ratios. A wide range of computer-based techniques compare the results with the spectra of known compounds enabling positive identification. Mass spectrometers may be combined with gas/liquid chromatographs, or used on-line to monitor gas composition in fermenters.

mass transfer A process that results in the movement of molecules from one place to another. In biological systems, mass transfer may result from diffusion, facilitated diffusion or active transport.

mast cell A type of cell found in connective tissue, characterized by strongly basophilic granules which accumulate serotonin, histamine and heparin. These compounds are released from the mast cells during anaphylaxis or inflammation, as well as in the immune response.

mating type One of a number of genetically distinct strains of fungi, yeasts, bacteria, algae, etc. that are needed for the successful formation of a viable zygote during sexual reproduction. Since the various mating types and their gametes are morphologically identical, male and female strains cannot be recognized. Various types of designation are adopted including + or –, a or b, etc.

matrix modifier A substance that is added to an electrophoresis gel in order to enhance the separation characteristics: for example, glycerol which reduces the mobility of DNA molecules and thus extends the separation range.

Maxam–Gilbert chemical sequencing A technique for sequencing nucleic acids based on the differential ability of the four organic bases to react with various reagent such as piperidine and hydrazine. It requires the use of end-labelled nucleic acid.

maxicell An *E. coli* cell that contains plasmids and a small amount of chromosomal DNA, used for the study of plasmid-encoded products.

maximum enzyme velocity (V_{max}) The theoretical maximum rate at which a given enzyme can catalyse a specific reaction when supplied with substrate at an infinite concentration. V_{max} is determined experimentally using, for example, Lineweaver–Burk kinetics.

maximum oxygen A measure of the fastest possible rate of uptake of oxygen by a growing culture expressed in terms of the volumetric mass transfer coefficient times the oxygen solubility.

maximum specific growth rate (μ_{max}) The theoretical maximum rate of growth of a culture under optimal conditions of nutrient supply. μ_{max} is determined experimentally from a double reciprocal derivation of the

Monod equation analogous to the Lineweaver–Burk plot for enzyme kinetics.

MCAF Human macrophage/monocyte chemotactic and activating factor; a cytokine that plays an important part in the human immune system. Also called MCP-1 (human macrophage chemoattractant protein-1).

MCP-1 Human macrophage chemoattractant protein-1. *See* MCAF.

MCPA 2-Methyl-4-chloro-phenoxyacetic acid; a synthetic auxin used as a weed killer.

mean detention time The average time that each unit volume of mixed liquor is retained in a bioreactor, fermenter or other vessel. The hydraulic mean detention time refers to the liquid portion of the liquor and the solids mean retention time refers to the solid portion. In a fully mixed system, the hydraulic detention time and the solids detention time are the same. Systems in which the biocatalysts or cell biomass are retained within the bioreactor, or in which cells are recycled, have a greater ratio of solids to liquid retention times.

medium A composite formulation of substrates, minerals, growth factors and vitamins used in the culture of microorganisms (bacteria, yeasts, fungi), animal cell lines or plant tissue cultures. Media are liquid or solidified with polymers such as agar or gelatin.

medulla The central region of an organ or tissue.

medulla oblongata The hindbrain. It contains centres for the regulation of blood pressure, respiration and other functions controlled by the autonomic nervous system.

medullary ray In plants, a vertical plate of tissue formed from parenchymatous cells lying across the vascular tissue.

megagram One million grams; equal to one metric tonne.

megaspore The larger of the two kinds of haploid spore produced by vascular plants; the smaller kind is called a microspore. In seed plants, the megaspore develops into the embryo sac (female gametophyte), whereas the microspore gives rise to the pollen grain (male gametophyte).

MEIA *See* magnetic enzyme immunoassay.

meiosis The reduction division associated with the formation of gametes. In this process, the cell nucleus divides into four daughter nuclei, each containing half the parent chromosome number (somatic number). The entire meiotic process involves two separate divisions (meiosis I and meiosis II). The first division is a true reductive division with the chromosome number being halved, whereas the second division is mitotic. In both divisions, various stages have been named on the basis of the appearance of the nuclear material and/or chromosomes. Division starts in an interphase cell in which the chromosomes are in a resting stage as far as division is concerned. The major sequence of divisions is then described as: prophase I; metaphase I; anaphase I; telophase I; interphase I; prophase II; metaphase II; anaphase II; telophase II; interphase II. The changes that occur during the prophase I are: (1) leptotene, the chromosomes begin to shorten and become visible under a microscope; (2) zygotene, the two identical or homologous chromosomes associate by the formation of synapses along their length, and the nucleolus becomes visible; (3) pachytene, synapsis is nearly completed along the length of the chromosomes which continue to contract and thicken; (4) diplotene, the two chromatids of each chromosome become visible and the paired chromosomes begin to separate from each other, with points of very close association called chiasma becoming visible; (5) diakinesis, the centromeres push farther apart and the doubled chromosomes take on the appearance of rings. The chromosomes continue to contract and the nucleolus begins to disappear. The chromosomes move to the centre of the cell and become arranged on the metaphase plate, and the centromeres attach to spindle fibres. In anaphase, the chromosomes begin to move towards the poles, but the centromeres do not split, hence the chromatids associated with each centromere move as a unit. The actual reduction in chromosome number occurs at this stage. In telophase I, the chromosomes form into new nuclei surrounded by a nuclear membrane and new cell walls are formed. Each nucleus is now $1n$ rather than $2n$. The duration of the interphase differs with the species. The second division then follows the normal mitotic sequence, except that in anaphase II the centromeres split lengthways in the chromosomes with one chromatid attached to each half. These may now be considered to be new chromosomes and separate to form new nuclei, and finally a quartet of four reproductive cells.

melanin In a general sense, all deep brown and black pigments of natural occurrence. True animal melanins (eumelanins) are formed by the polymerization of indole-5,6-quinone, which arises from the amino acid tyrosine, through the action of the tyrosinase enzyme complex. Some plant melanins, such as those formed on damage to cells of fungi or sugar beet, are eumelanins, whereas other plant melanins are catecholmelanins, since they yield catechol on alkali digestion.

melanism The occurrence of dark coloured individuals in a population of animals owing to excessive production of melanin.

melanocyte-stimulating hormone (MSH) A peptide hormone produced by the pituitary gland that stimulates the production of pigments in animal cells.

melanoma A particularly virulent type of skin cancer resulting from the proliferation of abnormal, highly pigmented cells.

melanophore A cell containing high levels of melanin.

melatonin A hormone produced by the pineal gland of vertebrates that regulates the dispersal of melanin in the skin.

melibiose 6-O-α-D-galactosyl-β-D-glucopyranose; a disaccharide comprising a galactose molecule linked to glucose through a (1,6)-link. It is found in plant exudates where it arises from the action of invertase on the trisaccharide raffinose.

melting The denaturation by heat of a double-stranded DNA molecule yielding two single-stranded DNA molecules.

melting curve A graphical plot of the change in absorbance at 260 nm, as a function of temperature, that occurs when a solution of DNA is heated. Heating results in denaturation owing to breaking of the hydrogen bonds between the bases and dissociation of the two strands of the double helix. The absorbance of double-stranded DNA is always lower than that of a single-strand DNA, which is lower than that of an equivalent amount of free nucleotides in solution. The form of the melting curve is characteristic of certain features in the primary and secondary structures of nucleic acid. Increases in temperature have no effect on absorbance until the transition point is reached. If the primary structure is homogeneous, a sharp transition is noted; otherwise the shape of the curve is affected by the frequency of the different base pairs since A–T pairs are easier to disrupt than are G–C. In molecules in which the helical structure is not complete, the transition occurs over a wider temperature range.

melting domain *See* denaturant gradient gel electrophoresis.

membrane In most plants and animals, a bilayer of lipids (e.g., phospholipids, glycolipids and sterols) in which globular proteins are embedded. The lipids of the bilayer have hydrophobic (non-polar) and hydrophilic (polar) moities; molecules are arranged so that their hydrophobic tails point towards each other, with the result that both surfaces of the membrane are composed of the hydrophilic heads. The bilayer is stable in an aqueous environment, since the surfaces readily associate with water. Both the proteins and the lipids are free to move and are in constant motion.

The proteins are divided into three types: (1) those that penetrate the bilayer from one side or the other, but do not pass through it; (2) those that pass through the membrane and thus have part of their structure exposed to the aqueous environment on either side of the bilayer; (3) those that are totally embedded in the hydrophobic core of the membrane. Important types of membranes include: the plasmalemma, which bounds the outer surface of the cell; the tonoplast, which bounds vesicles; the endoplasmic reticulum, composed of an extensive network of interconnected tubules and vesicles that extend through the cytoplasm; the Golgi apparatus, or dictyosomes, which is associated with the synthesis and secretion of enzymes and parts of the cell wall in plants; membranes associated with the chloroplasts, mitochondria and other organelles; the nuclear membranes.

membrane affinity separation A high-speed separation technique based on the highly specific binding that occurs between certain biomolecules. The system uses hollow-fibre membranes that are wide enough to allow convective throughflow of solutions. The membrane matrix contains a network of tiny pores. Affinity ligands that selectively bind to target protein molecules are attached to the matrix. This system enables clarification, purification and concentration of a sample to be consolidated into a single process, increasing yields as well as reducing separation time. It can be up to 100 times faster than conventional chromatographic techniques.

membrane filter bioreactor A bioreactor in which the fermenting broth is circulated continuously through a membrane filter. The product diffuses from the reaction zone through the membrane and is withdrawn continuously. This method is also applied to enzyme and resting cell reactors. The hollow fibre filter fermenter is one variation of this type of bioreactor.

memory cell A white blood cell, usually producing antibody, that survives for a long period following exposure of animals or man to a foreign chemical substance, an invading microorganism or a virus.

Mendelian inheritance The inheritance of genetic characteristics according to the laws proposed by Gregor Mendel (1822–84). The characteristics under consideration must be the result of expression of pairs of alleles, with one allele dominant to the other. The first concept (law of segregation) states that genes are present in pairs of somatic cells and that each gamete contains only one gene from each pair. The second concept (law of independent assortment) states that, if more than one pair of genes is considered, each pair segregates independently of any other pair. Although these ideas form the basis of modern genetics, they are not always correct and apply only to genes that are not modified by the effect of other genes at other loci and to pairs of genes that are not on the same chromosome. The segregation of genes on the same chromosome is affected by the degree of crossing-over.

Mendelian population An interbreeding group of organisms sharing in a common gene pool.

Mendelism *See* Mendelian inheritance.

meninges Layers of tissue that enclose the brain and spinal cord of vertebrates.

mercaptoethanol Monothioethylene glycol; a sulphydryl reagent used in the extraction of enzymes to protect SH groups and in the preservation of readily oxidizable compounds such as tetrahydrofolic acid and coenzyme A.

meristem In plants, region of tissue in which the cells are undergoing rapid mitotic division followed by differentiation into new tissues, resulting in growth.

merozygote A partially diploid cell arising as a result of transduction, transformation or conjugation in bacteria.

Mes *See* zwitterionic buffer.

mesencephalon The midbrain; the central of the three hollow dilations of the neural tube found in embryonic vertebrates.

mesentry A layer of the peritoneum that secures the stomach and intestines of vertebrates to the dorsal body wall and contains the various blood vessels, nerves and lymph vessels serving the gut.

mesocotyl The shoot axis between the coleoptile and the embryo of grasses.

mesophile A microorganism with a temperature optimum for growth at about blood heat (37°C) and which will grow over a range of temperatures from 20 to 50°C. Most organisms associated with mammalian and avian disease are mesophilic. Both aerobic and anaerobic mesophiles are used in the biological treatment of wastes.

mesophyll The region of parenchyma cells, often containing chloroplasts, found in leaves of higher plants. In dicotyledons, it is divided into an upper palisade mesophyll layer consisting of closely packed columnar cells and a lower spongy mesophyll layer with numerous air spaces permitting gaseous exchange. In C_4 plants, the chloroplasts of the mesophyll layer are unable to fix carbon dioxide, since they lack rubisco (the enzyme associated with the reductive assimilation of carbon dioxide).

mesophyte A plant that inhabits environments of reasonable moisture content. *Compare* halophyte, xerophyte.

mesosome A membrane structure found in the cells of some gram-positive bacteria associated with the development of new cell walls.

messenger RNA *See* mRNA.

messenger splicing The 'editing' of the primary transcript of a gene from a higher organism to excise the non-coding intervening sequences. This leaves a continuous coding sequence specifying the protein in question.

mestom sheath An inner layer of cells associated with the bundle sheath of some grasses.

Met An abbreviation for the amino acid methionine used in protein sequences and elsewhere.

metabolic heat Energy lost as heat during the growth of an organism. In aerobic biocatalysis and fermentation processes, knowledge of the amount of heat produced is important in bioreactor design since provisions have to be made to remove the heat. Heat production may be calculated from an enthalpy balance for a growing culture. However, for aerobic systems the amount of heat released can be derived on the basis of oxygen consumption. In general, 460 kJ of heat are released per mole of oxygen consumed. In fermentation, to produce ethanol, around 70 kJ are produced per mol of glucose converted to biomass or to ethanol.

metabolic pathway A series of enzyme-catalysed reactions that function as a whole to transform one compound to another. In prokaryotes, the genes that code for the enzymes associated with a pathway may be linked on operons. In some systems, the enzymes are structurally grouped together, often on membranes.

metabolic rate A measure of the rate of chemical reactions in an organism. For instance, in an aerobic organism, it may be expressed as the rate of oxygen consumption.

metabolism The overall biochemical reactions that take place in a living organism. It includes the building of more complex molecules (anabolism) and the breakdown of molecules to provide energy (catabolism).

metabolite A substance that acts as a substrate for or is produced by a metabolic process or enzyme reaction.

metacentric Descriptive of a chromosome in which the centromere is positioned centrally.

metafemale An individual that has a greater dose of female determiners than do normal females; also called superfemale.

metalloprotease An enzyme, containing an atom of zinc as a prosthetic group, that hydrolyses proteins. They are divided into neutral and alkaline enzymes. Neutral proteases of microbial origin are specific towards hydrophobic amino residues on the amino side of the cleavage point. Metalloproteases are inhibited by metal-chelating agents.

metalloprotein A protein that contains a metal as a prosthetic group.

metalloproteinase See metalloprotease.

metamorphosis The transformation from a larval to an adult form through the rapid rearrangement of tissues. The process occurs in insects and amphibians.

metaphase The second stage of cell division (mitosis or meiosis) during which the chromosomes arrange themselves in a random manner on the equatorial plate or central plane of the cell. By the start of this stage, the nuclear membrane and nucleolus have disappeared. The centromeres become attached to the spindle fibres which are associated with the directional chromosomal movement during further stages of division.

metaplasia The transformation of cells in a tissue or other types that are not normally present. It is an abnormal process which may be associated with tumour formation, hormonal imbalance or exposure of the cells to unusual conditions or chemical stimulants.

metastasis The transfer of cancer cells from one part of the body to another via the circulation or lymph ducts.

Metazoa A subkingdom of animals that includes all multicellular species possessing a nervous system. It comprises all animals except Protozoa and Parazoa.

methaemoglobin An oxidized form of haemoglobin that is unable to bind oxygen because the ferrous atoms of the haem group have been oxidized to their ferric state.

methanamide See formamide.

methane (CH_4) Natural gas; a major component of biogas produced by methanogenic bacteria from carbon dioxide, hydrogen and acetate.

methane digester A synonym for anaerobic digester.

methanogen A strictly anaerobic bacterium that is capable of producing methane. Methanogens include the genera *Methanobacterium*, *Methanobacillus*, *Methanococcus* and *Methanosarcina*. Methane bacteria are found in anaerobic soils (marshes and bogs), sewage sludge, landfill sites and anaerobic digestion systems. They also play an important role in the metabolism of ruminants.

methanogenesis The final step in the production of methane during which acetate, hydrogen and bicarbonate are converted to methane as a result of the activity of methanogens.

methanol The simplest alcohol, obtained by oxidation of methane. It is produced in large quantities from natural gas. It is also known as 'wood alcohol' or 'wood spirit'.

methionine (Met) One of the 20 amino acids commonly found in proteins. It is an essential amino acid for man.

Methionine $CH_3SCH_2CH_2CH(NH_2)COOH$

methionine production Methionine is produced commercially using strains of *Corynebacterium glutamicum*.

methyl violet Crystal violet or gentian violet. A stain used in histology to identify nuclei.

methylene blue Methylthionine chloride or 3,7-bis(dimethylamino)phenazothionium chloride; a stain used in histology to identify nuclei.

Methylophilus methylotrophus A fermentative bacterium that can be grown on methanol to yield single-cell protein.

methylotroph A bacterium that can use methanol as both the carbon and the energy source for growth. Methylotrophs have been used commercially to form single-cell protein (e.g., *Methylophilus methylotrophus*) and co-enzyme Q (e.g., *Pseudomonas* species).

4-methylumbelliferyl phosphate *See* 4-MUP.

4-methylumbelliferyl-β-D-galactopyranoside *See* 4-MUG.

metre (m) A unit of length equal to 3.2808 feet or 39.37 inches.

metric character A trait that varies more or less continuously among individuals, which are therefore placed into classes according to measured values of the trait. It is also called quantitative character.

mg An abbreviation for milligram.

Mg An abbreviation for megagram.

micelle A colloidal particle formed by the reversible aggregation of dissolved molecules. Charged micelles form colloidal electrolytes such as soaps and detergents.

Michaelis–Menten equation *See* Michaelis–Menten kinetics.

Michaelis–Menten kinetics A generalized description of enzyme kinetics based on a model that assumes formation of an intermediate enzyme–substrate complex, which has a greater tendency to dissociate forming the product rather than to release the unchanged substrate. A plot of rate of reaction against substrate concentration gives the right-angled hyperbola. This indicates dependence on substrate concentration at low concentrations and a maximum rate of reaction (V) at a saturating concentration, above which any further increase in substrate has no effect (or may even cause inhibition). The rate v for the reaction is given by:

$$v = (V[S])/(K_m + [S])$$

where K_m = the substrate concentration for half-maximal velocity of the overall reaction. This is the Michaelis–Menten equation.

mickle tissue disintegrator A type of bead mill.

microaerophilic Descriptive of a microorganism that grows best in the presence of only low concentrations of molecular oxygen.

microbe *See* microorganisms.

microbial biomass *See* biomass.

microbial film A thin layer of microorganisms absorbed on to a supporting surface.

microbial floc Particles formed by the aggregation of bacterial, yeast or microalgal cells. In general, the formation of flocs is a function of the chemical structure of the cell wall or capsule. In many cases, the formation of such flocs is a genetic characteristic and is dependent on the calcium concentration of the medium. Cells that form flocs are of value in some fermentation since they make clarification of the medium or separation and recycling of the cells easier. Certain anaerobic digesters, such as the sludge blanket reactor, depend on flocculation to form the stable sludge bed.

microbial leaching A method of recovering metals such as copper and uranium from ores of low content. Leaching involves cycling reactive chemical solutions through the ore to extract metal from its matrix. In microbial leaching, the process is designed to encourage growth of organisms that help directly or indirectly in the extraction. This is carried out using bacteria of the genus *Thiobacillus*, such as *T. thiooxidans*. These organisms grow chemoautotrophically on energy released by oxidation of sulphur compounds, generating sulphuric acid and copper ions. When the copper concentration is high enough, the metal is removed by electrolysis.

microbial metal accumulation All microorganisms accumulate metals from their environment since many are essential components of enzymes, pigments or intermediates of electron transport. In some cases, the amounts of metal accumulated are large and have been accumulated against a concentration gradient. Such metals may be complexed by extracellular polysaccharides, incorporated into components of the microbial wall or accumulated in vacuoles. Such processes may be applied to the removal of toxic heavy metals from dilute waste streams or used as the basis for the recovery of precious metals from dilute solutions.

microbial mining *See* microbial leaching.

microbial pest control A technique in which microorganisms (bacteria, fungi or viral cultures) or derivatives from them, such as the spore protein of *Bacillus thuringiensis*, are used in place of synthetic pesticides to kill harmful insects in particular.

microbial polysaccharide A simple or compound polysaccharide that is formed as a storage product, cell wall constituent or extracellular gum or slice by a bacterium, alga or fungus.

microbial sensor A biosensor in which the catalyst is a microorganism. For instance, a suspension of aerobic bacteria, such as *Pseudomonas fluorescens*, is immobilized in a collagen membrane and attached to an oxygen cathode. This is used to detect changes in rates of oxygen gas exchange, which in turn are proportional to the glucose concentration of any solution in which it is placed. Hence the sensor may be used to measure glucose levels. A similar approach is used combining an ammonia-sensitive electrode with cells that are capable of deaminating of amino acids, amines or urea.

microbial thin film A layer of active biomass formed by the growth of microorganisms on a solid support such as in a biological filter or an aerobic filter.

microbiology The study of microorganisms including their taxonomy, morphology, physiology, biochemistry and genetics.

microbody A small, spherical organelle enclosed by a single membrane found in animal and plant cells. Microbodies carry out oxidative reactions. They are further classified on the basis of their function. They include glyoxysomes and peroxisomes.

microcarrier A small, beaded material used as a support for the culture of anchorage-dependent animal cell lines. The beads are derived from silica, glass, dextran or similar materials.

microcarrier culture A technique in which animal cells are grown on the surface of small beads that are kept in suspension in a nutrient medium by gentle stirring. This method provides a very high growth surface-to-volume ratio, which enables concentrations of several million cells per millilitre to be produced. The products are harvested by allowing the beads to settle under gravity.

micrococcus luteus polymerase A DNA polymerase with 5' to 3' exonuclease activity, used to create short single-stranded regions in cloned DNA molecules.

microdissection The dissection of very small organisms or parts of organisms using a microscope to view the material.

microencapsulation *See* encapsulation.

microfibril A structural subcomponent of the cellulose fibres found in plant cell walls. It is composed of parallel cellulose chains held together by hydrogen bonding.

microfilament Fine filament found in bundles or individually in the cytoplasm of all eukaryotic cells. Microfilaments are involved in the process in cytoplasmic streaming, amoeboid movement and morphogenic changes. They are similar to the actin-containing filaments of muscle.

microfiltration A filtration process used to separate microscopic particles, such as bacterial cells of around 1 to 10 microns, from liquid media or airstreams. Microfiltration may be used to recover cells from fermentation processes, to sterilize culture medium or to maintain the quality of airflow in clean rooms or containment facilities.

microgram (μg) A unit of mass equal to 10^{-6} gram.

micrograph A permanent image obtained using a light microscope or an electron microscope in conjunction with a photographic plate or film.

microinjection A micromanipulation technique in which part of one cell is injected into another. The technique is used to inject the nuclei of sperm into an ovum, DNA in various forms into cells or nuclei, or organelles into cells.

micromanipulator A device that is mechanically or electronically controlled so that normal movements made by the operator, or movements programmed into a microprocessor, result in very fine responses in the tool being used. The operation is usually carried out under a microscope using very small tools that can hold, cut, squeeze, inject, retract, etc. Lasers may be used as cutting tools.

micrometre (μm) A unit of length equal to 10^{-6} metre.

micron Alternative, obsolete term for a micrometre.

micronucleus A small ancillary nucleus found in cells of some protozoa that functions in conjunction and sexual reproduction during which it undergoes mitotic division.

microorganisms Members of one of the following classes: bacteria, fungi, algae, protozoa or viruses.

micropipette A tool for accurately dispensing small amounts (μlitres) of liquids.

Typically a micropipette consists of a spring-loaded plunger or pump, activated by hand, filled with disposable plastic tips. Micropipettes, which may be single or multichannel, variable or fixed volume, are typically used in immunoassays, genetic manipulation, enzyme assays and for loading gels.

microplasts Sub-protoplasmic vesicles containing small portions of genetic material that can be introduced into whole protoplasts by fusion.

microplate *See* microtitre plate.

microplate reader A scanning photometer designed specifically to obtain numerical results from immunoassays carried out using microtitre plates. Results may be calculated directly using an on-line microcomputer and appropriate software designed to handle immunoassays based on enzyme, fluorescent or luminescent labels.

microprocessor An electronic device that accepts and processes coded instructions. Microprocessors are now being widely used in the fermentation industry; uses include, monitoring routine process variables, data logging, planning maintenance schedules, monitoring inventories to maintain delivery and shipping schedules, process documentation, generating process status information and sending appropriate alarms to operators, and automatic control of fermenter functions. *See* fermenter control.

micropyle A small pore in the outer coat of a seed that remains open as a result of the incomplete closure of the integuments around the ovule. In the ovule, it is the site of entry of the pollen tube during pollination and fertilization. In the mature seed, it may be the main route of imbibition of water during germination.

microscope An instrument used to produce a highly magnified image of a sample. In biology, electron microscopes and light microscopes are used. Light microscopes use visible (400–700 nm) or ultraviolet radiation (200–400 nm). In electron microscopy, a beam of electrons is used. Since these cannot be detected by the eye, various methods are employed to produce an image. A permanent image is obtained using a photographic film or plate exposed to the radiation, but for general viewing a fluorescent screen or a cathode ray tube is used. The magnification (degree of enlargement) and the resolution (ability to distinguish between two adjacent points or objects) are important factors for effective viewing. The theoretical limit of resolution is about half the wavelength of the radiation used. Hence the electron microscope with a wavelength in the region of 0.005 nm at 50 keV has much greater powers of resolution and hence magnification (up to 250,000 times) compared with the light microscope (up to 1500 times). The contrast obtained using both types of microscopes can be increased by staining the specimen. Additional techniques such as metal shadowing, negative staining and freeze fracture are used in electron microscopy. Various developments are available to improve the performance of light microscopes. (e.g., compound microscope, phase contrast microscope, ultraviolet microscope, dark-field microscope, polarizing microscope). Electron microscopes may be distinguished as transmission or scanning instruments.

microsequencing A technique used to increase the sensitivity of detection of products of the Edman reaction during amino acid sequencing of proteins. Techniques include the use of a radioactive label in the form of phenylisothiocyanate labelled with either radioactive carbon or radioactive sulphur, or the use of a protein that has been labelled with radioactive carbon during synthesis. An alternative technique is to use HPLC as a means of separating and quantifying very small amounts of amino acid.

microsome A structure consisting of ribosomes associated with fragments of endoplasmic reticulum produced during the isolation of ribosomes from tissue homogenates. Microsomes are probably artefacts and have no parallel *in vivo*.

microspore A haploid cell from which a male gamete is produced. *Compare* megaspore.

microtitre plate A plastic plate containing a number (usually 96) of small flat-bottomed wells arranged in rows. Microtitre plates are used for EIA and other immunological assays.

microtome An instrument used to prepare thin sections of biological material for examination under a light or electron microscope. For light microscopy, the material is first embedded in wax or a water-based polymer, or is frozen. This provides support, thus maintaining the tissues in position during the cutting process. For electron microscopy, the specimen is usually embedded in a hard epoxy resin. A ultramicrotome, fitted with a glass or diamond knife, is then used to cut the material into very fine sections (20–100 nm thick).

microtubule A straight cylinder found in the cytoplasm of most eukaryotic cells. Microtubules are of indeterminate length, but are at least several micrometres long, and have an external diameter of 24–25 nm. The wall of the cylinder is 5–6 nm thick, and the diameter of the apparently hollow lumen is about 12 nm. In cross-section, the wall consists of 13 circular subunits, each with a diameter of about 5 nm. Longitudinal views reveal a series of filaments made up of two types of subunit which occur alternately along their length. The filament has a periodicity of 8 nm, and the 13 filaments that constitute the microtubule wall exhibit a small displacement which results in a helical structure. The globular protein (molecular weight 120,000) that forms the filaments is known as tubulin. It consists of two subunits (α and β) of equal size, but different structure. Three broad categories of microtubules occur in cells: the microtubules that constitute the nuclear spindle in dividing cells; cytoplasmic microtubules; microtubules associated with the structure of flagellae and cilia.

microvillus A cytoplasmic projection from the free surface of an epithelial cell that increases the cell's absorptive surface area. Regions of dense, regularly arranged microvilli, such as are found in the linings of the intestinal tract, are known as brush borders.

middle lamella An amorphous layer that lies between the primary walls of plant cells. It is the first layer to be formed when a plant cell divides.

MIF See migration inhibitory factor.

migration See gene flow.

migration inhibitory factor (MIF) A lymphokine that inhibits the movement of monocytes and macrophages.

milligram (mg) A unit of mass equal to 10^{-3} gram.

Millon's reagent See Millon's test.

Millon's test A qualitative test for protein. The sample is heated with a solution of mercuric nitrate and nitrous acid (Millon's reagent). In the presence of protein, red precipitate of coagulated protein is formed.

mineral leaching See microbial leaching.

mineral requirements See trace element.

mineralocorticoid A corticosteroid hormone, such as aldosterone, that stimulates the re-absorption of salts and water in the distal tubules of the kidneys.

mini cell A small piece of protoplasm derived from a cell, usually from an in vitro cell culture, that contains less than the haploid number of chromosomes. Mini cells arise by reducing and expelling one or more chromosomes from the product of fusion of two unlike cells or protoplasts. Mini cells are also induced. They are fused with normal cells as a means of introducing one or more extra chromosomes.

mini Ti plasmid A derivative of the wild-type tumour-inducing plasmid of Agrobacterium tumefaciens, in which part of the DNA sequence that is not needed for infection and replication is excised. This leaves a smaller plasmid that may be used as a cloning vehicle for recombinant gene technology in higher plants.

minimal medium A growth medium that contains only the minimum nutrients required for the growth of a certain organism.

minimum inhibitory concentration The lowest concentration of a growth inhibitor, such as an antibiotic, in a dilution series that precludes the growth of an organism under standard incubation conditions.

minor base A nucleotide that differs in structure from the four primary building blocks of nucleic acid (A, C, T, G) and carries a substituent (usually a methyl group), or possesses a saturated bond or an isomeric form of the glycosidic linkage. Minor bases are found in RNA, the modifications being introduced after transcription has taken place.

miricidium The first larval stage in the development of endoparasitic flukes.

miscanthus A high productivity C_4 grass that can be used as an energy crop.

mismatch The presence of non-complementary bases in a length of DNA that otherwise shows base pairing.

miso A food product obtained by fermenting cereals, soybeans and salt with moulds, yeasts and bacteria. Organisms used in such fermentations include Saccharomyces, Torulopsis and Streptococcus.

mitDNA Mitochondrial DNA (also mtDNA).

mitochondrial ATPase An enzyme found on the inner mitochondrial membrane that catalyses the formation of ATP from ADP and orthophosphate. ATP formation is coupled to the free energy loss brought about by electron flow through the respiratory electron transport chain with the formation of

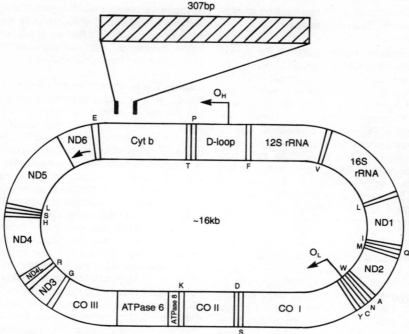

The mitochondrial genome of vertebrates

ATP. The mechanism of such oxidative phosphorylation has been ascribed to the chemiosmotic theory. The inner membrane of the mitochondrion has stalked particles on the surface facing the matrix. These particles, which have a head about 9 nm in diameter, contain the ATPase.

mitochondrial DNA A type of DNA contained in the nucleoids of mitochondria. It consists of several copies of a circular, histone-free DNA molecule (chromosome). The DNA molecules contain 15–75 kilobase pairs, and thus could code for 16–80 different proteins, assuming each comprises an average of 300 amino acids. However, part of this DNA is required to code for the rRNA, hence most mitochondrial proteins must be coded for by nuclear DNA.

mitochondrial enzymes The mitochondrial matrix contains all the enzymes of the TCA cycle, with the exception of the succinate dehydrogenase which is built into the inner surface of the inner membrane. Mitochondria also contain enzymes for fatty acid metabolism and interconversion of some amino acids.

mitochondrial membranes The two membranes of the mitochondrion differ in structure and composition. The outer membrane has a higher lipid content than the inner and a distinct enzyme complement. The two membranes also have different permeability characteristics; the outer membrane is freely permeable to low-molecular-weight compounds and to a number of proteins, whereas the inner membrane presents a barrier to many ions, low-molecular-weight compounds and proteins. The inner membrane possesses specific transmembrane transport systems.

mitochondrial mRNA mRNA transcribed from mitochondrial DNA.

mitochondrial replication The formation of new mitochondria by division of existing ones. Division is accomplished by invagination of the inner membrane.

mitochondrial respiratory chain A sequence of enzymes and proteins present in the inner mitochondrial membranes of eukaryote cells and in the cell membranes of prokaryotes. The chain receives electrons or hydrogen atoms derived from reactions of the TCA cycle. During passage of electrons through the chain, energy is conserved in the form of ATP by oxidative phosphorylation. Enzymes and carriers include dehydrogenase, flavoproteins (FAD, FMN), co-enzymes (NAD, NADP, co-enzyme Q) and cytochromes. *See* terminal electron transport chain.

mitochondrial ribosome A ribosome associated with the mitochondrion having a sedimentation constant of 70S. Mitochondrial ribosomes consist of a large subunit (50S) and a small subunit (30S). The large subunit contains at least two rRNA molecules, one of 23S and one of 5S, whereas the small subunit contains one rRNA molecule of 16S. These ribosomes are smaller than those in the cytoplasm. All the mitochondrion rRNA molecules are encoded by mitochondrial DNA.

mitochondrion An organelle that is the site of oxidative metabolism and phosphorylation found in all eukaryotic cells that carry out aerobic respiration. Mitochondria are specifically stained by the dye Janus Green B. They contain the enzymes of the TCA cycle and the respiratory electron chain. They are usually globular or cylindrical, may be branched with a diameter of about 0.5–1.5 μm and are rarely longer than 6 μm. A cell may contain several thousand mitochondria, but some algae and the yeast *Saccharomyces* have only one large mitochondrion per cell. The organelle is surrounded by a double-layered membrane or envelope. The inner membrane is folded to form a number of cristae. The envelope encloses a finely granular proteinaceous matrix that contains ribosomes and nucleoids; fibrous regions contain DNA.

mitogen A compound that stimulates the activity of lymphoid cells, leading to the production of soluble factors (e.g., lyphokines, interferon, etc.), changes in functional state and blast cell formation.

mitosis The process whereby a cell nucleus divides into two daughter nuclei, each having the same genetic complement as the parent cell. Nuclear division is usually followed by cell division. When the cell is not undergoing division, the cell is described as being in interphase. Mitosis may be divided into four active stages: prophase, metaphase, anaphase and telophase. In prophase, the chromosomes prepare for division by shortening and thickening. Chromatids can be detected and nucleoli seen. In metaphase, the chromosomes arrange themselves in a random manner on the equatorial plate at the central plane of the cell; by this stage the nuclear membrane and nucleolus have disappeared. The centromere of each chromosome becomes attached to the spindle fibre which is responsible for directional chromosomal movement during division. In anaphase, the centromere splits lengthwise and the chromatids begin to move towards the poles. The chromatids are now considered to be new chromosomes. In telophase, the chromosomes have completed their movement towards the poles and have began to disperse inside the new nuclear membrane. In plants, it is at this stage that the new wall is initiated.

mitotic index A measure of the proportion of cells present in a tissue or culture that are in a process of division. A value of 0.1 means that 10 per cent of the cells are dividing.

mixed culture A culture of microorganisms containing a number of species or genera. Many traditional food fermentation processes are dependent on the activities of mixed cultures.

mixed liquor (1) A mixture of the feedstock and active biomass in a bioreactor. (2) The effluent from a fully mixed system.

mob **gene** *See* mobilization gene.

mobile phase In chromatography, the carrier liquid that moves through the support to bring about separation.

mobility In electrophoresis, a measure of the rate at which a given component of a mixture moves through the support gel. The mobility generally reflects the charge and the mass of a molecule.

mobilization (*mob*) gene A gene that facilitates the transfer of plasmids from one cell to another. A plasmid must contain mobilization (*mob*) genes as well as transfer (*tra*) genes if it is to be capable of being transferred between cells. Experimental plasmids may have their *mob* and *tra* genes deleted in order to prevent the possibility of mobilization of recombinant plasmids in the event of accidental release into the environment.

modification enzyme *See* restriction enzyme.

modification methylase An enzyme that catalyses the chemical alteration of certain bases of DNA by methylation of nucleotides within restriction recognition sites corresponding to their own restriction enzymes. This protects their own DNA against attack.

modification methylase M.Eco RI An enzyme used in molecular biology to methylate foreign DNA to protect it against restriction enzyme *Eco* RI.

moiety One of two subunits of a macromolecule, each subunit being approximately the same size.

molal Descriptive of a solution that contains one mole of a compound dissolved in one litre of water or 1000 grams of solvent.

molality The expression of the number of moles of solute per litre of solution.

molar (M) Descriptive of a solution that contains one mole of a compound to give one litre of final solution.

molar extinction coefficient The absorbance (extinction) of a 1 M solution using a 1-cm light path or the absorbance of a solution containing 1 mole per millilitre using a 1-cm light path.

molasses A concentrated syrup that contains a significant amount of low-molecular-weight fermentable sugars. Molasses is produced as a byproduct of the sugar, paper pulp, fermented beverage and fuel alcohol industries, but the term is mainly applied to byproducts of the sugar industry. In this case, molasses is produced from the mother liquor that remains after the crystals of sugar have been removed by centrifugation from the masscuite. Alternatively it consists of a concentrated, inverted preparation of cane juice (high test molasses). Molasses is described in terms of its origin as sugar beet molasses, black strap molasses (produced during the processing of raw cane sugar) or cane refinery molasses. The various forms differ in the content and nature of fermentable sugars, nitrogen compounds, vitamins, minerals (ash content) and inhibitory substances. Molasses is used as a raw material for a wide range of industrial fermentations. However, the rather uncertain aspects of its composition and the possible presence of inhibitors make it more suitable as a substrate for the production of low-value bulk products (e.g., alcohols, organic acids, single-cell protein) rather than for high-value pharmaceuticals or speciality chemicals. Molasses is also used as an animal feed supplement and may be added to or partially refined in the production of speciality syrups and treacles.

molasses composition The composition of molasses varies quite widely. Typical values for the major are:

	Cane	Beet
	(% of total solids)	
Sucrose	45	64
Raffinose	–	2
Invert sugar	22	–
Other sugars	5	2
Other organic	15	22
Inorganic (ash)	12	10

mole The molecular weight of a substance expressed in grams; a gram molecule.

molecular biology The study of the chemistry of nucleic acids and proteins, especially in relation to the mechanisms of gene expression and gene manipulation.

molecular cloning *See* gene manipulation.

molecular weight The average weight of a molecule of an element or compound measured in units based on one-twelfth of the weight of an atom of carbon-12. It is the sum of the atomic weights of all the atoms in a molecule of any compound. Molecular weight may be expressed in terms of the dalton.

molecular weight marker A protein, polypeptide, nucleic acid, oligonucleotide, etc. used as a reference material in analytical techniques such as gel filtration chromatography, electrophoresis and density gradient centrifugation.

molecule A grouping of defined atoms, joined in a particular way.

Molisch test A quantitative test for the presence of carbohydrates in a biological sample. Drops of α-naphthol are added to the sample and concentrated sulphuric acid is then poured down the side of the test tube. The presence of carbohydrate is indicated by the formation of a violet ring at the juncture of the two solutions.

monoamine oxidase (EC 1.4.3.4) A mitochondrial enzyme that catalyses the oxidation of a wide variety of amines with the production of aldehydes. Monoamine oxidases are found in high concentrations in mammalian liver, kidney, intestine and pancreas. The enzyme's functions include the detoxification of poisonous amines and the breakdown of adrenaline at adrenergic nerve endings. These oxidases are flavoproteins; molecular oxygen acts as the hydrogen acceptor and becomes reduced to hydrogen peroxide.

monocistronic Descriptive of a length of DNA that codes for only one peptide, in contrast to transcriptional units which may code for several related peptides or enzymes. Monocistronic DNA is typical of eukaryote genes.

monoclonal antibody (Mab) An antibody produced by culturing a single type of cell. It therefore consists of a single species of immunoglobulin molecules. Such cell lines are produced by fusing cells capable of forming antibodies with myeloma (cancerous) cells which are capable of sustained division and growth. The immune response to a known antigen *in vivo* is highly heterogeneous, which means that the antiserum produced contains a mixture of antibodies. These are produced by different lines of B lymphocytes and correspond to the antigenic determinants of the antigen. If it were possible for a particular line of lymphocytes to be maintained *in vitro*, the resulting clone would produce a single type of antibody. In contrast, myelomas can produce abnormal antibodies in large quantities, but the antigen against which they are directed is not known. If a mutant strain of such myeloma cells that has lost the ability to produce antibodies is fused with a line of cells producing an antibody, the resulting hybridoma would be capable of producing a single antibody characteristic of the non-malignant cell. Such cells may then be injected into animals of the same line as produced the original cells for the fusion. Tumours develop in these animals and produce a monoclonal antibody, corresponding to the clone, which accumulates in high concentrations in the animal serum. Alternatively, a sample of the clone can be grown *in vitro*, and the antibody it produces harvested from the culture medium. A wide range of monoclonal antibodies have been produced by what is now a routine technique. These antibodies have been targeted against a very wide range of proteins, haptens, viruses and cell membrane components. Monoclonal antibodies are used in diagnostic (immunochemical) assays (e.g., in screening kits for hormones, allergens, certain types of cancers, viral diseases, bacterial infections, etc.). Other applications include the localization of specific proteins in histochemical investigations, labelling of cells for automatic sorting and use in affinity chromatography, as well as the targeting of anticancer and other drugs.

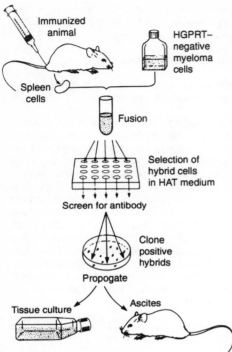

Immunized animal

HGPRT-negative myeloma cells

Spleen cells

Fusion

Selection of hybrid cells in HAT medium

Screen for antibody

Clone positive hybrids

Propogate

Tissue culture

Ascites

Production of monoclonal antibodies

Monocotyledonae The more advanced of the two major subgroups of the angiosperms. Monocotyledons are characterized by the presence of a single cotyledon in the embryo. In general, these plants do not possess a vascular cambium, hence they do not show secondary thickening. The leaves generally have parallel veins and the floral parts are typically present in threes. This group is of particular economic importance since it contains major food crops such as wheat, rice, maize, barley, oats, sugar cane, sorghum, etc., as well as the palms which are important sources of vegetable oils. Other monocotyledons include the lilies and orchids cultured as flowers. Most C_4 plants are monocotyledons.

monoculture (1) A culture of microorganisms, plant or animal cells that contains cells of only one species, strain or clone. (2) A method of farming or forestry in which large areas of land are planted with a single species of crop plant.

monocyte A large phagocytic white blood cell found in vertebrate blood. Monocytes may be around 10 μm in diameter and stain with basic dyes such as methylene blue. These cells ingest bacteria and in inflammatory conditions migrate from the blood to the tissues as macrophages.

monocyte chemotactic and activating factor *See* MCAF.

Monod kinetics A theoretical expression of the rate of growth of microbial systems which is analogous to the Michaelis–Menten theory of enzyme kinetics:

$$\mu = \frac{\mu_{max}s}{K_s + s}$$

where μ = specific growth rate, μ_{max} = maximum possible growth rate attainable at high substrate concentration, s = substrate concentration and K_s = saturation constant.

monoecious Descriptive of a plant in which separate male and female flowers are produced on the same individual.

monogenic diseases Genetic diseases associated with a single gene (e.g., sickle cell anaemia).

monohybrid An organism that is heterozygous for one pair of alleles.

monokine A type of cytokine secreted by monocytes and macrophages.

monolayer A single layer. Anchorage-dependent cells form a monolayer of cells over the surface of the support matrix on which they are grown.

monomer A single unit; a building block for constructing the chain of a larger compound on a repetitive basis.

mononucleotide A compound consisting of a pentose sugar, phosphoric acid and a nitrogenous base that forms one of the units from which nucleic acids are synthesized. The base is either a purine or a pyrimidine, and the sugar is either D-ribose or deoxyribose. Mononucleotides, such as AMP and co-enzyme A, are also important regulatory compounds or cofactors.

monophyletic Descriptive of a group of organisms that have a common ancestor.

monoploid *See* haploid.

monopodial growth A type of growth in plants, characterized by a branching system in which the primary apex continues to grow and remain dominant.

monosaccharide The simplest group of carbohydrates. Monosaccharides which are generally known as sugars, are classified in a number of ways. (1) The number of carbon atoms in the molecule (C_3= triose, C_4= tetrose, C_5= pentose, C_6= hexose, C_7= heptose). (2) The configuration at C–1 and C–2 (aldoses with an aldehyde group, ketoses have a keto group). (3) The stereoisomerism, the form of the sugar being termed D or L. This is decided by the configuration of the highest numbered asymmetric carbon atom and is related to the configuration of glyceraldehyde (atriose). D-glyceraldehyde has the same absolute configuration as the related amino acid D-serum or organic acid D-lactic acid. Natural sugars are generally in the D-form. (4) The internal interaction of the carbonyl group with the hydroxyl group on C-4 (to form a furanose) or C-5 (to form a pyranose). (5) The arrangement of the hydroxyl groups such that a sugar solution may bend light to the right (+) or left (−) (i.e., be dextrorotatory (*d*) or laevorotatory (*l*). (6) The hydrogen atom at position 1 may be above (α-form) or below the ring (β-form). In the free form, the aldehyde (–CHO) or ketone (>C=O) group has reducing properties and gives a positive reaction in the chemical (Fehling's) test for reducing sugars.

monosodium glutamate A flavour enhancer produced on a large scale by fermentation. *See* glutamic acid.

monosomic Descriptive of a cell or an organism that has lost one of a pair of homologous chromosomes ($2X-1$).

monozygotic twins Identical twins; two organisms derived from the same fertilized ovum.

Mops *See* zwitterionic buffer.

morgan In genetics, a unit of linkage equal to one hundred map units.

morphactin One of a number of structurally diverse compounds that possess plant growth activity and react synergistically or antagonistically with endogenous plant growth substances, possibly as inhibitors of auxin transport. These compounds may block the cellular efflux of auxin, but do not stop its influx. This results in an accumulation of auxin which leads to inhibition of phototropic and geotropic response, stunted growth, fusion of plant parts and loss of apical dominance. In roots, the opposite reaction occurs – the growth of primary roots is stimulated, whereas the elongation of lateral roots is inhibited.

morphine A benzylisoquinoline-based alkaloid obtained from the poppy *Papaver somniferum*.

morphogenesis The development of the structure of an organism.

morphology The study of the structure of organisms in terms of their form, and the interrelationship of their internal parts.

morula A solid group of cells derived from a fertilized animal cell that gives rise to the blastula.

mosaic Descriptive of an organism that consists of two or more genetically distinct cell lines.

motor neurone An efferent neurone that connects to an effector such as a muscle.

mould *See* fungi.

moulting *See* ecdysis.

moulting hormone *See* ecdysone.

mRNA Messenger RNA; a form of RNA that transfers the coding information for protein synthesis from the nucleus to the ribosome. mRNA contains between one and ten thousand base pairs. The mRNA is formed from a DNA template by transcription. On the ribosome, the sequence is converted to the required amino acid sequence through translation. In prokaryotes, the mRNA may be a direct copy of the DNA template. In eukaryote cells, the initial transcription product contains extra portions derived from parts of the DNA known as introns. This intermediate heterogeneous nuclear RNA (HnRNA) is processed to produce the mRNA by removal of the surplus portions which may serve a control function.

MSH *See* melanocyte-stimulating hormone.

MSW Municipal solid waste.

mtDNA Mitochondrial DNA (also mitDNA).

mucilage A gum-like complex carbohydrate-based substance produced by both plants and animals.

mucin A glycoprotein; a major component of mucus.

mucopeptide A macromolecular heteropolymer containing two amino sugars (*N*-acetylglucosamine and *N*-acetylmuramic acid) and a number of amino acids (alanine, glutamic acid, diaminopimelic acid, lysine). Mucopeptides are found associated with prokaryotic cell walls.

mucopolysaccharides A polysaccharide that consists of a disaccharide, one moiety of which is an amino sugar. Mucopolysaccharides include hayaluronic acid, heparin and chondroitin.

Mucor A genus of moulds, members of which are used in the production of enzymes such as amyloglucosidase and artificial rennet.

mucosa A layer of moist epithelial tissue lining the internal cavities in vertebrates. It occurs in the respiratory, intestinal and urigenital tracts.

mucous membrane *See* mucosa.

mucus A glycoprotein secreted by globlet cells of the mucosa.

4-MUG 4-Methylumbelliferyl-β-D-galactopyranoside; a fluorogenic substrate used together with the enzyme β-galactosidase in fluorogenic EIA releasing the fluorescent 4-methylumbelliferone.

Müllerian duct The oviduct of vertebrates.

multicellular Descriptive of organisms or organs that contain many cells. *Compare* unicellular.

multiple alleles Groups of alleles, any two of which may occupy the same position on homologous chromosomes in diploid cells. The presence of a series of multiple alleles may be associated with incompatibility.

multiple allelomorph The characteristic produced by a multiple allele.

multiple effect *See* evaporator.

multiple effect evaporator *See* evaporator.

multiple factor inheritance The determination of a phenotypic trait by genes at more than one locus.

multivalent antigen An antigen that has more than one antigen determinant or epitope.

4-MUP 4-Methylumbelliferyl phosphate; a fluorogenic substrate used together with the enzyme alkaline phosphatase in fluorogenic EIA releasing the fluorescent 4-methylumbelliferone.

murine Pertaining to mice.

muscle A tissue with contractile properties that produces movement or provides tension. Muscles may be classified as voluntary (striated), involuntary (smooth) or cardiac. Striated muscle is responsible for the voluntary movements of skeletal parts and is of particular importance in locomotion. In vertebrates, it consists of elongated muscle fibres formed from multinucleate cells with a characteristic banding pattern. This reflects the presence of numerous myofibrils which are grouped into sarcomere units. The sarcomeres contain protein filaments which form the contractile part of the muscle. Cardiac muscle forms the vertebrate heart. It comprises a network of branched multinucleate cells and undergoes continuous rhythmic contractions.

mutagen An agent that alters the genetic information leading to a change in an expressed characteristic. Such agents fall into two groups: chemicals and ionizing radiation. Chemicals may induce loss or addition of basis in the DNA, or may be incorporated into DNA.

mutagenesis The production of mutations.

mutant An organism or a gene carrying a mutation.

mutation A change in the structure of DNA or the number of genes or chromosomes in a cell that results in an abnormal characteristic being expressed. Mutations arise naturally or are brought about by chemical mutagens or ionizing radiation. Mutations occur in gametes or somatic cells. Mutations in somatic cells are not inherited. Inherited mutations occur at the level of the gene or of the chromosome. Chromosome mutations include polyploidy, aneuploidy, inversion, duplication, translocation and deficiency. These can usually be detected by examining the nuclei of suitably stained dividing cells under the light microscope. Gene mutations, which usually occur in only one chromosome of a homologous pair, result from a change in the base sequence or base composition of the DNA and are not detectable by microscopic examination. Gene mutations result in an alternative reading of the genetic code, with the substitution of one or more amino acids in the protein for which the gene codes. This results in an ineffective protein or one that differs from the original in some specific property. Mutations are be recessive and/or deleterious. Advantageous mutations may become dominant as a result of selection pressures.

mutation rate The frequency with which a mutation occurs in a given organism or gene. In general, mutation rates vary between one in 10^4 and one in 10^8 per genome per generation.

mutator gene A gene that increases the mutation rate of other genes in the same organism.

muton The smallest unit of the gene capable of mutation; a base pair in DNA.

mutualism An association between two organisms that results in benefit to both. Examples include the algal/fungal complex found in lichens or the *Rhizobium*/legume association of nitrogen fixation.

mycelium The vegetative part of a filamentous fungi. It consists of a mass of hyphae.

mycobiont The fungal partner of a lichen.

mycoherbicide (1) A compound produced by or isolated from a fungus that shows potent antiplant activity. (2) A preparation based on or derived from a fungus that is used to control weeds (e.g., *Colletotridium gloeosporioides f* species *aeschynomene* which is used against curly indigo disease of rice and soybeans).

mycology The study of the fungi.

mycoplasmas A group of very small, nonmotile bacteria with flexible cell walls. It includes pathanogenic types and the organisms known as pleuropneumonia-like organisms (PPLO).

mycoprotein A single-cell protein produced by the fungus *Fusarium graminearum* and used as a food product.

mycorrhiza Soil fungus that infects roots of higher plants. Mycorrhizae absorb and translocate phosphate and other nutrients, and make them available to the plants. Also they produce antibiotics that protect the host roots from infection.

mycosis A disease associated with the presence of pathogenic fungi in or on the body.

mycotoxin A toxic substance produced by a fungus. The most important mycotoxins are the aflatoxins.

myelin sheath A structure that surrounds the axons of most vertebrate neurones. It is formed from double layers of plasma membrane that are derived from the membranes of Schwann cells.

myelinated nerve fibre A nerve fibre enclosed within a myelin sheath.

myeloid cell An undifferentiated bone marrow cell from which platelets, monocytes, neutrophils, eosinophils, basophils and red blood cells are derived.

myeloid tissue The tissue of vertebrates in which red blood cells and polymorphs are formed. In a foetus, this function is carried out by the liver and spleen. In adult vertebrates, the myeloid tissue occurs in the red marrow of some of the skeletal bones.

myeloma cell A malignant tumour cell, derived from B lymphocytes, that secretes antibodies.

myofibril The structural unit of a striated muscle cell. It consists of sarcomeres surrounded by mitochondria and the sarcoplasmic reticulum.

myoglobin A protein formed from a single polypeptide chain (molecular weight 17,000). It carries a haem group and acts as an oxygen carrier in muscle fibres of vertebrates.

myohaemerythrin An oxygen-carrying pigment derived from lower invertebrates used in immunological studies.

myo-**inositol** A stereoisomer of the carbohydrate inositol.

myosin One of the proteins found in muscle.

myrosinase An enzyme that hydrolyses glucosinolates to yield an unstable glucone that breaks down to give a range of products such as nitriles, isothiocyanates, oxazolidine, thiones, etc.

myxobacteria A group of bacteria, characterized by the lack of a rigid wall and the ability to produce a complex multicellular stalked fruiting body.

Myxomycetes The moulds; a group of fungi characterized by a plant body consisting of a plasmodium.

N

15N A non-radioactive heavy isotope of nitrogen that is used as a marker in cell biology and in studying the biochemistry of protein synthesis and nitrogen fixation.

n orientation Descriptive of the situation in which the vector and the inserted fragment of DNA have the same orientation. *Compare* u orientation.

N protein *See* lytic pathway.

N terminal The end of a protein or polypeptide chain that contains a free amino group (NH_2), hence the abbreviation N.

NAA *See* α-naphthaleneacetic acid.

NAD Nicotinamide adenine dinucleotide, oxidized form; a co-enzyme that functions as a hydrogen carrier in oxidation–reduction reactions associated with fermentation and aerobic respiration. NAD accepts hydrogen atoms from suitable substrates in reactions catalysed by specific dehydrogenases to produce the reduced form NADH. The reducing equivalent is used in intermediate metabolism to reduce other compounds or oxidized to water via the terminal electron transport chain.

NADH Nicotinamide adenine dinucleotide, reduced form. See NAD.

NADP Nicotinamide adenine dinucleotide phosphate, oxidized form; a co-enzyme that performs a similar function to that of NAD. It is particularly important in the oxidation–reduction reactions of photosynthesis.

NADPH Nicotinamide adenine dinucleotide phosphate, reduced form. *See* NADP.

naematolin A coronary vasodilator produced by *Naematoloma fasciculare*.

nanometre (nm) A unit of length equal to 10 angstroms or 10^{-9} metre.

nanotechnology Engineering at the nanometre level. Atoms and molecules are sculptured or arranged using particle beams or tunnel effect devices. Nanotechnology and increased knowledge of the charged and polar surfaces of carbohydrates and proteins may lead to the combination of biological and electronic semiconductor-based devices.

α-naphthaleneacetic acid (NAA) A synthetic plant growth substance with auxin-like activity.

narcotic A substance that induces stupor or sleep.

nascent Descriptive of nucleic acid (DNA or RNA) that has been newly synthesized.

nastic movements In plants, non-directional movement. Some nastic movements are fairly rapid, not depending on cell or cell wall growth, but reflecting changes in turgor pressure of certain cells. Other slower nastic movements depend on cell growth. *Compare* tropism.

native DNA Double-stranded DNA isolated from a cell with its hydrogen bonds between the strands intact. *Compare* denatured DNA.

natural group A group of organisms descended from a common ancestor.

natural selection A hypothesis concerning the mechanism of evolution proposed by Charles Darwin (1809–82). The theory suggests that natural variation in the genetic characteristics of a population results in phenotypic expression of characteristics which give certain individuals an advantage over others. Selection pressures brought about by competition between individuals for limiting factors (e.g., food or space), as well as the ability to withstand changes in the environment, will lead to the eradication of those individuals less suited to the conditions. When the survivors breed, their advantageous characteristics are passed on to future generations, leading in time to the formation of new species.

near infrared (NIR) An analytical technique using fibre or crystal optics to determine the chemical composition of an unknown sample. Light is reflected from or transmitted through the sample at wavelengths of 600–2500 nm. The amount of light absorbed by the sample varies according to the composition of the sample and the frequency of the wavelength. NIR is the only region of the spectrum that enables a large volume, unprepared (in its original form) sample to be studied. NIR is nondestructive and provides rapid and reliable simultaneous measurements of chemical and physical properties on-site.

nearest neighbour analysis A technique used in the structural analysis of oligonucleotides. It is based on the fact that when a new nucleotide is added to the growing point of a transcript, the α-phosphate on its 5′-hydroxyl is linked to the 3′-hydroxyl of the preceding nucleotide. If labelled (^{32}P) NTP is used and the resulting material hydrolysed by alkali, the ^{32}P will be transferred to the nearest neighbour which can thus be identified.

necrotrophic Descriptive of fungi that grow on dead host cells.

nectar A sugary substance secreted from the nectaries of a flower. It attracts animals (insects in particular) that cause pollination.

nectary A glandular structure found in the flowers of animal-pollinated plants.

negative interference The effect that one crossing-over event during nuclear division has on the probability that another crossing-over will take place in the same region of the chromosome. The result of such interference is that double cross-overs within a short length of a chromosome are less fre-

quent than would be expected from observations on the frequencies of single cross-overs.

negative staining A method of treating specimens for examination using light or electron microscopy. Only the background is stained so that the unstained specimen shows up clearly against a dark background. The capsules of bacteria may be revealed by this technique.

Nematoda Roundworms (nematodes). They are widely distributed in water, soil and as parasites in animals and plants. Some species cause serious disease in man or are significant pests in crop production.

Neodiprion sertifer **nuclear polyhedrosis virus** A baculovirus isolated from the larvae of the pine sawfly *N. sertifer*. Used in the manufacture of biological control agents for pine sawfly.

neomycin An antibiotic produced by the bacterium *Streptomyces fradiae*. It is an inhibitor of protein synthesis affecting gram-positive organisms. It acts by binding to ribosomes, resulting in a misreading of the genetic code. It is used to treat intestinal or skin infections.

neomycin resistance The ability to survive treatment with the antibiotic neomycin carried on a plasmid (pUB11O) specific to *Bacillus* species.

neoplasm A tumour or swelling in an organism caused by the abnormal or uncontrolled proliferation of cells. Tumours may be benign (the cells do not invade other tissues) or malignant (cancerous). In the latter case, the cells proliferate and pass around the body forming new tumours.

nepholometer An apparatus that measures the turbidity of a sample of cells or particulate material in suspension. A beam of light is passed through the suspension and the extent to which this light is scattered at right angles is measured. Nepholometers are used in microbiology to measure the growth of unicellular organisms. Since turbidimetric measurements can be made only with homogeneous suspensions, the technique is not suitable for use with filamentous organisms. Accurate measurements require cell suspensions of quite high density (more than 10^7 cells per millilitre).

nephridium An excretory organ found in many invertebrates consisting of a tubular ingrowth of the ectoderm.

nephron A unit of the vertebrate kidney comprising a malpighian body from which leads a uriniferous tubule. The malpighian body consists of the glomerulus (a knot of capillaries) surrounded by the Bowman's capsule.

nerve One of the main structures of the nervous system consisting of a bundle of nerve fibres enclosed in a sheath of connective tissue.

nerve cell *See* neurone.

nerve cord The central major strand of nervous tissue found in the nervous system of animals. In vertebrates, the nerve cord consists of a single hollow tube lying in a dorsal position. In invertebrates the nerve cord generally consists of a double ventral strand that connects ganglia associated with each segment of the body.

nerve ending The end portion of a neurone. In sensory neurones, it is the site at which external stimuli are transformed into signals. This occurs either in association with a receptor or through a system of ramifying branches. The nerve ending of a motor neurone is the site of transmission of an impulse to an effector, such as the end plate on a muscle.

nerve fibre The axon of a neurone surrounded by its myelin sheath through which nerve impulses are transmitted.

nerve impulse *See* impulse.

nerve net The simple nervous system found in some invertebrates.

nervonic acid 15:16-Tetracosenic acid; a naturally occurring unsaturated fatty acid containing 24 carbons found in marine oils and brain tissue.

nervous system A system of interconnecting cells (neurones) found in all multicellular animals (Metazoa). It coordinates activity between different tissues or parts of the body, receiving and transmitting information in the form of nerve impulses. The information comes from receptors which sense the environment and is passed to effectors which produce the response to the stimulus. Neurones make contact with other neurones through synapses. Synapses are generally made between the fine terminal branch of the axon of one cell and the dendrites of another cell. Although the membranes of the two cells become closely apposed, they remain separated by a narrow synaptic cleft. Transmission of an impulse across this gap depends on a chemical mechanism mediated by a neurotransmitter. The simplest nervous system is the nerve net, whose capabilities are restricted because of the limited range of receptors and the localization of synapses in ganglia. The most advanced systems are divided into two separate but interrelated, parts (central nervous system and peripheral nervous system). In the majority of animals, the anterior ganglion collects most information and becomes dominant. The brain is the dominant nervous centre found in the vertebrates. It is associated with the sense organs of the head and collects and processes most of the sensory inputs to the nervous system. The brain also controls motor output patterns throughout the system, as well as being the site of long-term memory and the learning processes.

neural arch An arch of bone that encloses the spinal cord of vertebrates.

neural crest A band of ectodermal cells formed on either side of the neural tube in vertebrate embryos. It gives rise to the dorsal root ganglia of the spinal nerves.

neural network An interconnected group of nerve cells able to accept and respond to signals in any direction through a multi-synaptic pathway. *Compare* reflex arc.

neural network based model A computer system based on artificial networks. Neural networks are used for the prediction of key variables of a bioprocess, consisting of many interconnected elements (neurons). Each neuron has several input connections and one or more outputs. Each input is weighted and the sum of all weighted inputs gives the activation level of the neuron. The output of the neuron is calculated from this activation level and a transfer function. The transfer function is logistic (fermi or sigmoid). Such networks are suitable for modelling of non-linear processes. To model a system, the neural network must be trained by choosing weights such that the output of the network matches the response of the system being modelled to any given input.

neural plate The embryonic ectodermal tissue that gives rise to the central nervous system in vertebrates.

neural spine A projection from the neural arch found in some vertebrae that acts as a point of attachment for muscles.

neural tube A tube of tissue formed from the neural plate in vertebrate embryos that gives rise to the brain and spinal cord.

neuroblast An embryonic cell that gives rise to nervous tissue.

neuroendocrine system The combined system of nerves and endocrine glands that interact to coordinate the activities of multicellular animals.

neurohormone A peptide-based substance released from specialized nerve cells and transported through the blood stream to produce an effect at a distant site. The main site of production of neurohormones is the hypothalamus which produces a number of peptides that control hormone synthesis and secretion by the pars distalis of the pituitary gland.

neurokinin A biologically active peptide; one of a class of peptides known as tachykinins.

neuromuscular junction The synapse between a motor neurone and a muscle cell

membrane. It is similar in structure and function to the synapse between neurones.

neurone The main type of cell found in the nervous system. A neurone consists of a central cell body and contains one or more long unbranched processes (axons) as well as a number of short branching processes (dendrites). The axon forms the conductive region which transmits impulses over long distances within the body. Neurones are grouped together to form nerves which provide an integrated communication system serving the whole body. The neurones make contact with other nerve cells, receptors and effectors through synapses. Information is conveyed from one cell to other cells using neurotransmitters released from the presynaptic membrane.

Neurospora A genus of fungi that includes species used in the production of cellulase.

neurotransmitter A chemical that is secreted by a neurone and mediates the transmission of a nerve impulse across a synapse. Compounds identified as neurotransmitters include acetylcholine, noradrenaline, adrenaline, dopamine, aminobutyric acid and serotonin.

neurula The stage of development of the vertebrate embryo that follows the gastrula. It is characterized by the development of the neural tube from the neural plate and marks the first appearance of the nervous system.

neuter (1) An organism that does not have sex organs. (2) The removal of sex organs from normal plants or animals.

neutrase A protease derived from *Bacillus subtilis* that may be added to cheese to accelerate the maturation process.

neutrophil A phagocytic amoeboid white blood cell (polymorph) comprising 55–60 per cent of the white cells found in human blood. Neutrophils accumulate in large numbers in the blood during infection.

Newtonian fluid A fluid whose viscosity is constant and independent of the rate of shear at constant temperature and pressure. All gases and many homogeneous liquids exhibit newtonian characteristics.

NHP *See* non-histone protein.

niacin *See* nicotinic acid.

nick A break in a single strand of DNA.

nick-closing enzyme A form of DNA polymerase that can restore base sequences. A nick is introduced adjacent to an incorrect base. The base is then removed and the correct base inserted.

nick-translation A method used to obtain a labelled DNA probe. Although translation in molecular biology generally refers to the process of protein synthesis, this meaning does not apply here. Instead the term refers to the movement, or translation, of a nick along a duplex DNA molecule. Nicks can be introduced at widely separated sites in DNA by gently treating with DNase I, resulting in the exposure of free 3′-hydroxyl groups. DNA polymerase I of *E. coli* incorporates nucleotides at the free 3′-hydroxyl groups in a successive sequence. At the same time, hydrolysis of the 5′-terminal by the 5′-3′-exonuclease activity of polymerase I releases 5′-mononucleotides. If the system is incubated with radioactive (^{32}P) deoxynucleoside triphosphates, the reaction progressively incorporates the label into a duplex that is unchanged except for movement of the nick along the molecule. Since the original nicks occur at random, a DNA preparation becomes labelled to a degree that reflects the specific activity of the nucleotides used and the extent of replacement of the bases.

nicking The production of breaks in a single strand of double-stranded DNA. Such nicks may be produced by the endonuclease DNase I.

nicotinamide adenine dinucleotide *See* NAD.

nicotinamide adenine dinucleotide phosphate *See* NADP

nicotinic acid Pyridine-3-carboxylic acid; a B complex vitamin essential to man. Deficiency causes the disease pellagra.

nif genes A set of genes that encodes the information needed for the formation of enzymes and other proteins associated with the fixation of atmospheric nitrogen. These genes have been studied in detail in *Klebsiella pneumoniae*, which is closely related to *E. coli* to which the *Klebsiella* nif genes can be transferred. At least 17 genes are involved in nitrogen fixation. They are located in one gene cluster distributed on 7 operons. Some functions of nif genes are known; nifK and nifD code for the subunits of component I of the nitrogenase, and nifH codes for the subunits of component II. nifJ and nifF are involved in electron transport. The operon nifAL regulates the expression of the whole nif region. Normally, the *Klebsiella* nif region is transcribed and the nitrogenase complex synthesized only if fixed nitrogen is needed. Strains of *Klebsiella* that have constitutively expressed nif regions (nif derepressed) may be constructed by genetic manipulation. Gene-manipulated strains are currently being investigated for a number of purposes: (1) developing ammonia- and hydrogen-evolving strains; (2) developing *Rhizobium* strains able to nodulate the host legume in competition with resident strains of *Rhizobium*; (3) improving the characteristics leading to higher levels of nitrogen fixation; (4) increasing the efficiency of the nitrogen-fixing process (e.g., by recycling the hydrogen produced during fixation through the action of a coupled hydrogenase); (5) developing fertilizer plants (i.e., non-leguminous plants such as corn, rice or wheat), which is a much more complex problem requiring a transfer of plant genes involved in the symbiotic process from legumes to non-leguminous plants.

ninhydrin reaction A chemical test or spray used in chromatography to detect amino acids. A chromatogram is sprayed with a 0.2 per cent solution in acetone or an acidified 0.5 per cent solution in butanol. When the chromatogram is heated at 105°C, all compounds containing a primary or secondary amino group attached to an aliphatic carbon give a purple colour. However, α-amino acids will react more specifically in about 3 hours at room temperature to give similar colours. The reagent is also used to measure protein hydrolysates or other mixtures of amino acids following separation by column chromatography. A combination of automated column chromatography with photometric determination of the colour formed with ninhydrin is the basis of some automated amino acid analysers.

NIR *See* near infrared.

nitrate assimilation The conversion of nitrate to ammonia. For most plants in their natural environment, nitrate is the usual source of nitrogen. Nitrate must be converted into ammonia before it is incorporated into carbon compounds with the formation of amino acids and other cell constituents. The process in plants is termed assimilatory nitrate reduction in order to distinguish it from the respiratory use of nitrate as an electron acceptor rather than molecular oxygen. Assimilatory nitrate reduction is also found in many bacteria, fungi, yeasts and algae. The process occurs in two stages: (1) nitrate is reduced to nitrite by nitrate reductase; (2) ammonia is formed by nitrite reductase.

nitrate reductase An enzyme that catalyses the conversion of nitrate to nitrite. Eukaryotic nitrate reductase is an enzyme complex containing flavin (FAD), haem (cytochrome b557) and molybdenum. Electrons are provided by NAD(P)H derived from photosynthesis or carbohydrate oxidation. Prokaryotic nitrate reductase is a smaller protein containing molybdenum, but no haem or cytochrome. The enzyme has a fast rate of turnover and is present at high concentrations when nitrate is available, but is repressed by the presence of ammonium ions.

nitrification The conversion of ammonia, liberated from decaying organic matter in the soil, to nitrate. Two genera of bacteria are involved; *Nitrosomonas* converts am-

monia to nitrate and *Nitrobacter* converts nitrite to nitrate.

nitrite reductase An enzyme that converts nitrite to ammonia. Plants and photosynthetic prokaryotes possess a ferredoxin-linked nitrite reductase which accepts electrons from reduced ferredoxin, but not from NAD(P)H. The enzyme contains a tetranuclear iron–sulphur centre and a special haem (siro) similar to that found in sulphite reductase. Nitrite is reduced directly to ammonia without the formation of free intermediates.

nitrocellulose filter A flat sheet of paper-like material made from cellulose nitrate, a nitric ester of cellulose. Cellulose nitrate binds DNA strongly and can be permanently fixed by baking at 80°C.

nitrogen A chemical element present in amino acids and proteins and hence important in the diet of animals and man. It forms about 80 per cent of the atmosphere.

nitrogen cycle The overall circulation of nitrogen through the biosphere. The cycle involves the nitrogen-fixing organisms (bacteria and cyanobacteria), organisms that produce ammonia from decaying matter, the nitrifying bacteria which oxidize ammonia to nitrite or nitrate and plants which assimilate nitrogen as ammonia or nitrate and form amino acids, as well as the denitrifying bacteria which convert nitrate back to nitrogen gas through nitrite.

nitrogen fixation The assimilation of gaseous (atmospheric) nitrogen by reduction to ammonia and incorporation into amino acids. Only some groups of organisms (soil bacteria and some cyanobacteria) are capable of nitrogen fixation. The bacteria include mainly those of the genus *Rhizobium*, which develop a symbiotic relationship with higher plants forming nodules on their roots. Such associations are formed mainly with leguminous plants. Some other plant genera such as alder (*Alnus*) also form symbiotic relationships with nitrogen-fixing bacteria of the genus *Frankia*, and ferns such as *Azolla* contain symbiotic cyanobacteria (*Anabaena*). Free-living bacteria that fix nitrogen are known from over 25 different genera including *Clostridium*, *Klebsiella* and *Azotobacter* and the photosynthetic bacteria including *Rhodospirillium rubrum*. Certain nitrogen-fixing bacteria are found in close association with the roots of C_4 grasses and other plants with high photosynthetic rates which exude carbohydrates into the rhizosphere. This relationship has been termed associative fixation or biocoenosis. Bacteria of this type include *Beijerinkia* species, *Azotobacter paspali* and what was known as *Spirillum lipoferum* (found in association with sugar cane), but which is probably two species of *Azospirillium* (*A. lipoferum* and *A. brasilense*). The basic requirements for nitrogen fixation in all organisms are the presence of the enzyme complex nitrogenase, a strong reducing agent (reduced ferredoxin, flavodoxin, NADH or NADPH), an energy source (ATP–Mg^{2+}) and a low or zero oxygen level.

nitrogenase An enzyme complex that catalyses the reduction of atmospheric nitrogen (dinitrogen) to ammonia in nitrogen-fixing organisms. The enzyme has two major components, each of which has two or four subunits. The larger component contains molybdenum, non-haem iron and sulphur, and the smaller contains iron and sulphur. The enzyme, which is strictly anaerobic and is easily inactivated by molecular oxygen, also acts as a hydrogenase. Hydrogen production is a wasteful reaction, and those species with a low level of hydrogen production are more efficient nitrogen fixers. The two reactions catalysed are:

1. Nitrogenase:
$$N_2 + 12ATP + 6e^- + 6H^+ \rightarrow 2NH_3^+ + 12ADP + 12P_i$$

2. Hydrogenase:
$$4ATP + 2e^- + 2H^+ \rightarrow H_2 + 4ADP + 4P_i$$

where P_i = inorganic phosphate. The ammonia formed is assimilated into amino acids through the GS/GOGAT reaction.

nitrosoguanidine   *N*-Methyl-*N*′-nitro-*N*-nitrosoguanidine; one of the most potent chemical mutagens. It can produce a high yield of mutations coupled with a high survival rate.

nitrous acid A mutagen. Cells are treated by suspending them in an acidic buffer and adding sodium nitrite. Mutagenesis is controlled by varying the length of time the cells are treated.

NK cells Natural killer cells; a lymphocyte subset activated by interferon and other substances that are capable of mediating cellular cytolysis without specific antigen–antibody reaction.

nm Abbreviation for nanometre.

NMR spectroscopy *See* nuclear magnetic resonance spectroscopy.

Nocardia **species** A genus of actinomycetes used for the bioremediation of soils contaminated by phenols and/or iron.

node (1) In plants, the part of the axis to which leaves are attached. (2) In vertebrate nervous systems, a region of exposed axon that occurs between adjacent Schwann cells of myelinated nerve fibres.

nodulation and fixation genes The genes involved in the *Rhizobium*–legume symbiosis, which is one of the most effective nitrogen-fixing systems. Identification of some *Rhizobium* nif genes has been achieved by hybridization with the nifYKDH fragment of *Klebsiella pneumoniae*, with cloning and analysis of special *Rhizobium* nif fragments in *E. coli*. Fixation and nodulation genes can also be identified by transposon mutagenesis. By this technique it is possible to analyse the whole symbiotic process, and hence to identify the genes involved by cloning the genes in *E. coli*. The next step is to alter the fixation and nodulation genes by genetic engineering techniques in order to construct *Rhizobium* strains that are more effective in nitrogen fixation.

nodule bacteria *See Rhizobium*.

nodulins A collective term for proteins that occur in the root nodules of nitrogen-fixing plants.

non-coding strand That strand of double-stranded DNA that is complementary to the coding strand, but is not used as a source of information for synthesizing a molecule of protein.

non-competitive inhibition A form of enzyme inhibition in which a compound binds at a site other than the substrate binding site, causing a reduction in enzyme activity. This may be a form of allosteric inactivation or it may be due to irreversible damage to the enzyme.

non-disjunction An abnormality that occurs during anaphase I of meiosis when both members of a bivalent migrate to the same pole. This results in aneuploidy with one daughter cell becoming trisomic whereas the other is monosomic.

non-endemic disease A disease that is normally completely absent from a community because it is excluded by control measures or because the community is isolated from carriers.

non-histone protein (NHP) A protein, other than a histone, that is found in the nucleus of a eukaryotic cell. NHPs include the polymerases and other regulatory enzymes involved in the control of transcription.

non-homologous Descriptive of chromosomes or chromosome segments that contain dissimilar genes and that do not pair during meiosis.

nonident P-40 A detergent used to solubilize proteins and to reduce the number of non-specific hydrophobic interactions that occur during protein blotting and ELISA.

non-ionic surfactant A detergent that is uncharged in solution. Typical commercial products are obtained by condensing ethylene oxide on to the polar end of a fatty acid, fatty alcohol or alkyl phenol to provide a polymeric ether chain that terminates in a hydroxyl group.

non-isotopic probes A nucleic acid sequence used for DNA hybridization using enzyme, chlorogenic, fluorogenic or other non-radioactive label. Non-isotopic probes are used for gene mapping and diagnostic applications such as the detection of genetic abnormalities.

non-random mating A mating system in which the frequencies of the various kinds of matings with respect to some trait or traits are different from those expected according to chance.

nonsense codon A base triplets (UAA, UAG or UGA) that does not code for any amino acid and that leads to termination of a polypeptide chain.

nonsense mutation A mutation that results in the termination of a polypeptide chain.

nopaline See opine.

noradrenaline 1-(3,4-Dihydroxyphenyl)-2-aminoethanol; a neurohormone also known as norepinephrine, released from the adrenal medulla. It acts as a neurotransmitter in the sympathetic nervous system at postganglionic effector junctions; effects include powerful vasoconstriction.

norepinephrine See noradrenaline.

northern blot A technique similar to the southern blot procedure used for elution of RNA fragments from gels.

notochord A rod of tissue that lies dorsally along the length of the bodies of members of the phylum Cordata. In vertebrates, the notochord is partially or totally replaced by the vertebral column.

NPV See nuclear polyhedrosis virus.

NTP See nucleoside triphosphate.

nuclear magnetic resonance (NMR) spectroscopy A technique that provides structural information. The sample is subjected to a magnetic field which causes the nuclei of various atoms to orientate in one of two energy levels. If energy is applied to the nuclei, they will change their orientation. The energy wavelengths that cause this transition correspond to radio frequencies, and the precise frequency depends on the environment of the nucleus (i.e., its relationship to other nuclei or atoms in the molecule). The technique is generally used to determine the position of hydrogen (proton NMR) or carbon (using ^{13}C-labelling) atoms.

nuclear membrane A double membrane that surrounds the nucleus of eukaryotes and is continuous with the membranes of the endoplasmic reticulum. Each unit membrane is 8 nm thick and separated by a perinuclear space 15 nm wide. It is perforated by numerous nuclear pores.

nuclear polyhedrosis virus (NPV) Any of a number of viruses of subgroup A of the genus Baculovirae. Most NPV isolates have been obtained from Lepidoptera. NPVs have also been reported in Coleoptera, Diptera, Hymenoptera, Neuroptera and Trichoptera. Since NPVs have high pathogenicity for their insect hosts, several have been used for commercial production of biological pest control agents.

nuclear pore An annular-shaped hole that occurs in nuclear membranes; usually large numbers are present. The inner and outer membranes of the nucleus become fused together at the annulus. Nuclear pores are the site of active transport of materials into and out of the nucleus. Nuclear imports include the nucleotide precursors of DNA and RNA, histones and ribosomal proteins, whereas exports include mRNA, tRNA and ribosomal subunits.

nuclease An enzyme that cleaves nucleic acids. *See* DNase, nuclease SI, restriction endonuclease and RNase.

nuclease SI A very specific nuclease that degrades single-stranded nucleic acids or splits short single-stranded stretches in DNA, but does not attack any double-stranded structure. It is used in gene manipulation for converting sticky ends of duplex DNA to form blunt ends or to trim off single-stranded ends after conversion of

single-stranded cDNA to the double-stranded form. It is also used to cleave duplex DNA at A–T-rich sequences following partial thermal denaturation.

nuclease-free reagent A chemical used to extract or purify DNA or RNA that has been tested to ensure very low levels of ultraviolet-absorbent material and enzymes capable of denaturing or hydrolysing nucleic acids (RNA and DNA).

nucleic acid Either of two types of macromolecule (DNA or RNA) formed by polymerization of nucleotides. Nucleic acids are found in all living cells and contain the information (genetic code) for transfer of genetic information from one generation to the next, as well as for the expression of this information through protein synthesis.

nucleic acid hybridization *See* annealing.

nucleic acid sequence analysis A technique for determining the sequence of bases in a specific nucleic acid and from which the amino acid sequence of the protein for which it codes can be determined. It is also used in determination of taxonomic relationships between viruses and other organisms, as well as determining control sequences governing initiation and termination of transcription. *See* Maxam–Gilbert chemical sequencing.

nucleoid The region of a prokaryotic cell in which the DNA is situated. It is analogous to the eukaryotic nucleus, but is not enclosed within a membrane at any time. Similar regions containing fibrils of nucleic acid are also found in chloroplasts and mitochondria.

nucleolus A small, spherical structure found within the interphase nucleus; cells may have several nucleoli. Nucleoli disappear at metaphase and reappear at telophase. Under an electron microscope, they appear granular, are composed of particles of about 15 nm in diameter and lack a limiting membrane. They are rich in protein and DNA, and contain much of the nuclear RNA. The rRNA component of the cytoplasmic ribosomes is transcribed in the nucleolus. Ribosomal proteins synthesized in the cytoplasm move to the nucleolus where the characteristic 80S ribosome is assembled by attaching the 18S, 28S and 5.8S rRNAs together with 5S RNA which originates independently in the non-nucleolar region of the nucleus.

nucleoplasm The nuclear equivalent of cytosol, with which it is continuous through the nuclear pores.

nucleoprotein A complex formed from nucleic acids and protein. In eukaryotes, nuclear DNA is associated with histones and protamines.

nucleoside A compound consisting of a purine or pyrimidine base linked to D-ribose or D-deoxyribose. The common nucleosides in biological systems are adenosine, guanosine, cytideine, thymidine and uridine.

nucleoside triphosphate (NTP) A general term used to include all the triphosphates of biological importance (i.e., ATP, CTP, GTP, ITP, TTP and UTP).

nucleosome The basic unit of structure of chromatin. It consists of histones, basic proteins and acidic non-histone proteins associated with DNA. The nucleosome has a base core of two molecules, each of four different histone species which contain a DNA chain of about 140 base pairs. The nucleosome particles are connected by linkers that contain strongly folded DNA and one molecule of another histone (H1), which determines the spacing of the nucleosomes.

nucleotide A compound consisting of a nitrogenous base, a pentose sugar and phosphoric acid. Nucleotides are the basic building blocks from which nucleic acids (DNA and RNA) are constructed. The major nucleotides found in living cells are those derived from the purines adenine and guanine, and the pyrimidines cytosine, thymine and uracil. The sugar is either D-deoxyribose (in DNA) or D-ribose (in RNA).

Nucleotides also occur free in the cell as mononucleotides (AMP) or as dinucleotides (NAD, FAD).

nucleus The central organelle found in almost all eukaryotic cells (with the exception of mammalian red blood cells and plant sieve tube elements). It contains the inheritable information (genetic material) in the form of DNA which during cell division becomes organized into the visible chromosomes; the chromosomes cannot be distinguished in non-dividing cells where they are represented by the chromatin. The nucleus is 2–8 μm wide and is surrounded by two unit membranes each 8 nm thick separated by a perinuclear space which is continuous with the lumen of the endoplasmic reticulum. The membrane is perforated by nuclear pores. In fungi and many lower plants, the nuclear membrane remains intact during division. In higher organisms, it fragments and is reformed around the daughter nuclei. Within the nuclear membrane is nucleoplasm, embedded in which are chromatin and nucleoli. The nucleoli are the sites of ribosome synthesis. Some protozoa possess two types of nuclei: a larger meganucleus which is polyploid and contains most of the DNA and nucleoli; a small micronucleus which functions in conjugation.

nullisomy A condition in which the chromosome number of a cell or organism is reduced because of the absence of both members of a homologous pair.

nurse callus A callus that is plated out on a medium seeded with plant cells to provide essential nutrients and stimulate cell division.

nutrient An element or compound that is needed by an organism to provide it with energy and building material for growth. Nutrients include the major elements, trace elements and a wide range of carbon sources, as well as (to varying degrees) essential metabolites including vitamins, amino acids, fatty acids and other growth factors.

nutrient agar A nutrient broth solidified by the addition of agar.

nutrient broth A medium used in the culture of pathogenic and other bacteria that contains peptone, meat extract and sodium chloride.

nutrient film technique A method of plant propagation in which plants are grown in a trough through which a shallow layer of nutrient solution is recycled. The lower part of the root is immersed wholly in the solution. The top part of the root, however, protrudes above the surface and is covered in a thin film of solution. This allows for adequate root aeration whilst optimizing nutrient uptake.

nutrient limitation The condition in which growth of a culture is limited by the availability of a nutritional requirement. The lack of a carbon source or any of the essential elements, vitamins or other compounds leads to a cessation of growth. Lack of other nutrients may produce changes in metabolism. For example, a lack of nitrogen in the form of ammonia can induce the derepression of other pathways of nitrogen uptake, as well as increased formation of both endo- and exo-polysaccharides. A phosphate deficiency can lead to marked changes in wall composition of some gram-positive bacteria and changes in the phospholipid content of gram-negative cells, as well as changes in phage-binding capacity and the ability to retain plasmids within the cell. Lack of sulphur or magnesium can cause changes in wall structure and composition. Lack of potassium affects the respiration of gram-negative organisms, leading to excretion of partially oxidized metabolic intermediates, whereas lack of iron can lead to excretion of iron-chelating compounds as well as a loss of phage binding capacity in *E. coli*.

nutritional requirement The minimal nutritional need for the proper growth and maintenance of an organism or culture. It includes both macronutrients and micronutrients (trace elements, vitamins, essential amino acids, etc.).

nyctinastic movement Movement that occurs in plants on a daily basis in response to changes in light and/or temperature. Examples include the opening and closing of flowers and the movement of leaves to aid or avoid the direct interception of sunlight.

nymph The immature form of an insect.

nystatin An antibiotic produced by *Streptomyces noursei*.

O

obligate Descriptive of an organism that requires a certain environmental condition or nutrient for growth or survival.

obligate aerobe An organism that will only grow in the presence of oxygen.

obligate anaerobe An organism whose growth is inhibited or that is killed in the presence of oxygen.

occlusion body A protein crystal containing virus particles observed in insects or mites infected by nuclear polyhedrosis viruses.

ochre mutant In phage, a suppressor-sensitive mutation that blocks transcription because of the presence of the nonsense codon UAA.

octopine An opine, the formation of which is induced in plant cells infected with some strains of Ti plasmids from *Agrobacterium tumefaciens*.

octyl glucoside A detergent used to solubilize membrane-bound proteins.

odontoblast A cell from the periphery of the pulp cavity of a tooth, characterized by long cytoplasmic processes that extend into the canals of the surrounding dentine.

oesophagus The passage through which food passes from the mouth to the stomach in vertebrates.

oestradiol-17β Oestra-1,3,5(10)-triene-3, 17β-diol; a major natural oestrogen produced and secreted by mammals.

oestrogen An 18-carbon steroid hormone produced by the ovaries, testes, placenta or adrenal cortex in vertebrates. In mammals, oestrogens stimulate the growth and maintenance of the female reproductive organs. They also determine the female secondary sexual characteristics, affect reproductive function and behaviour, and regulate the expression of genes by stimulating the synthesis of specific mRNAs and proteins in the target tissues. The predominant oestrogen found in most mammals is oestradiol-17β. Other oestrogens of importance include oestriol and oestrone.

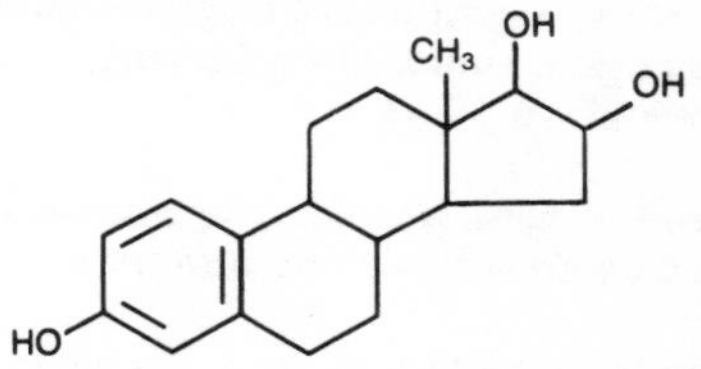

Oestriol

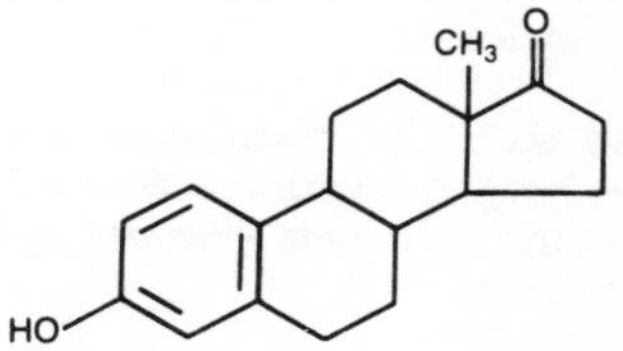

Oestrone

oestrous cycle The reproductive cycle that occurs in sexually mature, non-pregnant female mammals. The process is regulated by the hypothalamus which releases factors that stimulate the periodic secretion of pituitary gonadotrophins. These promote the production of oestrogens and progesterone. Ovulation occurs during the end of the first phase of the cycle known as oestrus, during which the lining of the uterus proliferates. This is followed by metoestrus, dioestrus and pro-oestrus during which the corpus luteum first develops and then regresses if fertilization has not taken place. If fertilization does occur, the cycle becomes suspended in the metoestrus phase for the duration of pregnancy.

oil overlay A thin film of oil added to a slant culture or liquid stock culture of microorganism to reduce the rate of dehydration of the culture due to water loss from the surface.

oil shale An oil-bearing rock in which the hydrocarbon is not liquid and therefore cannot flow. The rock has to be mined, crushed and heated to obtain the hydrocarbon, called 'kerogen'.

Okazaki fragments Small molecules of 100–2000 bases that are formed during replication of double-stranded DNA. *See* DNA replication.

oleagnus Descriptive of a cell that accumulates large amounts (over 20 per cent of the dry weight) as lipids.

oleandomycin A macrolide antibiotic produced by *Streptomyces antibioticus*.

olefin A hydrocarbon homologous to ethylene, having the general formula C_nH_{2n}; also known as an alkene.

oleic acid *cis*-9:10-Octadecanoic acid; an 18-carbon fatty acid with one double bond. It is one of the most widely occurring long-chain fatty acids.

oleochemical An industrial chemical based on or derived from naturally occurring lipids or fatty acids.

oleoresin A natural mixture of essential oils and a resin.

olfactory organ An organ of smell. In vertebrates, olfactory organs are paired structures located in nasal cavities that communicate with the exterior environment through the external nares. In invertebrates, olfactory organs include structures such as the antennae of insects.

oligodeoxyribonucleotide An oligonucleotide that contains deoxyribose; a short length of DNA.

oligomer A chain of a few monomeric units, the length of which need not be closely defined.

oligonucleotide A macromolecule consisting of a short chain of nucleotides; a short length of DNA or RNA.

oligonucleotide synthesizer An automated machine designed to synthesize short polynucleotide chains (oligonucleotides) similar in structure to DNA or RNA. These machines use solid-phase synthesis in which one nucleotide at a time is added on to a growing oligonucleotide chain. Each nucleotide is added using the same sequence of chemical reactions with an appropriate derivatized purine or pyrimidine base. The chemical reactions used and the details of operation vary with the different machines commercially available. The most widely used method is based on the phosphoramidite method of DNA synthesis.

oligopeptide A peptide chain made up of a few amino acids.

oligoribonucleotide An oligonucleotide that contains ribose in the backbone; a short length of RNA.

oligosaccharide A carbohydrate containing a few monosaccharides.

oligotrophic Descriptive of a stretch of water in the natural environment that has a low concentration of nutrients, and thus a low productivity. *Compare* eutrophic.

omasum The third chamber in the stomach of ruminants.

ommatidium One of the small units that make up the compound eye of arthropods.

omnivore An animal that feeds on animal and plant material.

oncogene A gene, which may be carried by a virus, that affects the normal metabolic control and metabolism of a cell in such a way that it becomes cancerous.

oncogenic virus A virus that carries an oncogene which may be inserted into the genetic elements of an infected host cell or organism resulting in abnormal development. Both RNA and DNA viruses may be oncogenic. They include adenoviruses, leukoviruses and papovaviruses. Oncogenic viruses are also capable of inducing cell transformations *in vitro*.

Oncornavirinae A group of viruses which include the HTLV that cause leukaemia in humans.

on line Descriptive of the continual transfer of data from a recording device to a data logger, chart recorder or microprocessor.

one gene–one enzyme hypothesis A supposition that the gene is equivalent to the amount of genetic material required to encode the sequence for one specific enzyme. However, this is now known not to be correct, since some genes do not encode protein structures and many enzymes are composed of several subunits which may be coded for by separate genes. A more correct interpretation would be one gene–one polypeptide chain.

ontogeny The development of an individual during its lifetime.

oocyte The egg cell, contained in an ovary, which undergoes meiosis to form an ovum and a polar body (a cell with little cytoplasm). The first division of meiosis occurs in a primary oocyte which generates the secondary oocyte. This then undergoes the secondary meiotic division to produce the ovum. In some species, the cell released from the ovary and with which fertilization occurs may be at the oocyte stage.

oogamy The fusion of two gametes of unequal size. These are generally a small, motile male sperm and a larger, sedentary female ovum, which contains the food reserves for the early development of the zygote.

oogenesis The formation of an ovum.

oogonium (1) A structure found in some algae and fungi that bears the ova, which may be termed oospheres. (2) A primordial germ cell that gives rise, by mitosis, to oocytes, from which the ovum and polar bodies develop by meiosis.

oosphere A female gamete that develops inside an oogonium. Characteristically an oosphere is a large, spherical, sedentary, haploid gamete that contains food reserves for the early development of the zygote.

oosponal A hypotensive produced by *Gloeophyllum striatum*.

oospore A thick-walled resting spore that develops from a fertilized oosphere.

opal mutant In phage, a suppressor-sensitive mutant that prevents transcription because of the presence of the nonsense codon UGA.

open circular DNA A circular double-stranded DNA molecule in which one of the polynucleotide strands has been nicked and the double helix therefore assumes a non-supercoiled (relaxed) state. *See* covalently closed circular DNA.

operator In the DNA of an operon, a nucleotide sequence that is recognized and bound by a repressor protein, which, in turn, inhibits transcription of the operon. *Compare* promoter.

operator gene A structural gene present in an operon that regulates protein synthesis.

operon The genetic unit that regulates the expression of inducible enzymes in prokaryotes; a group of closely linked genes that code for enzymes associated with the same biosynthetic pathway. Although the genes are present, they are only expressed if there is a need for the metabolic pathway to operate following a change in the environment. The genes are switched on through a complex control mechanism. An operator gene acts as an on/off switch controlling the transcription of mRNA for all the enzymic proteins coded for by structural genes and a regulator gene produces a repressor which prevents the synthesis of mRNA by the operon by binding specifically to the DNA of the operator locus.

opiate A chemical that induces sleep; a soporific.

opine A guanidoamino acid. The opines octopine and nopaline are formed by plant cells following infection by the Ti plasmid, and may be used as genetic markers.

opioid peptide An opioid peptide with opiate-like activity that acts directly on narcotic receptors.

opportunistic infection A disease caused by an organism that is not usually associated with the particular host (e.g., infection of humans with dry rot fungi, or the wide range of organisms that exploit the loss of immune resistance in the disease AIDS).

opsonin An antibody that reacts with the surface antigens of bacteria and promotes phagocytosis.

optic nerve The second cranial nerve in vertebrates. It passes from the retina of the eye to the brain.

optical activity The rotation of the plane of vibration of a beam of polarized light when passed through a solution of an optically active compound. Compounds that contain one or more asymmetric carbon atoms can exist in two different configurations known as enantiomers, which are mirror images of one another. One enantiomer rotates the beam of polarized light to the left (*l*-form or laevorotatory) and the other rotates the beam to the right (*d*-form or dextrorotatory).

optical isomerism A form of isomerism in which the isomers differ in their optical activity.

optical rotation The angle through which the plane of polarized light is rotated when passed through an optically active substance.

optimum temperature range A narrow range of temperature, which may cover only two or three degrees, in which cultures of an organism show maximum growth rate. Below the optimum growth rate, the rate in general declines only slowly with the decrease in temperature, whereas at temperatures only a few degrees above the optimum a precipitous decline in rates to zero may occur.

optrode An optical biosensor in which an enzyme and a pH-sensitive dye are immobilized on to a probe. The enzyme reaction causes a change in pH which in turn causes the dye to change colour.

orbit The cavity in the vertebrate skull that houses the eyeball.

order A grouping used in the classification of plants or animals consisting of closely related families. Orders are grouped into classes.

ore A metal-bearing mineral or rock.

organ A part of the body of any multicellular organism that forms a distinct structural and functional unit made up of several different types of tissue.

organ culture The growing of organs, usually of embryonic origin, *in vitro*.

organelle A subcellular structure associated with a specific cell function or metabolic role. Organelles include the nucleus, mitochondria, chloroplasts, microbodies, ribosomes, Golgi bodies and the endoplasmic reticulum. Most organelles are bounded by or composed of one or more limiting membranes. The metabolism of the cell is apportioned between various organelles in such a way that competing reactions, or reactions proceeding in opposite directions, are kept separate. For instance, respiration is largely confined to the mitochondria, whereas photosynthesis occurs in chloroplasts. Metabolic pathways may involve the interaction of the activities of several different types of organelles. For instance, photorespiration requires the interaction of chloroplasts, peroxisomes and mitochondria.

organic compound A chemical compound containing one or more carbon atoms.

However, carbon dioxide and carbon monoxide are not classified as organic compounds. The term derives from the original discovery of organic compounds in living organisms.

organic solvent A liquid organic compound used to dissolve materials.

organism A complete and intact living entity.

organogenesis The period during embryogenesis when the major organs are formed.

organometallic compound An organic compound that contains one or more metal atoms.

organotherapy The use of extracts of organs (enzymes and hormones) for therapeutic purposes.

organotroph An organism that grows on organic material.

ori *See* origin of replication.

origin of replication (ori) A base sequence that is recognized as the position at which the replication of a molecule of DNA should begin. In bacteria, plasmids and viruses, there is usually only one such position. Lengths of DNA that contain the sequence for the origin of replication may be termed replicons.

ornithine $(H_2N(CH_2)_5CH(NH_2)COOH)$ A basic amino acid that functions as an intermediate in the ornithine/citrulline (urea) cycle and is a precursor of pyrroline alkaloids.

ornithine/citrulline cycle A cyclic metabolic pathway in which ornithine condenses with carbamoyl phosphate to form citrulline, which is then converted to arginine via argininosuccinate, and arginine is converted back to ornithine with the liberation of urea. The process is also known as the urea cycle.

orthologous genes Homologous genes that have become differentiated in different species derived from a common ancestral species. *Compare* paralogous genes.

osmiophilic globules Small lipid bodies that stain with osmium tetroxide.

osmium tetroxide An oxide of osmium used in histology to identify fats which it stains black. Osmium tetroxide is also used as a fixative in microscopy.

osmoregulation The process by which animals maintain the correct concentration of water, salts and other solutes in their bodies. This is carried out by nephridia, malpighian tubules or kidneys in multicellular organisms and by the contractile vacuole in protozoans.

osmosis The tendency of a fluid or solvent to pass through a semipermeable membrane from a solution of lower solute concentration to one of higher solute concentration, thus equalizing the conditions on either side of the membrane. In living cells, the semipermeable membranes involved are usually the plasma membranes and/or the tonoplast and the solvent water. These membranes are selectively permeable and also contain transport mechanisms that are capable of selectively transporting a variety of ions, as well as low-molecular-weight and high-molecular-weight compounds, across the membrane. Movement of ions in particular is used to adjust the osmotic pressure of cells and induces small movements such as the opening and closing of stomata in leaves.

osmotic potential The maximum osmotic pressure that could develop as a result of osmosis in a solution separated from pure solvent by a semipermeable membrane.

osmotic pressure The pressure that must be applied to a solution in order to prevent the flow of solvent through a semipermeable membrane separating the solution from one of a lower osmotic pressure. The osmotic pressure increases as the concentration of solutes increases and is dependent on the number of ions or molecules rather than the molecular or ionic species involved.

osmotic shock disruption A cell disruption technique in which a steep osmotic gradient is created across the outer membrane of a cell, causing water to flow into the cell. The pressure on the cell membrane increases until it ruptures and the intracellular material is released.

ossification The replacement of connective tissue by bone. It is characterized by the invasion of tissue, such as embryonic cartilage, by osteoblasts which deposit successive layers of bone and become trapped as osteocytes in the bone matrix.

osteoblast A cell derived from a connective tissue layer beneath the periosteum that is responsible for the deposition of bone.

osteoclast A cell involved in the remodelling or repair of damaged bone. Osteoclasts act by resorption of existing bony tissue and the laying down of new bone.

osteocyte A cell found in the bone matrix that is derived from osteoblasts. Osteocytes become trapped during mineralization of the bone. They release calcium from the bone into the blood stream.

ouabain A glycoside that inhibits adenosine triphosphatase obtained from the wood of *Acokanthera ouabio* or seeds of *Strophanthus gratus*. Ouabain is used as a selective agent in the production of hybridomas.

oudenone A hypotensive produced by *Oudemansiella radicata*.

outbreeding The crossing of individuals of the same species that are not closely related.

ovalbumin Egg albumin.

ovary (1) In animals, the main female reproductive organ. There are two ovaries in vertebrates and these produce ova and steroid hormones under the control of gonadotrophins produced in the pituitary. Production of ova occurs as part of the oestrous cycle. The mammalian ova develop within the so-called graafian follicles which arise from one of the many oogonium-containing follicles enclosed within a stroma of connective tissue. The mature ovum is released at ovulation and the residual cells of the graafian follicle contribute to the formation of a temporary endocrine gland known as the corpus luteum which secretes progesterone. If fertilization does not occur, the corpus luteum degenerates as the ovary enters the next oestrous cycle. (2) In plants, the basal portion of a carpel, or carpels, which contains one or more ovules carried on a placenta. The two types of structure are distinguished as an apocarpous gynoecium (a monocarpellary ovary) or a syncarpous gynoecium (a polycarpellary ovary). In the latter, two or more carpels are fused to form a single structure bearing ovules or placenta corresponding in number to the number of carpels. The ovary may possess a single loculus, or several loculi.

overdominance The condition in which the heterozygote exhibits a more extreme manifestation of the trait (usually fitness) than does either of the homozygotes.

overflow continuous fermentation *See* cascade fermentation.

overlapping genes A phenomenon in which the same portion of a DNA sequence contains the message for two different proteins, translation of which may be achieved by shifting the reading frame by only one or two nucleotides.

over-producer A mutant cell that produces large quantities of a chemical that is not usually accumulated. This is due to a fault in metabolic regulation. Over-producers generate large amounts of secondary metabolites or produce intermediates of central metabolism. Many industrial fermentations are carried out using mutants or strains that are over-producers.

oviduct The tube that transports ova from the ovary to the uterus in viviparous animals, or to the outside in other species.

oviparity A form of reproduction that occurs in most invertebrates, and many vertebrates (with the exception of mammals), in which the fertilized eggs are spawned. These eggs contain poorly developed embryos which are supplied with a large food supply in the form of yolk.

ovoviviparity A form of reproduction in which the embryos develop within the parent animal but do not form a placenta or make contact with the maternal body in any way for nutritional purposes.

ovulation The discharge of an ovum or oocyte from a mature follicle in a vertebrate ovary.

ovule A structure found in higher plants (gymnosperms and angiosperms) in which the female gamete develops. It consists of a short stalk bearing one or two integuments which enclose the nucellus (a small mass of sporophyte tissue) leaving a small pore (the micropyle) due to their incomplete closure. A single cell at the micropyle end enlarges to become the megasporophyte which undergoes meiosis to produce a megaspore. This in turn gives rise to an embryo sac. This produces the archegonia in gymnosperms or the functional gametic nucleus in angiosperms. After fertilization, the ovule matures to form the seed.

ovum An unfertilized, non-motile female gamete produced in an ovary.

oxidase An enzyme that catalyses an oxidation (e.g., glucose oxidase).

oxidation The removal of electrons, such as the oxidation of ferrous to ferric iron:

$$Fe^{2+} \rightarrow Fe^{3+} + e^-$$

Oxidation may also be regarded as the removal of hydrogen, such as the oxidation of lactic acid by lactate dehydrogenase:

$$lactate + NAD \rightarrow pyruvate + NADH$$

oxidation pond A system for treating liquid waste in which the effluent is stored in shallow open lagoons. The rate of BOD removal is enhanced by the growth of algae which release oxygen during photosynthesis; this in turn enhances the growth of aerobic heterotrophic bacteria.

oxidation–reduction potential (E) The electrode potential of a half cell containing a mixture of oxidized and reduced forms of the reactants. In practice, E_0 is used as the electrode potential when the concentrations of the oxidized and reduced forms are equal. In biological reactions, the potential is determined at pH 7.0 and is denoted as E_0'.

oxidative phosphorylation The synthesis of ATP from ADP and inorganic phosphate coupled with electron transport along the respiratory electron transport chain. This process occurs in mitochondria during aerobic respiration. There are three sites in the chain where ATP can be formed. The energy is derived from reduced co-enzymes, including NADPH and FADH generated by oxidation of intermediates of the TCA cycle. NADPH is produced during the oxidation of pyruvate, isocitrate and malate giving a ratio of ATP formed to oxygen consumed (P/O ratio) of 3. The formation of FADH during the oxidation of succinate bypasses one of the sites of phosphorylation; hence succinate gives a P/O ratio of 2. Phosphorylation is associated with the activity of complex membrane protein aggregates termed coupling factors with ATPase activity. Oxidative phosphorylation is uncoupled from electron transport by various chemicals and antibiotics. The concept of the mechanism of phosphorylation known as the chemiosmotic theory is now generally accepted.

oxidoreductase An enzyme that catalyses oxidation–reduction reactions (i.e., electron transfer). Oxidoreductases include the dehydrogenases associated with NAD, NADP, flavins, cytochromes and quinones in respiratory and photosynthetic electron transport. Oxidoreductases are one of the main groups (EC 1) used in enzyme classification:

    1.1 Acting on CH–OH of donors
    1.2 Acting on CHO or C=O of donors
    1.3 Acting on CH–CH of donors
    1.4 Acting on CH–NH_2 of donors
    1.5 Acting on C–NH of donors
    1.6 Acting on NADH or NADPH as donor

1.7 Acting with nitrogen compounds as donors
1.8 Acting on S groups of donors
1.9 Acting on haem groups of donors
1.10 Acting on diphenols as donors
1.11 Acting on H_2O_2 as acceptor
1.12 Acting on hydrogen as donor
1.13 Oxygenases
1.14 Hydroxylases.

oxim A chemical compound containing a divalent group N(OH) joined to a carbon atom.

oxygen concentration The amount of oxygen, expressed in terms of equivalent volume under standard conditions. It is expressed as moles or weight per unit volume of gas or liquid phase.

oxygen debt A condition that occurs in animals that are normally aerobic if insufficient oxygen is available in the tissues. This may occur during periods of high activity during which metabolism is switched to an anaerobic pathway by the activation of the enzymes lactate dehydrogenase. As a result, pyruvate is converted to lactate, which accumulates in the muscles. When aerobic metabolism is re-established, the lactate is transported to the liver and oxidized.

oxygen electrode An electrochemical cell in which the current generated is proportional to the activity of oxygen present in a solution. In principle, the electrode consists of a platinum/silver junction with potassium chloride as the electrolyte. An electrical potential (polarizing voltage of about 0.65 V) is applied across the wires, with the platinum made negative with respect to the silver. The magnitude of the current is linearly proportional to the oxygen activity of the solution. This may be amplified electronically and recorded on a chart recorder or digital readout. In electrodes designed for biological use, the electrode is protected from contamination by a thin oxygen-permeable membrane, usually made of Teflon.

oxygen quotient The rate of consumption of oxygen by an organism or tissue measured in terms of volume of oxygen consumed per unit weight per unit time.

oxygen transfer The transfer of oxygen from air into solution in a fermenter. This is expressed in terms of the volumetric oxygen transfer coefficient (k_La). In practice, rates of oxygen transfer are expressed in terms of millimoles of oxygen transferred per litre-hour, which is equal to $k_La \times c^*$, where c^* is the equilibrium concentration of dissolved oxygen in the liquid phase, expressed in millimoles of oxygen per litre.

oxygen transfer rate A measure of the rate at which oxygen passes from the atmosphere into solution. Such rates are determined using an oxygen electrode or by measuring the rate of oxidation of a solution of sulphite to sulphate in the presence of a metal catalyst (cobalt or copper).

oxygen uptake rate A measure of the actual rate of oxygen use by a culture expressed on a volumetric basis. It is dependent on the cell concentration times the average rate of oxygen consumption for that culture.

oxygen yield The amount of biomass and/or end products produced in an aerobic reaction expressed as a function of the amount of oxygen consumed.

oxygenic reaction A reaction carried out in a reactor in which oxygen, rather than air, is introduced. In fermentation, such a reaction may use commercial-grade oxygen to provide the dissolved oxygen required for biochemical oxidation by the aerobic organisms.

oxyhaemoglobin A bright red form of haemoglobin produced when the iron atom in haem binds with molecular oxygen. In many vertebrates, oxyhaemoglobin is used to transport oxygen in the blood.

oxytocin A peptide hormone secreted by the pituitary that causes contraction of the smooth muscle of the uterus and the cells surrounding the alveoli of the mammary gland.

P

P_1 The parental generation used to produce the F_1 progeny.

P_{660} *See* PR.

P_{680} A chlorophyll a–protein complex that functions as a trap for photosystem II in non-cyclic photophosphorylation.

P_{700} A chlorophyll a–protein complex that functions as the trap for photosystem I in cyclic and non-cyclic photophosphorylation.

P_{730} *See* PFR.

P_i An abbreviation denoting inorganic phosphate.

Pab *See* polyclonal antibody.

pacemaker (1) A group of muscle cells or neurones, the spontaneous electrical activity of which drives the cyclic activation of an effector organ. The major pacemaker is the group of cells in the sinus venosus of the vertebrate heart which activates the contractions of the cardiac muscle. (2) An artificial electronic device which may be implanted in the body to perform the same function.

pachytene A stage in prophase I of meiosis.

packaging The re-introduction of a recombinant DNA molecule into a phage particle. The required phage DNA is produced in a concatemeric form, using a rolling circle replication mechanism. This is encapsulated *in vitro*. In the presence of phage head precursor, the concatemeric DNA is cleaved into monomers, and nicks are introduced in opposite strands 12 nucleotides apart at each *cis* site to produce the linear monomer with its cohesive termini. The head is formed and then assembled with the tail structure. The principle of *in vitro* packaging is to supply the DNA with high concentrations of phage head precursor, packaging proteins and phage tails. This is achieved using a mixed lysate of two induced lysogens, one of which is blocked at the pre-head stage, whereas the other is blocked for head formation. This can be done by using amber mutants. In the mixed lysate, genetic complementation occurs and the exogenous DNA is packaged.

packed bed reactor A tubular bioreactor that is filled with a solid matrix. It contains trapped cells or enzymes, or is coated with cells or enzymes. It is run as a plug flow reactor, with the medium entering at one end and percolating through the matrix, during which time the substrate is converted to product, which emerges in the effluent from the column.

packed cell volume A technique used to determine the relative growth of a cell culture. An aliquot of cells is taken and spun in a centrifuge at a defined speed for a fixed time. A calibrated capillary or test tube is used. The volume of cells is recorded and expressed as volume of packed cells per volume of medium.

PADGEM Platelet activation dependent granulocyte external membrane protein; a glycoprotein that is presynthesized by platelets and endothelial cells. PADGEM appears immediately on the cell surface following stimulation by thrombin or histamine attracting white blood cells to the site of tissue damage. It is also known as CD62 or GMP-140.

PAF *See* platelet-activating factor.

PAGE *See* polyacrylamide gel electrophoresis.

pairing The process by which members of each pair of homologous chromosomes form a close association at prophase I of meiosis.

palindromic sequence A symmetrical repeated sequence in DNA molecules such that the sequences in the two strands are the same if read in the same polarity. For example

$5'$ $3'$
        CATTATATAATG
        GTAATATATTAC
$3'$ $5'$

Short palindromic sequences occur frequently in DNAs, and palindromic sequences of several hundred base pairs have been identified in some molecules. Restriction endonucleases cut DNA at palindromic sequences.

palisade mesophyll The main region of photosynthetically active cells found in the leaves of dicotyledons. The palisade layer is characterized by long, closely fitting columnar cells containing many chloroplasts.

palmitic acid Hexadecanoic acid; a long-chain fatty acid containing 16 carbon atoms.

pancreas A gland that lies between the spleen and the duodenum. The exocrine tissue, which makes up the bulk of the gland, forms and secretes a number of enzymes including trypsinogen, amylase, maltase and lipase. These are released into the pancreatic duct where the pancreatic juice is formed which flows into the duodenum. The secretion is controlled by the vagus nerve and the peptide hormones secretin and pancreozymin. Glucagon and insulin are secreted by the endocrine tissue (islets of Langerhans).

pancreatin A preparation containing all the enzymes of the pancreatic juice. It is obtained from animal tissue and used as a therapeutic or digestive aid.

pancreozymin A peptide hormone released from the mucosal cells of the duodenum that stimulates contraction of the gallbladder and secretion of digestive enzymes by the pancreas.

panmixia *See* random mating.

panning A selective cell purification method, based on affinity chromatography, in which a specific cell type pretreated with monoclonal antibodies is bound to antigens adsorbed on to polystyrene dishes.

pantothenic acid A B complex vitamin required in the diet of vertebrates including man. It is a precursor of co-enzyme A.

papain A proteolytic enzyme isolated from papaya.

papaverine An alkaloid derived from opium that relaxes the involuntary muscles of the gastrointestinal tract and other smooth muscle.

paper chromatography A technique generally used for the separation of low-molecular-weight compounds such as amino acids, sugars and organic acids. Two-dimensional paper chromatography was used, in combination with radioactive ^{14}C, to elucidate the mechanisms of the photosynthetic carbon reduction cycle and subsequently widely used in studies on central metabolism. An extract, often obtained by alcoholic extraction, is concentrated and placed in one corner of the chromatogram. This is developed by allowing the solvent to migrate through the paper in the first direction. The paper is then dried, turned through 90° and developed in a second solvent.

paper raft A square of filter paper resting on an actively growing callus that is used to culture single plant cells. The callus provides essential growth factors that facilitate plant cell division.

papilla A small projection or pimple occurring in animals or plants. Papillae include small protuberances concerned with the senses of touch, taste and smell, the vascular process at the root of a hair in mammals or small blunt hairs found in plants.

papilloma A tumour of the skin or mucous membrane that develops as a papilla.

papillomavirus A type of papovavirus responsible for the formation of warts and similar skin lesions or tumours.

papovavirus A class of tumour-forming viruses, characterized as naked icosahedral bodies of two types: (1) papillomaviruses which are about 55 nm in diameter; (2) smaller polyomaviruses of about 45 nm in diameter.

paracentric inversion A chromosomal inversion that does not include the centromere.

paralogous genes Homologous genes that have arisen through gene duplication and that have evolved in parallel within the same organism. *Compare* orthologous genes.

parasexual hybridization Any of a number of processes resulting in non-meiotic genetic recombination in vegetative cells, for example, conjugation, protoplast fusion, transduction, transformation and mitotic recombination.

parasite An organism that lives on (ectoparasite) or in (endoparasite) another organism – the host – from which it obtains its nourishment. Parasites and their hosts are usually of different species. Many parasites have complex life cycles which involve several generations, each with a distinct host. Such mechanisms enable the wider distribution of the parasite.

parasympathetic nervous system Part of the vertebrate autonomic nervous system characterized by cholinergic peripheral nerve endings.

parathyroid glands Endocrine glands that lie close to the thyroid glands and secrete calcitonin and parathyroid hormone in vertebrates. They regulate calcium and phosphorus metabolism.

parathyroid hormone A peptide hormone secreted by the parathyroid glands in response to low levels of blood calcium. It stimulates the resorption of bone, the intestinal absorption of calcium and the reabsorption of calcium salts by the kidney.

parenchyma A tissue formed of thin-walled living cells that forms the ground tissues of the plant. Parenchyma cells, which are the least modified type, resembling meristematic cells quite closely, act as storage tissue for sugar, starch and some oils. The cells also function in the movement of water and metabolites.

parental type An association of genetic markers, found among the progeny of a cross, that is identical to an association of markers present in a parent. *Compare* recombinant type.

parthenocarpy The formation of fruits without the occurrence of fertilization or seed development. Parthenocarpy is induced artificially in some commercial crops by spraying with plant growth substances such as auxins and gibberellins. This can lead to the normal development of the ovary wall and other floral parts that contribute to the formation of false fruits.

parthenogenesis A process found in animals in which an egg cell develops normally without being fertilized by a male gamete. Parthenogenesis, alternating with generations showing normal sexual reproduction, is common in some insects including plant pests such as aphids. The advantage of parthenogenesis is that it accelerates the rate at which offspring are produced. A similar process is also quite common in plants (*see* parthenocarpy).

partially mixed digester An anaerobic digester in which only part of the contents is mixed. This may operate as a two-stage system: a lower solid, unmixed layer in which acidogenesis occurs; an upper, mixed layer where methanogenesis occurs.

particle porosity A measure of the volume of space taken up or available to a liquid and/or enzyme or microorganisms within a biomass support particle.

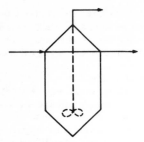

Partially mixed continuous digester

partitioning effect A localized change of environmental conditions (e.g., pH, product concentration) in the vicinity of an immobilized enzyme brought about by diffusion limitations, that may cause the repulsion or attraction of substrates, products or inhibitors altering the rate or equilibrium of the reaction, which then differ from those in the reaction catalysed by the free enzyme.

parturition The expulsion of the foetus at the termination of pregnancy in mammals.

passage The subculturing of a cell line.

passenger DNA Foreign DNA sequences introduced into a cloning vehicle.

passive immunity A condition brought about in one individual by the administration of an immunoglobulin produced by another individual, usually by injection. The serum is obtained from an animal or another human. The effectiveness is only moderate or low, but is immediate. However, the effects are short-lasting. Reactivation may be dangerous because of anaphylactic shock. The technique is used for therapy and as a prophylactic measure.

passive immunization The administration of a preparation, containing an antibody, to an animal or man. It neutralizes a toxin or combines with an invading organism or virus.

Pasteur effect A decrease in fermentative ability exhibited by some yeasts on aeration. It is a metabolic response to the increased availability of oxygen, which in turn permits the onset of oxidative phosphorylation promoting the rapid conversion of ADP and inorganic phosphate to ATP. Hence, alcohol production ceases as the activities of the TCA cycle come into operation.

pasteurization A heat treatment used to kill pathogenic microorganisms that might be present in foods and beverages.

pathogen A microorganism that infects another plant or animal to produce disease symptoms or a toxic response.

pathogenic Descriptive of a substance or organism that produces a disease.

pathology The science that studies the origin, nature and course of disease, or the conditions and processes of a particular disease.

pBR322 An artificial plasmid used as a cloning vector. It is one of the most versatile and widely used of the artificial plasmids. The following history gives an indication of the complexity of the construction of artificial plasmids. A plasmid r7268 was isolated in 1963 and renamed RI. A variant of this, derepressed for mating transfer, was isolated as RI drd19. The Ap transposon from this plasmid was transposed on to another known as pMB1 to form pMB3. This plasmid was reduced in size using the restriction enzyme *Eco* RI to form a very small plasmid (pMB8) which carries only colicin immunity. The enzyme *Eco* RI was then used to generate a number of restriction fragments from another plasmid pSC101 and were combined with pMBS opened at a unique *Eco* RI site, and the resulting chimeric molecule was rearranged by *Eco* RI activity to generate pMB9. Another element known as Tn3 was transposed to pMB9 to form pBR312. This was rearranged to form pBR313 from which two fragments were isolated and ligated to form pBR322. The plasmid is 4362 base pairs long and has been completely sequenced. There are eleven known enzymes which cleave the plasmid at unique sites. These include *Hind* dIII, *Bam* HI and *Pst*. The *Pst* I site is useful since it produces 3'-tetranucle-otide extensions which are suitable for reaction with terminal transferase. Hence this site is excellent for cloning by the homo-polymer tailing method.

PCR *See* polymerase chain reaction.

PDGF *See* platelet-derived growth factor.

peat A highly organic acid soil that occurs in bogs or marshy regions. It is composed of partially decomposed vegetable matter. It may be cut out, dried and used as a fuel directly or converted by anaerobic digestion to biogas.

pectic enzyme *See* pectolytic enzymes.

pectic substances Polysaccharides extracted from plant cell walls by prolonged treatment with boiling water. They are formed largely from galacturonic acid, arabinose, galactose and methanol covalently linked to other polysaccharides and cell wall components. The galacturonan of higher plants is of commercial value in the food industry, being used under the name of pectin as a setting agent in jam making.

pectin *See* pectic substances.

pectin esterases *See* pectolytic enzymes.

pectolytic enzymes Enzymes capable of degrading pectic substances. Pectolytic enzymes, which occur in a wide variety of bacteria and fungi, are divided into two classes: (1) depolymerizing enzymes; (2) saponifying enzymes or pectin esterases. The depolymerizing enzymes are classified into several groups. (a) Hydrolases: endo-hydrolase (endo-polygalacturonase) or exo-hydrolase (galacturonopolygalacturonase or digalacturonogalacturonase). (b) *trans*-Eliminases: endo-*trans*-eliminase (endo-pectic acid *trans*-eliminase or endo-pectin *trans*-eliminase) or exo-*trans*-eliminase (exo-pectic acid *trans*-eliminase or oligoga-lacturonide *trans*-eliminase). Commercial enzymes are generally obtained from *Aspergillus niger* or *Sclerotinia libertiana* grown on solid substrate fermentations.

Pectolytic enzymes are used extensively in the clarification and depectinization of fruit in order to obtain higher concentrations of juice. They are also used in the removal of the mucilagenous coating in coffee bean preparation and in the curing of cocoa, tea and tobacco. An additional use is in the retting of flax, hemp or jute.

pedigree A diagram showing the ancestral relationships between individuals of a family over two or more generations.

PEG *See* polyethylene glycol.

penetrance The extent to which a given gene is expressed in an organism. It is calculated as the percentage of the organisms of a given genotype that shows the character in the phenotype. In mendelian genetics, penetrance is assumed to be 100 per cent. Variations in penetrance are due to the modifying effects of other interacting genes.

penicillin An antibiotic that disrupts cell wall synthesis in gram-negative bacteria. The parent molecule (penicillin G) is produced by *Penicillium notatum*. A wide range of synthetic analogues has been produced by chemical modification of this basic structure.

penicillin acylase An enzyme that removes the benzyl group from penicillin G, forming 6-aminopenicillanic acid.

penicillin resistance The property possessed by some bacteria, actinomycetes, yeasts and cyanobacteria that enables them to grow in the presence of penicillin. This is often associated with the presence of the enzyme penicillinase, which is carried on some natural, wild-type plasmids.

penicillinase β-Lactamase; an enzyme that inactivates natural penicillins and occurs in some resistant organisms.

Penicillium A genus of moulds, a member of the ascomycetes. The vegetative stage consists of a much-branched mycelium, which produces conidiophores bearing tufts of non-motile spores (conidia). These stores

Penicillin K   Penicillin F

Natural penicillins

Oxacillin   Methicillin

Semisynthetic penicillins resistant to penicillinases

Semisynthetic penicillins orally administered

on germination give rise to further mycelia. Sexual reproduction is common, although many strains are heterothallic. The asci usually develop in clusters, enclosed by a loose layer of hyphae. In addition to the production of penicillin, fermentations based on various species or strains of *Penicillium* are used in the production of enzymes and the curing of cheese.

pentose A monosaccharide containing five carbon atoms.

pentose phosphate pathway An oxidative metabolic pathway, the enzymes for which are present in the cytosol. The overall process is divided into two parts. The first phase is physiologically irreversible, whereas the second phase is reversible. Phase I commences with the oxidation of glucose-6-phosphate to D-gluconolactone-6-phosphate with the reduction of NADP to NADPH. The lactone is then hydrolysed to 6-phosphogluconic acid and oxidatively decarboxylated to ribulose-5-phosphate, again using NADP as the oxidant. As a result, two molecules of NADPH are produced per molecule of glucose phosphate. In the second phase, ribulose phosphate is converted back to hexose phosphate in a complex series of reactions. The cycle has three main functions: (1) generation of NADPH in non-photosynthetic tissue; (2) generation of pentoses which are required for the synthesis of nucleotides and nucleic acids; (3) generation of a four-carbon sugar phosphate which is required for the formation of shikimic acid, the precursor of many aromatic ring structures. The pentose phosphate pathway occurs in germinating seeds, root tips and other areas of active biosynthesis in plants. In animals, it occurs in tissues associated with the synthesis of steroids and fats (e.g., liver, mammary glands, adipose tissues and adrenal cortex). In general, the reductant (NADPH) is used in synthetic reactions and is not used in phosphorylation.

pepsin An endopeptidase; a proteolytic enzyme produced by glands of the vertebrate stomach.

peptidase An enzyme that hydrolyses peptides, releasing the constituent amino acids.

peptide A compound consisting of two or more amino acids linked covalently through peptide bonds. A peptide of three or more amino acids is called an oligopeptide if the peptide chain is short, whereas longer peptide chains are called polypeptides or proteins.

peptide bond A covalent link that joins the individual amino acids to form peptides and proteins. The peptide bond is formed from the α-carboxyl group of one amino acid and the α-amino group of the next by elimination of a molecule of water.

peptide hormone A peptide that shows hormonal activity.

peptone A fragment produced by the partial digestion of protein.

per cent transmission An expression of the amount of light that passes through a sample as measured in a spectrophotometer or colorimeter.

per cent yield The yield of a chemical reaction or fermentation process in which the result is given in terms of the amount (weight) of product expressed as a percentage of the amount (weight) of reactants or substrates used or consumed.

percolating filter A system of aerobic wastewater treatment based on a plug flow fixed film bioreactor.

percolation The slow movement of a liquid through a bed of solid particles.

perennating organ A structure or organ that is adapted to overwintering. Perennating organs include seeds and underground storage organs (e.g., tubers, corms, bulbs and rhizomes) which serve as a means of vegetative propagation for the plants and as a source of food for animals, including man. Most of the substrates used in large-scale fermentations are derived from sugar beet, potato, cassava root, etc.

perennation In plants, a method of overwintering.

perennial A plant that continues to grow from year to year.

perfusion bioreactor A continuous culture system in which mammalian cells are grown on microporous beads. The beads provide a large surface area for cell growth and facilitate the continuous supply of nutrients and removal of wastes. This allows the cells to be cultured for several weeks at a time.

perfusion chromatography A high-speed chromatographic process in which the separation column is packed with porous particles. Perfusion systems have similar resolving power and capacity to conventional chromatography systems but are up to ten times faster. This increased speed is the result of the pore structure. This consists of throughpores that transect the perfusion particles allowing convective flow of sample molecules. The throughpores are lined with smaller diffusive pores that provide a large surface area for absorption.

perianth The structure of a flower that surrounds the sexual parts. It usually consists of two whorls of leaf-like parts. In dicotyledons, these may be dissimilar consisting of an inner corolla (the petals) and an outer calyx (the sepals). In monocotyledons, the two whorls are similar and are coloured in insect-pollinated species, or much reduced in wind-pollinated species.

periblem In plants, the part of the apical meristem that gives rise to the cortex.

pericardial cavity In vertebrates, the space enclosing the heart.

pericardium A fibrous membrane structure that surrounds the vertebrate heart.

pericarp The wall of a fruit which is formed from the ovary wall. The pericarp is divided into three layers: the outer exocarp; the middle mesocarp; the inner endocarp.

pericentric inversion A chromosomal inversion that includes the centromere.

periclinal In plants, descriptive of the plane parallel to the surface of an organ.

pericycle A layer of parenchyma that lies between the stele and the endodermis. In roots, the pericycle forms the meristems from which lateral roots arise.

periderm The outer protective tissue of the roots and stems of woody gymnosperms and angiosperms.

peridium The outer layer of the spore-producing body of a fungus.

periodontal membrane Connective tissue that connects the roots of teeth to the cavities in the jaw bone.

periosteum A membrane of connective tissue that encloses bones and provides attachment for tendons and muscles.

peripheral nervous system The network of cranial and spinal nerves that connect the central nervous system (brain and spinal cord) to various effectors and receptors throughout the body.

periplasm The fluid in the space between the cytoplasmic membrane and outer membrane in gram-negative bacteria.

perisperm A seed storage tissue that develops from the nucellus.

peristalsis A series of muscular contractions that passes along tubular organs, such as the oesophagus and intestines, caused by sequential contraction of circular and longitudinal muscles. This results in the contents of the tube being moved in front of the wave of contraction.

perithecium In fungi, a flask-shaped ascocarp lined with a layer known as the hymenium, which produces the spore-containing asci.

peritoneum A layer of epithelium that lines the abdominal cavity of vertebrates.

permeation chromatography *See* gel filtration.

permissive condition *See* conditional lethal mutation.

peroxidase An iron-porphyrin-containing enzyme that catalyses a reaction in which hydrogen peroxide is an electron acceptor. Most peroxidases are found in plants. However, at least two peroxidases (lactoperoxidase and myeloperoxidase) occur in animals. The overall reaction is:

$$AH_2 + H_2O_2 = A + 2H_2O$$

where AH_2 may be a phenol, p-aminobenzoic acid, p-phenylenediamine, ascorbic acid or ferrocytochrome. Leuco forms of oxidation–reduction indicators may also be used as substrates.

peroxisome A microbody present in the photosynthetic cells of higher plants. They are important, together with chloroplasts and mitochondria, in the photorespiration and contain a wide range of enzymes, including catalase and those associated with the metabolism of two-carbon compounds and the re-assimilation of ammonium ions. Large numbers of peroxisomes occur in the photosynthetic tissues of C_3 plants, which show higher levels of photorespiration, compared with those in the C_4 plants. In C_4 species, peroxisomes occur more frequently in the bundle sheath cells, which are also potential sites for the production of phosphoglycollate, the initial substrate of the C_2 pathway.

pest A disease-inducing organism, often applied to organisms that cause disease or attack agricultural crops.

pesticide A chemical compound or biological agent used in the control of pests and disease.

petri dish A flat, shallow circular container made of glass or clear plastic used for the culture of bacteria, fungi or tissues on nutrient media which often include agar as a support material.

PF *See* phytochrome.

PFGE *See* pulsed field gel electrophoresis.

PFR The form of phytochrome that absorbs red light resulting in rapid conversion to the PF form.

pH A measure of the degree of acidity (pH below 7) or alkalinity (pH above 7) of a solution. Pure water has a neutral pH. pH is defined as the negative logarithm of the proton concentration:

$$pH = -\log_{10}[H^+]$$

This convention is used since the actual concentration of the hydrated proton is very small, and it is awkward to handle very small negative powers.

pH electrode The primary standard used for measurement of hydrogen ion concentrations. It is a platinum electrode which is immersed in the solution to be measured with gaseous hydrogen bubbled over its surface at a pressure of 1 atmosphere. The electromotive force of this electrode in 1.0 M H_3O^+ ions is zero. The potential difference between the electrode and a standard electrode (e.g., a calomel electrode) is measured and used to calculate the H_3O^+ ion concentration. This type of electrode is not suitable for everyday use and is generally replaced by a glass electrode surrounded by a reference electrode with a potassium chloride solution forming a salt bridge. This design gives a practical, compact and simple probe which is electrostatically screened over most of its length.

pH meter A device that combines a pH electrode with electronic circuits in order to determine the pH of a solution.

Phaeophyta The brown algae, some of which are used as a commercial source of alginic acids.

phage *See* bacteriophage

phagocyte A cell that is capable of ingesting extracellular particles such as bacteria. Phagocytes include both polymorphs and macrophages, which play an important role in disease control in vertebrate tissue, and free-living protozoans.

pharmacokinetics The study of the quantitative activity of pharmacological agents.

pharmacology The study of drugs, their preparation, uses and effects.

pharynx A part of the vertebrate alimentary canal that lies between the buccal cavity (mouth) and the oesophagus.

PHB *See* poly-β-hydroxybutyrate.

Phe Abbreviation used to denote the amino acid phenylalanine in protein sequences and elsewhere.

phenazine methosulphate (PMS) An artificial electron acceptor that reacts directly with reduced co-enzymes and prosthetic groups such as flavins and pyridine nucleotides. It is used in studying respiratory and photosynthetic electron transport.

phenocopy A non-hereditary phenotypic modification that mimics a similar phenotype due to a gene mutation.

phenol extraction The initial stage in the purification of DNA or RNA. A cell extract is mixed with one part phenol and one part chloroform and then centrifuged. Protein is precipitated at the interface between the organic phase and the aqueous phase that contains the RNA and DNA.

phenotype The observed characteristics of an organism that are the result of the interaction between the genetic characteristics (genotype) of the organism and its environment.

phenotypic variance The variance among individuals with respect to some phenotypic trait or traits. *Compare* genetic variance.

phenylalanine (Phe) One of the 20 common amino acids that occur in protein. It is an essential amino acid for man.

Phenylalanine   CH₂CH(NH₂)COOH

phenylketonuria An inherited disorder of metabolism that results in an inability to metabolize the amino acid phenylalanine to tyrosine. It is carried as a single recessive gene, and if not detected can result in severe mental retardation. The symptoms can be minimized by a diet low in phenylalanine.

pheromone A chemical excreted by animals, and insects in particular, which results in specific reproductive, behavioural or developmental responses in members of the same species.

phialocin An anticoagulant produced by *Phialocephala repens.*

phloem In higher plants, the vascular tissue responsible for the movement of organic compounds. It is a composite tissue containing cells of several types. These include the sieve tubes which conduct the material and the companion cells which contain large numbers of mitochondria and provide the energy for active transport.

phosphate A chemical group containing atoms of phosphorus and oxygen.

phosphate triester synthesis A technique used in the production of oligonucleotides which uses protected monotriethylammonium salts of nucleotides. In the presence of a coupling agent, such as mesitylenesulphonyl nitrotriazole, the triester is incorporated into the growing chain of an oligonucleotide.

phosphate/oxygen ratio *See* P/O ratio.

phosphatide *See* phospholipids.

phosphatidic acid A simple glyceride composed of two long-chain fatty acids esterified to a molecule of glycerol phosphate.

phosphite synthesis A technique used in the production of oligonucleotides in which solid-phase synthesis is achieved using diiosopropyl phosphoramidites.

6-phosphogluconate dehydrogenase (EC1.1.4.4) An enzyme that catalyses the second dehydrogenation step of the pentose phosphate pathway. It converts 6-phospho-D-gluconic acid to D-ribulose-5-phosphate.

phosphoglyceride A fatty acid ester of glycerol phosphate with an alcohol group esterified to the phosphate. Common phosphoglycerides cephalin and lecithin contain ethanolamine and choline, respectively. The plasmatogens found in brain and heart tissue also belong to this group. These compounds are typified by an unsaturated fatty aldehyde and a carboxylic acid esterified to the glycerol molecule and a base such as ethanolamine esterified to the phosphoric acid group.

phospholipids A polar lipid found in plant and animal membranes. Phospholipids consist of two groups: phosphoglycerides and sphingomyelins. The molecules of phospholipids are amphipathic, comprising a polar head made up of phosphate and ancillary alcohol, sugar or amino compound and a hydrophobic tail formed by the long-chain fatty acids.

phosphomannan A polymer produced by *Hansenula* species.

phosphoramidite method A chemical synthesis used in the production of oligonucleotides. The method is performed with the growing nucleotide chain attached to a solid support so that excess reagents in the liquid phase can be removed by filtration. The process is a cyclic one in which five separate reactions are carried out each time a nucleoside is added. The nucleoside is attached to a silica solid support through a spacer attached at the 3'-hydroxyl; the 5'-hydroxyl is blocked with a dimethoxytrityl group. The first step of the cycle is the removal of the dimethoxytrityl group which frees the 5'-hydroxyl for the addition reaction. The next step (activation) creates a highly reactive nucleoside derivative, which reacts with the hydroxyl group by simultaneously adding the phosphoramidite derivative of the next nucleoside and a weak acid (tetrazole) to the reaction chamber. The phosphoramidite is blocked at the 5'-hydroxyl with the dimethyoxytrityl group. The next step – capping – blocks off any chains that have not undergone addition (usually less than 5 per cent) and have a free hydroxyl group by acetylation. This step is not needed for the synthesis itself, but reduces impurities. The internucleotide linkage is then converted from the phosphite to the more stable phosphate using iodine as the oxidizing agent and water as the oxygen donor. The dimethyoxytrityl group is then removed and the cycle repeated until elongation is complete. At this point, the oligonucleotide is still bound to the support and has protecting groups on the phosphates and the exocyclic amines of the bases A, G and C. To produce biologically active oligonucleotides, the methyl protective groups are removed by treatment with thiophenol. The chain is then cleaved from the support by treatment with concentrated ammonium hydroxide. Finally, the protecting groups on the exocyclic amines are removed by treatment with ammonium hydroxide. The material is purified by HPLC or gel electrophoresis.

phosphorescence The emission of visible electromagnetic radiation from a molecule following stimulation by radiation of a specific wavelength, which continues after the exciting radiation has been removed. *Compare* fluorescence.

phosphorylation The formation of ATP from ADP and inorganic phosphate. *See* chemiosmotic theory, oxidative phosphorylation, photophosphorylation.

phosphorylation potential The relationship between the levels of ADP and ATP, which controls the balance of anabolic and catabolic processes in living organisms, tissues, cells or organelles. Rates of phosphorylation are stimulated by high ADP levels and suppressed by high ATP levels.

phosphotase An enzyme that catalyses the hydrolysis of monophosphate esters.

photoautotroph An organism that uses light energy in photosynthesis to form nutrients from inorganic substrates (carbon dioxide, water, nitrate, sulphate, etc.). Photoautotrophs include the euglenophytes, algae and higher plants that contain chlorophyll a and form oxygen from water.

photobiological hydrogen production A system that uses light and a biocatalyst to form hydrogen and oxygen. Four different systems exist. The first type of reaction, catalysed by photosynthetic bacteria, uses organic compounds as substrate. The other methods all produce hydrogen by the photolysis of water. These reactions are carried out by cyanobacteria, green algae and artificial systems reconstituted from chloroplast membranes, iron–sulphur proteins and microbial hydrogenases. In all cases, the hydrogen is produced by diverting reductants generated through the normal light reactions and intermediate electron transport systems from carbon reduction to a hydrogenase. The objective of these systems is to produce hydrogen for use as a fuel or chemical feedstock. They are still at the experimental stage with low efficiencies and poor stability. A further problem arises from the fact that the water-splitting systems also produce oxygen.

photoheterotroph A photosynthetic organism that uses organic compounds as electron donors. Photoheterotrophs include the green, purple and brown bacteria that do not form oxygen.

photolysis The cleavage of water during the light reactions of photosynthesis.

photometer A device for measuring light intensity.

photomultiplier An electronic device used to measure low light intensities. Photons pass through a window and strike a series of dynodes arranged in a cascade form across which a high potential is applied. At each dynode secondary electrons are produced, thus amplifying the size of the signal that arrives at the anode. The size and/or shape of the signal is then analysed and quantified using electronic circuits. Photomultipliers are used in spectrophotometers and scintillation counters.

photonasty Nastic movement that occurs in plants in response to stimulation by light.

photoperiodism The response of an organism to the length of a light period. The most notable photoperiodic responses occur in plants where flowering, bud dormancy, leaf fall, tuber formation, etc. are controlled by day length. Plants are distinguished as long-day, short-day or day-neutral, depending on their response to variations in the period of darkness to which they are subjected. The responses in plants are the result of phytochrome-mediated phenomena; a reaction to red light may be reversed by a flash of far red light, and vice versa. Many animals also show photoperiodic responses.

photophosphorylation The formation of ATP from ADP and inorganic phosphate that occurs during photosynthesis. Two distinct processes may be distinguished experimentally: (1) cyclic photophosphorylation, which is associated with the activity of photosystem I and does not produce a reductant or involve the splitting of water; (2) non-cyclic photophosphorylation, in which the formation of ATP is associated with the splitting of water and evolution of oxygen in photosystem II, the reduction of ferredoxin in photosystem I and the passage of electrons through the intermediate electron transport chain that links photosystem I and photosystem II.

photoreactivation A type of DNA repair mechanism that requires the presence of light. For example, ultraviolet irradiation can cause the formation of dimmers between adjacent thymine bases in the same strand of DNA. These may be cleaved enzymically in the presence of visible light.

photoreceptor A sense organ that responds to the stimulus of light.

photorespiration A light-dependent process that occurs in the green leaves of higher plants. It is characterized by the uptake of oxygen and the release of carbon dioxide, as well as the formation of ATP. Compounds containing two carbon atoms, derived from phosphoglycollate (produced in the oxygenase reaction catalysed by rubisco), are converted back to a three-carbon compound which re-enters the photosynthetic carbon reduction cycle. The initial stages of the metabolism of phosphoglycollate (the C_2 pathway) occur in the peroxisomes, where it is metabolized through glycollate, glyoxylate and glycine. Two molecules of glycine are then converted to one molecule of serine, with the formation of ATP and the release of carbon dioxide in the mitochondria. The three-carbon amino acid serine is converted back to phosphoglyceric acid in the peroxisome. Photorespiration also involves a complex pattern of nitrogen metabolism in order to maintain a low concentration of otherwise inhibitory ammonium ions, which are released during the formation of serine. The metabolism of nitrogen depends on the re-assimilation of ammonia by cytoplasmic glutamine synthetase and the reformation of glutamate by a chloroplastic aminotransferase. The nature and magnitude of photorespiration reflect the kinetic characteristics and oxygenase properties of rubisco. The overall result of photorespiration is the loss of up to 30 per cent of the carbon fixed in photosynthesis. The complex metabolism of phosphoglycollate represents a way of returning part of the fixed carbon at least to the chloroplasts. Under some conditions of high light, high temperature and low carbon dioxide concentration (or high oxygen concentration), photorespiration may represent a protective mechanism that prevents damage to the chloroplast. Photorespiration appears less important in C_4 plants as indicated by low rates of light-dependent carbon dioxide release. However, these plants do contain the necessary enzymes and display light-dependent oxygen uptake. It is possible that the higher rates of carbon dioxide assimilation seen in C_4 plants reflect the refixation of carbon dioxide produced in the bundle sheath cells as it passes through the mesophyll layer.

photosynthesis The reduction of carbon dioxide using light energy absorbed by chlorophyll and other photosynthetic pigments, with the formation of organic compounds. In green plants, a wide variety of algae and the cyanobacteria, the hydrogen donor is water and oxygen is evolved. Some bacteria (Chromataceae, Rhodospirillaceae and Chlorobiaceae) also carry out photosynthesis, but the process differs from that in higher plants because other electron donors are used and oxygen is not produced. Also the chlorophylls of the pigment systems are different (acteriochlorophylls) and only one photosystem is present. With the exception of the cyanobacteria, all oxygen-forming photoautotrophs contain chloroplasts. The overall process is divided into the light-dependent reactions which are largely carried out on the inner membranes of the chloroplast and the dark reactions which are catalysed by enzymes contained in the amorphous stroma. The light reactions produce energy (ATP) and reducing power (NADPH) to drive the dark enzyme reactions. Light is absorbed by antennae pigments which are grouped in photosynthetic units of about 300 molecules associated with a reaction centre. Absorbed quanta are transferred by a random walk process to either one of the two reaction centres or traps which consist of chlorophyll–protein complexes known as P_{700} and P_{680}, the numbers indicating the wavelength of maximum absorption of light by these complexes. These traps are associated with photosystem I (based on P_{700}) and photosystem II (based on P_{680}). Photosystem I and photosystem II are linked by an intermediate electron carrier chain to form the so-called Z scheme. Charge separation at the trap results in the formation of high-energy electrons which are accepted by electron carriers. Electrons from photosystem II flow down the intermediate electron

carrier chain to replace the electron lost from photosystem I. The electron flow is coupled to non-cyclic photophosphorylation, resulting in the formation of ATP. The electron from photosystem I passes to an iron–sulphur protein – ferredoxin – which in turn replaces NADP to produce the reductant required for the dark reactions using a proton derived from water. At the same time, electrons from water are donated to the trap of photosystem II with the release of oxygen. The initial reaction in the reductive assimilation of carbon dioxide in all plants is catalysed by the enzyme now known as rubisco. Because of competition between carbon dioxide and oxygen, the carbon substrate ribulose-1,5-bis-phosphate (RBP) is converted to two molecules of 3-phosphoglyceric acid (3-PGA) or to one molecule of 3-PGA and one of phosphoglycollate. 3-PGA is then reduced to a three-carbon sugar which is exported from the cytoplasm, used in the regeneration of RBP or stored in the chloroplast as starch. The regeneration of RBP involves the interaction of a number of complex reactions that make up the photosynthetic carbon reduction (PCR) cycle. The PCR cycle represents the only mechanism for reductive assimilation of carbon in photoautotrophs. Plants possessing this pathway alone are known as C_3 plants. In C_4 species and CAM plants, this process is supplemented by a reaction in which carboxylation of phosphoenolpyruvate results in the formation of a four-carbon acid (oxaloacetic acid).

photosynthetic efficiency A measure of the extent to which light energy intercepted by a leaf, leaf canopy or photosynthetic cell suspension is converted into organic matter. Efficiency is expressed in terms of total incident light or photosynthetic active radiation (PAR). For a crop, the overall efficiency (E) in terms of total incident light is the product of the interception efficiency of the canopy (E_i) and the biological efficiency with which absorbed light is converted into cell products (E_b) (i.e., $E = E_i \times E_b \times PAR$). Typically $E_i = 0.8$, $E_b = 0.29$ and PAR = 0.5, giving a maximum efficiency of photosynthetic carbon dioxide fixation to the level of carbohydrate at about 11 per cent using normal solar radiation. This is reduced owing to dark respiratory processes to about 6 per cent. In C_3 plants, maximum efficiency is reduced by photorespiration to about 4 per cent. These theoretical efficiencies may be compared with observed short-term and annual efficiencies:

	C_3	C_4
Short-term	1.9–3.3	2.9–4.3
Annual	0.4–1.4	0.7–2.4

photosynthetic pigments Chlorophylls, carotenoids and phycobilins. All of these classes of pigments occur as chromoproteins (pigment–protein complexes). All oxygen-producing plants possess chlorophyll a. Higher plants also contain chlorophyll b, and other forms (chlorophylls c and d) are found in algae. The carotenoids and phycobilins are accessory pigments.

photosynthetic productivity An expression of the yield, in terms of harvested dry weight, produced by a given crop or within a given ecosystem. Productivity is usually expressed in terms of tonnes dry weight produced per hectare per year. Short-term productivities are expressed in terms of dry weight accumulated per square metre per day. Typical annual and short-term productivities are:

	C_3	C_4
Short-term (g/m²/day)	20–40	30–60
Annual (t/ha/yr)	3–40	5–80

The short-term productivities extrapolate to over 100 dry tonnes per hectare per year. However, such annual productivities are not recorded because of environmental limitations, pests, disease and genetic characteristics of the plant, although yields of intensely managed sugar cane grown under ideal conditions may approach such values because they show C_4 photosynthesis and because they possess an indeterminate growth habit and a long growing season.

photosynthetic rate A measure of the capacity of a leaf or plant to carry out photosynthesis. It is expressed as the amount of carbon dioxide fixed or oxygen evolved in relation to leaf area, leaf weight, chlorophyll content, protein content, area of land occupied by the plant, etc. Net rates of photosynthesis are obtained by subtracting short-term rates of dark gas exchange (respiration) from those observed in the light, or determining the rates of increase in dry weight over a period of time. For unicellular organisms such as algae, cyanobacteria and photosynthetic bacteria, rates may be expressed in terms of cell number or packed cell volume. Typical rates of photosynthesis are as follows:

Plant type	Photosynthetic rate (mg CO_2/dm²/h)
C_3	20–50
C_4	70–100
CAM	5–10

Gas exchange rates may be expressed in weight, moles or fractional volumes (parts per million, ppm). These may be converted as follows:

mg CO_2/dm²/h × 0.0278 = mg CO_2/m²/s
mg CO_2/dm²/h × 0.6312 = µm/dm²/s
mg CO_2/m²/s × 22.72 = µm/dm²/s

phototroph An organism that uses light as an energy source. Phototrophs are divided into two groups: photoheterotrophs and photoautotrophs.

phototropism In plants, a response to the stimulus of light. Most stems are positively phototrophic (i.e., grow towards a light source) whereas roots are negatively phototrophic.

phragmoplast The region containing the cell plate between the daughter nuclei of a dividing cell.

phycobilin One of the main classes of photosynthetic pigments that occur in Rhodophyceae, Cyanophyceae and Cryptophyceae. Phycobilins consist of the bilins, phycoerythrobilin and phycocyanobilin, which are open tetrapyrroles, covalently bound to two protein molecules of molecular weights of 19,000 and 21,000 that occur in a 1:1 ratio. Each subunit carries one to four molecules of phycobilin.

phycobilisome A particle formed by the aggregation of phycobilins, on the photosynthetic lamellae of cyanophytes and in the chloroplasts of red algae and members of the cryptophyta.

phycobiont The algal partner in a lichen.

phycocyanin A blue phycobilin pigment.

phycoerythrin A red phycobilin pigment.

Phycomycetes A diverse group of lower filamentous fungi. Most species are aquatic and have motile cells within the life cycle, but also included are the genera *Rhizopus* and *Mucor* which are terrestrial and have non-motile spores (Zygomycetes). These are used in fermentations, the production of microbial rennets and cheese manufacture.

Phycomycotina A synonym for the Phycomycetes.

phylogenetic Descriptive of a classification system that is based on the evolutionary relationships of organisms.

phylogeny The history of the evolution of a given species or type of organism.

phylum A primary division of the animal or plant kingdom. It consists of a number of classes with characteristics in common, which suggests that they have a similar evolutionary origin.

physical map A pictorial representation of the position of genes that have been located by experimental means, such as determination of linkage, use of DNA probes or use of mutants.

physiology The study of the functions of organisms.

phytase An enzyme used to supplement animal feed. Phytase increases the digesti-
bility of phosphorus-containing organic compounds (phytic acid, polyphosphate) and therefore reduces the phosphate content of manures.

phytoalexin A phenolic compound that contributes disease resistance in plants.

phytochrome A chromoprotein found in plants. The prosthetic group of phytochrome is an open tetrapyrrole related to phycocyanobilin. This molecule mediates many physiological responses in plants which are initiated by the absorption of a low dose of red light (660 nm) in an overall dark environment and reversed by a low dose of far red light (730 nm) in the same conditions. The inactive form (PR) is converted to the active form (PFR) by illumination with far red light.

phytohaemagglutinin A lectin that binds to surface glycoproteins of some animal cells stimulating cell division.

phytohormone A plant growth substance.

phytokinin A naturally occurring kinin.

pickling A lactic acid fermentation process used to preserve vegetables (usually small cucumbers, onions, cabbage or olives).

picornavirus A naked icosahedral virus that contains single-stranded RNA. This group includes the enteroviruses and rhinoviruses which cause disease in humans and are the agents responsible for foot and mouth disease in ruminants.

piezoelectric sensor A mechanical device based on the piezoelectric effect. Piezoelectric materials when subjected to mechanical stress produce a potential difference whilst application of an electric field to the material results in a dimensional change. The application as sensor transducers is based on their ability to generate and transmit acoustic waves in a frequency-dependent manner. In one type, a bulk wave is transmitted from one face of a crystal to the opposite face; other (acoustic wave) devices operate by transmitting waves along a single crystal face from one location to another. Applications involve a specially coated oscillating crystal acting as a sensitive detector of changes in surface mass, which may be brought about by the complexing of an antigen to an antibody immobilized on to the piezoelectric crystal.

pilot plant An intermediate production facility used to study scale-up and other production problems between bench-scale experiments and full commercial production.

pineal gland An endocrine gland embedded in the vertebrate forebrain that secretes melatonin and vasotocin.

pinocytosis A process by which a cell engulfs extracellular particles. It usually occurs by an intucking of the plasma membrane to form a vesicle.

pitressin *See* vasopressin.

pituitary gland An endocrine gland of vertebrates attached by a short stalk to the hypothalamus that secretes peptide and glycoprotein hormones. The pars distalis secretes growth hormone, lipotrophin, thyrotrophin, luteinizing hormone, follicle-stimulating hormone, prolactin and ACTH. The pars intermedia secretes melanocyte-stimulating hormone, and the pars nervosa secretes oxytocin and vasopressin.

placenta (1) In mammals, a temporary organ that develops within the uterus and establishes a close contact between the blood circulations of the foetus and the mother. The placenta also produces hormones (gonadotrophins, oestrogens and progesterone). Following parturition, the placenta is shed from the body as an afterbirth. (2) In plants, the part of the ovary to which the ovules are attached.

plant cell culture *See* plant tissue culture.

plant cloning vehicle A vector used in gene manipulation to carry foreign DNA and insert it in an inheritable manner into plant cells. Possible vectors include the Ti plas-

mid of *Agrobacterium tumefaciens* and the DNA plant viruses. *See* plant DNA virus, Ti plasmid.

plant DNA virus A virus that contains DNA and infects plants. There are two groups: the caulimoviruses which have double-stranded DNA and the geminiviruses which have single-stranded DNA. The first group includes the cauliflower mosaic virus (CaMV) which has been studied in detail. It consists of isometric particles about 50 nm in diameter.

plant growth substance A natural or artificial substance that when present in low concentrations in a plant will affect its growth. *See* abscisic acid, auxin, cytokinin, ethylene, gibberellins.

plant row A row of plants that represents the random progeny from a single plant following a cross. For example, F_3 plant rows would be the progeny from a single F_2 plant.

plant tissue culture A technique used for the growth of undifferentiated plant cells *in vitro*. Such cultures are classified on the basis of their nutritional requirements as photoautotrophic (carry out photosynthesis and require no additional nutrient) or chemotrophic (require a source of carbon, usually glucose, supplemented with various growth factors). Such cultures are further classified as callus cultures (blocks of undifferentiated amorphous cellular tissue) or suspension cultures. Cultures are usually initiated by excising small pieces of meristematic or embryonic tissue from plants, which are surface sterilized and transferred to a suitable medium under sterile conditions. Callus tissue is usually grown on solid agar containing glucose, other nutrients and plant growth substances or artificial analogues of these. Coconut milk is often used as a general source of amino acids, vitamins, minerals and growth factors. Treatment of callus with auxin and kinetin results in the formation of differentiated tissue and the formation of roots and shoots. Treatment with gibberellins induces the proliferation of meristems and differentiation into whole plants. Suspension cultures consist of single cells or small clumps which are kept in suspension by agitation. Again these may be induced to undergo embryogenesis by adjusting the level of plant growth substances in the culture. Such techniques are used for the rapid propagation of plants of commercial importance (e.g., oil palm) and some ornamental flowers, the production of sterile or virus-free cultivars for introduction into new regions and the propagation of new strains (since the culture conditions often result in genetic abnormalities). Tissue culture techniques are also of importance in some of the methods that are being developed for plant gene manipulation. Techniques of protoplast fusion or introduction of foreign DNA, using suitable vectors, into plant protoplasts require the subsequent regeneration of the whole plants. This is achieved in some species through tissue culture techniques if the protoplasts are capable of reforming walls and dividing to form calluses.

plant vector *See* plant cloning vehicle.

plantlet A small plant; used to denote such a plant derived from a tissue culture.

plant/nif gene transfer A procedure used to transfer *Klebsiella* nif genes directly to plants in order to establish them in the plant nuclear genome. This involves the following steps: (1) transferring the *Klebsiella* nif region to *E. coli*; (2) cloning the whole nif gene cluster in a multicopy plasmid cloning vehicle; (3) introducing the *Klebsiella* nif gene cluster into the nucleus of a plant protoplast; (4) regenerating the whole plant thus leading to the expression of the nif genes. The transfer of the nif gene cluster to a plant nucleus is accomplished using the Ti plasmid of *Agrobacterium tumefaciens*. Regeneration of whole plants from protoplasts has only been achieved for a limited number of plant species, few of agricultural importance. Expression of the nif genes in the eukaryotic system is a serious problem. For example, *Klebsiella* nif genes do not function in the yeast cell. Even if expression were successful, the problem of oxygen protection is unsolved.

Finally, it is not known whether electron transport proteins of the plant cell can couple to a functioning nitrogenase complex.

plaque (1) In microbiology, an area of lysed cells produced in a film of susceptible bacteria grown on an agar plate following infection with a lytic bacteriophage. (2) In oral hygiene, a deposit of polysaccharides and bacteria on the surface of teeth that contributes to the development of dental caries.

plaque count A technique used to determine the number of phage particles or infected bacterial cells in a suspension. The suspension is spread at appropriate dilutions on to the surface of an agar plate that is evenly inoculated with a thin suspension of a susceptible bacteria. The number of plaques formed is then counted.

plasma The clear, colourless fluid component of vertebrate blood; the fluid that remains when the white and red cells are separated from fresh uncoagulated blood.

plasma arc spectroscopy A technique used to determine the level of metals and other elements in a sample. The sample is introduced into a plasma arc at a high temperature (above 5000°C) and the ultraviolet emissions passed through a diffraction grating to fall on a series of detectors. The signals are treated electronically and the quantity of a given element present is printed out directly.

plasma growth factor *See* somatomedin.

plasmagene A self-replicating cytoplasmic entity that carries genes which are independent of the cell nucleus (e.g., the genomes of the chloroplasts and mitochondria of eukaryotes or the prokaryotic plasmids).

plasmalemma The outer membrane that surrounds the protoplasm of a cell.

plasmatogens *See* phosphoglyceride.

plasmid A circular molecule of DNA (molecular weight 10^6–2×10^8) that carries 1–3 per cent of the cell genome and codes for important genetic traits which are not normally coded for by the bacterial chromosome. Plasmids, which are found throughout the prokaryotes, are replicons that are stably inherited in an extrachromosomal state. They include prophages which are maintained in an extrachromosomal state and the replicative forms of filamentous coliphages, but not those forms that are integrated into the host chromosome. Plasmids to which phenotypic traits have not been ascribed are known as cryptic plasmids. Some of the phenotypes that have been identified as being conferred on the host cell by plasmids are antibiotic resistance, antibiotic production, degradation of aromatic compounds, haemolysin production, sugar fermentation, enterotoxin production, heavy metal resistance, bacteriocin production, induction of plant tumours and hydrogen sulphide production. Plasmids are of two types – conjugative or non-conjugative – depending on whether they carry the tra genes that promote bacterial conjugation. Plasmids can also be distinguished on the basis of whether they are maintained in the host cell in multiple copies (relaxed plasmid) or as a limited number of copies (stringent plasmid). Plasmid replication is usually regulated independently of chromosome replication, and copy number can be controlled by a plasmid-borne regulatory system. Plasmids are now used as cloning vehicles or vectors for the introduction of foreign DNA-containing genes that do not normally occur in the host cell.

plasmid incompatibility The inability of two different plasmids to co-exist in the same host cell. Groups of plasmids that are mutually incompatible are considered to belong to the same incompatibility class. Over 25 incompatibility groups are known for *E. coli* and over seven for *Staphylococcus aureus*.

plasmid pBR322 *See* pBR322.

plasmid purification The separation of plasmid DNA from other forms of prokaryotic DNA and cellular components. The first stage is cell lysis. This should be gentle so that the plasmids are released without the release of too much contaminating chromosomal DNA. High-molecular-weight DNA and cell debris are removed by high-speed centrifugation to give a cleared lysate. Pure plasmid DNA is then produced using isopycnic centrifugation in caesium chloride containing ethidium bromide which binds by intercalating between the DNA base pairs and in so doing causes DNA to unwind. A covalently closed circular DNA such as a plasmid has no free ends and can only unwind to a limited extent, thus limiting the amount of ethidium bromide bound. Linear DNA molecules derived from fragments of the chromosome have no such constraints, and hence bind more of the ethidium bromide. The density of the complex decreases as more ethidium bromide is bound, hence the circular molecules which have a higher density are separated from the linear forms of DNA. An alternative method is to separate the DNA by chromatography on hydroxyapatite.

plasmid replicon A base sequence that acts as an 'origin of replication' that has been isolated from a plasmid and is used in the construction of cloning vehicles.

plasmid rescue A technique used for transforming *Bacillus subtilis* in which an inactive donor plasmid interacts with a resident plasmid to effect a transformation. In practice, foreign DNA is ligated to monomeric vector DNA and the recombinant inserted into cells containing a homologous plasmid. The resident plasmid combines with the inserted plasmid resulting in transformation.

plasmid vector A plasmid involved in the transfer of a gene or genes carried on a length of foreign DNA into a host in which they do not normally occur. This is one of the techniques used in what is known as *in vitro* genetic manipulation, gene (genetic) engineering or genetic manipulation. The plasmid used is a vector or a cloning vehicle. Plasmids are not the only cloning vehicles used, but are important since some plasmids have many of the properties required of an ideal vector. A low molecular weight makes the plasmid easier to handle. In addition, low-molecular-weight plasmids are often present in multiple copies which facilitates their isolation and leads to gene dosage effects for all cloned genes. They are also less likely to have multiple sites for endonuclease activity. This is important since one of the first steps in cloning is to cut the vector and the DNA to be inserted with the same endonuclease. If the vector has more than one site of activity, several fragments will be produced. The ability to confer a recognizable phenotypic trait on the host is necessary in order to recognize transformed cells (e.g., by their resistance to specific antibiotics).

plasmin An enzyme that attacks and dissolves blood clots. It is present in blood as the inactive precursor plasminogen.

plasminogen A precursor of plasmin.

plasminogen activator A system or compound that induces or enhances the production of plasminogen. Such activators include the enzymes urokinase, streptokinase and tissue-type plasminogen activator/fibrin complexes.

plasmodesma A narrow tube in the wall of plant cells through which the protoplasm of one cell is kept in contact with the protoplasms of the adjacent cells.

plasmodium A multinucleate protoplasmic form of the vegetative stage of the slime fungi (Myxomycetes).

Plasmodium The generic name of the sporozoan that causes malaria.

plasmogamy The fusion of protoplasts that occurs in the formation of a heterokaryon.

plasmolysis The loss of water from a prokaryote or plant cell that occurs when it is placed in a hypertonic solution.

plastid An organelle found in plant cells that is enclosed in a double membrane (envelope). Plastids vary in form and function and include chloroplasts which are the site of photosynthesis and their precursor form, which develops in plants kept in the dark, known as etioplasts. Some plastids accumulate pigments including carotenoids. These are known as chromoplasts and are generally derived from chloroplasts. They occur in flowers and fruits, where they contribute to the colour of these organs. Leucoplasts are colourless plastids that are modified for the storage of food reserves and can be classified according to the nature of the reserves: amyloplasts (starch); elaioplasts (lipids); proteoplasts (proteins). Plastids divide in synchrony with cell division or arise by differentiation of proplastids located in meristematic cells.

plastocyanin A copper-containing protein that functions as an electron carrier in the photosynthetic electron carrier chain.

plastogene A self-replicating genetic entity associated with a plastid. It is a type of plasmagene.

plastoglobulus A lipid-containing droplet that occurs in chloroplasts. In aged chloroplasts, or during the transition of chloroplasts to chromoplasts, the plastoglobuli increase in size and number, and accumulate carotenoids.

plastome The genetic material contained in cytoplasmic organelles. *See* chloroplast genome, mitochondrial DNA.

plastoquinone A quinone that functions as an electron carrier in the intermediate photosynthetic electron carrier chain of chloroplasts.

plate count *See* viable count.

platelet A component of mammalian blood, about 2 μm in diameter, that plays a role in the clotting of blood.

platelet activation dependent granulocyte external membrane pancreatin *See* PADGEM.

platelet-activating factor (PAF) A factor released by mast cells and white blood cells in an immune response. PAF causes platelets to aggregate and facilitates the release of substances such as histamine from within them.

platelet-derived growth factor (PDGF) A protein dimmer derived from platelets that modulates cell growth.

plating A technique used to obtain pure cultures of microorganisms (bacteria, yeasts and fungi) that produce a distinct colony when grown on solid medium (a nutrient medium solidified with agar or similar agent in a petri dish). A suspension of organisms is then streaked on to the plate using a sterile loop dipped into the culture. A series of parallel, non-overlapping streaks across the surface of the medium are made. With each successive streak the number of cells is diluted so that the final streaks will yield separate colonies. An alternative method is the pour plate method. A portion of the medium containing the cells is added to a liquid agar medium at about 45°C. This is then poured into a petri dish to harden, resulting in a solidified medium with colonies scattered throughout. Cells from individual colonies, which represent clones of the same cell, can then be isolated for further culture.

pleiomorphism A type of polymorphisms in which different forms of a given species develop sequentially during the life cycle of an organism.

pleiotropy Descriptive of a single gene that is expressed in several different ways in the phenotype, causing the development of a number of apparently distinct and unrelated characteristics. An example in humans is the recessive gene responsible for phenylketonuria.

plerome Part of the apical meristem that gives rise to the tissues internal to the cortex.

pleura In mammals, a serous membrane that covers the lungs and lines the wall of the chest cavity enclosing the pleural cavities.

pleuropneumonia-like organisms A mycoplasma.

plexus A diffuse network of neurones.

ploidy The number of times a complete set of all the individual distinct chromosomes are repeated in the nucleus of a particular cell. The following terms are used to describe the indicated number of times the set of chromosomes occurs: one, haploid; two, diploid; three, triploid; four, tetraploid; n, polyploid.

plug flow digester An anaerobic digester that consists of a long tube or an elongated covered pit that is treated as a plug flow reactor. The material to be digested is introduced at one end and overflow occurs at the other. Since these digesters have a high liquid content and internal mixing occurs, or may be deliberately carried out, the kinetics of reaction only approximate to those of a true plug flow reactor.

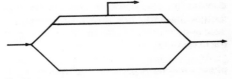

Plug flow digester

plug flow fermenter A version of the dialysis fermenter in which a dense plug of cells is maintained between two support plates. Medium is pumped through the plug under high pressure and rapid fermentation takes place. Easily fouled membrane filters are not suitable; instead a layer of kieselguhr filter aid over a porous frit support plate is used. Kieselguhr is also mixed into the plug to prevent dense packing of the yeast which would halt the flow.

plug flow reactor A reactor, often tubular in form, in which the substrate passes through an essentially unmixed system which may consist of an unstirred liquid phase or a system in which the biocatalyst consists of a stationary matrix such as immobilized cells or enzymes, or packed cells. The substrates enter the column at one end and the products emerge in the effluent at the other. Under suitable conditions of biological activity and residence time, very high conversion efficiencies may be achieved since the incoming substrate is not mixed with the outgoing product stream. In the case of a perfect plug flow reactor, no axial mixing occurs and no mixing occurs between a given portion of the influent and any liquid that entered the reactor either before or after the material under consideration. Thus for a steady-state system, all fluid entering the reactor has the same residence time within the reactor. Hence

$$\tau = V/F = 1/D$$

where τ = residence time, V = volume of fluid in the reactor, F = volumetric flow of the fluid and D = dilution rate.

plumule (1) In plants, the apical bud of a seedling that occurs above the node of the cotyledon. (2) In birds, a feather.

PMS (1) *See* phenazine methosulphate. (2) *See* pregnant mare serum.

P/O ratio In oxidative phosphorylation (aerobic respiration), the ratio of phosphate incorporated into ATP to the oxygen consumed.

Podbielniak extractor A type of centrifugal countercurrent liquid extractor commonly used for large-scale recovery of antibiotics from fermentation broths.

poikilothermic Descriptive of cold-blooded animals. They are unable to regulate their body temperature, which changes with that of the environment. With the exception of mammals and birds, most organisms are poikilothermic. *Compare* homoiothermic.

point mutation A mutation involving the alteration of a nucleic acid sequence in which one nucleotide is replaced by another, leading to a different amino acid occurring at the relevant position in the protein. This in turn will alter the protein structure and may affect catalytic activity.

polar bodies The smaller cells that are produced during meiosis in oogenesis and that do not develop into functional ova. *Compare* spermatid.

polar mutation A mutation of one gene that affects the expression of the adjacent non-mutant gene on one side, but not of that on the other side.

pole The outer region of a dividing cell, or the end of the spindle, towards which the chromosomes move in the later stages of cell division.

polishing A final process applied in the treatment of water, beer, fermentation broth or other liquid to completely remove contaminants or particulate matter.

pollen The mature microspores of gymnosperms and angiosperms. Pollen is transferred by mechanical means within a flower, or from flower to flower by wind pollination or animals, often insects.

pollen culture The propagation of haploid plants from immature pollen.

pollen sac A part of the anther (microsporangia) of angiosperms or gymnosperms in which pollen develops.

pollen tube In angiosperms, a filamentous tube that grows out from a pollen grain during fertilization after it lands on a receptive stigma. The pollen tube grows between the cells of the style and enters the ovule, often through the micropyle. The pollen tube usually contains three nuclei: a vegetative nucleus and two generative nuclei. One generative nucleus fuses with the ovum to produce a zygote. The other generative nucleus disintegrates or fuses with a polar nucleus to form a primary endosperm nucleus. This gives rise to the endosperm tissue which acts as a food reserve material for the seedling.

pollination The transfer of pollen from the anthers to the stigma of an angiosperm, or from the male cone to the female cone in gymnosperms. If the transfer occurs in the same flower, it is termed self-pollination; if it occurs between two different flowers, it is termed, cross-pollination. Some plants have evolved complex incompatibility mechanisms in order to ensure cross-pollination. Such outbreeding leads to greater genetic variation.

pollution The release of natural or manufactured products into the environment in such a way as to cause harmful effects. The release of energy in the form of heat may also be regarded as a form of pollution, as may the production of unacceptable levels of sound or vibration. Major problems are associated with water and with air pollution. The release of organic matter, such as sewage and farm manure, into water may result in contamination with pathogens or parasitic eggs, as well as the depletion of the oxygen content due to the activity of bacteria which decompose the material. The extent of pollution is described in terms of the biochemical oxygen demand (BOD), or the chemical oxygen demand (COD); greater BOD or COD values indicate higher levels of pollution. Lakes and rivers may be polluted by high levels of inorganic nutrients (due to run-off of fertilizers from agricultural land). This favours the growth of algae due to eutrophication of the water. Detergents, pesticides, insecticides, halogenated compounds, xenobiotics and heavy metal contamination from industrial processes or mining operations also create problems. The major air pollutants arise from the burning of fossil fuels in industry, the home or internal combustion engines. These processes result in the release of oxides of sulphur and nitrogen (which form acids resulting in so-called 'acid rain') and partially combusted hydrocarbons. Further problems may arise from the release of lead derived from anti-knock additives in high octane petroleum. All these products of combustion can have deleterious effects on plant, animal and microbial life.

pollution control The reduction of the level of pollutants in the environment. Biological clean-up procedures include: the anaerobic digestion of sewage sludge, organic industrial wastes, farm manures and farm wastes;

the use of aerobic microbial treatment, including activated sludge processes; the use of organisms that selectively accumulate materials such as heavy metals or that are capable of metabolizing xenobiotics. *See* activated sludge, anaerobic digestion, deep shaft system, trickle filter.

poly A Polyadenylate; an oligonucleotide formed from adenosine residues.

poly (A) tail A sequence of polyadenylic acid residues added to the 3'-end of the majority of eukaryotic mRNAs following transcription.

poly (U) sepharose An affinity matrix composed of poly (uridylic) acid and agarose used for the purification of mammalian mRNA. The poly (U) acid selectively binds to the poly (A) tail of mammalian RNA molecules by complementary base pairing.

polyacrylamide   gel   electrophoresis (PAGE) An electrophoretic procedure in which polyacrylamide is used as the support matrix. In general, two types of polyacrylamide gel electrophoresis are carried out. (1) A one-dimensional procedure using either intact proteins or proteins solubilized with sodium dodecyl sulphate (SDS). This is carried out on cylindrical rods of gel (disc electrophoresis) or as parallel separations on a slab of gel. (2) A two-dimensional separation, with the native protein separated in the first run. The plate is then treated with SDS and the sample separated in the second direction. Various proteins are separated the first time, whereas the second development separates the individual subunits of the protein. Similar techniques are used to separate components of ribosomes.

polyadenylate *See* poly A.

polyadenylation The non-transcriptive addition of poly A to the 3'-end of eukaryotic RNA.

polyamine A compound that contains two or more amino groups. A number of polyamines occur in biological systems, including putrescine ($NH_2(CH_2)_4NH_2$), cadaverine $(NH_2(CH_2)_5NH_2)$ and spermine $(NH_2(CH_2)_3NH(CH_2)_4NH(CH_2)_3NH_2)$. These compounds are associated with DNA helices in some viruses and bacteria in a way that is analogous to the histones of eukaryotic cells.

polybrene 1,5-Dimethyl-1,5-diazaundecamethylene polymethobromide; a reagent used in the sequencing of proteins.

polycistronic Descriptive of a length of DNA that codes for several proteins or peptides, often with associated enzymic functions.

polyclonal antibody (Pab) An antibody produced in the normal immune response to an antigen consisting of a number of closely related, but not identical, proteins. The variation in polyclonal antibodies reflects the fact that they are formed by a number of different lymphocytes, in contrast to monoclonal antibodies which are formed by a clone of identical cells. *Compare* monoclonal antibody.

polycross In breeding, a cross in which selected individuals are allowed to mate at random.

polycyclic aromatic hydrocarbons Complex organic compounds consisting of linked ring structures. Many such compounds occur in coal tar and may be highly carcinogenic.

polydeoxyribonucleotide A short length of DNA; an oligonucleotide.

polyembryony A process, such as the production of identical twins, in which more than one embryo develops from a single zygote. The process is common in some plants and invertebrate animals.

polyester foam A foam produced from polyester; a synthetic polymer in which the structural monomers are linked by ester groups, formed by condensation of carboxylic acids with alcohols.

polyethylene glycol (PEG) Used to minimize aggregate formation during protein refolding.

polygene One of a number of genes, the expression of which results in a single phenotypic characteristic. The action of polygenes often results in a continuous variation in such a characteristic, each gene having only a small effect on the trait in question. For instance, seed colour in grains such as maize and wheat can vary from white, through a range of pinks, to dark red.

polygenic inheritance The circumstance in which the expression of several different genes results in the expression of a single recognizable trait in the phenotype.

polyhedrin A protein that forms the matrix of occlusion bodies produced by nuclear polyhedrosis virus infections.

poly-β-hydroxybutyrate (PHB) A thermoplastic polyester consisting of $-CH_2CHOHCH_2COO-$ that is accumulated as an energy reserve by a wide variety of microorganisms including *Alcaligenes*, *Azotobacter*, *Bacillus*, *Nocardia*, *Pseudomonas* and *Rhizobium* species. Under nutrient limitation, some species can accumulate up to 70 per cent of their weight as this material. The polymer may be of commercial value, being recovered from fermentation by cell breakage followed by solvent extraction into halogenated hydrocarbons.

polylinker A synthetic oligonucleotide DNA sequence with several different restriction sites. Polylinkers are introduced into vectors so that they can be used to clone DNA fragments generated by a variety of different restriction enzymes.

polymer A long chain of monomeric units, the precise number not being defined.

polymerase An enzyme that catalyses the synthesis of a polymer. *See* DNA polymerase, RNA polymerase.

polymerase chain reaction (PCR) An *in vitro* method for the enzymatic synthesis of specific DNA sequences, using two oligonucleotide primers that hybridize to opposite strands and flank the region of interest in the target DNA. PCR is based on repeated cycles of denaturation, oligonucleotide primer annealing and primer extension by a thermostable DNA polymerase, which results in the exponential accumulation of a specific fragment whose termini are defined by the 5'-ends of the primers. Since the primer extension products synthesized in one cycle can serve as a template in the next, the number of target DNA copies approximately doubles at every cycle. A typical PCR medium includes the DNA sample to be amplified, pH buffers, gelatin, deoxynucleotide triphosphates, primers and the polymerase. The reaction is carried out in a thermal cycler programmed to run at, typically, 95°C for 20 seconds to denature the double-stranded DNA sample, at 55°C for 20 seconds to anneal the primers to their complementary sequences, and at 70°C for 30 seconds to allow extension of the annealed primers by the polymerase. The technique has been applied to sequencing, engineering of DNA, mutation detection, gene expression, construction of genetic maps, evolutionary analysis, diagnosis of monogenic disease, DNA typing, disease susceptibility, forensic fingerprinting, detection of human infectious diseases and detection of oncogenes. PCR was patented by Cetus Corporation and is licensed by Perkin Elmer. *See* amplification, polymerase, primer, thermal cycler.

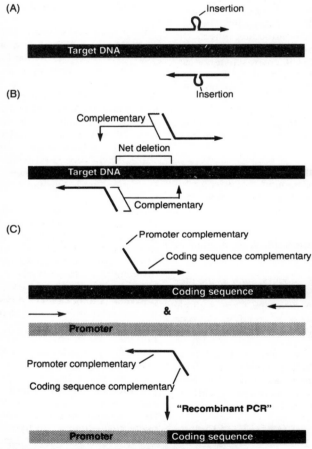

Insertion, deletion and sequence recombination via polymerase chain reaction (PCR)

polymorph A polymorphonuclear leucocyte; one of a group of white blood cells, with phagocytic activity, that includes neutrophiles, eosinophils and basophils. These represent up to 65 per cent of the white cells in human blood.

polymorphic Descriptive of species in which adult individuals occur in any of two or more forms. Polymorphism is common in animals in which the male and female differ in secondary sexual characteristics.

polymorphism The occurrence at a significant frequency, of at least one per cent, or two or more variants at a particular genetic locus. The existence of polymorphisms can be shown by analysis of gene products or by direct analysis of DNA sequences. Examples of polymorphisms in human populations are the ABO and rhesus blood groups. *See* RFLP.

polynucleotide A polymer consisting of many nucleotides. Both RNA and DNA are polynucleotides, as are synthetic nucleotide sequences which may consist of polymers of only one nucleotide species such as poly U (uracil).

polynucleotide ligase *See* DNA ligase.

polyomavirus A type of papovavirus that includes SV40.

polypeptide A polymer consisting of a number of amino acids linked by covalent bonds (peptide links). *See* oligopeptide, protein.

polypeptide hormone A hormone comprising a short amino acid sequence; amino acids may be present in unusual forms. Polypeptide hormones affect cells by binding to the outer plasma membrane and activating adenyl cyclase to initiate or stimulate the production of cyclic AMP, which in turn induces a change in cellular gene expression.

polyploid Descriptive of an organism in which the basic haploid number of chromosomes (or genomes) is multiplied by a whole number (usually three, four or five). Polyploids arise naturally, as a result of unusual crosses or hybridization, or are induced by treating cells with colchicine or other similar chemicals.

polyribonucleotide A short length of RNA; an oligonucleotide.

polyribosome *See* polysome.

polysaccharide A high-molecular-weight polymer formed from sugar units (monosaccharides) joined through glycosidic linkages. Polysaccharides include storage carbohydrates (starch in plants, glycogen in animals), structural compounds (cellulose and hemicellulose in plants, chitin in insects and mucopolysaccharides in other animals) and many gums of commercial importance produced by higher plants, algae and bacteria (agar, agarose, alginate, dextran, xanthan, guar, carrageenans, etc.).

polysome An association of a variable number of ribosomes with a single mRNA molecule that is used in translation. Polysomes occur free in the cytoplasm or are bound to the surface of the endoplasmic reticulum or the outer membrane of the nucleus.

polysomic Descriptive of a cell, tissue or organism having one chromosome represented three or more times.

polytene Descriptive of a giant interphase chromosome that results from the lengthwise aggregation of chromatids formed by a number of rounds of DNA replication without accompanying nuclear divisions. Polytenes reveal a specific banding pattern of the chromatin.

polytran An exopolysaccharide produced by *Sclerotium glucanicum* used in oil recovery, ceramic glazes, printing inks and seed coatings.

porasil *See* porous silica.

porous glass A support material used in chromatography. It is prepared from sintered alkali borosilicate glass that is tempered to form a two-phase micro-heterogeneous matrix. One phase is then leached out to form a continuous system of uniform channels, the diameter of which depends on the tempering conditions. Porous glass is used for gel filtration in aqueous or organic solvents, if adsorption effects are minimized by pretreatment with hexamethyldisilazane which blocks accessible hydroxyl groups. Commercial preparations are available (Corning porous glass) covering a molecular weight range of up to 9×10^6.

porous silica A support material used in chromatography. It is produced by fusing silica microstructures so as to form beads within microcavities. Porasil is a commercial preparation.

porphin A tetrapyrrole structurally related to porphyrinogen with methine rather than methylene bridges. Substitution at C-1 to C-8 yields protoporphyrin IX, a key intermediate in the synthesis of chlorophyll and haem.

porphyrin A tetrapyrrole. It is important as the organic part of the metalloporphyrins, which are formed by chelation of either iron or magnesium. Iron porphyrins are prosthetic groups of the cytochromes and haemoglobins. Magnesium porphyrins are the chlorophylls.

porphyrinogen A compound formed from four pyrrole residues joined by methylene bridges at their α-carbon atoms.

portal vein A blood vessel that connects two capillary beds, as in the hepatic portal system or the renal portal system (found in amphibia).

position effect The alteration of the phenotypic expression of a gene when its position on a chromosome is changed by translocation, inversion or crossing-over.

posterior Descriptive of the part of an animal that is furthest from the head, or the part of a plant organ that is nearest to the main axis.

post-transcriptional changes Modifications made to HnRNA following transcription. *See* heterogeneous nuclear RNA.

post-translational protein modification The cleavage of a signal sequence that directs the passage of the protein through a cell or organelle membrane.

potable Descriptive of a liquid that is fit to drink (e.g., water that has been purified for such a purpose). The term is also applied to fermentation ethanol to distinguish it from synthetic ethanol derived from ethylene.

power input The amount of energy put into a system, for instance as electrical energy used to drive a fermenter impeller. The energy input will increase with the viscosity of the solution, which in turn will increase the amount of energy dissipated as heat into the culture.

power number (N_p) A dimensionless group of relevance to the stirring of fluids in fermenters that represents the inertial forces transmitted to the fluid.

$$N = P(\rho N^3 D^5)$$

where P = impeller power input, N = impeller speed, D = impeller diameter and ρ = density of continuous phase.

PPG An artificial β-glucan with high affinity for β-glucan receptors on macrophages. PPG increases the ability of white blood cells to attack pathogens and the amount of monocytes and neutrophils in the blood. It is being developed as an anti-infective and a vaccine adjuvant.

PPLO Pleuropneumonia-like organisms. *See* mycoplasmas.

PR The form of phytochrome that absorbs far red light, resulting in its rapid conversion to the PF form. PFR also decays slowly to the PF form in the dark.

precipitate A solid formed from a solution as the result of precipitation.

precipitation A method of removing a substance in solution from a liquid by treating the liquid in such a way that the required compound forms an insoluble precipitate. Precipitation of biological materials is achieved by addition of salts, organic solvents, chelating agents, etc., by changes in pH or by heating or cooling. The solid material is then removed by filtration or centrifugation.

precipitin An antibody that complexes with and precipitates a soluble antigen.

precursor A compound that is formed prior to, and converted into, the compound of specific interest. An example of a precursor is trypsinogen which is converted to trypsin.

pregnant mare serum (PMS) A blood serum obtained from pregnant mares for use in cell culture.

prenatal Descriptive of an event before birth.

preproinsulin A protein comprising 109 amino acids that is a precursor of proinsulin. Preproinsulin is formed in the β-cells of the pancreas where the first 23 amino acids serve as a signal protein to permit the passage of the molecule through the cell membrane.

pressure A force normal to the surface on which it acts.

pressure cycle fermenter A fermenter in which the contents are kept agitated or mixed. Gas exchange is enhanced by circulating through an exterior limb and returning to the bottom of the main vessel where the contents are re-injected under pressure. Such fermenters may be built in the form of towers. As a result of the increased hydrostatic and/or operating pressure, the rate and efficiency of oxygen transfer is increased.

presumptive Descriptive of cells or tissues that are assumed to give rise to a specific organ or structure in latter developmental stages.

presumptive test A procedure used to establish the possibility of contamination of

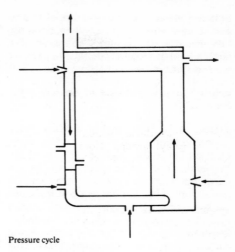

Pressure cycle

water by faecal matter. The water sample is inoculated into tubes of lactate broth, which are incubated at 37°C. The production of gas is taken as an indication that the water has been contaminated. This may be confirmed by further culture on EMB agar.

Pribnow box A sequence of bases found in prokaryotes that binds RNA polymerase and may function as a promoter region.

primary cell culture A cell culture derived directly from the tissue of an organism. Primary cell cultures are generally heterogeneous and are frequently subcultured to produce secondary cell cultures.

primary metabolite A metabolite that is formed by a microbial culture during log phase growth.

primary oil production The early stage of the working of an oil well in which oil reaches the surface under the pressure of the reservoir or is brought up by pumping.

primary production In ecology, a measure of the total amount of organic matter generated by primary producers.

primary sex ratio *See* sex ratio.

primary sexual characteristics The reproductive organs, ovaries and testes. *Compare* secondary sexual characteristics.

primary structure The structure of a compound that depends on covalent bonding. For instance, the primary structure of a nucleic acid or protein is defined in terms of the sequence of bases or amino acids.

primed *in situ* **labelling of nucleic acids** *See* PRINS.

primer A substrate that is required for a polymerization reaction and that is structurally similar to the product of the reaction. Primers are used in the synthesis of DNA *in vitro*. For enzyme synthesis, they correspond to the initiation sequence. For chemical solid-state synthesis, they may consist of a single protected nucleoside bonded to the support by the 3'-hydroxyl group. Some enzymes, especially those that catalyse the synthesis of oligosaccharides, have a short oligosaccharide primer as a prosthetic group on the enzyme.

primitive streak A longitudinal band of mesodermal cells that develops along the dorsal groove of the gastrula.

primordium A group of cells that subsequently develop into a specific tissue, organ or part of the body.

PRINS Primed *in situ* labelling of nucleic acids; a technique used to visualize unique DNA sequences, allowing high-quality cytogenic mapping and Q-banding. Hybridization of synthetic oligonucleotides or short DNA fragments to the complementary nucleic acid sequences *in situ* followed by primer extension in the presence of biotinylated or digoxigenin-labelled nucleotides by a suitable polymerase. Fluorescence labelled avidin or antidigoxigen Fab fragments are used to visualize the labelled site. The sensitivity of PRINS is virtually independent of probe length.

prions Also known as unconventional agents and slow viruses; a protein found in brains of sheep and other mammals suffering from spongiform encephalopathies. Concentrates from brain tissue show high infectivity, suggesting a central role for prion proteins in transmission of spongiform encephalopathies. Prions exhibit unconventional biological and physical properties, including a strong resistance to physical inactivation processes, which are efficient in inactivating other classes of virus.

Pro An abbreviation used to denote the amino acid proline in protein sequences and elsewhere.

probe (1) In nucleic acid dependent analysis, a length of RNA or DNA used in molecular hybridization to detect complementary sequences, by base pairing, in the presence of a large amount of non-complementary DNA. The probe is always labelled, usually with a radioactive element or with a enzyme, chromogenic or fluorogenic marker to enable it to be detected. Commonly, the position of a radioactive probe, on a southern blot for example, may be detected by autoradiography. (2) A mechanical device, electrode or biosensor, used for real-time on-line process control or measurement.

probiotic A preparation of living organisms included in animal feeds or dietary supplements in order to increase the digestion and assimilation of nutrients or to promote health.

process control The overall control and integration of the many individual components of a complex process. It is often achieved electronically.

prochymosin *See* chymosin.

procion blue H-B *See* cibacron blue 3G-A.

producer In ecology, an autotrophic organism that forms complex organic compounds by photosynthesis. These compounds are used by heterotrophic organisms.

product recovery membrane fermentation An experimental system that has been proposed for continuous ethanol recovery from fermenter broth employing selective membrane separation techniques. Ethanol is more soluble in the extractant, so diffuses across the membrane and is carried away, whereas the sugar substrate is retained in the fermenter until completely utilized.

Since only a small amount of extractant leaks into the broth, the requirements for non-toxicity, immiscibility and non-emulsion-forming properties are reduced. Polypropylene glycol p-1200 has been identified as a suitable extractant.

productivity A measure of the total amount of biomass, or other product, formed in a given time. Productivity in cell cultures is expressed in terms of cell mass, cell weight, cell number or on the basis of unit reactor volume in relation to time. For example, the productivity of a yeast culture may be expressed in terms of the volume of ethanol produced per fresh weight of cells per unit time, or in terms of the volume of ethanol produced per unit fermenter volume per unit time.

progeny The offspring produced in any generation.

progeny testing A technique in which the offspring are investigated to establish the genetic characteristics of the parents.

progesterone A steroid hormone produced by the corpus luteum of the mammalian ovary and to a lesser extent by the testis, placenta and adrenal cortex. It is an intermediate in the synthesis of most steroid hormones, as well as being important in regulation of the oestrous cycle and maintenance of the uterus in pregnancy.

progestogen A substance that displays progesterone-like effects on the female mammalian reproductive organs.

prohormone A large polypeptide that is formed as a precursor to the formation of a peptide hormone (e.g. proinsulin is a precursor of insulin).

proinsulin A polypeptide comprising 86 amino acids formed from preproinsulin by the removal of a peptide containing 23 amino acids. The proinsulin molecule folds to bring the first and last segment of the chain together. The central part of the chain, which serves to align the two peptides (A and B chains), that form insulin, is then excised.

prokaryote Lower organisms that lack a well-defined nucleus and contain genetic material in the form of double-stranded DNA attached to the plasma membrane and not enclosed within a membrane of its own. Mitochondria, chloroplasts and other membrane-limited organelles are absent; the enzymes involved in energy metabolism are distributed through the cytoplasm. The intermediates of respiratory electron transport are associated with membranes, as in photosynthetic species are the pigments and intermediates of photosynthetic electron transport. Prokaryotes, which are mainly bacteria, but include the cyanobacteria, may be obligate anaerobes, facultative anaerobes or fully aerobic.

prolactin A protein hormone, also known as lactogenic hormone, that is secreted by the pars distalis of the mammalian pituitary gland and maintains lactation. It consists of a single chain of 198 amino acids, with three disulphide linkages. It is structurally related to growth hormone.

prolamellar body A quasicrystalline structure composed of interconnected membranous tubules in a regular array that occurs in etioplasts. These bodies are the precursors of the lamellae of the chloroplast which develop when the plant is exposed to light. The prolamellar bodies are composed of a basic repeating unit consisting of four short lengths of tubule joined at a central point in a tetrahedral fashion. Each of the four arms of the tetrahedron link with those of an adjacent tetrahedron to build up a three-dimensional lattice.

prolamine A simple plant protein, such as gliadin (a component of gluten), which is only soluble in aqueous ethanol.

proline (Pro) One of the 20 common amino acids found in proteins.

Proline

promiscuous plasmid A plasmid that is capable of promoting its own transfer to a wide range of gram-negative bacteria and of being stably maintained in these diverse hosts. These plasmids generally belong to the incompatibility classes known as P and Q. Such plasmids offer the possibility of readily transferring cloned DNA molecules into a wide range of organisms.

promoter A DNA sequence that promotes transcription of a gene to produce mRNA and may be the attachment site for RNA polymerase (transcriptase). *Compare* operator. *See* Pribnow box, TATA box.

proofreading The ability of DNA polymerase to read sequences of DNA and to repair mistakes made in the course of copying the template. This ability accounts for the fact that the actual accuracy of replication is much higher than would be predicted from considerations of stereochemistry alone. All three polymerases found in *E. coli* possess this ability. If a wrong nucleotide is incorporated, it causes a slight distortion in the duplex and also in the structure of the polymerase that stimulates the exonuclease activity and the removal of the mismatched nucleotide(s) from the 3'- end. Functioning again as a polymerase, the enzyme then replaces the eliminated nucleotide(s) with the correct complementary ones.

prophage The state of a phage genome in a lysogen; a phage attached to a specific site on a bacterial chromosome in the process of lysogeny. Under these conditions, the phage becomes indistinguishable in behaviour from the bacterial chromosome with which it is reproduced. The lysogenic conditions confer on the cells immunity to infection by that phage, but not to infection by other different phage. Occasionally it may revert to form an active phage, resulting in lysis and the release of infective particles. However, the free phage particles cannot kill the rest of the population owing to its specific immunity. Their presence can be detected if a sample of the culture is plated on a sensitive non-lysogenic strain of the same bacterial species – termed an indicator strain.

prophase The first phase of nuclear division in either mitosis or meiosis.

prophylactic A preventive agent used to protect against disease before it occurs.

prophylaxis The prevention of disease. This may include the study of the biological behaviour of disease-causing agents and applying a series of measures against them.

proplastid A small organelle between 0.5 and 1.0 μm in diameter found in meristematic cells of plants. It differentiates to form plastids.

propylene A three-carbon alkene.

prostaglandin A hormone-like substance, formed from a fatty acid, which occurs in mammalian tissues. Prostaglandins possess a wide spectrum of biological activity with specific effects on smooth muscle, causing vasodilation and vasoconstriction, as well as stimulating contraction and relaxation of the uterus. Prostaglandins also modify levels of cyclic AMP in the body and are released during inflammatory tissue response. The analgesic effect of aspirin is associated with inhibition of prostaglandin synthesis.

prosthetic group A non-protein molecule that associates with a protein to form a complex. Examples include co-enzymes such as flavins and pyridine nucleotides, as well as lipids and polysaccharides, which are the prosthetic groups of lipoproteins and glycoproteins, respectively.

protamine A low-molecular-weight basic protein that is associated with nucleic acids.

protandry Descriptive of flowers in which the stigma matures prior to the pollen. *Compare* protogyny.

protease An enzyme that catalyses the hydrolysis of proteins to amino acids.

protected nucleoside *See* protected nucleotide.

protected nucleotide A synthetic derivative of one of the purine or pyrimidine bases found in DNA or RNA that is used in the chemical synthesis of oligonucleotides.

protein A macromolecule made up of one or more chains of amino acids joined covalently through peptide bonds. Proteins vary greatly in molecular weight from a few thousand to several million daltons. There are 20 common amino acids found in proteins, and these are arranged in specific sequences that reflect the base sequence of DNA in the gene from which the protein is encoded. All enzymes are proteins. However, not all proteins show catalytic activity. Other proteins serve regulatory (hormones), protective (antibodies), structural (muscle) or storage functions. Proteins may be classified in a number of ways. Early systems of protein classification were based on solubility of proteins: (1) albumins, soluble in water and dilute salt solution; (2) globulins, insoluble in water, but soluble in salt solutions; (3) glutelins, insoluble in neutral solutions but soluble in dilute acids and bases; (4) prolamins, insoluble in water, but soluble in 70–80 per cent aqueous ethanol. In general, these are simple proteins in contrast to conjugated proteins which include a non-protein prosthetic group. Both functional and structural properties are determined by the conformation of the protein, which is defined at four levels of complexity. The primary structure defines the sequence of amino acids. The secondary structure is determined by the nature and extent of hydrogen bonding, which often results in regular coiling of the molecule in the form of an alpha-helix or a beta-plated sheet. Tertiary structure is formed by the folding of the amino acid chain and is maintained by the formation of disulphide bridges and non-covalent attractive forces, such as hydrophobic interaction. Large or complex proteins may be composed of a number of subunits, each formed from a separate polypeptide chain. In any given protein, these subunits may be identical or consist of two or more different forms, which may vary in size, complexity or even in the type of genome in which they are encoded (e.g., the rubisco from higher plants consists of eight large subunits encoded in the chloroplast genome and eight small subunits encoded by nuclear DNA). The arrangement of the subunits is described as the quaternary structure of a protein.

protein A A protein produced by *Staphylococcus aureus* that has a broad range capacity to bind immunoglobulin G, and hence is used to measure cell-bound antigens and antibodies. Protein A binds to the antibodies without disturbing their binding of antigen. Protein A is used in an immobilized form in affinity chromatography for the separation of subclasses of immunoglobulins, as well as in various types of immunoassay.

protein determination A technique used to measure the amount of protein in a sample. This is performed using a spectrophotometric protein determination, the Kjeldahl method, the Lowry method or the Biuret reaction, or on the basis of the sum of the peptides or amino acids detected by fingerprinting or using an amino acid analyser.

protein engineering A technique used in the production of proteins with new or artificial amino acid sequences. This may be achieved using solid-state polypeptide synthesis and linking the polypeptides to form a protein. Alternatively, new proteins are produced by transcription and translation systems to form proteins from synthesized lengths of DNA or RNA with novel sequences.

protein refolding The reformation of the tertiary structure of protein molecules following denaturation.

protein sequence phylogenetics A technique used to determine the genetic relationship between various organisms. The method is based on determination of the amino acid sequence of a comparable protein, often cytochrome c. Knowledge of the genetic code makes it possible to calculate the minimum number of nucleotide changes necessary to produce the change in the amino acid sequence. It is assumed that the greater the differences, the less the phylogenetic relationship between the two organisms.

protein sequencing An analytical method used to determine the sequence of amino acids that make up a peptide or protein. Information is obtained by a combination of chemical or enzymic hydrolysis followed by fingerprinting or amino acid analysis. Fully automated solid-state systems are available.

protein synthesis The production of a protein from its constituent amino acids. This takes place in association with specific organelles known as ribosomes. The information that determines the amino acid sequence of a protein is carried in the DNA sequence of a gene. This is transferred to a base sequence on a molecule of mRNA in the process known as transcription. The information is encoded in specific sequences of three bases (nucleotide triplets) known as codons. In eukaryotes, the mRNA migrates to the cytoplasm and associates with a number of ribosomes to form a polyribosome. Polyribosomes are also formed in prokaryotes and the plastids of eukaryotes. The mRNA acts as a template for the formation of the protein, with each amino acid being transferred to the growing peptide in turn. The correct sequence is achieved as a result of the amino acids forming a complex with tRNA, which carries a specific anticodon (base triplet) that can recognize and bind with the respective codon in the process of translation.

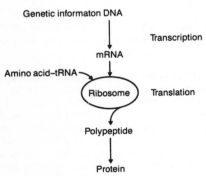

Protein synthesis

protein targeting The addition of a short leader sequence to a protein to facilitate its passage through a target membrane (e.g., the membrane of a specific cell organelle).

proteinase A proteolytic enzyme that partially hydrolyses protein to form small peptides.

proteoglycan An extracellular matrix macromolecule in which unbranched glycosaminoglycan side chains are linked to the serine residues of a core protein.

proteolysis The hydrolysis of proteins into amino acids. Proteolysis is catalysed by a number of different types of enzymes known as proteases or proteolytic enzymes. These include both endopeptidases (e.g., renin) and exopeptidases (e.g., trypsin and chymotrypsin), as well as cathepsins.

proteolytic enzyme An enzyme that hydrolyses proteins to amino acids. *See* cathepsin.

proteoplast A plastid which is modified to act as a storage organelle for protein.

prothrombin A glycoprotein present in normal blood plasma. It is the inactive precursor of thrombin.

Protista A kingdom of single-celled organisms, distinct from plants or animals, which includes the bacteria, unicellular algae, protozoans and some fungi. The prokaryotic members are known as the Monera.

protoclonal variation Phenotypic variation between plants regenerated from cells cloned from a single plant protoplast.

protoderm The meristematic tissue of the apical meristem that gives rise to the epidermis.

protogyny Descriptive of flowers in which the pollen matures prior to the stigma. *Compare* protandry.

proton/oxygen ratio The ratio of protons released to the amount of oxygen consumed in respiration.

protoplasm The living contents of a cell, including the cytoplasm and the nucleus, as well as various organelles and plastids.

protoplast The total contents of a cell, excluding material outside the plasma membrane. Protoplasts are prepared from plant cells using cellulase or lysozyme. Protoplasts are used in cell fusion and as acceptors for vectors in genetic engineering.

protoplast fusion A technique used to produce hybrid organisms in which protoplasts derived from two different (plant) sources are fused to produce a single cell which may then be induced to form a new cell wall, callus tissue and finally new plantlets.

prototroph A strain of organism capable of growth on a defined minimal medium from which it can synthesize all of the more complex biological molecules it requires. *Compare* auxotroph.

Protozoa A phylum comprising unicellular microscopic animals. *See* protozoon.

protozoon A member of one of the lower orders of animals, the Protozoa, usually microscopic in size and unicellular, although colonial forms exist. Parts of the cell may be specialized as cilia or flagella.

provirus A latent virus genome that is present in a host chromosome, but is not expressed.

proximal The part of an organ or tissue that is closest to the point of origin or attachment. *Compare* distal.

pseudoallele A gene that appears to function as a single unit but within which crossing-over can occur.

pseudodominance The apparent dominance of a recessive gene (allele), owing to a deletion of the corresponding gene in the homologous chromosome.

pseudogene A sequence of DNA that is similar to a structural gene sequence, but is not apparently transcribed.

pseudomonad Any genus of polarly flagellated, gram-negative, rod-shaped bacteria. These include the fluorescent pseudomonads, which produce a water-soluble greenish-yellow fluorescent pigment and the marine luminous bacteria.

Pseudomonas A genus of rod-shaped, motile, aerobic bacteria that is widely distributed in both soil and water.

pseudo-plastic fluid A fluid in which the apparent viscosity decreases, but subsequently becomes linear. Such behaviour is characteristic of many cultures of moulds or actinomycetes.

psychrophile A microorganism with a temperature optimum for growth of between 0°C and 30°C. Psychrophiles are associated with spoilage of refrigerated food and occur widely in temperate soils and water.

pteroylglutamic acid *See* folic acid.

PTFE Polytetrafluoroethylene; a material used to manufacture filters.

Pth Phenylthiohydantoin.

Pth amino acid An amino acid derivative in the form of phenylhydantoin used in protein sequencing.

ptyalin An amylase found in saliva.

puff A swelling found in the giant polytene chromosomes of the salivary glands of some dipterans.

pullulan An uncharged microbial polysaccharide found in *Pullularia pullulans* and composed of glucose. It is highly viscous and forms clear oxygen-impermeable films and fibres used in foods, food packaging and adhesives.

pullulanase An enzyme that catalyses the hydrolysis of α-(1,6)-glucosidic links at a branch point, as well as in a linear chain of a number of oligo- and polysaccharides. It degrades pullulan to maltotriose and is active on amylopectin, glycogen and β-dextrins.

pulse chase experiment A technique used to follow the metabolism of a compound. A radioactive substrate is fed for a short time, the non-radioactive substrate is then introduced and samples are taken at intervals. The movement of the radioactive label is followed as it moves from one compound to the next.

pulse shape discrimination A technique used to distinguish different types of ionizing particles (α-particles, β-particles, protons, etc.) on the basis of the amplitude and lifetime of the signal.

pulsed field gel electrophoresis (PFGE) A method of separating high-molecular-weight DNA fragments. Electric fields are periodically applied at varying angles across an agarose gel. This causes the DNA molecules to change direction repeatedly, enhancing differences between their relative mobilities and thus increasing the sensitivity with which they can be separated.

pupa A non-feeding, non-motile stage in the life cycle of an endopterygote insect, in which metamorphosis occurs.

pupil The opening in the iris of the eye in vertebrates through which light enters.

pure culture A culture of a microorganism that contains only one strain or species.

pure line A true breeding (homozygous) genotype, or a continuous series of generations of an organism, that is consistently homozygous for one or more characteristics. Pure lines are produced by inbreeding animals or by self-pollination in plants.

purification A process used to increase the proportion of a given substance in a mixture; a procedure that results in an increase in the specific activity of an enzyme.

purine A nitrogenous base, derivatives of which are constituents of nucleic acids, nucleotides and co-enzymes. The most abundant purines are adenine and guanine.

puromycin An antibiotic that causes premature release of partially formed protein chains from ribosomes by displacing

the chain with a molecule of puromycin attached. It inhibits protein synthesis in bacteria, algae, protozoa and mammalian cells.

Puromycin (stylomycin)

putrefaction A decomposition, catalysed by the growth of microorganisms. It is characterized by the formation of evil-smelling end products which are generated as the consequence of the breakdown of proteins.

PVDF Polyvinylidine fluoride; a material used to manufacture filters.

pyranose A monosaccharide that exists as a six-membered heterocyclic ring comprising five carbon atoms and one oxygen atom.

pyrenoid A small body found in the chloroplasts of algae that is associated with the storage of carbohydrates.

pyrethrin An insecticide derived from the plant *Chrysanthemum cinerariaefolium*.

pyridoxal phosphate A co-enzyme derivative of pyridoxine that participates in transamination and other reactions of amino acids.

pyridoxine Vitamin B_6; a precursor of the co-enzyme pyridoxal phosphate. It is an essential growth factor in the culture of many microorganisms.

pyrimidine A nitrogenous base, derivatives of which are constituents of nucleic acids and nucleotides. The most abundant pyrimidines are cytosine, thymine and uracil.

Q

Q_{10} *See* temperature quotient.

Q-banding A chromosome banding technique used in demonstrating areas of heterochromatin, especially the Y chromosomes. Q-banding involves the use of quinacrine dyes.

quadrivalent Four completely or partially homologous chromosomes that are associated by pairing from prophase to metaphase of the first meiotic division.

quantitative character *See* metric character.

quantitative precipitin reaction An immunochemical test in which the amount of precipitate formed as a result of reaction between antigen and antibody is determined by measuring the amount of protein using optical density at 280 nm or microKjeldahl analysis.

quantum efficiency *See* quantum yield.

quantum number A measure of the number of light quanta required for completion of a given photochemical reaction. In photosynthesis, a measure of the number of light quanta required for the assimilation of one molecule of carbon dioxide or evolution of one molecule of oxygen. The theoretical minimum quantum requirement for photosynthesis, if the two photoreaction Z scheme is correct, is eight. The quantum number is determined experimentally as the reciprocal of the quantum yield.

quantum speciation The rapid rise of a new species, usually in small isolates, with the founder effect and random genetic drift playing important roles. It is also called saltational speciation.

quantum yield In photosynthesis, the number of moles of carbon dioxide fixed, or oxygen evolved per light quantum (Einstein) absorbed. It is determined experimentally from the initial slope (α) of a plot of photosynthetic rate against light intensity. The theoretical minimum quantum requirement is 0.125, but best values recorded are around 0.08 and field values may be around 0.002.

quaternary structure Used to describe the packing of folded polypeptide chains in a complex protein.

quench correction A method used to correct the observed counts per minute produced by a scintillation counter to give a true value in terms of disintegrations per minute. Methods fall into three groups: (1) internal standard calibration, where the experimental sample is counted once, a standard of known radioactivity is added and the sample recounted; (2) external standard calibration, where the sample is counted twice. The second time after bringing an external gamma-ray source into close proximity to the sample; (3) channels ratio method, where the counting channel is split into two parts such that quenching causes a proportional change in the ratio of the counts recorded in one channel to those counted in the other.

quenching A process that reduces the number of photons which impinge upon the window of the photomultiplier of a scintillation counter. Quenching results in a counting rate (counts per minute, cpm) that is lower than the true disintegration rate (disintegrations per minute, dpm). The difference is due to dilution effects, or effects of coloured quenchers or chemical quenchers. Diluters reduce the frequency with which the ionizing radiation hits the scintillator molecules. Colour quenchers intercept the photons before they can strike the photomultiplier. Chemical quenchers react preferentially with excited solvent molecules, dissipating the energy as heat before it can be transferred to the scintillators.

quinacrine Derivative of acridine used as an antimalarial drug and in cancer chemotherapy. Quinacrine dyes (e.g., quinacrine mustard, quinacrine hydrochloride), which fluoresce under ultraviolet light, are used as chromosome stains. *See* Q-banding.

R

R factor A resistance factor. R factors are similar to the F factors. They are a class of plasmids that are capable of transferring antibiotic resistance from one strain of bacteria to another through conjugation or transduction. In general, R factors are extrachromosomal and do not undergo reversible integration into the cell chromosome.

R loop A region of a double-stranded DNA molecule in which one DNA strand is displaced and paired with a complementary strand of RNA.

race A population or group of populations distinguishable from other similar populations of the same species by the frequency of genes, chromosomal arrangements or hereditary characteristics. A race that has received a taxonomic name is known as a subspecies.

racemate A mixture of equal parts of both optically active compounds (*d* and *l*). A racemic mixture does not possess any optical activity.

radial immunodiffusion A quantitative immunological test in which the antiserum is incorporated into a gel (e.g., agarose or agar). The antigen is placed into a well in the gel. Diffusion of the antigen from the well into the gel results in formation of a precipitate. This results in a ring or halo of precipitate being formed, the area of which is proportional to the antigen concentration. The concentration of antigen is quantified by comparison with a set of antigen standards, run at the same time.

radicle The embryonic root, continuous with the hypocotyl, that occurs in germinating angiosperm and gymnosperm seedlings.

radioactive Descriptive of elements, compounds or materials that emit ionizing radiation.

radioactive decay The breaking up of a radioactive atom with the emission of particles or gamma-rays. Decay is associated with the loss of the radioactive isotope and the formation of another isotope of the same element but of lower mass, or the formation of one or more different elements. The rate of decay is proportional to the amount of the radioactive isotope present in the sample and is characterized in terms of its half-life. The half-life is the time taken for the radioactivity to decay to 50 per cent of its original activity.

radioactive decay correction A compensation made for the loss of radioactivity due to decay that occurs during the course of an experiment. For isotopes with long half-lives (e.g., ^{14}C) this may not be necessary. However, if the half-life is short and is similar to the duration of the experiment, a correction is required. The percentage isotope remaining at any time may be calculated as follows:

$$\log(N_o/N_t) = 0.3010(t/h)$$

$$\text{percentage isotope} = 100 - \text{antilog} \ [0.3010(t/h)]$$

where t = time of decay, h = half-life, N_o = radioactivity at start, N_t = radioactivity at time t.

radioactive half-life The time taken for a radioactive isotope to lose half its radioactivity. *See* radioactive isotope.

radioactive isotope An unstable element that decays with the emission of gamma-rays, beta-particles or alpha-particles. Some of the most common isotopes used in biological studies are listed together with their properties.

Element	Mass	Half-life	Energy (MeV) Particles	γ-rays
Hydrogen	3	12.1 years	0.0185	–
Carbon	11	20.5 min	0.95	–
Carbon	14	5100.0 years	0.156	–
Phosphorus	32	14.3 days	1.71	–
Sulphur	35	87.1 days	0.169	–
Calcium	45	152.0 days	0.260	–
Iodine	125	60.0 days	–	0.035
Iodine	131	8.1 days	0.605	0.637
				0.363
			0.25	0.282
				0.080

radioactive label A radioactive compound or element. It is used as a means of marking a compound and following it in a biological system.

radioactive labelling (1) The synthesis of a chemical compound in such a way that one, or more, of the normal stable atoms is replaced by a radioactive atom of the same element with a high specific activity. (2) The labelling of individual organisms or cultures by feeding with food or substrates that contain specific radioactive elements. The radioactive compounds are used to trace the metabolic fate of the molecules or atoms concerned. *See* radioactive tracer.

radioactive standard A specimen containing a known quantity of a radioactive isotope with a known rate of decay. It is used for the calibration of instruments employed in the measurement of radioactivity.

radioactive tracer A radioactive isotope of one of the elements commonly found in living tissue. The most common tracers include tritium (^{3}H), ^{14}C, ^{35}S and ^{32}P. They are used to elucidate complex metabolic pathways, to obtain mass balances in culture, to follow enzyme kinetics or to determine reaction mechanisms.

radioactivity The spontaneous disintegration displayed by certain elements or isotopes due to the composition of their atomic nuclei.

radioallergosorbent test (RAST) An immunological test used to measure IgE antibody specific for an allergen which is bound to an insoluble carrier. The serum is reacted with the insolubilized allergen and the particles washed and reacted with a radiolabelled antibody to human IgE; the amount of radioactivity is proportional to the amount of IgE antibody specific to the antigen in the test serum.

radioautograph *See* autoradiography.

radiobiology The branch of biology concerned with the effects of radiation on living organisms and the behaviour of radioactive biological materials. It is also concerned with the use of radioactive tracers in biological systems.

radiochemistry The study of radioactive elements and their use in the investigation of chemical processes.

radioelement An element that is naturally radioactive or a radioisotope.

radiograph An image produced by the action of X-rays or other radiation from a radioactive substance on a photographic plate.

radiography The process of production of radiographs.

radioimmunoassay (RIA) A widely used analytical technique, based on immunological reaction, for measuring proteins (e.g., antibodies, antigens, peptide hormones, enzymes, etc.). Although many different systems exist, their main feature is that a radioactive label is used to follow the reaction and the use of the interaction of an antibody with an antigen. The assays, which often employ proteins that have been labelled with ^{125}I by iodination, may be based on direct binding, with the amount of radioactivity in the antibody–antigen precipitate being measured An indirect approach may also be used. For instance, the assay may be based on the ability of an unlabelled protein to compete with a known standard in binding to an antibody. The protein concentration of the sample is determined by comparing the degree of inhibition with that produced by a series of standards containing known amounts of the protein being measured. The technique has particular advantages in terms of sensitivity, specificity and precision. Kits that use specific monoclonal antibodies are available for a wide range of diagnostic purposes.

radioimmunoelectrophoresis An immunoelectrophoretic process in which radiolabelled antibody or antigen is used, followed by autoradiography, to quantify the reaction.

radioisotope *See* radioactive isotope.

radiolabelling *See* radioactive labelling.

radiology The science dealing with X-rays and other radioactive emissions, and their use in biology and medicine for the examination or photographing of organs in particular.

radioluminescence Luminescence caused by radiation from a radioactive material.

radiolysis The chemical deposition of a substance following treatment with radiation.

radiometer An instrument used for detecting and measuring small amounts of radiant energy.

radionuclide An unstable atomic species, characterized by a given mass number, atomic number and energy state, that decays emitting radiation (alpha, beta and gamma-rays).

radio-opaque A compound or material that is opaque to radiation and is therefore visible using X-ray photography.

radiotherapy The treatment of disease, usually tumours, using X-rays or radioactive substances.

ramp-time The time taken for the temperature to change between successive steps in a PCR reaction.

random amplified polymorphic DNA *See* RAPD.

random genetic drift A variation in gene frequency found from one generation to the next due to chance fluctuations.

random mating The formation of crosses with no deliberate choice of parents in terms of their genetic characteristics.

random sample A sample obtained in a system in which there is no conscious choice for a particular type or characteristic.

range of reaction The range of all possible phenotypes that may develop, by interaction with various environments, from a given genotype.

RAPD Random amplified polymorphic DNA. A method used to search for variations in DNA in the construction of genetic maps. The RAPD method uses a series of synthetic ten-base-long chains as probes. Polymorphisms result in different patterns following restriction and separation by gel electrophoresis.

raphe (1) A line of junction in organs, such as the line of fusion between the funicle and integument in a plant ovule or the junction between the two halves of the vertebrate brain. (2) The narrow slit on the valve face of the frustule of a diatom.

RAST *See* radioallergosorbent test.

rate zonal centrifugation A separation technique in which molecules or small particles are sedimented through a gradient of increasing density or viscosity usually formed from sucrose. Separation is based on molecular size and conformation. The degree of separation depends on the duration of the sedimentation.

reactive blue 2 *See* cibacron blue 3G-A.

reading frame A nucleotide sequence from which translation occurs. Since the code does not contain punctuation marks, it is possible for two different proteins to be coded for by the same sequence that contains overlapping genes. This phenomenon is found, for example, in small viruses such as θ x174 in which the sequence ATCCGCGCTTCGATAAAA corresponds to Met–Arg–Ala–Ser–Ile–Lys. By shifting the reading frame one nucleotide to the left, the same sequence corresponds to Ala–Arg–Phe–Asp–Lys–Asn–Asp.

read-through The continuation of transcription by RNA polymerase beyond the normal termination codon.

re-association The base pairing of complementary single-stranded DNA to form a double helix following melting. *See* melting.

receptor An organ, cell or part of a cell specialized to respond to a stimulus from an external or internal change in environment by producing a local graded membrane potential which may initiate a nerve impulse. Receptors are classified according to the effective stimulus: for example, photoreceptors (light); chemoreceptors (chemicals).

receptor potential A graded depolarization elicited in a receptor cell as a response to a stimulus. This potential triggers a burst of propagated impulses, the frequency of which reflects the intensity of the stimulus.

recessive Descriptive of a trait or gene that is expressed in homozygous but not in heterozygous cells; a member of a pair of alleles which does not show its effect in the phenotype in the presence of any other allele.

recipient An organism that receives nucleic acid, tissues or organs from another individual, which may be of the same or a different species, in processes such as grafting.

reciprocal cross A pair of crosses or matings used to determine whether the sex of the parents has any effect on the phenotypic expression of the alleles of interest in the offspring. For instance, the offspring of a male of genetic make-up AA and a female aa may be compared with the offspring of a male aa and a female AA.

reciprocal translocation An exchange of chromosome segments between two non-homologous chromosomes.

recircularization The tendency for a plasmid that has been cut using a restriction enzyme to re-establish its circular form.

recognition sequence *See* recognition site.

recognition site A sequence of base pairs that is recognized by a restriction endonuclease.

recombinant A cell whose DNA comes from more than one source.

recombinant DNA DNA formed when single-stranded DNA combines by complementary base pairing to form a new DNA double helix. This process occurs *in vivo* during crossing-over in meiosis and between the chromatids during normal cell division (mitosis), as well as during conjugation and transformation in bacteria. It forms the basis of *in vitro* gene manipulation or genetic engineering.

recombinant DNA technology *See* gene manipulation.

recombinant type An association of genetic markers, found among the progeny of a cross, that is different from any association of markers present in the parents. *Compare* parental type.

recombination The formation of a zygote that contains genes which are combined in a different way from that found in either parent. Recombination is the result of crossing-over during meiosis in eukaryotes or of DNA exchange in prokaryotes. Recombination may also involve the addition of new sequences to an existing molecule of DNA. Recombination is an important means of producing genetic variation *in vivo*, leading to new genotypes which through the effects of selection pressure can result in evolutionary change.

recon The smallest unit of genetic information that can undergo recombination. Theoretically this corresponds to a single base pair in a DNA molecule. However, in general, recombination occurs between longer sequences or involves complete genes.

red blood cell *See* erythrocyte.

redox potential A measure of the ease with which a given compound can accept or donate electrons. It is expressed in volts with reference to the normal hydrogen electrode. In biological systems where a pH of 7 is assumed, the oxygen couple (O_2/H_2O) has a value of +820 mV and the hydrogen couple a value of –420 mV. The redox potentials of some important biological couples are as follows:

NAD/NADH –320 mV
NADP/NADH –320 mV
favoprotein –50 mV
Cytochrome b +40 mV
Cytochrome a +290 mV

These values are for an equilibrium midpoint (50 per cent reduced) and differ *in vitro*. For instance, the redox potential of NADPH (90 per cent reduced) is –400 mV.

reduction The addition of electrons. For example, the reduction of ferric to ferrous ions:

$$Fe^{3+} + e^- \rightarrow Fe^{2+}$$

Reduction may also be regarded as the addition of hydrogen. For example, the reduction of pyruvic acid to lactic acid:

$$CH_3COCOOH + NADH \rightarrow$$
$$CH_3CHOHCOOH + NAD$$

reduction division *See* meiosis.

reflex An immediate or involuntary response to a stimulus that is inborn and unconscious, and does not require a learning process. In many animals, simple reflex actions are mediated through a reflex arc. However, in animals with more advanced nervous systems, additional interneurones are involved between the afferent and efferent pathways permitting more complex responses.

reflex arc A simple arrangement of nerve cells in association with a receptor and an effector which results in reflex responses. An impulse evoked by a stimulus perceived by the receptor is transmitted along an afferent nerve directly to an efferent nerve in a monosynaptic pathway.

reflux A method of extraction in which a condenser is attached to a vessel containing a boiling liquid. The apparatus is arranged so that the condensed vapour flows back into the vessel through a sample. Material soluble in the condensate is gradually leached from the sample.

regeneration The regrowth of parts of an organism which have been lost through injury.

regulator gene (1) A gene that regulates or modifies the activity of other genes. (2) A gene that codes for an allosteric protein which (alone or in combination with a corepressor) regulates the genetic transcription of the structural genes in an operon by binding to the operator. *Compare* structural gene.

relative centrifugal force (g) The force generated in a centrifuge at any point from the centre of rotation. It is dependent on the speed of rotation, where

$$g = 1118 \times 10^{-8} \times R \times N^2$$

where R = radius in centimetres from the centre of the rotor to the point at which the relative centrifugal force value is required and N is the speed of the centrifuge in revolutions per minute.

relative viscosity A description of the flow behaviour of a fluid expressed as the ratio of the dynamic viscosity of a solution, or of a dispersion, to that of the solvent, or continuous phase, measured at the same temperature.

relaxed plasmid A plasmid that is maintained as multiple copies per cell.

relaxin A peptide hormone secreted by the mammalian ovaries, placenta or uterus during the later stages of pregnancy. The action of relaxin is associated with the breakdown of collagen and cartilage associated with the relaxation of the pelvic ligaments.

release factor A factor that facilitates the release of completed polypeptide chains from mRNA following transcription. Also called termination factor.

released control The replication of plasmid DNA in a situation where concomitant protein synthesis is not required.

renin An enzyme secreted by the kidney. It is associated with the formation of angiotensin from a liver globulin.

rennet (1) The membrane that lines the fourth stomach of a calf. (2) The secretion from the stomach of the calf that contains rennin. (3) A commercial preparation or extract of the rennet membrane used to curdle milk as in the making of cheese, junket, etc. Two phases can be distinguished. In the primary phase, which is enzymic, the protective colloid of the caesin is broken down with a glycopeptide being split off. The secondary phase is non-enzymic consisting of coagulation under the influence of calcium ions. The primary phase has a Q_{10} of about 2, whereas the secondary stage has a Q_{10} of about 15. This permits continuous systems of clotting with the first stage being conducted at low temperature. In the second stage, warming clots the milk.

rennin An acid protease; an enzyme that coagulates the casein in milk. It is the active ingredient of rennet and is secreted from the stomach wall of young mammals. Renninlike acid proteases are also produced by *Mucor*, *Endothia* and *Trametes* species.

repair enzyme An enzyme that catalyses the insertion of a correct base or nucleotide into a sequence where the wrong base pair has been previously inserted. Repair enzymes include polymerases, endonucleases and glycosidases. *See* DNA repair.

repeat A chromosomal duplication in which the duplicated segments are adjacent (in tandem), inverted or not; also called tandem duplication.

repetitious DNA DNA in which the base sequences are repeated many times in the genome of any cell; in highly repetitious DNA the base sequences may be represented more than 1000 times. Such DNA is concentrated in heterochromatin and in chromosomes where it is located in the region of the centromere. Moderately repetitious DNA includes the genes for rRNA and tRNA, as well as structural genes coding for the synthesis of histones.

replacement vector A cloning vehicle in which part of the native DNA has been replaced by a foreign DNA sequence. This type of vector may be produced from a plasmid that has two restriction sites. *Compare* insertional vector.

replica plating A technique in which the pattern of colonies growing on a culture plate is copied. A sterile filter paper is pressed against the culture plate and then lifted. Next the filter is pressed against a second sterile plate. This results in the new plate being infected with cells in the same relative positions as the colonies in the original plate. Usually the medium used in the second plate will differ from that used in the first (i.e., it may include an antibiotic or lack a growth factor). In this way, transformed cells can be selected.

replicase An enzyme (e.g., a polymerase) that catalyses the replication of macromolecules such as RNA and DNA.

replication The production of two double-stranded molecules of DNA from a double-stranded DNA parent molecule. Replication requires the splitting of the parent molecule, followed by synthesis of new strands of complementary DNA. *See* DNA replication.

replication fork *See* DNA replication.

replicon A length of DNA that is replicated as a unit from a single initiation site. An origin of replication sequence in a DNA molecule is required for its replication. In bacteria and viruses, there is usually one replicon per genome, whereas each eukaryotic chromosome contains many replicons. In genetic engineering, fragments of DNA bearing the required genetic characteristics are attached to a suitable host-specific replicon to form a vector or cloning vehicle.

repression The mechanism that prevents the expression of a gene (and hence the synthesis of a particular enzyme). *See* repressor.

repressor A protein that binds to the operator in an operon, preventing synthesis of mRNA and consequently protein synthesis.

reproductive isolating mechanism (RIM) A biological property of an organism that interferes in its breeding with organisms of other species.

reproductive isolation The inability to interbreed due to biological differences.

research kit A package that contains all the required reagents, in a suitable form, to carry out one or more specific assays which may be based on immune, chemical or enzyme-catalysed reactions. A research kit uses a procedure or reagents that have not been validated or accepted by health authorities.

reserpine 3,4,5-Trimethoxybenzoyl methyl reserpate; a tranquillizer that reduces blood pressure. It releases catecholamines from tissue.

resin Any of a number of acidic substances based on terpenes or phenols produced by many trees and shrubs, and conifers in particular. Resins occur as solids or dissolved in essential oils forming balsams such as turpentine.

resistance plasmid A plasmid that confers antibiotic resistance to a host bacterium.

resolution (1) In chromatography, a measure of the effectiveness with which one solute is separated from another. (2) In microscopy, the ability to distinguish two adjacent and separated points or objects. The theoretical limit of resolution of a microscope is about half the wavelength of the radiation used. Therefore the shorter the wavelength, the higher the resolution. The best light microscopes give magnifications of 1500 with a resolution of 200 nm, whereas an electron microscope can give a resolution of 0.5 nm at a magnification of up to 250,000 on the screen.

respiration The overall oxidative metabolism of food materials to produce metabolic energy. In general, the term is applied to aerobic (oxygen-requiring) processes, although the term anaerobic respiration may also be used. Various partial processes in animals associated with respiratory gas exchange are also referred to as respiration: for inhalation and exhalation (breathing) or the overall processes by which carbohydrate and oxygen interact to produce carbon dioxide and water with the generation of ATP (i.e., the combined action of glycolysis and the respiratory electron transport chain).

Reserpine

respiratory chain *See* electron transport chain.

respiratory pigment A compound that increases the oxygen-carrying capacity of an animal's circulatory system. The pigment occurs in solution in the plasma or is confined to cells (corpuscles). Respiratory pigments include haemoglobin, haemocyanin and haemerythrin.

respiratory quotient The ratio of the volume of carbon dioxide produced by an organism during respiration to the volume of oxygen taken up. The respiratory quotient varies according to the type of food reserves being oxidized. The theoretical values for various classes of substrate are as follows: carbohydrate, 1.0; protein, 0.8; fats, 0.7. In practice, however, these values are modified owing to the interconversion of metabolites and the creation and discharge of an oxygen debt.

respirometer An instrument used to measure the rate of respiration or gas exchange of a culture or tissue. Most respirometers use manometric principles or are based on oxygen electrodes.

response The reaction to a stimulus.

resting nucleus *See* interphase.

resting potential A steady-state potential difference across a biological membrane when it is not excited by a stimulus or metabolic activity associated with energy conversion or active transport. The potential results from the unequal distribution of ions between the fluids on either side of the membrane.

restriction The protection of a bacterial cell from the effects of foreign DNA entering the cell. This is brought about by site-specific endonucleases (restriction endonucleases) which make double-stranded cuts in the DNA. Normally the DNA of a cell that synthesizes a restriction enzyme is protected from the action of the enzyme because these cells also synthesize a modification enzyme. The modification enzyme alters the structure of the DNA sites that are usually recognized by the endonuclease. If a cell with an active modification system is infected by a bacteriophage whose DNA has not previously been modified, the unmodified DNA is broken into fragments – the number of fragments is a function of the number of sensitive sites – and the fragments are then degraded by exonucleases. The probability of the phage DNA initiating an infection is several orders of magnitude less than if the phage DNA has been modified.

restriction endonuclease An enzyme capable of breaking down foreign DNA molecules. *In vivo* endonucleases are important in protecting cells from invasion by foreign DNA. Two main types of restriction enzymes are known. Type 1 restriction endonucleases recognize a specific site and then make a double-stranded cut somewhere nearby, but without any specificity as to the nucleotide sequence that is cut. Type II restriction endonucleases recognize a site and cleave specifically at that site. Type II enzymes are of particular use in molecular cloning, genetic mapping and DNA sequence analysis. The recognition sites of restriction enzymes are palindromic sequences. The double-strand cut is either staggered or aligned along the axis of symmetry. Staggered cuts create so-called 'sticky ends' which may be re-annealed with each other and covalently closed by the enzyme DNA ligase. Several hundred different restriction enzymes from different species and strains of bacteria have now been purified and their cleavage sites determined.

restriction endonuclease nomenclature The discovery of a very large number of restriction enzymes has necessitated a uniform method of nomenclature. All restriction enzymes have the general name 'endonuclease R' followed by a system name. In general, the following rules are adopted in determining the system name. The species name of the host organism is identified by the first letter of the genus name and the first two letters of the specific name to form a three-letter abbreviation used in italics (e.g., *Escherichia coli* = *Eco*). The strain, type of virus or plasmid associated with the specific enzyme is indicated, generally by a single letter, which in early systems was put as a subscript, but is now written on the line. Where a particular host strain has several restriction and modification systems, these are identified by Roman numerals. For example, one of the restriction enzymes from *Haemophilus influenzae* is known as endonuclease R *Hin* dIII. The corresponding modification enzymes are designated as methylase M (e.g., methylase M *Hin* dIII).

restriction enzyme *See* restriction endonuclease.

restriction fragment length polymorphism *See* RFLP.

restriction map A pictorial representation of the sites on a chromosome or DNA sequence that have been shown experimentally to be cleaved by specific restriction endonucleases.

restriction site A sequence of base pairs in a DNA molecule that is recognized by a restriction endonuclease. Type II restriction endonucleases recognize and break DNA within particular sequences of tetra-, penta-, hexa- or heptanucleotides that have an axis of rotational symmetry. For example, *Eco* RI cuts at the following positions:

$$
\begin{array}{c}
\overset{*}{} \\
5'\text{-G} \;\Big|\; \text{A A T T C} \\
3'\text{-C} \;\; \text{T T A A} \;\Big|\; \text{G} \\
\underset{*}{}
\end{array}
$$

where * indicates the base modified by the corresponding specific methylase in the process of modification. The target sites of some of the more commonly used restriction enzymes are tabulated (note that only one strand is shown and the site is written from the 5'- to the 3'- end reading from left to right; | indicates the point of cleavage).

restriction site mapping A technique in which genomic DNA is cleaved with restriction endonuclease into hundreds of fragments of varying size. The fragments are

Origin	Name	Recognition site
Anabaena variabilis	*Ava I*	C|TCGGG
Bacillus amyloliquefaciens H	Bam *HI*	G|GATCC
Bacillus globigii	*Bgl* II	A|GATCT
Escherichia coli RY13	*Eco* RI	G|AATTC
Escherichia coli R245	*Eco* RII	|CCAGG
Haemophilus aegyptius	*Hae* III	GG|CC
Haemophilus influenzae Rd	*Hin* dII	GTT|GAC
	Hin dIII	A|AGCTT
Klebsiella pneumoniae	*Kpn* I	GGTAC|G
Providencia stuartii	*Pst* I	CTGCA|G

separated by gel electrophoresis and blot-transferred to a cellulose nitrate film. Radioactive RNA or denatured DNA complementary in sequence to the required gene is applied to the blot and detected by autoradiography. By using several restriction enzymes singly and in combination, a map of restriction sites can be built up.

restrictive condition *See* conditional lethal mutation.

reticulocyte An immature erythrocyte that is formed from an erythroblast. Reticulocytes are anucleate, possess a net-like cytoplasm and stain with basic dyes such as methylene blue.

reticuloendothelial system The system of macrophages found in vertebrate tissue.

reticulum The second chamber of the ruminant stomach.

retina The innermost sensory layer of the eyes of vertebrates and cephalopods. It consists of a layer of photosensitive cells, distinguished as rods and cones, that are linked to the optic nerve.

retinal *See* retinene.

retinene Retinal; an aldehyde derivative of vitamin A that combines with the protein opsin in the rods of the retina of vertebrates to form the light-sensitive pigment rhodopsin.

retinol Vitamin A₁.

Retinol (vitamin A₁)

retro-inhibition *See* feedback inhibition.

reverse osmosis A technique used to concentrate solutions. The sample to be concentrated is passed under pressure through a system bounded by a semipermeable membrane. The pressure forces water through the membrane, but larger molecules are retained, and hence their concentration increases. The membranes may be supported on a tubular matrix or on large flat plates in order to give a large surface area.

reverse passive haemagglutination An agglutination test in which an antibody is bound to the surface of red blood cells.

reverse transcriptase An enzyme, found in RNA tumour viruses, that copies RNA into a DNA molecule. It is used in genetic engineering to produce specific cDNA molecules from a purified preparation of a specific mRNA, which may then be incorporated into plasmids as artificial genes. The action of reverse transcriptase is similar to that of other DNA polymerases, using deoxyribonucleoside triphosphates as substrates. However, it cannot initiate polymerization; it requires a primer which it extends by adding nucleotides to the 3′-hydroxyl.

reverse transcription The production of a molecule of DNA from an RNA template. *See* reverse transcriptase.

reversion A second mutation that restores the genetic information altered by a first mutation.

RFLP Restriction fragment length polymorphism; an analytical technique used to detect genome polymorphism by comparing restriction maps of DNA from individuals. Variations in the position of restriction sites will result in different length restriction fragments which can be identified using southern blotting with suitable hybridization probes. Such DNA sequence variations display mendelian inheritance and can be used as genetic markers in linkage studies, including studies of defective genes that cause inherited disease, or beneficial genes which relate to desirable characteristics in plants or animals. Hence, RFLP can be used as a tool in commercial breeding overcoming the time delay associated with breeding experiments to produce conventional linkage maps.

rheogram A pictorial representation or graph illustrating a rheological relationship (e.g., a plot of shear stress as a function of shear rate).

rheology The study of the deformation and flow of materials, solutions and, in particular, suspensions.

rheopectic fluid A fluid or solution that when subjected to a constant shear stress shows an apparent viscosity that decreases with time.

rhesus system One of the blood group systems based on the antigens present on the surface of the red blood cells. Human blood is rhesus-positive or rhesus-negative.

Rhizobium *See* nitrogen fixation.

rhizome A horizontal underground stem that functions as a means of vegetative propagation in some vascular plants. It may also function as a storage organ.

rhizomorph A root-like structure, derived from a large number of vegetative hyphae, that is formed in some parasitic fungi.

rho (ρ) factor A protein which has a specific effect on the termination of transcription. The rho factor recognizes a stop signal and prevents RNA polymerase from continuing to copy the template beyond this point. However, it appears that both rho-dependent and rho-independent termination sites exist.

Rhodophyta The red algae; multicellular algae that show an alternation of generations and possess phycocyanin and phycoerythrin as accessory pigments. They are the source of several important plant gums, including agar, produced by *Gelidium* and *Gracilaria* species, which is used as a matrix for microbial culture, as well as the sulphated polysaccharides known as carrageenans.

rhodopsin The light-sensitive pigment found in the rods of the vertebrate eye. It is composed of retinene, an aldehyde of vitamin A_1, attached to a protein opsin.

RIA *See* radioimmunoassay.

riboflavin Vitamin B_2; a 7,8-dimethylisoalloxazine ring linked at position 10 to the $1'$-carbon of the alcohol D-ribitol. Riboflavin is an essential nutrient for mammals, functioning as a precursor of the coenzymes FMN and FAD.

Riboflavin (vitamin B_2; lactoflavin)

ribonuclease *See* RNase.

ribonucleic acid *See* RNA.

ribosomal biosynthesis The assembly of ribosomal particles from RNA and protein components. This is coordinated in such a way in eukaryotes and prokaryotes that neither excess protein nor nucleic acids accumulate. In *E. coli*, the control of the synthesis of the proteins is at the level of transcription with the genes for ribosomal proteins organized into several transcriptional units that function like operons. The exact control mechanisms are very complicated; more so in the case of eukaryotes where rRNAs are synthesized in the nucleus and ribosomal proteins in the cytoplasm.

ribosomal protein One-third of the mass of prokaryote ribosomes, and half the mass of eukaryote ribosomes, is made up of protein molecules. There are 21 different proteins in the 30S subunit of the bacterial protein and 34 in the 50S subunit. All these proteins have been isolated and characterized for *E. coli*. In eukaryote ribosomes, the proteins show considerable species variation with between 36 and 40 associated with the large subunit and from 29 to 32 associated with the small subunit. The molecular weight of these varies between 8000 and 40,000.

ribosomal RNA *See* rRNA.

ribosome A particle found within all cells that is made up of RNA and protein. The ribosome is the site of protein synthesis. Ribosomes are classified on the basis of their rate of sedimentation in svedberg units (S). Two types may be distinguished. The heavier type, or 80S ribosome, is typical of the cytoplasmic ribosomes found in eukaryotes. It is made of two subunits of 60S and 40S. The lighter 70S ribosome (with subunits of 50S and 30S) is typical of prokaryotes, but is also found in chloroplasts and mitochondria of eukaryotes. The RNA/protein ratio is 2:1 in the 70S ribosomes and 1:1 in cytoplasmic ribosomes of eukaryotes. The smaller subunits contain one RNA molecule, whereas the large subunits contain several different types of RNA. *See* polysome, protein synthesis, rRNA.

ribulose A five-carbon keto sugar important as a mono- or bisphosphate in the photosynthetic carbon reduction cycle.

ribulose bisphosphate A five-carbon sugar phosphate. It is the substrate in the primary carboxylation reaction common to all photosynthetic and many chemosynthetic auto-trophic organisms. *See* ribulose bisphos-phate oxygenase/carboxylase.

ribulose bisphosphate oxygenase/car-boxylase (rubisco) (EC 4.1.1.39) The enzyme responsible for the assimilative reduction of carbon dioxide to the level of carbohydrate in all photoautotrophs and most chemoautotrophs. It is identical to the main constituent of fraction I protein. At one time it was known as carboxy dis-mutase, and latterly as ribulose diphosphate (or bisphosphate) carboxylase. The EC nomenclature is 3-phospho-D-glycerate carboxylase. It catalyses a carboxylation and an oxygenase reaction:

1. Carboxylation:

Ribulase bisP + CO_2 + H_2O → 2(3PGA)

2. Oxygenase:

Ribulose bisP + O_2 + H_2O → 3PGA +
P glycollate

The oxygenase and the carboxylation reac-tions compete with each other. It contains two subunits (A and B) with a quaternary configuration of A_8/B_8 in higher plants. Subunit A has a molecular weight of 500,000 and is encoded by chloroplastic DNA, whereas subunit B has a molecular weight of 15,000 and is encoded by nuclear DNA. Synthesis of these subunits is carried out on chloroplastic 70S or cytoplasmic 80S ribosomes. During the synthesis of the sub-unit B, a larger precursor is transported across the chloroplast membrane and cleaved in the stroma prior to assembly with the large subunits. The concentration of the enzyme present in leaves can reach over 10 milligrams protein per gram fresh weight, giving a concentration of about 240 mil-ligrams of enzyme per millilitre of chlo-roplast stroma, or 0.4–0.5 mM enzyme. This makes it the most abundant protein in the world. Such high protein concentrations are needed to achieve reasonable rates of carbon dioxide assimilation, since the enzyme has a low turnover rate. The affinity of the enzyme for the various substrates (K_m

values) also restricts the rate of assimila-tion. The oxygenase reaction represents the initial step of the C_2 or photorespiratory pathway. Hence attempts have been made to identify varieties of plants with a lower ratio of oxygenase to carboxylase activity on the basis that their use will lead to a grea-ter productivity. In C_3 plants the enzyme is located in the stroma of all the chloroplasts, whereas in C_4 plants it is restricted to the chloroplasts of the bundle sheath.

ribulose bisphosphate oxygenase/car-boxylase activation Carbon dioxide is not only a substrate for this enzyme, but also functions as an activator or regulator of the carboxylation reaction. Carbon dioxide reacts with an amino group of a lysine mol-ecule in the active centre. Magnesium is also required as a cofactor.

ricin A highly toxic plant protein derived from the castor oil plant. It consists of a toxic polypeptide (A chain) attached to a cell-binding polypeptide (B chain). The B chain is a lectin that binds to galactose-containing glycoproteins or glycolipids on cell surfaces.

rickettsia A small, rod-shaped obligate prokaryote parasite. Rickettsiae are similar to large viruses, but possess a bacterial-like wall containing mucopeptides. They breed in arthropods such as fleas and lice with-out apparently harming them. However, if transmitted to mammals, including man, they can cause severe diseases such as typhus, Rocky Mountain fever and Q fever.

rifampicin An antibiotic that is a potent inhibitor of *E. coli* RNA polymerase and phage DNA synthesis. Replication in some organisms is rifampicin-insensitive since they contain a different form of polymerase.

rifamycins Aromatic and aliphatic anti-biotics produced by *Nocardia mediterranei*.

RIM *See* reproductive isolating mechanism.

Ringer's solution An aqueous solution of calcium, potassium and sodium chloride, buffered with bicarbonate or phosphate, of such a pH and osmotic strength to be a suitable medium in which to suspend living cells or tissues under investigation *in vitro*.

RNA Ribonucleic acid; a polymer composed of alternating units of the sugar D-ribose and phosphate. Attached to each sugar is one of the four bases adenine, cytosine, guanine or uracil. Uracil (which is analogous to thymine) is the only major base that occurs in RNA but not in DNA. Certain forms of RNA may include a variety of minor bases. A number of different types of RNA exist, most of which are associated with the synthesis of proteins. These include mRNA (messenger RNA), rRNA (ribosomal RNA), tRNA (transfer RNA) and HnRNA (heterogeneous nuclear RNA). RNA is normally the product of transcription from a DNA template, but some viruses can form DNA from an RNA template using the enzyme reverse transcriptase, the RNA acting as the bearer of inherited information. Some forms of RNA can fold into double-stranded regions of complementary base pairing, whereas other types are substantially single-stranded and are not base paired.

RNA phage A phage containing RNA.

RNA polymerase An enzyme that catalyses the formation of RNA via transcription of DNA. Using nucleoside triphosphates as substrates, they build up polymers by joining the α-phosphate group of the incoming nucleotide in the phosphodiester linkage to the 3'-hydroxyl of the proceeding one, splitting off a molecule of pyrophosphate. Synthesis proceeds from the 5'-end to the 3'-end.

RNA primer A short length of RNA that binds on to the lagging strand of the replication fork prior to ligation of Okazaki fragments.

RNA replicase *See* RNA replication.

RNA replication The copying of the genetic information contained in the RNA of a viral genome. This reaction is catalysed by RNA replicases. The new molecules of RNA formed then serve as a template for the synthesis of progeny RNA molecules.

RNA sequence analysis The determination of the base sequence in an RNA using enzymes in a method directly analogous to the Maxam–Gilbert DNA technique, except that base-specific ribonucleases are employed that cleave specifically next to G, A, or A and U, or are specific for pyrimidines.

RNA transcriptase The enzyme responsible for transcribing the information encoded in DNA into RNA; also called transcriptase or RNA polymerase.

RNA virus A virus in which the genetic information is carried in RNA. These include the picornaviruses, the aboviruses and the myxoviruses.

RNA-dependent DNA polymerase *See* reverse transcriptase.

RNA-PRINS *See* PRINS.

RNase Ribonuclease; an enzyme that catalyses the breakdown of RNA. Most RNases require a divalent cation as cofactor (e.g., Ca^{2+}, Mg^{2+}, etc.). Hence activity can be blocked by addition of EDTA.

RNase-free agent *See* nuclease-free reagent.

Robertsonian change A chromosomal mutation due to centric fusion or centric fission.

rocket electrophoresis ELISA A type of immunoassay in which electrophoresis of an antigen sample is carried out across a layer of agar containing specific antibodies. This results in the formation of rocket-shaped patterns the height of which corresponds to the concentration of antigens in the sample.

rod A light-sensitive cell present in the retina of most vertebrates.

roentgen *See* röntgen.

roller bottle apparatus A culture system that is used for the propagation of anchorage-dependent cells or liquid cultures of aerobic organisms. The culture is placed in a sealed bottle that is placed horizontally on a set of revolving rollers which, by turning the bottle slowly round on its longitudinal axis, keeps the particles in suspension.

rolling The movement of white blood cells along the surface of the vascular endothelium before cell-to-cell adhesion.

rolling circle replication A DNA replication mechanism in which a circular chromosome is replicated to form a linear one. Initiation begins with the cleavage of a phosphodiester bond in one strand of the parental circular molecule to produce a nick. The complementary strand then serves as a template for synthesis of the new strand which is covalently attached to the 3'-hydroxyl of the nicked parent strand. As this new strand is formed, the other strand is displaced from the template to form a 'tail'. Synthesis of a complement to the tail then occurs. As replication proceeds, two daughters are produced – one circular and one linear. This mechanism is characteristic of some bacteriophages and plasmids. It also occurs during oogenesis in some eukaryotes.

röntgen (r) The quantity of X- or gamma-radiation that corresponds to 5.24×10^{13} eV of energy.

röntgen equivalent The dose of radiation that produces the same amount of energy dissipation per gram of tissue as the absorption of one röntgen in one gram of dry air (i.e., 83.8 ergs per gram of tissue).

root The part of the axis of a higher plant that is concerned with the absorption of water and mineral nutrients from the soil, as well as providing anchorage and support for the shoot or stem.

root nodule A small swelling containing nitrogen-fixing bacteria formed on the roots of legumes following infection by *Rhizobium* species.

rosette A rose-shaped cluster formed by red blood cells adhering to the surface of a T-lymphocyte.

rotor fermenter A continuous pressure dialysis reactor in which the usual simple fixed membrane is replaced by a rapidly rotating membrane cylinder. Feed and air are pumped into the annular fermentation zone, pressurized to ensure that the filtrate flows continuously through the membrane, where cells grow and are retained. The centripetal force developed at the membrane surface by rotation causes large molecules impinging on the surface to be thrown back to the annular zone so only a thin cake develops and high filtration rates, and hence productivity, can be maintained.

roundworm *See* Nematoda.

Rous sarcoma A virus-induced tumour that occurs in domestic fowl.

rpm Abbreviation for revolutions per minute.

rRNA Ribosomal RNA. rRNA is found in the small and the large ribosomal subunits. The smaller subunits contain one molecule of rRNA, which in prokaryotes has a molecular weight of 500,000 and a sedimentation coefficient of 16S, whereas eukaryotic rRNA is larger with a molecular weight of 700,000 and a sedimentation coefficient of 18S. The prokaryotic 50S particle contains a 23S RNA molecule with a molecular weight of 1.05×10^6 and a small RNA species (5S) which contains 120 nucleotides and has a molecular weight of 36,000. The 60S subunit of the eukaryotic cytoplasmic ribosome contains a larger RNA molecule; its molecular weight varies between 1.3×10^6 and 1.7×10^6 in different species, and it has a sedimentation coefficient of about 28S. In addition, there are two small RNA species in this subunit: a 5S RNA of the same size as that of the prokaryote ribosome and a 5.8S RNA with a molecular weight of 47,000. With the exception of the 5S RNAs, all forms contain some substituted bases.

rRNA synthesis In prokaryotes and eukaryotes, the production of mature rRNA molecules depends on post-transcriptional processing of the transcripts from nuclear DNA. In prokaryotes (e.g., *E. coli*) the genes for the 16S, 23S and 5S rRNAs are closely linked and are transcribed from a common promoter as a single unit, or pre-rRNA. The 5'-end of the pre-rRNA contains the 16S rRNA, followed by the 23S and 5S molecules. As transcription proceeds, the nascent pre-rRNA is modified by sequence-specific methylation of certain bases and is subsequently cut by processing enzymes to yield the mature RNA molecules. During the maturation process each rRNA molecule becomes associated with specific proteins. In eukaryotes, the 18S and 28S rRNA molecules are also transcribed from a common promoter to form a pre-rRNA that is processed by methylation enzymes and nucleases. However, the 5S rRNA of eukaryotes is transcribed separately from its genes, which may not be linked to the rRNA genes.

rubisco *See* ribulose bisphosphate oxygenase/carboxylase.

rumen The first chamber of the ruminant stomach.

ruminant A mammal that is a member of the suborder Ruminantia, characterized by the ability to use cellulosic materials as a major proportion of its diet. These animals (e.g., cattle, sheep, goats and antelopes) have a complicated digestive tract that includes a four-chamber stomach consisting of the rumen, reticulum, omasum and abomasum. The rumen contains a wide range of anaerobic microorganisms, including bacteria and protozoa, that are capable of converting cellulose to volatile fatty acids, carbon dioxide and methane. The fatty acids are absorbed by the host which uses them as a source of energy and carbon for growth.

runaway replication Uncontrolled plasmid replication that occurs when growth temperature is raised. The copy number of a runaway plasmid can increase from around 15–20 at 30°C to several thousand at 40°C.

rusts A group of parasitic basidiomycetes of the order Uredinales, many of which are important pests of grasses (grain crops in particular). The rusts have complicated life histories usually involving a secondary host.

S

S *See* svedberg unit.

S phase A phase of the cell cycle during which each chromatid is duplicated.

S value A measure of the size of macromolecules, viruses and subcellular particles on the basis of their rate of sedimentation during ultracentrifugation. It is a function of the weight and the shape of the molecule or particle. The S value is defined in terms of the svedberg unit.

S1 nuclease An endonuclease, usually derived from *Aspergillus oryzae*, that cleaves single-stranded DNA or RNA to yield mononucleotides.

saccharification The hydrolysis of a polysaccharide to produce a sugar solution.

Saccharomyces A genus of ascomycetous yeasts that normally reproduce asexually by budding. Some species (e.g., *S. cerivisiae*) periodically undergo sexual reproduction in which four ascospores are formed in a single ascus derived from a single cell. Zygote formation takes place immediately after germination of the haploid ascospores. Diploidy is then maintained throughout the next vegetative growth period. Other strains used in brewing are polyploids and seldom, if ever, enter a sexual phase. Strains of *S. cerivisiae* are the principal agents used in beer production, wine making, production of potable and fuel ethanol, and the production of single-cell protein. Other species used in beer include *S. uvarum* (*S. carlsbergensis*).

sacrophyte An organism that obtains its nutrients in the form of organic matter in solution from dead or decaying plant or animal tissue.

saliva The secretion produced by the salivary glands. It consists of mucus and amylases, such as ptyalin, which initiate the digestion of starch.

salivary gland An exocrine gland that secretes saliva. In vertebrates, these ectodermal glands are derived from the buccal cavity.

Salmonella A genus of gram-negative, rodshaped bacteria that are aerobic or facultative anaerobes. Many are pathogens, occurring in spoilt food and contaminated water. The many species and strains are distinguished by antigenic properties. *S. typhi* can infect man only and causes a unique severe fever – typhoid. Other diseases caused by these bacteria include paratyphoid and gastroenteritis. Recovery from infection, or vaccination, confers a variable degree of resistance, and antibiotic therapy is generally successful. However, the recovered patient may become a chronic carrier.

salt A compound which on dissociation yields cations of a metal and anions of an acid radical; the product of a reaction of an acid and a base. In common use, the term is applied to sodium chloride.

saltational speciation *See* quantum speciation.

salting out *See* ammonium sulphate precipitation.

salvarsan A drug specially designed for the treatment of syphilis. Although effective against the causative bacterium (*Trepomena pallidum*) it has undesirable side effects on the patient.

sample oxidizer An automated analyser used in the preparation of samples containing radioactive carbon or hydrogen for scintillation counting. The sample is ignited electrically in oxygen and fully oxidized to carbon dioxide and water vapour. These gases are trapped – the water by condensation and the carbon dioxide in a solution of amine – and introduced automatically into separate vials. The method is used with particulate samples, large samples of low activity or samples of liquid that are immiscible with the scintillation cocktail.

sandwich assay A type of immunoassay in which the detection system includes two different antibodies and the avidin–biotin reaction as follows. The solid phase is coated with capture antibody and incubated with the antigen-containing sample. The biotin-labelled antibody targeted at a second antigen epitope is added to form a sandwich layer. After washing, labelled streptavidin with an enzyme or luminescent marker is added. This binds to any available biotin. A relevant substrate (dependent on the type of label used) is added and the reaction is then assessed photometrically.

Sanger sequencing *See* dideoxy sequencing.

sapogenin A C_{27} sterol in which the side chain has been modified to produce a spiroketal. Sapogenins occur naturally as saponins.

saponification The hydrolysis of glycerides using an alkali, such as potassium or sodium hydroxide, to yield glycerol and the salts of the fatty acids (soaps).

saponin A 3-*O*-glycoside of sapinogenin. Saponins include the digitonin, which is obtained from *Digitalis*. Saponins have detergent properties and cause disintegration of membranes, and hence are capable of bringing about haemolysis of erythrocytes.

saprophyte An organism that feeds on dead and decaying organic matter. Saprophytes excrete enzymes that digest such organic residues externally, the low-molecular-weight compounds formed then being absorbed. Many fungi and bacteria are saprophytes.

saprozoic Descriptive of heterotrophic organisms that feed on organic materials obtained in solution rather than solid organic matter.

Sarcodina A class of protozoa, characterized by the possession of pseudopodia which are used for food capture and locomotion. They include the amoeba.

sarcoma A highly malignant type of tumour that arises in connective tissue as a solid mass of cells.

sarcomere A unit of structure in striated muscle.

satellite DNA A fraction of DNA that separates from the bulk of the DNA when native DNA is separated using caesium chloride density gradient centrifugation. The buoyant density at equilibrium is dependent on the G + C content of the DNA; the higher the G + C content, the higher the buoyant density. Eukaryotic DNA has an average G + C content of 30–35 per cent, hence fractions of DNA with an unusually high or low G + C content form such satellites. Chloroplast, ribosomal, mitochondrial and centromeric DNA can all form satellites.

sauerkraut A fermented food product produced by the lactic acid fermentation of shredded cabbage.

sausage fermentation A bacterial fermentation catalysed by species of *Lactobacillus*, *Leuconostoc* and *Pediococcus*, as well as strains of *Micrococcus* (which reduce nitrate to nitrite) aiding preservation of these meat products.

Sc *See* Schmidt number.

scale-up The development of a full-scale production facility from an initial laboratory concept or experiment.

Scatchard plot A method for analysing the interactions between small molecules which bind ions and the ions themselves.

SCCL Small cell carcinoma of the lung.

Schizomycetes In some classifications denotes the bacteria.

Schizophyta In some classifications denotes a group comprising the bacteria and Cyanophyta.

Schizosaccharomyces A genus of yeasts characterized by their method of asexual reproduction, which involves fission rather than budding.

Schmidt number A measure of the fluid properties of a system expressed as a dimensionless group that relates viscosity and the density of the fluid to the diffusivity of a solute in a solvent.

$$Sc = \mu/(\rho D_{AB})$$

where μ is the viscosity, ρ the density of the fluid and D_{AB} the diffusivity of solute A in solvent B.

Schwann cell A glial cell that forms the myelin sheath which surrounds the axons of some vertebrate nerve cells.

scintillation counter An analytical device used to quantify the radioactive content of a labelled sample, usually a weak beta-emitter. The sample is dissolved in an organic scintillator solution, or suspended in a gel (e.g., water/Triton X-100/toluene emulsion). The scintillator is excited by absorption of a beta-particle and decays emitting a weak flash of light (a scintillation). The intensity of the scintillation is proportional to the energy of the particle. The scintillations are detected by a pair of photomultipliers, which operate in such a way that noise is eliminated. The pulses from the photomultipliers are amplified and counted electronically. As pulses of varying sizes can be distinguished, it is possible to use double-labelling techniques (e.g., a mixture of tritium and carbon, or carbon and phosphorus). The number of pulses per minute is the same as the number of scintillations detected, which in turn is proportional to the number of disintegrations per minute multiplied by a quench factor. The degree of quenching is determined using an automatic standardization procedure or by adding an aliquot of known radioactivity as a standard. If the specific activity of the labelled material used is known, results can be calculated in absolute terms.

scintillation counting The use of a scintillation counter to determine the radioactive content of a radiolabelled sample. Various methods exist for incorporating the radioactive specimen into the scintillator solution: (1) as a simple solution in toluene (for steroids, fats, hydrocarbons and some gases such as carbon dioxide); (2) chemical digestion to render the sample soluble in toluene; (3) as a suspension in a gel formed from finely divided silica powder, or in an emulsion formed by addition of the detergent Triton X-100; (4) chemical oxidation to carbon dioxide (for ^{14}C) or water (for ^{3}H).

scintillator A chemical substance that emits a weak flash of light when struck by an ionizing particle. Scintillators used in liquid scintillation counters are defined as primary or secondary. Secondary solutes are added to increase the matching between the fluorescence emission and the photomultiplier response. 2,5-Diphenyloxazole is one of the most often used primary solutes. In gamma-counters, scintillators are generally impregnated into wells made of transparent plastic.

sclerenchyma A plant tissue, characterized by thick walls. The main function of sclerenchyma is to provide mechanical support. The cell walls are generally lignified, and at maturity the cells have lost their living contents. Sclerenchyma consists of both long tapered fibres and other forms grouped as sclerids.

sclerids *See* sclerenchyma.

scleroglucan An uncharged microbial polysaccharide composed of glucose found in *Sclerotium glucanicum*; also known as polytran. It is highly viscous and pseudoplastic, stable to pH and temperature, and lacks sensitivity to salt. It is used in drilling muds and latex paints, and to enhance oil recovery.

scleroprotein A simple protein that is insoluble in most solvents and forms an important part of skeletal and connective tissue in animals. Scleroproteins include collagen, elastin and keratin.

sclerotium A hard-walled resting body produced by some fungi including the ascomycete *Claviceps purpurea* which is parasitic on rye. The sclerotia produced on rye are known as ergots and contain alkaloids that are related to LSD and ergotamine.

SCP *See* single-cell protein.

Scrapie An infectious agent, the exact identity of which is not known, causing a usually fatal disease in sheep, goats and deer. *See* spongiform encephalopathy.

screening The isolation of sought-after microbes from a mixed population by obtaining a clone from each individual and testing it separately for the desired property.

scrubbing The cleaning of a gas stream by removal of particulate matter and/or chemical constituents. Chemical contaminants are removed from gas streams by a variety of methods: physical absorption by a liquid; chemical reaction with a liquid; physical absorption on a solid; chemical reaction with a solid; membrane separation; compression, chilling and cryogenics; biological scrubbing (i.e., using the growth of a microorganism to remove selectively an impurity).

scum A layer of floating solids formed on the surface of a mixed liquor. It may occur during fermentation as a result of inefficient mixing or be produced deliberately during clarification.

scutellum A part of the embryo of grasses that is appressed to the endosperm in the seed, acting as an absorptive organ. It is formed from the cotyledon or the complete embryonic axis.

SDS *See* sodium dodecyl sulphate.

sebaceous gland An exocrine gland, derived from the epidermal malpighian layer, that opens on to the hair follicle and secretes sebum.

sebum A mixture of fatty acids, triglycerides and steroids secreted by the sebaceous glands. It lubricates the hair of mammals and acts as a waterproofing agent.

secondary cell culture A cell culture created by the repeated passage of a primary cell culture.

secondary fermentation A fermentation reaction that occurs during the manufacture of dairy products in addition to the main fermentation process (i.e., the breakdown of lactose into lactic acid). These secondary reactions give dairy products their distinctive flavours. For example, the flavour of some types of cheese is imparted by a secondary fermentation producing propionic acid.

secondary metabolite A compound, often complex in chemical composition or structure, that is not an essential intermediate in the central metabolism and is formed as a byproduct. Although not essential for growth, secondary metabolites perform a wide range of protective functions. These include the production of gums, oil, fats and resins that protect against dehydration, toxic compounds, poisons, pigments, etc. In some cases, especially in microorganisms, the formation of secondary products is associated with the slowing down or stopping of active growth and cell multiplication. Many of the products formed by microorganisms and plants, and utilized by man, are secondary products.

secondary (oil) production The obtaining of more oil from a reservoir after primary production has ceased. This is achieved by injecting water or gas to increase the underground pressure and to drive oil from the rock into the well bore.

secondary sex ratio *See* sex ratio.

secondary sexual characteristics Sexual characteristics of adult animals other than the primary sexual organs (e.g., facial hair, breast development, antlers, horns, feather colour, etc.).

secondary structure Those aspects of the structure of macromolecules that depend on hydrogen bonding. These include the helical arrangement found in DNA and the alpha-helix or beta-pleated sheet structures found in proteins.

second-generation anaerobic digester A sophisticated anaerobic digester with high rates of gas production at short retention times.

secretin A peptide hormone secreted by the duodenal mucosa that stimulates the release of pancreatic juice. It is a straight chain of 27 amino acids and is similar in structure to glucogen.

secretion (1) The discharge of molecules, which have been formed intracellularly, into the surrounding medium. (2) The molecules that are secreted. These may include hormones, enzymes, glycoproteins, lipids or waxes, ions and sugars. The usual mechanism of secretion depends on exocytosis in which the material is released through the plasma membrane in small membrane-bound vesicles. Other mechanisms exist; in the sebaceous glands, the entire contents of the cell are lost (holocrine secretion).

seed (1) In general, the propagative part of a plant, including true seeds, bulbs, corms, stem cuttings, etc. (2) Specifically, the structure that develops from an ovule after fertilization and contains the embryo plant plus food reserves. (3) A microbial culture held back as a starter for subsequent cultures.

seed plants The Spermatophyta; plants that form true seeds. These are divided into two groups: the Gymnospermae and the Angiospermae.

segregation The separation of a pair of alleles on homologous chromosomes during meiosis so that only one member of each pair is present in the gametes.

selectin *See* LECAMs.

selection The isolation of specific microorganisms from a mixed culture by allowing growth to occur in an environment that favours those clones required. *See* artificial selection, natural selection.

selection coefficient *See* coefficient of selection.

selection differential In artificial selection, the difference in mean phenotypic value between the individuals selected as parents of the following generation and the whole population.

selection gain In artificial selection, the difference in mean phenotypic value between the progeny of the selected parents and the parental generation.

selection pressure The product of the various forces, which reflect environmental conditions or nutrient availability, favouring the growth of some individuals and preventing the growth of others. This can lead to a change in the degree of variation in the population under pressure.

selective value *See* adaptive value.

self-annealing The process in which complementary single-stranded sequences at either end of a DNA duplex fuse through base pairing to produce a molecule of circular DNA.

self-antigen A compound produced by an organism that stimulates its own autoimmune system, resulting in damage to its body.

self-fertilization The union of male and female gametes produced by the same individual.

selfing Breeding by self-fertilization.

self-replicating Descriptive of plasmids and other extrachromosomal molecules of

DNA or RNA that are able to control the timing and rate of their own synthesis without any control by chromosomal DNA.

self-sterility A condition found in some plants and animals that prevents the fertilization of a female gamete by a male gamete produced by the same organism. The process usually involves incompatibility mechanisms in plants, and social or behavioural patterns in animals.

self-transmissible Descriptive of plasmids that contain transfer genes allowing them to transmit their DNA by conjugation.

semen A fluid containing spermatozoa and secretions produced by the male of animals in which internal fertilization occurs.

semiconservative DNA replication The copying of DNA that results in two daughter molecules, each containing one strand derived from the parent and one newly synthesized strand. This mechanism may be compared with a conservative replication mechanism which would require the parent molecule to be retained in its original form and the daughter molecule to be formed of entirely new material. The proof that the actual mechanism of DNA replication in living systems is dependent on a semiconservative mechanism was provided by Meselson and Stahl using cells grown in a medium enriched for the heavy isotope of nitrogen (^{15}N). They showed that when the heavy labelled cells were transferred to a medium containing the normal isotope of nitrogen, the isotope was diluted in each generation.

semipermeable membrane A porous membrane that permits the passage of small molecules such as water and inorganic ions, but does not permit the passage of larger molecules such as sugars and proteins. Most biological membranes are semipermeable.

semispecies *See* incipient species.

semisynthetic Descriptive of a compound that has been derived by the chemical modi-

fication of a biological product. Examples include some penicillins and steroids.

semisynthetic penicillins An antibiotic produced from penicillin by making some chemical changes to its structure.

senescence The terminal phase in the life cycle of an organism, during which degradation gradually takes place. In some organisms, senescence of discrete areas of the organism is part of the normal pattern of growth. Senescence may be a genetically programmed event and under hormonal control or may result from the accumulation of errors in genetic expression as the organism ages.

sense organ A collection of sensory receptors, together with any associated structures, that are specialized to respond to a particular stimulus.

sense strand A strand of duplex DNA that acts as a template for the synthesis of messenger RNA.

sensitization The stimulation of a reaction towards a specific antigen or hapten.

sepal One of the structures that forms the outer whorl of the perianth of flowers. Sepals are usually green and function as an outer protective layer in the bud.

separation factor The degree of separation in any process defined as the ratio of the concentration of the components in the product to those in the feed.

Sephacryl A cross-linked dextran polymer used as a gel filtration medium. Sephacryl is a registered trademark of Pharmacia Biotechnology AB.

Sephadex A gel produced by cross-linking selected dextran fractions with epichlorhydrin and marketed in bead form. Various types of gels are available, differing in pore size and swelling characteristics, according to the degree of cross-linking. Sephadex is used in gel filtration. Gels in which the matrix is a minor component are used for fractionation of high-molecular-weight substances; denser gels are used for separation of low-molecular-weight compounds. Sephadex is available in eight porosities which provide the fractionation of globular proteins with molecular weights up to 8×10^5 and linear polymers up to 2×10^5. Sephadex is a registered trademark of Pharmacia Biotechnology AB.

Sepharose A proprietary form of agarose supplied in bead form for use in gel filtration and other types of liquid chromatography. Sepharose is a registered trademark of Pharmacia Biotechnology AB.

sepsis A localized or general bacterial infection, especially such infections that are associated with a rise in body temperature (fever).

septic Infected; usually descriptive of pus-forming bacterial infection.

septic tank A container in which solid organic wastes or sewage are decomposed by anaerobic bacteria.

septicaemia Blood poisoning; infection by persistent pathogenic bacteria in the blood stream.

septum (1) A dividing wall or membrane that occurs in a plant or animal. (2) A membrane with semipermeable (osmotic) properties.

sequence map A pictorial representation of the sequence of amino acids in a peptide or of bases in a oligonucleotide.

sequencing *See* DNA sequencing, protein sequencing, RNA sequence analysis.

sequencing gel A polyacrylamide gel containing urea used for separating single-stranded DNA fragments. The use of a long (up to one metre) slab at an elevated temperature results in a high resolving power, permitting the separation of single-stranded DNA fragments that differ by only one nucleotide. These gels are used to separate radiolabelled DNA fragments in sequenc-

ing. *See* dideoxy sequencing, Maxam–Gilbert chemical sequencing.

sequestering agent A compound, such as EDTA, that complexes with metal ions in solution.

Ser An abbreviation used to denote the amino acid serine in amino acid sequences and elsewhere.

series CSTR fermenter *See* cascade fermentation.

serine (Ser) One of the 20 common amino acids found in protein.

Serine $HOCH_2CH(NH_2)COOH$

serological test A test in which antibodies are used in the detection of an antigen. The serum may be complexed to a fluorescent or radiolabelled marker to enable the extent of the reaction to be followed.

serology The study of blood serums and the interaction between antigens and antibodies. In particular, it is concerned with the *in vitro* study of three main types of reactions or serological tests known as agglutination reactions, complement fixation tests and precipitation reactions.

serotonin 5-Hydroxytryptamine (5HT); a neurotransmitter synthesized in nervous tissue.

serotype An organism or cell defined in terms of its serological properties.

serum The blood fluid that remains when coagulated blood is separated by centrifugation (i.e., plasma without the blood clotting factors).

sewage The waste matter that is collected by a sewerage system. It consists of wastewater, as well as solids of industrial and domestic origin. Raw sewage is characterized by a high concentration of pathogens of faecal origin.

sewage farm A place where sewage is treated. More specifically it is a process of aerobic treatment of sewage solids in which they are treated by being stacked and turned over periodically by mechanical means.

sewage sludge The active biomass recovered from an activated sewage plant.

sewage treatment A process designed to purify sewage, to remove the BOD and pathogenic bacteria, and to produce clean water. It may include filtration, chemical treatment, aerobic biological treatment and/or anaerobic biological treatment.

sewerage A system of sewers.

sex (1) The characteristic of being either male or female. It is used to distinguish between individuals of the same species in which sexual reproduction occurs on the basis of secondary sexual characteristics. (2) The process of genetic exchange between a male donor and a female recipient.

sex cell *See* gamete.

sex chromatin *See* Barr body.

sex chromosome A chromosome that is associated with the expression of primary or secondary sexual characteristics. In animals, there are two types of sex chromosome (X and Y). X chromosomes are, in general, similar to other chromosomes, whereas the Y chromosome is often much reduced in size. In diploid organisms the possibilities exist for a homogametic sex (XX) and a heterogametic sex (XY). In some species, the Y chromosome is missing so that the heterogametic sex is expressed as XO. In man and many mammals, the female is XX and the male XY, the Y chromosome carrying the genetic information for maleness. In some insects, although the same combinations lead to male and female, the sex characteristics are associated with the X chromosome. In extreme cases, the Y chromosome is missing; hence XX is female and XO is male. In birds and some fishes, the XX is male and the XY female. Many plants are hermaphrodites; however, a few (including the willows) do have an XX/XY pattern of sex determination, whereas others show the Mm/mm pattern (*see* sex determination).

sex determination A mechanism by which the sex of an individual is determined in genetics. A common approach is through the expression of characteristics carried on sex chromosomes with a homogametic sex (XX) and a heterogametic sex (XY or XO). Other mechanisms include those found in insects such as the mosquitoes which possess a single gene with two alleles concerned with sex determination. The gene exists in both the homozygous recessive condition (mm) and as a heterozygous form (Mm). The mm is often female and the Mm male. In many Hymenoptera, the female (queen) is diploid but the males are haploid.

sex factor A genetic element or plasmid found in some bacteria associated with the ability to conjugate. A copy of the plasmid is transferred from the donor (F$^+$) to the recipient (F$^-$) cell during conjugation. In some cases, the F factor undergoes recombination with the chromosome of the F$^+$ cell, in which case the F factor causes transfer of part or all of the chromosome. Strains with integrated F factors are termed Hfr.

sex pilus A fimbria-like structure formed by a male-type bacterium through which DNA is transferred during bacterial conjugation.

sex ratio The ratio of males to females in a population. It is usually expressed as the number of males per 100 females.

sex-limited gene A gene that is expressed in only one sex. The gene may be on any chromosome, but its expression is under the control, often indirectly through hormone action, of the sex-determining genes. Typical sex-limited genes are those associated with the expression of secondary sexual characteristics.

sex-linked gene A gene that is carried on one of the sex chromosomes, expression of which results in a characteristic appearing in only one sex. In those species in which there is no crossing-over between the X and Y chromosomes, the genes associated with the X chromosome are permanently linked. When there is crossing-over, only the unpaired part of the chromosome will carry sex-linked genes. These genes appear as homozygous alleles in the homogametic sex (XX) and are present as single genes in the heterogametic sex (XY). In man, abnormalities such as red/green colour blindness and haemophilia are due to sex-linked recessive genes.

sexual reproduction A method of producing new generations in which an organism arises from a zygote. The zygote is formed as a result of the fusion of two haploid gametes or nuclei. In general, one gamete will be produced by a male and one gamete by a female organism. Sexual reproduction represents a mechanism for genetic recombination and thus results in an increase in variation.

sexual selection A mechanism in which one sex (often the male) possesses exaggerated secondary sexual characteristics. Females are assumed to prefer to mate with the most extreme examples, whose characteristics are therefore inherited by their male progeny. Such sexual selection could account for the evolution of many of the highly exaggerated characteristics found in birds, fishes and mammals.

Sh *See* Sherwood number.

shear The movement of one layer relative to a parallel adjacent layer.

shear rate The rate of change of shear.

shear stress A component of stress parallel or tangential to the area under consideration.

Sherwood number (Sh) A measure of convective mass transfer expressed as a dimensionless number defined as

$$Sh = (k_c L)/D_{AB}$$

where k_c is the mass transfer coefficient, L the length of the system and D_{AB} the diffusivity of the solute A and the solvent B.

Shine–Dalgano sequence A short nucleotide sequence (AGGAGG) located upstream from the initiation codon of messenger RNA. It is complementary to a sequence at the 3'-end of 16S rRNA and acts as a ribosome-binding site.

shoot In vascular plants, the part (usually above ground) comprising the stems, leaves and buds.

short-day plant A plant that shows a photoperiodic response and flowers when subjected to 'short days' or more correctly an extended period of uninterrupted darkness. *See* photoperiodism, phytochrome.

shot gun cloning A procedure used to obtain a large number of clones that contain most of the genes present in a genome which has been cleaved using a restriction endonuclease and the resulting oligonucleotides inserted into a vector. The vector is then used to transform bacteria, producing a gene library.

shot gun technique *See* gene library, shot gun cloning.

shuffle clones Alleles that are recombined *in vitro* during PCR.

shuttle vector A vector that is able to replicate in two or more different organisms.

SI units An internationally agreed system of units used for scientific purposes (Système International d'Unités). It is based on the metre/kilogram/second (kgs) system and replaces both the metric (cgs) and imperial systems. It consists of seven basic units which may be used in combination to express other physical quantities. Basic units and derived units have special names and agreed symbols. The main and derived units include:

Quantity	Unit	Symbol
Length	metre	m
Mass	kilomgram	kg
Time	second	s
Electric current	ampere	A
Temperature	kelvin	K
Gram molecular weight	mole	mol
Energy	joule	J
Power	watt	W
Pressure	pascal	Pa
Electric charge	coulomb	C
Electric potential	volt	v
Electric resistance	ohm	Ω
Luminous flux	lumen	lm
Illuminance	lux	lx
Radioactivity	becquerel	Bq

Decimal multiples and submultiples are expressed using a set of standard prefixes, again with standard abbreviations.

Multiples

10 raised to the power of	Prefix	Symbol
1	deca	da
2	hecto	h
3	kilo	k
6	mega	M
9	giga	G
12	tera	T
15	peta	P
16	exa	E

Submultiples

10 raised to the power of	Prefix	Symbol
− 1	deci	d
− 2	centi	c
− 3	milli	m
− 6	micro	u
− 9	nano	n
− 12	pico	p
− 15	femto	f
− 18	atta	a

siblings Two or more individuals having the same parents.

sickle cell anaemia A human disease resulting from the inheritance of a defective allele coding for gamma-globin. It results in erythrocytes that assume a sickle-like form when the blood is deprived of oxygen. Affected erythrocytes are removed from the circulation resulting in anaemia.

sickle cell trait A phenotype recognizable by the sickling of erythrocytes exposed to low oxygen tension. It is determined by heterozygosity for the allele responsible for sickle cell anaemia.

sickle haemoglobin An abnormal type of haemoglobin found in carriers of the genetic defect that results in sickle cell anaemia.

sieve element A cell found in the phloem of vascular plants that functions in the translocation of dissolved organic nutrients. In angiosperms, the sieve elements have associated companion cells.

sieve tube An element of the phloem in vascular plants consisting of a vertical series of sieve elements.

sigma (σ) factor One of the five subunits of prokaryotic RNA polymerase. The polymerase consists of a four-subunit core enzyme with which the polypeptide sigma factor associates to form the active holoenzyme. The presence of the sigma factor enables the holoenzyme to recognize the correct template strand at the promoter site. Once RNA synthesis has begun, the sigma factor dissociates from the core enzyme, which continues transcription until it reaches and transcribes a transcription termination site on the DNA. A termination factor (rho) then acts to prevent further transcription.

signal compound A compound used in an affinity assay as a means of detecting the presence of a particular group. For instance, a fluorochrome or an enzyme linked to an antibody can function as a signal compound.

signal sequence A sequence of between 15–30 mainly hydrophobic amino acids added to the end of protein molecules that are to be secreted by a cell to facilitate their passage across the endoplasmic reticulum.

silent DNA *See* intron.

silica Silica dioxide. It occurs naturally in the form of quartz, sand, flint or agate.

silica gel A high absorbent gelatinous form of silica used as a drying agent and catalyst support.

silicate Any salt derived from silicic acids or silica.

silicon A non-metallic element, having both amorphous and crystalline forms, that occurs in a combined form in minerals and rocks.

silicone A compound made by substituting silicon for carbon in an organic substance. Silicones are characterized by greater stability and resistance to extremes of temperature than the parent carbon compounds. Among the silicones are oils, greases, resins and a group of synthetic rubbers.

silicosis A disease of the lungs that results from inhalation of siliceous particles.

Simian Virus 40 *See* SV40.

simple continuous stirred tank reactor (CSTR) A simple variation on the standard batch process. Pasteurized feed is pumped continuously into an agitated vessel containing active cells. Most of the sugar is consumed with the production of secondary products and/or new cell mass. A uniformly mixed liquor flows continuously from an overflow port in the side of the fermenter. Air is sparged through the fermenter base to maintain the optimum oxygen tension. In the case of ethanol production, the specific productivity is limited because of ethanol inhibition. A high concentration of ethanol both in the fermenter and the overflow product is maintained to reduce distillation costs. Low cell densities may occur owing to wash-out of cells, counteracting new cell growth, limiting total productivity. Using high productivity cultures, ethanol output is about three times that of the conventional batch system.

single-cell isolation A technique used in microbiology to obtain a pure culture. This entails the physical isolation of a single cell from a colony or liquid medium using a micromanipulator, or the use of serial dilutions of a culture until samples containing only a few cells are available for inoculation of fresh medium. This second method is suitable for use with fungal spores where the germinating spore may be recognized and isolated from an agar plate.

single-cell protein (SCP) The product obtained from a wide variety of processes in which yeasts, bacteria, fungi or algae are grown for their protein content. SCP is used as food or animal feed as it also contains carbohydrates, fats, vitamins and minerals. Possible substrates for single-cell protein production include agricultural and food-processing wastes, byproducts such as molasses and cheese whey permeates, n-alkanes and other petroleum-derived raw materials, alcohols such as methanol or ethanol, and gases such as methane, carbon monoxide, hydrogen or carbon dioxide. In addition, biomass produced as a byproduct of anaerobic waste treatment processes has been considered as SCP. Several attempts aimed at the large-scale production of SCP using fossil fuel-based substrates have failed. This has been due in part to real or imaginary concern about possible health hazards associated with the products, but to a greater extent it has been due to economic constraints during the late 1970s when there was a rapid rise in oil prices and increased production of low-cost agricultural surpluses. At the same time, there has been a great increase in soya bean production, as well as more corn gluten feed being produced as a byproduct of the US fuel and other ethanol programmes. SCP production is capital-intensive and, with the exception of photosynthetic algae, energy-intensive. At present, SCP processes for the production of animal feed are attractive only where soya bean and fishmeal have to be imported. The use of organisms for human consumption is limited to those accepted by regulatory and public health authorities. In many cases, SCP has to be processed in order to lower the nucleic acid content to acceptable levels.

single-cell protein (algal) Algae are of interest as a source of SCP since they can be grown in large quantities in open ponds using sunlight as an energy source. Productivity, and thus the economics of the process, depends on the intensity and duration of illumination. Hence successful systems have been associated with subtropical or tropical regions, especially desert areas. Algae of the genera *Chlorella* and *Scenedesmus* have been used as food in Japan, and *Spirulina* is being produced in Israel, USA, Mexico, Thailand and elsewhere. Part of the commercial production is being sold as a 'health food'. Algal SCP production is of potential where it is associated with the production of shellfish, shrimps, fin fish, etc.

single-cell protein (bacterial) Bacteria are of interest as a source of SCP because of their high growth rates and the amino acid spectrum of their protein. The large-scale propagation of bacteria as a source of animal feed protein is a fairly recent technology, having been developed in the late 1970s to early 1980s. Plants have been built using both methane and methanol as feedstocks. The major investment has been by ICI in the UK using the methanol-utilizing bacterium *Methylophilus methylotrophus* to produce Pruteen. Cellulose wastes have been used as substrates with bacteria of the genera *Cellulomonas* and *Alcaligenes*. The use of photosynthetic bacteria such as *Rhodopseudomonas gelatinosa* has also been proposed, in which case production techniques would be similar to those used for algal single-cell protein.

single-cell protein (fungal) A wide variety of fungal mycelia have been grown as SCP in aerated, agitated deep-tank cultures, in tower fermenters or using solid substrate fermentation. A variety of fungi, mushrooms in particular, have traditionally been used as food. Some SCP is derived from mycelia of organisms such as *Agaricus*

campestris or *Morchella* species. Other fungi, including species of *Mucor*, *Aspergillus*, *Trichoderma*, *Gliocladium*, *Verticillium* and *Fusarium*, have been used, grown on wastes, molasses or artificial media based on glucose syrups.

single-cell protein (yeasts) Yeasts have been used in baked and fermented foods for generations. Dried brewers' yeast, a byproduct of the brewing industry, has an established use as an animal feed. In recent years, a number of yeast-based SCP processes, using agitated, aerated deep-tank cultures, have been developed. These include the growth of *Saccharomyces cerevisiae* on molasses, *Saccharomycopsis lipolytica* on n-alkanes, *Kluyveromyces fragilis* on cheese whey and *Candida utilis* on starchy wastes. The main yeast used on n-alkanes is *Candida lipolytica*, otherwise known as *Endomycopsis lipolytica*.

single-stranded DNA A form of DNA that is not base paired with a second strand of DNA or RNA, and thus can hybridize with other suitable polynucleotides.

site-specific drug A therapeutic agent, the action of which depends on the specific interaction with a recognition site on the target enzyme or organism.

skin The outer covering, made up of epithelial cells, found in the vertebrates. It consists of an outer epidermis and a underlying dermis. The skin acts as a protection, a means of conserving water, a generalized sensory organ and in warm-blooded animals is important in temperature regulation.

slant culture A method used for maintaining stock cultures of a microorganism. The cells are plated on agar contained in a sealed bottle. The bottle or tube is held at an angle while the gel sets.

slant tube fermenter A modification of the tower fermenter giving a higher flow rate capacity. A 3 centimetre diameter tube 14 metres long is mounted at 45° to the horizontal, and sugar solution is pumped through the tube from the base. Fermentation takes place progressively up the tube. As the cell settling depth is very shallow, high flow rates are possible. Cells settle on the lower tube wall and roll down, while the carbon dioxide evolved rises to the upper tube wall and bubbles rapidly up out of the fermenter. There is thus a three-phase flow. A bank of many slant fermenter tubes operated in parallel from a single pump could in theory achieve industrial-scale production, but a special flow distributor system would be required to maintain an equal flow in all the tubes.

SLFIA *See* substrate-labelled fluorescence immunoassay.

slime fungi Myxomycophyta.

slow virus *See* prions.

smile A curved distortion that occurs in autoradiographs of DNA sequences.

smooth muscle A type of muscle found in vertebrates. Unlike striated muscle, it has no obvious ultrastructure and produces slow contractions. Smooth muscle occurs in sheets around hollow organs such as blood vessels and the intestines. It is under the control of the autonomic system.

smuts Fungi of the order Ustilaginales (basidiomycetes) that are important as disease agents for many crops, including most grains.

soap A mixture of salts of long-chain fatty acids produced by saponification of glycerides.

sodium azide An antimicrobial agent. It is used at 0.2 per cent to prevent infection of chromatography columns and gel suspensions. It interferes with fluorescent protein markers and the anthrone reaction, as well as inhibiting some enzymes.

sodium dodecyl sulphate (SDS) An ionic detergent used for denaturation of protein and in electrophoresis of protein subunits.

sodium lauryl sarcosine An ionic detergent with properties similar to sodium dodecyl sulphate, but soluble in high salt concentrations, thus enabling its use in caesium chloride gradient centrifugation.

sodium pump An active transport mechanism associated with cell membranes. The pump moves sodium ions out of the cell against a concentration gradient producing the resting potential across the membrane. The sodium pump is important in neurones.

soft rot A plant disease caused by pathogenic coliform bacteria often of the genus *Erwinia*. The bacteria produce pectinase which dissolves the intercellular cement of plant tissues, allowing the spread of the bacteria through the organism.

sol particles An aqueous dispersion of inorganic colloidal particles (e.g., gold), used as a label.

solid substrate fermentation The growing of microorganisms, often fungi, on a solid material rather than a liquid medium. Such techniques can be divided into two basic types: thin layer and deep bed. In the former system, the organisms are grown on the surface of the substrate, which is spread on shallow trays about 2–4 cm deep; the trays are incubated in air-conditioned rooms or cabinets. The simplest deep bed systems consist of heaps of substrate that are stirred periodically by hand. More sophisticated, fully automated systems include rotating drums, conveyor belt systems, which pass through air-conditioned tunnels, or deep tanks through which air is blown. The substrates used are generally based on wheat bran.

solid-phase hybridization A technique in which one of the hybridizing species is complexed with an insoluble support.

solid-phase sequenter A device used in amino acid sequencing of proteins in which the sample is covalently attached to a solid-phase support of derivatized glass or polystyrene beads and packed into a microcolumn, prior to initiating the Edman degradation.

solids detention time *See* mean detention time.

solid-state synthesis A technique used for the chemical synthesis of polypeptides or polynucleotides. The growing chain is linked to a solid support by one of its ends and elongation proceeds at the other. The excess reagents and byproducts of each cycle of the process are eliminated by washing. At the end of the process, the polymer is detached, purified and its sequence checked. The technique forms the basis of automatic peptide and gene synthesizers. When used to form polynucleotides, artificial synthesis differs from that catalysed by DNA polymerase since the latter requires a template. In the chemical synthesis, it is possible to introduce variations as required.

somaclonal variation Variation that occurs in plants propagated from cell or tissue cultures.

somatic Descriptive of non-reproductive cells and/or cell divisions.

somatic hybridization A procedure in which diploid (somatic) cells or protoplasts are fused *in vitro*. *See* cell fusion, protoplast fusion.

somatic motor nerve A peripheral motor neurone that in vertebrates supplies striated muscle.

somatomedin A polypeptide, also known as plasma growth factor, produced by the liver under the stimulation of growth hormone.

somatoplasm A term proposed by A. Weismann (1834–1914) as part of his germ plasm theory, which distinguished between the germ plasm (sex cells and the cells from which they arise) and the somatoplasm which comprises all other parts of the body. The somatoplasm is equivalent to that part of the body consisting of somatic cells.

somatostatin A peptide hormone, consisting of 14 amino acids, produced by the hypothalamus. It stimulates the release of insulin and growth hormone.

somatotrophin *See* growth hormone.

sonication The use of ultrasonic energy. May be used to break cells or to aid cleaning of surfaces with surfactant.

sorghum *See* sweet sorghum.

sour cream A fermented milk product manufactured by ripening pasteurized cream of 18 per cent fat content with lactic acid- and aroma-producing bacteria. Rennet and sodium citrate may also be added. The latter is metabolized by *Streptococcus lactis* and *Leuconostoc cremoris* to produce more aroma compounds such as diacetyl.

souring A drop in pH associated with the production of an organic acid due to microbial growth. In anaerobic digestion, it involves a switch from methanogenesis to acid fermentation.

southern blot A technique used in genetic manipulation for hybridization tests. An agarose gel containing denatured DNA fragments is placed between a filter paper and a cellulose nitrate filter saturated with buffer. The DNA is eluted from the gel on to the cellulose nitrate to which it binds. This filter is then used for complementary hybridization tests which reveal the nature of the sequences in the blotted filter and thus in the original gel. If the filter is placed in a solution of radioactive RNA or denatured DNA, the regions of hybridization can be detected by autoradiography. The method is very sensitive and can be used to map restriction sites around a single gene sequence in a complex genome.

soy sauce A fermented product manufactured by fermentation of a mixture of soya beans and cereal, usually wheat, with salt. The process is complicated and uses a sequence of fungi and bacteria. *Aspergillus oryzae* may be used as a starter, salt is added later and further fermentations are carried out using *Pediococcus soyae* and various yeasts (*Saccharomyces rouxii*, *Torulopsis* species). The resultant cake is then pressed to produce the liquid sauce which is pasteurized.

soya bean meal A residue obtained as a result of processing soya beans or extracting oil from soya beans. The meal is rich in protein and is widely used as an animal feed supplement. Alternative sources of animal protein, such as single-cell protein, may be compared with soya bean meal used as a standard in terms of its amino acid composition and nutritive value.

spacer A chemical, for example a short alkyl chain of up to C-12, used in construction of an affinity chromatography absorbent. A spacer is added in order to avoid problems of steric hindrance between the ligate and the matrix that would otherwise prevent correct binding.

spacer DNA DNA that is located between the regions containing the information used to determine the actual amino acid sequence in proteins. These regions may or may not be transcribed by RNA polymerase.

spacer group Compounds chemically bonded to a stationary phase to provide sites for derivatization in production of modified phases for affinity chromatography.

sparger An orifice that introduces air or oxygen into a reactor.

SPDP *See* *N*-succinimidyl 3-(2-pyridyldithio)propionate.

specialization The tendency of organisms to evolve and become adapted to a specific environment. Extremes of specialization are found in parasitic organisms (endoparasites in particular) where the organism is only able to survive in a specific host and requires a specific sequence of alternative hosts in order to reproduce.

speciation The formation of new species.

species A unit used in the classification of living organisms. Members of the same species resemble each other closely and are capable of interbreeding with the production of fertile offspring of similar appearance and genetic make-up to the parents. Each species is based on a representative

sample, or holotype, and is named according to the system of binomial nomenclature.

specific activity (1) In radioactive work, the ratio of radioactive atoms to stable atoms in a given compound. It may be expressed in terms of becquerels (the previously used microcurie or curie is now obsolete) per gram or per mole. (2) In enzymology, a measure of the ratio of enzymically active protein to total protein. It may be expressed in terms of millimoles of substrate converted per second (or minute) per milligram of protein.

specific enzyme activity The activity of an enzyme expressed in terms of the amount or number of moles of substrate converted per unit time by unit weight of protein.

specific growth rate constant (μ) A proportionality constant for the growth of unicellular microorganisms undergoing binary fission. In a well mixed batch culture system, growth is proportional to the biomass concentration:

$$\mathrm{d}x/\mathrm{d}t = \mu x$$

where $\mathrm{d}x/\mathrm{d}t$ = the rate constant and x = biomass concentration on a dry weight basis. Under conditions where μ remains constant:

$$\ln x = \ln x_0 + \mu t$$

where x_0 = biomass concentration at zero time and t = time. Hence

$$x = x_0 \mathrm{e}^{\mu t}$$

When $\ln x$ is plotted against time, a straight line with slope μ is obtained. Hence

$$\text{generation time} = (2.303 \times \log 2)/\mu$$

The value of μ is identical to the dilution rate for a continuous culture at equilibrium.

specific production rate The rate of formation of an end product from a fermenter expressed in terms of the amount formed per unit of time per unit of another variable (cell volume, wet cell weight, number of organisms, volume of reactor, etc.).

specific rate of reaction The rate of product formation, or substrate utilization, expressed in terms of unit mass of the microorganism involved, or per unit weight of biomass or enzyme.

specific viscosity The difference between the viscosity of a solution or dispersion and the viscosity of the solvent or continuous phase measured at the same temperature.

specificity The ability of an enzyme to catalyse only a restricted type of reaction with a limited range of substrates.

spectinomycin An inhibitor of protein synthesis. It is used for plasmid amplification in organisms that show chloramphenicol resistance.

spectrophotometer An analytical device consisting of a light source, diffraction grating, sample holder and detection system that is used to measure absorption spectra or changes in absorbance at fixed wavelength. The light source is a lamp producing radiation in the region of 200–360 nm (ultraviolet) or 360–760 nm (visible). This is diffracted so that a narrow beam (1 or 2 nm wide) can be passed through the sample. The degree of attenuation is measured using a photomultiplier, and the signal presented on a chart recorder or cathode ray tube. Fully automated systems are now available that can calculate kinetic constants, concentrations, etc. on the basis of measurements made at fixed wavelength, and can manipulate spectra produced by scanning samples.

spectrophotometric protein determination A technique used to measure the amount of protein in solution. The extinction of a diluted protein solution is measured at 260 and 280 nm, and the ratio of the extinctions calculated. This is used to correct for the presence of nucleic acid contamination using standard tables.

spectrophotometric terms The absorbance or extinction is defined in terms of the molar extinction coefficient (ε) of a compound measured for a 1 M solution (i.e., 1 mole per litre) using a 1-centimetre light path. It has the dimensions of $M^{-1}\,cm^{-1}$. For substances that absorb visible light or ultraviolet light strongly (e.g., purines, pyrimidines, flavins, porphyrins, nicotinamide nucleotides, etc.) ε is of the order of 10^3–10^4. An alternative definition expresses concentration in moles per millilitre. In this case, the molar extinction coefficient is the absorbance of a solution containing 1 mole per millilitre using a 1-centimetre light path. It has the dimensions cm^2/mol and is of the order of magnitude of 10^6–10^8.

$$A = E = -\log T = \log I_0/I = \varepsilon l c$$

where A = absorbance, E = extinction, T = transmittance, I_0 = intensity of incident light, I = intensity of transmitted light, ε = molar extinction coefficient, c = concentration (mol/litre) and l = length of optical path (cm).

spectroscopy The use of a spectrophotometer.

sperm An abbreviation for spermatozoon, the male gamete.

spermatid A haploid cell produced in the animal testis as a result of the second meiotic division in spermatogenesis which matures to form a functional spermatozoon. *Compare* polar bodies.

spermatocyte A diploid cell located in the seminiferous tubules of the testis that undergoes meiosis to form the haploid spermatids.

spermatogenesis The formation of spermatozoa.

spermatogonium A primordial germ cell that gives rise, by mitosis, to spermatocytes, from which the spermatozoa develop by meiosis.

Spermatophyta The taxonomic group that consists of the seed plants (gymnosperms and angiosperms).

spermatozoon A motile male gamete formed in the testes of animals.

spheroplast A protoplast that retains some wall material.

spherosome An organelle, derived from the endoplasmic reticulum and bounded by a single membrane, that is the site of synthesis and/or storage of lipids in some eukaryotic cells.

sphincter A circular band of muscle associated with the inlet or outlet of a hollow organ. Contraction of the sphincter can partly or wholly close the lumen.

sphingolipid A lipid comprising a fatty acid residue, a base and a sphingosine residue.

sphingomyelin A phospholipid found in brain tissue.

Sphingomyelin (bovine)

sphingosine A lipid alcohol that is a component of the sphingomyelins, gangliosides and cerebrosides.

spina bifida A genetic disease in which the spinal chord does not develop correctly.

spinal cord The part of the central nervous system of vertebrates that is enclosed within the vertebral column. The spinal column is derived from the embryonic neural tube.

spinal nerves Segmentally arranged paired nerves that arise laterally from the spinal cord of vertebrates. The nerves arise from a dorsal afferent and a ventral efferent root. These then fuse to form the mixed nerves that constitute the peripheral nervous system.

spindle An ellipsoidal microtubular structure that forms during meiosis or mitosis and is involved in the separation of homologous chromosomes, or sister chromatids. The organization of the spindle in animal cells is associated with the activity of the centrioles.

spinning cup sequenter A device for the liquid-phase sequencing of peptides or proteins. The reaction vessel consists of a glass cup spinning at 1200–1300 rpm fitted with a vacuum system to remove volatile chemicals. A solution of the sample is added to the cup and then dried as a thin film on its interior surface. Reagents are added to dissolve the sample and to effect degradation. Excess reagents, byproducts and the required amino acid anilinothiazolines are removed by evacuation and solvent extraction.

spiral filter A filter consisting of semicircular spiral channels. Fluids passing through the channels are subject to centrifugal forces and turbulence, enhancing the efficiency of the filtration process.

spirochaetes A group of bacteria characterized by a long, slender spiral shape with thin flexible walls. The spirochaetes move by flexing the cells. Some species are free-living in water, others including *Treonema pallidum* (syphilis) cause serious disease in man.

spleen A large lymphoid organ situated in the intestinal mesentary of vertebrates. It is associated with the storage and destruction of blood cells, as well as the removal of foreign bodies from the blood stream. The spleen also produces lymphocytes.

splicing (1) The enzyme-catalysed joining of fragments of DNA in gene manipulation. (2) The joining of conserved sections of mRNA following excision of introns.

splicing enzymes A ligase associated with joining of lengths of DNA or RNA *in vivo* or *in vitro*.

spongiform encephalopathy An infectious disease that causes characteristic brain damage, leaving a spongy vacuolated texture to diseased tissue. Spongiform encephalopathies include Scrapie (primarily sheep and deer) and BSE (primarily domestic cattle) in animals and Gerstmann–Straussler–Scheinker syndrome (GSS), Kuru (associated with ritual cannibalism) and Creutzfeldt–Jakob disease (thought to be primarily associated with improperly sterilized surgical instruments and organ transplantation) in man. Spongiform encephalopathies are characterized by a slow evolution and the absence of any immune reaction, as well as major proteic metabolism dysfunctions, including the accumulation of two normal proteins of the central nervous system, one of neuronal and one of glial origin. *See also* prions.

spore A small reproductive form of a microorganism. It is typically very resistant to harsh environmental conditions.

sporophore A spore-bearing structure.

sporophyte The diploid, asexual generation that produces the spores by meiosis in plants in which a sexual (haploid) generation alternates with an asexual (diploid) generation. *Compare* gametophyte.

Sporozoa A class of parasitic protozoa that includes the malaria parasite, *Plasmodium.*

sport An organism with unusual characteristics produced as a result of a naturally occurring mutation.

spray drier A device for recovering dry solids from an aqueous solution or suspension. The liquid is atomized in a chamber into which a stream of heated air is blown. Moisture evaporates into the air stream and the dry powder is collected.

stacked plate reactor A reactor consisting of circular glass or stainless steel plates mounted on a central shaft and immersed in a growth medium. This provides a large surface area for the extensive culture of mammalian cells.

staining A procedure used in the preparation of samples to be examined by microscopy that enhances the contrast. In light microscopy, the specimens are coloured using various dyes, many of which are selective in that they stain a specific type of tissue. Several stains may be used in sequence to produce a counterstained sample. Stains are classified as acidic, basic or neutral, depending on the nature of the coloured radicals of the stain. Acidic stains tend to react with cytoplasm, whereas basic stains are taken up by nucleic acids. In electron microscopy, the term may be applied to electron-dense materials such as salts of osmium, uranium and lead that bind to and increase the electron density of various cell constituents.

stamen The microsporophyll of angiosperm flowers consisting of the pollen-producing structure (anther) borne on a filament.

staminode A sterile stamen.

standing crop The total quantity of organic matter (biomass) available, including both the useful part of the crop to be harvested (e.g., grain) and residues such as leaves and straw. It is often expressed in terms of tonnes per hectare.

Staphylococcus A genus of spherical non-motile gram-positive bacteria. They may form short chains, but do not form spores. Some are pathogens causing abscesses, wound infections and meningitis, and are implicated in some forms of food poisoning (*S. aureus*). Other species are used in fermentation of meat products.

starch A high-molecular-weight polysaccharide consisting largely of D-glucose units linked through an α-(1,4)-link, forming a spiral chain with only one terminal reducing moiety per chain. It consists of two fractions: amylose (25 per cent) and amylopectin (75 per cent). It is the major storage carbohydrate in higher plants, where it accumulates in the form of grains. The grain structure and composition are characteristic of a given plant species.

Starch serves as a major source of calories for human and other non-ruminant animals. Starch from maize, and to a lesser extent that from potatoes and wheat, is used as starting material for the manufacture of glucose, glucose syrups and high fructose syrups, as well as in the production of potable and fuel ethanol.

starch sheath A layer of endodermal cells that surrounds the stele in some leaves and stems of dicotyledons.

start codon A trinucleotide in an mRNA at which translation is initiated and which sets the reading frame. In eukaryotes it is AUG which is decoded as methionine. In prokaryotes it is usually AUG giving N-formyl methionine. However, GUG, decoded as valine, may also occur as a start codon in prokaryotes.

starter culture A carefully prepared authentic preparation, or stock culture, of a known organism; in particular, cultures used to initiate industrial fermentations. It may consist of a growing liquid culture, a lyophilized culture or a frozen culture.

starter rotation The use of different inoculant cultures in rotation during the manufacture of dairy products to limit the risk of a bacteriophage specific to any one of the cultures becoming established.

start-up The first stage of operation of a continuous fermentation or anaerobic digestion process, during which the process is brought to steady running conditions.

state-of-the-art An idiomatic phrase used to imply that the most recent or up-to-date technology has been used or is being described.

stationary phase (1) In chromatography, the solid packing or support material, that may be in powder, gel or sheet form. (2) In cell culture, the period during which there is no growth, following the exponential phase.

stearic acid n-Octadecanoic acid; an 18-carbon long-chain fatty acid that is widely distributed in natural oils and fats. Storage fats of ruminants contain high levels of stearic acid.

stele The primary vascular tissue in plants. It consists of the xylem and phloem, as well as the pericycle and endodermis.

stem The part of the axis that bears the leaves, axillary buds and flowers.

stereoisomers Chemical substances that contain the same number and types of atoms, linked identically but for their three-dimensional configuration.

sterigma A small projection from a basidium that bears the basidiospore.

sterile (1) In microbiology or health care, descriptive of an object or solution that is free of living microorganisms. (2) In reproductive biology, descriptive of an organism that is incapable of producing offspring. (3) In botany, descriptive of a flower that fails to develop or flowers that lack properly formed and functioning stamens and/or pistils. (4) In agriculture, descriptive of a very poor soil that is incapable of supporting normal vegetation.

sterile operation A procedure or series of procedures that use materials free from infection or contamination with microorganisms in conditions that prevent such infection or contamination.

sterility The property of being sterile.

sterility test There are two main groups of sterility tests: indirect and direct. Indirect tests include the monitoring of temperature and time, and the use of bioindicators. In direct tests, sterile substances are passed through the system and are then checked to ensure that no contamination has occurred.

sterilization The eradication of all forms of living matter; the removal of the power of reproduction is also implied. The difference between these two usages is not real because reproduction is one of the innate properties of living matter. Thus an organism unable to reproduce is biologically essentially dead.

sterilize (1) In microbiology, to carry out a procedure that is designed to kill microorganisms, usually by bringing to a high temperature with steam, dry heat or boiling liquid. (2) In reproductive biology, to destroy the ability of an organism to reproduce by removing the sex organs or inhibit their function.

sterilizer An autoclave or similar heated container used to sterilize growth media, biochemical or health care reagents and solutions, small apparatus or instruments, etc. The design of sterilizers for liquid media is based on the death kinetics of microorganisms. The inactivation by heat involves a loss of viability but not physical destruction. At a specific temperature, the rate of inactivation of microorganisms is

$$dN/dt = -k_d N$$

where k_d = temperature-dependent rate constant, N = number of potentially viable organisms and t = time. The effect of temperature on the rate equation is given by the Arrhenius equation

$$k_d = \alpha e^{-E/RT}$$

where α = an empirical constant, E = activation energy, R = gas constant and T = absolute temperature. Hence

$$dN/N = \alpha e^{-E/RT} dt$$

In sterilization of culture media, a compromise may be necessary since over-exposure of the medium to heat may result in adverse effects on medium quality. For this reason, heat-sensitive components of culture media may be sterilized using ultrafiltration and then added to the bulk heat-sterilized medium.

steroid A lipid characterized by a complex seventeen-carbon perhydrocyclopentanophenanthrene nucleus. Steroids include a wide range of compounds with biological activity (e.g., sterols, hormones and vitamin D).

Numbering of steroid carbon atoms

steroid bioconversion A process in which one type of steroid, or a precursor, is converted to a related molecule using enzymes or cells as catalysts. Such transformations include the hydroxylation of progesterone using *Rhizopus arrhizus*, which introduces an oxygen atom at C-11. Microorganisms are also used in the conversion of raw materials, such as diosgenin from yam roots and stigma sterol from soya beans, by cleavage of their side chain to produce the aglycone.

sterol A steroid alcohol. Examples of sterols include cholesterol and ergosterol.

sticky ends The self-complementary single-stranded ends of a DNA molecule that has been cut using a restriction endonuclease.

stigma In angiosperms, the receptive surface of the gynoecium to which pollen grains adhere. It is usually borne on a style. The epidermis of the stigma exudes a sugary solution that induces the germination of compatible pollen and initiates fertilization.

stilboestrol A synthetic hormone; the parent substance of a group of oestrogenic agents.

still A distillation apparatus or a distillery. A simple still consists of a vessel, in which a liquid is heated and vaporized, and a cooling device or coil to condense the vapour.

stimulus An event in the internal or external environment that incites a biochemical

One-step biotransformation of steroids (11ß-hydroxylation)

1) side chain removal
2) 3β–OH→3-keto
3) Δ⁵ — Δ⁴
4) Δ¹

Cholesterol

Δ¹,⁴ -3,17-dione

One-step multienzymne biotransformation of steroids using *Mycobacterium* species

CH₂OH
CO
- - OH

Curvularia lunata
(11ß)

Reichstein compound S

CH₂OH
CO
····· OH

HO

Hydrocortisone

or physical response in a living organism or biological process.

stipe A stalk or other slender support in non-seed plants and fungi; for instance, the stalk of the fruiting bodies of mushrooms and toadstools or the stalk of the large brown algae (Phaeophyta).

stirred tank fermenter The most widely used type of fermentation vessel. It consists of a tank fitted with cooling coils, or cooling jacket, and a mechanically driven impeller, as well as various ports for input and output of liquid and gases. The degree of sophistication varies and includes fully automated and instrumented systems.

stirred tank reactor *See* stirred tank fermenter.

stock (1) In breeding, the race or strain of plants or animals from which a particular group of offspring has been obtained (breeding stock, pedigree stock). (2) In horticulture, the stem, tree or plant that furnishes slips or cuttings or a stem in which a graft is inserted and that is its support.

stoichiometric Descriptive of a reaction mixture in which the ingredients are present in the exact amounts required for the reaction to go to completion without any of the reactants being left.

stoichiometry The calculation of the quantities of chemical elements or compounds involved in chemical reactions.

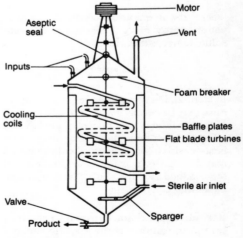

Stirred tank fermenter

Stokes' radius The radius of a spherical volume occupied by a macromolecule in solution.

stolon A horizontal stem of a plant that grows along the surface of the ground and takes root at the nodes where a new shoot arises. It is an organ of vegetative propagation.

stoma A small pore found in the epidermis of the aerial parts of plants through which gas exchange occurs. Stomata provide the main route of photosynthetic gas exchange and of water vapour loss in transpiration. Each stoma is bounded by a pair of guard cells that control the size of the aperture through changes in cell shape resulting from changes in cell turgor. When the turgor of the guard cells is low, the two cells are closely appressed and the pore is closed. When the turgor is high, the pore opens as a result of the differential thickening of the cell walls. The change in turgor is the result of water moving in and out of the cells in an osmotic response to changes in potassium concentration.

stomach Part of the anteria region of the alimentary canal in animals. The oesophagus leads into the stomach, and the stomach discharges its contents into the duodenum. In vertebrates, the stomach secretes hydrochloric acid and pepsin, which initiates digestion of protein. In birds, the posterior end of the stomach forms the gizzard. In ruminants, the stomach is divided into four chambers to facilitate the digestion of cellulose.

stomatal movement Stomatal movement causes changes in the pore size of the stomata in the epidermis of higher plants. These changes control both the rates of photosynthetic gas exchange and the rates of water use (loss) through transpiration. In general, stomata close in response to water deficit and open in response to low concentrations of carbon dioxide. Stomata also respond to changes in light intensity and in temperature, as well as showing both blue-light and phytochrome-type responses. Closure is affected by the plant growth regulator abscisic acid.

stomium A weak area found in the wall of certain plant structures, such as the anthers. It is the site of rupture on dehiscence.

stomodaeum In embryology, an anterior invagination that opens into the archenteron and later gives rise to the buccal cavity of vertebrates.

stop codon A trinucleotide sequence that terminates protein synthesis as there are no complementary tRNA molecules and hence an amino acid cannot be inserted into the polypeptide chain at that site. There are three stop codons: UAA, known as ochre; UAG, known as amber; and UGA, known as opal.

strain (1) In fluid mechanics, the degree of deformation relative to a reference length, area or volume. (2) In microbiology, a set of cells or cultures of common origin that are of similar genetic make-up; a pure culture of organisms composed of descendants of a single parent organism. (3) A pure breeding variety of a plant or higher animal.

strain stability A measure of the tendency of change to occur in the genetic make-up of succeeding generations of the descendants of a single cell or variety of breeding stock.

strand polarity The organization of the base sequence in a single-stranded nucleic acid. A molecule with positive polarity contains the same base sequence as the related mRNA. Negative polarity molecules have a base sequence complementary to the positive strand.

stratum corneum The outer layer of the vertebrate epidermis consisting of dead keratinized cells.

streak plate *See* plating.

streamline flow *See* laminar flow.

Streptococcus A genus of spherical, non-motile, gram-positive bacteria. These bacteria do not form spores and typically appear under the microscope as long chains. Many species are pathogens, causing both pyogenic and haemolytic symptoms, and are common causes of infection of the respiratory tract, leading to sore throats, as well as more serious diseases such as scarlet fever (*S. pyogenes*). The principal cause of bacterial pneumonia is *S. pneumoniae*. If the infected subject has no immunity, the toxins may produce a skin rash. Virulent strains may produce impetigo, puerpural fever, rheumatic fever and endocarditis. Most infections are curable with penicillin. The haemolytic streptococci are common contaminants of milk and milk products, but are destroyed by pasteurization. Some species and strains are used in the production of yoghurt (*S. thermophilus*), cheese (*S. durans*), buttermilk (*S. lactis*) and other fermented dairy products.

Streptomyces A genus of actinomycetes used in the production of antibiotics. They are also the source of some industrial enzymes such as pullulanase, protease (*S. griseus*) and glucose isomerase (*S. phaeochromogenes*).

streptomycin An aminoglycoside antibiotic obtained by fermentation using *Streptomyces griseus*. Streptomycin is an inhibitor of protein synthesis inhibitor. It binds to the 30S bacterial ribosomal subunit

Streptomycin

causing mRNA to be misread. This results in nonsense peptides.

streptomycin dependence The need to include streptomycin in a growth medium that is found in some mutant organisms. Protein synthesis is blocked in the absence of the drug. The inhibitor causes distortions in reading of the mRNA, that are compensated for by the streptomycin-induced distortion. The dependence is alleviated by mutations in the formation of ribosomal protein.

streptomycin resistance The ability to survive treatment with the antibiotic streptomycin, mediated through a chromosomal mutation, that results in an altered 12S ribosomal protein that will not bind the antibiotic.

stress Force per unit area.

striated muscle A type of muscle, characterized by a transverse banding pattern, that is responsible for voluntary movements of skeletal parts and movement in particular. The banding pattern reflects the structure of the sarcomere units that make up the myofibrils.

stringent control Descriptive of replication of chromosomal DNA that only occurs in the presence of protein synthesis.

stringent plasmid A plasmid that will only induce the formation of one or a few copies per cell.

striped muscle *See* striated muscle.

structural gene A gene that codes for a polypeptide. *Compare* regulator gene.

style An elongation of the carpel that bears the stigma.

Styragel A polystyrene support material used in gel filtration chromatography with lipophilic solvents. *See* Bio-beads S.

subarachnoid space In vertebrates, the space, containing cerebrospinal fluid, that lies between the arachnoid mater and the pia mater meninges of the brain and spinal cord.

subcutaneous tissue The hypodermis; in vertebrates, a layer of connective tissue that lies beneath the dermis.

suberin A polymeric substance similar to cutin that covers the epidermal cell layer of the underground parts of higher plants. It is built up of both saturated and unsaturated dicarboxylic acids ranging from 16-carbon to 22-carbon, the main one being octadec-9-en-1,18-dioic acid.

submerged culture A process or fermentation in which the cells develop below the surface of a liquid medium.

subspecies A taxonomic unit that is a subdivision of the species. Members of one subspecies are distinguishable from other subspecies by the frequency of genes, chromosomal arrangement or hereditary phenotypic characteristics. Subspecies may result from the spatial separation of one breeding stock from another. This may be a natural process, due to geographical isolation, or may reflect a defined breeding programme. Subspecies sometimes exhibit incipient reproductive isolation, although not sufficiently to make them a different species.

substrate (1) The substance on which an enzyme acts. (2) The food on which a microorganism grows.

substrate conversion efficiency The ratio of the amount of end product recovered from a biological reaction to the amount of substrate used or introduced into a fermenter.

substrate-labelled fluorescence immunoassay SLFIA A type of homogeneous immunoassay.

subtilisin carlsberg A protease produced by *Bacillus licheniformis* used extensively in biological washing powders.

subunit One of a number of particles that associate to produce a whole unit or structure. Many enzymes are composed of several polypeptide subunits. These are grouped in a specific combination to form a single entity with catalytic ability. Numerous structures, such as microtubules, flagella and cilia, are composed of a number of subunits.

succinate dehydrogenase A constituent enzyme of the TCA cycle found in mitochondria of all aerobic cells. It contains FAD as a prosthetic group and requires no separate co-enzyme. The enzyme catalyses the formation of fumaric acid from succinic acid, coupled to the reduction of FAD.

N-**succinimidyl 3-(2-pyridyldithio)-propionate (SPDP)** A bifunctional chemical reagent used to covalently link biological molecules such as proteins. It is used in the labelling or targeting of biologically active molecules by conjugation with antibodies, enzymes, lectins, etc. SPDP reacts specifically with the primary amino group of a protein to introduce 2-pyridyl disulphide residues into the molecule. Such proteins may then be linked by the formation of intermolecular disulphide bonds. If required, the proteins may be cleaved subsequently by reduction.

succus entericus The material secreted by glands in the wall of the small intestine of vertebrates. It contains digestive enzymes that have amylase, lipase, peptidase and protease activity.

sucrose A white crystalline disaccharide that occurs as the major transport carbohydrate in most plants and as a storage carbohydrate in sugar cane and sugar beet, from which it is isolated commercially. It is readily hydrolysed to the constituent monosaccharides (glucose and fructose) by dilute acid or the enzyme invertase. Sucrose is a major source of carbon in many commercial microbiological processes, where it may be supplied in an impure form as molasses. A number of microorganisms, however, do not produce invertase, and hence require prior inversion of feedstock. World production of sucrose is around 100 million tonnes per annum.

Sucrose

sugar (1) A synonym for sucrose. (2) Any monosaccharide or disaccharide.

sulfate *See* sulphate.

sulfazecin A β-lactam antibiotic produced by *Pseudomonas acidophilus*.

sulphate A chemical grouping, containing atoms of sulphur and oxygen.

sulphide A chemical compound that only contains atoms of a metal and sulphur. Metals are often found in ores in this form.

sulphite liquor A byproduct of paper pulp production. Liquor from hardwoods contains about 2–3 per cent fermentable sugars, of which 80 per cent are pentoses and 20 per cent are hexoses. In contrast, liquor from softwoods contains about 80 per cent hexoses and 20 per cent pentoses. This material is used as a fermentation substrate, for instance in the production of *Candida utilis* or *Paecilomyces varioti* as feed (single-cell protein).

sulphonamide An antibacterial drug made by chemical synthesis from the dye sulphanilamide. Sulphonamides are competitive inhibitors of the synthesis of folic acid from *p*-aminobenzoic acid.

sulphuric acid A strong mineral acid that contains atoms of sulphur, oxygen and hydrogen.

supercoil *See* supercoiled DNA.

supercoiled DNA A strongly twisted form of DNA that develops during unwinding of a double-stranded, closed circular genome, as found in many prokaryotes. Free rotation of the strands is not possible, as is the case for a linear molecule. Hence, for each turn that the helix is unwound, a twist occurs in another part of the molecule. This effect is overcome by untwisting enzymes that can remove superhelical twists and can thus restore or preserve the original helical structure of the DNA.

supercritical extraction A method of recovering products using a supercritical fluid as the solvent.

supercritical fluid A substance maintained as a fluid below its normal freezing point.

superfemale *See* metafemale.

supergene A DNA segment that contains a number of closely linked genes affecting a single trait or an array of interrelated traits.

superhelical DNA A twisted form of DNA that is wound around the proteins of the nucleosome core particles in eukaryotic chromosomes. Each particle of 16 × 11 × 5.7 nm is surrounded by 1.75 turns of DNA.

superinfection Infection of a host organism by a virus that has already been infected by another virus. Is it the virus or the host that has already been infected?

supernatant The liquid that collects above the solid layer after centrifugation or sedimentation.

superovulation The production of a greater number of ova per oestrus cycle than occurs normally. This can be induced by hormone treatment and is used to obtain a large number of zygotes for transfer to surrogate mothers as a means of increasing the rate of breeding of rare strains or endangered species, or as a means of overcoming some types of infertility.

superoxide dismutase An enzyme that catalyses the reduction of the superoxide radical to hydrogen peroxide.

superoxide radical A highly active form of oxygen produced when an oxygen molecule loses an electron.

supported growth system A culture method in which growth of cells depends on the presence of a surface to which the cells become attached. *See* anchorage-dependent cell.

suppressor *See* intergenic suppressor, intragenic suppressor.

suppressor-sensitive mutation A mutation (sus) whose phenotype is suppressed in a genotype that also carries an intergenic suppressor of that mutation. A phage carrying a sus mutation can produce progeny when it infects one strain of host cell (carrying a suppressor gene – the permissive condition), but fails to produce progeny when it infects another strain of host cell (lacking a suppressor gene – the restrictive condition).

surfactant A chemical substance capable of dissolving in water and in fatty materials, thus helping fats and oils to mix with water. Detergents behave similarly.

suspension culture A cell or tissue culture in which single cells or small clumps are grown in an agitated liquid medium.

SV40 vectors The SV40 virus is an attractive cloning vehicle or vector for several reasons. (1) The genome consists of a single, covalently closed circular DNA molecule that has been fully sequenced. (2) The regions of the genome responsible for various functions have been accurately located in respect to the physical map. (3) The viral genome can multiply either vegetatively or as an integral part of a cellular chromosome. However, wild-type SV40 cannot be used as a vector because the addition of exogenous DNA would result in a DNA molecule that was too large to be packaged into the viral coat. Mutants that lack the late region can be propagated in mixed infection with a helper virus and used to construct vectors. The usual restriction endonuclease/ligase-based techniques are then employed to add additional DNA coding for the required gene or genes to a fragment of SV40 that contains the origin of replication, the regions at which splicing and polyadenylation occur and the entire early region required for complementation by a helper virus. Using such techniques, foreign genes have been expressed in monkey cells during lytic infection with a recombinant SV40 genome.

SV40 virus A small DNA-containing virus of the group papovavirus. The name is an abbreviation for Simian Virus 40, which reflects the fact that the virus was first isolated from cell cultures of tissues derived from an African green monkey. The virus, which can induce cellular transformation, is widely used in research. The genome has been sequenced and shown to code for five proteins. The capsid is constructed from 420 subunits of a 47,000 dalton polypeptide VP_1, with small amounts of two other polypeptides (VP_2 and VP_3). When the virus infects a suitable cell, about 1 per cent of the particles multiply in a conventional lytic cycle, culminating in the production of new virus particles. When SV40 infects a mouse or hamster cell, no progeny are made, but some cells become transformed.

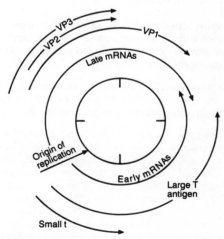

SV40 DNA
genetic Map

svedberg unit A unit of sedimentation. The svedberg unit (S) is a sedimentation coefficient of 1×10^{-13} seconds. S values are usually expressed for the solvent water at 20°C.

sweat A watery fluid, produced by the sweat glands of mammals, evaporation of which assists in cooling the body surface.

sweat gland An exocrine gland that occurs in the skin of mammals and produces sweat.

sweet sorghum A tall grass traditionally grown as an animal feed that is now being planted as an energy crop.

Symba process A fermentation process that produces single-cell protein. It uses starch wastes, that are fermented by a combination of two yeasts: *Saccharomyces* (*Endomycopsis*) *fibuligera* and *Candida utilis*.

symbiosis A close relationship between two organisms, that may be related species or totally different organisms. The use of the term is often not very exact and may refer to parasitism, commensalism or mutualism. More specifically, it is a relationship between organisms in which both obtain some benefit in terms of nutrients or physical protection, and neither causes any harm to the other.

sympathetic nervous system The part of the autonomic nervous system of vertebrates concerned with homeostasis and emergency responses.

sympatric Descriptive of populations or species that inhabit, at least in part, the same geographic region. *Compare* allopatric.

synapse An area of functional contact between neurones, or a neurone and an effector. Synapses usually occur between the terminal branches of the axon of one cell and the dendrites of the next. There is no physical contact between the membranes, the information being transferred across the synaptic gap by means of a chemical neurotransmitter (e.g., adrenaline, acetylcholine).

synapsis The pairing of chromosomes at meiosis.

synaptinemal complex An organelle, present during meiosis, that mediates close pairing between homologous regions of chromatids.

synchronous culture A culture of microorganisms, plant tissue or animal cells, treated in such a way that all the cells undergo nuclear division at the same time. Photosynthetic cells may be synchronized by subjecting cells to alternating periods of light and dark. Heterotrophic cultures may be synchronized by nutrient limitation or temperature shock.

Syndyphalin 20 Highly active enkephalin analogue. Sequence (Tyr–DMet[o]–Gly–Phe–ol)

synergism The interaction of two or more substances or stimuli that have the same effect when used on their own, but when used in combination produce a response that is greater than the sum of the individual effects.

Synthetase *See* ligase.

synthetic medium *See* defined medium.

synthetic plasmid A circular DNA molecule that is constructed from a replican and one or more gene DNA sequences. The synthetic plasmids have a genetic make-up that differs from wild-type plasmids. They are used as cloning vehicles.

syntrophy A microbiological phenomenon in which there is an interaction between two different organisms plated on the same medium, such that their combined activities are quantitatively or qualitatively different from the sum total of their activities when they act separately in the same environment.

systematics A synonym for taxonomy.

systole The contractile phase of the heart beat in which blood is expelled into the aorta and pulmonary aorta.

T

T *See* thymine.

2,4,5-T 2,4,5-Trichlorophenoxyacetic acid; a synthetic auxin used as a herbicide. Some preparations contain dioxin and other impurities that may induce teratogenic activity.

T antigen A protein induced by polyomavirus following infection and cell transformation. T antigen binds to the viral DNA and is necessary for the replication of the viral genome.

T cell *See* T lymphocyte.

T lymphocyte A type of lymphocyte that matures in the thymus gland. These cells are responsible for the cellular immunity processes, such as direct cell binding to an antigen, thus destroying it. T lymphocytes also act as regulators of the immune response as helper T cells, or suppressor T cells.

T$_3$ *See* triiodothyronine.

T$_4$ *See* thyroxine.

T$_4$ DNA ligase *See* DNA ligase.

tachykinins Peptides with biological activity that have the N-terminal sequence –Phe–X–Gly–Leu–Met–NH$_2$. They bring about contraction of smooth muscle.

tailing The modification of some forms of HnRNA following transcription by the addition of between 10 and 20 adenosine residues to the 3′-end. This additional sequence survives the removal of any introns during the processing of HnRNA to mRNA, hence most mRNAs are tailed.

tandem duplication *See* repeat.

tannin Originally a compound present in some plants that was used to tan animal skins to produce leather. The term is now used to define two main groups of high-molecular-weight plant phenolics. Hydrolysable tannins contain a core of a polyhydric alcohol, usually glucose, esterified with gallic acid or hexahydroxydiphenic acid. Condensed tannins are made up only of phenols of the flavone type and never contain sugar residues. On treatment with hydrolytic agents, condensed tannins do not yield low-molecular-weight products, but tend to polymerize to yield amorphous phlobaphenes.

tanning The treatment of animal skins with tannins to produce leather. An extract of the bark of oak trees is a common tanning agent. A good tanning agent has a molecular weight of between 500 and 3000, and contains sufficient phenolic hydroxyl groups (one or two per 100 molecular weight) to form crosslinks with protein. Simple phenolic compounds are too small to form effective crosslinks, whereas compounds of higher molecular weight are ineffective, since they cannot penetrate between the collagen fibres of the animal skin.

***Taq* polymerase** A thermostable polymerase derived from *Thermus aquaticus*.

tar sand A mineral deposit in which a tarry mixture of hydrocarbons is entrapped in sands or sandstones.

target site A recognition site of known chemical structure that may be used in the modelling of drugs for a specific purpose.

taste bud A receptor responsible for the recognition of taste in vertebrates. Taste buds consist of a number of sensory cells usually grouped together on papillae situated on the tongue, or associated with the epithelium of the mouth. Four types of taste buds exist which can identify bitter, salty, sweet or sour tastes.

TATA box A sequence of DNA, where T=thymine and A=adenine, associated with the initiation site of many gene sequences. It has the property of binding RNA polymerase and can function as the promoter region.

taurine An amino acid that contains a sulphonuic acid residue. Taurine is a component of the bile salt taurocholate.

taurocholate *See* taurine.

taxon A unit of classification at any level.

taxonomy The science of classification of living organisms.

TCA cycle *See* tricarboxylic acid cycle.

TDP *See* thymidine 5'-diphosphate.

TDS *See* total dissolved solids.

techoic acid A polymer consisting largely of the phosphate esters of a sugar alcohol (either ribitol or glycerol) together with glucose and alanine. Techoic acids are constituents of the cell walls of gram-positive bacteria.

teleology The belief that design or purpose is part of, or apparent in, natural processes.

teleost Belonging to the Teleostei.

Teleostei The bony fishes in which the skeleton is composed, in part at least, of bone rather than cartilage.

teliospore A resting spore produced on a dikaryotic hyphae by the fungi known generally as rusts and smuts. On germination, the nucleus of the spore undergoes meiosis to produce a single basidium with four basidiospores.

telocentric Descriptive of a chromosome in which the centromere is in a terminal position.

telomere The end of a chromosome in which the DNA is looped back.

telophase The final stage of either meiosis (I or II) or mitosis.

TEMED *See* tetramethylethylene-diamine.

temperate phage A bacteriophage that becomes integrated into the chromosome of its host rather than inducing a lytic cycle. *See* lysogeny.

temperature quotient (Q_{10}) The ratio of the rate of reaction at a given temperature to that of the same reaction carried out at a temperature is that $10°C$ lower. In chemical reactions, including those catalysed by enzymes, the rate roughly doubles for each 10-degree increase in temperature; thus such reactions have a Q_{10} of about 2. Physical reactions, which are diffusion-limited, usually have much lower temperature coefficients.

temperature-sensitive genes A gene that is not expressed when the temperature to which it is exposed falls outside certain specific limits (e.g., $25–35°C$). Temperature-sensitive genes have been used in gene engineering to improve the production of unusual secondary products that may impair the growth of host cells. This is achieved by incorporating two origins of replication into the plasmid vector: a weak marker that leads to the production of only one or two copies of the gene per cell; a strong marker that, when activated, leads to the production of hundreds of gene copies. During growth at a low temperature, the strong marker is kept switched off by a suppressor protein encoded by the temperature-sensitive gene. However, the cells do produce enough copies of the plasmid to maintain one in each host cell. When sufficient cell concentration has been achieved, the temperature is raised above the temperature that inhibits expression of the repressor protein for the strong marker, and hundreds of copies of the plasmid are formed. Each plasmid contains the gene for the required product, hence the cell commences active synthesis of large amounts of the required product. *See* thermoinducible lysogen.

temperature-sensitive mutation A mutation leading to a gene that is functional at a low (high) temperature, but is inactive at a higher (lower) temperature. Such mutations produce a normal phenotype at one temperature, but a mutant at another.

template (1) In general, a pattern or mould against which a complex product is made. (2) In molecular biology, base sequences found in nucleic acids that serve as the basis for the synthesis of complementary strands of DNA or RNA.

tendon A tough, dense, inelastic white fibrous tissue that connects a bone to a muscle. Tendons are composed of collagen fibres, interspaced with rows of fibroblasts.

tendril A filiform, leafless organ found in climbing plants that twist around an object in order to support the plant. Most tendrils show haptotropism.

tensile stress The stress of a body or material under tension.

tension A state in which a body is stretched or increased in size in one direction with a decrease in size in a specific ratio in the perpendicular direction.

tentacle ion exchanger An ion exchanger designed for use in HPC columns. Functional groups are carried along flexible polymer chains rather than rigidly fixed to a solid matrix. The flexibility of the tentacle exchangers greatly reduces the risk of structural deformation of biomolecules in the separation column and subsequent loss of biological activity.

tequila An alcoholic beverage distilled from alcohol produced by fermentation of a 9 per cent sugar solution obtained by pressing tissue cut from the agave or mezcal. The yeast-based fermentation is carried out in a batch fashion for a period of about 38 hours to give a 4.5 per cent ethanol solution. The tequila is then obtained as a 76–110° US

proof spirit using a pot still. White spirit may be drunk without aging, or the spirit may be aged in wood for about a year.

teratogen An agent that causes foetal abnormalities. Teratogens include chemical agents such as thalidomide and X-rays, which cause chromosome damage.

teratogenic Descriptive of a substance or treatment that leads to the production of foetal abnormalities.

teratology The study of malformations in plants or animals.

teratoma (1) A tumour of embryonic origin that often contains differentiated tissue. (2) A discrete, hard tumour formed on plants in response to infection with *Agrobacterium*.

terminal electron transport chain A series of redox couples located in the inner membrane of eukaryotic mitochondria. The terminal electron transport chain serves as a mechanism for the oxidation by molecular oxygen of high-energy reduced compounds, such as NADH and succinate. During the flow of electrons through this chain, a high proportion of the free energy liberated from the oxidation of carbohydrates in the TCA cycle is conserved by using it to generate ATP from ADP and inorganic phosphate in oxidative phosphorylation. The terminal electron transport chain removes a pair of electrons from the high-energy reductant, which has a negative E_0' value of about −0.32 V, and passes them through a sequence of redox systems, whose E values become progressively more positive, until they reach oxygen and reduce it to water at an E_0' of +0.817 V. With the exception of co-enzyme Q, all the components of the chain are proteins with characteristic prosthetic groups. They are of three kinds: the flavoproteins, which have prosthetic groups of FMN or FAD; the cytochromes which have haem prosthetic groups; and the iron–sulphur proteins, in which the prosthetic group consists of non-haem iron ligated to cysteine or inorganic sulphur. The components of the chain are classed as electron carriers or hydrogen carriers, and as one-electron or two-electron carriers. The sequence of such carriers found in animal mitochondria is as shown in the diagram below. The components of the terminal electron chain are organized within the inner membrane of the mitochondria in such a way that a potential gradient is formed across the membrane. This potential is associated with the formation of ATP. *See* chemiosmotic theory.

terminal transferase An enzyme that adds oligonucleotides, such as oligo-(dT), to the 3'-ends of double-stranded DNA. The terminal deoxynucleotidyl transferase from calf thymus is used in gene engineering.

terminalization The movement of chiasmata towards the ends of homologous chromosomes during metaphase I of meiosis.

termination factor *See* release factor.

termination sequence A DNA sequence sited at the end of a transcriptional unit that signals the end of transcription.

terminator *See* termination sequence.

terpene A compound that contains an integral number of five carbon units of the following basic structure:

$$H_3C \diagdown$$
$$C{=}CH{-}CH_2{-}$$
$$-H_2C \diagup$$

Terpenes are classified according to the number of such units present in the molecule:

Type	No. of C atoms	Example
Hemiterpene	5	Isoprene
Monoterpene	10	Geraniol
Sesquiterpene	15	Farnesol
Diterpene	20	Geranlygeraniol
Triterpene	30	Squalene
Tetrterpene	40	Phytoene
Polyterpene	1000s	Rubber

Terpenes are important metabolic intermediates in the formation of a wide range of secondary products and biologically active compounds, including vitamins, steroids, pigments and polymers. Monoterpenes are

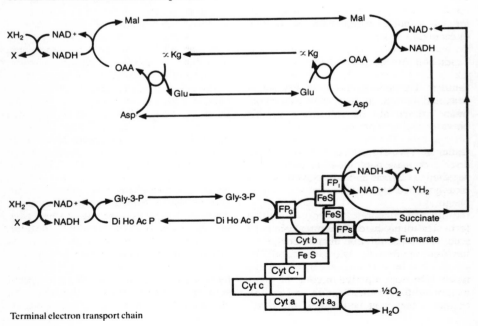

Terminal electron transport chain

widespread in plants, and their strong smells have made them important in the perfumery industry. They often occur as components of essential oils.

terpenoid Any of a large number of compounds with varying numbers of carbon atoms, but which are clearly derived from five-carbon precursors (*see* terpene). Terpenoid quinones and chromonols include phylloquinone (vitamin K), plastoquinones, ubiquinones, and tocopherols. Many are important intermediates in electron transport systems.

terramycin A synonym for the antibiotic now generally known as oxytetracycline.

tertiary (oil) production The phase in the working of an oil reservoir after secondary recovery (pressure maintenance) is complete. Tertiary recovery requires the injection of carbon dioxide or of water containing surfactant or polymer in order to sweep the remaining oil towards the production wells.

tertiary sex ratio *See* sex ratio.

tertiary structure Three-dimensional folding of a polypeptide chain or protein molecule.

Tesla coil An electrical discharge device that is used to establish the presence of a vacuum. The device checks that a sealed culture ampoule is properly evacuated, which is essential if the culture is to remain viable over a long period.

test cross The mating of an F_1 hybrid with a double recessive parent in order to establish whether the hybrid is homozygous or heterozygous for a particular trait seen in the phenotype.

testa The outer hard protective coat of a seed formed from the integuments after fertilization.

testes The reproductive organs of male mammals that produce sperm and steroid hormones. In most vertebrates, the testes

are paired, and in mammals, they are born outside the body in the scrotum that helps to maintain them at a temperature below the normal body temperature. Testes are composed of seminiferous tubules, lined with germinal epithelium, which contain the spermatogonia that produce haploid spermatozoa. Androgen-producing interstitial cells lie between the tubules. The production of Androgens is under the control of the pituitary gonadotrophins.

testosterone A steroid hormone; the main androgen secreted by the mammalian testes.

tetracycline An antibiotic produced by *Streptomyces*. Tetracycline and chlorotetracycline bind to the small subunit (30S) of bacterial ribosomes blocking the subsequent binding of aminoacyl-tRNA and thus inhibiting protein synthesis.

Chlorotetracycline

Oxytetracycline

tetracycline resistance The ability to survive treatment with the antibiotic tetracycline. It is mediated through a membrane protein that inhibits cellular transport of the drug. Tetracycline resistance is a common marker used in cloning vectors.

tetrad A group of four haploid cells formed as a result of the meiotic division of a diploid cell.

tetrad analysis A technique used to analyse the products of meiosis in haploid phases of ascomycete fungi (e.g., *Neurospera*). The position of the spores within the ascus reflects the separation of the chromosomes at the earlier meiotic division. Hence analysis of the genetic characteristics of the ordered spores can be used to determine the extent of crossing-over.

tetrahydrofolic acid A derivative of pteroylglutamic acid (*see* folic acid) which is a co-enzyme of importance in the metabolism of C_1 groups and in the synthesis of the purine and pyrimidine bases of nucleic acids.

tetramethylethylenediamine A catalyst for the polymerization of polyacrylamide gels.

tetraploid Descriptive of a cell or organism having four times the haploid chromosome number (i.e., $4n$).

tetrapod A vertebrate that has four limbs. Tetrapods include the amphibians, reptiles, birds and mammals.

tetrasaccharide A polysaccharide comprising four linked monosaccharide units. Such compounds include stachyose (two galactose units plus one glucose and one fructose) which occurs in many genera of the Leguminosae and Labiatae. Maltotetrose consists of four glucose units formed during the acid or enzymic hydrolysis of starch. It is a significant component of low dextrose equivalent glucose syrups.

tetrasomic (1) Descriptive of a cell or organism in which there is a gain of two chromosomes giving a chromosome number 2X + 2. (2) Descriptive of a cell or organism having one chromosome represented four times.

tetrazolium salts Complex organic molecules that change colour on mild reduction with the formation of insoluble formazans. All such compounds are characterized by a heterocyclic ring structure containing one carbon and four nitrogen atoms, one of which is quaternary. Two types of salts exist: monotetrazoles with one heterocyclic ring; ditetrazoles with two such rings. Tetrazolium salts are used as qualitative markers of oxidative enzyme activity, and in tissue sections, this enables enzyme activity to be localized.

tetrose A monosaccharide that contains four carbon atoms (e.g., erythose).

thalamus The posterior part of the brain in higher vertebrates. It is associated with consciousness and the relay of sensory information to higher centres.

thalassaemia An inherited human disease in which the body fails to produce enough haemoglobin. There are many different types of thalassaemia.

Thallophyta A major subkingdom of plants. It includes all those forms not differentiated into roots, stems and leaves (e.g., algae, fungi, lichens).

thallus A plant body that is not differentiated into roots, stems or leaves; characteristic of the multicellular members of the Thallophyta.

thaumatin An intense sweetener derived from the fruit of *Thaumatococcus danielli* and marketed under the trade name Talin.

theoretical plate In chromatography, the bed length that brings about the same relative change in concentration in a solute as would be obtained on equilibrating with fresh stationary phase. The number of theoretical plates (N), obtained by dividing the column length by the height of one theoretical plate, determines the efficiency of chromatographic separation. For a given solvent, $N = V_e/\sigma$, where V_e is the peak elution volume and σ the standard deviation reflecting zone broadening. The theoretical plate concept is based on the fractional distillation theory.

thermal cycler A programmable cyclical temperature control system used for PCR processes.

thermal denaturation A change in the conformation of a molecule induced by heating. Most proteins and nucleic acids are sensitive to temperatures above 60°C, and may show some sensitivity if exposed for prolonged periods to temperatures of over 40°C. Thermal denaturation of nucleic acids is used in some techniques of hybridization and in the determination of Cot values.

thermistor A semiconductor, the resistance of which changes rapidly with change in temperature. Thus it can be built into electronic circuits for measuring or monitoring temperature.

thermoinducible lysogen A strain of bacterium that contains a prophage whose repressor is temperature-sensitive. Raising the temperature of the culture leads to induction.

thermonasty A nastic response to temperature.

thermophil A microorganism with a temperature optimum for growth of between 40°C and 70°C, or higher. Thermophils are generally associated with hot springs. Extreme thermophils have been isolated from the depths of the Pacific Ocean which, under pressure, can grow at temperatures of over 200°C. They are used in waste treatment and fermentation of lignocellulose substrates, where higher rates of metabolism are an advantage. Thermophils are also used in the production of heat-stable enzymes for industrial use.

thermoplastic Descriptive of a compound, usually a polymer, that becomes soft and pliable when heated without undergoing any changes in its chemical structure.

theta replication A mechanism of DNA replication, found in prokaryotes, in which initiation of a circular molecule of DNA occurs at a certain point and leads to the formation of a replication bubble that grows as replication proceeds in two directions around the chromosome. This method of replication converts a circular chromosome into two circular daughter chromosomes.

thiamine Vitamin B_1; a precursor of the co-enzyme thiamine pyrophosphate. A deficiency of this vitamin leads to beriberi in man.

thiamine pyrophosphate A co-enzyme involved in reactions concerned with carbohydrate and amino acid metabolism. These reactions include those catalysed by transketolase, α-keto acid decarboxylases and acetoactate synthase.

thin layer chromatography *See* chromatography.

thin layer gel filtration A technique in which molecules are separated on a flat plate (typically 20 × 20 cm) on which a layer of xerogel 0.5–1.0 mm thick is spread. Samples are applied to the horizontal plate, and irrigation is started by inclining one end of the plate. After development, the chromatogram is dried in an oven at 50–60°C when the xerogel matrix strongly adheres to the plate. The separated compounds are then detected by suitable staining procedures or visualized under ultraviolet light.

thinning The reduction of the viscosity of a starch suspension by partial hydrolysis of glycosidic links. Thinning may be achieved using either acid or enzymes.

thixotropic fluid A fluid which when subjected to a constant shear stress exhibits an apparent viscosity that decreases with time. A thixotropic gel becomes liquid when shaken or stirred.

Thiamine pyrophosphate

thoracic duct A lymph vessel that collects lymph from most of the vertebrate body and empties into the posterior vena cava close to the heart. It is the main route by which lymph enters the blood stream.

Thr An abbreviation used to denote the amino acid threonine in amino acid sequences and elsewhere.

threonine (Thr) One of the 20 common amino acids found in protein. Threonine is an essential amino acid for man.

Threonine $CH_3CH(OH)CH(NH_2)COOH$

threshold A critical level; the point at which a stimulus becomes perceptible or is of sufficient intensity to produce an effect.

thrip A small insect of the order Thysanoptera, which has piercing and sucking mouth parts and feeds on plant sap. Thrips are serious plant pests causing physical damage and transmitting disease.

thrombin An enzyme with proteolytic activity that catalyses the conversion of fibrinogen to fibrin during the clotting of blood. It is formed from an inactive precursor, prothrombin, in the presence of blood platelets, calcium ions and thromboplastin.

thromboplastin A protein associated with the conversion of prothrombin to thrombin during the clotting of blood.

thylakoid Originally denoted the basic subunit of the chloroplast lamellae, which in cross-section has the appearance of a vesicle surrounded by a single lipoprotein membrane. Although it is now known that the internal membranes of most chloroplasts are derived from only one or two highly folded or convoluted sheets, the term is still used for convenience. The appearance of thylakoids in cross-section varies in the different groups of plants. In red algae, the thylakoids are single and lie parallel to one another. In other algae groups, the thylakoids are paired or occur in threes. In green algae and higher plants, the thylakoids become appressed in stacks

known as grana. An early concept of the chloroplasts of higher plants suggested that the thylakoids were of two types: larger intergranal thylakoids, which ran from one end to the other of the chloroplast; small granal thylakoids, which formed the stacks. This concept suggested that each thylakoid contained a discrete lumen. It is now known that the folded chloroplast lamellae system in fact divides the stroma from a single complex cavity. The thylakoid membranes contain or have associated with them the intermediates of light-harvesting systems, the reaction centres and other intermediates of photosystems I and II, the intermediates associated with water splitting and oxygen production, components of the intermediate electron transport chain, the iron–sulphur proteins and enzymes associated with the reduction of NADPH and an ATPase known as coupling factor associated with the process of photophosphorylation.

thymidine A nucleoside consisting of thymine and D-ribose linked through a β-glycosidic bond.

thymidine 5′-diphosphate (TDP) A nucleoside diphosphate based on thymine.

thymidine 5′-monophosphate (TMP) A nucleotide derived from the base thymine.

thymidine 5′-triphosphate (TTP) A nucleoside triphosphate derived thymine; one of the bases used in the synthesis of DNA.

thymine (T) A pyrimidine base, derivatives of which are constituents of nucleic acids and nucleotides.

Thymine

thymus An endocrine gland situated ventrally in the lower neck region of vertebrates. It is associated with cell-mediated immunity and allergic aspects of the immune response. The gland decreases in activity with maturity.

thyroglobulin A precursor protein from which the thyroid hormone is derived.

thyroid A paired endocrine gland located on either side of the trachea in mammals. It is the site of secretion of calcitonin, as well as thyroid hormone, which controls metabolic rate. The growth of the thyroid and secretion of thyroid hormone is stimulated by thyrotrophin.

thyroid hormone A mixture of two iodine-containing amino acid-based compounds, triiodothyronine (T_3) and tetraiodothyronine (thyroxine, T_4), which are secreted by the follicles of the thyroid glands of vertebrates. Thyroid hormone increases oxygen consumption and energy production, as well as stimulating developmental changes such as moulting and metamorphosis.

thyroid-stimulating hormone *See* thyrotrophin.

thyrotrophin A glycoprotein secreted by the pars distalis of the pituitary gland in vertebrates that has hormonal activity. It stimulates the growth of the thyroid gland, as well as the secretion of thyroid hormone.

thyroxine (T_4) Tetraiodothyronine; a thyroid hormone.

Ti plasmid *See Agrobacterium.*

tick An ectoparasite that is a member of the Acarina. It is characterized by a small, round body formed from a fused cephalothorax and abdomen.

tissue A group of cells and associated intercellular substances that combine to perform a particular function in multicellular organisms. Tissues are combined to form organs.

tissue culture The culturing of plant or animal tissues *in vitro* on a prepared medium. *See* animal tissue culture, cell culture, plant tissue culture.

tissue plasminogen activator (TPA, t-PA) An enzyme that converts plasminogen into the enzyme plasmin which dissolves blood clots. Recombinant TPA is being tested as a treatment for heart conditions.

tissue typing A process for characterizing the antigen in a tissue that provokes the production of antibodies in other animals of the same species.

tissue-type plasminogen activator A plasminogen activator produced by the host organism, in contrast to artificial plasminogen activators, such as streptokinase and urokinase.

titre A measure of the amount of antibody present in a serum. It is estimated by determining the greatest dilution of the serum that causes agglutination as a result of the required antigen–antibody reaction. The titre is expressed as the reciprocal of this dilution.

TLC Thin layer chromatography. *See* chromatography.

TMP *See* thymidine 5'-monophosphate.

TMV *See* tobacco mosaic virus.

TNF *See* tumour necrosis factor.

tobacco mosaic virus A rod-shaped plant virus consisting of a single-stranded RNA molecule of 6500 bases surrounded by a helical array of 2130 identical protein molecules.

TOC *See* total organic carbon.

tocopherol A compound of similar basic structure to Vitamin E, the best known of which is α-tocopherol. These compounds are chromonols in which the isoprene units of the side chain are saturated.

δ-Tocopherol (R=H)
γ-Tocopherol (R=CH₃)

Tocopherol

TOD *See* total oxygen demand.

tonoplast The membrane that limits vacuoles in plant cells.

torque The rate of increase in the moment of momentum in the rotary motion of a body around an axis, such as an impeller in a stirred tank reactor. Torque is equal to the product of the momentum mass times velocity and the normal distance from the axis.

torula yeast A yeast that contaminates various dairy products. Food grade torula yeast is produced as a dietary supplement for humans and animals.

total carbon The total amount of carbon in a chemical compound.

total dissolved solids (TDS) The mass recovered from a filtered solution when dried at 105°C. *Compare* total suspended solids.

total organic carbon (TOC) A measure of the carbon content of a sample. It is used as an indication of the amount of organic pollution in a water sample. The technique can be automated and rapid, using electrical pyrolysis followed by infrared gas analysis of the carbon dioxide liberated.

total oxygen demand (TOD) The amount of oxygen consumed in the combustion of all the organic carbon in a sample at about 900°C.

total solids The amount of material obtained by drying a representative sample to constant weight at 105°C.

total suspended solids (TSS) The mass of the solid material retained following filtration and drying at 105°C. *Compare* total dissolved solids.

totipotent Descriptive of embryonic cells before they become irreversibly differentiated. Such cells can develop into any type of tissue provided they are stimulated appropriately.

tower fermenter A tubular bioreactor in which the height is several times the diameter. Many tower fermenter designs have been developed. A typical system consists of a vertical cylinder with a conical base, topped by a large-diameter settling zone fitted with baffles. Nutrient solution is pumped in at the base. In general, flocculent yeast or filamentous fungi is used, since these will tend to form a plug which is retained in the lower part of the vertical tube when the fermenter is run as a continuous system. Thus there is no requirement for a mechanical separation and recycling of the biomass. Productivity may be up to 80 times that for simple batch fermenters. A disadvantage is encountered when oxygen or air is supplied by direct sparging at the base of the column, since the resulting turbulence can prevent the cells settling. The system is very simple. The energy requirement to pump liquid up the tower is offset by the saving on agitation. High productivity means that smaller fermenters may be used with savings in both capital and operating costs compared with conventional batch processes. Throughput can be increased by packing the fermenter with support materials on which the biomass can grow, forming a thin film providing high cell density, even at increased flow rates.

toxic shock syndrome (TSS) A relatively rare disease thought to be caused by certain strains of *Staphylococcus aureus* which produce toxic shock syndrome toxin-1 (TSST-1). TSS is associated with tampon use by young menstruating women, but it has also been reported in men and non-menstruating women. Symptoms include muscle pain, high temperature and a scarlet fever-like rash. They can be mild to severe and sometimes fatal.

toxin A biological poison.

t-PA *See* tissue plasminogen activator.

TPA *See* tissue plasminogen activator.

TPN Triphosphopyridine nucleotide; the now obsolete synonym for NADP.

tra **gene** *See* transfer gene.

trace element An element that is required in low concentrations to support growth of all living organisms. Trace elements participate in metabolism as cofactors in enzyme reactions, electron transport and membrane transport phenomenon. In culture of cells and microorganisms, iron, zinc, copper and manganese concentrations of about 10 milligrams per litre are required. Other trace elements are required by specific organisms such as photosynthetic cells, nitrogen fixers and methanogens. Correct composition of trace elements are essential for good growth; many commercial processes have suffered from inattention to the microelement requirements of the organism used.

tracer A marked compound introduced into a culture or used as substrate for any reaction carried out *in vitro* as a means of following the course of growth or metabolism of the compound. Radioactive or heavy isotopes of the normal elements found in living organisms are often used as tracers.

trachea (1) In vertebrates, the windpipe which leads from the larynx to the lungs. (2) In insects, one of the many branched tubules, open to the atmosphere through the body wall, via which air diffuses into the tissues. (3) In plants, a xylem vessel.

tracheid An elongated, empty lignified xylem cell that acts as a transport vessel for the water flow associated with transpiration and as a component of the tissues that provide mechanical support.

trait A phenotypic characteristic associated with the expression of a single gene.

trans (1) In chemistry, one form of a molecule showing *cis–trans* isomerization. (2) Descriptive of the location of two alleles on different chromosomes. *See cis–trans* test.

transaldolase An enzyme involved in carbohydrate metabolism that catalyses the transfer of a dihydroxyacetone residue from a keto to an aldo sugar. The products of the reaction are an aldose derived from, but three carbon atoms shorter than, the donor ketose, and a ketose derived from, but three carbon atoms longer than, the acceptor aldose. The reaction, which does not involve a cofactor of any type, is freely reversible. However, neither free dihydroxyacetone nor its phosphate can be used as substrate.

transaminase An enzyme that transfers an amino group from an amino acid to a keto acid with the production of a second keto acid and a new amino acid. All transaminases contain pyridoxal phosphate as a co-enzyme. The amino group is initially transferred to the co-enzyme to form the intermediate pyridoxamine phosphate, from which it is transferred to the second keto acid.

transamination The transfer of an amino group from one amino acid to another catalysed by transaminase.

transcriptase A general term for polymerases that catalyse the formation of nucleic acids. *See* reverse transcriptase, RNA transcriptase.

transcription The process whereby information contained in a nucleotide sequence of DNA is transferred to a complementary RNA sequence. Genes coding for either mRNA or tRNA are transcribed into a precursor RNA which is then modified to the final forms of RNA. In eukaryotes, structural genes (i.e., sequences of DNA coding for proteins) are transcribed initially into heterogenous nuclear RNA (HnRNA) which is processed after transcription by removal of the introns to give mRNA. In prokaryotes, mRNAs are short-lived, and transcription of many genes can be switched on or off in response to environmental changes. In eukaryotes, the profile of mRNA is fairly constant, and the molecules are more stable. The mechanism of mRNA synthesis also differs. In prokaryotes, genes for enzymes of one metabolic pathway may form an operon, transcription of which is regulated by a single control mechanism. In eukaryotes, the mRNAs are monocistronic. Transcription produces an exact copy of a continuous DNA sequence, the fidelity of which depends on a specific start point, correct copying and a specific termination. The reaction is catalysed by DNA-dependent RNA polymerases.

transcription unit A cluster of genes that determines functionally related RNAs or proteins. All the genes are expressed together. For instance, the rRNA genes in *E. coli* are present in a unit that contains the nucleotide sequences coding for the three rRNAs separated by spacer regions that code for tRNA genes as follows:

Direction of transcription

16S RNA   23S RNA   5S RNA

tRNA   tRNAs

Structure of the ribosomal RNA transcription unit in *E. coli*

In eukaryotes, the genes for 18S, 5.8S and 28S RNA are present in one transcription unit, whereas the 5S rRNA gene is transcribed independently.

transducer A device that converts a measurement into an electrical signal, the magnitude of which is proportional to the magnitude of the measurement. *See* biosensor.

transduction The transfer of bacterial genes from one bacterium to another by a phage.

transfection The transformation of a cell with DNA from a virus.

transfer (*tra*) gene Referred to as mobilization gene.

transfer RNA *See* tRNA.

transfer room A small room that can easily be kept clean and sterile. It is used for the critical transfer of inoculum to new medium.

transferase An enzyme that catalyses reactions in which a group is transferred from one compound to another. Transferases are one of the main groups (EC 2) used in enzyme classification:

2.1 transferring one-carbon groups
2.2 transferring aldehydic or ketonic residues
2.3 acyltransferases
2.4 glycosyltransferases
2.5 transferring alkyl groups
2.6 transferring nitrogenous groups
2.7 transferring phosphorus-containing groups
2.8 transferring sulphur-containing groups.

transferrin A serum protein that transports Fe^{3+} ions.

transformant A bacterial cell that has been transformed. *See* transformation.

transformation A permanent genetic change induced in a cell following incorporation of new DNA. Some bacterial species can take up exogenous DNA and do not discriminate between uptake of DNA from a similar species or from a completely different organism. Exogenous DNA may also be taken up by plant and animal cells, but may not be incorporated into nuclear material in a heritable manner. Such transformation is often associated with infection by virus particles which induce changes in growth and adhesion to neighbouring cells, similar to those changes associated with the formation of tumours. Some transformed cells are malignant. The objective of gene engineering is to achieve a transformation in a host cell that is restricted to the expression of one or more carefully selected genes.

transgenic organism An organism that has had novel DNA introduced into its genome.

transgenosis The artificial transfer of genetic information from bacteria to eukaryotic cells by means of transducing phages.

transit peptide A peptide attached to a protein which guides that protein to a specific intracellular or extracellular destination.

transition A mutation in which one purine or pyrimidine is replaced by another, leading to a change between the base pairs A–T and G–C. *Compare* transversion.

transketolase An enzyme of carbohydrate metabolism that catalyses the transfer of a two-carbon ketol moiety from a keto sugar to an aldo sugar. The products of the reaction are an aldose-derived from, but two carbon atoms shorter than, the donor ketose and a ketose derived from, but two carbon atoms longer than, the acceptor aldose. Transketolase requires thiamine pyrophosphate and magnesium. The reaction is freely reversible.

translation A stage in protein synthesis associated with the activities of ribosomes. The information contained in the nucleotide sequence of an mRNA molecule is used as a template to build a polypeptide or protein molecule. Several ribosomes bind to a molecule of mRNA to form a polysome. Each nucleotide triplet (codon) of the mRNA specifies an amino acid. However, there is no direct interaction between a codon and the amino acid it represents; the association is mediated by tRNA. There is at least one unique species of tRNA for each of the 20 amino acids. The amino acid binds with its specific tRNA to form an aminoacyl-tRNA. Base pairing occurs between the codon of mRNA and the anticodon of tRNA, bringing the amino acid into the right position for it to be added to the growing polypeptide chain on the ribosome. All polypeptides are synthesized beginning at the N-terminal and progressing to the C-terminal, and are initiated with a methionine using $tRNA_{iMet}$; this methionine may be cleaved before translation is complete. In prokaryotes, the initiating methionine has the N-terminal blocked by a formyl residue, which is cleaved from the N-terminal methionine residue once synthesis has begun. Methionines within the polypeptide are inserted by a second form of methionine-specific tRNA. Both forms of methionine tRNA have the same anticodon which pairs with the methionine codon AUG. The initiation of polypeptide synthesis begins with the attachment of the small ribosomal subunit to a binding site on mRNA that includes the initiating codon AUG. The initiating tRNA

then pairs with the AUG codon. The formation of the first peptide bond is catalysed by peptidyl transferase, which is part of the larger ribosomal subunit. The ribosome then moves along the mRNA by one codon, to which the next tRNA binds and the next peptide bond is formed. The deacylated tRNA is then dissociated from the mRNA and the next codon utilized. Polypeptide synthesis continues until a termination codon is reached.

translocation (1) In genetics, chromosome mutation in which a section of the chromosome breaks off and is replaced in an abnormal position, which may be on a different chromosome or the same one. (2) In plants, the movement of compounds or water through the conducting elements, consisting of phloem and xylem. The phloem conducts mainly organic materials, whereas the xylem is the site of movement of water and mineral salts.

transmission In spectroscopy, the amount of radiation transmitted through a sample expressed as a percentage. *See* spectrophotometric terms.

transmittance In spectroscopy, a measure of the amount of light that passes through a sample. *See* spectrophotometric terms.

transpiration The loss of water, mainly from the leaves, as vapour diffusing through the stomatal pores. Some water is also lost from the surface of the plant in cuticular transpiration. If the rate of transpiration exceeds the rate of water uptake, the plant may wilt, and under extreme conditions die. The rate of transpiration increases with temperature, low humidity and high air speed across the leaf. Stomata generally close in response to wilting, thus restricting gas exchange and hence lowering the capacity for photosynthesis. Under these conditions the rate of photorespiration in C_3 plants may increase; stomatal closure and photorespiration together result in significant yield decreases.

transpiration stream The flow of water from the soil through the xylem of the roots

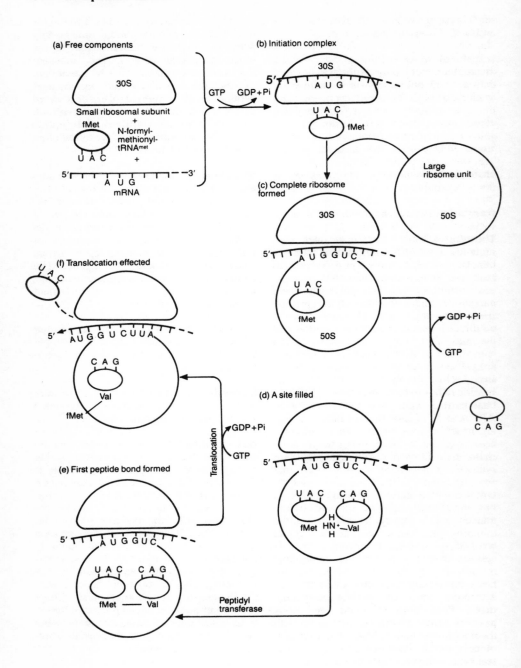

Translation: polypeptide synthesis

and stems to the leaves. The movement of water is the result of loss from the leaves due to transpiration.

transplant A part of a tissue or organ transferred from one organism to another in grafting or organ transplantation.

transplantation antigen An antigen that initiates the immune response that leads to the rejection of a tissue or organ transplant.

transposition A translocation of a chromosome segment from one position to another without a reciprocal exchange. *Compare* reciprocal translocation.

transposon A DNA element that can insert at random into plasmids or the bacterial chromosome independently of the host cell recombination system. In addition to the genes involved in insertion, transposons carry genes that confer new phenotypic properties on the host cell such as resistance to antibiotics (e.g., ampicillin, kanamycin, etc.).

transversion A mutation in which a purine is replaced by a pyrimidine (or vice versa) in a base sequence of DNA. This results in a change of A–T for T–A, G–C for C–G or A–T for C–G. *Compare* transition.

trehalase An enzyme that catalyses the hydrolysis of trehalose to two molecules of glucose.

trehalose A storage disaccharide composed of two molecules of glucose joined through an α-(1,1)-glycosidic linkage.

tribe In taxonomy, a subdivision of large subfamilies of plants.

tricarboxylic acid (Krebs) cycle A respiratory pathway located in the mitochondria that oxidizes acetyl-CoA derived from pyruvate (formed by glycolysis) completely to carbon dioxide. The TCA cycle commences with the condensation of the acetyl residue of acetyl-CoA with oxaloacetic acid (OAA) to form the tricarboxylic acid citric acid. The reaction is catalysed by citrate

synthase. The enzyme aconitase then converts this acid to isocitric acid, which is subsequently oxidatively decarboxylated by isocitrate dehydrogenase to α-ketoglutaric acid with the formation of reduced NAD. A second oxidative decarboxylation then converts the keto acid to succinyl-CoA, which is converted to succinic acid by the enzyme succinate thiokinase. The free energy liberated in this reaction is conserved in the coupled phosphorylation of ADP (in plants) or GDP (in animals). This is the only substrate-level phosphorylation associated with the TCA cycle. At this stage, two atoms of carbon have been lost as carbon dioxide. Of the four remaining atoms of succinate, two are derived from the acetyl unit and two from the central carbon atoms of OAA. The succinate is then used to regenerate OAA in a series of reactions that form fumaric acid, malic acid and OAA in sequence. During these reactions, energy is conserved in the form of reduced FAD (succinate to fumarate) and NADH (malate to OAA). During one turn of the cycle, two carbon are lost, equivalent to the two carbons of the acetyl derived from acetyl-CoA, hence there is no net loss or gain of carbon. At the same time, three molecules of NADH are generated. These are re-oxidized by the terminal electron transport chain, with the three electron pairs passing down the chain producing three ATPs for each pair. Two ATPs are formed from the FADH and one during the substrate-level phosphorylation. Thus the total number of ATPs formed per turn of the cycle, or metabolism of one acetyl unit, is 12.

2,4,5-trichlorophenoxyacetic acid *See* 2,4,5-T.

Trichoderma A white rot fungus widely used in the production of cellulases.

Tricine *See* zwitterionic buffer.

trickle filter A mechanical device in which liquid is sprayed on to, and allowed to percolate through, a bed of particulate material on which a layer of biomass is grown. A device of this type may be used for the purification of wastewater.

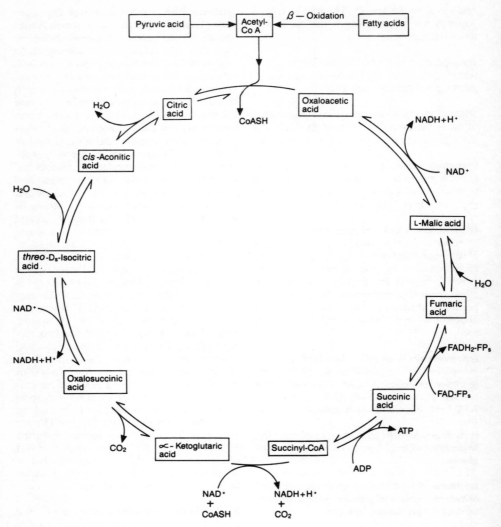

Krebs (tricarboxylic acid) TCA cycle

tricuspid valve A valve found between the atrium and ventricle of the mammalian heart.

triglyceride A compound consisting of three long-chain fatty acids esterified to a molecule of glycerol. Triglycerides are major components of animal fats.

triiodothyronine (T$_3$) A component of thyroid hormone.

triose A monosaccharide containing three carbon atoms. Trioses include dihydroxyacetone and glyceraldehyde, both of which occur as phosphorylated intermediates in glycolysis, the photosynthetic carbon reduction cycle and other pathways of central metabolism.

triplet code The way in which information is encoded in DNA. Each group of three nucleotide bases signifies an amino acid.

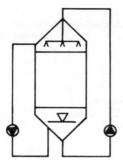

Trickling filter

The order of the groups of three bases in the DNA is the same as that of the amino acids in the proteins.

triploblastic Descriptive of an animal that develops from three embryonic cell layers: the ectoderm, endoderm and mesoderm. Most metazoa are triploblastic.

triploid Descriptive of a nucleus, cell or organism that has three times the haploid chromosome number. Triploid organisms are usually sterile owing to problems associated with the lack of homologous chromosomes.

tris *See* tris(hydroxymethyl)amino-methane.

trisaccharide An oligosaccharide consisting of three linked monosaccharide units. The most common natural trisaccharide is raffinose (galactose–glucose–fructose) which occurs in sugar beet and beet molasses, where it may inhibit crystallization of sucrose. Maltotriose is a trisaccharide consisting only of glucose units formed during acid or enzyme hydrolysis of starch. It is a significant component of low dextrose equivalent glucose syrups and may be present in high fructose corn syrups.

tris(hydroxymethyl)aminomethane (tris) A widely used buffering agent in many biological assays and in the isolation of enzymes and subcellular organelles. Tris buffers are prepared by combining the base with hydrochloric acid.

trisomic Descriptive of a cell or organism that has gained one of a pair of homologous chromosomes (i.e., $2n + 1$). A number of human genetic abnormalities are caused by trisomy resulting in a chromosome number of 47 rather than 46. These include: Down's syndrome, caused by chromosome 21 being present three times; metafemales, trisomic for the X chromosome; Patau's syndrome (that results in cleft palate and hare lip, as well as other usually fatal abnormalities), trisomic for chromosome 13; Edwards' syndrome (which results in usually fatal abnormalities in most organs), trisomic for chromosome 18.

tritium (^{3}H) A radioactive isotope of hydrogen of atomic mass 3 that undergoes radioactive decay with the emission of a beta-particle and the formation of a stable isotope of helium. The half-life of tritium is 12.26 years. Tritium is widely used as a tracer in biological studies and as a label in microautoradiography, where it is highly suitable since the low-energy beta-particles travel only short distances from their point of origin in a photographic emulsion, thus giving a high resolution.

Triton X-100 A non-ionic detergent used to dissolve cytoplasmic membranes without denaturing protein, as well as to break up hydrophobic protein aggregates. It is also used as a gelling agent in liquid scintillation counting of radioactive compounds.

tRNA A RNA with 75–90 nucleotides that carries and matches a specific amino acid to its correct codon (base triplet) on mRNA during translation (protein synthesis). There is at least one unique species of tRNA for each of the 20 amino acids. They are designated as tRNA$_{Phe}$, tRNA$_{Ser}$, etc. The various tRNAs differ from one another in nucleotide sequence and in their content of certain rare nucleotides that are found only in tRNA and are formed by post-transcriptional enzyme modification of the standard base. All prokaryotic and eukaryotic tRNAs have similar sedimentation characteristics (4S) and similar secondary and tertiary structures. The structure can be generalized in terms of a clover-leaf configuration as shown in the diagram.

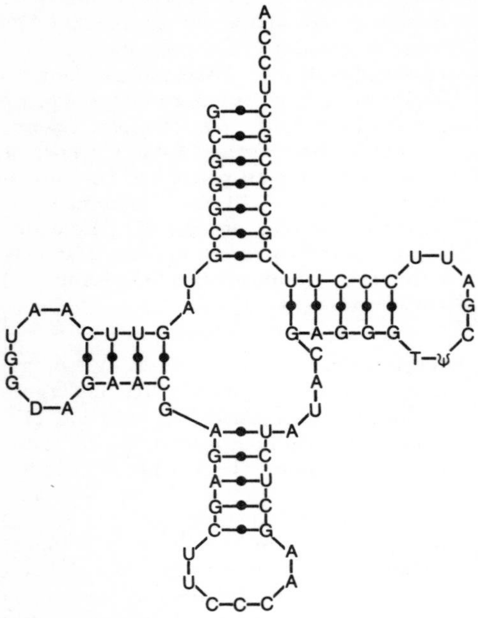

tRNA gly *(E. coli)*

All tRNA molecules share two important properties. (1) At the 3'-end of the molecule, they possess the terminal sequence –pCpCpA, which serves as a covalent attachment site for an amino acid. (2) Internally each molecule bears a loop containing three nucleotides comprising an anticodon, which is complementary to one of the specific codons that code for a specific amino acid. Each amino acid combines with a specific aminoacyl-tRNA synthetase in a reaction requiring ATP. The activated synthetase complex then reacts with a specific tRNA molecule to reproduce an aminoacyl-tRNA.

tRNA precursor A form of tRNA that is about 20 per cent larger than the mature molecules and contains extra sequences at both the 5'- and the 3'-ends. In prokaryotes, these are removed by specific enzymes, RNase P and RNase Q, which cleave at the 5'- and 3'-ends, respectively.

tropism In plants, a directional growth movement that occurs in response to a directional stimulus. Growth towards the stimulus is termed positive, and growth away from the stimulus negative. Stimuli causing tropic growth (and the responses) include light (phototropism), chemicals (chemotropism), gravity (geotropism), water (hydrotropism) and touch (haptotropism).

tropomyosin A protein that occurs in the I filament of striated muscle.

troponin A protein that occurs in the I filament of striated muscle.

tropophase *See* exponential phase of growth.

Troughton viscosity *See* elongation viscosity.

Trp An abbreviation used to denote the amino acid tryptophan in protein sequences and elsewhere.

trypan blue *See* dye exclusion test.

trypsin A protease that is secreted by the pancreas of vertebrates in the form of an inactive precursor trypsinogen.

trypsinogen An inactive precursor of the pancreatic protease trypsin. Trypsinogen is converted to trypsin by the removal of a polypeptide in a reaction catalysed by the enzyme enteropeptidase.

tryptophan (Trp) One of the 20 common amino acids that occur in proteins. An essential amino acid for man.

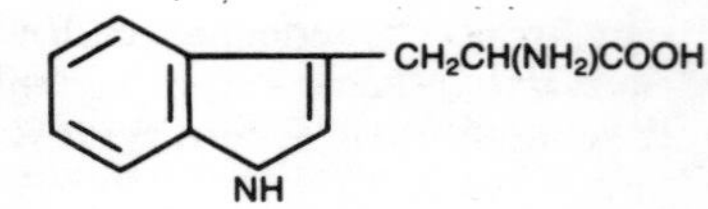

TSH Thyroid-stimulating hormone. *See* thyrotrophin.

TSS *See* total suspended solids, toxic shock syndrome.

TSST-1 *See* toxic shock syndrome.

TTP *See* thymidine 5'-triphosphate.

tuber An underground storage and/or perennating organ. Both stem tubers (e.g., potato) and root tubers (e.g., dahlia) occur.

tubulin *See* microtubule.

tumour An abnormal or morbid swelling in any part of the body. It consists of new tissues that are autonomous and differ in structure from the part of the body in which they are growing. Neoplasms, which often result from the uncontrolled growth of cells, serve no useful purpose. Tumours that proliferate, invade and ultimately destroy other parts of the body are malignant or cancerous, whereas non-invasive tumours are benign.

tumour necrosis factor (TNF) A monokine that induces leukocytosis, fever and weight loss. Synthesis of TNF can be induced in mononuclear phagocytes by a variety of agents including lipopolysaccharides. TNF facilitates the destruction of RNA and DNA viruses by macrophages and induces differentiation in myeloid cells. *See also* ELAM-1.

turbidimeter A device used to measure the turbidity of a sample. In general, a light beam is passed through the sample and the turbidity measured in terms of the decrease in absorbance. A nephalometer is a specialized turbidimeter.

turbidimetry A technique in which the turbidity of the sample is measured. It is commonly used to estimate the growth of microorganisms. *See* nephelometer, turbidimeter.

turbidity A measure of light scattering due to microscopic matter suspended in a fluid.

turbidostat A continuous culture fermentation system in which fresh medium is introduced in order to maintain a constant culture turbidity.

turbulent flow Flow in which motion at any point varies rapidly in direction and magnitude.

turgor pressure The hydrostatic pressure that occurs within a cell as the result of uptake of water by osmosis, conferring rigidity on the cell.

Turner's syndrome A human sex chromosome abnormality that occurs in some females who have a complement of XO rather than XX. The syndrome may result in mental retardation, infertility and reduced stature.

turnover number A measure of the activity of a catalyst. The turnover number is the number of molecules of substrate converted to product by each molecule of catalyst (enzyme) per unit time.

two-phase Descriptive of a system composed of two immiscible fluids such as air and water, lipid and water, etc. Two-phase systems are used in extraction and/or purification of organic substances. More complex two-phase systems are used for fractionation of cells, particles, viruses and macromolecules. For instance, a mixture of dextran and polyethylene glycol in water can give a two-phase system within which such particles will partition on the basis of their molecular weight and other physical properties.

two-stage digester An anaerobic digester in which the acidogenic (acid-forming) are separated from the methanogenic reactions. The two reactions may take place in the same tank or in separate vessels, the effluent from the first stage acting as feed for the second. The technology used in the two stages may differ. For instance, a high solids, fully mixed first stage may be linked to an anaerobic filter as the second stage.

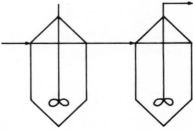

Two-stage digester

type specimen A synonym for holotype.

typing phage A bacteriophage used in the identification of a bacteria species subdivision or serotype based on the host specificity.

Tyr An abbreviation used to denote the amino acid tyrosine in protein sequences and elsewhere.

tyrocidine A polypeptide antibiotic produced by *Bacillus brevis*.

tyrosine (Tyr) One of the 20 common amino acids that occur in proteins. Tyrosine is a precursor of noradrenaline, adrenaline, melanin, thyroid hormone and various alkaloids.

Tyrosine   HO$-$⬡$-$CH₂CH(NH₂)COOH

U

U *See* uracil.

u orientation Descriptive of the situation in which the vector and the inserted fragment of DNA have opposite orientations. *Compare* n orientation.

UAA A codon that does not code for any amino acid. It is termed a nonsense codon and its function is to stop translation.

UAG A nonsense codon. *See* UAA.

ubiquinone *See* co-enzyme Q.

UDP *See* uridine 5'-diphosphate.

UDPG Uridine 5'-diphosphate D-glucose. *See* uridine 5'-diphosphate.

UGA A nonsense codon. *See* UAA.

ultracentrifuge A high-speed centrifuge that is used for the preparation or analysis of cells, membranes, subcellular particles, proteins, nucleic acids and other macromolecules. The effect of the high forces generated in an ultracentrifuge is to sediment the particles at a rate that depends on the viscosity and/or density of the medium through which they move, as well as on the shape, density and molecular weight of the particles. The molecular weights of nucleic acids and proteins may be determined from their rates of sedimentation. The particles are centrifuged through a density gradient, where they will reach an equilibrium position equivalent to their density. The separation of a mixture of particles is improved by using a step-wise or discontinuous gradient system. *See* density gradient centrifugation.

ultrafilter A filter used for the separation of small colloidal particles. For instance, it is employed to concentrate protein solutions

during the preparation of enzymes. The filter consists of a flat plate or tubular membrane with semipermeable properties, through which the filtrate passes under pressure or suction. Ultrafilters are also used for removing bacteria from water or other solutions, thus making them sterile.

ultrafiltration The separation or concentration of colloidal substances and other compounds using an ultrafilter.

ultrafiltration fermenter A continuous fermentation system run in conjunction with continuous ultrafiltration, such that the low-molecular-weight product of the reaction is removed, thus reducing the effect of feedback inhibition.

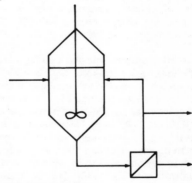

Ultrafiltration fermenter

ultramicroscope A light microscope in which the resolution is increased using diffraction effects.

ultramicrotome An instrument used to cut very fine sections for viewing in a transmission electron microscope. The sample material for sectioning is usually embedded in a hard resin and cut with a glass or diamond knife.

351

ultrasonic Descriptive of a sound wave, or regular periodic disturbance in a medium, that is above the audible limit of around 20,000 hertz.

ultrasonic cell disintegration A technique used to disrupt cells by bombarding them with ultrasonic waves.

ultrasonic cleaning A method of cleaning in which the sample is immersed in a liquid, which may contain a detergent, and ultrasonic waves are passed through.

ultrastructure The fine structure of a cell as revealed by an electron microscope.

ultraviolet disinfection The destruction of microorganisms in close proximity to an ultraviolet light source of 253 nm. The technique is used in contained environments and clean rooms.

ultraviolet light Electromagnetic radiation with a wavelength of 200–400 nm, continuous with the blue region of the visible light spectrum. A wide range of organic molecules including nucleotides, nucleic acid and proteins absorb ultraviolet light. *See* ultraviolet spectroscopy.

ultraviolet microscope An optical microscope that uses ultraviolet radiation as the light source. It has the advantage of greater resolution, since ultraviolet radiation has a shorter wavelength (200–400 nm) than visible light (400–700 nm). However, this light is damaging to living cells and to the eyes, thus living material can only be inspected for short periods, and an indirect method of visualization is important. The radiation is made visible by projecting it on to a fluorescent screen, using a closed circuit television device or recording the image using a photographic plate. Ultraviolet microscopy is especially useful for examining chromosomes and other material containing nucleic acids, which absorb ultraviolet light strongly.

ultraviolet mutation The production of a mutation in a microorganism using ultraviolet light with a wavelength of 200–300 nm. Such light is generated by a low-pressure mercury vapour lamp. These effects can be reversed by photoreactivation on exposure to longer wavelengths of ultraviolet light and the visible spectrum.

ultraviolet spectroscopy A spectroscopic technique in which ultraviolet light is used as the radiation source. A wide range of biological molecules absorbs ultraviolet light, including co-enzymes, proteins, nucleic acids, nucleotides, phenolics and some pigments. Ultraviolet spectroscopy is employed in a scanning mode to obtain spectra that are used to identify or characterize molecules. Using fixed wavelengths, ultraviolet absorbance is used to determine the concentration of proteins or nucleic acids. The course of reactions catalysed by dehydrogenases, which involve the oxidation or reduction of pyridine nucleotides (NAD or NADP) is often followed spectrophotometrically by measuring the change in absorbance at 320 nm.

ultraviolet visualization A technique used to detect the position of proteins, nucleic acids and other compounds that absorb ultraviolet light, or fluoresce in the presence of ultraviolet light, on paper, gel or thin layer chromatograms, or on electrophoretic gels. In some cases, the matrix is sprayed with a suitable reagent prior to inspection to permit visualization of the compounds.

UMP *See* uridine 5′-monophosphate.

unconventional agent *See* prions.

uncoupling agent A compound that breaks the interdependence of electron transport through the respiratory terminal electron transport chain, or the photosynthetic intermediate electron transport chain, and phosphorylation.

undefined medium A growth medium containing some components that are unknown.

ungulates A group of hoofed, grazing mammals that comprise the odd-toed ungulates, Perissodactyla, which include the horse, and the even-toed ungulates, Artio-dactyla, which include pigs and ruminants.

unicellular Descriptive of an organism (e.g., bacteria, protozoa, some algae) that consists of one cell only.

unisexual Descriptive of a plant or animal having only one set of reproductive organs, either male or female. *Compare* hermaphrodite.

univalent A single chromosome produced when there is a failure in the production of the chiasma. This results in failure of a homologous chromosome to move on to the spindle equator in meiosis. Univalents frequently form micronuclei and are lost, or may divide at first anaphase to be included as single-stranded chromatids in telophase nuclei. In this case, they are incapable of movement from the equator at second anaphase and are again lost as micronuclei at this second division.

unsaturated fatty acid A long-chain fatty acid that contains double bonds.

untranslated sequences A region of mRNA that is not used in the synthesis of an amino acid sequence of a given peptide or protein. They usually appear at either end of the sequence that codes for the amino acid sequence.

untwisting enzyme An enzyme that preserves or restores the helical structure of double-stranded DNA during replication of circular DNA molecules. These enzymes produce a nick, allowing free rotation, and then reseal the nicked DNA strand once the supercoils have been removed.

unwinding enzyme A protein that binds to DNA strands at the growing point of the replication fork during replication of double-stranded DNA. A large number of proteins binds to the site where the double helix is unwound before the formation of new DNA. As the site moves along the template, some of the molecules of the unwinding protein become detached to clear the way for the DNA-synthesizing enzymes, and for the DNA-synthesizing enzymes, and

become attached again to a more distant site on the template.

upflow sludge blanket An advanced anaerobic digester in which the cells form flocs which are kept in suspension in the lower part of the reaction tank in the form of a bed. The system is used with a liquid feed for waste material in solution. The feed stream is introduced at the base of the fermenter so that it passes slowly up through the bed.

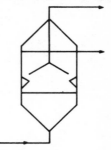

Upflow sludge blanket

upstream In a manufacturing plant, descriptive of those parts of the process that come before the fermenter or bioreactor. *Compare* downstream processing.

uracil (U) A pyrimidine base that is a constituent of one of the four nucleotides of RNA. *See* nucleotide, nucleoside.

urea (H_2NCONH_2) The main nitrogenous waste product of deamination of amino acids in mammals. It is synthesized in the liver via the ornithine/citrulline cycle, and excreted in solution from the body by the kidneys.

urea cycle *See* ornithine/citrulline cycle.

urease An enzyme that catalyses the conversion of urea to ammonia and carbon dioxide.

uric acid An end product of purine degradation that is sparingly soluble in water.

uridine A nucleoside consisting of uracil linked to D-ribose by a β-glycosidic bond.

uridine 5'-diphosphate (UDP) A nucleotide that, in combination with different sugars, acts as an intermediate in carbohydrate metabolism. The sugars include arabinose, galactose, mannose, glucose and xylose.

uridine 5'-monophosphate A mononucleotide comprising uridine and D-ribose.

uridine 5'-triphosphate (UTP) A nucleotide that is important in the synthesis and interconversion of many saccharides and carbohydrates.

urocanic acid A substance produced microbiologically from the amino acid histidine. Uracanic acid absorbs ultraviolet light and is used for that purpose in suntan lotions.

urokinase An enzyme that catalyses the formation of plasmin from plasminogen.

UTP *See* uridine 5'-triphosphate.

UV Abbreviation for ultraviolet (light).

V

vaccination The administration of a vaccine by ingestion or injection.

vaccine The agent containing antigens, produced from killed, attenuated or live pathogenic microorganisms. It is used to stimulate the immune system to produce antibodies and antibody-containing lymphocytes, thus conferring immunity against specific diseases such as smallpox, cholera, tetanus and diphtheria.

vaccinia An animal DNA virus; a source of live vaccine for the immunoprophylaxis of smallpox. Vaccinia recombinants have been used as vectors, since vaccinia has a large capacity for foreign DNA. Vaccinia virus recombinants are formed by infecting cells with vaccinia virus and then transfecting with a plasmid recombinant vector which fuses to the vaccinia promoter. Within these infected cells, homologous recombination between the virus genome and plasmid DNA results in insertion of the foreign gene into the vaccinia virus genome. The recombinant genome is replicated and packaged into infectious progeny virus. The total progeny virus from transfected cells is then screened for virus recombinants.

vacuole An intracellular body containing fluid within a membrane envelope. A large, central vacuole containing cell sap and bound by a membrane (the tonoplast) is a feature of most mature plant cells. In addition, the cells of most organisms contain numerous small vacuoles that transport macromolecules between various parts of the cell and the plasmalemma.

vacuum drier An apparatus used to remove moisture from solids. The rate of evaporation is increased by reducing the pressure within a sealed container. The material to be dried is spread on trays or tumbled during drying.

vacuum fermentation A fermentation system developed for the continuous production of ethanol and other volatile products. The reaction is run under reduced pressure so that the volatile product leaves the fermenter continuously in the exhaust gas. The method, which is of interest for thermophilic fermentations, is still largely at the experimental stage.

vacuum pan An apparatus used to concentrate a solution by removing the liquid. The rate of evaporation is increased by lowering the pressure within a sealed container. Vacuum pans are used for controlled crystallization of solids from their mother liquor.

Val An abbreviation used to denote the amino acid valine in protein sequences and elsewhere.

valine (Val) One of the 20 amino acids found in proteins. Valine is a precursor of pantothenic acid.

Valine $(CH_3)_2CHCH(NH_2)COOH$

valine production Valine is produced by fermentation using either wild-type bacteria (*Aerobacter, Escherichia*) or auxotrophic and regulatory mutants (*Serratia, Corynebacterium glutamicum*) that are capable of over-production.

variable number tandem repeat *See* VNTR.

variance A measure of variation, calculated as the sum of the squares of the differences between the value of each individual and the mean of the population.

variation The phenotypic differences exhibited by individuals within a population or species due to the interaction between environmental influences and genotype. *See* continuous variation, natural selection.

variety A subgroup of a species that displays an identifiable set of variations. The term is generally applied to cultivars, many of which are hybrids that must be propagated vegetatively since they do not breed true.

vascular tissue (1) In plants, longitudinal strands of conducting tissue, consisting mainly of xylem and phloem. (2) In animals, fluid-filled system of vessels, such as the blood vascular system.

vasoconstriction Contraction of the smooth muscle walls in blood vessels, in particular arterioles and capillaries. This restricts the flow of blood to the capillary network.

vasodilator A compound or hormone that causes the muscular walls of blood vessels to relax, leading to an increase in volume.

vasopressin Antidiuretic hormone (ADH); a peptide hormone secreted by the posterior pituitary gland. Its effects are mediated by cyclic AMP, and include vasoconstriction and stimulation of water re-absorption by the epithelial cells of the distal sections of uriniferous tubules. It is also known as pitressin.

vasotocin A peptide hormone secreted by the posterior pituitary gland of lower vertebrates and by the mammalian foetus. It is structurally similar to vasopressin and oxytocin.

vector A replicon used for the transformation of cells in gene manipulation. Small plasmids, viruses and bacteriophage are suitable vectors, since they are replicons in their own right. Artificial vectors are constructed by cutting and joining DNA molecules from different sources using restriction enzymes and ligases.

vegetative pole In animals, the point on the ovum furthest from the nucleus.

vegetative propagation A form of asexual reproduction in which differentiated multi-

cellular portions of the parent organism become detached.

velocity gradient The derivative of the velocity of a fluid element with respect to a space coordinate.

velocity profile A description of the change in velocity in a mixture or flowing solution in a plane normal to the direction of flow.

vermiculture The culture of earthworms. It is used as a method of treating farm and household waste, with the production of compost, or as a means of producing feed protein.

vernalization Low-temperature treatment required by some plant species before they will break bud or flower. The response is thought to be mediated by hormones, and gibberellins have been shown to initiate the response in some cold-sensitive plants.

Verticillium lecanii A fungus marketed as an anti-aphid biopesticide.

vesicular arbuscular (VA) mycorrhizae A form of endomycorrhizae that occurs on many crop plants and temperate trees. The fungi are present in most soils and are not host-specific.

viable Capable of growth.

viable count A determination of the number of cells in a population capable of growth and reproduction. For bacterial culture, a sensitive method is to count the number of visible colonies that develop on a plated culture of a very dilute suspension grown on agar so that single cells are spatially separated.

vinca alkaloids Compounds obtained from the Madagascar periwinkle that are used as anticancer drugs.

vinegar The product obtained in an acetic acid fermentation of any ethanol-containing solution. A large proportion of vinegar is produced by fermentation of distilled spirits of variable quality. Superior vinegars are described in terms of the starting material (e.g., wine, cider, malt, whey, sugar, glucose, rice). *See* vinegar production.

vinegar production An oxidative fermentation in which dilute solutions of ethanol are oxidized by *Acetobacter*, with the oxygen or air, to produce acetic acid and water. Most production uses a specific strain with a high tolerance for acetic acid, derived from the firm of H. Frings in Germany. Early systems of production used trickle fermentations in which beechwood shavings were used as carriers. More recently submerged systems have been developed. *See* Frings aerator.

viral insecticide An insecticide in which the active ingredient is based on a virus or viral protein. Viral insecticides are often derived from a nuclear polyhedrosis virus.

virion The infectious particle or native virus consisting of a nucleic acid core surrounded by a protein coat. *See* virus.

viroid A very small virus-like agent that exists as a single strand of RNA of about 200 base pairs. Viroids may act as pathogens in plants.

virulent phage A bacteriophage whose infection invariably kills the host cell rather than conferring lysogeny. *Compare* temperate phage.

virus A minute infectious agent made of nucleic acid (DNA or RNA) and protein that is totally inert outside the host cell. On infection, the virus causes a change in the nucleic acid and protein metabolism of the host cell. As a result, some or all of the viral genes are transcribed and/or translated, and the host cell may be killed. A mature virus is termed a virion and consists of a shell of protein units (capsomeres) arranged around a central molecule of nucleic acid. Many viruses have their subunits arranged in the form of a polyhedron of 20 triangular faces; these are known as *icosahedral* viruses. Other viruses have a cylindrical form and are known as helical viruses. A third group includes the bacteriophage and are charac-

terized by the possession of a DNA-containing head and a long tail. Viruses are divided into those that infect vertebrate animals, angiosperms, arthropods or bacteria. Infection of other groups of plants or animals either does not occur or is very rare. Only the bacteriophage possess an apparatus for injection of the nucleic acid into the host cell; other viruses are taken up intact into the host cell.

viscoelastic Descriptive of the property of a compound or solution which results in partial elastic recovery when a deforming shear stress is removed.

viscosity The property of a fluid in relation to resistance to change in the shape or arrangement of its components during flow, and the degree to which this property exists in a fluid.

vitamin An essential foodstuff that an organism requires in small quantities, but is unable to make for itself. Vitamin requirements vary in different organisms.

vitamin A A fat-soluble vitamin derived from plant carotenes. The physiologically active form of vitamin A is the aldehyde retinene, which is a component of visual purple (rhodopsin).

vitamin B complex A large group of water-soluble vitamins that function as precursors of co-enzymes. The group includes B_1 (thiamine), B_2 (riboflavin), B_6 (pyridoxine) and B_{12} (cyanocobalamine), as well as nicotinic acid, pantothenic acid, biotin and folic acid. These vitamins are usually obtained from yeast or liver extract.

vitamin B$_1$ *See* thiamine.

vitamin B$_2$ *See* riboflavin.

vitamin B$_6$ *See* pyridoxine.

vitamin B$_{12}$ *See* cyanocobalamin.

vitamin C *See* ascorbic acid.

vitamin D A group of closely related fat-soluble steroids that includes calciferol (D_2), a deficiency of which leads to skeletal abnormalities. The precursors of vitamin D are derived from plant products (ergosterol and 7-dehydrocholesterol) which are converted to the vitamin in the presence of ultraviolet radiation.

vitamin E A fat-soluble vitamin consisting of a group of related tocopherols. It occurs in plant material, including wheat germ.

vitamin K A fat-soluble vitamin consisting of a mixture of plant phylloquinones.

Vitis The generic name for the vine that produces grapes, which are used in the production of wine. Quality wine is produced only from varieties of *V. vinifera.*

VNTR Variable number tandem repeat; a DNA fingerprinting technique used to determine inheritance patterns and interrelationships between individual members of a family.

vodka A neutral spirit distilled from fermented grain or potato starch and treated with activated charcoal.

void volume (V_o) In chromatography, the elution volume of a substance that is not retarded in any way during passage through the column. It is identical to the volume of the interstitial liquid between the particles and the bed. In gel filtration, V_o is determined by measuring the elution volume of a special marker of high-molecular-weight blue-dyed dextran which is eluted from the column immediately after the volume of mobile phase surrounding the gel has been displaced.

voidage The space occupied by a gas and/or liquid in a fixed or fluidized bed.

volatile fatty acid An aliphatic acid containing two to five carbon atoms. These compounds are the end products of the decomposition of organic matter by many fermentative bacteria.

volatile solids The organic fraction of a sample of biological material determined by measuring the difference between dry weight (total solids) and the ash content. This is the weight after drying at 105°C less the weight of residue after incineration at 450 or 600°C.

volumetric distribution coefficient (K_d) In gel filtration, the fraction of the solvent accessible volume within the gel that is available to the solute. It is independent of amount of gel, the dimensions of the bed and the packing density of the column. It is determined from elution data as follows:

$$K_d = (V_e - V_o)/V_i$$

where V_e = elution volume, V_o = void volume and V_i = internal volume. The value of K_d varies between zero for excluded solute and one for solutes able to permeate the gel with similar facility to the solvent. Values greater than one may be obtained if binding forces between solute and matrix occur.

volumetric loading rate The rate of addition of raw materials to a fermenter or anaerobic digester, expressed in terms of weight of material added per unit volume per unit time. (e.g., kilograms per cubic metre per hour).

volumetric oxygen demand A measure of the maximum potential oxygen requirement by a fermenter broth. It is equivalent to the product of the maximum cell growth rate, or the number of cells in a steady-state system, and the specific rate of oxygen consumption per cell, expressed in terms of unit volume of bioreactor or culture medium.

volumetric oxygen transfer coefficient (k_La) A measure of the capacity of an aeration system to transfer oxygen from air into the liquid phase of a fermenter. It is expressed in terms of k_L (the oxygen transfer coefficient) and a (the interfacial area between air bubbles and liquid) per unit volume of liquid.

volumetric rate of reaction The rate of substrate utilization or product formation expressed in terms of unit volume of the bioreactor or fermenter, or unit volume of culture medium.

volutin Water-insoluble metaphosphate polymers that accumulate in distinct granules in the cytoplasm of many eubacteria.

W

Warburg apparatus *See* manometry.

western blot A technique similar to the southern blot procedure used for elution of RNA fragments from gels. *See* immunoblotting.

whey A byproduct of cheese making that arises following the separation of curds (the solidified casein and butter fat). The exact composition of whey differs according to the animal from which the milk was obtained and the type of enzyme (rennet) or lactic fermentation used. Coagulation using rennet yields sweet whey with a high lipid content, whereas coagulation by lactic fermentation yields acid whey, containing smaller quantities of lactose and proteins. The solids content of whey is around 6–8 per cent, with lactose the major component (4–5 per cent). This lactose represent 70–80 per cent of the total dry solids, with protein at 10 per cent the only other major component. Thus whey is a suitable substrate for fermentation by some organisms and is available for such use as untreated liquid cheese whey or concentrated either to a molasses at 70 per cent solids or as dry whey powder.

whey fermentation A process that uses whey, or whey permeate, as the substrate for the production of food yeasts, single-cell protein, ethanol, etc.

whey molasses A viscous liquid produced by concentrating whey to around 70 per cent solids, often using reverse osmosis followed by evaporation.

whey permeate A liquid containing about 35–50 grams per litre of lactose produced as a byproduct of whey protein recovery.

whey powder A dry powder produced by concentrating whey to 50 per cent solids by evaporation followed by spray drying. The whey may be partly or totally demineralized by electrodialysis or ion exchange and/or deproteinized by ultrafiltration.

whey protein A protein recovered from cheese whey using ultrafiltration, protein precipitation (at the isoelectric pH and 90–95°C) or ion exchange resins.

whirlpool separator A hydroclone used for the separation of cells from the effluent of fermentations. The overflow from a continuous cell recycle reactor is pumped tangentially into a vertical cylindrical vessel. The cells are deposited in a central cone, where they accumulate before they are recycled. The energy requirement for the whirlpool separator is low.

whisky A distilled spirit derived from a fermented mash of grain. A number of variants are produced, characterized by the starting material, the length and method of storage of the distilled spirit, and the extent of blending. Bourbon, rye, wheat or malt whiskies are produced from maize (corn), rye, wheat or malted barley, respectively. The yeast used may be a commercial pure culture or a culture preserved in-house, often *S. cerevisiae*.

white blood cell A cell that circulates in the blood and is involved in defence against foreign invaders. There are a large number of different types of white blood cells. *See* basophil, eosinophil, lymphocyte, monocyte, neutrophil.

wild type Descriptive of a member of a species that possesses the dominant genotype which naturally occurs in the normal population.

wine An alcoholic beverage, generally based on yeast fermentation, in which the starting material is a sugar solution derived from the juice of fruit, the sap of trees (including palms) or hydrolysed plant carbohydrates. More specifically, the term is applied to the product of yeast-fermented grape juice. The type and quality of wine depends to a large extent on the type and quality of grapes used, as well as the method of production of the juice, and the rapidity of treatment of the 'must' with sulphur dioxide. The extracted juice, obtained by pressing, is clarified by centrifugation, filtration or sedimentation. Fermentation is brought about by natural yeast, or yeast is added after pasteurization. Red wine is produced if the initial fermentation includes the skins, so that colouring matter is extracted. For champagne, a dry white wine undergoes a secondary fermentation, after addition of sugar and a pure yeast culture, in a closed bottle.

wine spoilage The result of infection of wine with rapidly growing lactic acid- or acetic acid-producing bacteria.

wine yeasts In some areas, pure yeast cultures are used commercially. However, in general, wine production is based on the spontaneous fermentation by naturally occurring yeasts. Grape are the habitat of various types of yeast while still on the plant. The yeasts are transferred to the grapes by insects, including species of *Drosophila*, which are attracted by volatile aromatics developed during maturation of the grapes. Genera of yeasts so transmitted include *Kloekera, Torulopsis, Candida, Hansenula* and *Pichia*. Although these may be present at the start of the fermentation, they are displaced by stronger fermenting strains of *Saccharomyces* and *Kluveromyces*. The shift in yeast flora is caused by the addition of sulphur dioxide to the crushed grapes or 'must' and the increasing ethanol concentration which favours the more tolerant yeasts. The most important yeasts in this second stage include *S. cerevisiae, S. bayanus* and *S. uvarum*.

wobble *See* wobble hypothesis.

wobble hypothesis An explanation for the fact that tRNA may complex with two or three different codons that differ in their third letter. For example, the tRNA for tyrosine (containing anticodon GUA) can recognize both codons UAU and UAC for this amino acid. No wobbling is allowed in the first two letters of the codon.

wood alcohol *See* methanol.

wood spirit *See* methanol.

wort The raw material in the production of beer. It is derived mainly from barley malt and hops. The more important fermentable components are maltose, glucose and maltotriose. Non-fermentable carbohydrates account for about 20 per cent of the total wort solid; these are dextrins, pentose sugars and other polysaccharides. The wort also contains 3–6 per cent nitrogenous compounds (amino acids, peptides, proteins, nucleic acids). The polyphenols or wort tannins are derived mainly from the malt and include hydrolysable and non-hydrolysable tannins. Specific polyphenols are also derived from the hops in the form of an essential oil, which contains mainly terpenes, and resins which produce the bitter flavour. The most abundant vitamins present are those of the B complex. The major inorganic ions are calcium, sodium, chloride and sulphate, which are mainly derived from the water used.

X

X chromosome One of a pair of chromosomes found in diploid organisms in which sex determination is linked to specific chromosomes. *See* sex chromosome.

xanthan A microbial anionic polysaccharide, composed of glucose, mannose, glucuronic acid, acetyl groups and pyruvate, formed by *Xanthomonas campestris*. It is highly viscous, pseudoplastic, displays suspending ability and compatibility with acids and bases, forms gels with galactomannans, but is not thixotrophic. It is used in the preparation of salad dressings, oil well drilling muds, acid and alkali cleaners, and in enhanced oil recovery.

Xanthomonas A genus of the pseudomonads which includes important plant pathogens. *X. campestris* is used in the production of xanthan gum.

xanthophyll Any of a number of structurally related plant pigments based on a tetraterpene structure that contains oxygen functions such as hydroxyl groups borne on the cyclic ends of a carbon chain consisting of a series of conjugated double bonds.

xenobiotic A chemical compound that is not normally produced or metabolized by, or associated with, living organisms; a compound synthesized by man.

Xenopus laevis The African clawed toad. An animal extensively used in embryological, immunological and gene expression studies.

xenotransplantation The transplantation of organs and tissues between different species.

xerogel A solution of linear molecules whose movement, relative to one another, is restricted by cross-linking or physical interaction, producing a three-dimensional space network of solvated polymer chains. A given polymer matrix only forms xerogels in the limited range of solvents in which the individual polymer chains are inherently soluble.

xerophyte A plant adapted for growth under dry conditions.

x-gal A lactose analogue that gives a blue colour when it is broken down by β-galactosidase. It is used to differentiate between transformants with the β-galactosidase gene and those without.

X-ray (1) Electromagnetic radiation with a wavelength less than 0.1 μm produced from any man-made machine. *Compare* gamma-ray. (2) A picture generated by passing X-rays through an object on to a photographic plate or film.

X-ray crystallography A technique for determining the structure of crystalline materials, or macromolecules that show repeat structure. The possible structure is deduced from the diffraction patterns generated when a beam of X-rays is passed through the sample. The use of X-ray crystallography is important in the determination of the structure of proteins and nucleic acids.

X-ray therapy The treatment of disease, such as cancer, using controlled levels of X-rays.

xylan A polymer of xylose; a component of hemicellulose in plants. Xylans are used in the production of furfural, which is used in the manufacture of plastics.

xylem The water-conducting tissue in plants.

xylene Any of three aromatic hydrocarbon

isomers, structurally derived by methylation of benzene, that are obtained by distillation of coal, tar or oil. Xylene is used in fixing specimens for microscopic examination and as an intermediate in the manufacture of dyes.

xylitol A sweetener that occurs naturally in fruit, vegetables and wood. It is produced commercially from hemicellulose. Xylitol is isosweet with sucrose but is non-cariogenic.

xylose An aldopentose sugar that occurs in hemicellulose.

xylose isomerase An enzyme that catalyses the interconversion of the pentoses xylose and xylulose. The enzyme occurs in a large number of microorganisms and has been developed commercially for use as a glucose isomerase.

Y

Y See yield coefficient.

Y chromosome One of the pair of sex-determining chromosomes that occurs in organisms that have chromosomal sex determinants. In man, it is the male chromosome.

yeast Any fungus that exists generally in the form of single cells and that reproduces by budding or by fission. The grouping of such organisms as 'yeasts' cuts across the normal taxonomic classification of fungi. Important genera include *Saccharomyces*, *Kluyveromyces*, *Torulopsis* and *Candida*, which are used in the production of alcoholic beverages, fuel alcohol (ethanol), enzymes, single-cell protein and in baking.

yeast autolysate An autolysate produced using yeast as the starting material. The autolysates are the result of the action of intracellular enzymes, primarily proteases, on polymeric substances in the cells. The process is carried out at a temperature (between 40 and 55°C) that kills the yeast, but does not inactivate the enzymes. The process is initiated by the addition of plasmolysing agents. The final product is pasteurized and concentrated. Such autolysates are produced from spent brewers' yeast or primary grown bakers' yeast. The process is valuable since it produces meat-like flavours. The product is used in culture media and foods.

yeast classification Yeasts that show a sexual stage (forming ascospores or basidiospores) are classified in the appropriate group. Asporogenous yeasts are classified with the Fungi Imperfecti. In some instances, equivalent species can be found in both the ascosporogenous yeasts and in asexual species.

yeast extract A yeast autolysate that has been further treated to remove solids by filtration. Such extracts are completely water-soluble and form clear coloured solutions.

yield The net recoverable amount of the desired product from a reaction or process. This may be expressed in terms of the percentage yield or the ratio of final product to starting material.

yield coefficient (Y) A number that relates the amount of product generated for a given input. Coefficients are calculated on the basis of the assumed biochemical pathways and metabolic activities of the culture under question. For instance, for yeasts the substrate yield coefficient (Y_s) is 0.075 for an anaerobic system and 0.54 for an aerobic system using glucose as substrate. Under aerobic conditions, Y_s values for biomass production from various raw substrates are as follows: acetate 0.36; methanol 0.4; ethanol 0.68; n-paraffins 1.03. Values for Y_O (grams of cells per gram of oxygen used) range from 0.5 for n-paraffins to over 1 for glucose. Y_{cal} is used to denote the weight of cells in grams per kilocalorie of heat evolved.

yield stress The value of shear stress below which there is no flow.

yoghurt A fermented milk product that is produced from a standard mix of whole, partially defatted milk, condensed skimmed milk, cream and non-fat dried milk. Alternatively, milk may be partly concentrated by removal of 15–20 per cent water in a vacuum pan. The culture organisms are a mixture of *Lactobacillus bulgaricus* and *Streptococcus thermophilus*.

Z

zanflo A polysaccharide produced by a Tahitian soil bacterium. It is an anionic microbial polysaccharide comprising glucose, galactose, glucuronic acid, fucose and acetyl. It is highly viscous and pseudoplastic, suspends and stabilizes emulsions, and is compatible with salts and cationic dyes. It is used in textile printing and paints.

zearalenone An oestrogenic compound produced by *Gibberella zeae*.

zeatin A cytokinin derived from maize grains.

zonal centrifuge A centrifuge used for preparative-scale density gradient centrifugation. The gradient is formed as a series of concentric rings in a circular rotor, and the sample is spun to equilibrium.

zoogloeal mass A microbial floc or film normally associated with a biological wastewater treatment process.

zwitterion An ion bearing both a negative and a positive charge.

zwitterionic buffer A buffer that has many uses in biological investigations.

zygospore A thick-walled resting stage formed in some microorganisms following fusion of gametes to form a zygote.

zygote A diploid cell that results from the fusion of two gametes.

zygotic induction Induction of the lytic cycle that produces progeny phage particles in a non-lysogenic bacterium following its conjugation with a lysogenic bacterium.

zygotine A stage in the prophase of the first division of meiosis.

zymogen An inactive precursor of an enzyme.

zymogen granules Protein bodies that occur in the exocrine cells of the pancreas and contain a mixture of precursors of the enzymes carboxypeptidase, trypsin and chymotrypsin.

Zymomonas A genus of fluorescent pseudomonads that carries out an ethanol fermentation through the Etner–Doudoroff pathway. *Z. mobilis* is a suitable organism for use in industrial ethanol fermentation in immobilized systems.

Buffer	pH range
2-(*N*-Morpholino)ethanesulphonic acid (Mes)	5.8–6.5
N-(2-Acetamido)-2-iminodiacetic acid (Ada)	6.2–7.2
3-(*N*-Morpholino)-propanesulphonic acid (Mops)	6.5–7.9
N-2-Hydroxyethylpiperazine-*N'*-2-ethanesulphonic acid (Hepes)	7.0–8.0
N-Tris(hydroxymethyl)-methylglycine (Tricine)	7.6–8.8
N, *N*-Bis(2-hydroxyethyl)-glycine (Bicine)	7.8–8.8
3-(Cyclohexylamino)-propanesulphonic acid (Caps)	9.7–11.1